DEATH ·MUST DIE

A Western Woman's Life-Long
Spiritual Quest in India
with
Shree Anandamayee Ma

Based on
The Diaries of Atmananda

Ram Alexander

INDICA

Cover illustration: *Anandamayee Ma ca. 1945*

1st edition: 2000
2nd edition: 2002
3rd edition: 2006

Published by

Indica Books
D 40/18 Godowlia
Varanasi - 221 001 (U.P.)
India

email: indicabooks@satyam.net.in

ISBN: 81-86569-32-4

Printed in India by *First Impression*, New Delhi
Ph. : 011-22484045, 09811224048

To Ma

May She find it pleasing

Sri Anandamayee Ma - circa 1970

FORWARD

It is a matter of great pleasure that this new edition of *Death Must Die* is coming out. It is very interesting to know of Ma's teachings as recorded by Atmanandaji. She stayed closely by Ma for many years (almost 40) and has written with an open mind of her relationship with Ma and of her life in the ashram.

Atmananda accepted Ma as her Guru. Ma's teachings are all embracing and She would respond to each individual according to his or her unique disposition and character. In this context, when someone would ask Ma if they could accept Her as Guru, Ma would reply: "I am whatever you think". Ma performed this role of Guru, and even *Ishta*, for Her devotees in order to lead them on the path of perfection. In Atmananda's relationship with Ma as Guru, Ma was the Absolute in which all faiths and beliefs, all dualism and non-dualism — everything was included: *One Purna Akhanda Whole where even the minutest part cannot be excluded.*

During my stay in Dehradun I found Atmananda always busy translating Ma's words. In this she was extremely sincere, minutely trying to understand the subtle meaning of each word. She would scrupulously ask various Bengali devotees about this to ensure that her translations were as accurate as possible. She would persevere in this work, often under trying and adverse conditions, always doing it in a spirit of true dedication and humility.

Ma had asked Atmananda to maintain a diary for her introspection, and She thought that it could be of great value for *sadhakas* (spiritual aspirants) in the future. I hope that spiritual seekers will derive great benefit from going through this book.

Ma bless you all.

Swami Bhaskarananda

Swami Bhaskarananda
Spiritual Head and General Secretary
of the Shree Shree Ma Anandamayee Sangha

PREFACE

Monday, 14th February, 2000

I am happy to give this brief preface to this account of the spiritual journey of a western seeker in India, the ancient land of spirituality and God-realisation. I personally knew Atmananda and had seen her in the divine company of worshipful Shree Shree Anandamayee Ma. The account of inner questing of a sincere aspiring soul is always a source of inspiration and encouragement to all others who are upon the path to liberation. It also provides many valuable insights and some practical guidance in the life spiritual. As such, this present publication is sure to serve as a helpful reference book and companion upon this onward and upward ascent that culminates at the pinnacle point of spiritual perfection and enlightenment.

Sri Ram Alexander is doing a very valuable service to the world of seekers. I wish this publication all success and wide circulation.

JAI MA!

Swami Chidananda

Swami Chidananda
President, Divine Life Society
Sivananda Ashram
Shivananda Nagar - 249 192
Distt. Tehri Garhwal

Table of Contents

All pictures of Anandamayee Ma, unless otherwise indicated, are Anandamayee Ashram photos from the editor's personal collection.

Special mention should be made here of the late Br. Gadhadar (Gary Empie), an exceptional Western devotee of Anandamayee Ma, who played a crucial role in the preservation of these rare photos of her.

Prelude

"Forget the forgetting. Death must die."
Sri Anandamayee Ma

When the author of these diaries, the Austrian woman known as Atmananda, died in India in 1985, her frail saffron-robed body was placed on a flower-decked funeral bier, carefully seated upright in a cross-legged yogic position, and taken in procession through the ancient pilgrimage town of Hardwar. The body was carried to the Ganges where it was ritually immersed in a special area reserved for *sanyasis* —orthodox Hindu renunciates [1]. She was one of the few women and perhaps the only westerner to ever be given this honour. This book is essentially the story of how a modern western woman —a respected pianist and educator— arrived at this destination.

Atmananda's diaries are an intimate record of her spiritual odyssey in close association with several of this century's most important spiritual figures, particularly her Guru, the great Bengali mystic —Sri Anandamayee Ma. They also give a unique account of her fellow travellers, other western artists, intellectuals and spiritual seekers who, like herself, made the journey to the East in the first half of the 20th century and who were the precursors of the many young Americans and Europeans who from the late 60's on have flocked to India in search of spiritual fulfilment.

Atmananda's journey began in Vienna on June 7th, 1904 where she was born into a wealthy Jewish family and given the name Blanca. Her childhood was seriously marred by the death of her mother when she was only two, shortly after the birth of her younger sister, and the two girls were raised by their grandmother and a series of tutors. Blanca's father, although often away on business, took a keen interest in his daughters' education and was

---

[1] *Sanyasis* are the only Hindus who are not cremated as they are considered to have died to the world while still alive and are thus free of karmic defilements. So there is no danger of the soul lingering near the body after death. The gradual reintegration of such a purified body into the elements is considered auspicious.

13

determined that they should have the best of everything. Thus there was one governess who spoke only French to them until they became fluent and another who spoke only English until the same result was achieved. Upon discovering that Blanca had musical talent, a grand piano was purchased and the best teachers provided. She turned out to be something of a prodigy, giving her first acclaimed public recital at sixteen.

Her father encouraged Blanca's immersion in the extraordinarily rich cultural life of Vienna, then the capital of the sprawling Austro-Hungarian Empire. This was the Vienna of Freud, Mahler, Gustav Klimt and Richard Strauss, which for one giddy moment had arrived at a pinnacle of Western civilisation. But all this splendour would soon come crashing down under the guns of the First World War, during which at times she, along with much of the rest of the city, would undergo near starvation conditions.

It was amidst the ruin and devastation of this period and its aftermath that the seeds of Blanca's life-long mystical quest were sown. She began reading the spiritual writings of Tolstoy, the sermons of the Buddha and Meister Eckhart, the mystic poetry of Rilke and the esoteric novels of Herman Hesse and Gustav Meyrink. Then one day, when she was sixteen, while walking alone through a park pondering the senseless destruction around her, one of the defining moments of her life occurred. Suddenly, all matter —trees, rocks, the sky, water— was vibrantly alive and filled with a divine light in which there was no separation between the seer and the seen, but only an ecstatic unity which was by definition eternal love. For one timeless moment all this was overwhelmingly revealed to her and this revelation was to be the driving force of her life from then on.

She soon discovered Theosophy which gave an organisational structure and expression to her experience. Blanca immersed herself in this new religion at a time when it was at the peak of its popularity as a dynamic spiritual movement. She attended the 50th Anniversary convention at the Society's headquarters in South India in 1925 and later lived in a large Theosophical community in Holland for several years. In post World War I Vienna, not unlike America in the 1960's, the old social, moral and religious structures had been discredited and discarded and youth was a law unto itself. Many found, or thought that they had found, the answers they were seeking in the transcendent wisdom of Eastern mystical philosophy and yoga. But very few had the courage and the vision to pursue the quest as Blanca did.

Through Theosophy Blanca came under the influence of its reluctant messiah, J. Krishnamurti, and ultimately left the West for good to teach at his school in Benares. Meanwhile a fellow Austrian had come to power in Berlin who would embark on a path of destruction and hate-filled racism that would annihilate once and for all the world she had been born into, taking most of her friends and relatives with it.

In time Blanca became disillusioned with what ultimately she felt to be, for her at least, the inadequate teaching of Krishnamurti and her search took her to the ashram of the well-known South Indian sage, Ramana Maharshi. Although she found great solace with him, her destiny lay elsewhere and her quest was finally fulfilled at the feet of a divinely beautiful woman, the sublime God-intoxicated Bengali mystic worshipped throughout India by Her followers as an incarnation of the Divine Mother: Sri Anandamayee Ma. From 1945 until her death, Atmananda's life became ever more focused on her relationship with this extraordinary woman, a relationship whose sole purpose was to reveal the innermost truth of her own existence.

* * *

Shri Anandamayee Ma [2] (1896-1982) is one of the most outstanding religious figures of modern times and was the last great representative of the Hindu Renaissance that began with Sri Ramakrishna Paramahansa (1836-1886). Although India has always been a land of saints, during this period leading up to her independence from Great Britain in 1947 there seemed to be an exceptional number of these great ones and Atmananda had the exceptional good fortune to have close contact with several of them.

---

[2] 'Sri' or 'Shree' is a respectful title; 'Anandamayee' means permeated with bliss and 'Ma' is Mother. The name may be written with the word 'Ma' placed either before or after 'Anandamayee'. Her followers more often refer to her affectionately as 'Ma' or 'Mother'.

Anandamayee Ma seated in Siddhasana - late 20's

Regarding herself, Anandamayee Ma would say that she is whatever one thinks her to be, and that her consciousness was completely merged in the Divine (*Parabrahman*) —the state of absolute non-duality— which manifests in the relative appearance of each individual as his or her *Atman*. In this sense she would sometimes say to people that she was their *Atman* and, indeed, to be in her presence was to become intensely aware of one's indwelling divinity. To have a relationship with her was to come into contact with something that is, far more so than anything else, uniquely one's own and not something outside of or separate from oneself. This cannot be expressed in words and thus it is difficult to describe her. She is not to be known so much through her words or teachings, but through personal relationship —a relationship that is fundamentally, by its essential nature, nondual. This is the great mystery and secret of the ancient Indian Guru tradition which she embodied.

Anandamayee Ma was born in a remote village in East Bengal (now Bangladesh) on May 1st, 1896 [3] into a poor Brahmin family and given the name *Nirmala* —'stainless purity'. Before her birth her mother had received various signs and omens that this would be no ordinary child. From childhood on she radiated an uncanny beauty and was doted on by all the people in the village. The world she came out of was pervaded with religious devotion and worship. Her father would often go off for weeks on end with groups of ecstatic wandering religious minstrels, while her mother remained at home performing the extensive worship of the family deities as had been done by her forbears for centuries. A special room was set aside in their simple dwelling for the images of these Gods and Goddesses and the daily routine centred around their festive worship as it did in all traditional Hindu households. Anandamayee Ma would later say of this idyllic world of her childhood that it was a place where there was perfect harmony and order where everyone, of whatever caste or religion (the village was over half Muslim), knew exactly what

---

[3] Hindus are not as concerned with the solar birth date, which is not considered astrologically significant, as with the lunar date, which varies from year to year. In Anandamayee Ma's case this normally falls in the month of May.

his or her role or '*dharma*' was, and was at complete ease with this. This was an order based on mutual respect and on a deep awareness of the fundamentally spiritual nature of life which had been defined and refined over millenniums —a world still unpolluted by the modern opium of the masses: political panaceas and mass media manipulation.

As was the custom, Nirmala's marriage was arranged when she was 13 years old, although it was several years before she actually lived with her husband who was quite a bit older than her. When they did finally set up house together in 1914 there was never any question of normal marital relations between them. Difficult as it may be for some to understand, the quality of spiritual energy which she continually radiated, automatically and quite naturally precluded the possibility of her husband having such desires.

Bholanath, as her husband was called, got far more than he bargained for with Ma and undoubtedly this was not always easy for him. Nevertheless he persevered in this most unconventional relationship and was ultimately transformed into an outstanding yogi. During this period of her life it was noted that outwardly Nirmala was a model housewife, performing all her myriad domestic duties to perfection. Inwardly, however, something quite different was going on and at times, even in the middle of her household chores, she would go into a trance-like state, sometimes becoming unconscious and having to be brought around by others. She never gave any explanation as to what was going on at these times, however, and her demeanour was always joyous and radiant. She was always perfectly obedient and did not seem to have any personal desires. She was extremely beautiful but this was a beauty —as was the case throughout her life— that transformed the mind of the beholder into the highest spiritual awareness.

After some time Nirmala and Bholanath moved to the village of Astagrama where he had found employment. Here she became the object of veneration of an 'eccentric' local man who was both well-educated and highly religious. He was convinced that she was an incarnation of the Divine Mother. One day, when bowing before her, he spontaneously prophesied: "Now only I call you Ma; one day the whole world will do so!" [4]

In 1918 Bholanath found employment as an estate manager for the Nawab of Dacca in a place called Bhajitpur. It is here that what is referred to as Ma's *'sadhana leela'* (the play of ascetic spiritual practices) began in earnest. Ma always emphasised that she was in a state of perfect spiritual illumination since birth, that for her there was nothing to be attained or sought after spiritually as she had always been immersed in that timeless state. Nevertheless, shortly after moving to Bhajitpur, the idea occurred to her to 'assume the role of a *sadhaka'* —one who practices spiritual and yogic disciplines— although she had no training in this regard and almost no formal education. In the evening when her work was finished, she would light incense and sit quietly, repeating one of the holy names. Very soon her body would assume an advanced yogic meditation posture and she would go into a deep spiritual trance-like state. Bholanath, tired after a hard day's work, would sit on his cot, sometimes smoking his hookah, while watching her with rapt fascination until he finally fell asleep.

These states of mystic absorption began occurring with ever greater frequency and Bholanath worried about leaving Nirmala alone. The neighbours began to talk about these strange happenings and at length he consulted a renowned physician who also had some knowledge of yoga. The doctor assured him that she was in a very exalted spiritual condition.

On the full moon night of August 3rd, 1922, what is referred to as Ma's 'self-initiation' took place. In the evening after Bholanath had retired she sat down as usual for 'meditation' when spontaneously from deep within her an esoteric initiatory process occurred in which she experienced herself as both Guru and disciple. She then entered into *samadhi*, the state of ecstatic mystical absorption in which all duality ceases.

For the next several years her 'play' of *sadhana* continued unabated and she was often in *samadhi* for days on end —a state in which all outer signs of life such as breath and heart-beat came to a virtual standstill. She had the *darshan*, or vision, of various Divinities who would then immediately merge into her —the rela-

---

[4] From *The Life of Sri Anandamayee Ma*, Bithika Mukerji, p.18.

tive duality of worshipper and worshipped melting into absolute non-duality. Ma said regarding this period that she fully experienced every conceivable spiritual practice —both 'Hindu' and otherwise and followed each one through to its completion, although this was accomplished with tremendous rapidity. Normally it would take years or lifetimes to reach the end of even one of these practices. Later in her life she said that she had never revealed even a thousandth part of what she had experienced then. "During that time her days were not divided into mornings, evenings and nights —there was only one prolonged period of indescribable bliss. Sometimes, while engaged in performing an intricate yoga *asana*, her long black tresses would get entangled with her limbs and the hair was torn out by the roots, but she had no sense of bodily pain. Hunger, thirst, sleep or other demands of the body remained in total abeyance for days."[5] During this period Bholanath looked after her as a father would a helpless child.

In April of 1924 Bholanath and Ma moved to Dacca, the principal city of the region and the seat of the local British administration. Here Bholanath became manager of the Nawab's extensive estate, the Shahbag Gardens. It was at this time that Ma first became known to the world at large. Her divine ecstasies intensified at Shahbag and she emanated a spiritual radiance that others found irresistible. Those who now began coming to her came from the highest echelon of Indian society. They were doctors, lawyers, government officials and aristocrats from this relatively sophisticated modern city. They were not people of a particularly strong religious bent, many having virtually given up the old ways, but they experienced something overwhelmingly uplifting in Ma's presence —something that ultimately was not outside of themselves but which revealed the essence of their own innermost divinity.

At first it was mainly women who came, as it would have been considered highly irregular at that time for a young married woman to even show her face to male strangers. But Bholanath felt intuitively that she was meant to be the Mother of all and was prepared to let go of strict adherence to social conventions and

---

[5] Ibid., Bithika Mukerji, p.27.

Anandamayee Ma with Bolenath - mid 1930's

Anandamayee Ma in samadhi - early 1920's

any feelings of personal possessiveness. In 1925 when, after she had completed a lengthy period of silence[6], Bholanath urged her to speak to all those who had come to her, Ma warned him: *"You must think twice before you open the doors to the world in this manner. Remember that you will not be able to stem the tide when it becomes overwhelming."*[7]

Soon the tremendous authenticity of her spirituality became so obvious to all that the conventional social considerations were abandoned and both men and women flocked to her. It is impossible to convey here in this brief introduction the atmosphere of the magical and the miraculous which surrounded her constantly at this time. There were innumerable healings, both physical and emotional, and people discovered meaning in their lives that they had never dreamed possible. The elements of nature literally seemed to obey her and people were (and are) convinced that she was an incarnation of the Great Goddess —the Divine Mother of the universe. Some became so inspired as to renounce the world entirely and take up the intense practice of yoga and meditation. Often these were highly educated people who had to face serious social opprobrium, particularly as it was unheard of to receive such guidance from an uneducated village *woman*. In the not too distant future, the very greatest pandits, scholars and yogis of India would come to sit at her feet in awe, verifying that she was indeed a font, an embodiment, of the very highest wisdom as laid down in the Indian scriptures over thousands of years.

By 1926 her period of *sadhana leela* was coming to an end. No longer was she a shy village girl who kept her face covered with her sari in public; she had begun to assume the role of the great spiritual teacher she obviously was. Nevertheless her *bhavas* (states of spiritual ecstasy in which her body would exhibit various supernatural signs and movements) continued during *kirtans*[8] and at other times. Her devotees continued to increase and they made an ashram for her at Dacca. She refused to allow herself to be chained by her followers, however, and began to go on pilgrimage all over India.

---

[6] This lasted for 3 years and was only rarely broken for some important reason.

[7] *Life and Teaching of Sri Anandamayee Ma*, A. Lipski, p. 15

[8] Group devotional singing.

23

At times, in order to escape the increasing throngs who wanted to possess her, she would quietly announce that she was leaving immediately, often in the middle of the night, much to the complete dismay of those who felt that their lives depended on her. She would not give any indication of where she was going or when, if ever, she might return; but proceeding directly to the train station, sometimes taking only one person with her (who had been given only a moment's notice and who was often not allowed to bring any money or belongings with him), she would board the first available train, completely oblivious as to where it was going. Once inside, she would sink into *samadhi* as the train flew across India.

Gradually through the course of her almost ceaseless peregrinations she acquired large numbers of devotees throughout India. Kings, prime ministers, generals, scholars and saints bowed down before her. But however much worldly power a person might wield, when they were before Ma they were stripped naked as before God —their innermost Self— and it was always an awesome experience. In her presence one saw clearly that the primary purpose of life is spiritual and that the full recognition and understanding of this Reality is the sole reason of our existence. Before such overwhelming spiritual truth, the grandiose, competitive designs of the ego which are the source of our pain-filled sense of separation, dissolve.

Ultimately ashrams were built and an organisation formed. Ma, herself, tried to remain aloof from all this, but in any case, in time, things became more structured. She, however, always remained as she had ever been —completely untrammelled and free. By the time Atmananda began to get close to her in 1945, Anandamayee Ma had become one of the best known spiritual figures in India. [9]

---

[9] Information on the life of Anandamayee Ma is scattered throughout the diaries. Important incidents from Her early life can be found particularly in Chapter 23. See also entry for 18th Feb., 1955

Anandamayee Ma in samadhi - mid 1920's

Introduction

The Art of the Guru

Atmananda's diaries provide us with a unique in-depth study of the Guru-disciple relationship and the particular problems that arise when a westerner enters into this. The presence of J. Krishnamurti, the 20th century's most outspoken and eloquent anti-Guru Guru, throughout the book serves to highlight and to confront many popular misconceptions on the subject (many for which he is directly responsible), and we are ultimately treated to a face to face meeting between him and Anandamayee Ma —the Guru par excellence. The traditional function of the Guru has been widely misunderstood and misrepresented in the West, and Atmananda's quest —from Theosophy to Anandamayee Ma via Krishnamurti and Ramana Maharshi— gives us a rare balanced picture of the subject.

Although many seek the "consolation of religion" in their lives and some have found solace in Eastern philosophy, yoga and spiritual teachers, not many have ever seriously embarked on an authentic Guru-disciple relationship, which is *something fundamentally different*. Inherent in this relationship is a particular structure and discipline that effects an inner alchemy —a specific transformation process that, like every art, demands a degree of talent and a strong commitment from the practitioner if it is to be perfected. Aside from the great difficulty of finding a qualified Guru, very few are prepared to undergo the rigors such a relationship demands —the sine qua non of which is the journey beyond death, the death of the ego. From the point of view of the individual mind this is the same as physical death and the disciple must have complete faith in the Guru in order to successfully make this transition. This ego death entails abandoning all of one's beliefs and concepts that make up one's passionately held idea of who one is. Thus, unlike conventional religion, it is not and cannot be something that augments and gives comfort to our lives

26

as they are, but rather sweeps away completely our conditioned identity and makes it seem as a corpse in comparison with the absolute wholeness and ecstatic unity that is revealed as the authentic nature of our humanity. What is so often misunderstood is that this is not the loss of individuality *but the complete fulfilment of it*. In this state there is perfect harmony with all others and not the slightest possibility of egoity or selfishness, as one experiences one's neighbour as not other than oneself and the ecstatic recognition of this absolute unity as divine love. This is not a placid mindlessness but a state of radical clarity. It is not something to be accepted on faith but to be fully recognised through experience. It is one thing to have a momentary revelation of this, which all too often simply ends up becoming one more possession of the mind-ego complex, and quite another to become fully integrated into it. It is the Guru's job to reveal the way to this integration.

Another popular misconception regarding Gurus is that somehow only the weak-willed or spiritually less advanced individual would become 'caught up' in such an 'authoritarian' relationship. The truth, as these diaries amply illustrate, is completely the opposite. Only those people who, like Atmananda, have gone very deeply into the matter of spirituality and self-analysis and who are prepared to make a commitment based on tremendous strength of character and maturity, are qualified to embark on this path. In this regard it is said that although a qualified Guru is rare, a qualified disciple is even rarer. The contemporary and essentially western phenomenon of the cult guru, where the follower becomes a sort of slave to an organisation or to a group ideology, is absolutely contrary to the radical fulfilment of individuality based on direct one on one contact with the teacher that is the hallmark of the authentic guru tradition. In fact it is particularly when gurudom is taken out of its Indian cultural context and transplanted in modern societies that such travesties sometimes occur. The mind-set of Western culture has great difficulty escaping the straight-jacket theology of a *simplistic* monotheism with its obsessive proselytising and intolerant exclusivity, even when it turns to non-traditional forms of religious expression. The pathological religious attitudes and behaviour this often engenders are inconceivable within the all-inclusive monism that has always been the dominant characteristic of Indian spirituality [1], whether in its more abstract and philosophical practice of self-inquiry or through devotional forms of mystical absorption. Particularly within the initiatic process of the Guru-disciple relationship, the emphasis is always on personal transformation through experiential self-awareness rather than dependence on any salvation oriented belief systems.

The Guru is a powerful aid to Self knowledge in which, it is considered, lies the ultimate truth of one's existence. Each person's way to this inner realisation is uniquely his own and thus there is little in the way of outer dogma on this path. But fundamental to this process of Self-discovery is the essential philosophical conviction that until and unless one directly experiences the knower as the known, all outer objects of knowledge (including God to the extent that he remains a dualistic concept) can only be less than authentic. This is not to say that devotion and surrender to God are excluded, but it is through an authentic experience of the all-pervading Divine as the essence of one's individual being that one becomes initiated into an intense process of devotion to what alone IS. As we see in Atmananda's training with Anandamayee Ma, she pursues both Self-knowledge as well as devotional surrender; and under the guidance of the Guru a number of devotional and yogic practices (*mantra* and meditation) are given to facilitate this. As both Anandamayee Ma and Ramana Maharshi tell her: Only when the Self is known can one truly know God and vice versa.

Far from being the stuff of contemporary cult manipulation, the realisation that the true nature of the individual self is an absolute, all-encompassing, transcendent unity is not only the basis of Hinduism and Buddhism but also of the dominant school of the Western philosophical tradition: Idealism — extending from the pre-Socratic philosophers, Platonism and Neoplatonism

---

[1] Certainly Christianity also has a profound mystical wisdom tradition represented by such outstanding figures as Meister Eckhart and St. Theresa of Avila (not to speak of Jesus himself) that has much in common with Indian spirituality. (The same can be said of Kabbalistic and Hassidic Judaism as well as Islamic Sufism). But this view has always been in the minority.

through the contemporary Phenomenology of Husserl and Heidegger. But whereas in the West philosophy has in modern times been relegated to the domain of sterile academic speculation, in India (as in ancient Greece) it is a spiritual discipline passionately engaged in by the serious seeker of Truth under the charismatic tutelage of the Guru.

That state which the Guru embodies and to which the disciple aspires is one of permanent transformation of his or her ego structure in which a total cosmic integration occurs. In this is revealed both the ultimate humanism and the supreme individualism, in that all creation, all others, are experienced as having a fundamental integrity that is divine and in no way separate from oneself. In this state of sublime non-duality the experiencer is one with the experienced, such that the only possible response at any level of relationship is infinite love and compassion as all beings are experienced literally as oneself. To be in the presence of one who is established in this consciousness is to have this Reality awakened in oneself to some degree and this is clearly understood to be the truth of one's essential nature and not something imposed from without. There is a fundamental authenticity about this experience, inherent in all that is most worthwhile in the human experiment, that is totally beyond any external authority or belief system, although it is the source of all true religion [2]. When the Guru has fully succeeded in his job of awakening the disciple, he ceases to exist as 'another' and thus there can be no question of dependence or servitude of the disciple, although he will always feel overwhelming gratitude to his teacher for revealing the way.

The Guru guides those prepared to make this journey beyond death by holding up a mirror that uncompromisingly reveals one's desperate clinging to the circular patterns of ego-cherishing and simultaneously reveals the individual's true Self in which the lie of the false ego and one's fearful clinging to it are dissolved. To be sure, not all gurus, or would-be gurus, are equally qualified and a great guru can achieve with a glance, or the withholding of one, what a lesser guru does (less effectively no doubt) with hours of haranguing the indolent or rebellious disciple. This relationship

---

[2] The religious systems of India are unique in that they have always honored and based themselves on this principle.

is a process that is fundamentally beyond words and the 'teachings' of a great Master can never be understood only from his recorded sayings. This explains why sacred books and scriptures are often so woefully misinterpreted and taken totally out of the context in which they were originally expounded, once the Master is no longer. The transformative presence of a living Guru is by definition a great threat to the status quo of the ego, whereas the written words of a deceased teacher can easily be turned into just another prop with which one can feel spiritually safe.

A mature psychological balance and a well developed sense of morality and integrity are essential for the prospective disciple, without which he cannot possibly make significant progress in this endeavour. For the ethically and psychologically unprepared, to attempt to practice serious esoteric disciplines can often produce disastrous results. It is particularly for this that substantial association with the Guru is important so that he can closely observe the disciple and discern exactly what he may require and what he is able to absorb at each particular stage of his spiritual evolution.

To be in the presence of the Guru is, for the committed disciple, to be in the presence of God; which is to say that the profoundly magnetic spiritual presence of the Guru activates the spiritual centre within the disciple making him aware of the transcendent divinity within himself and all others in a much more intense way than he could normally do on his own. The disciple utilises this intensity to develop and deepen his meditation and to help him to clearly discriminate between right and wrong action —to see clearly the unceasing tricks of the ego as it desperately fights for its survival. Whatever heightens this inner state of transcendent awareness is seen as good and desirable, and whatever detracts is to be avoided. In this way a clear path of action opens out. Here also frequent contact with the Master is very helpful in intensifying and clarifying this process of discrimination in which one is attempting to 'bring down' and 'stabilise' a more fundamentally subtle level of awareness. It is particularly to protect and effect this all important subtle energy transformation that the serious aspirant needs to live (for some time at least) in a controlled and isolated environment —ideally the Guru's ashram— in order to maintain the proper 'laboratory conditions' in which to perfect his work.

Obviously a passionate commitment and effort on the part of the disciple are essential and this is invariably the result of he or she fully comprehending that the perfection of this self-transformative art is the ultimate —indeed the sole— purpose of their existence. Thus, far from being an escape from life, the disciple is convinced that only in doing this spiritual work is he taking full responsibility for his existence and that of the world. Again this has absolutely nothing to do with any belief system or organised doctrine imposed from without; which is not to say that there is not a structure and method which is revealed through the mystical process of the Guru-disciple relationship —a relationship that is inherently beyond all others until all 'others' have become precisely 'That'.

Of course it is understood that the Guru is only an outer manifestation of one's innermost Self, the in-dwelling Divinity within all, to which everyone has his own unique access. However, except for the rare phenomenon of the born saint or *avatar*, it is extremely difficult if not impossible to remain on the path of illumination, referred to in the *Upanishads* as the 'razor's edge', without the guidance of one who can shed light on the way. In any case, one can only begin exactly where one is at the moment, working with the inner Guru until, as it is said: "When the disciple is ready, the Guru will appear." [3] Although a great master may give his blessing to many, there are few whom he or she would consider qualified to seriously embark upon this path and such a disciple is severely tested before being accepted. This is the ancient time-honoured Guru tradition of India.

This book is the story of such a relationship. It is the story of a modern, artistic woman who had a life-long obsession to know the ultimate meaning and purpose of life and whose quest led her to India at an early age. It is an odyssey of someone steeped in western culture who ultimately abandoned it for total immersion in that of the East. Along the way she encountered some fascinating fellow travellers, often artists and intellectuals like herself, who shared her quest. Most importantly it is a record of her intense encounter

---

[3] See Anandamayee Ma's beautiful explanation of the Guru in the entry for 19th October, 1951. Also Atmananda's profound exposition in the last paragraph in the entry for 17th Sept., 1946 (also the 3rd paragraph in the entry for 23rd Oct., 1947).

with several of the greatest Indian saints of modern times who led her ever more deeply into that which she so ardently sought.

* * *

By the time I met her in 1972, Atmananda had long since found refuge in her Guru and the passionate struggles recorded here were already a distant memory. She was then deeply involved in the translation and editing of books on the life and teachings of Anandamayee Ma, which she strongly felt to be her life's work. It is ironic that these diaries, by far her greatest work, were written with the firm intention that no one other than herself should ever see them.

At the time of my first meeting with Atmananda, in spite of the great difference in our ages (I was 23 and she 68), she immediately treated me like an old friend. As it turned out, I was to spend most of the next 12 years in India, the major part of it as a monastic disciple of Anandamayee Ma, living in her ashram at Kankhal (Hardwar). During this time I saw a great deal of Atmananda and sometimes helped her with the ashram magazine of which she was the editor. Shortly before her death in 1985, she confided in me that although she had always intended to destroy her diaries (indeed, instructions to this effect are written at the beginning of each of the volumes in the event of her death), having recently gone through them after many years, she felt that they "might be of some value to others". To this end she asked me to carefully look them over and see what I thought. Unfortunately I had to leave India around this time and before I returned to comply with her request, Atmananda had passed away.

When I came back to India several months after Atmananda's death, her friend and long-standing fellow disciple of Ananda-mayee Ma, Melita Maschman [4], presented the diaries to me with the words: "I believe these are meant for you", although she was completely unaware that Atmananda had already chosen me for this work. Melita handed me a large bundle containing the 10 hand-written cloth-bound volumes which she had only recently rescued

---

[4] Melita Maschman is a renowned German author who has lived in India for the last 35 years. Her account of her wartime experience, *Fatzi* (published in English as *Account Rendered*) is considered a classic of the genre.

from oblivion. As I opened them I found pressed between many of the pages flowers that had been given to Atmananda by Anandamayee Ma, perfectly preserved after more than 40 years!

I had all but forgotten about the diaries by the time they unexpectedly came to me, but as soon as I began reading I realised what a great treasure they are. I was immediately struck by their evocative narration which unfolded almost like a novel, revealing the story of a heroic spiritual odyssey. It was clear to me that they had a life of their own with a special destiny to fulfil.

The first three chapters of this book tell of Atmananda's spiritual search before she meets up with Anandamayee Ma in 1945. The diaries open with an account of her intense youthful involvement with Theosophy during the 1920's and we are given a rare insider's glimpse of some of the more esoteric meditation practices and activities of this influential spiritual movement in its heyday. After J. Krishnamurti (who had been hailed as the Theosophical Messiah) abandoned the organisation in 1929, Atmananda eventually followed him to India where she became a teacher at his school at Rajghat outside of Benares as well as a popular radio performer of classical music. The diaries record her anguish and frustration with what she eventually felt to be the inadequacies and contradictions in Krishnamurti's teachings although she had great love for him and held him in high esteem. Nevertheless he infuriated and exasperated her and in 1942 she made a daring break with the highly insulated westernised India of Krishnamurti's followers, not to mention the British Raj, and visited the South Indian ashram of the renowned Hindu sage Sri Ramana Maharshi. He made a powerful impression on her and had it not been for wartime restrictions, she would have moved to South India in order to be close to him.

Some time after her return to Benares the English poet-*sadhu* Lewis Thompson came to stay at Rajghat school and became a close friend and mentor of Atmananda. The diaries give a poignant portrayal of her unique relationship with this unusual man whom Edith Sitwell hailed as a "poet of genius" and this is the most complete portrait that exists of him. It was particularly due to his influence that she seriously sought out the woman who was to become her Guru and the culmination of her spiritual search.

Atmananda in the mid 1950's (photo by Richard Lannoy)

The major part of the diaries deal with the evolution of Atmananda's relationship with Anandamayee Ma and her concomitant spiritual development there-in. This unfolds gradually even though she has, in a very real sense, been preparing for it for many years. Nevertheless everything she has done up to this point is mere spiritual dilettantism in comparison and she must be progressively weaned from the world into this altogether deeper level of spiritual commitment. Along the way she abandons much of her Western cultural conditioning as well as the physical and social comforts that are an inseparable part of it. A detailed account of meditation instructions are recorded which, although meant exclusively for Atmananda, have an essentially universal application and this is one of the rare instances in which such systematic instructions given by Anandamayee Ma (which are normally kept secret between Guru and disciple) have been disclosed.

The re-emergence in Atmananda's life of J. Krishnamurti in the late 1940's created serious conflict for her and her struggle to reconcile his fashionably modern iconoclastic 'way' with the seemingly more traditional and devotional one of Anandamayee Ma constitutes a central tension in her story. The diaries give an intimate, and at times highly critical, perspective of a man widely regarded as one of the most profound and influential thinkers of modern times.

Atmananda was very much an independent contemporary Western woman and, as she often repeats in the diaries, from childhood on she had been trained to question everything and never to accept anything on blind faith. She rigorously, often stubbornly, adheres to this in her exploration of the mystical, cautiously questioning and testing every step she takes. Only when she is completely convinced does she make the necessary leap beyond the intellect, and the diaries recount how such an essentially rational, pragmatic European becomes gradually transformed into a contemplative renunciate living in an orthodox Hindu ashram.

Hindu orthodoxy was one of the most traumatic problems that Atmananda had to confront and learn to cope with. The world of traditional Hinduism was so far removed from the modern Western world out of which she came as to be almost literally in another dimension. It was pervaded by a living spirituality in the same way that science and technology pervade our world today. For a westerner, to penetrate this spiritual world of traditional India as Atmananda did required a radical cultural transformation that is almost unimaginable. The orthodox Hindu felt even the touch of a foreigner to be polluting —seriously interfering with the fundamental spiritual harmony of his world. As irrational or superstitious as this may appear to us, it would seem to have a justifiable wisdom when one considers the damage done to traditional spiritual cultures by the death embrace of Western materialism.

One of the most unique aspects of the diaries is that this detailed record of mystical transformation does not take place in the isolation of a convent, but is set against the rich backdrop of Benares in the 1940's and Atmananda's close personal relationships within this ancient sacred city. There is a degree of plot and character development as her story unfolds, unusual in a work of this kind, and an evocative picture is given of a generation of Western spiritual seekers, artists, and intellectuals then living in or visiting Benares, who like Atmananda, found the siren call of India irresistible. Many of these people were quite exceptional and some later gained renown from their writings etc. The diaries invoke the milieu of these expatriate spiritual explorers at the twilight of the British Raj and are a rare tribute to them.

A vital undercurrent running throughout the book is the continual cross-cultural interplay taking place between India and the West. Theosophy was a conduit for bringing Eastern ideas to the West but it also brought many Westerners to the East (including its Western founders). Paradoxically, Mahatma Gandhi was introduced to the *Bhagavad Gita* via Theosophy while studying law in London. India's epic struggle for independence from Britain is the historical back-drop against which the main part of the diaries unfold (although it is rarely mentioned). Both Krishnamurti and Sri Aurobindo were highly Westernised Indians who spent their formative years in England immersed in the study of Western thought and culture. Both became exemplars of the Indian wisdom tradition, yet their quite different philosophies have a decidedly Western spin to them. The world of Atmananda and her friends is saturated with this cross-cultural fertilisation. Thus she takes out her mother's damask tablecloth, one of her few possessions, when meticulously preparing a dinner party in her room overlooking the Ganges for Krishna Prem, an Englishman who had been a professor of English literature in India at a leading University but who had by this time become a renowned Hindu ascetic and worshipper of Krishna.

The latter part of the diaries covering the years 1953-1962 is primarily made up of Atmananda's record of conversations and sayings of Anandamayee Ma. She was in a unique position to compile these as she was by then the principal translator for western visitors to the ashram. By this time she had virtually ceased to note down any personal problems as she seems to have at last found her peace in a totally committed spiritual life under the guidance of her Guru.

In the last chapter of this book I tell of Atmananda's life from the time my association with her began until her inspiring end in 1985.

* * *

Although Atmananda was Austrian by birth and never visited England or America, from the beginning she wrote her diaries in English —even before her first trip to India in 1925. This was undoubtedly related to her involvement with the Theosophical Society for which English was the language of choice. Although her grasp of English is very good, it is not perfect and there are many minor grammatical errors which for the sake of clarity needed correcting. Occasionally I have had to rewrite entire paragraphs but always the voice, style and syntax are hers. To this end I have left her slightly accented English even when it is not always perfectly grammatical. The original manuscript is contained in 10 notebook volumes of arbitrary length comprising over 2,000 handwritten pages in all, in which there are occasional passages in German as well as Hindi [5]. For the book this has been divided into chapters into which it falls naturally.

---

[5] These have generally been translated into English and there is a glossary of Sanskrit terms which have been italicized in the text.

The diaries in their unedited form were never intended to be read by anyone other than Atmananda. There are many things in them that would be incomprehensible and open to serious misunderstanding for anyone without direct experience of life in India and orthodox Hinduism. For the sake of clarification I have inserted commentaries throughout (always clearly set off from the text). I have also attempted to fill in the inevitable gaps in Atmananda's story with biographical information and background data and have taken special care to put a little flesh on the bones of her friends and acquaintances in Benares and Almora during the 1940's. These were exceptional individuals and unsung spiritual explorers and it would be a shame if they were completely forgotten.

Although a thorough and complete record of Atmananda's spiritual development, the Diaries are at times fragmented in other respects and we must assume that she confides elsewhere, in volumes assumed to be lost, important personal information which is only mentioned in passing here. In spite of this we are still provided with a rich picture of Atmananda and her world. This comes out particularly in her dreams and reminiscences. Thus she records taking refuge as a child in the protective folds of her orthodox grandmother's bilious black skirts, or describes particular streets in pre-war Vienna or else wandering through the labyrinthine lanes and gullies of her beloved Benares. At times the names of casual acquaintances are mentioned without any further explanation. This is either because nothing more is known about them, or more likely because their importance to the story lies solely within the incident being related.

In 1983 Atmananda wrote a memoir of Anandamayee Ma entitled *As the Flower Sheds its Fragrance*. This is comprised primarily of Ma's answers to questions posed by devotees as well as other observations made by Her, which Atmananda culled principally from her diaries. In this work she scrupulously chose not to include any of her own private conversations with Anandamayee Ma or the many instructions Ma had given her regarding her personal spiritual practice and development, which comprise the principal theme of the present work. In the latter part of this book there is some overlapping with the earlier work with the notable difference that the material presented here appears in its original form and format which is often more spontaneous than the later re-worked translations which were taken out of their original context.

The diaries of Atmananda could not, nor were they ever meant to, stand alone as a book. The introductory material, commentaries, final chapter and footnotes are intended as an essential and integral part of the whole work. I have always seen this book as a collaboration between Atmananda and myself in the service of Ma, and have found it to be a profound *sadhana* and true *darshan* of Her.

A Word of Caution:

It is important to keep in mind that Atmananda is always writing about events more or less as they occur, one day praising someone and the next day condemning them. This is particularly true regarding J. Krishnamurti. Her stormy relationship with him forms one of the main themes of the book and it would be a grave error to quote her out of context on this and other matters, such as her attitude towards orthodox Brahminism, without fully understanding the essentially positive conclusions that she ultimately reaches regarding them. I would advise the reader to enter into the flow of Atmananda's narrative from the beginning, as the development of her story and spiritual growth therein might otherwise be missed.

Sri Anandamayee Ma making mystic hand gesture

Prologue

Question: Am I right to believe that you are God?

Anandamayee Ma:
There is nothing but God; everything and everyone is only a form of God. In your shape also He has come here to give *darshan*.

Question: Then why are You in this world?

Ma: In this world? I am not anywhere. I am within myself.

Question: Why am I in this world?

Ma: He plays in infinite ways. It is His pleasure to play as He does.

Question: But I, why am I in this world?

Ma: That's what I have been telling you. All is He. His play is in numberless forms and ways. But to find out for yourself why you are in the world, to find out who you really are, there are various *sadhanas* [1]. You study and you pass your exam; you earn money and you enjoy the use of it. But all this is in the realm of death in which you go on life after life, repeating the same thing over and over again. But there is also another path —the path of Immortality, which leads to the knowledge of what you are in reality.

Question: Can anyone help me or must each one find out for himself?

Ma: The professor can teach you only when you have the capacity to learn. Of course, he can give you help but

---
[1] Spiritual methods or practices.

you must be able to respond. You must have it in you to grasp what he teaches. It is you who study and you who pass; you who earn and you who spend.

Question: Which is the best path?

Ma: All paths are good. It depends on a man's *samskaras*, his conditioning, the tendencies he has brought over from former lives. Just as one can get to the same place by plane, ship, train, car, cycle, etc., so also different ways suit different types of people. But the best path for each is the one which the Guru points out for him.

Question: I am a Christian.

Ma: I am also a Christian, a Mohammedan, anything you like.

Question: How can I get happiness?

Ma: First tell me whether you are willing to do as I bid you.

Question: Yes, I am.

Ma: Are you really? All right, suppose I ask you to remain here. Will you be able to do it?

Questioner: No. (Laughter)

Ma: You see, happiness that depends on anything outside of you, be it wife, child, money, fame, friends —whatever it is— cannot last. But if you find happiness in God who is everywhere, all pervading, who is your own Self —that is real happiness.

Question: Is there no substance to me as an individual? Is there nothing in me that is not God?

Ma: No. Even the form of not being is only God alone. Everything is He.

Question: Is there no justification in professional or any other worldly work at all?

42

Ma: Occupation with worldly things is like slow poison. Gradually, without your noticing it, it leads you to death. Should I advise my friends, my fathers and mothers [2], to take this road? I cannot do this. I say tread the path of Immortality, take any path that suits your temperament which will lead you to the discovery of your Self.

But you can do one thing: Whatever work you do throughout the day, try to do it in a spirit of service. Serve Him in every form, regard everyone and everything as manifestations of God and serve Him alone through whatever work you undertake. If you live with this attitude of mind, the path to Reality will open out before you.

Question: What is your work?

Ma: I have no work. For whom can I work since there is only ONE.

---

[2] Anandamayee Ma generally referred to people as Her mothers and fathers, or brothers and sisters according to their age.

J. Krishnamurti in the mid 1920's
(Krishnamurti Foundation, India)

I - Theosophy and J.K.[1]

Although the bulk of Atmananda's diaries deal with her relationship with Shree Anandamayee Ma, it would be impossible to understand her life without knowing something of her early involvement with Theosophy and J. Krishnamurti. At the time of her first diary entries in 1925, Blanca was approaching her 21st birthday and already steeped in Theosophy [2].

The Theosophical Society had been founded in New York in 1875 by Henry Steele Olcott, a civil war colonel and lawyer, and the extraordinary Russian mystic, aristocrat and adventuress —Helena Petrovna Blavatsky. Its stated objectives were: 1) To form a nucleus of the Universal Brotherhood of Humanity. 2) To encourage the study of comparative religion, philosophy and science. 3) To investigate unexplained laws of nature and the powers latent in man. The headquarters were soon moved to India where it took on a decidedly Eastern philosophical tone under the tutelage of Madame Blavatsky's Masters who were believed to reside in Tibet and with whom she claimed to have more or less constant psychic contact.

The Society soon became popular both in India and in the West and by the time of her death in 1891, Madame Blavatsky had attracted a number of capable disciples. The most distinguished of these was Annie Besant (1847-1933) who had already achieved renown as a social reformer, lecturer and feminist. She succeeded Colonel Olcott as President of the Society in 1905. Not only was she the author of numerous books on theosophical subjects, but she was also a prime mover in the early days of the Indian independence movement (being briefly imprisoned by the British for

---

[1] All through the diaries names and sometimes organisations are usually referred to only by their initials. This seems to have been a common Theosophical practice and Atmananda usually refers to Jiddu Krishnamurti as J.K. although occasionally she uses the more affectionate name of Krishnaji.

[2] For a description of her early life see the Prelude of this book.

her efforts) as well as the founder of several important Indian educational institutions. Under Annie Besant the Society became ever more aligned with contemporary Hindu philosophical ideas and ideals, to which were added elements of the western hermetic mystical tradition as per the original formula of Madame Blavatsky. In this way it became a true meeting place of East and West, influencing such westernised Indians as the young 'Mahatma' Gandhi and Jawaharlal Nehru, as well as Westerners such as Thomas Edison and William Butler Yeats.

At this time the Society was very concerned with the advent of the 'Coming World Teacher', and to this end in 1911 Annie Besant's trusted confidant, the 'highly clairvoyant' Charles Webster Leadbeater (1847-1934), claimed to have discovered the 'vehicle' for the World Teacher in the form of an emaciated 16 year old Brahmin boy whom he spotted walking along the beach outside the Theosophical headquarters compound at Adyar, Madras. The boy's name was Jiddu Krishnamurti and by the time Blanca first met him (possibly on his first visit to Vienna in 1923) he had already spent over ten years in the West, mainly in England, receiving a 'proper English education', as directed by the Masters via Leadbeater. He had been hailed as the future World Teacher by Theosophists around the world since the time of his discovery. And, indeed, this handsome, refined and debonair young Indian was about to come into his own as one of the most influential spiritual teachers of the 20th century. He would play a crucial role in Blanca's life, both positive and, apparently, negative.

The diaries open with a detailed account of a visit to the Vienna branch of the Theosophical Society by George Arundale [3], a leading Theosophist, and his young Brahmin wife, Rukmini [4]. We

---

[3] George Arundale (d. 1945) was to become president of the Theosophical Society after the death of Annie Besant in 1933 —a position he held until his death in 1945.

[4] Rukmini Arundale (1904-1986) became one of India's most celebrated classical dancers and choreographers and composed several ballets based on Indian mythology. She also founded the Kalakshetra School of the Arts in Madras —a major cultural institution. In 1977 she was asked to be President of India but declined on grounds of poor health. In the early 1980's she confirmed in private conversations with me that Atmananda had been a member of the inner circle of young theosophists in the 20's as well as a personal friend whose musicianship she greatly admired.

are given a unique glimpse into the inner workings of the more esoteric side of the society as it was in its heyday. At that time there were over 40,000 members world-wide spread throughout 40 different countries. For Blanca Theosophy was a very serious spiritual movement to which she was prepared to dedicate her life.

* * *

Vienna, 21ˢᵗ April, 1925

Central planning meeting with George and Rukmini Arundale, and discussion about my work. [George Arundale is the speaker] [5].

"Brood over music. Do not say you cannot play without written music set out in front of you. You can compose music which represents the growth of the soul. At the Initiation ceremony there is always a musical background. The *Gandharvas* [6] express what you have been and what you are; and as the monad [7] takes the vow they see his future and express what he will become through their music.

"You should do the same as Cizek does with music. Try to get away more and more from the static form. Express yourself on the piano. You may begin by using other composers, that does not matter; gradually you will get away from that. You must try to hear people, not only see them. Imagine their dominant note and then express it in sound. At the Initiation ceremony there is music all the time; you hear what you have been and what you will be in the future. The *Gandharvas* produce wonderful music of triumph. Creative music is very important. I have lectured about it once, but don't know where a copy of it is now. Try to express moods — for instance, "endeavour" (he showed me on the harmonium)—; it may be entirely different for you, that does not matter. Don't say that you can't compose; you have got to do it!

"Find your own way. Don't stick to any rules or restrictions. Go into the soul of things.

---

[5] All explanations have been placed in brackets throughout to distinguish them from words in parenthesis, which are part of the original text.

[6] Celestial musicians in Hindu mythology.

[7] Theosophical term for the individual soul or consciousness.

22nd April, 1925

Notes on G.A.'s talk [Arundale is again the speaker]:

"Even when only in Vienna I can sense the psychic atmosphere of the whole country, and can travel about in bodies other than the physical to gain more information when needed. I find that the spirit of Brotherhood is quite good in Vienna, but the other parts of the country are much more backward. Your group is influencing the atmosphere of Austria. Even if the Theosophical Movement here is small, it helps all the ultra theosophical movements, that means any group which propagates spiritual brotherhood.

"I don't bother about methods, but only results. Elly's work has a soothing, mellowing effect and makes it easier to breathe the Austrian air for the Master. So does yours (Kitty, John, Blanca [8]). You are the heart of the Brotherhood movement in Austria with two or three others on the fringe. You should make the shape of your group more definite, make it a focus through which the force of the Masters can play. Make it truly a group of the Masters, not just of yourselves. No rules but life. Judging from your eyes and a general feeling (I don't look at features), I take it that you have done this already. Reassert it by service. Throw yourselves into the work. Follow John's [9] example. He has made his place; whether the Masters find it convenient to take him into personal contact in this life or in the next is of no vital importance. But you should try to draw near to the Masters. Remember that your work depends very much upon that."

Later :

"Try to link up the Vienna branch decisively with Master the Count [10]. We'll determine to meet this night at His [sic] house [on the astral plane] during our meditation. Upon arriving we will cough loudly to confirm our presence there and He will then decide whether he wants to link you up or not."

---

[8] Kitty and John were to remain her life-long friends and like Blanca, Kitty spent much of her life in India.

[9] John Cordes, senior Theosophist and head of the Austrian Order of the Star. He was a close associate of J. Krishnamurti at that time.

[10] This refers to the mysterious Prince Ragoczi, the Compte de St. Germain, a Hungarian aristocrat and a shadowy historical figure who was a diplomat in France before the French Revolution and who was reputed to be an alchemist who knew the secret of immortality.

(We attempted this but no one remembered except Rukmini, who told us afterward that we were indeed there listening to Him and doing our meditation practices. So we don't know what has happened exactly but anyhow He has deigned to deal kindly with our group, and we felt this very strongly at our next group meeting on 26th April. On that night I slept very little but had the most wonderful unique experience of hearing a marvellous symphony rising from my soul for about an hour, so strongly that it seemed to burst out from inside. It comes to me that I should try to reproduce and strengthen this experience in order to get to my true work, just as Elly made contact with her Deva [11] on that particular afternoon at Ehrwald).

"There is nobody in the outer world who can take disciples other than Annie Besant and C.W. Leadbeater. Our two Masters [12] don't take any more pupils as They have reached Chohanship [an extremely high level], but they take them on probation for the two *Arhats* [Besant and Leadbeater]. The Masters will then switch them over to the *Arhats* if and when the disciples have become Adepts. But no one else is great enough to be a Guru [13]." [end of Arundale's talk].

Lotusnacht, 7th May, 1925

For a few days there has been such strong spiritual outpouring —completely overwhelming. Vaisak [14] is coming. Perhaps this time it will be so strong as to completely overwhelm us.

18th May, 1925

Music is the bodily clothing of the Devas. When one looks behind the notes of the music, one comes into contact with them. In every great composition lies potential contact with the highest

---

[11] Demi-god —in this case, a kind of muse or guardian angel.

[12] The two principal Masters, Master Morya and Master Kuthumi (KH), of the Theosophical Society who were believed to live in Tibet and who revealed themselves to chosen disciples via their occult powers.

[13] This was soon to change with Arundale becoming the prime mover behind an initiation mania in which he and his closest associates were all elevated to the very highest levels virtually overnight, setting the stage for the future rift between Krishnamurti and the Theosophical Society.

[14] Birthday of the Buddha, of special occult significance to the Theosophists.

truth. By studying the great musical masterpieces one can come into touch with this Reality. So if someone is studying piano with me, I can help him to enrich his life by guiding him to the great truth that is hidden behind the sounds.

20ᵗʰ May, 1925

While reading "Religion & Music" by Annie Besant I got several very inspiring ideas about my work, which made me extremely happy:

"Thus by music can the subtle body be made a help to the steadying of consciousness instead of being, as it usually is, a hindrance. This calming and steadying then is one of the services that music can render to meditation".

To invent music which makes the bodies quiet instead of rousing them to activity seems to me the best service that can be done for religion by music —soothing music that harmonises the bodies and makes them fit for the reception of higher things. Now we must do the same as did the old church composers almost 2000 years ago. They made a new type of music, the roots of which lie in Hebrew and Greek music. We have to create a new type of music for the sixth sub-race, the culmination of which lies in the sixth root race [15]. The music of antiquity had a monody, that of Christian culture, harmony. The next thing is collective creation.

The Deva in the blue temple gives an arpeggio which is the dominant tone. Everyone in his own unique way tunes himself to this and then the collective expression of it creates a new and transcendent harmony. What does Cizek do? He plays a dominant theme, say "Joy", and every pupil tries to express it in painting or sculpture.

15ᵗʰ June, 1925

The happiest time of my life (even though I have been extraordinarily happy at other times as well).

P.R. came from Zagreb with a letter from J.K. [J. Krishnamurti]

We have never known a life similar to that which we have been leading since then.

---

[15] The terms 'sub-race' and 'root race' have to do with Theosophical concepts of cosmic evolution as expounded in Blavatsky's magnum opus *The Secret Doctrine*.

Shivers of delight, especially on 11th June, the Feast of Corpus Christi. Now it is slowly drifting away. It is very easy to live and to help when one is so full of joy. For the first time I am really so possessed with this idea that I am not able to think of anything else. I am glowing with thankfulness to the Masters.

20th June, 1925

This night I had a very funny dream. I went down the stairs from the T.S. [Theosophical Society] and there was Master K.H. coming out of John's room followed by John. The Master looked very kind and said to him most graciously (but I can't remember the exact words any more, though I could when I woke up) : "I see that you are full of (good?) activities but you are not yet in perfect harmony with Me." John smiled and said that he was very grateful for that hint, and that he would work harder to achieve this. And I thought: "How kind of the Master to come to John's lodging."

Vienna, 7th November, 1925

In the night of the 1st to 2nd of November [All Saints Day] the Master deigned to take me on Probation as a disciple. May I ever spread His Love and His Blessing, may I become ever a better transmitter for His Power and may I bring many others to His Feet. May I ever do, and do only, what He wants me to do. Amen.

On the 1st of November George and Rukku [Arundale] were in Vienna again. We had the Consecration of the Altar, High Mass in English (I played the organ), Confirmations (Kitty and myself too), Baptisms and Admissions.

* * *

Between his first visit to Vienna in 1925 and his return there six months later, George Arundale was to become very involved in esoteric Christianity via what had become virtually a Christian branch of Theosophy —the Liberal Catholic Church. This was a direct derivative of the Dutch Old Catholic Church which (very importantly and esoterically for the high ranking Theosophist who received ordination) maintained a direct bishopric succession through the Roman Catholic Church which traces its lineage to St. Peter, the first Bishop of Rome. "The Mass followed the Roman Catholic ritual, but the liturgy, which Mrs. Besant helped Leadbeater compose, was in English; there was no confessional; and celibacy was not required of the clergy. The priest as well as the bishops were decked out in gorgeous vestments." [16]

This Theosophical Christianity was to be a major influence on Blanca over the next few years.

* * *

After the services we all had lunch together —fourteen people in all—, then Benediction and then back to the T.S. by car — George and Rukku, John, Elly, Kitty and I. Had a talk about the 'triangle' for Austria, about the best workers here and about 'bringing myself along' [17]. George asked me who my Master is and who is my link, about my work and many other things. Then he took my hands and asked whether I was conscious of my weaknesses. Of course. He told me that my temper was uncontrolled and that I deceive myself sometimes. Then we were interrupted.

While everybody was waiting outside during the E.S. [18] meeting, George called me in alone and told me: "The Master will take you on Probation tonight. We have asked Him and He is satisfied with you. You have done well; but you must do much better still. You need a good push forward. John has supported it and as he is the leader of the Austrian group, it will be done." John told me then to kneel and the Bishop (George) pressed my hand heartily. Then Rukku told me that my chief work was to help Lisl. [19] "She is not yet so far along as to become a pupil, but you must help her, you know!" I said: "I will". Rukku: "I knew you had been accepted when I saw you this morning. You must have tried very hard". I said yes but I did not realise that I had succeeded. (Indeed I thought myself very far from that during the last weeks. I even thought that I would be of no use at the T.S. Headquarters in Adyar). I

---

[16] Quoted from *Krishnamurti: The Years of Awakening*, by Mary Lutyens (p.150) to whom I am indebted for much of the information presented here on the history of the Theosophical Society.

[17] Theosophical speak for spiritual advancement.

[18] The 'Esoteric section' of the Theosophical Society. This was exclusively meant for those who had been accepted as initiates into secret meditation practices under the guidance of the spiritual Theosophical hierarchy.

[19] Another of Blanca's life-long friend who would later join her in India.

asked her to help me and she promised to do so. At the E.S. meeting George read a message of the Mahachohan and one of The Lord Maitreya.[20] I did not hear much of it as I was so happy. Then we went with George and Rukku and she showed us her jewels and told us by Whom [sic] some of them had been magnetised. We had dinner together and went to the station. Rukmini asked me to make up my mind to remember the proceedings of my acceptance ceremony which would transpire during the night on the astral plane, but I could not. So the next day I was not completely sure, but I felt that I really could give the Blessing of Him to others. On Tuesday I got a cable from Florence, Italy: "Hearty congratulations to Blanca from Rukmini and George." So it was true!

I think this has been done for the sake of Austria and I am expected to work and work and work (more than meditate and study etc). Well, I will do what is wanted. Perhaps if I do my duty, my weaknesses that hinder me in serving Him will fade away presently. I don't care any more about anything, as long as I can do His work. I am utterly calm and peaceful and thankful and I am filled with two wishes: to give His Blessing to everyone, in order to prepare in a tiny way His coming; and to bring all our members to His Feet. Not even now can I grasp the glorious fact that I have approached the Feet of that Holy One, yet I feel so changed and so happy that I am longing to share this feeling with others. I know that it is as yet only a time of test, yet I feel so marvellously safe.

Tonight I will take the pledge of the First Degree, tomorrow become a Knight of the T.R. [Theosophical Roundtable].

PLEDGE

I pledge myself to make Theosophy a living power in my life and to support the Theosophical Movement before the world.

I pledge myself to maintain a constant struggle against my lower nature, to abstain from all untruthful and injurious speech and to be charitable to the weaknesses of others.

---

[20] The Mahachohan was the embodiment of one of the very highest levels within the cosmology of Theosophy as was the Lord Maitreya who was considered to be the great World Teacher. The Theosophists believed Krishnamurti was to be the 'vehicle' for the Lord Maitreya, whose descent was awaited with great anticipation.

I pledge myself to do all in my power, by study and otherwise to prepare myself to help and teach others.

I pledge myself that I look for the Coming of the World Teacher and will endeavour to prepare myself for His Coming.

I pledge myself to obey the Rules of the School and of the Discipline I have entered.

I pledge myself to preserve inviolable secrecy as regards the documents and passwords of the School and all that passes at its meetings and to return all papers that I have received at the request of the Outer Head or her appointed agent. I expressly agree that should I hereafter be expelled from the School or resign from it, this obligation as to secrecy is binding on me for my whole life.

I pledge myself to cooperate with unswerving loyalty to the Outer Head for any object which she declares to be the work of the Masters and to resign from the E.S. if I feel such cooperation is impossible for me. To all this I pledge my Word of Honour invoking my Higher Self.

10th November, 1925

After a wonderful week, I have been living like a pig for three days. Of course it is better than before, but I am very ashamed to misuse the unspeakable kindness of my most adored and beloved Master and I have made up my mind to try hard to become a real *chela* (disciple). Whatever may happen, I will endeavour with all my power to become worthy of this tremendous privilege.

I got a letter from Bishop Arundale about the 'triangle', and about our group. He wants us to become really big. John thinks perhaps Lisl and myself could do better. He said that I had missed opportunities, i.e. with the church, and therefore had created some bad *karma*. Give up lukewarmness. I think that I should have helped Lisl instead of yielding myself to depression as I did last winter. John says I must follow every hint eagerly.

* * *

Shortly before George Arundale's return visit to Vienna (during which Blanca was accepted on probation by the Masters) an 'extra-ordinary series of initiations' had taken place at Ommen, a Theosophical centre in Holland and the headquarters of the Liberal Catholic Church. Not only was Arundale ordained a priest and then a bishop within a few days, but also he and his wife and several others claimed to have received a series of initiations on the astral plane which had heretofore been received only by Annie Besant, C.W. Leadbeater and to a lesser extent by Krishnamurti. Normally the exceptional student might hope to receive these over a series of lifetimes according to the prevalent Theosophical practice. Thus, whereas there had been only two arhats *previously, there were now seven.*

Although Annie Besant was privy to these "extraordinary occult happenings", Leadbeater, who was himself a bishop and who was considered to be the ultimate authority in such matters, was not pleased with the rapidity of the ordinations and was very sceptical about the higher initiations. Krishnamurti, who was at the time tending his seriously ill brother at the Theosophical retreat at Ojai, California, was at first incredulous and then appalled by these events which he felt to be a cheapening of those things which at that time were still held sacred by him. No doubt he also found the excessive emphasis being placed on the new Christian ritual not at all to his taste. He was moving in an evermore iconoclastic philosophical direction which would eventually cause him to deny the very existence, or at least the relevance, of the Masters —ultimately undermining the essential cosmological structure upon which Theosophical belief was based. Thus were sown the seeds of a rift that would virtually destroy the society four years later.

Very soon they would all be meeting at the Theosophical World Head-quarters in Madras for the 50th Anniversary convention to be held in December of 1925. While en route Krishnamurti received news that his beloved brother, Nitya, to whom he was very devoted and who had been his constant companion on his incredible odyssey since the time of his discovery in 1911, had died of tuberculosis. This was a very crucial turning point in his life and his loss of faith in the Masters, who had promised him that his brother would live, stems from this event.

Blanca was also to attend the convention and one can imagine her excitement on her first visit to India. There she would mingle with the elite and chosen ones of the Theosophical world. Mary Lutyens describes the atmosphere of the convention as follows: "Although the discord between the leaders of the T.S. was naturally kept very private, no secret was made of the fact that great things were expected to take place at the Convention; hundreds of members expected to see the Masters in person if not even higher beings. The New

York Times and the Times of India and lesser Indian papers all published articles about the arrival of delegates from all over the world... More than three thousand people attended the four day convention in the greatest discomfort, for it rained nearly the whole time..." [21]

* * *

22nd November, 1925

On board S.S. Orama from Naples. Dorothy Codd sharing our cabin told us some interesting things and gave us the following message:

In the Service of the King

Message from the Elder Brethen delivered at the Meeting of Members of the Brotherhood and Pupils held on September 24th 1925 at 78 Lançaster Gate, London.

"Go steadily forward, joyous in the new work lying before you, eager to share your increased power with all who need strength and courage. Have no anxiety about the success of the work, that is Our care. Yours the task to work hard, in full confidence, for often where you see failure, We see achievement. Leave Us to judge. Trust in Our guidance, as We trust you to grow ever more and more whole-hearted.

Nearer to you than ever are your Elder Brethen, for They too come to prepare the way for Their Mighty Brother. Think constantly of Us, unite your consciousness with Ours and remember that your work is Our work, and that we are all dedicated to the common service of the world. There is but one work and one service, one life and one goal, one power and one purpose."

* * *

5th-8th December

In Colombo we were privileged to do a lot of work for Him, by helping to keep up a bit the blessings that the seven Arhats [22] had brought there some days ago. We put on a performance for

---

[21] *Krishnamurti: The Years of Awakening*, p. 241.

[22] This refers to the visit of the top Theosophical leaders, including Krishnamurti, A. Besant, Leadbeater, and the Arundales.

the children of the Theosophical girls' college and by absorbing the Buddhist atmosphere, we got a better understanding of the problems [23] of this island.

Adyar, 10th December

10th December morning arrival.

Met C. Jinarajadasa [24] who recognised me at once, and George. J.K. shook our hands and C.W. Leadbeater spoke to us for about ten minutes outside Annie Besant's rooms. I saw her passing by as well as many of C.W.L.'s people and J.K.'s group. There was Mass by Rev. Thompson. Then we visited J.K.'s room; had an Indian lunch at Lady Emily's [25] together with Rajagopal, Shiva Rao, Edith Kollerstrom, Ruth, Monika, Mrs. Roberts, Betty, Mary, Rosalind, Koos, Muriel Beaufroy etc. [26] We ate off of banana leaves on the floor in traditional Indian fashion.

I paid a visit to Rukku and George at their home and saw also Sri Ram and his family [27]. I was introduced to Theodor Saint John (etc., etc.).

11th December, 1925

Morning prayers at Headquarters Hall, 7 a.m. Hindu chanting led by J.K., Buddhist by C.J., Parsee (Aria), Sikh, Jain, Jewish (Cohen), and Javanese. "O Hidden Life" was read by Annie Besant and repeated by the Chorus; then there was First Ray Benediction —most powerful vibration. Great impression of A.B. [Annie Besant]. Got introduced to Her. She was most kind to everyone. Mass by George. (Communion is always given in both forms). Great difference from yesterday.

In the afternoon we went to Madras in Aria's car and then attended J.K.'s lecture about India. I sat immediately behind J.K.

---

[23] Colonel Olcott, one of the founders of the Theosophical Society, was instrumental in reviving Buddhism in Ceylon where it was seriously undermined by colonial missionaries. He is revered as a national hero by the Singhalese to this day.

[24] A leading Theosophist who became president after George Arundale in 1945.

[25] Lady Emily Luytens was the wife of Sir Edwin Luytens and the mother of Betty and Mary. She was a prominent Theosophist and like a mother to Krishnamurti.

[26] These formed an elite group of young people around Krishnamurti.

[27] Sri Ram became T.S. president in 1953 after C. Jinarajadasa. His daughter Radha is the present head of the society. Rukmini Arundale was his sister.

and Annie Besant —wonderful overwhelming atmosphere! In the evening C. J. gave the Lantern Lecture about "Thought Forms" at the Headquarters building.

12th December, 1925

After morning prayers, I met Prince Miersky and Joe. Fell in love with the prince at once. Afternoon at the Shrine-Room.[28] Most thrilling hour of my life, I think. The atmosphere is not to be compared to anything else.

13th December, 1925

8.00 a.m. Meeting of the Esoteric Section —First, Second, Third Degrees in the Great Hall. Annie Besant was standing before the statue of Madame Blavatsky as she spoke. Near her were all the six *Arhats*. C.W.L. was studying the audience continuously.

"Think about why you are at this Convention —first of all, to help those who are not E.S. You must work as a huge channel all together and feel yourself as part of it. What we can do is not very important, but rather what the Masters can do through us. Make a habit of repeating every day in your meditation: 'I offer myself humbly as a channel that Their force may play through me unobstructed.' Try to become a real channel. Wishing to be useful is not enough; make yourself efficient. Do your best —only then have you done enough for Them. It is not fair to offer anything to Them that is not our best. Do this well in small things and then you may be ready to do a great thing."

1st January, 1926

Made up my mind to dedicate this year to the Master's service. Attended Morning Prayers and a most unique Mass— C.W.L. celebrating with five *Arhats* and a lot of Initiates present.

2nd January, 1926

Foundation stone laying for the Church.
Star meeting [29] 4.45p.m.

---

[28] In which there is an urn containing the ashes of Madame Blavatsky.

[29] Order of the Star in the East, a special branch of the T.S. presided over by Krishnamurti in his role as the World Teacher.

J.K. spoke about the Order of the Star of the East not being something definite and fixed and how he did not want it to be so because then it cannot be used by the Teacher. The period of preparation (for the Coming) is over and now we should be prepared. "Be without feeling and keep your mind empty. Those who really believe don't need lectures. Now we are entering a new period of our work. There can't be any struggle and failure anymore, but only achievement and perfection."

Annie Besant spoke about the charge they had taken of J.K. in 1911 and how recently on the 28th they had gone to the Himalayas and surrendered it to the Lord.

* * *

It was during this period that for the first time Krishnamurti spoke of himself in the first person when referring to the coming World Teacher for whom he was the "intended vehicle". Although there was no grand pronouncement those present at his talk noted a remarkable transformation. This was an event of no small importance to Theosophists around the world who had been awaiting this ever since his discovery in 1911 and for which he himself had been preparing all these years. Initially 'the Presence' was with him only briefly each day but this would become ever stronger until within a year or so he would claim to have become one with it. Most of the Theosophical leaders would find it hard indeed to accept what their long awaited Master then had to say.

* * *

3rd January, 1926

Annie Besant to the E.S.: "The motto for the E.S. should be: *There is no power greater than love.*"

7th January, 1926

George to the E.S.: "You have got an added power now because you have been in Adyar. You have got the peace of Adyar. Carry it with you and think of it when back in your countries and give it to others."

10th January, 1926

C.W.L. to the E.S.: "A group of people who know what they are doing have done spiritual work on you here and everyone of you, whether you feel it or not, has been raised into his higher bodies. Try to keep this higher standard, don't slip back into the turmoil of the world. But you can only keep it if you pass it on. Then it will not only not diminish, but will increase. There is more work to do than there is force available so pupils are expected to be very economical with it. See to it that you are a real transmitter. The force which is sent forth by the Great Ones affects our higher bodies and the Devas. Although our lower physical bodies cannot fully assimilate this power, we can be transmitters."

11th January, 1926

In the evening I talked with Jack and Oscar. It seems that the Gandharvas spoke to them and said that they want a harpist now, and later on, some very fine pianists. May be I am going to be one of them. Oscar and Jack want people who can express themselves artistically. I must not give up my music.

18th January, 1926

Since the celebration of the Baptism of Christ on the 15th of January, I am playing the organ at Church, often alone with Bishop Wedgewood celebrating. I like it best of everything.

Yesterday Jack said to me: "Before doing the meditation exercises wipe everything off of your mind and offer yourself to the Higher Self. Call a sheet of Egoic fire down into yourself and bring yourself into relation with the Creative forces of the Earth. The whole process is very much a matter of the Holy Ghost. Then think of an occasion on which you have realised how wonderful our true being is and try to retire into your Self and see things from that point and bring yourself into a creative attitude. Get a small group of people to work along that line and don't let them stop whatever may happen. Make your movement more airy and light and simple. The Deva that looks after these things has a link with everyone who wears the stone."

On board S.S. 'Orama', 5th February, 1926

Resume of the Impressions of Adyar:

I have learned to appreciate Greatness in fundamentally different manifestations. Everyone of the *Arhats* has His own way, His own opinions. One can't follow Them all simultaneously.

For the first time I have lived in an atmosphere of Reality and sensed what real Greatness means. It is the contrary of narrowness. There are no such things as principles which can be applied generally. Greatness can be hidden in every possible form.

Therefore don't judge. I have seen *Arhats* doing things for which I formerly despised ordinary Theosophists for doing. Everybody has his own way which is best for himself.

The Master Himself obviously overlooks so many outer things, even in His pupils. All embracing Tolerance seems to me of utmost importance now. There is no such thing as good and evil.

Don't depend upon anybody, but experience for yourself. Nobody can really tell you what is best for you to do. Before I went to Adyar I always was eager to be told by others what is right and what I ought to do. Now I am eager to experience for myself and to find out things for myself. Mistakes do not matter at all. It is only the fear of making ourselves appear petty in our own eyes that makes us ask others before we do a thing which to us seems right. Be independent in your judgement and think out things for yourself.

The great lesson of this trip has really been Oscar for me. He does not care about anybody's judgement and is honest with himself. He did exactly the contrary of what I expected of an *Arhat*.

The matter of belief is a very delicate one. Blind belief is no good, even in a Great One unless He is a Master. Even an *Arhat* may err. The best thing seems to be not to judge, and to find out for oneself. This is the most difficult problem that exists.

I have experienced that it is very possible not to recognise Him when He comes, if one does not have the right attitude.

Vienna, 13th February, 1926

Back in Vienna on the 11th of February after a pleasant journey alone with John. On the boat I spoke about Theosophy to some people who were already favourably disposed toward it. Then there were others who had just begun to read about it; also the Salvation Army and a crazy prophet who hopes to convert the German Emperor in order to establish the 'Kingdom' in Jerusalem. Then there was an English merchant from Calcutta who was in doubt as to whether he is the prophet Daniel or not! On the whole very interesting, again an opportunity to widen my horizon.

At first I found it enormously difficult to do anything in this grey, dull city and felt very much as in a dream. Then our dear Theosophists gave us a grand welcome and I saw that the light in this place of darkness and inertia is these people who seem to have worked so marvellously and I feel this so intensely that I do not want to retain anything for myself but to give them all and everything.

Now of course it seems that Lila and I are the only pupils because Kitty and Elly stayed on in Benares.

18th February, 1926

Theo Rhythm: At present the world is dark but there are points of light. We must make the whole world Light. That's what we are trying to do —penetrate into the heart of our real Self and look down on our body as a magnificent instrument to spread that Light on the physical plane. Therefore we have always laid so much stress on making these movements flow from the centre, which symbolises our Higher Self. Imagine that from that centre deep within Light flows into the whole body, coming through the arms, and emanates finally from the fingers, drawing lines of intense light around us. Maintain this attitude all the time whilst making the movements.

26th February,1926
Jewish Association:

Reasons:

(1) There are 6 million Jews in the world. The World-Teacher comes to them too. (2) C.W.L. said that everyone is born into the religion which is best for him. J.K. said we must all become priests, each in his own religion. (3) In the Theosophical world-university Hebrew theology is mentioned also. Create a beginning for that.

Austria in particular: No other section has perhaps as many Jews as Austria. If we really start a group, let us make it original. Not merely study books, but music, art etc.

There are no Jewish Master-pupils as far as I know except the two van Geldern who have a Jewish father, and Kitty and myself. Krishnaji says that we should all be priests in the religion in which we were born and infuse it with the universal light of Theosophy [30].

---

[30] This is, of course, very much out of character with what he will soon be saying and the general anti-authoritarianism that would characterise his mature philosophy.

27th February, 1926

I read a copy of a letter written by George to his Indian colleagues saying that through being a Bishop he can better work for His Buddhist friends, since by entering more deeply into one religion, he enters more deeply into them all, as they are all rays from the same central Truth.

<u>Self-preparation Group</u>

Application:

(1) I fully accept the ideal laid down by Krishnaji and will earnestly and unceasingly strive to carry it out in my daily life. (2) I have rendered practical service as follows: through the (a) Theosophical Society (b) The World Religion (c) The World University (d) the Revival of the Mysteries. (3) I choose from among the four lines of service mentioned in Rule 2 one of the categories as my special line of work. (4) I promise to obey the rules... (5) I promise to return my admission card and other documents entrusted to me in case I should cease to be a member of the Self Preparation Group.

The Ideal

by J. Krishnamurti

I intend this Group to be entirely composed of those who have but One desire, One thought, and One purpose in life —to tread the noble Path that leads to glorious Enlightenment and perfect Peace. They must be prepared to sacrifice themselves utterly for their idealism and to attain their goal at all costs, irrespective of all other considerations. They must be prepared to give up their petty personalities for the great work and to carry out in their daily life the teachings and the knowledge they may obtain in years to come. Their purpose in life must be to become perfect by following the Plan laid down by God for Humanity and to achieve that perfection as soon as possible. Their whole life, their entire energy, their utter devotion, however small or great must be consecrated at the altar of sacrifice to the Master. [31]

---

[31] This again expresses sentiments quite contrary to what would soon become his dominant philosophy and in this sense, it is a rare document.

Camp Huizen, 12ᵗʰ June, 1926

Arrived here on the 7ᵗʰ of June. Before coming here after Vaisak had a most ghastly time till after my birthday. Tried to help Lisl and probably succumbed to her state in order to understand her. Now since two days I am getting better; atmosphere here terribly strenuous. I am feeling quite mad.

* * *

For the next three and a half years Blanca stayed at Huizen, the head-quarters of the Liberal Catholic Church and a major Theosophical centre located in Holland. Here she became a full time worker for the Society, particularly as church organist and musical director. This was a 'new age' community composed of dedicated young people involved in what they felt to be a great spiritual mission. While she was immersing herself in esoteric Theosophical ritual via the Liberal Catholic Church, she was simultaneously becoming ever more influenced by Krishnamurti's increasingly radical iconoclasm which was ultimately to reject all forms of spiritual hierarchy and structure. This could only lead to an inevitable explosion.

Huizen was situated only a few miles from Castle Erde, a beautiful 18th Century moated castle. This along with an adjoining 5,000 acres of woodland interspersed with lakes was given to Krishnamurti in 1921 by Baron P. von Palvandt. The annual Theosophical camps were held at Ommen which was part of this large estate. Later Krishnamurti would return this extraordinary gift.

Mary Lutyens describes the Ommen camp of 1926 as follows:

"The Convention, which opened on July 24, was attended by about 2,000 people of practically every nationality. There was one huge tent for meetings, several tents for meals, rows of sleeping tents... Everything was extremely well organised. In the middle of the camp an amphitheatre had been built... Meetings were held there in good weather, and it was there that a great bonfire was lit every evening. K. [Krishnamurti] was at his best when talking at the campfires. The smell of burning pine was a delicious accompaniment to these evening meetings which began just as the sun was setting. K. wore Indian dress and as the 15 foot high pyramid of wood was lit, he would chant a hymn to Agni, God of fire." [32]

* * *

[32] *Krishnamurti: The Years of Awakening*, p. 250.

Bergerac (near Huizen), 4th July, 1926

Arrived on Friday 2nd of July. Attended a rehearsal of the play which is to be performed at the Castle Eerde. They want me to play the harmonium. This evening the whole of Bergerac is invited for dinner at Roelvink.

Saturday: Meditation at Church with Flo. Went onto Avenue of the Initiates —tremendous atmosphere!

The altar of Lady Mary is something marvellous. We must get that influence in our church too.

The Young Theosophists look very promising.

10th July, 1926

On Friday night I played at the Bishop's Compline. I also arranged the flowers for the newly built church.

We must get some magnetised stones (opal, turquoise and pearl) for Lady Mary's altar.

27th July, 1926

Pupils Meeting at Castle Eerde.

Be accurate. Much depends on small things. Don't fidget. Make only movements which mean something. Learn not to hear noises that have nothing to do with you. You can work surrounded by noises if you know that they do not really matter to you.

The astral body of a trained disciple is white, with delicate colours floating about it, but which flash up when directed by a thought.

Star Camp, Ommen, 6th August, 1926

Last night 1st degree and 2nd degree initiations in the E.S. — altogether seven candidates.

Tonight next step. Next day further still.

Since the Camp began there have been ordinations of eight acolytes, five Subdeacons, six Deacons, six Priests, over twenty Confirmations. The Chief gave two talks, Hugh did the Benediction with a procession of nearly three hundred people —myself playing the organ.

10th August, 1926

I have been hard at work lately to make my astral body a calm, pure, white mother-of-pearl-like thing and to direct it by raising my emotions onto the buddhic plane. As long as the astral body feels too strongly and enjoys itself too much, either by joy or grief, part of the force of the Master is lost for its own selfish amusement.

3rd September, 1926

Just as Hugh said in the meditation class yesterday, there is no time for petty things now. Let us dedicate ourselves body, soul and spirit to the Lord and realise that we have to be His servants in this life. Perhaps even my sluggishness served some purpose in giving others the opportunity to help me get out of it.

Star Camp, Ommen, 10th August 1927

I also have found my peace, I have found my happiness and my tranquillity. Krishnaji has opened my heart. There I stand completely stripped, alone with myself. I may lose this vision again, no doubt I shall; but I can never be as I was before. For I have touched the Eternal, for one moment I have quenched my thirst at the deep fount of Life, I have caught a glimpse of Truth. The world has changed, everything is new. I must begin afresh as a little child.

* * *

Almost 3,000 Theosophists attended the camp of 1927. From Mary Lutyen's description one is reminded of a 'new age' festival of the late 1960's. It was observed that: "Representatives of more races, creeds and sects than had ever before been gathered into one place" were gathered there. Typical of the devoted followers was "a young Bulgarian who could not afford the railway journey and had taken 6 weeks to walk to Ommen from his native country." A collection was taken up for his return journey which he declined as he decided to stay on and so was made camp custodian for the winter.

On August 7th Krishnamurti gave a talk entitled Who Brings the Truth *in which he dealt with the question of the Masters and the rest of the occult hierarchy. He is now speaking with the words of a full-blown mystic:* "I have found what I longed for, I have become united, so that henceforth there will be no separation, because my thoughts, my desires,

my longings —those of the individual self— have been destroyed...
Until now you have been depending on... [the Theosophical leader-
ship]..., on someone else to tell you the Truth, whereas the Truth
lies within you, in your own hearts, in your own experience... I
have been united with my Beloved and my Beloved and I will wander together the face of the earth... [but] you will not understand
the Beloved until you are able to see Him in every animal, every
blade of grass, in every person that is suffering, in every individual."[33]

In this and other talks given at this time, he was now openly denying the
value of all spiritual authority and hierarchy, including that of the Masters
and indeed of Theosophy itself, and encouraging those to whom he spoke to
"break all dependence" on these things. and experience the truth directly within
themselves. However, the inevitable result of this could only be to enhance his
own authority no matter how much he might deny it. Thus he would say:
"No one can give you liberation. You have to find it within but
because I have found, I would show you the way." [34]

Needless to say this marginalising of the Masters was to have a pro-
found effect on Blanca and, indeed, on all Theosophists, and would seriously
undermine the fundamental structure of the Society. However, for the time
being, the organisation, no matter how disturbing his pronouncements, was
still hailing J. Krishnamurti as its Messiah.

Thus these revolutionary rumblings still lay beneath, though quite near
to, the surface, and outwardly Theosophy had reached the peak of its popular-
ity. Krishnamurti had long since attained international celebrity. The press
frequently noted gossip about him and the following May he spoke at the
Hollywood Bowl to an audience of 16,000.

* * *

Huizen Epiphany, 6th January, 1928

Today I heard that Miss E. had been suspended. It gave me a
tremendous shock at first and I thought that I could not go on
existing if such a thing happened to me. Is not participating in this
great spiritual experiment here the only thing that matters? I have
gone into myself and mused about it and found that the Master

---

[33] *The Years of Awakening*, M. Lutyens, p. 268-9.
[34] Ibid, p. 263.

and I are not two but one. He reigns within me and if He ceased to exist in me, I would cease to exist. The outer name of Pupil —if there is an outer side to it at all— means nothing to the supreme fact of this mystical Oneness.

Since the Camp when I was for once stripped of all my little gods, and in darkness, pain and nakedness touched the One Life, nothing can happen to me anymore because I am the Eternal. I can err, I can fall, I can be overwhelmed, I can be blind, I can forget, I can commit crimes, I can be unfaithful to my friends, I can go through agonies —but this all is as nothing to what I truly am. These are only phases defined by time and space, the by-paths into which my erring soul may lose itself —but this has no part in who I really am— it does not belong to Me, for I am Not, I am not a separate self, I am He Who is all.

One night at a Rose Cross service I had another wonderful experience. I knew suddenly, in a flash, that it was foolish to seek the Christ in that little thing that I call myself, that is really less myself than anything else. I knew then that all the people, all the objects in the hall were just as much me, nay —much more than me, than that little thing that sat at the organ. I cannot reproduce now the actual experience of being All, but I know that it is more real than anything else.

Krishnaji [35] has given my liberation. I have seen the vision and there can be no rest until it be fulfilled.

8th April, 1929

More than anything in the world it seems to me that I want to be a perfect woman. I have worried myself out as to what my purpose in life is, music or occultism. After all, I have come to the conclusion that it is neither. It is ideal womanhood.

* * *

On the morning of 2nd August, 1929, at the opening of the Ommen Camp in an atmosphere of great expectation, Krishnamurti with Annie Besant by his side formally dissolved the Order of the Star —the organisation created in 1911 by Mrs. Besant to herald the coming of the World Teacher— of which Krishnamurti was the head. This was not completely unexpected and thou-

---

[35] Krishnamurti.

sands of Theosophists around the world anxiously awaited his pronouncement.

In his epic speech to the huge crowd of Theosophists that had gathered there he said: "I maintain that Truth is a pathless land, and you cannot approach it by any path whatsoever, by any religion, by any sect... A belief is purely an individual matter and you cannot, must not, organise it... Of what use is it to have thousands [of followers] who do not understand, who are fully embalmed in prejudice, who do not want the new but would translate the new to suit their own sterile, stagnant selves?... Because I am free, unconditioned, whole... I desire those who seek to understand me to be free, not to follow me, not to make out of me a cage which will become a religion... Again you have the idea that only certain people hold the key to the Kingdom of Happiness... No one has the authority to hold that key. That key is your own self." [36]

* * *

Huizen, 8th August, 1929

Two years ago I eagerly took in the first rays of the sun. Last year I burned myself, but this year I have become a volcano. Life is stirring so strongly in me that I am afraid of bursting whatever I touch.

9th August, 1929

This morning during church I got absolutely clear. There is no choice; there is only one way or rather there is no way. We are in the fire and we have got to burn whether it hurts or not. It's no use trying to avoid it because there is only that.

16th August, 1929

I know now without the shadow of a doubt that I am never going to take part in a church service again.

17th August, 1929

The ritual of the future is going to be collective self-expression without a set frame, but merely with a keynote that will be expressed by each person in his own way.

---

[36] *Years of Awakening*, p. 293-6

* * *

Krishnamurti's annihilation of Blanca's Theosophical belief structure was to have a devastating effect on her that would take her the best part of the next 20 years to come to terms with (as we shall see). However heroic his uncompromising stance may have been, it caused great distress to his many followers in the organisation that it threatened to shatter. Although Theosophy, which had essentially created him, had no problem in accommodating Krishnamurti's philosophy, which was fundamentally not different from traditional Indian non-dualism that formed the basis for both Vedantic-Upanishadic Hinduism as well as Buddhism, he did not feel that there was any common ground with its hierarchical structure and chain of initiations, etc. Annie Besant, who was deeply devoted to him, emphasised that "only a fragment of the Lord's consciousness manifested itself through K."[37], and that there were many paths that led to the Truth. But he seemed to see with a blinding clarity that had no room for anything other than his own vision and there was no question of other paths.

The devastation felt by loyal Theosophists such as Blanca is summed up by Mary Lutyens in explaining the feelings of her mother who had been like a second mother to Krishnamurti since he first left India: "...for Lady Emily and others like her, there were to be years of desolation ahead. They had been prepared to leave their homes, forsake their husbands, neglect their children, and work themselves to the breaking point for the Lord both before and after his Coming, and now it seemed he had no need of them."[38]

---

[37] Ibid., p. 288
[38] Ibid., p. 301

II - Ramana Maharshi

When we next meet up with Blanca, almost thirteen years have gone by. She is now a mature woman of thirty-seven and has been living and teaching for the last seven years at Krishnamurti's school on the outskirts of Benares, at Rajghat, situated in a beautiful pastoral spot on the Ganges. The school, which was influenced by Maria Montessori (who also came to India in connection with Theosophy), was originally intended to be a sort of experimental community where students and teachers lived together according to Krishnamurti's philosophy. Blanca had also established herself as a successful classical pianist, frequently performing on All India Radio which was to offer her the job of director of European Music, a considerable position at that time.

In early 1930 she had returned to Vienna from Huizen, Krishnamurti having shaken to the roots her faith in Theosophy and its Masters. Her once wealthy father had been ruined in the great depression of 1929, like so many others, and in general the city was on the verge of anarchy. It must have been hard for her to find work as a piano teacher and performer and the next five years would be a difficult and depressing time for Blanca. Nazism and anti-semitism were on the rise, and she no doubt jumped at the chance offered her in 1935 to return to India as a teacher at the recently opened Rajghat school. But it was a very sad farewell that she bid her father, grandmother, relatives and friends, most of whom would be betrayed into Hitler's gas chambers. But, of course, such a thing was utterly inconceivable when she left.

Through following Krishnamurti, Blanca was wrenched from the religious structure and spiritual community of Theosophy (although as the Theosophical avatar Krishnamurti could never really escape the continued adulation of many in that movement). But 'J.K.' (as she generally refers to him from here on) had shown her clearly that this was at best a comforting illusion.

In his discourses with his followers Krishnamurti advocated a self-analysis and reflection wherein the discursive mind is profoundly stilled and from this stillness spontaneously arises a more fundamentally authhentic level of consciousness. If Blanca were serious in her quest for this deeper Reality, she had to be prepared to die to all her past conditioning in order to be alive to that to which he pointed to with such overwhelming charisma and eloquence. With great seriousness and intensity Krisnamurti attempted to jolt the mind of those who sought his guidance into a state of direct cognition beyond the conditioned ego. She found his ideas irresistible and inspiring, and she heroically tried to give her life to his teachings just as she had to Theosophy. But ultimately, although she was extremely devoted to him, she found Krishnamurti's way impossible to follow.

In her diary entry for 1ˢᵗ October, 1945 Blanca refers to the last time she saw Krishnamurti at his school in Rishi Valley, South India in 1939 [1]: "I had to leave... because I knew I should break or go mad if I continued to follow J.K. and yet it still holds me." Both the teachings and, particularly, the man continued to exert a profoundly seductive fascination on her mind which is the source of one of her principle conflicts throughout the diaries. But there was something fundamentally flawed for her in the way that his teachings were stated with such compelling authority, rejecting all approaches other than his own; yet he refused all responsibility for those who followed him. He encouraged them to have essentially free and experimental life-styles but gave very few guidelines other than to reject all outer authority. This complete lack of outer structure plus Krishnamurti's increasing inacessibility (brought about by his self imposed exile in America throughout much of the 1930's and 40's) created a profound state of spiritual unfulfillment in Blanca for which she held him responsible. As she acquired a deeper understanding of the ancient culture of her adopted homeland, she could not help but note the apparent hypocrisy of his scorn of the great Indian spiritual tradition of which he himself was essentially a product (but about which he professed to know practically nothing), and this was particularly upsetting to Blanca later on when she felt that it was his arrogance in this regard that

---

[1] She would not meet him again until his return to India at the beginning of 1949.

blinded him to the profundity of the great Hindu masters with whom she was to have close contact.

Although at times she feels that the problem lies within herself rather than with Krishnamurti, she nevertheless felt the need for more compelling inspiration and guidance than he was able to give her. As Blanca became more aware of the futility of the attempts she and her colleagues at Rajghat school were making to create a community based on his teachings, she became ever more aware of the profound wealth of the dynamic spiritual culture of her adopted homeland.

Thus, in 1942, she made a daring break with the highly westernised, insulated world of Theosophy and Krishnamurti, and sought guidance from the great South Indian Mahatma, Ramana Maharshi, at his ashram on the slopes of Arunachala, the sacred mountain of Shiva, about 100 kilometres south-east of Madras. This was a leap into the unknown —the real India!

* * *

Sri Ramana Maharshi [2] is one of the most renowned and respected Hindu sages of modern times. He was born in 1880 to Brahmin parents and led a normal life until the age of 16. Then suddenly one day, while alone in his room, he was seized with the certainty that he was dying. Although at first afraid, he began to detachedly observe and analyse what was going on. In his own words: *"I said to myself mentally: 'Now death has come. What does it mean? Who is it that is dying? This body dies... but I am still very much aware of the full force of my personality. So what I call 'I' must be pure spirit transcending the body. The material body dies, but the spirit or the True Self cannot be touched by death. I am therefore 'That'. This was not a feat of intellectual gymnastics but came as a flash of living truth. Fear of death vanished at once and forever. This total absorption in the Self has continued uninterruptedly from that moment on."* [3]

Six weeks later he secretly left his home in the South Indian temple town of Madurai and made his way to the sacred mountain of Arunachala, worshipped for thousands of years as an in-

[2] Maharshi = *Maha Rishi* —great sage.

[3] *Sri Ramana, the Sage of Arunachala,* Aksharajna, p. 29. Published by Sri Ramanasramam.

carnation of Shiva, situated near the town of Tiruvannamalai. Upon arriving there he threw away whatever money and few possessions he had with him and abandoned himself to absorption in *samadhi*, a state of ecstatic oneness in which the individual personality dissolves into the infinite ocean of pure Being —the ALL. He remained immersed in this state of absolute silence for several years, completely oblivious to his physical well-being while staying at different places on the great hill of Arunachala. Gradually serious aspirants came to him for guidance and he began to instruct them, first through writing and later by speaking.[4] In time, as his fame spread, a community of seekers arose around him. From 1932 onwards, partly as a result of a popular book written by Paul Brunton entitled *A Search in Secret India* in which the Maharshi, as he was now known, figured prominently, Westerners began to seek him out.

Although, like Krishnamurti, Ramana Maharshi maintained that the ultimate Reality could only be known when the mind was utterly still and one's innermost being stood revealed, he had none of the cynical rejection of devotional and yogic approaches to meditation which characterised Krishnamurti and which Blanca found disturbing. In fact he considered certain yogic practices such as *japa* (repetition of a *mantra*, or *pranayama* (control of the breath through various exercises), as useful aids to the stilling of the mind as long as the correct perspective was maintained.[5] In this he was solidly within the mainstream of modern Hinduism, particularly the ancient tradition of *jnana* (wisdom), of which he was such a shining exemplar.

* * *

Ramanashram, Tiruvannamalai, 17th May, 1942

I left Benares on the 10th May. As the train approached Tiruvannamalai, I suddenly felt blissfully happy, thinking: "Now all struggle is over, there will be only peace. The prodigal son has returned to his father's house." After some time this passed.

---

[4] He always maintained however that his primary teaching was through silence (see *Be As You Are. The Teachings of Sri Ramana Maharshi*, David Godman, pp. 2-3.)

[5] See *Be As You Are. The Teachings of Sri Ramana Maharshi*, Godman, op. cit.

Upon arriving, my first reaction was to run away. The ashramites and the prostrations and adoration of the Guru seem all mad to me.

I wrote a letter to Ramana Maharshi asking him to straighten the twists in me. In his presence there is a deep peace, the same that I have felt ever since I decided to come here. But I am still saturated with Theosophy and J.K. and that conditions my attitude. Whatever happens I am influenced by what J.K. says. I have no freedom, that is my standard. I criticise others, considering myself far above them. I am terribly important. Isn't that part of the twist?

One thing seems sure, one can't get things suddenly or quickly, but only through patience, through experimenting and daring to risk one's happiness. Nobody can help one to attain Realisation otherwise.

26th May, 1942

Yesterday afternoon while sitting in the hall, the question of sex arose in my mind totally uninvited. At first this disturbed me but then I felt like meditating to get to the root of it and shut my eyes. It suddenly came to me to direct the energy from the sacrum up the spinal cord and let it stream out through the head in adoration. I did this and it relieved the strain at once. I went on doing it at intervals and before going to sleep.

At about 12.30 a.m. I woke up and had a strange experience, which I cannot put into words. It was not imagination and seemed beyond the mind altogether, but I was wide awake. I realised a fiery 'being' of terrific power without form of any kind and I understood what it is that one worships and why people prostrate in front of the Maharshi. It has nothing to do with him as I see him daily, but it seemed to be simultaneously him, God and also myself. What I usually call myself was ridiculous at that moment, so petty and insignificant —as was also the body of the Maharshi. I could not imagine that I would ever be the same hereafter. This state was very real. I was wide awake for hours and it persisted for sometime. The song: "Holy Lord, God Almighty... Casting down their golden crowns" —but I can't remember the whole anymore— came into my mind and I was consumed in adoration. I felt like writing down what I had perceived, or like reading

Tolstoy's *Gospel*.[6] I felt that now I shall understand. But I was too lazy. In the morning I could not recall or reproduce the experience. I only remembered what I had thought about it.

Later however I thought: "What is the value of such an experience if it does not carry over into my relationship with other people?" I am used to judging everything by that. This experience seems to have nothing to do with my ordinary self. How strange.

30th May, 1942

Last night I walked round the hill of Arunachala in the full moon with a *sadhu*, Premanand Saraswati, who I discovered had been an active Theosophist for 14 years. The hill has such a powerful magical presence. I'm told it has been worshipped as an emanation of the god Shiva for thousands of years. The traditional form of receiving its blessing is to walk around it, which took us nearly four hours. What a wonderful experience! The day before this I had the *darshan* of a *sadhu* living near Annamalai Tank, where Parvati [Shiva's wife] is supposed to have been immersed in penance for 1000 years.

It seems to me that I must put myself wholeheartedly into this atmosphere while I am here. So far I have mostly resisted and compared. I am all the time frightened to go away from J.K. and get caught here. But it is so silly. Whenever I read only a little of his talks I get upset.

3rd June, 1942

Today I asked Sri Ramana:

"In one of the books of your dialogues you say that such thoughts as: 'Is this a good thing to do or is that', should not be allowed. How can one live and decide without such considerations?"

He replied: *"If you surrender to the Supreme Will, there will be no question of decision or choice."*

Question: But I don't know the Supreme Will. I do not know to whom to surrender. How do I know the Supreme? I may deceive myself.

---

[6] Like many of her generation Tolstoy's more spiritual writings were a great inspiration for her from early adolescence on.

Bhagavan Ramana Maharshi (photo Sri Ramanasramam)

Answer: *It is the mind that deceives itself. At least you must admit that you exist. Either you accept the Supreme or at least you inquire as to the true nature of your Self. Who are you? Knowing or not knowing belongs to the mind and therefore all your so-called 'knowledge' is really ignorance. You identify yourself with the mind and that is the cause of the confusion. Enquire more deeply into the true nature of your individuality (i.e. Who is it that possesses a mind?). If you perceive that in fact, the mind does not exist at all, then it will vanish along with the confusion, and what truly is will stand revealed. When you look at your reflection in the water and believe it to be an accurate representation of yourself, then you are troubled when the movement of the water disturbs the reflection. But when you realise that this has no reality to it, then your worries cease. You cannot get rid of your shadow, but you need not believe that it is who you really are.*

Question: I feel as if I were two and not one.

Answer: *No, there is only the Self, there cannot be two. But if you focus only on the form of the bangle, you may forget that it is made of gold [7]. Yet the form of the bangle is dependent on the gold. It cannot exist without it and ceases to exist when the gold is melted down; but the gold itself remains constant. By deluding yourself into identifying solely with the mind, you deny your true Self. This is worse than suicide, because there you only kill the body; but here you are murdering the Self. Seek the Self and the ego will vanish.*

By solving one mind-created problem you only create new ones.

When you cut off one leaf, four new ones sprout out. Only by killing the root of the tree, can you prevent the leaves from growing.

Later:

There is nothing for me but Krishnaji. He is my prison. Not understanding him and having thrown away everything else, I have made him into my God and my chains. Bhagavan [8] helps me to understand J.K. but his way cannot satisfy me. Shall I ignore my dilemma by simply looking the other way? No, face the devil and he cannot bear your gaze. For me there is only one thing: love — and till it comes? Perhaps gazing at the Self.

---

[7] This is a classical Vedantic analogy.

[8] A respectful term meaning 'Lord' often given to Hindu holy men. It was one of the names by which followers of Ramana Maharshi often referred to him.

6th June, 1942

Faith is not beyond reason. If I reason it out, the only thing I know for sure is that 'I' am alive, I exist, and this 'I' is something that is ultimately beyond the limitations of the body, mind, time and space. That is faith. If I am truly alive, then everything else must be also. We forget this all the time. One must remind oneself of it constantly. That is surrender. Let the mind dwell on this fact and it will get enlightened and lose its pride.

My life is only love. But romantic entanglements, no matter how well intentioned, invariably degenerate into self-love —identification with body and mind. Forgetting that 'I' am truly alive, and being centred in the mind and body only, keeps me in a state of separation and ignorance. The moment I realise the cause of the confusion and drop what prevents me from truly loving, i.e. this false identification, then the mind created separation will go and with it the problem.

This is what I have to thrash out here through and through and then I shall know how to live. This was the purpose of my journey to Arunachala.

"*Self-Realisation*". Copied from "Crumbs from his Table" by Ramananda Sivarnagiri:

Disciple: Can I get knowledge of the Self, i.e. can I experience direct realisation of the Self?

Bhagavan: *Who is there without a knowledge of the Self? Everyone has experience of the Self.*

Disciple: But I don't realise it.

Bhagavan: *The fact is, that you are always in the state of knowing the Self. How can self not know the Self. Only you have got into the habit of thinking that you are this, that and the other. It is this wrong notion that produces and constitutes viparita bhavana* [false sense of separateness], *and that is why you say you do not know the Self.*

Disciple: How to get rid of this *viparita bhavana*? Can any ordinary man get rid of it? If so, how?

Bhagavan: *Yes. So many ways —Bhakti, Karma, Jñana Yoga, etc.*[9] *But the main way is simple.*

---

[9] The Yogas of devotion, of selfless service, and of wisdom.

Bhagavan Ramana Maharshi seated in front of the sacred
mountain of Arunachala (photo Sri Ramanasramam)

Disciple: But I am ignorant of the method and of the Self.

Bhagavan: *Who is ignorant of what? Ask the question and pursue the enquiry as to who it is that is said to be ignorant. Once you put the question, and begin to probe into the nature of the 'I', the 'I' disappears; then what survives is Self-Knowledge or Self-Realisation.*

Disciple: But how to get at that? Is not a Guru's help needed? Is not God's help needed?

Bhagavan: *Why? These are all only the means to the end. But once the goal is reached, the methods used to get there are found to be the goal in themselves. The Guru turns out ultimately to be God and God turns out to be your own real Self.*

Disciple: But is not Guru's or God's grace necessary for one's progress in this Enquiry?

Bhagavan: *Yes. But the very vichara* [enquiry] *that you are making is actually the Guru's grace or God's grace itself.*

Disciple: I would request you to bless me with your Grace.

Bhagavan: *You go on with your enquiry.*

Disciple: How? I do not know how to proceed.

Bhagavan: *Who does not know how to proceed? You say 'I' and yet you do not know 'I'. Can anyone be ignorant of himself? Is not that ludicrously impossible? If there is something else to be attained or known, then you may feel difficulty in attaining it. But in the case of the ever-present, inescapable 'I', how can you be ignorant of it? You have constantly to find out and get rid of your false notions of 'I', one after another. Do that.*

Disciple: In that, is not a Guru's help necessary and useful?

Bhagavan: *Yes, to start your enquiry. But you yourself must pursue your enquiry.*

Disciple: To what extent can I rely on Guru's grace in this? Up to what point is the enquiry itself to be carried on?

Bhagavan: *You must carry on this demolition of wrong identification by enquiry till your last false notion is destroyed —till the Self is realised.*

Disciple: How can I help others?

Bhagavan: *Who is there for you to help? Who is the 'I' that is to help others? First clear that point and then everything settles itself.... "*

9th June, 1942

My mistake was that I wanted to understand J.K.'s teaching, rather than J.K., and was trying to do this with my mind. This is exactly the wrong way round. On top of that, I identify myself with the mind. I love myself, i.e. the mind, and therefore get more and more imprisoned in mental constructs and become self-centered, so that I can't really love others. By living in His presence continually, the mind is bound to become clarified.

If one lives completely in the present, one cannot hold any theories, opinions. So you can only live in the present when all these concepts which constitute the mind are destroyed.

10th June, 1942

The mind itself is not the illusion, but rather the mind that sees itself as separate. Culture is being sensitive to the awareness of who one is and who others are.

This evening Mrs. Sujata Sen took Miss M. and me to see 'Shiva-Shiva' Sadhu. He lives in the woods near Durga Seva Ashram in a tiny house of stone near a pond. He has not spoken a word for twelve years. He looks like God. What eyes, what a smile, what a face! Body tall and thin. I went into ecstasy straight away. I remember the Theosophical saying about the Master K.H.: "In his holy Presence every wish fades away except the one to be like him". I could sit and look at his face for all eternity. That is bliss.

14th June, 1942

That *sadhu* lived in a small cave for seven years and came out only once a month. He is so beautiful. I am always afraid to let go of the world and yet the beauty I seek is only an expression of the Supreme Reality that is not of this world. I play the piano, not for the sound in itself, which can even be ugly on a piano that is out of tune, but for the hidden something that I contact through it. Yet I cling to the world. Again the confusion of the mind that will not give up its 'knowledge' which is actually ignorance.

From "*Maha Yoga*" [10]:

"*The world is real, but not as we see it —like the rope mistaken for the snake, like dreams and like a mirage in a waste land.*

---

[10] A book of Ramana's sayings.

"Mere theoretical knowledge can never dissolve this world of appearance; only the actual Experience of the Self can do so."

15ᵗʰ June, 1942

'I' don't really see anything, it is habit that sees. I don't know anything for myself and until I do everything is dead. What a strange thing to discover! How exciting life becomes when one begins to think for oneself, to question everything, to try and find out about everything that one has taken for granted — like a child, coming to everything new. Who would still want to go to the cinema or to any amusement when he has got this eternal amusement within himself all the time?

16ᵗʰ June, 1942

Meditation on Hitler. Who is Hitler? I hold Hitler in my heart and keep still.

Hitler must not be killed. He must be turned round and made to see. Hitler is creative power turned downward. His God is Race. Why does he want to kill the Jews?

Our whole civilisation is based on the fallacy of looking at the world from the wrong end —from the outside material standpoint and not from the spiritual centre. Hitler's function is to destroy this. He is the match that lights the funeral pyre and burns itself up in the process.

17ᵗʰ June, 1942

Question: When I asked you how to solve the problems of life, you said 'self-surrender'. How can one surrender without danger until Self-Realisation has been achieved, as the mind may create its own God to surrender to? The most cruel things in the world are done in the name of God.

Maharshi: *The mind and all of its creations come from the same source. Self-inquiry and self-surrender are the same. As you proceed in Self-inquiry you automatically surrender (as you become nearer to the Divine Source). The person that surrenders to a mind-created God will have to bear the consequences of his actions and suffer for them. But even the thought of God, however false, will take you to the Supreme Truth of the Self ultimately. The man who has realised knows that the thought of a separate God is utterly false. But until then one cannot help it. When you are totally still, you are the Self. When we think, we are forgetting God. Self-inquiry leads back to Him (who is none other than the Self).*

Question: Ultimately, but it may take a long time!

Maharshi: *There is no time, you may have it even now.*

Someone else's question: If the Self is one, why is it necessary to approach a Guru?

Maharshi: *In reality it is not necessary, but because we are dreaming on the physical plane, the presence of the realised man is necessary to wake us up — to remind us of ourselves. When the proud elephant dreams that a lion comes, he gets a shock and wakes up suddenly. As we are all dreaming, the help of the Guru, within this dream, is necessary in order to force us to wake up. The eyes of the Guru disperse the dream.*

Question: The physical eyes?

Maharshi: *There are only 'eyes', not physical or otherwise.*

Miss Merston's question: From where does the 'resolve' come to start the Self-inquiry?

Maharshi: *From the mind, like all other thoughts. But by having only one single thought, this thought finally also gets absorbed. You need not follow your thoughts, the more you think the more thoughts there will be. But rather take each thought back to its source; that is surrender and enquiry at the same time.*

It is not Theosophy that twisted me, or J.K. that broke me by tearing me away from it. The twist in my mind, which has caused this powerful false identification with the physical rather than with the True Self, began much earlier — either in my childhood or else I was born with it. But Theosophy did nothing, or nothing fundamental, to clear this error. The centre was merely shifted from one thing to the other within the dream of life. The shock which J.K. gave me was so great that I was knocked out completely for these 14 years; but what does it matter.

Maharshi told how he tried to get away from the Ashram and food and so went into the woods for a day, but he met so many devotees and was offered so much food that he was worse off than before.

Questioner: Why are you unable to refuse when others prevail on you for this or that? Are you not free of *karma* and therefore able to do as you like?

Maharshi: *There are 3 types of karma :*
(1) Made by one's own actions and desires.
(2) Inevitable karma like Government (world circumstances beyond your personal control).
(3) The karma of others taken on himself by the man who is free of his own karma.
Questioner: Is it like Christ, who suffers for the sins of others?
Maharshi: *Yes. There is no freedom, it is merely a word.* (i.e. even Christ or the Realised Saint, still must fulfil his destiny outwardly —although inwardly he is fully liberated).

18th June, 1942

We went to see Shiva-Shiva Sadhu again. I asked him whether he knew Kallahali *Mudra* [an esoteric yogic discipline], being a Malayalam. He declined disgustedly. Then he drew a circle on the ground with a dot at the centre and rays coming out from it like the spokes of a wheel, and said: "All the rays represent different ways, but I remain in the centre. All letters are derived from 'OM' only. Dwell in that."

All knowledge is in his eyes, eyes that have gazed only within for years, not seeing the sun except once a month. That is the whole secret. And we fools think air, sun, freedom of movement etc. are necessary for health and mental development when in reality it is only God that we need and nothing else.

20th June, 1942

Walked round Arunachala by myself. Wherever we may go, whatever we may do, as long as we move within the mind, what is the use? What we need is a "shock" to push us out of that vicious circle. A shock of beauty, a shock of pain, any shock. J.K. gives the greatest shocks. Even nature seems merely an escape that gives me only a momentary satisfaction. The longer I am here, the smaller I get. When shall I stop existing altogether? Wish I could burn up soon.

21st June, 1942

The mind forgets its own Nature in activity.
This evening I went to see Skandashram,[11] Virupaksha cave

---

[11] The place where Ramana Maharshi lived for many years, further up on the hill.

and some other caves where the Maharshi lived. What an atmosphere at Skandashram. I was very deeply moved on entering these caves where such great beings have received illumination. They are awesome. The yogis and mahatmas live here without air, sun, water, food, books, art, nature, clothes; and we make millions of people sweat to provide the 'necessities' of life. And then we complain that there are Hitlers and misery and war. In a glimpse I saw the whole madness of our lives. And then we have the cheek to talk about God, profundity and to criticise the Maharshi and others who <u>know</u>, when we haven't even done with the mere surface of life. We think ourselves superior in our sophisticated nescience and look down on the simple coolie, who has at least the sense to humble and prostrate himself before such a sublime being.

22ⁿᵈ June, 1942

A *sadhu* came today and sang hymns to Subramaniam [12]. He is one of the oldest devotees of the Maharshi and famous for his songs. He looks ridiculously like the statues of Ganesh [the elephant-headed son of Shiva], beard tied in a knot and tummy enormous. Most uncanny. He brought his whole family with babies to act as the chorus. It was like a fairytale, Arabian nights.

24ᵗʰ June, 1942

On the 22ⁿᵈ evening Sujata took us to a strange temple in the wild jungle. I had decided to climb up on Arunachala the next day, but had no one to go with. Pathak turned up in the evening unexpectedly with a local boy, so we went together the next morning —then on to Skandashram for two hours; after that we visited Shiva-Shiva Sadhu who taught us how to coordinate our breath in conjunction with meditation on *Om*. In the evening Merston read me a letter from Gerald Heard [13] to Sorrenson [14], where he mentions that writing is his trade, but his central activity is six hours of meditation daily. He is writing a book *Man, the Master*. He also says that Aldous Huxley and Krishnaji like each other

[12] A popular South Indian god, son of Shiva.
[13] British author and philosopher of the period, a close friend of Christopher Isherwood, Aldous Huxley, and Krishnamurti.
[14] An eccentric Danish *sadhu* who called himself Sunya Baba. See intr. to chap. III.

very much, but J.K. still will not have anything to do with methods and Huxley leans more toward Heard. Heard envies Sorrenson
his Himalayan retreat and says J.K. would also prefer India and
silence, but has chosen the U.S.A. and words instead.

25th June, 1942

Yesterday my old agony of restlessness returned, and with
it my fear of being caught here and of losing J.K. (is he my possession?!). I had back-ache, head-ache and tummy-ache and utter misery. It all came from reading a few lines by J.K. and also
seeing Shiva-Shiva Sadhu and feeling frightened that the Ashram
might find out and not approve. This in turn made me resentful
at feeling somewhat bound. But this morning I suddenly got back
my peace after deciding to talk to Bhagavan and to ask him why
I can't get rid of my egotistical resistance. As I asked him the
question tears came. The answer was: "*Take the resistance into your
heart [15] and keep it there*". I have to do everything from the heart.
Let the heart see, hear, think, speak, eat, sleep —everything—
and not do anything else. Though I do not know the Lord of my
Heart, whoever He is, I must surrender to him and leave all else.
It is very difficult to do in practice. I am still not clear about J.K.
and until I am I won't have any peace. I shall take him into my
heart and will clear this problem by the time I leave. That is the
real reason for my visit.

From the *Ashtavakra Gita* [16]: "*When the mind is freed from such
pairs of opposites as 'this is done' and 'this is not done' it becomes
indifferent to religious merit, worldly prosperity, desire for sensual enjoyment and for liberation.*

*The one who abhors sense-objects avoids them, and one who cov-
ets them becomes attached to them. But he who does not accept or reject, is neither unattached nor attached.*

*He who has an egoistic feeling even towards liberation and con-
siders even the body as his own, is neither a jnani nor a yogi. He only
suffers misery.*"

---

[15] For Ramana Maharshi the heart was the seat of the Self —the absolute unchanging Reality of non-dual awareness.

[16] A classic advaitic text attributed to the semi-mytholgical sage Ashtavakra.

26th June, 1942

Krishnaji [17], as I know him, is my own creation. I have not understood him with my heart. I did what I thought he had asked me to do, but he himself refuted it. Then what am I afraid to lose? What I have never had? And perhaps when my imaginary image of him is lost, the reality might take its place.

27th June, 1942

Upon reading King Janaka's story in the *Ashtavakra Gita* about how the Rishi Ashtavakra taught him Self-realisation after Janaka had accepted him as his Guru and surrendered completely to him, a sudden surrender to the Maharshi arose in me spontaneously and his outer form vanished.

I feel more and more that Madras (which is so much closer to Ramana) will be better for me to live in than Delhi. The company of the Wise, whilst we are yet ignorant, is the most precious thing to seek.

Rajghat, 3rd July, 1942

On the 28th —last day at Tiruvannamalai— I wanted to know how I should live after leaving there. The answer came in the form of an experience in which the Maharshi's head suddenly seemed to go inside me and he said: "You, ego, get out. I am now dictator here and whatever I tell you, you have to do. Not a breath without my order. I am your Self until you have realised It". To my own surprise I loved the dictator. That is what I have always wanted. I am going to cling to him every moment and I shan't rest till he has absorbed the last atom of me. Then I shall again be where I want to be —with J.K! That's the great mystery.

In the train my thoughts stayed in Tiruvannamalai. When the train crossed the bridge, Mother Ganges told me a secret: You will not always be with the Maharshi.

---

[17] Affectionate name for Krishnamurti.

III - Benares

*"Benares is older than History,
older than tradition, older even than legend"* [1]

Mark Twain

Benares is one of the oldest continuously inhabited cities on earth and has an unbroken cultural continuity going back almost 3,000 years. It is the sacred city of Shiva and anyone dying within its confines is guaranteed Liberation by Him. The ritual worship and bathing in the Ganges go on there today much as they have for millenniums, although when Blanca was there in the 1930's and 40's it must have been far more pristine than the squalid over-crowded noisy place it is today. But even now when one sits by the river or walks through the old town with its labyrinth of narrow winding lanes it is easy to experience its timeless sanctity. The German traveller and philosopher, Count Herman Keyserling, writing a generation before Blanca described it thus:

"Benares is holy. Europe, grown superficial, hardly understands such truths anymore... I feel nearer here than I have ever done to the heart of the world; here I feel every day as if soon, perhaps even to-day, I would receive the grace of supreme revelation... The atmosphere of devotion which hangs above the river is improbable in its strength; stronger than in any church that I have ever visited." [2]

The Rajghat school, where Blanca was to live and work for almost 20 years, is located about 5 miles north of town at a particularly beautiful spot on 200 acres of land overlooking the Ganges. The ancient pilgrims' path to Sarnath, the deer park where the Buddha gave his first sermon after his enlightenment in the 6th Century B.C., runs through the grounds which are strewn with the ruins of temples and fragments of statues —all that remains of the ancient city of Kashi, as Benares was called in its earlier incarnations. Krishnamurti was particularly taken with

---

[1] Mark Twain, *Following the Equator*, p. 496

[2] Count Herman Keyserling, *India Travel Diary of a Philosopher* pp. 118-22, (as quoted in *Benares, City of Light*, Diana Eck, p.17).

the beauty of the place and wrote: *"This path is a very ancient way; many thousands have trodden it, and it was rich in tradition and silence. It wandered among fields and mangoes, tamarinds and deserted shrines..."* [3]

Benares has always been a magnet for India's wandering holy men as well as learned pandits. In Blanca's day a small international community of intellectuals, artists, and spiritual seekers had sprung up there. The British Raj was still very much in control in India (although, after the war, their hold on power would quickly unravel) and this crowd of sophisticated Western Indophiles and would-be Hindus must have been quite an enigma to them.

The uncrowned king of this new caste was the French Indologist, musician and aesthete, Alain Daniélou, who together with his close companion, Raymond Burnier, inhabited a massive 18th Century palace on the Ganges in the old city. Daniélou wrote numerous books on Indian religion and culture and was particularly instrumental in introducing Indian Classical music in the West. He was an accomplished pianist and a serious student of the *veena* which he studied under a renowned master in Benares for many years. He was particularly proud of having received initiation from a famous ultra-orthodox swami and this he felt, aided by his fluency in several Indian languages, gave him a unique perspective on Indian culture. Not far from Daniélou lived the Swiss painter and patron of Indian Arts, Alice Boner, who was highly influential in the rediscovery and popularization of classical Indian dance as well as being an authority on Hindu Temple architecture. They were part of an elite and hearty group of adventurous western cultural explorers who immersed themselves in the richness of this ancient Hindu city and its great spiritual tradition. This could not be done in a classroom, but only by becoming attuned to Hindu sensibilities and etiquette, and by being prepared to abandon what was seen by the Indians as arrogant and barbaric western attitudes and customs. Only then could one hope to be allowed even partial entrance into this vast, profound, but carefully guarded heritage.

---

[3] From *Commentaries on Living*, p. 17 as quoted by Mary Luytens in her second volume of her biography of Krishnamurti *Krishnamurti: The Years of Fulfillment*.

Two river views of Benares (photos by Ram Alexander)

One of the most respected of these spiritual adventurers was the Englishman, Ronald Nixon, better known by his Hindu monastic name, Sri Krishna Prem. He had been a fighter pilot during the First World War and after the war had come to India as a professor of English Literature at the University of Lucknow. Like Blanca, he had been influenced by Theosophy early on and had become very interested in Indian spirituality. Imagine his surprise when he discovered that the elegant Bengali wife of the University Chancellor was, in fact, a great mystic. He became her disciple, shaving his head and donning the ochre robes of a renunciate. Ultimately they founded an ashram in the Himalayas where he lived a life of the strictest asceticism.

Other prominent members of this group of foreign scholars and seekers were the German Tibetan Buddhist, Lama Anagarika Govinda, who would later become well known for his books on Tibetan Buddhism and his travels in Tibet; and the eccentric Austrian monk-scholar, Agehananda Bharati, whose story is told in his colourful autobiography, *The Ochre Robe*. Later on Blanca became friends with the young Colin Turnbull, then studying in Benares, who would become one of the most prolific and respected anthropologists of his generation.

There was also the Swiss explorer, Ella Maillart, who in search of ancient silk roads crossed the Gobi desert through China and into Tibet and India in the 1930's as related in her book *Forbidden Journey*. She would cross Blanca's path in Benares on a visit to her friend and *gurubhai* [4], the English poet Lewis Thompson, who was to play an extremely important role in Blanca's life.

On her annual migration to the Himalayas in the summer of 1943, a ritual journey made by almost all Europeans living in India at that time to escape the heat of the plains, Blanca had her first meeting with Anandamayee Ma at the insistence of her friend, the Danish *sadhu*, Sorrenson —better known as Shunya Baba. Shunya Baba was quite a character who dressed in rather shabby Indian *kurta* and pyjama with a kind of turban that made him look more like a coolie rather than a European Sahib. Wherever he went he was accompanied by his inseparable companion, a little Tibetan dog named Wuji (the name roughly translates as

---

[4] Literally, 'guru brother', i.e. a fellow disciple of the same teacher.

'Honorable Emptiness'), whom he was convinced was the reincarnation of a fallen mahatma. When I met him at his home in the
Himalayas near the town of Almora in 1976, he told me that he
had originally come to India in 1922 at the invitation of the Nobel
Prize winning poet, Rabindranath Tagore. He had met Tagore
while working as a gardener in England when the latter asked
him to come and "teach mysticism" at Shanti Niketan —his experimental university in Bengal. He told me that although he had
been 'a natural mystic' since childhood, he only fully realized
this when, upon meeting Ramana Maharshi, Ramana said to him:
"We have always been aware, haven't we, you and I". This pro-
voked a deep and lasting realization in him and Blanca knew
enough to pay attention when he urged her to meet Anandamayee
Ma as she relates in Chapter IV.

Krishnamurti spent the war years in relative seclusion in California at his retreat at Ojai where his influence was felt by a
number of leading artists and intellectuals, particularly Aldous
Huxley who became a close friend. But the absence of his dynamic inspiration had caused the quality of the Rajghat school to
deteriorate [5]. It was not the progressive, idyllic educational community originally envisioned by him. Although Blanca had close
friends there and loved the beauty of the place, she felt the community's general stagnation and was ripe for a change. As she
says in many places, her life is nothing if not an intense spiritual
search, and she could never be satisfied in any environment that
did not provide ample scope for this quest.

Thus upon returning to Benares from Tiruvannamalai, she
had the intention of making a clean break with her past and join-
ing the ashram of the Maharshi. She was obviously deeply affected
by her contact with Ramana Maharshi and made a sincere effort
to put into practice what she had learned from him. He had given
her a taste of the real India which made Krishnamurti and Theosophy seem lacking by comparison. However, as it was the middle of the Second World War, her movements were severely re-

---

[5] Today the Rajghat educational complex is one of India's better known educational institutions, comprising a large co-educational primary and secondary school, a woman's college, a farm, an agricultural school and a free hospital which caters to the needs of the many surrounding villages.

stricted by the British authorities and she was unable to get permission to make the move. Being Austrian she was technically an enemy alien in British India, but she seems to have been treated quite leniently, no doubt because she was Jewish. In this she fared far better than Lama Govinda who spent several years in a British detention camp in North India.

* * *

Rajghat, Benares, 3rd July, 1942

At 12 p.m. walking from the station to Rajghat I felt stronger than ever the terrific peace of this place. It is quite equal to Tiruvannamalai. There Daniélou was right. In the morning I had a short note from Kitty about the job in Jaipur. It was like a slap in my face. The whole mess of our relationship came up. I wrote to her in the afternoon and cried so hard I could hardly breathe.

* * *

Throughout her years in India Blanca remained close to her friend Kitty whom she had known since her earliest Theosophical days in Vienna. They had come to India together for the Theosophical Convention of 1925 and Kitty had stayed on, eventually marrying into a prominent Theosophical family of South Indian Brahmins. Her husband, Siva Rao (frequently referred as S.R.) was a prominent journalist who later became a member of Parliament. His brother Sanjiva founded the Rajghat School, and anotther brother, Sir B.N. Rao, was one of the framers of tthe Indian Constitution. All tthree, especially Siva Rao, were very close to both Annie Besant and J. Krishnamurti. Through her close friendship with Kitty, Blanca became like a member of this tightly knit family. Kitty and her husband were very much in Krishnamurti's inner circle of followers and were very involved with his educational work as well as other projects in India. Whenever Krishnamurti came to New Delhi, he stayed at their home.

* * *

4th July, 1942

The school is dead and utterly neglected. There is even less life than before.

In the train I met a man who was going to see a pandit at Lucknow who reads one's past and future out of a book [6]. He is to

---

[6] The 'book' referred to here is the *Brighu Samhita,* an ancient astrological text that several pandits in India claim access to. It is written on parchment-like

have said that Russia will be defeated by October and Hitler will die through suicide. The war will end next March. I also met the botanist Sani of Almora on the Madras train. I like Madras.

Delhi, 18th July, 1942

"In ancient times music was something other than mere pleasure for the ear; it was like an algebra of metaphysical abstractions, knowledge of which was given only to initiates, but by the principles of which the masses were instinctively and unconsciously influenced. This is what made music one of the most powerful instruments of moral education, as Confucius had said many centuries before Plato." (G. de Mengel, *Voile d'Isis* [7]) copied from Daniélou's manuscript.

In Benares I heard Basu [8] play the *veena* and tried to listen without preconception. Indian music seems formless in our sense of the word.

Raymond Burnier [9] came to Rajghat of his own accord and then listened every day for an hour to my playing and made suggestions for the radio program.

Rajghat, 24th August, 1942

Reading W.H. Bates, *The Cure of Imperfect Sight by Treatment Without Glasses*: "The physician has continually to struggle against the idea that to do anything well requires effort. This idea is drilled into us from our cradles. The whole educational system is based upon it... It is as natural for the eye to see as it is for the mind to acquire knowledge, and any effort in either case is not only use-

---

leaves which are believed to have been recorded thousands of years ago, and are arranged according to an astrological filing system. When a petitioner arrives, an astrological time chart is drawn up for the moment of his arrival and, ideally, a leaf matching that configuration will be found for him. This will give specific information about his present, past and future, detailing his present problems, what he did in previous lives to bring this about, and what means can be taken —spiritual practices, etc.— to alleviate the problem. Obviously, as the prediction about the war indicates, it is not always accurate.

[7] A journal closely associated with the French 'traditionalist' philosopher, René Guénon.

[8] A famous musician who was Daniélou's teacher.

[9] Wealthy Swiss photographer and aesthete who lived with Daniélou and later married Radha Shastri, the current president of the Theosophical Society.

less but defeats the end in view. The mind, when it remembers one thing better than all other things, possesses central fixation, and its efficiency is thereby increased, just as the efficiency of the eye is increased by central fixation. In other words, the mind attains its greatest efficiency when at rest and it is never at rest unless one thing is remembered better than all other things."

Rajghat 8th November, 1942

S.R.[10] says there may be a possibility of my becoming Director of European Music in Delhi, if I pursue the matter. My first impulse was to write: "Please pursue the matter very seriously", but I decided not to write until I had slept over it. I spent a fairly sleepless night and now have begun to ponder over it and wonder what to do. It is not really what I want. But it is understood that I cannot get *that* straight away. It is good for me to learn to deal with people. But also I want to be near the Maharshi. That job hardly ever gives a holiday. The real attraction is my friends in Delhi. By getting what I have been so keenly desiring, will the desire finally be satiated? Or is there another method: to see the underlying Reality so that then all attachment and desire are seen for what they really are —mere illusion.

* * *

At this point there is a break in the diaries of over two years and it is not known if they are lost or whether they were destroyed by Blanca. In any case there seems to have been a fairly predictable continuity in her life during this period and one can piece together some details based on passing references she makes later on. She remained at her job teaching at the Rajghat school and continued her radio performances. Undoubtedly her commitment to the spiritual quest remained paramount as it did throughout her life. During this period she had what was for her a very important relationship with a man referred to only as 'X'. From other sources we know that he was a prominent Indian, very much in Krishnamurti's elite inner circle. As often happens, since she was unable to possess the unpossessable teacher, her affections were transferred to someone particularly close to him. In any case, they parted company by the time we next meet up with her.

---

[10] Siva Rao, Kitty Rao's husband. Throughout the diary she refers to him as S.R.

It was during this time that her first meetings with Anandamayee Ma occurred and that Lewis Thompson came to stay at Rajghat school — events that will be dealt with in the next chapter.

* * *

"To speak of one's emotions without fear or moral ambition, to come out from under the shadow of other men's minds, to forget their needs, to be utterly oneself, that is all the muses care for." (Yeats)

12th February, 1945

Dreamt of J.K. There were five people with him including myself, and J.K. said to us: "*I choose you for my group. Think of me* (or the Lord?)" —I forget which, as I did not write it down at once due to laziness— "*Think of me all the time and leave all else*". I felt extremely happy and elated and wondered why I was among the five. I knew who they were, but have forgotten. I believe there was one other European and the other three were Indians, but can't be sure now. I went on dreaming for sometime about how I obeyed his command, which was more than a command, more like an inner joyful compulsion. My eyes became very fiery and intense, burning with radiance.[11]

The dream was very vivid. I woke up from the noise of the water overflowing in the tank and went downstairs to tell the caretaker at about 6 a.m. and wrote this down afterwards.

(The next day Miss Masani offered me the job as Director of European Music).

---

[11] This dream was extremely important for her and she refers to it often.

IV - First Meetings with Ma

Although Atmananda first met Anandamayee Ma while spending her summer holidays in the Himalayan 'hill station' of Almora in the summer of 1943, it was not until she came under the influence of Lewis Thompson that she began to seriously consider her.

In her 1983 memoir of Anandamayee Ma entitled *As the Flower Sheds its Fragrance*, Atmananda describes these early meetings. Although she had heard Ma highly spoken of for some time, she evidently did not feel particularly drawn to her and it was not until her friend, the Danish *sadhu* Shunya Baba, urged her to do so that she made the effort to meet Ma while on a visit to Almora. She describes their first meetings thus:

"Mataji was sitting on a string cot in the open, with a few people squatting around Her [1] on the grass. She seemed all joy and beauty, with Her long black hair falling loosely over Her shoulders and back, Her radiant face smiling. She addressed a few words to me and I noticed that She did not treat me as a stranger, but as if I were well known to Her. 'She certainly looks very lovely,' I thought, 'but that alone will not help me.' I could not see any way of getting to know more about Her. I knew no Bengali and only some colloquial Hindi, not nearly enough for a serious conversation.

"There was another factor that was against me. I was wearing European dress, a sun hat, shoes and socks and carried a hand-bag in one hand and a mountaineering stick in the other. My appearance seemed to clash painfully with Mataji's surroundings and I was sensitive to the curious glances of the people who were grouped around Her. Nevertheless I remember distinctly being struck by the inward beauty and purity that shone in the faces of two or three

---

[1] Throughout the diaries Atmananda capitalizes all pronouns referring to Anandamayee Ma.

of these people. After about fifteen minutes, I got up to go. Mataji remarked about my leaving so quickly, but I said it was getting late as I had to walk about three miles to the cantonment."

The second meeting with Ma took place a few months later after her return to Benares:

"On a Sunday, I went to see some friends at Assi Ghat and intended to visit also Sri Harihara Baba who had a tremendous reputation as a great mahatma and lived in a houseboat on the Ganges near Assi Ghat. The famous *veena* player, Sri Basu, happened to be at the house of my friends. He said they were all going to see Sri Anandamayee Ma, who was somewhere quite near at the moment and would I care to accompany them. I readily agreed.

In spite of the dense crowd around Her and the loud devotional singing and dancing which disturbed me, I distinctly felt that there was something very special about Mataji which I could neither gauge or define, but which had a fascination that was undeniably worth pursuing.

In the winter of 1944 an English *sadhaka*, Lewis Thompson, who had lived in South India for a number of years, came to stay at Rajghat School. Being the only other European, I was requested to receive him and see that he was comfortable. It did not take me long to find out that he was a quite unusually earnest seeker after Truth, in fact, ruthlessly single-minded. He had come to Ceylon at the age of 23 and one year later proceeded to South India in quest of spiritual guidance which he had sought in vain in England and France. He had stayed in Sri Ramana Maharshi's ashram for seven years with intervals and had received initiation from a well-known Guru, a *jnani* of the South. He had made it a point to meet and study closely everyone who was believed to be highly advanced spiritually. He had been to the Sri Aurobindo Ashram twice for some length of time, had met Swami Ramdas and Mother Krishnabai, J. Krishnamurti, Sri Yogaswami of Ceylon and a number of others who are difficult to approach and known only to a very few. He had obviously developed an authentic intuition as to what was real knowledge and attainment rather than mere book learning.

To my question as to why he had come to North India when he had found so much in the South, he gave as one of his reasons that he had seen a photo of a Holy Mother who travelled in the North for whom he had immediately felt a strong attraction. He consulted his Guru who said: 'Yes, go and meet Her.' He showed me the picture. 'Oh', I exclaimed, 'this is Sri Anandamayee Ma. I have had Her *darshan*.' He said; 'Yes, this is the name by which She is known.' I told him that She was presently in Benares. The next morning Thompson set out to meet Sri Sri Ma and was not seen again at Rajghat that day.

It must be made clear that Thompson had a very sharp, critical intellect and was extremely difficult to please. Only the very best, the highest, interested him and he coldly would dismiss everything else. To my amazement, I found him all but in raptures when I asked him about his impression of Sri Anandamayee Ma. 'As soon as I saw Her', he said, 'I knew that my intuition had been correct —except that I found far more than I had expected. I simply could not tear myself away. When She retired for Her meal and rest, I spent the time somewhere near by and went back to see Her again in the evening and remained till late at night. I have never seen anyone like Her. There is not the slightest trace of ego to be detected in Her'. 'How can you possibly judge in one day?', I questioned, 'you cannot even have talked to Her.' (Thompson did not know either Hindi or Bengali). 'I am quite certain,' he declared with emphasis, 'I have spent many years studying the great mystics of India and have developed some insight in this respect. There is no need to talk. I watched Her very carefully; I have never before come face to face with such perfection; there is no flaw in Her, none whatever.'

It naturally made a deep impression on me to hear someone talk in this strain, particularly one whom I had found to be utterly unemotional, detached and one-pointed. I could hardly help wanting to know Mataji for myself and at close quarters. But the opportunity did not offer itself so quickly.

Mataji can sometimes be heard to say: *'There is a time for everything. No one can come to me until the time is ripe.'* Almost two years after I had had my first *darshan* of Her, it seemed my time had come at long last to make closer contact with Her.

100

Anandamayee Ma around the time of
Atmananda's first meeting with her

In the second half of March 1945, Thompson received a letter from a Buddhist *bhikkhu* [2] —an old Ceylonese friend of his who had come to Sarnath— asking him to meet him there. By road Sarnath was then about 10 miles from Rajghat, but by footpaths across the fields, only 4 or 5. Thompson walked to Sarnath that evening, announcing that he intended to return the next morning. He did not take anything with him, but stayed away the whole of the next two days. When he did not come back even in the afternoon of the third day, the Principal of the school and myself decided that he must have fallen ill. There had been a case of cholera in the servants' quarters opposite to where he stayed at Rajghat. There was then no phone at Sarnath. The only thing was to go there and see what had happened. Equipped with some medicines from the school dispensary, I went there by cycle rickshaw.

I found Thompson sitting very happily in the room of one of the *bhikkhus*. To my astonished inquiries, he replied: 'Sri Anandamayee Ma is here. My friend and I went for Her darshan the evening I arrived. I had no intention of talking to Her, but She Herself started by asking me about myself. There is an excellent translator here, such as I have rarely come across... Every morning Mataji, J.C. Mukerji [the translator], and myself have been discussing in private for two or three hours. She Herself offered me this unique opportunity. How could I possibly leave before I had put before Her every point that was puzzling me.'

I spent that evening in Mataji's presence on the roof of the Birla Dharmasala. At Sarnath no crowd thronged round Mataji — only a few of Her companions, and some of the *bhikkhus*. It was an informal and quiet gathering and this time I did not feel out of place; everything seemed friendly and congenial.

Sarnath [3] had been my favourite place of pilgrimage and rest ever since I had come to Rajghat nearly ten years before. On many Sundays I used to walk there early in the morning and spend the day reading Buddhist scriptures, sitting either in the library or in the open near the *stupa*, enjoying the peace, solitude and the natu-

---

[2] Buddhist monk.

[3] Sarnath is the park outside Benares where the Buddha gave his first sermon. It is one of the holiest sites for Buddhists and even today remains an oasis of peace and meditation dominated by the remains of an ancient *stupa*.

ral beauty of the setting, wondering how it was that, even after millennia, the presence of the Lord Buddha could still be felt so strongly. Ever since my adolescence I have felt drawn towards the Buddha; in fact I had read his talks first in German translation when I was 15 or 16 years old. But little did I dream that Sarnath, where the Buddha had delivered His first sermon after He had attained illumination, would be the setting for the most decisive and important turning-point in my life.

Sri Mukerji asked me whether I wished to make use of his services as an interpreter, but I just wanted to sit quietly and imbibe the atmosphere. I returned to Sarnath the next evening on foot, stayed for the night and walked back at early dawn to be in time for school. This I repeated almost daily. Occasionally, however, I found that Mataji had gone to Varanasi and would not be returning to Sarnath until the next day.

The 24th of March was a Saturday and I came prepared to remain for the weekend. I asked a question during the evening gathering and late at night had a long private talk with Mataji. What She said was so completely convincing that there was no room for doubt. In fact I felt it was not another talking to me, but my higher Self conversing with my self. This cannot be explained. It was an experience beyond words, but all the more real for that. What Mataji said was only the outer expression of something that took place simultaneously on a much deeper level." [4]

* * *

Sarnath, 24th March, 1945

Alone, with J.C. Mukerji, High Court Lawyer from Allahabad as my translator, I put the following questions to Anandamayee Ma after first explaining my spiritual history and background to Her:

Question: Why is it so difficult to decide between two or three courses of action and how is one to know which is the right thing to do?

Anandamayee: *It is the nature of the mind in its present state to be fickle and divided, to be attracted by one thing and repelled by an-*

---

[4] Quoted from the introductory 'prelude' of Atmananda's book *As the Flower Sheds its Fragrance*, published by the Shree Shree Anandamayee Sangha.

other. As long as the mind is in this state this difficulty must persist. But if the mind is steadied and raised to a higher level beyond this fickleness, where it can view things quietly from above, the choice will become clear.

Question: How is the mind to attain to that state?

Anandamayee: *By dwelling on that which is permanent. Constant change is in the nature of this world and if the mind dwells on this world, it must also be ever changing.*

Question: Then in order to achieve this calm state of mind should I seek solitude?

Anandamayee: *No, for the present it is not necessary to leave the world and its activities. The call for solitude will come at some stage, when it will be so imperative that you must obey. For the present, if you do some 'sadhana' for some hours every day, it will slowly change your attitude towards your work and you will then be in the world, but not of the world.*

Question: What kind of *sadhana* do you suggest?

* * *

Anandamayee Ma gave different spiritual instructions to each person according to their particular needs and temperament as discerned by her. For certain people she would recommend a devotional practice; for others a method of philosophical inquiry, while for others, some form of yoga and meditation for stilling the mind. In fact, these three would usually go together, as in the case of Blanca, but with one aspect being emphasized more than another according to the need of the individual. She did not give spiritual instructions automatically, but only to those with whom she had a certain 'connection' (for lack of a better word), or as She put it —for whom She had 'kheyal'. *This is a key concept in trying to understand Anandamayee Ma and signifies a sort of spontaneous Divine inspiration which She claimed was the basis for all of Her actions, rather than their being determined by any personal desire or will. Most importantly, when She did give instructions based on Her* 'kheyal', *a subtle but quite profound power was transmitted through which the recipient would be able to fulfil these instructions. Thus, for Blanca, the Guru-disciple relationship had now begun.*

* * *

Anandamayee: *Give about three hours daily to meditation. Start with half an hour at least and increase slowly, without straining. One hour in the morning and —as you are not taking a heavy meal in the evening— two hours at night, will be excellent.*

First put yourself into the right state of mind by thinking of yourself as part of the One Life that pulsates in every animate being, including the Theosophical Mahatmas, Krishnamurti etc. Imagine that the Divine Light and Grace are showered on you, that you are bathed in them. Become enveloped in this great calm and quiet. Then when you have become very still and absorbed in this, concentrate on your breathing. Do not hold or force your breath, but simply watch the natural inhaling and exhaling. If your thought wanders, bring it back to your breath.

Along with this, practice 'viveka' [discrimination as to the ultimate nature of Reality], or 'vichara' [inquiry into the true nature of the Self], all day long. When irrelevant thoughts come into your mind, remember that what really interests you is Self-Realization and therefore dispel them.

Throughout the day try to remember that you are part of that greater Life and see your work as part of a greater activity. Do not tell anyone about this meditation. Keep a diary and write down daily what experience you have had, how you feel about yourself and your work and your surroundings, how your outlook changes. This will in time become the account of a mystic. As a businessman keeps account of his money, so keep account of the spiritual wealth that will come to you. Keep whatever spiritual wealth you get like a miser keeps his money.

Keep this diary entirely to yourself. Don't let anyone read it. If you have any experiences in your meditation, do not bother about them. Note them, look at them like a spectator, and just go on with your sadhana. If you feel dejected that you are not getting anywhere, do not bother about that either, but just go on.

If this meditation produces conflicts in your life, so that work and the company of people become distasteful, do not bother about this either. And do not give up your sadhana because the conflict is taxing. If you should feel called to stop all activity and to live a purely religious life in time, do not blame me, for you have asked me for a 'sadhana'. Meanwhile do your work just as you take your bath or change your clothes, as a necessity that has to be attended to. It will then become less irksome and it won't worry you. Think of your work as part of a larger whole. Just as when you wash your ears or brush your teeth, you do it for your whole body, so your work should be thought of as a service, which is part of a bigger service. Avoid physical contact with others as far as possible. By touch bad qualities may pass from one person to another. Keep aloof from others, but don't let them feel it. Inasmuch as the thought of superiority comes into your mind, you are pulled down. Keep the thought of God realization with you as a companion day and night.

If at present you are free of responsibilities for others, do not acquire new ones or bother about new activities and better jobs, but stay quietly in Benares, which is a good place, and get on with your 'sadhana' as this is your primary interest.

When you meditate, sit in any comfortable position. You may change it if necessary, but slowly try to increase the time in which you can comfortably remain in the position which suits you best. You may go on with this even when you are indisposed or unwell. When you get tired, lie down and continue your meditation and fall asleep with it.

Whatever sadhana you do has to be done for God and not for your own benefit.

Question: If I notice that thoughts belonging to a certain particular type keep on disturbing the mind, should I attend to this matter or just dismiss them?

Anandamayee: *Have you any strong attachment?*

I reply: Music —not for fame, but because it is a natural gift, that should be perfected.

Anandamayee: *Things like that are not a serious problem, but what is most difficult to get rid of is attachment to persons. These are serious obstacles in this kind of meditation. If it is not affection, it may be repulsion, which is equally bad. Try to realize that the physical is temporary and subject to destruction at any moment and concentrate on that in others which is beyond the physical.*

(I admit that there has been very strong attachment to a person, but that it seems over).

Anandamayee said that the marks are still left and stay for a long time. She also said: *"I noticed on seeing you for the first time a strong tendency towards mysticism, which I could detect from the shape of your foot; but I also noticed the attachment which is in the way."*

I tell her about Lewis Thompson and that he has helped me greatly to get rid of attachment. I also ask her whether I may tell him about my discussion with her. She says: *"Yes, that is all right. Discuss spiritual matters with him as much as possible. But do not talk to anyone else about this as that will be detrimental."*

I wrote down all I could remember from my discussion with Her on the 25th morning. Then Mukerji and I went to Her and he translated most of it to Her to see whether I had remembered properly. She added and slightly changed a few things. Of course there must be some of Mukerji's interpretation in it, as he had to translate. I then copied this from a paper into this book on March 29th).

Sarnath, 25th March, 1945

I tried to follow Anandamayee Ma's instructions on meditation. It is difficult to imagine myself part of all life. But calling down the Divine Grace and Bliss and Peace gets a terrific response that drives away naturally all disturbing thoughts. I want to remain in this blissful state, which is so different from what I am in at other times. Concentrating on the breath seems to centre consciousness in the region of the solar plexus.

Rajghat, 26th March, 1945

Trying to meditate after 10 p.m. The concentration of the breath produces an increasing longing like love sickness, but not for a person, rather for that which seems the origin of breath.

V - Lewis Thompson

" Every attempt at Presence is an effort of Absence."
"For the Thusness of Reality all mental forms and
relations whatever are *absolutely insane.*"
"All human work is, spiritually, stupidity or evasion.
The friends of God in a secular age are rogues and vagabonds."
"For understanding is also a veiling, not the naked presence of
the Truth that reduces all else to ash... Can't each one of us say:
My secret is so simple that I can't tell it to myself?" [1]

Although Blanca was greatly impressed by her meeting with
Anandamayee Ma at Sarnath, she is still very much in the initial
stage of her involvement with her. The more devotional and yogic
methods of meditation suggested by Anandamayee Ma are quite
different from the philosophical inquiry and self-analysis she has
been practicing with both Ramana Maharshi and Krishnamurti,
and it takes her a while to adjust to it. There is still much in her
social life at Rajghat that both interests and distracts her —not the
least of which is Lewis Thompson.

There is great charm in her description of her friendship with
Thompson as it develops over the next chapters —be it intense metaphysical discussions over tea, reading Cocteau together, or late-night
walks along the Ganges. She is infatuated with and idolizes him.
Thompson was an intense spiritual aspirant with profound insight
based on many years of hard-won personal experience with some of
India's greatest modern spiritual teachers. He was also a writer of
great sensitivity whom Edith Sitwell referred to as "a poet of genius". However, he had an uncompromising nature with little patience
for anyone who did not measure up to his exacting standards. [2]

By the time that he came to the Rajghat school, where he held
the position of librarian for several years, Lewis Thompson was in
the midst of a traumatic metaphysical dilemma that would haunt
him until the end of his short life. He had spent a number of years

---

[1] *Mirror to the Light*, Lewis Thompson, pp. 159, 118, 54, 70 edited with an
introduction by Richard Lannoy, Coventure, 1984. See also *Black Sun. The
Collected Poems of Lewis Thompson*, Hohm Press, 2001.

[2] Note Earl Brewsters comment about Thompson in the introduction to ch. VI.

with a south Indian Vedanta [3] Guru, but had been abruptly dismissed by him shortly before having come to Benares at the end of 1943. This was due in part to intrigue instigated against him by jealous fellow followers of the Guru, but there was a deeper underlying cause and his inability to resolve the rift in this all important relationship weighed very heavily on him.

Thompson, both as a *sadhaka* and an artist, was an individual of tremendous seriousness of purpose whom, as Atmananda tells us, cannot be dealt with lightly. Although he had a deep commitment to Eastern mysticism and the rejection of ego implied therein, at the same time he very much saw himself as an artist within the Western Romantic tradition (he was for example particularly influenced by and identified with the poet Rimbaud). As Atmananda later speculated [4], this fundamental artistic narcissism would seem to have been at the core of his troubled relationship with his Guru. He never seemed to fully come to terms with what he undoubtedly deeply understood: that only in letting go completely of his great desire to be a divine artist —a transmitter of the supreme truth— could he possibly hope to attain this goal, i.e. as long as the desire remained an egoistic attachment it could only be an obstacle to the pure transcendence that he so ardently sought. But no one was more aware of this than Thompson himself and his writing, which he considered his principal *sadhana*, could be said to be an intense poetic meditation on this theme. In any case it was precisely in walking a tight-rope over such perilous paradoxes that he derived his inspiration, as his work amply illustrates. Very few have ever grappled with this fundamental poetic dilemma more heroically than Thompson, or walked further down the path of its solution.

Blanca's relationship with Lewis Thompson is multi-faceted. At times she imagines that she is in love with him, especially when they are apart, although his total absorption in himself and his *sadhana* precluded any serious emotional involvement, particu-

---

[3] The classical school of non-dualist philosophy called Advaita Vedanta, systematized by the great 9th century Hindu reformer Shankaracharya.

[4] She expressed her opinion on this to me at some length in our last conversation, in December of 1984, shortly after she had carefully gone through Thompson's recently published book of aphorisms *Mirror to the Light*.

larly with a woman. Indeed, he is almost as unattainable for her as is Krishnamurti of whom he reminds her. At other times she feels motherly towards him (he is five years younger than her), and prides herself on having the 'good fortune' to look after such an 'exceptional individual'. But the most important aspect of their relationship for her, and also the role to which he was best suited, was as a very special friend and mentor, a kind of secondary guru whose profound assistance she felt to be invaluable. He was, as she says, someone from her own culture with whom she could relax and speak freely, someone whom she felt to be several steps further along than her and who could brilliantly explain the way.

Initially, as we see in this chapter, Blanca is extremely submissive to Thompson and clearly in awe of what she considers his artistic and spiritual superiority —which in any case he seems always ready to remind her of. But as time goes on and he observes the profound transformation wrought in her through her association with Anandamayee Ma, he acknowledges his respect for her as a very serious spiritual seeker.

* * *

Rajghat, 27ᵗʰ March, 1945

As menses have started, I don't feel up to concentration. During the day doubts about Anandamayee Ma cross my mind as to whether she is really what Lewis thinks. Also they have in some mysterious way to do with J.K.'s aversion to meditation, etc. But is not what she advised me to do completely in line with the pantheistic experience of my adolescence in which I saw everything infused with an all-pervading Divine life force? So many thoughts cross my mind, it is difficult to keep account of them. Lewis suggests I should always keep paper and pencil with me and note down on the spot.

29ᵗʰ March, 1945

I must learn Hindi, so as to talk directly to Anandamayee Ma and Sharananandji.[5] I am not really interested in Realization. I am too slack. How can one make this longing so overwhelming as to

---

[5] A great Mahatma who was blind with whom she often conversed.

Lewis Thompson - late 1940's
(photo courtesy of Washington State University)

sweep everything away? Even here I am half-hearted like in all my other activities.

31st March, 1945

Went to Sarnath, but found Anandamayee Ma gone to Benares. Walking there something about surrender got clear. Sanjiv Rao [6] writes I should accept the Delhi job, but says that his decision is not completely impersonal, as he can't take the responsibility of my refusing such a good (?) offer. He says music is my *dharma*, not teaching. It seems to me that neither is my *dharma*, but reading over my diary I come across a saying by Brahmajna Ma [7]: "By the term *'dharma'*, I understand the effort to cross the sea of this world. That one has come into this world at all is in itself a wrong notion; to give up this confused idea and realize one's source —one's true home—, this is *dharma*."

Having been busy with Truth since my childhood, is not this 'Search' my *dharma*, and everything else incidental? Why did I say "I want to love everyone" when J.K. asked me in what I am interested. Music did not enter my mind then.

It is not true that where one stays and where one goes do not matter. It does, as long as one is bound and weak. Where would I be had I not gone to Tiruvannamalai?

1st April, 1945

I woke up in an awful confusion about this question. There is some attraction in the Delhi job. I met Bholia early this morning and asked him again to look up my horoscope. There is also a lot of resistance against putting the mind to sleep by meditation. I am not doing it properly.

I have never followed my heart more than half way. Why not go into it wholly this time and risk not going to Delhi. It is not

---

[6] Founder and principal of the Rajghat School and a close friend of Atmananda. He was Kitty's brother-in-law.

[7] A great Bengali woman saint (1880-1934), in the *jnana* (non-dualist) tradition. Swami Paramananda, the chief *sanyasi* disciple of Anandamayee Ma and head of the Anandamayee Sangha for many years, had been a close follower of Brahmajna Ma until her death after which he devoted the remainder of his long life to the service of Anandamayee Ma.

music that takes me away from the Real Thing, but clinging to a person. Now that the problem has come up again here, I better stay with it and not start it all over again somewhere else.

2ⁿᵈ April, 1945

My real activity should not lie in the physical at all. Therefore it is better to remain where I am. As Lewis quite rightly says, since I have asked Anandamayee Ma, I am bound to obey Her.

4ᵗʰ April, 1945

The resistance against sitting down and meditating is very great, but when I manage to overcome it, the bliss is indescribable.

6ᵗʰ April, 1945

Visit to Anandamayee Ma.

Asked about concentration on breath. She says that its purpose is only to still the mind and generate a state of inner rest and peace (*shanti*); it is only to prepare the ground for deeper spiritual revelation.

She told a young married man with a child, who wants to give up working and renounce the world, that he should continue to work as he still had worldly *karma* to fulfil.

On the way back it occurred to me: The body belongs to the world, and so does the mind. The 'I' is far removed from all that. Where am 'I'?

Mother [8] says that I did not tell her my name, so she has called me Ramdasi, then changed it to Ramanandi. She asked me which I prefer and I replied "Ramanandi". It is a lovely name. She said: "*I thought you wanted 'anand' [bliss].*" Of course I do.

8ᵗʰ April, 1945

My sister's death anniversary. [9] My attitude is changing already. I live more inside myself and outer things are losing their

---

[8] She generally refers to Anandamayee Ma as Mother, Mataji, or Ma.

[9] Her sister who was two years younger than her, died at the age of 17 of diphtheria which she contracted while working with underprivileged children in post World War I Vienna.

attraction. As Lewis says, one is like an iceberg —only a small peak shows on the surface and the bulk is under water.

I hardly think of X nowadays. He doesn't mean anything to me now. Is it because the sea separates us? Or will it last? Strange how things change.

10th April, 1945

Visit to Anandamayee Ma at Sarnath.

Sleeping there on the roof [10] near Her feet is really extraordinary. What an atmosphere of love and eternity.

13th April, 1945

Started meditating at Ghoshal's in a room full of people and got so far away that I found it difficult to walk afterwards.

Ella Maillart [11] came on the 10th. There is something hard and disagreeable in her face. On the 12th Kitty wrote about father's stroke. I am angry with S.R. for not having informed me at once.

17th April, 1945

Ella M. left today. I did not like her influence, but for Lewis it seems to have been very healthy. It was like a holiday for him. Strangely, I actually missed her after coming back from the station. Funny how habit works and how painful any change is. But it is so peaceful here without her. She is worldly, practical and too clever. L [12] is quite different with her. She calls out another aspect of him. I really cannot manage socially when left alone with a new acquaintance. I am only comfortable when we are three. How awkward I am. I never feel at home and at ease in this queer world. It is like being in exile. I seem to call out the saint and ascetic in L., on the other hand he longs for relaxation and gets it from the boys at school and tea.

I do not particularly like it at Anandamayee Ma's ashram at Bhadaini [13]. So much noise and disturbance. She is different there.

---

[10] One of the great joys of life in India is the custom of sleeping under the stars during the hot season, often on the flat roof tops.

[11] Swiss explorer and authoress, see introduction to Chapter III.

[12] Throughout the diaries, she refers to Thompson as L. or Lewis.

[13] The ashram is situated on the Ganges in the part of Benares known as Bhadaini.

I must concentrate inside and not run after these people, but make a sustained effort myself. Somehow Ella Maillart's influence has taken me off *sadhana*. Didn't Anandamayee Ma tell me to avoid contact with others? Now I feel immediately turned inwards since she has gone.

Delhi wants me again and the police seem to assent also this time. Well, if I must go, I must. But willingly I shan't. I do not want to be with S.R. and Kitty now. There are too many strains on our friendship at present. Sanjiv has resigned [14]. How pertinent my dream was.

My poor father is paralyzed and I did not even write to him.

18th April, 1945

At breakfast this morning with Lewis I realized that I must be more by myself and follow Anandamayee Ma's advice. He told me that neither the physical nor the emotional or mental is my centre, but something beyond. None of these three outer spheres have any real interest for me and to the inner one I don't attend to enough. I feel this is because of my attachments. L. says that I also —not only Ella— keep him from his own world. I realize that. At the same time, I do get a glimpse of that world now and then and it fascinates me beyond measure. It is right for me to keep quiet in his presence and to let his world be imposed on me. Being with him means so very much to me; I shall not go away voluntarily. Is that again attachment? If it is, it is of a higher form anyhow. I feel that I should foster this affection to the utmost of my capacity.

19th April, 1945

Lewis behaved impossibly today at lunch. He read while I ate, and ate when I had finished and then made tea. I wonder what it is in me that makes him react in this way. There is something very wrong with me and my attitude to food. I must observe it. But I won't stand this behaviour from him and shall eat alone hereafter.

---

[14] As principal of the Rajghat school.

20ᵗʰ April, 1945

It occurs to me that even thinking of Eternal Life or anything at all belongs to the life of the Ego. Whereas concentrating on the breath seems to lead to a void beyond. Perhaps that is why it is so frightfully difficult. Yet having asked for Her advice, I must carry it out to the utmost.

21ˢᵗ April, 1945

Last night menses and a terrific storm. Could not sleep and felt wretched and read part of the night.

Somehow ate again with Lewis. He again behaved in the same upsetting manner, like an iceblock. I have put all cups and things in his room. Now he must eat there. I am beginning to see why no one can stand him. I am so upset I wish I had taken the Delhi job. After all my chief reason for staying was really him, not Anandamayee Ma, which is wrong and I shall have to pay for it evidently. I am not ready for *sadhana*. I want to have a good time, according to my own liking of course, which is in any case not what most other people like. Really, if L. continues to behave in this way and things go wrong all round, as they have been doing with Sanjiv resigning, illnesses etc., the only thing left will be for me to turn inside which will be for the best.

In any case it was better to stay here, because in Delhi there would have been too many distractions. Miss Masani still hopes to get me and offers me broadcasts in May or June or any time I want.

22ⁿᵈ April, 1945

I feel miserable this morning. How I depend on Lewis' mood. It makes me realize how dependent I am on others for happiness. In my meditation, however, I feel steady and serene. I am very tired and not too well.

Evening:

Manu was here and L. was extremely fascinating. Why does he never talk to me like that anymore? He said something to the effect that, when thought is completely satisfied, it stops of its own accord. It occurs to me that it is my trying to follow Anandamayee Ma's advice that has separated me from him. That is why he is so icy, because I do not respond to him as I used to. I am not looking to things and people for anything except for relaxation, which I need to have.

I tried to play the piano today but that also is extremely irksome. This visit to Anandamayee Ma has really brought to the surface a number of problems and made me conscious of extreme dissatisfaction. As I have asked Her what to do, I must follow her advice, if only as an experiment to see what happens. Be reckless and don't bother how much trouble it may cause and how much you may have to give up. After all, when you have fixed the goal, you must get there in spite of, and notwithstanding, anyone or anything.

25th April, 1945

Yesterday asked Lewis about J.K.'s teaching regarding stopping thought and bringing it to an end naturally. He says J.K.'s method is too intense for my nature, that I have too much inertia; that only something mad, something overwhelmingly intense, can take one out of the daily rut of ordinary thought. Only a strong interest will call out spontaneous concentration. "If you take Anandamayee Ma to be The Great Mother and obey Her, She will become for you what you put into Her. Even if you see later that She is not that, no harm will be done. But you can't go far wrong with Her."

L. is marvellous when he talks on these subjects, utterly lucid and illuminating. But at present he seems to be in depression. It affects very much. I wake up miserable every morning. I believe it is largely due to him. How suddenly we are cut off from each other.

I saw Anandamayee Ma yesterday. She was gracious as usual but I seem out of gear. The resistance of habit is very great. Lewis is quite right. I have been utterly lost in mediocrity and ordinariness so far.

26th April, 1945

This morning I imagine myself in J.K.'s presence and get great bliss. I intensely wish to find my own self. Words cannot express this at all. I find myself dumbfounded.

28th April, 1945

Discussing with Lalji how Lewis changes in the company of various people, it struck me that it is my attitude that makes him so stony. I was wrong to preach to him about money. The only reaction to my reprimands was that he immediately lost the only 10 rupees that he had left. A person who has done so infinitely much for me, who has changed my life altogether, cannot be judged in this ordinary way. If he has a weakness or two, why take any notice of it at all. I shan't do it anymore. He is evidently going through a period of spiritual torture and all he needs is someone who will see only the God in him and lavish the utmost affection and tenderness on him. Something that is beyond me works through me the moment this is my attitude. This morning in my meditation I had a glimpse of what an instrument of the Eternal might be. One must first stop every activity, every emotion, every thought and become utterly empty to be able to receive the Divine Life, which is waiting to be released. It is so utterly different from what one is used to. The people around one are all moving in the reverse direction. In this way one finds oneself compelled to retire into solitude where one can proceed with this process of transforming oneself and remain there until the transformation is complete.

30th April, 1945

I am in a state of intense doubt, I should call it creative, joyful doubt. I know nothing at all. Who am 'I'? Who thinks? Who sees? I see the wisdom of Anandamayee Ma's telling me simply to watch the breath in order to stop the aimless movements of the mind. As an experiment, try to be utterly still. It takes one so far away from everyone and everything ordinary. What else is important but to know why I am here, what life is, what everything is. Until then what can one possibly think or do that is of any meaning at all.

Evening:

Lewis showed me what he wrote to his sister. How much joy and tenderness he felt when his younger sister had a heart-to-heart talk with him before he left England. He said this also makes my relation to him clearer. A long conversation ensued which touched me to the core. He then told me why I irritate him so —because I am obsessed with looking after him and he feels my 'weight' too much. I said that he is difficult to look after and that I am clumsy, and that I never stood such treatment from anyone before but have submitted to it from him because I am aware of and respect his spiritual authority. I feel a person of such uncompromising seriousness has to be allowed anything.

He said that I am not really a woman and have none of the tricks and playfulness of a woman. He used the example of his friend's wife who looks after him perfectly, instinctually and without her personality interfering. He told me that the greatness of woman is to be the impersonal 'WOMAN', *Prakriti*. This is her true *dharma* —something totally feminine and unrelated to masculine egoicity. Woman rules in her own domain and man is free in his, so that they compliment and mutually enhance each other. She gets *Purusha* through him, he *Prakriti* through her. [15] It establishes perfect balance. The western woman is ugly because she has an artificial, socially conditioned individuality. Both (modern men and women) are unhappy because they have come out of their own spheres and have obscured their archetypal identities.

This talk has done something to me. It is not ready to be put into words. I have always felt that what I want most is to be a perfect woman. Can it be done? It must. It will.

This talk was like a loving embrace and has brought us very much nearer. All this is far away from the physical— a very subtle meeting. The 'weight' is the negative attachment of which Anandamayee Ma spoke.

1st May, 1945

Awareness is a state, not an act. It goes on beyond time and beyond the ego. It seems to me that Sharananand's *Sharanagati* [16] and J.K.'s 'Awareness' are perhaps the same.

I do things for L. chiefly because I want or feel I need some-

---

[15] In Indian philosophy *purusha* (the male principle) is the unmoving, unmanifest aspect of God and *prakriti* (the female principle) is all manifested life, creation and movement.

[16] The book in Hindi written by Swami Sharadananda which she has been reading. The title refers to perfect surrender.

thing from him. I can hide this from myself under the pretext of attending to his needs. To wish for someone's company is attachment which binds and must inevitably lead to separation.

2nd May, 1945

Lewis showed me two new poems. He does live in a world which is far away from the ordinary. How really can he put up with the ordinary shallow colourlessness of all mundane existence. It must irritate him. And there is tension because I can't really meet him on his plane. It is the tragedy and greatness of the poet that he must ever remain alone and misunderstood by most, lest he lose the power to bring to the world what only he can conceive. I have not got the courage to let go and enter deeply into his world. It is too painful. Yet meeting him cannot be without meaning?

Rajghat, 4th May, 1945

I am still very interested in this world. Going to Almora tomorrow seems so important that it is difficult to concentrate on anything else. I feel that I am finally beginning to become aware of my attitude at least.

It is the cold, cruel inhuman aspect of Lewis that frightens me. I like a more human touch. But that kind of remoteness produces art. I am not really an artist.

VI - Almora

In the unbearably hot summer season the annual migration to the mountains was an indispensable ritual for the *sahibs* and *memsahibs* (Western men and women) during the British Raj. The entire government moved from New Delhi to the Himalayan city of Simla which became an exclusive European resort. Almora was a much more informal 'hill station', well suited to Blanca and her artistic friends. Situated at an altitude above 6,000 feet, it afforded the visitor panoramic views and walks in the crisp pine-scented mountain air. The houses were mostly stone cottages which were scattered on the hillsides at respectable distances from one another. These were always well staffed with servants —an inescapable part of life in India, particularly at that time, that even the poorest Westerner would take for granted. Life there seems to have consisted of leisurely reading, hikes in the mountains and plenty of tea and conversation.

Here we encounter many of Blanca's friends from Benares as well as some new ones. Most notable of these was Earl Brewster, an American painter then in his 60's who is best remembered today as a close friend of D.H. Lawrence. He accompanied Lawrence on a tour of Etruscan tombs in the mid 1920's and Lawrence later visited him in Ceylon. Brewster was also a major influence on Lama Govinda's life-long involvement in the East, dating from the time they were both painters together in Capri. Lewis Thompson also numbered among Brewster's close friends. In his introduction to Thompson's book of meditative aphorisms, *Mirror to the Light*, Richard Lannoy describes a meeting he had with Brewster at his home in Almora where he found him: "silver-haired and elegant in a black velvet jacket with purple cravat... We were served tea from Edwardian silver by a Pahari servant wearing trousers which had once belonged to Lawrence. 'I have known only two men whom I consider to have been giants.', Brewster told me. 'One was Lawrence

Atmananda in Almora - early 1940's
(courtesy of Swami Nirvanananda)

and the other was Thompson. Physically the two could have been brothers... Thompson expressed his views with the fierceness of the tiger.'" [1] Brewster was quite fond of Blanca, which says something for her own artistic sophistication and charm.

Sunya Baba also lived near Almora on top of a hill nicknamed appropriately Cranks Ridge by the locals. His place was next to the temple of Kesari Devi, across from which was the house of Dr. Evans-Wentz, the pioneer translator and popularizer of classic Tibetan texts such as *The Life of Milarepa* and *The Tibetan Book of the Dead*. Later Lama Govinda lived for many years in this house. To complete the picture, the ashram of Sri Krishna Prem was located a few miles further out near the village of Mirtola.

Anandamayee Ma's ashram is situated near the base of Cranks' Ridge adjoining the temple of Patal Devi —Goddess of the underworld. A local *sadhu* once tried to convince me that Patal Devi was the patroness of America as that country is located directly beneath India on the opposite side of the world!

* * *

Almora, 8th May, 1945

Germany surrenders.

Arrived here 6th evening. I am less conscious than in Benares and influenced by the people around me, who live as if there were only this funny world in which I am also evidently still interested. But it is apparently good food and general comfort that I need now. I notice how tense I am and what a relief the absence of L. is. The strain that he produces is probably the chief cause of my rash. I am taking yeast and calcium and homeopathic medicine and also tripholla [2]. I am very tired and sleepy. Reading *Experiment with Time* by J.W. Dunn and have decided to try and become conscious of my dreams by noting my first thought on waking. Bought a copy book for this.

Almora, 12th May, 1945

I am utterly silly here. The meditation is irksome and I have nothing to write into this diary. I am half asleep. In quite a differ-

---

[1] *Mirror to the Light*, p. 29.

[2] An Ayurvedic treatment.

ent state than in Benares. Am learning Hindi and teaching Lucinda the piano. Have stopped dreaming again.

Binsor, 15ᵗʰ May,1945

Walked to Binsor yesterday. Before leaving I had Martha's letter about father's death [3]. It rather upset me more than I expected. Poor old man, I hope he is at peace. I wonder whether he sees now the way in which I live and whether it disappoints him. It must be rather different from what he imagined.

Binsor, 21ˢᵗ May, 1945

Continue to be dull and empty, but since I have been staying with Alice Boner [4] it is better than at Levi's, where the physical is almost too pleasant and satisfying. Here it is dingy and unsatisfactory, which has the effect of driving one inside. I try to meditate again, with little success. Alice seems extremely depressed. I get the impression that she finds her life useless and unsatisfactory and that is why she always escapes into illness. I wonder whether one can help her? She has strong prejudices. This morning on my mentioning Anandamayee Ma, she said that she found it sickening to deify gurus no matter how great they might be.

Almora, 31ˢᵗ May, 1945

Last night at Dewaldhar, being alone in the house after Meyer left, something happened in my meditation which I cannot quite describe. I got into a new level of consciousness, but became frightened because it took me out of my usual state.

This morning I started at 4.30 a.m. for Someshwar. The first hour or so walking alone with an old coolie in the moonlight and the complete silence was a profound meditation. I entered into a luminous awareness quite different from my ordinary state, retiring into my true Self and losing identification with my ego. It was utter bliss. The time before the world awakens is really the time when one can have communion with *That* which is behind all things. The activities of the world do not disturb one then. I

---

[3] Although it is not clear, most likely he had been in a concentration camp and survived to reach America only to die shortly thereafter.

[4] See introduction to Chapter III.

must use this time. When the first rays of dawn appeared even in these lonely woods, it was much more difficult to turn inside. The night is more perfect and more concentrated than the distracting day. I understood why it is said that for the Realized Being, night is day and day night.

I must try to go back into this state which is beyond my ordinary self and abide in that, so that by and by my outer activities may be directed from within. It was painful later on to watch how the mind wastes and dissipates itself in endless repetition of irrelevant thoughts. How can there be surrender when the mind chatters all the time? It is strange that one is usually not conscious of this.

What a change from the silly atmosphere here with completely artificial people and their ever noisy, well trained servants. I need to be by myself in nature as much as possible.

While I waited for the bus in Someshwar, I was studying Hindi and a very nice Congress Party man, a wool hawker, came and taught me the meaning of all the words I had written down to ask about. He then treated me to tea and biscuits. I was quite touched. How delightfully simple and natural these people are, though the bazaar was full of flies, and dirty.

It is strange that I always seem to get profound insights when I live in dirt. Even L.'s great cleanliness seems to be an obstacle to going within oneself. There is a great temptation in outer orderliness and neatness, but if obsessive it can be counter-productive.

In Lucknow, years ago, when I got into a strange state of illumination I also lived in extreme dirt [5]. Cleanliness, comfort and civilization seem diametrically opposite to realization. In Sarnath also I lived in utter ascetic simplicity, using *dharmasala* [6] blankets and sheets etc. Tiruvannamalai was also very primitive. I wonder why the spiritual and the austere seem to always go together.

I must try and use nights or the very early morning before dawn for concentration and see whether that helps. When all are asleep one might get detached more easily from physical surroundings.

---

[5] A tantalizing glimpse into her time in India before 1942, not covered in the extant diaries.

[6] A traditional pilgrims rest-house, always very simple and austere.

1st June, 1945

When I walk by myself I become thoughtful. This morning even on the road I thought: "Why am I here? Why do I think? Why can't I remain without thought? Why was the mind created and why is it restless by nature? It must be seeking for something that it has to do; it must have a purpose.

3rd June, 1945

In the face of death it matters little whether one has been happy or comfortable. All that matters is whether one has found the purpose of one's life and fulfilled it; whether one's life has been one continuous worship of the Source of All Things or whether one has frittered away time and energy in useless enjoyment and movement. We are always facing death, but unless someone near to us dies or something else drastic happens, we forget.

4th June, 1945

Today I tried to wake at 4.30 a.m. but didn't manage until 5.30. Anyway at least that's quieter than later on. I met *sadhus* all day. First Bhatt's son expounded to me Sanskrit scriptural truths and told me, appropriately enough, that it is said if you want to find God, you must first control your tongue in taste and in speech! That's what I need to do certainly.

Then I went to Dr. Pande's shop and met Umeshanand of Anandamayee's ashram. In the afternoon Sorrensen [Sunya Baba] came to see me and stayed for two and a half hours. There was a strong earthquake while I sat and talked to him. The house rocked like a ship for perhaps a minute and again later also. So one really does always live in the face of death! After seeing off Sorrensen I met the old *swami* from the Ramakrishna Mission and the young one from Ahmedabad.

7th June, 1945

Borrowed Isidora Duncan's autobiography. Oh, it is fascinating. What an adventurous spirit with a fundamentally spiritual art, wonderful woman. I am not so courageous and adventurous as she, but I have a certain glimpse or inkling of the truest things, which are even beyond art and yet very likely the source of art.

9th June, 1945

Malati writes her condolences for father's death. How little people know what one feels. It seems almost funny or pathetic to receive all these letters of condolescence.

Lewis writes that sleeping after 4 a.m. increases one's *tamas*[7]

11th June, 1945

The night before last I read L.'s poem, which he had sent me some days ago, over and over again till I knew it by heart and had entered into its heart:

> "Moonlight.
> *Night of sapphire and camphor,*
> *Hard and suave like silver,*
> *Elusively resonant*
> *Living absence.*
> *Pressureless touch,*
> *Accentless blaze.*"

It had a peculiar effect and took me away into the heart of that moonlit night, that unending "accentless blaze". I could not sleep much, but was happy and full of love for the poem and its author. I wrote a few words about it and sent them to him. It helped me to wake at 5 a.m. I went out into the garden in the dark, before dawn, and remained in the particular hush of that hour, called 'Brahma Kala'.

13th June, 1945

My consciousness seems certainly changed, lifted from the earth somewhat, perhaps due to the leisure and quiet and many hours of reading daily. But I feel extremely exhausted. The effort of waking early and of meditation seems to cause great strain.

The Dance of Shiva by Coomaraswamy was extremely interesting and illuminating about India.

14th June, 1945

Last night I had a peculiar meditation. It struck me that I could not remind myself constantly of the oneness with the Supreme or

---

[7] Inertia.

127

call down the Divine Grace upon myself without calling down the crucifixion of the ego which means abject suffering. Somehow it struck me that this would come soon, that this calm and leisure could not continue for very much longer.

I then remembered L. and felt that it would come through him. To serve him is to serve the divine through him. I pray that I may always be attuned to the Divine will, no matter what the consequences, rather than to follow my own petty desires. Is the desire to serve Lewis 'His' bidding or due to my own desire to express myself as a woman, which I have had all these years and which was always frustrated? I shall soon know. Circumstances will speak.

I cannot sleep tonight. This always happens when I get in touch too closely with Lewis. He is the first man I have met who desperately needs affection and yet one has almost to force it on him, although even then he won't have it. He has almost contempt for women and that makes it all the more interesting for me; he doesn't lead you on, oh no, he cools you down incessantly and makes you more detached all the time. That's why I really love him better from a distance —the poet. When we are together everyday, we irritate each other. To what will this lead?

15th June, 1945

Yesterday cleaned Rama Rao's house, then went to see Anandamayee Ma, who is presently staying at Her ashram here. I got quite excited on arriving there at the prospect of seeing Her. She asked me some questions. I seemed sometimes to know beforehand what she would ask. Of course she wanted to know where the *Sahib* ' was (Lewis).

I met old Bhatt on the road and he told me that a Russian lady, who is the companion of the Rani of Bhopal, wants to meet me. I received a copy of Sri Aurobindo's *The Mother* from Brewster this morning by post and a letter. He says, "your visit was a blessing" and "come for the entire day". There was a strange moment of intimacy when I sat there with him —suddenly, like a presence that united us—, inexplicable to myself. It was sort of another consciousness —a sudden flash of understanding. I feel nearer to him since this. I felt such deep pity for the old man, all alone there. I wish he had a friend staying with him, like Valentine for instance.

"The mind of the Sage, being in repose, becomes the mirror of the universe" (Chuang Tzu). I feel like being a burning flame of love. This can't be for one only, but for the ONE which encompasses all.

17th June, 1945

Walking on the road this morning I suddenly felt how unreal the outer world is. The moment one turns within this seems so obvious.

I still enjoy food too much and simply increase the *tamas* by overeating.

Read Sorrensen's *Memory*, and what he wrote about Sri Yashoda Ma and Sri Krishna Prem [8]. It is interesting how his tendency of hiding himself and walling himself in, defending himself all the time against some aggressive egos as he puts it comes out in what he writes, as well as in his only visible activity: building houses to protect his silence.

18th June, 1945

Went to see Brewster. Just saved him from the irksome visit of Miss Chatterji. On my way sat in the woods near Eppworth Cottage, ate my lunch and had a very nice meditation. My body was quite apart from me, though I was fully conscious and awake. Even now I can feel the body as being quite a separate entity when I remain a witness to it. What is it that makes me feel the pain and sensations of this particular body and not of any other? Where is this special 'I' located? What is it that divides me from all other bodies and manifestations? If I am only a part of the vast Life that flows through all, why am I not conscious of the other parts? What is it that moves the body, the mind, and that feels? What is it that thinks and why in this particular way? Is this kind of inquiry what is meant by *vichara* [9] ? I suppose so. Isn't it mad to go on living unconsciously and taking everything for granted?

I was keen to read the new translation of the *Gita* by Christopher Isherwood to Brewster who had seen the book at the

---

[8] Yasoda Ma was the guru of Sri Krishna Prem. See introduction to Chapter III.

[9] The process of self-inquiry.

Ramakrishna Mission yesterday, but dared not ask for it. I had not been at Brewster's for an hour when the post brought that very book! A present from Bunting. I read the Introduction by Huxley and three or four chapters with great delight. How things flow into each other beautifully the moment one makes the slightest attempt at surrender!

Brewster returned L.'s letter to me. I read it on returning home. He is such an extraordinary creature. A great rush of love goes through me when I think of him. It is not personal. It is the Great Being that loves through me. Perhaps no love is ever personal, but by considering oneself and the beloved as separate individuals, one makes it personal and thereby perverts and degrades it. How I shall try to keep this love just as he expressed it: "Pressureless touch, accentless blaze" —most of all "Living absence".

20th June 1945

Yesterday I had a peculiar meditation. I seemed to ask for deep pain. I felt that I cannot get to the Highest without it. Afterwards I felt rather afraid of it. I later wondered where the pain would come from, could not imagine.

Just now I had a peculiar dream about a fire I wanted lit in my room, but thought it was not possible. Then someone said: "why not", and lit it. It seemed to symbolise my unresolved relation to 'X'. [10] There are hidden desires in me for physical comforts and a different physical life from what I am presently leading. At the end of the dream Dr. K. said "We are done for, there is nothing for us but to commit suicide". I seemed surprised, but then shared his despair. I also could not see a way out for myself.

I wonder whether this is where the pain is going to come from: the discovery that inside I am all rotten and a lie; all the dealings with saints and *sadhus* an escape, coming from a very deep dissatisfaction and a craving for things of this world which is suppressed. Anandamayee Ma told me about my attachment that keeps me back. It is still there and unfulfilled. What should I do about it? I must find out.

Later:

Keeping this diary and dreaming seems a great help in pull-

---

[10] See commentary on page 96 after entry for 8th November, 1942.

ing out unresolved complexes from within my psyche. I wonder whether I get so frightfully exhausted in my attempts to meditate because there are so many tied up, suppressed conflicts inside that get stirred up by the concentration? There is something in me that revolts violently against this effort.

When I consider Anandamayee Ma to be the Supreme MOTHER, it generates a deep joy that makes it almost easy to conquer *tamas* without effort. I saw Her yesterday. On my way there I felt that I was going to the Divine MOTHER. It is such intense joy to see Her.

Dr. Vyas read a commentary on the *Gita* in Hindi. I understood quite a lot, which made me very happy. I unfortunately ate not only the mango given by Anandamayee Ma in the evening, but also a whole melon and drank two glasses of water and fruit juice. This was far too much and disturbed my sleep. The greediness for enjoyment through taste is immense in me.

22nd June, 1945

Again waking up in a state of pure bliss having offered myself to the Supreme Mother before going to sleep. Somehow the Mother and L. seem connected or rather *I have the definite feeling that the Mother wishes to love him also through me.*

This morning's bliss was spoiled immediately by my thinking and worrying about Rama Rao's arrival.

I feel definitely a subtle change of consciousness (since the 20th, I believe). It is like a pregnancy of the spirit. I do not seem to be alone anymore. There is something that is beginning to absorb me, a subtle power, infinitely sweet and gentle, that seems to embrace and permeate me. I wonder whether this has to do with Lewis, or is it the influence of the Mother or are both the same.

One has to be careful to constantly be aware of the difference of the Self from the body. When the power from above begins to descend, if the body and mind are impure, there is a reaction of sexual excitement.

23rd June, 1945

Saw Anandamayee Ma yesterday evening. Sat there for one and a half hours. She seemed to draw me into Herself. I felt a tremendous attraction towards Her. I feel the same now thinking of Her.

When I sat and waited for the Rama Raos I suddenly realized how absurd it is to get angry. I saw it in a flash. Who gets angry and with whom? Surely it can only be the wilful personality that sees itself thwarted in its endeavours. Not having created anyone or anything in this world, what right has one to expect that people should fit in with one's own sweet will? If you surrender you cannot possibly be angry. How is it your business to correct and mind what the Creator allows to happen.

Read Lewis' letter to Rama Rao to him. How untrue and 'made' it sounds, painfully artificial. What a difference to his completely open letter to me. It struck me that he can be quite abnormal and difficult and he wants love very badly, which would undoubtedly smooth out all his difficulties. It is certainly worth a great deal of trouble, pain, anything, to attempt to give him this.

Read Anandamayee Ma's little book *Sad Vani* [11] in English. Some of it I liked very much, some not. Unfortunately there was no time to see Her in the evening.

27th June, 1945

I seem much less disturbed by noise and am able to ignore it and concentrate. If I realize that I am at all times in the Presence of the Supreme, nay part of Its creation, how can the mind waver for a moment even, and how can one speak of irrelevant things? How can one bother about what others think or say of one's behaviour? How can one ever forget this?

1st July, 1945

Saw Anandamayee Ma yesterday. There was *bhajan* by a Ramakrishna monk. She closed her eyes and sat, a picture of absolute stillness, wonderful to behold.

Brewster is not at all well. I found him saying the other day that separation gets more acute with time and that there seems to be no point in his life now [12]. He is a great darling. He also seems very fond of me.

---

[11] A little book of Anandamayee's sayings compiled by Her close disciple Bhaiji.

[12] His wife had recently died.

I started reading Meister Eckhart, his sermons etc. as collected by Franz Pfeifer. It is wonderful, wonderful, wonderful. Purest Indian philosophy. He did know God.

2nd July, 1945

It seems obvious to me that what keeps me back from direct and unhindered aspiration toward my Self or God is suppressed desire —as J.K. once told me. I still do not understand how to deal with it. But it certainly is a definite obstacle to my meditation. There is a hidden desire to remain in this world that makes full surrender impossible. Maybe this is what makes me so tired when I try to concentrate. I must deal with this, face it and see what can be done about it. For how many years have I carried this heaviness with me and not been able to deal with it. It is probably from my former life (as a monk?) where I must have made considerable progress spiritually (which seems obvious as I get tremendous response of Grace whenever I open myself to it), but evidently suppressed the sex question which remains even now unresolved. I ought to ask Anandamayee Ma about this, but how awkward with a translator. Shall I ever know enough Hindi to discuss such things directly? I certainly am not ready to live an entirely religious life until this problem has resolved itself. I must not rest but pursue this quietly, and patiently see it through. Then I shall be free to proceed.

I thought that Lewis, by his great purity, had helped me through this problem, but evidently not yet —or only very partially.

Brewster really seems to have taken a deep liking to me. He told me I reminded him much of his daughter. When I said good-bye he had tears in his eyes and kissed me on both cheeks. I still feel that if I could —even now— marry the right man, who would take me up into a purely spiritual life by his own depth and aspiration, and who would be to me all in all —the God and idol of the Hindu wife— however difficult and unhappy it might make my life in some ways... this would provide the right solution and make my life one-pointed.

Letter of 27th June from Lewis shows how very intuitive my criticism of his writing was. He mentions that he used "transcended crucifixion" (an expression I used in my letter) in two of his poems. I seem to be very near —almost inside of him— when we are away from each other. But when together, we clash. I am far too heavy, clumsy and coarse and he too elusive and subtle. Hardly a pinpoint of his consciousness seems present in this world of matter; only just enough to be able to give an inkling, to some extent, of all the richness —I would almost say effulgence— of his extraordinary and rare being. Has it not been infinitely worthwhile to subject myself to his difficult personality, to live in frustration in order to contact closely this genius; and beyond him, there can be only SILENCE - GOD, just like the little moonlight poem that is so much like him and in the end takes one up into Silence...

4th July 1945

Last night with Anandamayee Ma I felt like I had been in the arms of the Supreme Mother. It reminded me very much of the atmosphere of Skandashram at Tiruvannamalai about which I had written to Malati that it made me feel like a babe in her mother's arms. In any case it was so intensely sweet, so inexpressibly comforting, that one could not dream of desiring a lover after that — what a come down! And yet one forgets, and desires remain lurking —isn't it unbelievable!

Anandamayee Ma sent word through someone that I should see her before going to Benares. So I must go this morning, in spite of menses, dead or alive. I love following Her call.

Evening: Saw Mother. She was wonderful, she wanted me to travel with three of her devotees, that's all; but by way of parting said: *"Now it is the last time for a long time, but as everything is everywhere, if you think of someone, you are already with them."* Sorrensen came to see me after I got back.

I don't think I shall see Rama Rao again. My dream that he is dying seems right.

I am dead tired but how I enjoyed my visit to Patal Devi [Anandamayee Ma's Ashram at Almora]. I stayed there for at least two hours or more. Tomorrow to Ranikhet.

Forest Rest House, Ranikhet, 5th July, 1945

All worked perfectly. Julia Drummond fetched me in her car. The dentist says I should have a wisdom tooth out. I feel changed, very quiet and much more settled in myself, not dependent on others and circumstances for my happiness.

Atmananda in Almora with friends - early 1940's (courtesy of Swami Nirvanananda)

VII - Life at Rajghat

Rajghat, 8th July, 1945

Travelled in great comfort, but did not, as it turned out, look after Anandamayee Ma's devotees; they arrived safely though. Shared a compartment on the train with six Bavarian nuns. Borrowed from them *One with Jesus* by Jaeger (a Jesuit) —a mystical book just about like *Sharanagati* [1] in Christian garb. My rash is very troublesome, also the wisdom tooth (slightly) and constipation and disturbances all night. I feel very tired and troubled. The one luxury that I crave for is quiet and solitude.

10th July, 1945

Yesterday as I tried to dust Lewis' room, the sculpture of Durga fell over and broke in two. I wonder whether this is what I have been doing for him all along —helping him with physical, irrelevant things and destroying his Gods and his inner repose. I again feel very strongly that I must leave him alone. Physically we do clash.

I feel very tired and worn out. But there is a change all the same. It is a pity to bury it again by work. Like in the Christian book I read in the train, I (the ego) must get out and make room for the Divine Mother.

11th July, 1945

Lewis came yesterday. He did not mind the broken Goddess at all. He seemed glad to be alone there. My reaction to him is different now, but it is too early to say. He is a strange being. He comes and talks to me as much as possible. He needs contact with people. He lives in his own strange world so much. He is not aware of other peoples' world. He read Cocteau's *Opium* to me this evening. It depicts a strange, strange world and it is painful to get

---

[1] The book she had been reading in Hindi by Swami Sharanananda.

back to the ordinary. He showed me Henri Moore's pictures, which I could not really appreciate, chiefly I suppose because I have pre-conceived ideas. He said that if I could see the uniqueness of <u>everything</u>, then only can I come fresh to art and be able to see it from the artist's point of view.

13th July, 1945

There is a strange change in my relation to Lewis. Today he again read *Opium* to me. He looked so cold, like steel; I almost felt frightened and the world of Cocteau is so uncanny. This kills love.

I am very tired and not feeling fit. The noise here is too ener-vating and there are so many children. I crave for quiet and soli-tude. One day I shall get it.

16th July, 1945

The noise and confusion around me are simply a reflection of the restlessness in me. When I have a chance of being really quiet, I always find something that has to be done, and when it's done the outer quiet is over.

21st July, 1945

This noise and restlessness makes me withdraw from conscious awareness like a tortoise and I don't live at all, only vegetate. Had diarrhoea and was dreadfully weak. Could not meditate at all. Then Lewis got fever, so I have to get there early in the morning and won't be able to sit down and meditate. Last night again I dreamt I was interred in 'Zimmeran' whatever that means. I wish I had quiet. Often I feel sorry that I did not go to Delhi. It is so difficult here and I get ill all the time; the food is quite unsuitable.

22nd July, 1945

Lewis has had fever and I am busy with him. But I don't seem to do it in the right way. I get tired and annoyed. This evening we had a bust up over H. Krishna. I said I would not get things for him if he gave them to H.K. He says he is not responsible, there is no giving and taking and it is not in his power to hold on to things. He says: "When a vessel is already overflowing and you put in more water, that is what happens". I say: "It is like pouring water into a vessel with a hole in it." He says "Both are right" and that I am evidently attached, as Anandamayee Ma says. He told me to read the *Gita*. I opened it to the following (Annie Besant's translation):

"But the man who rejoiceth in the SELF, with the SELF is satisfied, and is content in the SELF, for him verily there is nothing to do. For him there is no interest in things done in this world, nor any in things not done."

23rd July, 1945

Deadlock with Lewis. I said so many hard things to him which I had kept inside me all these months that now he can't very well let me go on doing things for him. He still looks ill and weak. I asked him whether he wanted milk. He said: "No". Later I saw him go to the kitchen for it. Poor man. But what can I do? I keep on being so annoyed about the boÿs and also at his accepting everything from me as a matter of course, as if I were his 'elemental'. I feel cold and tied up. What a change to the love I felt last month! How temporary everything is. Can one expect anything to last? It is all of the moment.

28th July, 1945

I feel so strained, half mad. Lewis is getting too much for me. I do not understand his ways. He is ill and I feel desperately worried, but one can't look after him. He changes what he wants and expects everything to happen by itself. He has no servant and I have to send mine, whom I share with someone else in any case; but he does not wait till he comes, and runs about when he should rest. I find it impossible to collect myself because I am too worried. There he is right. He sends me a comic poem. I have no sense of humour anymore. I never think anymore. I have gone quite silly. I wonder whether Sanjiv Rao was right after all! But how could I go against Anandamayee Ma's advice and against my own wish and leave Lewis alone.

Read *Les Monstres Sacrés* by Jean Cocteau. It is a very fine drama of a strange triangle, very great and true. It brought back memories of my past very vividly.

29ᵗʰ July, 1945

Suddenly last night I saw how comic the situation is from one point of view. There is such a total deadlock in L.'s physical affairs, he must come to a complete solution soon. The water also stopped and could not be set right. Krishni also refused to lend her servant. But life goes on all the same from hour to hour. One has to look at it with detachment and not take oneself so seriously. Then it becomes very amusing.

31ˢᵗ July, 1945

Received a letter from Swami Paramananda [2] saying that Anandamayee Ma on hearing my letter said: *"Always try to meditate on God. Do not pass your time in vain."* She evidently knows in what a state I am.

Lewis is better and a servant found.

Seem caught in the restless atmosphere here. I must go to Sarnath next holiday.

8ᵗʰ August, 1945

The other day when Lewis read to me, I suddenly saw him differently. There was a kind of recognition, but so subtle and fleeting that I could not really grasp it. It was of the same stuff as a dream.

Yesterday he helped me to practice Mozart, explaining the interpretation to me in sensual terms. I suddenly wondered whether I have become so bland because I never had this experience really: just letting myself go without fear or guilt; whereas he experiences things purely artistically with an uncompromising drive to uncover their truth and beauty. My nerves have become dull, whereas his are alive to a pinpoint sensitivity. Have I been like that from the beginning, or have I been spoiled by life. I rather think the latter as I can imitate and reproduce this fineness and sensitivity when my finger is put on it by someone else. I believe I have been very violent with myself and have spoiled and suppressed a great deal. That is why I have become sort of disgusted with everything. It is not real renunciation. But then the very fact that I recognize this shows that I must have some genuine understanding of the real thing.

---

[2] Head swami of the Anandamayee Ma Ashram.

9ᵗʰ August, 1945

Wrote letters for Malati for three hours this morning. The restlessness at her place and the eternal calling of servants and doing fifty other things as well was very enervating. If I behaved like this at Sanjiv Rao's faculty breakfasts, then L. was quite right to avoid them and to reproach me so severely for being such a pain. I am glad he brought my attention to this. It is really most important to do only one thing at a time.

This evening I walked alone in the school garden. It is exquisite to watch a flowering tree. How wonderful it looks, it does not complain of the heat, it just exactly fulfils its Creator's intention and is happy. Nature's atmosphere is still very beautiful here, but what human beings are doing to it, oh dear!

13ᵗʰ August, 1945

Now I am again in tune with Lewis.

Last night meditating, I found that the Divine seems to be waiting to be let in; indeed I almost feel it as a sort of pressure on me. But the instrument is so impure, it just cannot absorb it. It is a great strain. This morning again I had a very successful meditation on Anandamayee Ma. She is quite right, I forget the Presence of God. Why am I so impure? This concentration makes me frightfully tired.

17ᵗʰ August, 1945

But I have grown very fond of L. again. Today he told me he might go to Ceylon. I feel quite desperate at the thought of separation for good. One day of course it will come, no doubt.

Last night I dreamt again my old nightmare of having to play a concert and not being able to find the music book etc. L. says it must have a deep symbolic meaning. I wonder whether it means the choice of the world or the eternal, music representing the world. Whenever I see J.K., it takes me away from music. The question I asked Anandamayee Ma was also whether or not to go to Delhi [for the job as music director]. She definitely said "No". In my Theosophical time this was also the great problem and I could never decide then either. When the church solved it[3], I had to give

---

[3] She played the organ and was music director at the Liberal Catholic Church in Huizen, Holland.

that up also. At present I feel terrified of going to Delhi in a few days, as I shall be alone at 7 Bharakambha Road [4] and the nightmare of last night still haunts me. Strange, it is music that keeps me in touch with this world —which seems right, if only I can surrender and do it in the correct way.

20th August, 1945

What nonsense is 'balance'. Balance with what? Fitting in with what and whom? Who am 'I', who is it that obeys the body's urge? This self-perpetuating stream of thought and deed must be stopped. Thought spins and spins, where? —to the grave and back to birth, what for? Nonsense, nonsense, nonsense. Who amuses himself with this? God's *Leela* [5]?

New Delhi, 26th August, 1945

I dislike Delhi more than ever. It is a sticky horrible place. This house full of political activities. Surroundings are very important. Thank God I did not accept the job here.

27th August, 1945

Everyone at the All India Radio tries to persuade me to take up the job of director. Strangely there is still a temptation in it for me. I say to myself that in any case I can't really meditate, so why not do something else instead. Yet I am afraid of starting on this Delhi life. It will take me far away into utter unreality.

Benares, 31st August, 1945

This is so much better than Delhi. Lewis talked to me for a long time about my playing which he criticized seriously. He said that instead of surrendering to the music I drive through it and impose myself on it rather than letting it flow naturally through me. I feel less and less interested in music. I am no longer really a musician. He agrees with me. Art has only a justification when it is a way of self-development, but with me this is no longer the case. It balances me as long as there are certain forces still potent

---

[4] The large family home of Kitty and Siva Rao and his two brothers.

[5] *Leela*, 'play 'or game. It is used in the sense that the world and all of creation are the 'play' of God. This idea is fundamental to Hindu spirituality and culture.

in me that need to be released. But it also upsets the calm of meditation. I must and will give it up but somehow I haven't the courage to do it yet. One has to take the plunge. But it can't be imposed from outside. Just like when I wanted to go to Tiruvannamalai, one must really be ready.

L. says that when he first met me I reminded him of a woman he had known when he was about 18. She was then about 45 - 50, had been a first class violinist and was still very beautiful and remarkable. One day she had dropped her art and became a devout Catholic, entered some order and started going about in a black cloak. She had switched over from one to the other in a minute. He also tells me about Kierkegaard, who was an artist by temperament and a mystic, and who says that there is no connection between the two but that one must make a leap. I have always felt that: the gap between music and what I really want. I cannot harmonise the two, yet cannot get out of music either — not yet.

Rajghat, 1ˢᵗ September, 1945

Malati is leaving suddenly —strange. She says that after having made the decision to go to Ramana Maharshi's ashram at Tiruvannamalai, she felt as if she were going home after having been far away. She does definitely seem changed and calm now. I feel happy for her. She is again as she used to be. She herself says she had become estranged from herself and a slave. Now she has been forced to break the spell and escape Kelkar's tyranny. Is Hitler finally dead now also at Rajghat?

L. says he dreamt of a fundamental change in me that would take place in the October holidays, he thought. How I wish that this were true!

Read in Sharananand's book about how eating should be a taking in of energy to feed the 'prana' (the subtle life energy) —that a *sadhaka* does not 'eat' at all in a physical sense. How difficult this is for me. At least I now remember mostly what I am out to do. In this way Delhi has helped. Change makes one more conscious.

The piano bores me dead stiff. Yet I have not the courage to decide against accepting the broadcasts in October. See what Kitty says —if anything.

Atmananda with Rajghat School faculty - late 1930's (courtesy of Swami Nirvanananda)

5ᵗʰ September, 1945

Malati left. Even though we are such good friends, I really feel nothing. At the very moment of saying goodbye, of course there was a surge of feeling; but nothing is real to me. Is it detachment or complacency? I believe I must have attained to a good deal of detachment in former births but got stuck somewhere.

I have written to Delhi. I can't give up the piano as yet. It will fall away by itself, as L. says.

8ᵗʰ September, 1945

It occurred to me today that if I really want to find out Who 'I' am, I must be at it all day and night and leave all else. Just to sit still for half an hour and then to live the same unconscious life as everyone else is rather ridiculous.

9ᵗʰ September, 1945

This morning I had an intense feeling of happiness when trying to meditate. I thought how wonderful it will be to surrender entirely, not to exist at all —to still that constant current of activity and excitement which I am now able to stand back from and observe.

Then I went to see Lewis. He knew that I would come and had kept tea for me. The barber was there. I had tea and then sat alone looking at a historical atlas of India while he was being shaved. Then he began telling me, of his own accord, of his experience of total disillusionment with a relationship that he had thought of as the deepest thing in his life and how that produced a complete void and made everything non-existent; how his friends quite rightly concluded he had committed suicide. After that, he said, one lives like a ghost, seeming to do things, but actually doing nothing.

I then told him that I had had similar experiences, but having gone to the verge of madness had grown back together again; that I often feel the ridiculousness of everything and yet can go on with my ordinary activity as if nothing had happened. To this he said that my nature was much too solid for the real madness (as though he felt threatened that another could share this secret treasure with him). But later he admitted that I was made in such a way that my mind could really break —that is, break through the brain barrier into 'Reality'. It is, as I always feel, that there is a tremendous power from on high waiting to enter, but my nature is equally strong in its own way and can't accept it. How to resolve this?

I then asked him about my difficulty in meditation which makes me so tired. He explained to me most beautifully how most Westerners attempt to concentrate with the will, which is the reverse of true meditation. He said that to meditate means to plunge completely into one's own being and to drop everything else —all the activities that wander in the mind stream which goes on continually— and to let go completely so that there is nothing left of this stream of mental activity which constitutes what we feel to be our whole life and the life of the whole world. The pictures on a cinema screen seem real, although without the screen —which in our minds corresponds to a sheet of white light on which thought is projected— they cannot exist. Yet we never think of the screen because we get too absorbed in the ever-changing scenes that move by so quickly. Meditation means to plunge into that screen, going beyond the constantly changing surface images, and hold on to it, not by an act of will, but rather by a kind of letting go or abandonment —something that is closer to imagination than to will.

He then told me not to shut my eyes, as that would provoke reveries, but simply to leave the eyes alone —not to stare blankly nor to concentrate on a particular point but to sit comfortably and to keep the spine and head erect and poised— he said that that was very important.

He also told me that only Anandamayee Ma, who had given the *sadhana*, could help me with my difficulties. I said that I felt one should not do these meditations at all unless one had someone near to watch and advise. But L. says: "If Anandamayee Ma asked you to do it, you are absolutely safe".

I sat in his room for nearly three hours. Then he came to mine after food for another hour. There was a very intimate sense of rapport between us, which continues. There is such a deep attraction, but utterly beyond the physical. When I look at him in terms of any physical attraction, it breaks immediately.

While he was in my room, a letter from Malati came thanking me for my understanding and sympathy. She is in the depths of hell at present.

145

I read in *Zen Buddhism* by Christmas Humphries: "If you are not determined to die in a last ditch effort to get realisation, you cannot understand". It is the same as Sharanananda's teaching.

Malati says: "How little one human being knows about another." Of course, we each are entirely different —and yet ultimately the same. Love makes us want to lose ourselves in the beloved. But until we have found our own centre and are fulfilled we can never really love.

Whenever I have some spiritual realization, the physical nature immediately tries to re-assert itself all the more strongly — wanting to eat and talk, or whatever it takes to restore its dominance. But if I dedicate eating, talking, everything to the One Supreme Purpose, it is bound to lead up to the One happening, instead of only increasing duality.

10th September, 1945

Last night I tried to follow Lewis' instructions when meditating. It was a great help. I could sit up straight for a long time without getting tired and got at something quite different from usual —I should call it colourless. What he told me about dropping everything and watching the mind stream from outside tallies with complete surrender. Only I find that the inner spiritual force contacted by such intense meditation is a power that must be dealt with carefully. This must be the *Kundalini* energy that I have read about in the books of Arthur Avalon [6]. If one is not able to channel this force correctly it can cause a negative reaction in the body which may not be ready for it. I felt very distressed about this and prayed fervently to the Mother to help me. I remember J.K.'s verdict to the effect that I was suffering from repressed emotions that block my energy; but now the energy seems ready to explode.

I woke up late feeling very depressed about this but when I meditated I was less tense and not so exhausted as I used to be. To

[6] Pen name for Sir John Woodroffe, noted English jurist and author and translator of seminal works on Tantric Yoga *sadhana* and philosophy. *Kundalini* is the primordial cosmic energy coiled like a serpent in the *muladhara chakra* located at the base of the spine. It is literally the energy of enlightenment and its awakened movement through the various bodily spiritual centres (or *chakras*) until it unites with the highest centre at the crown of the head brings about a total mystical awakening.

think that concentration is uttermost relaxation changes the whole thing. To collect one's mind in the centre point of one's being where it can completely rest —this is where its true home is.

This morning I had quite an experience of Anandamayee Ma's inner presence. It calls out a great love and takes away the heaviness.

I read a passage on how a *sadhaka* should eat in Swamiji's book *Sant Sangam*. It is evident that I must follow his advice. I wrote the whole thing out into my book of quotations. If I feed my body out of greed it will be built up in a way that is utterly antithetical to realization. It will always remain heavy. To take food as an offering to *prana* will purify and lighten the body and obliterate the sex impulse.

15th September, 1945

Lewis suddenly burst into an excited account of his trouble with Ella and his Guru. I am flabbergasted and stunned. It is really appalling. It is all on an altogether different plane. In the end authority is only a hindrance. One must find out and know for oneself. J.K. is right.

* * *

Lewis Thompson was closely associated for a number of years with Sri Krishna Menon, a highly respected South Indian master of Advaita Vedanta —the ancient Upanishadic philosophy of non-duality [7]. *It seems that Thompson, in the outspokenness of his passionate philosophical disputations with his teacher, had overstepped a certain line of fundamental etiquette and respect in his relationship with him. This rift was exacerbated by the jealousy of some of the other followers and ultimately the Guru asked him to leave.*

* * *

16th September, 1945

I am appalled at L.'s story. How can he live? Though I suppose we all live like that. There is something impossible in all of our lives that were we to really take it seriously we would have to

---

[7] Advaita Vedanta is the most completely monistic school of Hindu philosophy, akin to Buddhism in its denial that the material world or the individual mind has any inherent Reality.

solve it at once or perish. It occurs to me that however much one may appear to know, one really knows nothing previous to enlightenment; that the more one seems to know or thinks one knows, the more difficult it is to recognize how completely valueless this empty knowledge really is. L. needs a new dimension, a complete break in order to transfer knowledge from the mind to the heart —exactly what he tells me all the time.

23rd September, 1945

Reading Ramana Maharshi's books since yesterday. They are really the finest. He says that the mind is built up from the subtle substance of the food which one eats. This is indeed a very important matter.

25th September, 1945

Yesterday Lewis talked to me for nearly three hours about the ultimate non-existence of the visible world as postulated in both Indian and Western idealistic philosophies. This impressed me greatly.

He said to me: "How do you know that life is not a dream? You can't prove that it is not and you can't prove that it is unless you wake up." Can one wake up? Suppose I try, as an experiment, to imagine that everything is God —like my experiment at 16 where I loved the stones on which I walked.

What does it mean, 'God'? I shall try anyhow. See what happens.

26th September, 1945

Read some of J.K.'s talks. I notice some things that I never saw before. What he says is so subtle and I see it would have been quite impossible for me to get at it had I gone on as I had been. There is no question that I had to leave it alone for some time. I cannot say what 'awareness' and 'discernment' are in the state I am in. Besides, I haven't the strength of mind to deal with my problem in J.K.'s way. It is just impossible. He really —as Lewis says— is not aware of the *adhikara* (spiritual ability) that alone enables one to get benefit out of his teaching. Maybe I shall come back to it later.

27th **September, 1945**

I have doubts about Anandamayee Ma. Is she really completely divine? It is impossible for me to know. If I know nothing, how can I know this. However, I reason with myself that it is better to imagine that She is. I cannot manage by myself and She is obviously someone quite extraordinary. Of course I have accepted Her largely on the authority of Lewis who doubts the integrity of his own master! So where do I stand? L. also is not omniscient. He has extraordinary dreams which I feel are partly a kind of escape, as this physical world is so utterly unsatisfactory for him. His interpretation does not always seem quite right. Then also he is tense. His eyes are bad and, as Agarwal told him, this is due to his staring technique in meditation. He also makes an effort to see instead of allowing himself to see. All the same, he seems to be extremely near Self-realization.

My difficulties in the *sadhana* which Anandamayee Ma asked me to do:

(1) Having been nurtured on J.K.'s teachings, I have doubts as to whether it is right to coerce the body by making it completely still, to coerce the feelings by making them still, to coerce the mind by making it watch the breath instead of what it would like to do.

The mind likes to wander but if it becomes fascinated by something, it will focus on this of its own accord and without strain. Then also the emotions become satisfied and blissful and the body stays still and relaxed. The main thing therefore is to find an object of absorbing interest for the mind. When J.K. asked me: "In what are you interested?" I answered that I did not know and he said: "What a mess we have made of our lives!" I said: "I want to love everyone." J.K.: "Why don't you?" I: "Too often when one loves someone, it leads to physical attachment." He (shocked): "Oh no! If you truly love one, you love all."

However it seems to me that no thing and no one can absorb my whole interest for any length of time. The mind gets tired of even the most beloved people and things, and longs for a change. Is that not so because it is looking for the *Atma*, its own source, which is beyond the temporal? Mother told me to watch the breath or to meditate on the *Atma*, but I don't know how to do the latter. The Atma, not having any qualities, cannot be thought about. When the mind touches the *Atma*, it is gone. Any thought covers up the true *Atma* and when one really touches it, thought is annihilated.

(2) How can I imagine myself part of the life that pulsates through every being? Who am 'I'? Oh, now I see vaguely —this is what it is driving at: Forget about your body, thoughts, feelings, and experience yourself as not separate from that one life. (Before I was always unconsciously attempting to force myself as the ego to become one with all, rather than letting go of all personal effort and allowing that which is, to be).

(3) She said: *"Imagine that the Divine grace and light is showered on you."* On whom? Who am 'I' again? But here also I now see that, having imagined myself as part of the life that animates every living being, this is my starting point. In that state I merge into light and peace —no question of body. These visualizations are a technique that can jolt the mind into an altogether new and liberated perspective.

This writing down everything and analysing oneself is really a tremendous help. Anandamayee Ma knows what She's talking about. I must meet Her and discuss my questions with Her.

My intensity is not yet strong enough for Self-realization. That may be because some *samskaras* still have to be completed. Yet since it is my destiny to be without any encumbrances —no family, no liabilities—, isn't it an ideal opportunity for the Search?

"Cursed is this world and cursed is all that is in this world, except the remembrance of God and that which aideth it."

(sayings of Prophet Muhammad)

28th September, 1945

Last night had a very blissful meditation on the Mother. But it again reacted on the body. I must find out what to do about this. I am much more conscious now during the day and don't allow my thoughts to wander unobserved so much as I used to; but it is rather strenuous and produces eye strain and a slight headache. Yet just as by walking long distances at Almora, though I got over-tired, my muscles soon got into shape and then I could walk easily —so it may also be with training the mind.

29th September, 1945

Lewis talked to me for a long time in the evening about the waking-state and the dream-state. He said that to write down dreams was a discipline enabling one to remember and thus to become more conscious. Then one is able to throw out all the rubbish and open out to a deeper level. At present the consciousness is blurred by the mind that is stained like a dirty window. It has to be cleaned thoroughly. Then one discovers that the waking-state influences the dream-state and vice-versa. It is obvious that the dream-state is subjective in everyone, but we don't believe that the waking-state is as well. But he says when we become conscious, we discover that the waking-state also is only a dream; but we must take this dream very seriously, otherwise we don't get anywhere. The attitude that 'nothing really matters' is poisonous, it leaves you where you are. In order to 'realize' you have to suffer a crucifixion of the ego, which afterwards you find out did not really exist.

I am beginning to wonder what all this muddle is about inside me. The Theosophical confusion evidently had a deep significance. It occurs to me that perhaps Ramana Maharshi only very graciously helped me to straighten out this state of confusion, but otherwise His way is not at all my path? The real tangle seems to be between J.K. and the MOTHER, to both of whom I am very strongly attracted. Or will I see that they are one?

It seems to me that Lewis is a Godsend to help me out of this muddle. He also is in a state of suspension and most probably, as soon as it is over, will go back to his own teacher —and I to mine? Though I feel no physical attraction to him, there is still this beastly suppressed desire in me which I discussed with J.K. and it makes everything impure.

1st October, 1945

Am again fascinated by J.K. Strange how he holds me in his grip.

Went to the T.S. with Lewis to see Radha [8] dance and talk

---

[8] Radha Shastri comes from an important Theosophical family. She was married to Atmananda's friend, Raymond Burnier, and is today the current president of the Theosophical Society.

about Bharatnatyam [9]. In my dream where I told L. about my theosophical past, I had to stop at the Egyptian Rite and with Master K.H., as L. went away. Next day I tried to tell him in the waking state, but it did not come out somehow. I only told him my dream and that I thought some of my past still stuck to me. He said: yes, that may be the reason why you cannot proceed. I also told him that I had been told that I would be condemned because I had given up these rites. He said curses work mostly because some part of the cursed person believes in it. If one faces it completely, it has no power over one. He said I should take the whole matter apart and deal with it. I could become conscious of it in my dreams, perhaps.

There is a deadlock in my meditation since I began to think of J.K. again. It paralyses it. I now notice things in J.K. which I did not before. Strange how this fascination persists, even though I could not do anything with it all these years and remained stagnant and wasted all my time; still I find it has a strong effect. I had to leave Rishi Valley [10] six years ago, because I knew I should break or go mad if I continued to follow J.K., and yet it still holds me. But how can I believe that anything that comes from J.K. can be evil. Can it? Am I not in the same position as L.? Yet I seem calm and fairly happy on the outside!

Lewis seems the only point of light in all this chaos. He fascinates me. He talked to me about how when one is really in love the concentration on the beloved becomes so intense that he or she becomes like a devotional image in which the living deity is present and the individual vanishes. But there is always a point beyond which one cannot proceed, because every person is limited, no matter how sublime. Therefore it seems to me that the only salvation is to find a human being who is perfectly realized, that is Divine but appears to be human, a true Guru, so that there should be no limitation. One's devotion, love and concentration on that Being ought to be able to take one right into SILENCE.

---

[9] An ancient form of classical South Indian dance which Radha and particularly her aunt, Rukmini Arundale, were instrumental in reviving.

[10] The Krishnamurti school located near Bangalore which at that time was also a kind of ashram for his followers.

J.K. Talks 1940, p. 11: *"For thought is now the product of greed* [11] *and therefore transitory, and so cannot understand the eternal. That which can understand the immortal must also be immortal. The permanent cannot be understood through the transitory. That is, thought born of greed is transient and whatever it creates must surely also be transient and so long as the mind is held within the transient, within the circle of greed, it cannot transcend nor overcome itself. In its efforts to overcome it creates further resistances and gets more and more entangled in them."*

This seems to be exactly what Anandamayee Ma told me: As long as the mind is busy with transient things it must be fickle. Put it on that which lasts. So what she has asked me to do takes the mind out of this circle of greed.

2nd October, 1945

By reading J.K. I again got thoroughly upset. He exerts such a fascination on my mind —or is it that the mind tries to save its life by cultivating that which both stimulates it and fuels it's doubts. I go round in a circle. I am sick of it. This naturally upsets my endeavours in meditation as it causes me to doubt what Anandamayee Ma has told me.

3rd October, 1945

Last night tried to meditate and instead of watching the breath, which I always find tedious, tried to concentrate on God. As I do not know how to do this, it occurred to me to think of L. and go further. Such an intense love was the result that I almost felt frightened of it. Never have I felt like that for anyone. Is it because he has hardly any ego left? Unfortunately I did not write this down at once in spite of the impulse to do so. But waking in the night I pondered over it and could not go to sleep. There is great reluctance to put this down however. Why? L. says Sri Krishna Menon told him that he was a Tantric Yogi with many disciples in his last life. Was I one of them?

4th October, 1945

Last night read *Sat Vani*, the little book of words of Ananda-

---

[11] Greed here seems to mean the limited ego's fundamental need to possess, control and conceptualize, rather than allowing that which 'is' to be.

mayee Ma —the last bit being about breathing and contemplation becoming one. As a result I seem to have had some communion during sleep and woke up at 6.30 a.m. with the definite consciousness of the Bliss and Presence of the Mother. But within a few minutes the mind rushed in and destroyed the whole thing. I then tried to meditate in bed but was not very successful. The ever 'chattering mind' as J.K. calls it, destroys everything.

Yesterday received a letter from Walter. I was surprised to be reminded that I had asked S.R. to see about possibilities for me in the U.S.A. I have not the slightest wish left to go there, on the contrary. This time my journey to Jaipur and Delhi tomorrow hardly occupies me, while Almora seemed all important.

Had the most interesting conversation on evil with Lewis. He says Lucifer is nearest to God; that he sacrificed himself, as the necessary resistance needed to bring the world back to its source. Lewis said that he himself went through a period of being luciferic. A person who does not realize the devil in himself and come to love him cannot be complete. He says this is also in me, but hidden. I say I am terrified of it. The time has not yet come when I can safely embrace the devil without falling his prey. "That is precisely the way to be subject to it", he emphasized.

J.K. is also luciferic and many people describe him as such. It struck me that only the other day it had occurred to me that he can be evil —the Kali aspect of the Mother perhaps. I am really in the same boat as L.; I also don't know whether J.K. is a force for good or for evil. *But I do certainly know that he is empty, without ego, and is my own self when I am with him.* L. says that he must not be considered as a personal teacher, but only as a *sadhaka*, and that is the only relationship that he recognizes —between him and other *sadhakas*. My relationship to him is becoming more and more this and must become still more perfectly so. This is what my relationship to Kitty is really meant to be as is the case with 'X'. I remember now that from childhood I was worried about the problem of evil. And the only thing that I disliked in Tolstoi was that he says: "Do not resist evil." Whereas *At the Feet of the Master* [12] says: "You must actively resist the Evil". I liked the latter.

---

[12] A book attributed to the very young Krishnamurti, written when he was 16 years old and still completely under the influence of the Theosophical Masters.

Jaipur, 7ᵗʰ October, 1945

Miss Merston [13] saw me off at Kashi (Benares). She has just returned from Tiruvannamalai. She does not seem at all changed. Is that what J.K. means by saying: "All your Rishis and Maharishis are bunk".

Jaipur, 9ᵗʰ October, 1945

When I watch my new neighbour, Mrs. H., I find her just unbearably silly, self satisfied and bourgeoise. This is worse than any vice or destructive quality —it is death, completely living in the little idiotic circle of her I-ness. But it could not get on my nerves so if I hadn't something of it myself. I must seek *satsang*. Why must I go and play for the radio at all? Now that restrictions will be removed I can go where I like and need not bother with having an official excuse to travel.

Jaipur, 11ᵗʰ October, 1945

Travel restrictions are now nearly over. They have really kept me from one thing only: from going to Tiruvannamalai. Do I still want to go? Most certainly, but with one difference: then I wanted to go for a year or two and see what happens, now I am going for good —not necessarily to Tiruvannamalai— but to my real Home, and no one shall hinder me. It will all come by itself, slowly and quietly. What is the good of travelling about all over and meeting this and that person. No good at all.

Dr. H. is very nice and very capable, but one cannot really do anything revolutionary, vital and decisive and remain an ordinary bourgeois, polite, kind and easy-going person. One must set oneself apart, do something drastic. These nice humdrum, comfortable existences —the more satisfying they are, the more poisonous really. Not for nothing have I been with Lewis Thompson all this time.

---

[13] Daniélou states in his rather eccentric autobiography, *The Way to the Labyrinth,* that Juliet Merston was employed as a spy by the British authorities to keep an eye on European Indophiles such as himself and Atmananda. He relates that she worked as his secretary for several years and was so sympathetic to the interests of the people she was hired to watch that she always wrote glowing reports on them.

The net outcome of this visit of mine has been that another illusion is gone: meeting new people. Shall I use my newly-won freedom of movement to go visiting? Certainly not. Go deeper and deeper inside. Anandamayee Ma may not be too far from Benares. I might go to Her at Diwali. Yes.

Delhi, 13th October, 1945

In the train read Maharshi's *Sad-Vidya* and had quite a meditation on it. It changed me altogether. Some process seems to be going on inside me all the time: when outer conditions are favourable it becomes slightly visible, when unfavourable it hides, but rushes out the moment they are over. I felt the influence of the Mother and believe it must be from the Dussehra [14] feast at Rae Bareilly that is being celebrated now.

Delhi, 15th October, 1945

It is remarkable how true my dream was. Kitty disagrees with me on every point. I itch to have a talk with her, though, and find out how she lives. She really seems to be all 'make-up'. She is right not to want me in the house. It is definitely wrong for me to be near her. Fortunately she has given me a room far away from hers. She gets almost seasick when any spiritual person is mentioned. There is no relationship between her and me at all, there cannot be. She goes right, I go left —or rather reverse. It does not matter to me at all now, still I wonder how it is I used to call her my better half.

18th October, 1945

I killed a mosquito on my hand. Nothing was left but a black smudge. When I die, what will be left but a much bigger, more colourful, rotten smelling smudge! And this is the kind of thing one identifies oneself with. Isn't life a miracle. That flying, lively mosquito within a second becomes a black smudge. Where does the life go? Why? Why should one feel so much more for one's own smudge than for others? Perhaps it is necessary.

---

[14] Refers to the annual ten day autumn festival to the Goddess Durga. This is a very colourful and powerful pageant characterized by joyous singing and wild rhythmic drumming. Elaborate food and fruit offerings are made to a specially crafted life-size image of the Goddess. On the 10th day the image is immersed in the nearest river to dissolve back into the formless from whence She came.

Kitty does a lot of social work. This is her way of worship. She can only fulfil herself through outer activity evidently. Perhaps it satisfies her completely as being her way to Liberation?

Ours are two different universes. But the moment one respects the other person sufficiently to allow her entire freedom, there is no occasion for clash or quarrel.

I feel almost antagonistic towards J.K. He is not the World-Teacher. What I owe him, though, is no little thing and I have much to be grateful to him for.

Rajghat, 22ⁿᵈ October, 1945

My relationship with Lewis seems to have taken on tremendous dimensions. I am beginning to feel that I cannot go on like this. Either I must drop him completely or go into this completely and risk everything. I cannot do the first and I am terrified of the second.

23ʳᵈ October, 1945

On hearing that Anandamayee Ma is most probably in Benares I felt rather terrified and panicky, instead of happy. I feel frightened now to talk to her. I made plans to see Her at Diwali [15] and now that She has come here, I feel like hiding, instead of hurrying to Her. Is the ego afraid of being killed?

24ᵗʰ October, 1945

Went to see Miss Merston instead of going to Mother. She was very friendly. We talked about J.K., Shri Ramakrishna, etc. There must be a deeper reason for my not going to Anandamayee Ma. I was even more frightened before going to Tiruvannamalai.

Received a postcard from Swami Paramananda to say that Anandamayee Ma is at Vindhyachal near Mirzapur. So in this case the resistance to seeing Her seems to have had an element of intuition in it as She is not in Benares after all. I had planned to see her at Diwali and now am invited for Kalipuja on Diwali night. Having consecrated myself to the service of the Mother, I should trust my feelings more. She is guiding me. Since receiving the

---

[15] Diwali, the festival of lights, is perhaps the most popular Hindu festival of the year; gifts are exchanged and the Goddess Lakshmi, Patroness of the home, beauty and prosperity, is honoured.

postcard I feel strangely elated and near to Her. Somehow it also strengthens my affection for Lewis. Reading Ramakrishna's life [16], I came across an interesting passage where he tells his nephew, Hriday, not to go in for visions etc. as he needs someone to serve him, and promises him he will get all in that way.

This evening when playing the piano there was a strange unearthly overtone sometimes in my high tones.

25th October, 1945

When meditating I tried to imagine that the breath belonged to the MOTHER and I was taking into my body Her Life with every inhalation and throwing out the ego with every exhalation. I am capable of tremendous devotion really, but always feel that I still have work to do down here. At present I feel I must not leave L. I always feel that the MOTHER wants to love L. through a woman who will look after him.

I am again getting very weary of this school which is so utterly flat. Was too restless to play the piano tonight. Went for a walk meditating on the Mother. It is always fruitful to walk alone. When L. came back from the bazaar, I could not see his nice side at all. I vacillate between love and almost repulsion for him. What I love is so obviously not he, the visible one, but something far beyond that for which he is a focus; but it is so much easier from a distance. It is quite tantalizing. When he is far, I imagine him as something divine and highly desirable, but when I sit face to face, unless he talks about purely spiritual matters, it is flat and disappointing. What disturbs me and makes me try to hold on all the more is that I cannot grasp him, he is so ethereal that he cannot be held on to. Yet there is something behind that seems to be *The Thing* that I must get at! What madness!

---

[16] Paramahansa Ramakrishna (1836-1886), probably the most famous of the many great Indian saints of modern times. Like Anandamayee Ma he was born in a Bengali village, but spent most of his life as a temple priest in a suburb of Calcutta where he profoundly influenced a select group of followers, including many very westernized Indians living in what was then the second capital of the British Empire. His great disciple, Swami Vivekananda, created a tremendous sensation when he spoke at the First World Parliament of Religions held in Chicago in 1893.

29th October, 1945

L. brought me some white scented flowers this morning, saying: "The Mother of Pondicherry [17] uses these as a symbol of transformation."

I then sat down for my morning meditation, feeling that I really don't know how to do it. It occurred to me that if I consider Anandamayee Ma an incarnation of the Divine MOTHER and, as she told me to watch the breath, how can I look for something else that 'interests' me. Reading *Sri Ramakrishna's Life* made me realize a little what surrender is. When I surrendered to the Mother this morning in my meditation it was an effort to stop. It was such bliss. Unfortunately I had to go to school. I had a faint inkling of how one really cannot keep one's mind on work when one gets deeply absorbed in that kind of thing.

30th October, 1945

Last night went to Prahlad Ghat with Lewis and witnessed by chance the funeral of the *pujari* of the Hanuman temple behind our kitchen. It was a strange experience. Then read Sri Ramakrishna's life till late. It fascinates me greatly though there are some things —about 'woman' for instance— that I can't stomach [18], but I have a great desire to get in touch with this remarkable Being. I wonder whether I can? I feel rather anxious to hear from the police whether I can go to see Anandamayee Ma for Diwali; though I tell myself that I must not worry and surrender the whole affair into the hands of the MOTHER. She knows best —and yet I feel impatient.

2nd November, 1945

Last night while meditating I felt for a fraction of a second that my breath is God's breath which keeps this clay going. It was such a shock that I could not bear it for long.

---

[17] A French woman who was the chief disciple of Sri Aurobindo and who ran his ashram in Pondicherry while he spent the rest of his life in seclusion.

[18] Sri Ramakrishna used to constantly warn his disciples against "woman and gold". By "woman" he clearly meant lust and used the two words interchangeably in his recorded talks to his exclusively male monastic disciples. He also had a number of outstanding women disciples, first and foremost of whom was his wife, Sarada Devi.

Travel restrictions have been removed as of yesterday which was 'All Saints' Day' and 20 years after I was supposed to be put on Probation as a disciple of the Theosophical Master (whatever the reality of it was, to me it meant a great deal). I was able to meditate for 50 minutes in the morning practically without strain for the first time. Yet at school many things went wrong as a reaction.

I am quite wild with joy at going to Vindhyachal today to see Mother. This time I shall not return. Lewis' flowers, a symbol of transformation, are still in front of me, but now nearly faded.

There was after all no need to worry about permits. I am so half-hearted that I don't really have faith in the spiritual and always take precautions.

About two days ago L. showed me one of his friend's (Rajagopal) letters where he writes to him: "When I forget the whole world, you do not disappear. I am sure this is not sentimentality".

L. told me how and why Brewster misunderstood him. He expressed it rather beautifully, true or otherwise. Then I asked him how he thought I saw him. He said: "We have a static influence on each other. Your mind is of so different a type that I do not take into account at all what you say about me. What I appreciate in you is your humility etc." I felt so mortally hurt. I could have cried. But it is good. It makes me free. I need not worry that he wants my help in any way, far from it. It is significant that this should happen on the day I am leaving for the Mother. He said he dare not face Her, as he has not done what She told him. And it was he who told me I must obey her! And so to Vindyachal!

VIII - Vindhyachal

Vindhyachal is the ancient site of an important pilgrimage temple to the Mother Goddess situated in the Vindhya hills (between Benares and Allahabad) on a plateau overlooking a bend in the Ganges. The countryside has a wild vitality to it that puts one in touch with the *shakti* (divine power) of the Goddess. The ashram of Anandamayee Ma is on a hill outside of the town commanding a dramatic view of the river and plains below.

Anandamayee Ma spent most of Her public life (the better part of 60 years) wandering from one ancient holy place in India to another, rarely staying anywhere more than a few days or weeks. Gradually, as more and more people became devoted to Her, they constructed ashrams in some of these places where they might be better able to spend time with Her. To be in such a place with Ma was not only to receive Her blessing but to become initiated into the ancient power of the place itself which became profoundly activated and accessible through Her presence there. These ancient focuses of spiritual power are points on the energy grid that sustains the electro-magnetic field of Indian spiritual culture. Ma was particularly concerned with keeping this 'field' of sacred geography intact.

Although a proponent of the highest non-dual Indian philosophy, Anandamayee Ma had the feasts of all the popular Gods of modern Hinduism celebrated in Her ashrams with great *élan* and encouraged Her devotees in these popular devotions. Each God is considered a different manifestation of the Supreme Lord who lies within us and who is indeed our innermost Self. The devotee is free to choose the God or Goddess to whom he feels most attracted for his private devotion and no one deity is given preference or priority over another. On the festival day of a particular God or Goddess elaborate formal worship is done following ancient rituals which are performed with strict precision, exactly as prescribed in the ancient texts. Great attention is paid to observing rules of ritual purity —particularly for the officiating priests—and to performing the rite at the exact astrological moment. If all this is carried out correctly, it is believed that the participants will receive the blessing of the Deities and have their *darshan* (literally, vision). Paradoxically there is also a strong element of play to this, particularly as every devotee has the firm conviction, indeed experience, that simply being in Ma's presence —whatever the occasion— is the greatest blessing of all.

Perhaps no manifestation of God is more beloved by the Bengalis than the Goddess Kali —the dark terrifying Mother. To Her devotees, however, she is not frightening but is rather an incarnation of compassion because it is understood that she only destroys our egos —all that keeps us from true union with the Divine. On the night of the dark moon of November, when most of India is celebrating Diwali, the festival of light sacred to Lakshmi —Goddess of wealth, beauty and overall good fortune— the Bengalis worship their beloved Kali —the dark one— She who removes the darkness from Her devotees so that the light may be revealed. It was during the celebration of Kali Puja in Vindhyachal that Blanca had a profound initiatic experience. After this her name was changed to *Atmananda* —the bliss of the Self— and from this point on, she will be referred to thus.

* * *

Vindhyachal, 2nd November, 1945

J.C. Mukerji arrived the same day as I, and Mother at once took me to her room to talk. I voiced some of my difficulties with meditation, namely, getting exhausted, to which She said: *"It does not matter, later on it will become the reverse —work will tire you and meditation exhilarate you."* Then as to my half-heartedness, She asked: *"Is there any other sphere of activity which you feel would give you more complete fulfilment?"* I said: "No, but as a woman I am not fulfilled." I could not put this clearly, but during the night which was practically sleepless I got quite clear: most of a woman's life is, traditionally, service to her husband and children. I felt that this is necessary for me. Either I must get married (though the sex part of married life does not attract me any more) to a man who has the same ab sorbing interest and whom I can take care of and serve as a kind of Guru, or I must find a Guru whom I can physically serve. At present my life is dual and hypocritical, like an ordinary Christian who goes to church on Sunday and feels devotional and then lives an ordinary worldly life all through the week. I cannot offer all my present activities as a service to the Great Mother, because they are simply too complex and artificial, as teaching at the school must inevitably be. I cannot accept perfection unless it also embraces the physical, as long as I am still identified to some extent with the world. This side must be expressed to make my surrender true and real. It is this which makes the body restless. I cannot at present leave all physical activities, so these also must become a prayer.

In the general talk last night she explained that with every breath one should think of God and, thus gradually, identify breathing with one's *Ishta* (one's preferred form of God). One must feel that God is the atmosphere, the air, everything around you, and become conscious of that.

This is really what I felt even in my childhood. I must have had some realization of it in a former birth, but it was not complete. In fact it seems to me that this partial realization at the back of my mind acts as a hindrance to that burning desire that alone makes one achieve.

3rd November, 1945

Question: I feel the need for surrender through a deep spiritual relationship, either to a Guru or a husband who will be like a Guru and whom I can serve. At present what I do is not real service.

Ma: *You are intelligent and old enough to find out for yourself whom you can trust completely as a Guru. Look around, take any amount of time to test the person, man or woman; but once you have taken the plunge, it is for good, like a Hindu marriage —undissolvable— and you must accept his or her word for better or for worse and abide by it implicitly whether it appeals to you or not.*

Question: I find it very difficult to concentrate on the breath and also boring, and can only do it when I think of you as the Great Mother who has commanded me to do so. Yet I feel that you had a special reason for asking me to concentrate on the breath. If you can explain this to me I shall then be able to do it without difficulty.

Ma: *Through breath, 'Prana Vayu'* [vital energy, wind], *Conscious-ness pervades matter. Everything that is alive breathes. When breath stops, you die. Physical life depends on breath. It is through 'prana' that matter becomes alive. Desires and the wandering mind ('ichha' and 'vasana') make breath impure. Therefore I advise the practice of concentration on breath-ing combined with taking any one of God's names (mantra). If the breath and the mind become 'ekagra'* [one-pointed] *and steady, then the mind expands to infinity and all phenomena are included in that one all-inclu-sive point. If you think of God with the breath it will purify the 'prana', the physical sheath and the mind. You get ill because you spoil the body by impure 'prana' caused by desire, worries and pain due to unfulfilled de-sires. But do not think that when you start doing this meditation practice, you will immediately become well. If you have eaten bad food yesterday and pure food today, yesterday's food will still make you ill. If you breathe while thinking of God's name, you will feel the call through His Grace. It is by this Grace <u>only</u> that you can feel the Call to Him.*

You should practice the following daily: Sit still for a few seconds or minutes and calm yourself. Then breathe three times taking the name 'Atma'[1]. *The breathing should be done as follows: Inhale and then hold the breath for a count that is twice as long as that of the inhalation. Then exhale to a count that is four times that of the inhalation. Then meditate on the immanence of God as the Life that permeates every living being. Even if your thought of it is not truly the Reality of that Life, it will take you there. Just as you were told that I am at Vindhyachal and you ac-cepted that it was true and travelled all the way here, and thus you actu-ally found me; in the same way, your thought of the Immanence of God (the cause of everything) will take you to the Reality of This. During your work, every now and again, do this breathing exercise. Try to see that Life in everything as much as possible.*

Then there is also another way —the reverse of this: "Neti, neti"[2], *rejecting everything that can be an object of perception or thought as not God. That also leads to Him.*

Question: I take it for granted that you think that is not my way as you suggest the other?

She affirms.

---

[1] *Atma* —the Self, the indwelling non-dual Reality.

[2] Literally 'not this... not this' —the negation process through which one in-quires into the question of "Who am I"?

4th November, 1945

I was given food by myself on a dirty unswept verandah [3] and felt extremely upset and decided not to eat the next day. Somehow I mentioned this to someone who brought it to Anandamayee Ma's notice and she asked some ladies to eat with me. J.C. Mukerji talked and talked to me and asked me to have food. I was very upset and told him all about the dirty bathroom and the dirt all over and why is it that no one organizes the place. Later on I reflected that every time I have a somewhat spiritual revelation, it happens in extremely uncomfortable and dirty surroundings. This seems necessary to break the false sense of well-being that cleanliness and order give me. Here again it is the same.

5th November, 1945

Last night during the *Kali Puja* (10 p.m. to 3 a.m.) some change seemed to take place in me, and so I no longer mind the shabby surroundings anymore at all. It occurred to me that instead of remaining ensconced in my European ego I should share the life of the others here. If I adopt their customs and manner and outlook, they will forget that I am a foreigner and treat me accordingly. Unconsciously they must be repelled by my foreign dress and also by my attaching so much importance to the physical. A Mr. Dutt presented me with a white *dhoti*, which since I have begun wearing makes me feel quite different. I must not go to such places in frocks (which are outrageous to Indians). Immediately their attitude changed upon my adapting myself.

Last night during the Puja I found my mind getting extremely still and lucid. I began to reflect on the difference between matter, so-called mechanical, and true life, which occurred to me thus: The root cause creates both. But the first, like any mechanical device, runs its course blindly according to some inherent law, like a mechanical toy. Man has this mechanistic side which is the life that animates him and which repeats itself endlessly. But there is also the possibility of a new impulse of life that may come at any moment —life as pure consciousness. When the Divine Life prin-

---

[3] As a foreigner, the traditional rules of brahminical orthodoxy, still very much the norm at this time, would have normally precluded her eating with higher caste Hindus.

ciple comes into play, what was before mechanical and inert, now becomes alchemically transformed into True Meaning —spontaneous and new at every moment. Time, which is the mechanical repetition of the outward life impulse, stops.[4]

Towards the end of the *Puja* Anandamayee Ma suddenly looked quite different and extremely young and beautiful like a living Goddess. *I seemed to remember this sight from somewhere; she looked like someone, and suddenly it occurred to me that my mother looked like that when she was about 24, just before she died.* It made me cry.[5] Anandamayee Ma looked like an unearthly vision. At that moment I felt convinced that what Ramakrishna said about Himself to one of his devotees is true of Her also: "I assure you", he said, "that there is only God in this body, nothing else." She was changing at every second with a radiant spontaneity, beautifully smiling and altogether like a Goddess. It made me cry a lot and as I prostrated myself before Her, I felt within: "I have now seen <u>Who</u> you are". This occurred just as the Kali idol had become fully consecrated and at that moment it was overwhelmingly clear that Anandamayee Ma, Herself, was the Goddess.

At 4 a.m. Gurupriya[6] came and woke me up and brought me a meditation mat (*asana*) as a present from Mother. Mother was sitting in the tent outside my room and sent for me. She asked me whether I slept in a nightdress and then said: "*I thought of you today and am giving you this asana, so you should not feel cold.*" Of course she actually gave it as a help to steady my concentration. Then She sent me back to sleep.

Benares, 10th November, 1945

I am not lukewarm anymore.[7] I have fallen in love with Anandamayee Ma. She fascinates me so completely that at times I

---

[4] One of the titles of Kali is 'She who destroys time'.

[5] An essential part of the *sadhana* process with Anandamayee Ma was the unlocking and releasing of deep-seated psychological trauma.

[6] Anandamayee Ma's principal attendant and a very close disciple. She was often referred to simply as *Didi* (older sister). Her diaries, published by Anandamayee Sangha, are the most detailed account of Ma's early life.

[7] Thompson's dream in which he foresaw a fundamental change taking place during this period was correct; see entry for 1st September, 1945.

feel quite mad. Saw her again on the 7th and 8th at Her ashram in Benares at Bhadaini. She satisfies completely my longing for beauty and artistic sense. Also she is an ideal Woman and Mother to all of Her devotees. So She really personifies what I have longed for for the last 15 or 20 years. Now I see why I was not allowed to go to Tiruvannamalai for good. *Jnana* [8] is not my way. This time it will not fail.

She has also given me a new name. She told me that she has called me Atmananda because of the auspicious signs on my feet. The concentration on *Atma*, and on Her, has now become much easier and not tiring, quite the contrary. But the yearning for Her and God still reacts on the body. It is like lovesickness, pain and joy all at once.

I am reading *Sharanagati Tatwa* again. It means something so different now. It almost throws me into ecstasy.

I have almost forgotten Lewis. What he said to me about having a static effect on him, before I went to Vindhyachal, caused a real break. It was he who brought me to Anandamayee Ma really, and prepared me for this change. Strangely, he also brought me those flowers of transformation that remained fresh till I left for Vindhyachal.

Mother gave me two of her own saris and made me put one on at once. I shall drop frocks altogether along with this Rajghat work and adopt the dress she gave me —white saris. Strange that it never struck me how little comfort matters and that I should become Indian if I want to take shelter under the Indian tradition and remain here for the rest of this life. I am going to Her for the weekend, though I have a feeling She may be leaving today. (I could not stay for the weekend as she left the next morning, but slept there the night).

I have ordered a Bengali grammar.

Rajghat, 15th November, 1945

Sarnath. In the Chinese temple had a nice, but short meditation. A column of light seemed to stream from the Buddha through me.

I have now almost forgotten what Lewis said to me about

---

[8] The way of pure intellectual discrimination and self-analysis to the exclusion of all else.

having a static effect on him. I feel certain that he is practically a realized being. There is just the slightest something that keeps him from it and produces a terrific tension. He had a terrible outburst of temper yesterday, face all quivering and snow-white; no wonder he still feels shattered.

Concentration much easier. I am trying to keep silent from 6-7 p.m. as is done in Ma's ashram at Vindyachal. It occurred to me to imagine a stream of devotion and light going up from the bottom of the spine out through the head. It seems to help relieve congestion in the lower part of the body and has a very purifying effect on any sort of sexual restlessness. Emotion goes up instead of flowing partly down. I have felt rather calmer during the last few days, but somehow I believe it is the calm before a tremendous outburst of *bhakti* (devotion) when I go to Vindhyachal on Saturday.

It seems to me that the mind —as it is at present— has to be stopped at all cost and by any possible means made empty. Only then can a new mind with truly creative thoughts descend from above. That is when Real thinking will begin.

Vindhyachal, 19th November, 1945

She seems to become what one sees in Her, being completely empty Herself. But I notice that if you worship Her, She becomes an incarnation of your innermost aspiration and most cherished ideals.

I fluctuate between being utterly silly and clogged up, and having an intense desire to surrender —to be nothing but an empty shell that holds Her Life.

J.C. Mukerji says Gopinath Kaviraj [9], whom he considers the greatest living scholar and philosopher of India, says that Anandamayee is more than an *Avatar*, She is the Divine MOTHER of the universe Herself.

---

[9] Gopinath Kaviraj is recognized as one of the greatest authorities of this century on Indian Religion and Philosophy, particularly on the *Tantras*. He spent the last years of his life living in Ma's ashram in Benares where he died in 1976.

IX - Moonlight on the Ganges

Rajghat, 20th November, 1945

Yesterday at Vindhyachal the *Gita Puja* [1] of the fat Guru from Allahabad went on all day, sometimes deteriorating into people rolling on the ground, yelling etc., and She calmly withstood it and even took part. Incredible!

Left in the evening with Lewis. Was very annoyed with him because he kept on like a naughty boy, irrationally so, and made me pay for everything on top of it. We got a rickshaw at Mugalsarai, full moon night, at about 10.30 and were tightly packed in with luggage. We had to sit very close of course and quite uncomfortably. I was still annoyed but also amused at the comic picture of us and suddenly felt an impulse to take his arm, which he accepted for the first time. Immediately the strain left us both and I got into touch with his very delicate and exquisite presence. Partly this and partly the cold made me put my hand on his, which he submitted to in a half-passive way. It brought us much closer and had a most extraordinary effect. The whole landscape including ourselves and the smoothly moving rickshaw became utterly dreamlike, like a cinema film; my hand, his hand, they were no longer hands, but only a queer dreamlike sensation. What I always felt (and <u>saw</u> clearly when I looked at him in Mother's room the evening before), that he is not physical at all but only a kind of precipitation of thought, became an experience; and I entered into this ethereal sphere slightly. He really does not exist physically, it only seems so. I have never held a more subtle and refined hand. He said: "From your hand I can feel that you must open yourself to the Unknown." It occurred to me at once that he is the Unknown. I am not sure whether I also said it. I am so longing to open myself to the Unknown, but It is holding Itself back. Why?

---

[1] An elaborate devotional ceremony worshipping the famous Hindu scripture *The Bhagavad Gita*.

Probably the shock would knock me off my balance. This whole ride and walk over the pontoon bridge and up the hill was most exquisite. We were in total harmony with each other and we walked in step naturally. He told me how the *sukshma prana* (energy of the subtle body) of two individuals melts into one when they love each other, and at a certain point the bodies are left behind and one experiences complete union. He was referring to an experience he had had with a someone whom he loved. We both did not want to go home. The tiredness was gone. It was like one of the songs of Richard Strauss where a couple walk into the great Unknown, I forget the name and the words.

This was an extraordinary climax of our first journey together to Anandamayee Ma. That this should happen after I had again and again resolved to surrender myself completely to the Mother is probably significant. Isn't it a paradox to feel this strong attraction to a person so totally beyond the physical. How very difficult it is. How slow one has to be and how tactful and delicate and pure to be allowed to get into touch with this matchless purity. I have never known a hand that had a touch so pure. This contact has produced a definite and highly uplifting and refining change in my make-up. But is it the intention of the Mother or merely a temptation of my strong Ego? This friendship must become complete, we must have absolute understanding of each other; then we shall part —but only physically. There will be consciousness of communion across oceans, nay planets. Perhaps there always has been, but I have forgotten. If I become sufficiently pure and free from self, this ancient communion will shine forth again. Till then there must be longing, yearning and restlessness. He is so <u>entirely</u> different from anyone else and so completely fascinating —unfathomable, ever elusive, ever retreating, never to be grasped as a whole—; and yet that is exactly what has to happen —one day— for an eternal moment.

This evening we walked along the Ghats, very distant, both very tired —no contact. Yet the world looks different when walking by his side, indeed it is a new and fascinating world. Now that I sit here alone, I intensely feel the separation —physical only, yet as real surely as the thought that takes me there. This was not so before: I used to feel nearer to him the further away I was physically. His mind is so subtle and flexible, like a surgeon's instrument; his emotion so utterly refined, not a trace of grossness in it, a poet's emotion at all times; but his ethereal physical being appears so wounded. This seems to produce the disharmony.

All my life I have known that something is in store for me, a great miracle. *"Neti, neti"* [2] has been the keynote of my days. But now —has it really begun to manifest?— the miracle that has brought me to the feet of Anandamayee Ma and that may take me to Her very heart?

21ˢᵗ November, 1945

In the morning I woke up quite differently and calm. It is my impurity that prevents a complete communion. To get it I must become like an empty vessel, then it will come by itself, must come. The only way to approach L. is through devotion. He is almost completely empty, so God sits directly under his skin as it were and permeates the physical also; that is why he is different from others. I am in a peculiar mood. There is a growing sense of unity. But my meditation was disturbed last night because of overtiredness and this morning because a reply to an insolent letter of the Calcutta Radio was in my head. It may be a very good thing that I have to refuse my Christmas broadcasts. What does money matter!

23ʳᵈ November, 1945

Again last night desperately longed for L. He disturbs my meditation. This morning also, but then I got absorbed into the Mother when I meditated again at 10 a.m. Also I had a feeling that Anandamayee Ma was in Benares and I phoned to Sharma after school. I was right. We (Krishni and I) got to the ashram about an hour after her arrival. There I had a very intense meditation of surrender. But again after sometime began to ponder about L. *There is something that has to be finished off, before I can go to the Mother entirely.* I meant to bring him the garland She gave me this evening, but the light was out in his room when I returned. I had imagined this was the Mother's wish. So was I wrong after all? Is it only my

---

[2] In Upanishadic and Vedanta philosophy, *"neti, neti"* (not this, not this) is the method one employs in deconstructing the false 'I' when enquiring "Who am I".

own ego? I shall try again tomorrow morning. If it is merely my own desire, I shall not find him there.

24ᵗʰ November, 1945

Gave the garland to L. but the atmosphere I had imagined was not there. He resists certain things. We evidently live in two different worlds and can never really meet. I felt hurt and annoyed at his telling me how much he wanted to remain at Vindhyachal and meet some funny boy whom he had met in the train. So the drive in the moonlight which meant so much to me, means nothing at all to him. He says he does not "care for any individual in the world. All are symbols." All right. Why do I worry myself for this cold and heartless creature? The Mother evidently wants to teach me a lesson. I must and will withdraw more and more from him. My dream where we leave by trains in different directions will come true. (30ᵗʰ April 1946. Yes, he has gone to Almora and I am going to Calcutta). Why I always fall in love with people so utterly beyond my reach, God only knows.

Evening:

Went to Anandamayee Ma with Kamala Sahai. Upon arriving we found that She [3] had gone out on a boat and unfortunately we could not wait for Her to return, but we sat on the ashram roof for nearly two hours. Her Presence was so potent even though She was not there physically, that I almost preferred it. I had a very good meditation, visualizing myself as a vessel for the Mother and imagining how She thinks, feels and breathes etc. through my body. It was full of *ananda*. Since Diwali it is really much easier to meditate, only I get so frightfully hungry and eat butter and cream as never before. I do not concentrate on the immanence of God these days, but on the Divine Mother as revealed through Anandamayee Ma. It seems to me She is much greater than any conception I could possibly have of God. Besides, there is much more emotional satisfaction and therefore interest and concentration in thinking of Her, but the very intensity of Her profound inner presence can provoke a strong physical reaction which I must carefully observe. I suppose this will go in time as the lower na-

---

[3] From here on the diaries capitalize all pronouns referring to Anandamayee Ma.

ture ultimately becomes completely transformed by Her. It is as though the senses sense their potential extinction in the face of such overwhelming spirituality and thus desperately try and reinforce themselves.

25ᵗʰ November, 1945

It is just a week since I was at Vindhyachal. It seems like ages. I do not quite know why, but the whole nature of time seems to have changed.

Today did not see L. except in the kitchen, but did not speak. Complete deadlock continues. I feel nothing at all. It is very strange how one's feeling can change from one extreme to the other and one can hardly remember how one felt before.

26ᵗʰ November, 1945

This morning at 11 a.m. I had a phone message from the Cantonment station that Mother was leaving for Dehradun and had called me to see Her off. She was already at the station. If I had left just then, I could have probably made it on time. But I took it for granted that I could not leave the school and miss the practice for the anniversary celebration. Now I hear the anniversary won't take place as Rama Rao is dying. Next time if she calls me, I shall just run and not bother about anything else. Later: I am told the train was 40 minutes late. I could have got there. Rama Rao died today. He was only 45 years old.

3ʳᵈ December, 1945

Today, suddenly, it occurred to me that I am getting old and in a mad hurry to get 'there'. Where? I am there all the time but because I haven't known it for so long I have come to accept this state of being lost, and cannot bear to admit the truth that really I am always 'there'. If I can manage to think 24 hours without a break that I am only a part of the Mother, then I shall be 'there'. The 'I' is only a mechanism with no inherent Reality. What keeps it alive is SHE, who keeps everything alive. To imagine that She breathes through me, through everyone, is a terrifying and awesome thought.

5th December, 1945

Recently I have felt much drawn to Sri Bhagavan Ramana Maharshi and felt intensely that I want to go to Tiruvannamalai. Miss Merston came yesterday and talked to me during the time I usually meditate (about 6.30 to 7.15). I felt that I was in a different state, as if behind my talking I was actually meditating all the time. I got on quite well with her this time.

6th December, 1945

These days in my meditation I feel so utterly lost in the abyss of my ignorance and in my appalling taking everything for granted. How can one bear this state of affairs? The realization of this bottomless ignorance is so terrifying that one tries to cover it up and forget it immediately. I find myself eating to drug myself.

There is only one thing that one has to admit: That there is Being. Everything else is a great question mark. It is quite maddening.

Now I see why I could not go to Tiruvannamalai three years ago. I was not nearly ready for the strain of it. One has to go slowly or the body and mind will break. But I must steadily give up all distracting activities. I am 41 and who knows how much time I have left; certainly none to waste.

10th December, 1945

Malati sent me a reply from J.K. to the question: How can I know myself? He suggests keeping a diary and recording one's thoughts and feelings as they come into one's mind. J.K. always upsets me, but also causes me to think more deeply. Yet as I have decided to regard everything that comes to me as coming from the MOTHER, so I have to deal with this in that light also. It is extraordinary how much Lewis resembles J.K.

11th December, 1945

It suddenly occurs to me: Where can one go to find God? One has to dig and dig. As Mother said: "*Dig in one place and you will make a hole, but if you dig in many places you will never get anywhere.*" One must gather one's strength in one point. That is concentration. To become a focus for His Energy. Why does one dissipate one's energy all the time? Why is one drawn to socialize with others who are the same or worse? Why should this be 'relaxing'?

J.K. says controlling the mind makes it dull and narrow. I do not find that. What Mother has asked me to do has made me more conscious, more observant even of outer things. It has brought much to my notice, especially the appalling ignorance in which I am steeped. At the same time I am happier, more serene, more balanced, less concerned with the gross outer world. Lately also I am very much more determined to leave off distracting occupations and to attend only to what really interests me: to find out what life is all about and what its ultimate meaning is. Miss Boner asked me whether I would not want to go on a concert tour in India. No. This will only waste my time and take me away from my search.

12th December, 1945

I am conscious of my abysmal ignorance but at the same time I feel happy because to realize this utter ignorance and sense of being lost and having nothing to hold on to is surely necessary to destroy the state of dreaming in which the lostness and ignorance are mistaken for Reality. I am much more keen to find out the truth and more and more am losing interest in anything else. I want to keep silent for a week from Christmas to New Year to give expression to my awe of that ignorance which at present acts, speaks, thinks and feels. How dare it! What presumption.

Very stimulating conversation with Lewis on J.K.'s talks. We also spoke about people living completely in the mental orb of a great person like, Sri Aurobindo [4] for instance or, as I suggested, Guénon [5]. Very few have the capacity to think for themselves. Since I spent more time trying to meditate on the immanence of God, the awesome impossibility of the task becomes ever more evident. I must talk to Anandamayee Ma again, but I haven't formulated what I want to say. There is always the conflict between J.K. and

---

[4] See entry of 24th January, 1946.

[5] René Guénon (1886-1951), contemporary French philosopher who emphasized the importance of the world's great religious traditions and particularly the integrity and fundamental similarity of their metaphysical teachings. He spent the last part of his life as a Sufi in Egypt.

everything else —his saying: "Don't put the brake on." and She: "Bring thought back to one point."

Lewis fascinates me so, partly because he is so like J.K.

13th December, 1945

Suddenly got such an overwhelming sense of the immensity and beyondness of Truth: the Unspeakable, Inexpressible. How can one possibly strive for anything else but to become totally empty so as to be able to receive even the tiniest spark of that Stupendous Whole, about which every word or thought is blasphemy and ridiculous? Yet what else is there to be done but to attune one's body and mind to the Fullness of the Supreme. To think of Him or Her or whatever little the mind can conceive of, is to take 'That' into one's body with every breath. If the body gets tired because not used to this, one must be ever watchful to get back to it as soon as possible. Therefore it is of the utmost importance to cultivate the company of those that are completely that Supreme Perfection.

Repeating the name of God must attune the body to His vibration and makes impossible the gross vibrations that keep us completely caught in the illusion of our separate selves.

Evening:

Long walk with Lewis on the *ghats* and through the lanes. How fascinating —a whole world in itself which to truly experience would fill a whole life, or perhaps many. Lanes with strange shops and pictures on the walls, the mysterious *ghats* along the river in the moonlight with trees and houses all intertwined —in the mist it takes on the quality of a dream. The houses are closed and dark and seem deserted, yet must be seething with life and people. To go with Lewis is always extremely interesting, it takes away all fatigue and makes one feel fresh. He also felt the same. I always think of Ramakrishna's saying that Benares is made of pure gold. Unconsciously I must have imbibed it all.

What an enormous lot I have lived through since this morning. What changes of consciousness! Lazy in the morning, school, gossip restlessness and eating all afternoon, then suddenly a marvellous realization of the Unfathomableness of God and the walk with L.

How can I ever be lukewarm again? How can one waste one's time when such a tremendous thing —oneness with God— is to be achieved? At least it is worth trying, worth going mad over.

15th December, 1945

Yesterday Damodar burst out in such a way about Sanjiv Rao that I still feel quite seasick. The drain that smells so awful is only a symbol for the poison in people's hearts and minds here. This morning I could not help pondering over the problem of evil. How is dirt reconciled with God's immanence? Why has he created the capacity for desire, hate, revenge, etc. I must ask Anandamayee Ma about this.

There must be a way of grasping this. Fire and water eat each other. It is their nature and does not appear evil because there is nothing personal in it. The evil seems to arise simultaneously with the sense of egoicity. The lizard eats the mosquito. Is it evil? Yet the mosquito <u>must</u> fight for its existence with every means. A passive mosquito that accepted death from the lizard without trying to save itself would be contrary to nature. If there wasn't this personal identification, would we then act for and against each other like elements of nature? Does the thunderbolt hate the tree it kills? And does the tree hate the thunderbolt for being killed by it?

Evening & night, 12:30 a.m.:

Who is free from self-deception and what right have I to judge his motives. The whole trouble is that one forgets one's true nature and behaves as if everything and everyone were separate from us. What is evil? In Anandamayee Ma's presence certain things are impossible. Evil is simply to forget God, *and in Her presence this is not in the realm of possibility.* Indeed it is this that makes Her so completely irresistible.

"This world is cursed and everything in it except the remembrance of God and that which aideth it." [6] But as soon as one remembers, it becomes blessed. In whatever way one remembers, it aids and makes everything beautiful and alive.

When I walked home I could hardly recognize the path, partly because of the state I was in.

---

[6] From *The Sayings of Mohammed.*

During eclipse, 19th December, 1945

At 6.10 a.m., meditating, had a glimpse of how when the mind is full of pictures like a 'cinema' it forgets its source. How the mind has to be turned in on itself and contemplate the lamp that alone makes the show possible. When the lamp is not lit there is no show. I experience nowadays how the breath is influenced by thought in meditation, and that when the mind is still, the breath stops automatically.

Evening:

At the Chinese Temple at Sarnath it came to me immediately that I must have been with the Buddha. There is a kind of rapport between the Lord Buddha and myself —also the fact that I made contact with Anandamayee Ma at Sarnath.

Surrender is not mere passive acceptance, but is rather to consider everything that happens as coming from God.

20th December, 1945

Suddenly realized how cosmic consciousness projects the mind and the world. My own mind is also a projection of this consciousness. The deeper I enter into this primal consciousness the more significant everything becomes. Then each day is not only just a passing incident, but the crest of a wave in consciousness; just like the faintest glimmer of sunlight is an aspect of the sun itself. Where then is the senselessness of ordinary life? It becomes senseless only when one sees it from the outside as a jumble of fragmented events; but a profound harmony emerges when one enters more deeply into the source of these seeming fragments.

23rd December, 1945

All that we see is a modification of Consciousness and therefore not unreal as such. But when seen as fragmented phenomena independent of the whole, it becomes completely meaningless.

MOTHER appears as a column of light when I contemplate her. Having glimpsed such purity how can one still be engaged in thoughts about nonsense, that is, the world as it appears from its own plane.

25ᵗʰ December, 1945

How to get action right so that it leads back to the Centre instead of onto new activity that takes one further away —that is my great problem. Should I keep away from everything except what is absolutely necessary and spend all the rest of the time in contemplation? That seems the right thing. So I should avoid all visitors, which means curtailing my visits to others also. I must try and become more clear about right action. How can action become absolutely pure, that is, "without ego", so as to leave no residue, no *karma*, that just takes one round in a circle?

29ᵗʰ December, 1945

Kashi Railway Station (Waiting for the train to Dehradun).

It seems to me that I must change the whole structure of the mind. At present it is turned outwards and influenced by the senses and emotions. Now it has to be turned inwards so as to listen to that which is the source of emotions and sense impressions. But for now the mind is still a slave to these. Even when thoughts are disagreeable and recognizable as hurtful and useless, why does the mind turn to them. I must keep *viveka*, the sword of discrimination, intact and stay balanced all the time. Keep alert outside whilst remaining fully focused within on the source, penetrating always deeper and deeper.

X - "One Can't Remain on this Earth Looking at Her "

I feel extremely drawn to Her and feel like not talking to anyone here, but only concentrating on Her. She draws me irresistibly. Then again doubt comes. It is maddening. One does not know anything at all. She says to my question about doubt: "*If you have a Guru follow him and ascribe your doubt to the impurity of your mind.*" To this I say: "As my mind is impure, how can I know the Guru either?" She says: "*By accepting his word, you will slowly come to understand for yourself.*"

She also said: "*Don't listen to outward conversation and advice. Listen within and follow your own intuition.* At someone's question as to whether I had family, She said: "*Yes, she has father, mother, sister, brother, friends and everything because God is her all.*" I asked Her about diet and She told me not to eat eggs [1] as they are not conducive to meditation. I have wanted to give them up for a long time, but did not want to make a fuss. Regarding this Mother told me: "*If your aim is to please God you don't need to worry about pleasing anyone else.*"

31ˢᵗ December, 1945

In the night I felt quite lovesick for Her, as if I could put up with anything at all just to be with Her, and yet, just staying with Her is also not enough. I feel like crawling inside Her and ceasing to exist.

Evening:

She answered all my unasked questions in a general talk in the evening after the meditation. She obviously addressed it to me. She talked about the different paths. "*Do not get diverted from your own path. If you are trying to dig a well and you dig up earth a*

---

[1] It was taken for granted that meat was to be excluded from one's diet.

little here and a little there, nothing happens; but if you dig in one place,
you will eventually find water." She evidently meant to tell me that
my path is *Atma dhyana* (meditation on the Self), that is, no shape,
no form, but only making the mind empty (*shunya*) so that the
Atma may be revealed. *"Do not pay attention to anything outside,*
concentrate all the time on the Centre within. Once you are in the Cen-
tre you will look in all the four directions and see everything as it is. Do
not waste your time. Whatever you do —eating, drinking, working—,
think of Atma all the time; remain in the Centre (J.K.'s awareness!).
Don't let anything distract you. Don't drop your work, but keep on
with this meditation while you are doing it. Like that it will take you to
freedom. Think that He works through you. Surrender entirely to Him.
Become his 'yantra' [2]. *Pray that not your desire may be done, but His.*
Through 'prana vayu' [3] *he manifests in you. Think of Him with every*
breath. Remember that <u>He</u> breathes through you. That will cleanse you.
Do not waste time. The day that is gone does not return ever again. Do
not bother about other paths, stick to your own. Whether you are lying
down, sitting or walking, be aware of the Centre. When you talk, think
that He talks through you. When you meditate do not move, remain
absolutely still.

We are all connected through 'samskaras' [4]. *Whatever 'samskaras'*
take you to 'mukti' [5] *are your friends, but those which bind you are your*
enemies. If you have to meet people see the Atma in them. Whatever
situation you must encounter, look for the Atma in that also."

She told me not to talk to any male *sanyasi*. There is a rule that
they may not even look at the picture of a woman. *Sanyas* is very
difficult and once one has taken it on, one must observe the rules
strictly.

Kishenpur, 3rd January, 1946

My meditation in the jungle at Dunga very good. The chief
thing is to be one-pointed. The mind becomes empty of its own
accord if only my desire for God is strong enough. If I totally refuse

---

[2] Esoteric geometric representations of the deity.

[3] Subtle life-energy related to breath.

[4] Impressions carried over from our actions in previous lives that determine
and influence our present situation.

[5] Liberation.

to attend to anything else, the result is immediate. The thought that it is He who actually breathes, not I, that He moves every limb, makes the heart beat etc., just makes one die. The ecstasy of His presence is such that one can't bear to exist. Only He.

Last night suddenly it occurred to me that She told me: "*All sadhana must be done for God's sake, not for yourself*". I realize that unconsciously I nurture a thought of self-advancement and that is why I am not wholly successful. I feel that having shunned all worldly success etc, I feel I must make a success of surrender. But that is also not right. I get sometimes furious at J.K. for having driven me into romantic involvements. But perhaps this kept me from spiritual pride, which is a worse danger.

She asked me to come at 5.30 a.m. for *dhyana* with the others. I should keep to this hour daily. Also she asked me the other night to do *dhyana* before going to sleep. Evidently this is important to tune the mind for the long period of sleep.

I am sharing a small room with a Tibetan *sanyasini*, a former disciple of Sarada Devi [6]. She looks lovely, just like an old nun.

Kishenpur, 4ᵗʰ January, 1946

Yesterday washed all the windows of the meditation hall and oiled all the doors, thinking all the time: "May my mind's doors and windows get clean for Him to enter and may all the noises of the world stop so that I may listen to His voice only. Mother saw me and said: "*This cleanses the mind also, if you do it with the correct attitude*". In the evening I had a very good meditation in Her presence. She looked so entrancingly beautiful. She is utterly holy, just a miracle. In the night I cried a lot and am still crying this morning. I don't know why. They say tears wash away all sins. It must be for that!

It occurred to me to think *Om* instead of *Atma*, as it seems to have a more *mantric* effect. But the result was somehow disturbing, causing a rather frightening movement of *Kundalini*. I must obey Her implicitly and unquestioningly. She is so uncannily beautiful, one sometimes feels too beautiful to be true. She asked me this evening whether I wanted to talk to Her.

---

[6] The wife of Sri Ramakrishna and a great saint in her own right who after his death continued his spiritual work for many years.

5ᵗʰ January, 1946

Talk with Anandamayee Ma.

"When meditating sit still with the back straight. In order not to go to sleep think I am 'chetana' [pure consciousness]. *If you feel nothing at all, it is only an intermediary stage that will go after sometime. Think that blessing rains down on your head from above. The head is your root and the body the tree. When the root is well watered the whole tree becomes beautiful.*

"If you become angry, remember that the power you get in your 'dhyan' will become dissipated through anger. Don't react when others worry you or are cross, remain all the time dedicated to Atma, that will help your meditation. Do your work always with the thought that it is His work. Dedicate it to Him and think you are doing it to cleanse your mind, as you polished the windows here, so do all your work.

"Speak as little as possible, only what is absolutely necessary. When you mix socially with people who laugh and talk about worldly things, don't pay much attention to it and go away as soon as possible. Read only such books as will help your 'sadhana'. Meditate as much as you possibly can. Think that He lives in you through 'prana vayu'."

She looked unearthly beautiful as she lay on Her cot and talked to me. One can't remain on this earth looking at Her.

She also said: *"Atma is everything, there is nothing outside it. Bhagavan* [personalized God] *is like ice which is itself only frozen water, but Atma is like the water, formless".*

Rajghat, 7ᵗʰ January, 1946

Arrived here last night late. Jiten met me at Lucknow and I spent a lovely morning with him there as well as in the train that afternoon. Talked and talked and She has told me to talk as little as possible.

This morning meditation poor —cannot concentrate on anything but Her. I don't have any desire for Truth or anything else. Whoever She is, whatever She is, She has captured my heart and mind completely. I just want to be an atom of Her body, so as to be with Her all the time. I am aching to be with Her, nothing else. It won't be difficult to think of Her all day, and in the night I shall naturally be transported to Her feet the moment I go off to sleep. At present my wish to go to Tiruvannamalai or anywhere else is completely gone. I only want to sit at Her feet and absorb Her into my self, become one with Her so that there can be nothing else. That's all.

She said: *"Come again"* when I sat in the bus and She saw me off. I will.

All the time while teaching today I imagined that She was talking, playing, moving, breathing through me. I found this to be pure bliss; it makes work a pleasure. By thinking of Her I feel a profound link with Her body as though She is living within me and I am Her in some sense. *It is definitely not just my imagination.* But why not go and be with Her? Is it worthwhile taking leave for only three months as I now plan? And then how to go back to work? Can't I get so far as to resign my job by April? Not if I waste my time on irrelevant things.

8th January, 1946

Strangely I cannot imagine Her face. I see Her pictures but I can't remember how She looked at Dunga or Kishenpur. I wonder why this is. Must I get beyond Her physical veil?

During the procession with Rama Rao's ashes it suddenly came to me why the mind must be empty and the emotions transparent. One can only begin to listen to Him [God] when there is nothing else. As soon as one gets only the faintest glimpse of the sweetness that is beyond the distracting nonsense of the mind, one cannot help yearning for it more and more with all one's being. When this yearning becomes stronger one has to avoid the company of those who are immersed in the normal mind, as this interferes with one's contact with Him and this is too painful. One could rather stand any kind of pain than that.

Oh Mother, what have you done to me?
I am going madder every minute with longing for your sweet presence.
I am full of bliss just because of the tiny glimpse I have had of You
And yet one big ache because 'I' still exist.
How can one continue to exist beside you.
It is a sacrilege not to die immediately on the spot and forever. [7]

---

[7] Although she did not arrange these lines as verse in the diaries, I found the similarity to Classical Indian devotional lyrics striking, particularly to that of the Bengali poet-saint Ram Prasad.

This evening to my surprise I enjoyed the party at Assi Ghat. I felt it was His *rasa* [8] that made it enjoyable. But why go in for the part when you can become the All.

9ᵗʰ January, 1946

I speak far too much. But I am now able to think of Mother almost incessantly during my classes. When Lewis spoke to me this morning about his talk with Damodar, I tried to listen impersonally; that is, imagine that it was He (the Divine) speaking to me and that it was also 'He' listening through me. It caused a peculiar sensation of hearing the whole thing from a distance.

It is very important in meditation to keep aware of the fact that one is not the body. Then there can be nothing for sensual feelings to connect with. What then is the body? I must find that out. The life of the body is movement, work; so let it all be done by Her alone.

10ᵗʰ January, 1946

In the afternoon played the piano for about three hours without ever getting up, imagining all the time that She is listening. Every piece becomes a love-song to Her and was full of intense emotion. At times I cried. Her presence and my yearning became so intense. When L. came I felt irritated at his getting in between us, so-to-say. His playing seemed cold.

In this way I can make my music a *kirtan* [9]. It does not disturb my *sadhana*. On the contrary. It occurred to me to write and ask Her whether I may go to Delhi in March for a week. I wrote. But I have given up all idea of going South. I just want to stay with Her. Only now am I beginning to know what it is to be in love. One cannot rest until one ceases to exist apart from the Beloved. Everything is pain, except the Beloved.

The Force that created this body and wants to use it will also feed it and see that it is in good condition. So why worry about money? If only one surrenders to Him who created the body, He will look after it according to His wisdom. Who is it that craves for food and who enjoys it?

---

[8] The underlying sweetness one experiences when perceiving the presence of God in his creation; a key concept in Indian aesthetics.

[9] Hindu devotional singing.

Evening:

Saw Brewster, Alice Boner, etc. How empty everything is and no one's company satisfies me any more. Met J.C. Mukherjee at the Ashram. That is a real joy. I just love him. He is one of Anandamayee Ma's closest devotees together with Didi. The whole afternoon I could not get at Her with all these people round me, but going home in the rickshaw alone... there She was —suddenly I felt wrapped up in Her. What is life apart from Her? An abomination, nothing more.

13th January, 1946

This morning in my meditation again much wandering thought. I cannot maintain the same intensity that I had in Dehradun in Her presence. I must see Mother again soon somehow. To calm my mind I did *japa* [10].

While cutting the children's nails, I suddenly discovered the secret of impersonal action: that it is not I who cut the child's nail, but that it is done. There is neither I nor the child.

Read another of Sharanananda's books in Hindi in which a *bhakta* [devotee] is described as one who has no power to do anything except to love his Beloved. I intensely wish to be like that. Had a wonderful meditation, so much so that I feel almost giddy. Asked the Mother to do my *sadhana* for me and to bind me so completely that I cannot breath but when She breathes through me, not move but when She moves me, not think anything but Her own thoughts —in short, lose myself completely in Her. I see now that this transformation must be fairly slow so as to keep the physical intact. She will give the speed according to Her wish. I have only to obey implicitly. It is such bliss to do that.

15th January, 1946

In my morning meditation I imagined telling John [11] about Mother. I woke up this morning with the thought of him, telling him that only now do I know what it is to truly fall in love, and what being a *bhakta* really means.

---

[10] Mantra repetition.

[11] John Cordes, her old Theosophical mentor in Vienna.

16th January, 1946

Saw Sri Krishna Prem yesterday and Sharanananda [12]. I just love the latter. There seems no difference between him and Mother. He also seems to have that wonderful quality of egolessness. It was such a blessing to be with him.

Yesterday I tried all day long to keep in my mind a line of song she taught us at Dunga: "*Bhajo Radhakrishna, Gopala, Govinda, Gadhadara Ghirdari*" [13]. I find it creates a harmony of body, mind and spirit to keep one's mind occupied in this way. It keeps the mind in a mild ecstasy all the time. But I got very cross with the children all the same.

Evening:

Spent some hours with Swamiji Sharanananda. My Hindi has progressed to the point that I now understand 99.5% of what he says. I love His presence, but what He says is not always practical. The only one who says things that are completely practical and can be applied all the time with ease is Mother. Every moment that is not spent in contemplation and adoration of Her is wasted. Again there is this intense yearning to be absorbed by Her. Also when I am with Swamiji, although She and he seem the same, yet She is so much more satisfying.

Swamiji explained to me: "Sharanagati *is the process of purifying the mind and* sharanapan *is the fulfilment of the task and the merging into the Beloved.*" He also said: "*There are four stages in the spiritual path: first the unfoldment; second, the enjoyment of the result; third, to distribute it to others; and fourth, to realize that indeed there are no others.*"

17th January, 1946

To surrender to the Mother always brings bliss, but it seems that my enjoying food too much makes the body imbalanced. Today my meditation was disturbed as I had to think out how to receive Sri Krishna Prem [14] and his party this afternoon. Two thoughts occurred to me: I should take out my mother's dam-

---

[12] The blind Swami who is the author of the book she often refers to —*Sharanagati.*

[13] All different names of Krishna.

[14] See introduction to Chapter III.

ask tablecloth, and I must buy some garlands. The challenge is how to manage such things without disturbing one's inner absorption.

Night:

Party went off very well. I worked hard for it and enjoyed it. Then went to Noni Babu's *bhajan* [devotional singing] and then to Sharananand. He said: "*Seva* [service] is not work, it is *puja* [worship]". Lewis was there also but suddenly vanished. He walked home in spite of his septic foot and wrote a poem on the way. He came to tell me about it late at night. It is wonderful and drove tears to my eyes. It is the best he has written. I cannot help loving the poet in him. He seems much more perfect than Sri Krishna Prem, much more subtle and refined.[15]

18th January, 1946

Stayed with Sharanananda for nearly four hours. We came to talk about the subject of work. He said: "*When your work is over, leave it alone completely and get immersed in Ram [God]. You are doing your work badly because you don't know how to let go of it. Just as by sleeping you get the capacity to begin again the next morning, so by withdrawing completely from thought of work you get renewed energy to return to it at the appropriate time. Every work has to be done completely, that is, with skill and sincerity. One has to take trouble over it. When it is done completely, no thought of it remains. When you are completely absorbed in it, then there is no question of 'mind'. When the work is over, rest completely in God, then also there can be no mind.*"

He then spoke about *bhakti* and said: "*The bhakta is one with all. Anyone can be a bhakta, but a true bhakta does not do many things; he does only one thing; he remains in God at all times, he regards everyone as God's and every work as God's and therefore thinks, feels and does only one thing and not many.*" I then asked: "*Must one not drop that work that one cannot do with sincerity?*" He said: "*Exactly. Drop your work and become a bhakta. Wear what people give you, eat what they offer you and sleep wherever they put you.*"

---

[15] Krishna Prem was noted for his eloquence, grace and wit.

So I must not just take leave for three months, but go away all together. Let things happen. Don't talk about this to anyone, but keep it in the heart. He really told me exactly the same as Mother —to meditate on the immanence of God all the time—; the same as J.K. said in my dream: "Think of me all the time and leave all else."

It is too good to be true. I have always felt that at some point I shall leave everything and belong only to God. Now it is really about to happen.

He also said: "*The* bhakta *does the work that comes to him, but he does not look for work. He looks for God all the time in whatever he may do and wherever he may be.*"

20th January, 1946, 1.30 a.m.

Sri Krishna Prem was here all day. Most wonderful talk about *bhakti* and how he looked for a Guru. Talked a lot in Thompson's room.

In the evening I saw Sharananandaji. I asked him what an *avadhuta* was. He said: "*One who does not consider his body in the least, who is completely oblivious to it, who, like Anandamayee Ma, will not even take the trouble to eat*".[16] This is really my difficulty, that I want everything done well, clean and orderly for my body. That is why I have to go on doing this dreadful work for which I am quite unfit. Why should I earn money? I have no one for whom I am responsible. Just to keep this wretched body, which really has such few wants. If you are a *bhakta* and consider yourself only that, won't He who cares for all creatures also keep you, even without wasting your time in earning money. Why don't I give all my money and everything that I have to Mother and leave the rest of my life in Her hands. Yes, I will do that; but, how can I wait three and a half months more? This last fortnight has seemed

---

[16] Although attuned to the minutest detail in the daily running of Her ashram, etc. and to the practical realities in the lives of countless people who sought Her out, Anandamayee Ma could not, would not feed Herself. She said that She had no identification with Her body and remained in it solely to satisfy others' desires and needs. Thus it was up to them to maintain it as She had no will in that regard. Indeed, She had no egoistic desire whatsoever. So from 1922 until the end of Her life She was fed the little food She would accept by Her disciples.

like many years. The swamiji talked so wonderfully to Madhuri, Lalji's daughter-in-law, that I could not help crying. When she sang to him, she looked so radiant that I was struck with awe. Then he explained to her what her marriage meant. He advised her not to do too much, but to love much, to serve and renounce. He then gave her a prayer, which he copied for me. He said it was universal.

20th January, 1946

The Swami said that when there is *prem* [love], *dhyana* comes by itself. I prayed to the Mother to fill me so with Love for Her that I should be unable to perceive, think or feel anything else but Her. I feel intuitively that She either has come already or is coming to Benares.

Met Gopinath Kaviraj [17] and his spiritual companion, a Bengali girl with wonderfully magnetic eyes, and was extremely attracted to her. Her eyes seem to have gone inside me and are causing a very deep longing for Mother. Anandamayee Ma evidently sends me all these saints to learn from while She is away. I must use all my free time to learn Hindi and then Bengali.

Coming home I found my washed clothes all crumpled up and some had fallen down from the line and were soiled. I lost my temper badly, then realized that this comes only from my identification with the body. Millions of people have dreadful trouble all the time, but I am utterly oblivious of it. But when anything happens even to the clothes of this body, not to speak of the body itself, I behave as if the world was coming to an end. I think Mother sends me these incidents to teach me. Swamiji told me to disregard my body entirely.

Not being busy with anything this evening I again had this unbearable, mad and yet infinitely sweet longing for Mother.

21st January 1946

Met Gopinath Kaviraj and the wonderful Bengali woman, whom Lewis says is a real *Shakti*. [18] She has magnetic eyes that go right inside you.

---

[17] See footnote for entry of 19th Nov., 1945.

[18] A woman of great spiritual power and an adept at Tantric sadhana.

190

23rd January, 1946

I am not sincere, my surrender is only a farce. Therefore I cannot concentrate. Nowadays thoughts about the details of how I am going to drop work and what to do with all my things etc. creep into my mind. Then when I think of giving all I have to Her, it occurs to me that suppose I do not get on in the Ashram, what will I do? Suppose She won't give me money to travel with Her, etc. Is that surrender? But I feel happy to prostrate myself on the ground before Her and say: "Take all and make me the smallest particle of yourself".

Yesterday sat in the jungle and studied Hindi. It was quite a meditation. I must do this again. I have decided to resign definitely from July, whatever happens. If I sell my piano, music etc. I shall have quite a lot of money.

I went for a walk with twenty-three children and had to spank two as they drove me to desperation; then wondered how I could sit down to meditation after that. But I succeeded in the end and had a most wonderful *dhyan* on the greatness and immensity of the Centre of all things. From such a perspective this world of ours becomes so different. God divides himself into an infinite number of pieces and when the pieces forget their source they see no sense in their existence and become unhappy. This forces them to search for meaning which leads them back to Him. How can one bother about anything else but to get back there as quickly as possible. What does it matter what others say, what the body feels, where it is, what happens to it as long as one can get back to the Source. Who is going to waste time in work? What does work mean at all, except that which helps one to return. All else is nonsense and illusion. The physical by itself is nothing but a symbol of the great truth which lies beyond.

Lewis told me his real name last night. It is beautiful in sound and meaning. He broke his glasses frame this morning. His eyes are wonderful when not hidden by those silly glasses. Unforgettable.

24th January, 1946

I get a tremendous answer from Mother every time I ask for her Love and dedicate myself to Her in my meditation. Last night read Sri Aurobindo's journal *Advent*. I feel rather eager to see his Ashram.

* * *

Sri Aurobindo Ghosh (1872-1950) was one of the most famous saints and philosophers of modern India. He spent his formative years in England where he was a brilliant student. Only days before he was to receive his hard earned degree from Cambridge, which would guarantee him entry into the prestigious and elite Indian Civil Service, he turned it down essentially because he found his teachers to be petty racists. He then returned to his native Bengal, discovering his homeland for the first time and establishing a reputation for himself as a poet and scholar.

It was not long before he became India's leading revolutionary, a number of years before Gandhi appeared on the scene. Unlike Gandhi, Sri Aurobindo advocated the violent overthrow of British tyranny and ultimately he was arrested by the British on very serious charges involving a bomb plot. While in prison he practiced intense meditation and yoga and had a deep enlightenment experience. He then miraculously escaped conviction and after his release took refuge in the French colony of Pondicherry in South India.

There he renounced politics and his former involvement in the world as such and began his voluminous writings. The gist of his philosophy is that mankind's spiritual evolution is open-ended and that matter itself must ultimately be divinized. To this end he claimed to have brought down for the first time a new spiritual power that would enable the world to make the next great evolutionary leap. Although in this respect his teachings were quite novel, they were nevertheless very grounded in traditonal Indian yoga and mysticism and he wrote a number of commentaries and interpretations of ancient texts.

His principal disciple was a French woman known as Mother Mira. Already something of an adept before she met Sri Aurobindo, she was the driving force behind what became a large and famous ashram in Pondicherry, as well as the near-by international community of Auroville. She died in 1973.

* * *

Evening:
Went to see Gopinath Kaviraj's *'Shakti'*. She has a beautiful atmosphere of surrender about her that makes me wild with longing for Mother. She told me to ask her something, but I could not

think of anything. Finally the only thing that came into my mind was: "How can one know what God's will is?"

She said: "*You must fix a time when you meet with Him and sit still to find out. If you want to come to this house you must come by some road, be it straight or crooked, without a road you cannot get there at all.*"

It is strange that everyone tells me the same: Meditate.

Afterwards I felt a tremendous urge to know His will and nothing else. I suddenly understood how any kind of enjoyment or pleasure in the world takes one away from seeking Him. One must never rest until one becomes aware of Him day and night to the exclusion of all else. Then of course, all become He and the supreme pleasure of His company is to be had from all.

Instead of thinking how to manage after giving up my work and how to get the most money from the sale of my things, if I meditate on Him all the time and do nothing else, He will solve all these problems that are really only an unnecessary bother to me and waste my time.

26th January, 1946

Yesterday received a postcard from Abhaya with a message from Mother. She says: "*Do regular 'atmakriya'*[19] *of Atmananda. This little child is always with you. Remember that.*" I was so moved as to cry. Isn't it pathetic. She is always with me and in the helpless condition of a baby and I attend to other things. Had a very good meditation concentrating on Her in the evening. She knows what will move me: the thought of the Christ child that is helplessly waiting to be tended and we don't hear His cries.

She writes: "*You can go to Delhi for the work for which you previously went there*", and I do not want to go. Must I now go? I cannot decide. Isn't it a dreadful state to be in, not to know which is the right thing to do.

Kashi Station, 27th January, 1946

Afterwards I asked Lewis and decided not to go and tore up the letter I had written to the Radio people. At midday I heard Annapurna say to Prabha: "There will be no buses till February

---

[19] Explanation given in entry for 28th January.

1st." Immediately afterwards she read in the paper that Mother is in Bareilly. At once I decided to take the next train after fulfilling my promise to take L. to the Godowlia Mother. [20] It was a most extraordinary experience. I translated for L. That night I hardly slept afraid to miss the early morning train. All night I prayed to Mother: "Take possession of me completely. Don't let any particle of myself remain. Make me just an instrument of yourself. Do anything you like with me, only don't keep me apart from you. Help me to get out of this school work." I am burning with passion for Her. Now I have found out what Love is.

There was a young girl in a flame coloured sari with the Godowlia Mother, who is supposed to be very great. She is only ten years old now and looks nothing special to me. But the Guru is supposed to have said she is to be worshipped and that if she gets married she will die. What people one meets once one gets into the spiritual stream. The saints begin to grow like mushrooms these days.

Bareilly, 28th January, 1946

When I bowed to Her yesterday on arriving, I touched Her feet for the first time and she pulled my hair and made me sit next to Her.

I did not even feel dirty this morning after the train journey and went directly in to meditation sitting by Her side. There was *kirtan* going on for twelve hours yesterday with everyone walking and dancing around a make-shift tree-like alter to Krishna. I must say the people look transformed, 'verklart'.[21] I was wondering from where all these wonderful looking people had come. Abhay looked like a young God.

Evening:

It was very difficult for me to join the *kirtan* and She did not ask me to either. But, as I was sitting there so as to be near Her, I had to get up when She did and join the *parikrama* [22] along with everyone else. She may go to Delhi tomorrow. I feel worried about going to Delhi with Her. I could not quite listen to Her talk therefore.

---

[20] A local saint —probably the Bengali woman she has already mentioned.

[21] Divinely transformed.

[22] The circumambulation of a sacred object or place which is done to receive its blessings.

I asked Her about '*atmakriya*'. She said: "*Atmakriya is that which leads you to Atma [Self] realization. When the mind becomes clear, then you see yourself in the mirror. The Great Moment comes of itself and nothing and no one else can take you to this Realization; but through the shakti* [spiritual power] *of your Guru, you can be fully prepared for it when it comes.* [23] *But you must obey Him. He is your Guru whom you believe to be perfect and this faith is what makes Him your Guru.*"

Strangely, this morning Hariram Joshi told me that a glance is enough to transmit initiation from Guru to disciple. This evening at the climactic moment of the *kirtan* festival in which She seemed to become one with Sri Krishna Himself, She looked straight into my eyes so deeply I could hardly bear it. I have not yet found out what that look meant. But I guess it confirmed Her catching hold of my hair last night. I suppose I shall have to go to Delhi with Her. There must be a *samskara* left that has to be worked out. As soon as I decided not to go to Delhi for the Radio, at once the circumstances that brought me to Bareilly arose, and now I am going to Delhi after all.

Someone asked Her: "Have we not to destroy evil?" She said: "*Yes, you have to. But if there is no evil in you, then you do not see it in others. Things are evil from your point of view, but not from His.*

Then She was asked: "If my country needs me, isn't it selfish to only think of God? Reply: "*You work for your country, because you consider it yours, so that is also selfish. But if you can do the work for your country as a service to God, then it is all right. Whatever you can do as a service to Him is all right. The first duty is Atmachintan* [remembering the Atma]. *Atma cannot be thought of, but if you clean the mind by thinking of Him, you may then get Realization.*"

The thought occurred to me or else I dreamt that someone said: "J.K. may be the Antichrist." The thought sticks to me.

Dr. Vyas said to me: "*Atmakriya* referred to a brea' ag exercise which She must have given you." Another gentleman said: "No, these exercises can only be done b; *brahmacharis* [celibate monks]. In her case it means simply concent.ction on the Supreme Self."

This morning She said: "*Think before you act, once you have done something do not think of it anymore.*"

---

[23] This is a fundamental teaching of Anandamayee Ma.

195

Bareilly, 29th January, 1946

Hariram Joshi's house.

Slept at Her feet in a room with seven others, five men and two women, with the window ajar about two inches. During the morning meditation I said to Her within: "Now I have given myself to you entirely to do anything you wish with me. <u>You</u> do my *sadhana*, everything. If the whole world is your own body, then you are everyone. Hitler, Kitty, S.R., cats, dogs etc. You do everything that has to be done. I will keep entirely still and wait for you to burn me up."

This morning I could sit quite straight all the time. I cried during the *bhajan* but also joined in singing. What is it that makes me feel so reluctant to sing aloud or show any devotion or reverence in public? Evidently I do not have perfect faith. It is the mind's impurity that does not allow me to join the ceremony.

Kitty and S.R. are on my mind as Mother may go to Delhi today. In any case I shall stay with Her until my leave is over. I will go and see them if She gives permission. It occurs to me that even hate or contempt for Her is better than no thought at all. As Ramana Maharshi said: "Hate or love, it is all the same; the thought of Him will take you there."

Afternoon:

We are going to Hardwar after all tonight.

This morning I told Her that I would give up my work. She asked me whether I wanted to do anything else. I said I wanted to stay with Her, that I had a little money to begin with. I said 3 months was a long time to wait, but I could not leave before. She said: "*In any case I often go away and leave my own people for sometime, so wait these three months where you are.*" She also told me that I must lose anger altogether.

We then went to some place in the bazaar in a car where she sat so near me that what She had said in Her postcard "*This body will stay on your lap*" became literally true. Later I sat near Her and many people took me for the Mataji and touched my feet. It was very embarrassing. I am afraid of such things. I am not pure enough to bear this. We stayed away for about 4 hours or more. People are now very friendly with me and eat with me and allow me to touch Her things, etc.

Hardwar, 30th January, 1946

Last night in the train quite unexpectedly I again had the opportunity to sleep at Her Feet. She is just a marvel, Sri Krishna, Christ.

* * *

After Benares, Hardwar is the most important pilgrimage city for Hindus in North India. It is situated in a beautiful spot on the Ganges in the foothills of the Himalayas where, it is said, the sacred river comes out of the mountains to meet the plains. It is a town of many ashrams and temples.

* * *

Hardwar is wonderful. We are only a very few here and Udas [24] is the only other woman. It is just bliss to be here. I guarded Her while she seemed to sleep this morning, which moved me to tears; but then I found She had a headache because I let Her be in a draught. I am far too self-centered to be of any use, but She is teaching me very fast and I can learn quickly. I asked for some work, so She gave me a petticoat to stitch. But I see that it is really no use to anyone but to myself. I dare say all work is such until it is done purely and without ego. She sent me to bathe in the Ganges this morning and in the evening we sat on the *ghat* and heard some boys chanting Vedic hymns. I decided to send a wire and take one day more leave. It is so difficult to go away from Her at all. I sat at her feet today till my legs are lame.

Hardwar, 31st January, 1946

Slept at Her Feet. I want to ask Her whether I cannot contemplate Her, as that calls out Love; whereas Atma has not much meaning for me. Jiten arrived this morning.

Rajghat, 3rd February, 1946

Jiten asked me to stay on in Hardwar. I could really have done so, but when I got unwell with no place even to wash and was staying with a crowd of people in one room (some had arrived from Dehradun that morning), I felt I should not stay. But now I

---

[24] One of Anandamayee Ma's closest disciples who performed great austerities and was Her main attendant for many years.

see that it is only because I identify myself with the body. There was actually no need to return yesterday when there were no buses. I see now why I have to work —because I am still attached to various comforts. They mean more to me even than Her company, otherwise I would not have left!

When I took leave of Her, She was most gracious. She blessed me saying for farewell: *"Remain always Atmananda* [the bliss of the *Atma]"*.

I was extremely exhausted and could not meditate at all yesterday. I got out of the habit as I had not kept up my evening meditation at Bareilly and Hardwar. Yesterday Lewis told me: "Don't worry about anything, keep your mind on the Source and everything will be arranged from there."

Last night some children came to my room and it suddenly struck me that they are all Sri Krishna. I was pondering all day on what She had said at Dehra: "*The whole world is to me like my own body*". If one understood the meaning of only this one sentence, it would change everything. Fancy seeing Her in every body, in every animal, stone, plant etc.

She asked me whether I can cook. I said, "No, nobody will eat what I cook". She replied: *"But you will be alone, you must learn to cook for yourself. When you come to me I shall teach you to cook"*. She made me stitch a petticoat for Her. It struck me that I have had my petticoat lying cut and waiting for the tailor. Evidently She will teach me everything.

Evening:

Meditation better than usual. I see that the mind creates pictures because it is afraid to face that which lies yet deeper and which is nearer to Reality. I got some slight inkling of a terrific Being that is behind the outer appearance of Mother. As I surrender more and more to Her, She will show more of Herself. After meditating my left leg was so stiff it took three or four minutes of tapping it to be able to get up.

4th February, 1946

There is something that is beyond the chattering, picture producing mind. But as long as the mind produces images, it cannot show itself. When I meditate, Her image vanishes, but She remains —formless. Complete surrender means to cast out everything and make room for Her. The mind must be blank and merged only in Her, and the heart free from the slightest desire or craving, prepared to accept everything from Her only.

5th February, 1946

Went for a walk by the side of the Ganges and came to the house of a *sadhu* lady who lives there with her Guru. She gave me fruit and water.

I am reading *Srimad Bhagvat* [25] with great delight and I am making a practice of seeing Sri Krishna in everyone I meet. The children become very much less troublesome that way.

6th February, 1946

I can now concentrate on the breath for some time. It is still extremely difficult to sit out the whole hour; but I obey Her and do it. Let Her do what She will with me.

Lewis is in a terrible state. He feels he must do his Guru's work first but is somehow unable to do so. It seems to me he must, at all cost, go there and surrender to him.

7th February, 1946

If one sees Him everywhere the mind loses its restlessness, because where then is one to go? Movement becomes irrelevant. Read *Srimad Bhagavat* with great delight. Getting engrossed in Sri Krishna —a passage particularly struck me which said that even intense devotion cannot bring one to His Feet as quickly as hate! [26] It also says that one who is killed by the Lord in battle is enlightened at once. When walking on the road this evening in semi-darkness, stumbled over a stone and could have had a very bad fall, but She seemed to pull me back. She looks after me much better than I could. Even when I am thoughtless, She never is. Every breath, every movement, is Her's.

---

[25] One of the principal scriptures for Vaishnavas (devotees of Krishna).

[26] The principal villains in the myths of Rama and Krishna were actually great devotees. They were told before taking birth that if they would consent to being the primary antagonists of the Divine incarnations, they would attain liberation in only one life at the hands of their Lord whereas if they served him as devotees it would take several lifetimes.

8th February, 1946

Got in touch with Her on rather a higher level than usual. Ram means 'all pervading'. I repeated this for some time.

I become more and more mad for Her. I don't mind anything as long as I can be as near Her as possible, and I fully trust Her to deal with every detail. She will look after everything once I am merged in Her. Through the process of devotion and meditation I pray that She quickly brings about the necessary purification. Yes, I must leave this place and bathe my head in the dust of Her feet.

9th February, 1946

Now I get more and more in touch with Her. There is a great sense of effulgence where everything vanishes —I can hardly bear the bliss of it. She seemed to pervade my whole body and mind for a few minutes. Then again the body revolts and the mind wanders, though the sweetness of her contact is incomparable. She has become a totally addictive habit. I am dying to be with Her day and night, still thoughts about security when leaving work come up in my mind. What nonsense.

Lewis is in a difficult condition. I feel a great motherly affection for him and imagine his head bathed in light. It occurred to me this evening to pray to his Guru for him, as he himself seems unable to do so. The Guru seemed grateful that at last someone has approached him, as if he were only waiting for it and responded immediately. Is all this only imagination?

10th February, 1946

Went for a long walk along the Ganges, came to a lovely little temple. I thought much about J.K. and how many years I have given to him with no positive result. Now I will give myself entirely to Her and see what happens —for better, for worse, in sickness and in health. This is the first time I am able to do this and the first time that it is being accepted and responded to. So I will obey her implicitly and leave all else. She said: *"Atmananda raho"* [stay immersed in the bliss of the Self (*atma*)].

I shall not resign but take one year's leave, as the police might not like my loafing. Within that year I might be able to acquire British or Indian naturalization. Then only shall I really be free to

go where I like. I want to rent out the piano and music for that
year if possible.

11th February, 1946

Tremendous bliss this evening when I imagined Her breathing through me —but I can bear it only for a short while.

12th February, 1946

The mind now acquiesces to the fact that it has to go back to its
Source which is the Source of all things. In the beginning it revolted
at the idea of wasting its time on what it considered as doing nothing. Now it sees that all its outer activities are useless and vain.

In the evening walked to Sarnath with Lewis to see the Ceylonese
Buddhist monk Ananda Matreyi, who told us ghost stories and how
he had a vision of the Lord Maitreya and the Theosophical Masters.

L. is in a very bad mood and I am going to leave him alone.

13th February, 1946

The mind is now quite conversant with regarding Him as the
true life of all people and gets some kind of glimpse of this for a
minute or two during meditation; but it has yet to have a major
effect on the everyday life.

Sanjiv Rao is right. Lewis can become the instrument for evil.
He is so stubborn and has too much pride in his subtle knowledge. It is a difficult path he insists on treading.

15th February, 1946

Yesterday Sarnath. Concentrated on Sita-Ram on the way and
on *Atma* on the way back. It has a definite effect. Talked to Ananda
Maitreyi about J.K. and he told me about the Pratyeka Buddha,
who, having become fully realized, cannot teach others. He believes J.K. to be like that. It came to me during my meditation that
I must sever myself completely from J.K. and all that he represents —but then what about my dream?

Met the German Tibetan Buddhist monk Lama Govinda [27] at
Sarnath. He has beautiful blue eyes, but does not strike me as be-

---

[27] Anagarika Govinda 1898-1985, later to become a well known author of books
on Tibetan Buddhism.

ing terribly profound. That thought, however subtle, simply builds up my own ego.

Evening:

Reading *Sad Vani* I came across some passages which make it quite clear that the reasoning power and the critical intellect have to ultimately be surrendered. That seems an impossible task and I feel afraid to do it. Now I see why She wants me to concentrate on *Atma* —because that contains the idea of the absolute non-dual Self, which is all and everything, so that there is nothing to give up because in that is contained all. I must reason it out and get beyond doubt. It is no use leaving this place and going to Her if I am in this condition. That is, I dare say, why L. criticized the people round Her and very nearly Her also —because it is a reflection of a hidden thought in myself. It is the old problem of evil. *Is evil this fundamental reasoning power that creates division?*

16ᵗʰ February, 1946

Doubts about Mother again arise. Reading Vivekananda's [28] "Talks" with great pleasure. It gives my mind just the food it needs. I see now that the *buddhi* or reasoning is a fundamental part of the causal body or will, which has to be abandoned. That is the whole trouble —the ego's fear that it has to go. Vivekananda says: "Free will is a misnomer. Will can never be free. How can it be? It is only when the true self has become bound that this so-called will comes into existence and not before. The will of man is bound, but that which is the foundation of that will is eternally free".

17ᵗʰ February, 1946

Her Presence very strong today. If you are in the Presence of God, will you talk? Will you let your mind chatter? Will you not strain every nerve to concentrate on Him, to merge in Him, to forget yourself and your pettiness!

I asked Her interiorly to help me to get over my greed for food. The reply from within is: "Think that your body is not separate from mine. Whenever you eat remember that you feed me. With such care must you look on food."

---

[28] The great disciple of Sri Ramakrishna who brought his Guru's message to the West where he was enthusiastically received in the 1890's.

18ᵗʰ February, 1946

I feel Mother very near. She seems with me all the time. Again the desire to go South has risen very much and it is She who seems to tell me to go and says: "Don't worry about money, it will come. Consider all the money that goes through your hands as coming from me, spend it lavishly on others, very sparingly on yourself and you will get money to do all these things that you want to do."

21ˢᵗ February, 1946

As long as I eat for sense gratification instead of offering the food, I shall never purify my *prana*. The ego keeps itself alive partly through enjoying food eaten in the wrong way.

22ⁿᵈ February, 1946

Lewis came back last night from the Ashram in a towering rage as I am supposed to have said something about him. I was rather upset last night, but I feel innocent this morning. I should talk less.

23ʳᵈ February, 1946

Her lesson to me is evidently that if you are always in the living presence of God or Reality, you need nothing else. When I slept with Her and 8 people in that airless room at Bareilly, or when I stayed at the *dharmasala* ²⁹ in Hardwar where the room was both a corridor and also used as a kitchen by some strangers, I was happier than I had ever been in all my life. But when I got unwell, I went on strike and left. There the body was stronger than I and now I may not see her till May!

25ᵗʰ February, 1946

I get Her Presence more now. Today I had a glimpse of what the mind becomes when it has surrendered; how it watches Him animating all things, never identifying with the separate ego but being always a perfect instrument through which He alone acts.

---

²⁹ Pilgrim guest houses, usually free, found everywhere in India, particularly in holy places.

1st March, 1946

Wrote letter of resignation. L. seemed rather touched and I think A.K. is also. I feel sort of in a whirl, not at all elevated or peaceful. Never mind.

Mother's Presence is extremely potent now. The chief thing in meditation is to ask Her to pervade me with Her light, peace and grace. Yet sometimes I forget it.

2nd March, 1946, Shivaratri [30]

Went to the Vishwanath temple [31] and many other temples with Gopibai. Throwing flowers at Annapurna [32] I got such a response that tears came at once.

Sat for meditation afterwards. Mother's Presence is becoming ever more prominent. The only thing I can concentrate on is Her. It gives *ananda* and makes me forget myself and not mind what happens as long as I can be with Her.

A.K. yesterday asked me to take leave instead of resigning. I agreed, but I cannot really be bothered with this now. Let it be as it is. Mother will look after me and make things happen as they must.

3rd March, 1946

Last night very potent presence of Mother, but again was bothered by sensual thoughts. I believe this is due to having been touched and pushed by all sorts of people in the temple. When the spiritual becomes too intense there is an inevitable reaction and restlessness. I must go slowly.

Perhaps it will be better to take leave and then resign after some months and thus not appear to leave so abruptly.

5th March, 1946

I have communion with Mother now every time in meditation, for a few minutes at least; but then thought wanders to mat-

---

[30] Shivaratri is the 'Night of Shiva' during which Hindus traditionally fast and meditate all night.

[31] The principal temple in Benares and one of the most important shrines to Shiva in all India.

[32] 'The Goddess who feeds all'. There is a particularly beautiful image of her in a shrine near the Vishwanath Temple complex.

ters of this earth and it is like another world —a much grosser vibration that shuts me off from Her. I now unify or combine three things: Meditation on *Atma* —which I imagine to be Her— concentration on breath, which I also imagine coming from Her, and transforming my body and mind into a hollow vessel totally filled with Her grace. With every breath the I-ness goes out and the *Atma* comes in.

7th March, 1946

My liver is upset and it spoils my mind which somehow brings up doubt about Mother. Lewis, with whom I am again much more friendly, is very helpful with this. He told me that he did not consider Vishudhanand [33] a *jivanmukta* (a totally realized being) but a yogi who had attained to a very high level without taking the final step. To my question as to how one is to be protected from such Gurus, he said that the desire for *mukti* is the only true safeguard. If one has had even the faintest glimpse of Reality, one can never be satisfied by anything else. Even if one accepts a Guru who is not a *jivanmukta,* one will be forced to drop him again if one's aspiration for the highest is sincere. It is likely that the pure desire for *mukti* will not let one accept anyone who is less than that.

8th March, 1946

I know nothing at all, except that there is a body with which I identify myself. It feels hunger, cold etc. and there is something that thinks. What happens when this body dies, I do not know. It seems unreasonable to me that I should die with it, but even that may be only a *vasana* [product of thought with no inherent reality] and nothing else. There must be something that keeps this body together and that formulates the laws governing its existence.

To think all this out anew from the beginning I must seclude myself and live alone without responsibilities for some time at least. I need to be quiet and in nature with a few books that will stimulate this kind of inquiry or still better, to be with Mother — then I can get to the root of all this.

---

[33] A famous *siddha* (one who has occult powers) in Benares at that time and a principal mentor of Gopinath Kaviraj. He is mentioned in Paramhansa Yogananda's *Autobiography of a Yogi.*

The firm resolve that nothing less than complete *mukti* will do means that I have no duties other than the one of constant, uninterrupted concentration on that One which is beyond the ever revolving wheel of the world, beyond birth and death —be it Something or be it Nothing. It makes no difference as soon as one is resolved to get out of this nonsense and to the Ultimate at all cost.

I remember Kitty, who certainly has resolved the same, and therefore whatever she does must lead her out of this nonsense.

10th March, 1946

Intense doubt of everything. I do not know anything at all. There is nothing to hold on to within my knowledge, except that there are people like J.K. who say they have gotten out of this mess. But as he does not teach me how to do it, I must find another way. However he did tell me something clearly in my dream. Anandamayee Ma is the most profoundly spiritually attractive thing I have ever found and so I will trust Her entirely to lead me, with the firm resolve that I shall not rest until I have found out whatever there is to be found. This very resolve must lead me the right way. If there is nothing to be found, then from where does the desire to find it arise in everyone? There must be something either in the world or in the mind, or beyond both, that will either put sense into this nonsensical life cr take one out of it and beyond it.

All the time I feel connected with Kitty. Even in my meditation I think of her and she seems to share in all this. Mentally I tell her all I experience.

11th March, 1946

Can sit now for one and a half hours at a stretch in the morning. Tried to realize this morning what the body is, what its feelings are and what the mind is. The mind becomes anything it thinks of and when it desires something it identifies itself with the desired and becomes that. The mind can change at every moment. What is that which gives one individual identity, gives life and the energy to judge and discriminate? That something, is it the *Atma* ?

13ᵗʰ March, 1946

Did not meditate last night and this morning, but missed it a great deal. It caused great dissatisfaction. The mind at once tried to look for some enjoyment and outer contact. It shows how desires are born as a result of being out of tune with one's real state. Even the faintest contact with the higher Reality makes one indifferent to every other enjoyment.

This evening sat again for meditation. As soon as I concentrate on Mother She immediately lifts me out of my ordinary state. And yet why do I doubt? Lately I am afraid of the crowd round Her, and when I am not so well I have fear of how I shall stand the strain of the hard life in the ashram, vigils, discomforts etc. Then I want to remain in this comfortable place here. Strange. I imagine that She does not want me, but that is not true. It was always I who ran away, She never sent me.

14ᵗʰ March, 1946

Reading *Adhyatma Ramayan* in Hindi with delight. What I seek is completely apart from the world and everything that is connected with it.

If my search is due to His attraction and His wish, won't He provide me with all necessities! Need I worry that I can't put up with certain discomforts and bad food? Will He not see that I get everything that is necessary, as soon as I have no other wish, no other thought but of Him. It is my lack of faith that spoils everything. What is money? He that produces the cosmos with a mere gesture, won't He give a morsel of food and a quiet corner to His *bhakta*?

16ᵗʰ March, 1946

I feel now intense mistrust of the whole world, as I perceive it anyhow. It seems to have nothing whatsoever to do with Reality or Truth. It has to be entirely abandoned with all that is part of it —thought, choice etc.

XI - Thoughts of J.K.

Rajghat, 18th March, 1946, Holi [1]

This morning woke late and felt out of sorts. Sat for half hour only. Evening: extremely calm and blissful. I sit quite straight, head does not drop. I remembered what Lewis had told me about concentration: One cannot concentrate the mind, one must let go of it and relax in one's own centre —which is beyond the whole *leela* of thinking, feeling and action that constitutes both the world and the mind.

Reading what J.K. says in his 1940 Talks on meditation etc. I see that I now understand him much better, but I could have never understood anything without the help of Sri Ramana Maharshi, Lewis and Mother. J.K.'s way was too difficult, nay impossible for me. First the mind has to be cleared and made less dense and he does not give a method for this, then only can it get a glimpse of That, which has no connection whatsoever with this world or the mind.

22nd March, 1946

Spent one and a half days with Mother. From the moment she arrived I got into a strange mood, more or less like when I had to leave Huizen [2]. Seeing Her with such a big crowd etc., I thought: "What have I to do with all this?" I felt critical and had a strange feeling of nervousness in my stomach and cloudedness of mind, so that I could not see any light at all. This went on all day, except for sometime when I concentrated and got quiet and blissful. I then decided to talk to Her. I did so this morning for a very short time with many disturbances. It seemed to me that

---

[1] Holi is a festival connected with Krishna in which the participants gleefully throw coloured water and powder on each other.

[2] The Theosophical community in Holland where she had lived for several years but then abandoned due to Krishnamurti's influence as related in chapter I.

reading J.K. has shown me that my faith really has no base and all I am doing is built on authority and imagination and can be destroyed by the slightest thing.

When I told Her that I had dropped J.K. because I could not do anything with his way, She said: *"It is not necessary to leave. There are many masters, they have different ways, but they all lead to the same truth. Dedicate yourself completely to that great Power that illumines everything. Japa is only to keep the mind in check* [3]. *But the main thing is 'dhyan'. Do as much of that as possible, lying down, sitting, standing. Keep the mind empty. Make it one pointed."* Then she asked me to keep *satsang* [spiritual company]. When I told Her that I don't like *bhajan* and *kirtan*, She said: *"Then you don't need to do it. The name of God is sacred. You do dhyan but let others do kirtan. You should be in a quiet place and solitary."* She asked me not to resign now, but to take leave, and if after it is over I feel like resigning then I can do it. This was exactly my idea.

On the first day when I was in a black and critical mood, She seemed to studiously avoid me, unconsciously I expect. When Her gaze turned my way, Her eyes immediately diverted.

The next morning after I insisted on talking to Her it became different. In the train she became extremely gracious. She gave me a white garland that had been offered to Her and after keeping the yellow flower that was on it, said: *"Be of one colour! I have not given you all, I am keeping this one flower."* She blessed me with Her hands and touched me deliberately. Then she threw oranges to me when the train was already moving and I was watching Her depart from the platform. These two days were a dizzy experience.

I have to do the three broadcasts after all, but not in Delhi.

27th March, 1946

I don't feel up to much and therefore often get tired. However my mind does get quite still and void now, and I keep sitting quite straight. I call on Her always to keep watch over me. She knows what She is doing.

---

[3] Anandamayee Ma often explained that *japa* (repetition of a mantra), when done correctly, automatically leads to *dhyana* (meditative absorption). Her instructions here, as always, are geared to Atmananda's (or whomever She might be responding to) temperament and needs of the moment.

29ᵗʰ March, 1946

Maha Varuni *Mela*. [4]
Watching the endless crowds for hours. I never realized there were so many people in the world. When one thinks that each one of these moving specks is infinitely concerned with himself and his 'possessions' and that I am also one in this crowd, it makes me feel quite mad. What can one do? Isn't one animated by something that is evidently beyond this petty body with its little thoughts and little feelings. And then Anandamayee Ma says: *"I feel the whole world as my own body."* What a tremendous saying it is.

2ⁿᵈ April, 1946

Altogether I seem to have gone backwards a good deal. Is it really a fall or the aridity that is described in the "Dark Night of the Soul"?

3ʳᵈ April, 1946

Whenever my mind wanders to irrelevant things, I think of Mother and it is immediately raised to a level where these things don't exist and I can concentrate with ease and *ananda*.

5ᵗʰ April, 1946

Yesterday got J.K.'s 1944 *Talks*.
It is still very fascinating and I still do not understand. At least now he admits that one must retire from the world, also that stillness of the mind is absolutely essential. But his way of getting to that stillness, although inspiringly stated, seems impossible to achieve to me. I do not understand it. On the other hand when I meditate, even if I do not have such deep concentration, yet it does change me in that I don't get so immersed in outer things; I see more and more that this ordinary life is a mere waste of time and that I must not submit to it. Ramana Maharshi says what is the use of analyzing the rubbish that has to be thrown away in any case. J.K. says to watch every flutter of thought-feeling as it has its significance.
Nowadays I write nothing into my diary because I have again become more affected by my worldly surroundings. *Satsang* is of

---

[4] A large religious fair.

211

the utmost importance. Anyway I am now convinced that what has to be got at is beyond anything that can be known and that nothing that one can do or think can take one there; but when all thought and activity cease, then the way begins to open up. Mother told me not to drop J.K. I shall again talk this over with her. Perhaps I shall give him another chance when he comes, but then I shall go into it thoroughly and for a long time, with no work to distract me.

When I stay with Mother I must try and work as little as possible and also not get too involved in the Ashram. After all, am I there to reform them or myself! As you learn music by being with a musician and by listening to his playing and explanations, so I shall learn by being with One who is immersed in and radiates 'Reality'.

J.K. upsets me. The mind seizes on his saying: "No forcing will do" and then uses this as just the right excuse to perpetuate its restlessness.

What is the good of analyzing mental 'craving'? It is only a question of identification. The body-mind always craves something as it is by nature unfulfilled. It can only be fulfilled by annihilation of desire which is achieved through the process of surrender. If one gets absorbed in the Absolute there can be no craving, no separation.

7th April, 1946

Is 'awareness' not 'surrender' —a taking stock of everything that constitutes one's mind and emotions and burning it in the light of the Unthinkable.

Lewis said this morning that the total surrender to the Guru, who is Reality as such, is concentration on the Supreme which swallows up the mind. It is not an idea, but an intensely profound process.

What J.K. says is not a way. It is a work of art which conveys an experience which one has to make one's own. In doing this one creates one's own way and method.

The chief thing to me is total concentration, that one-pointedness that includes everything and destroys the separateness of everything, that is a burning fire which eats up desires and thoughts.

To be in close touch physically, mentally and emotionally with One who has attained the highest illumination enhances this concentration, awareness, and surrender a million times. Therefore it is so absolutely necessary, until one is strong enough to be alone. It always makes me breathless when I think of this.

Adi Shankaracharya [5] says that the objects perceived by the senses should be offered as oblations into the fire of the Self.

It all boils down to identification with the mind and body. What J.K.'s 1944 *Talks* say also amounts to that: (p. 4) "As long as we regard ourselves as individuals, apart from the whole, competing, obstructing, opposing, sacrificing the many for the particular or the particular for the many, all those problems that arise out of this conflicting antagonism will have no happy and enduring solution, for they are the result of wrong thinking-feeling."

"To understand, all denial or acceptance, judgement or comparison must be set aside. In becoming aware we shall discover what is honesty, what is love, what is fear, what is simple life and the complex problem of memory."

p. 78: "Just as a lake is calm when the breezes stop so when the mind has understood and thus transcended the conflicting problems it has created, great stillness comes into being. This tranquility is not to be induced by will, by desire, it is the outcome of the freedom from craving."

9th April, 1946

I woke up thinking that all work and all involvement with others is an escape, a distraction from the deep inner concentration which alone takes one to one's Self and which alone is the One thing worth doing. Yesterday when I went to see whether Lewis was all right, it was a kind thing to do, but it was also an escape, an excuse to take me away from what I really have to do.

I cannot meditate at all these days. My mind has got hold of J.K.'s words and is trying to use them as a means of diverting me.

Evening:

As there was no electricity, I lit an oil lamp and put it before Mother's picture for my meditation. This had a symbolic effect of

---

[5] Adi Shankaracharya, the great 9th century interpreter of classical Indian non-dualistic philosophy, was one of the principal shapers of modern Hinduism.

putting Her alone into light and everything else in darkness. Meditating on Her, the Reality behind the body, I got very good concentration and felt that it may not be necessary to be always with Her physically if I can keep Her in my mind in this way.

10th April, 1946, Ram Navami [6]

I find myself in a meditative mood and in touch with J.K. I told both Kelkar and Miss M. about it. I find that it seems to work inside me. It now has this power that the mere reading of him gives me the capacity to get at that awareness and that hush, that stillness, which is the 'awareness' of which he speaks. I understand him to mean that first and foremost there is that stillness, but simultaneously one takes the *vasanas* and common thoughts up into the stillness and surrenders them. When these rudiments of ego are absorbed, then there is real stillness because the root of the false ego, 'I', is dead. Once one has surrendered to this process he remains in an intense state of 'unknowing' until the Uncreated has absorbed whatever is left of ego impressions completely — until pure knowledge stands revealed.

When I was undoing the threads of my quilt this morning, it occurred to me that unravelling the mind is very similar. One goes on pulling out the threads, up and down and across and there seems no end to it, there are always more left; and when at last the threads have really all come out, there are still the impressions of the thread and the stitches, and they look very nearly like the thread itself.

The very thought of J.K. today drowns all other thought and elevates the mind. Was that what he meant in my dream last year? The power of even his writings has now become such that it is not only words but the Thing Itself and therefore even the reading of it takes one out of oneself —*or is it Mother's enchantment*, because she told me not to leave what I have already begun?

* * *

Anandamaye Ma, as Guru, would invariably bring to fruition all valid previous sadhanas (spiritual practices) already begun by her disciples before they came to her. This seems to be because, as she maintained that ultimately

---

[6] Birthday of the epic hero and avatar Rama.

there is really only ONE Guru, once she had assumed that role, all previous sadhanas *practised by her disciples under the guidance of other teachers (perhaps even those from previous lifetimes) were taken over by her so that the particular* karma *could be completed. This was often the experience of those under her direction.*

* * *

I now wonder whether my pet dream of living in a community that is out to "live the Life" will still come true. Somehow I feel it will.

11th April, 1946

I am now able to concentrate much better by simply thinking of Mother or of J.K. —which is the same. In either case I am drawn out of my stupid self. I must remember that no thought belongs to me. It is really the identification with thoughts or problems that make them potent. If one can look on as an observer, one just smiles at everything.

I now intensely desire to be with J.K.

12th April, 1946

Lewis had fever yesterday. I enjoy looking after him and he seems to be quite as sorry at the prospect of our parting at the end of the school term as I am.

There must be desire as long as there is the sense of I, the mind. 'Craving' (as J.K. puts it) seems to me to be really the only positive thing we have, because it compels us to destroy the barriers of the snug prison of the mind. Craving is really the urge to come back to perfect balance. We simply have to learn how to desire the proper things. The false sense of balance given by physical security within the context of separateness is poisonous and worse.

Perfection clothes itself with a physical body like Ananda-mayee Ma's in order to seduce us mortals whose perceptions are based on the physical senses. It uses physical attraction to captivate the senses and lure them into the fire of truth. Once we have become irrevocably attached to Her, She disappears and becomes 'That'—our innermost Self—, the ONE.

13th April, 1946

Reading J.K.'s early works, I see that by having met the other Great Ones and having read other things, I now feel that I understand what he means. But by itself in that form in 1928, it was really very misleading. I cannot be blamed. It was impossible to act on that. I was bound to be led by the nose. Even now what he says is, as L. says, to be taken as a piece of art, from the experience of which one creates one's own method.

14th April, 1946

It seems to me that playing the piano upsets me. The vibration is evidently not helpful to my *sadhana*. It seems to draw me into worldliness. I must give it up. I was much better when I spent my time learning Hindi instead of playing the piano.

Had only about 15 minutes to meditate as I was disturbed. But in those 15 minutes Her Presence was so potent that I vanished completely. She seemed to have taken possession of me. It was such bliss.

17th April, 1946

Anna came on the 15th evening. That night I found my mind all in a whirl from her influence. But today we had long talks about J.K., Mother, Ramana Maharshi etc. and now she does not seem to disturb me anymore, though I can't keep up my evening meditation and get less sleep. Anna seems extremely clear. Her touch is very pure. There is nothing sticky to her at all. This may be partly due to her strict diet and extensive fasting and also she told me today that J.K.'s camp at Rajghat in 1938-39 really killed her ego. It is quite likely, and in spite of appearance perhaps it never revived in the same way. Perhaps he does that to all of us. Perhaps Kitty is also really dead in this way but clings on desperately to a past which hardly exists anymore, just out of habit.

I somehow talked so much today that I had a sore throat. But as Anandamayee Ma says, if you talk, talk only about 'That'. So that is what I was doing. I feel Mother's Presence quite strongly now. She is presently in Dacca.

216

18th April, 1946

My meditation was disturbed by thoughts of my talk with Anna yesterday. Sometimes my thoughts become so intense that they possess me. I must find out how to become loose, so that I remain aware of myself while thoughts fly in and out like birds from a nest.

Lisl is my only friend from my childhood and said she wanted to meet Mother. I look forward to introducing her in Calcutta.

If I take Mother to be Reality, God, and surrender to Her decisions in all things, then all my troubles will be over. But can I? To be aware of every thought—feeling, as J.K. says,— does it not mean to surrender completely to that awareness, in other words to live in the presence of God.

Ramana calls all thoughts rubbish. Being a *jnani*, for Him the world does not exist. On the other hand, Sri Aurobindo takes the position that the physical also has to be Divinized.

25th April, 1946

One day I suddenly realized that there is no time. One cannot grasp it. The moment has no extension. It is already gone when one becomes aware of it. So time is only an invention of the mind to keep events on a string.

When in Lucknow for the broadcast from 19th-21st, I met Mira Ben —the famous follower of Gandhiji— and liked her very much. There seems much determination, quiet confidence and no nonsense about her. I treated the radio like a concubine. I feel now that it has been the piano that has all along kept me from India, from really plunging into it.

Lewis says that by meeting and studying as many of these realized Beings as possible, one comes to a deeper understanding of them. My wish to visit the Great Ones in the South persists. Also Mother said once that some *samskaras* are good and must be nourished and this desire seems to be one of that kind.

I am sorry to part from Lewis, though I see the fallacy of it because we are much nearer when we are apart physically. But still there is attachment. He always reacts to this with grumpiness.

26th April, 1946

I am still very interested in this world and therefore cannot make my mind truly empty; and I do not see why I shouldn't be interested. I want to read. I want to meet great people. There is still such a strong sense of the 'I'. Also it perhaps depends much on what I read. I am reading Romain Rolland's *Vivekananda*. Rolland is essentially muddled and therefore reading him makes me restless.

27th April, 1989

It will be good for me to travel with Mother for some time. This will kill my ego as I shall have to conform to ashram life and submit to others. The time for my being alone has evidently not yet come. Mother says, meditate on the One Life that pulsates through all. This brings the solution —only I am not doing it.

28th April, 1946

Lewis looks like a great Saint when asleep. I wonder whether he is in *samadhi* while sleeping. I watched him a little this afternoon when he slept in my room under the fan. That is why he need not worry about money or can even make mistakes over it and other petty things —because he is established in another realm, so ordinary rules of conduct are really not necessary for him. But one cannot imitate this state.

30th April, 1946

Yesterday saw Alice's painting of Krishna in Vishvarupa manifestation —the vision of Arjun in the *Bhagavad Gita* [7]. I meditated on it this morning and it was rather marvellous to do so. It depicts the whole world or rather the three worlds inside the huge figure of Krishna. If one could always keep in mind that every movement, every activity, every breath exist within Krishna, how wonderful life would be. Nothing could be trivial.

I attempted to remain aware of what Lewis had told me about my behaviour of following only my own thought associations and

---

[7] This exceptional painting along with other works of Alice Boner is today housed in the art museum at Benares Hindu University.

not being receptive to other people, and really Alice was much nicer and not so distant. It is true that I am rather oblivious of the other person in a conversation. There is something in me that is afraid of being crushed.

Tonight Lewis left for Lucknow and Almora. I felt it very much and cried all the way home from the station. At that moment I felt desolate and desperate at parting. I do not know when or whether at all we shall ever meet again. Is it possible to part forever from one you love. It must remain with one somehow and return in ever new shapes. Now an hour or two later I feel stable again. But I feel upset at parting all the same. Is not life strange! —nothing real, ever changing. But Lewis has changed my whole life from top to bottom, just by being what he is. There is no one like him.

3rd May, 1946

I have not read anything for days and been slack in meditation and have worries about the future, though I am only partly conscious of them. Even the packing of my numerous things gives me a headache. I feel like throwing away everything and managing like a *sanyasi*. But then again I need things, books etc.

I have a great wish to live in a kind of modern convent, with men and women who have the same aim and have given up the world. I suppose my search will take me to that. It is my old, old wish. I am tired of this nonsensical existence, but I cannot manage by myself. The original aim of Rajghat, which is what really attracted me to it, still haunts me. I suppose it will have to fulfil itself.

XII - The Plunge

A life of *sadhana*, a religious life, often appears to move toward the goal more in a spiral —sometimes quite a wide one— than in a straight line. Thus what may seem to the person in the thick of it to be regression after a period of 'progress', is more likely to be simply the next step in an essentially forward moving transformative process under the watchful guidance of the Guru. In the little more than a year since Atmananda first spoke to Anandamayee Ma at Sarnath, her rapid spiritual progress has not had to confront any serious obstacles. But now that she has taken the major step of taking a year's leave from her work so as to more completely immerse herself in this spiritual process, it is inevitable that her ego will be intensely confronted. It will find ample reasons to justify and rationalize rebellion in its struggle to survive. But Atmananda is by now as committed to the process of breaking the ego as Anandamayee Ma is to accomplishing this, and their relationship now moves into a new phase.

* * *

Anandamayee Mandir, Calcutta, 6th May, 1946

Arrived here yesterday after a strenuous train journey. I am having a very difficult time, but there is no doubt that Her Presence and Blessing make it much easier to go within. Read the *Bhagavad Gita* in the train and now find it easier to meditate on Krishna, who, it is said, upholds the worlds with a mere gesture of his finger. When I do this I do not feel the heat [1] nor the sleepiness nor the turmoil of the city, but otherwise it is hardly bearable. Now I see what it means to surrender myself and to leave all the arrangements to Him, accepting whatever comes. Is the experience of living in dirt and squalor necessary? I suppose if one is

---

[1] Calcutta is unbearably hot at this time of the year.

not to mind anything and not to have a sense of mine and thine, then one must be prepared to live under all sorts of conditions. How difficult it is for me to stand dirt. The Swamiji told me to accept whatever was offered with regard to food, clothes and accommodation. How excruciatingly difficult it is. And worst of all the noise!

Lewis is right, I should keep paper and pencil with me at all times. So many thoughts occur to me when I cannot write them down.

8th May, 1946

This morning again great depression and could hardly meditate and was worrying where to go. Then it suddenly struck me that I must leave it to Her. It came to me that She will settle it even without my asking Her. In the afternoon during the *kirtan* it occurred to me that the only way is to regard Her as God, or my own Self, which has revealed itself as the Guru. Then all will become easy. Of one thing I am certain: that She is beyond the human level and transforms whatever one puts into Her into a unique revelation of one's own innate Divinity. Therefore the best way for me is to surrender to God through Her and stop criticizing anything. After all, the ego has to go and perhaps it is good for me not to sleep so much. I almost do not even feel tired.

10th May, 1946

Yesterday I felt that She is utterly divine and I could feel Her inside me. I feel a distinct change of my metabolism. I feel much lighter and refined and almost rarefied. Yet again in the evening when I tried to meditate and dedicate myself to the Divine in Her form, there seemed a block of doubt in my mind and I could not proceed. Last night I went to a devotee's house to see the picture of a yogi who is supposed to be 450 years old. The picture looks like a woman. I had a strange feeling of having seen him before.

Yesterday I felt Mother to be like the Christ, then it crumbled again into doubt.

12ᵗʰ May, 1946

I am very much influenced by my surroundings and I still find the world attractive. My hold on the Spiritual is as thin as a hair. I miss L. very much. I am very dependent. My own judgement does not function. I had rather a good meditation outside of Mother's room; but there is some doubt about Her in my mind. It seems to me that I have to go South. I cannot get rid of this wish. [2] I must talk it over with Her. I want to study quietly and also satisfy my mind. Sometimes I am utterly blank and don't see the point of all this and want to drown myself in activity. Who knows whether I shall not have to go back to Rajghat again to work. The controversy between the *sadhana* which Mother gave me and J.K.'s method —though I cannot do it— still goes on. I always remember my dream and somehow feel I shall go back to J.K. though I don't know how.

18ᵗʰ May, 1946

At Lisl's heard wonderful Beethoven by Schnabel and Toscanini. It <u>does</u> seem to be the Vedanta [3] of the West. When I had decided to stay on an extra day there, fate made me leave. Rudi talked about impending riots and within a few minutes someone offered a lift in a car. [4] So I am guided. Still I have no faith. Every day I dedicate my life and heart and soul to Him and still I worry.

Again today I worry whether I shall get the opportunity to talk to Mother before She leaves and ask Her whether I should go South or stay with Her. I have not the nerve to leave it to the last moment and I hesitate to tell Her. Yet definitely there is the wish to go, otherwise I should just follow Her and not bother. I got the letter from school yesterday about my leave. It was important to know I have fourteen months and not only five. Why shouldn't I spend three of these months on seeing the different Great Ones in the South?

---

[2] She had wanted to return to South India since her visit to the ashram of Ramana Maharshi in 1942, but had been unable to do so due to wartime travel restrictions that were only recently lifted.

[3] The ancient wisdom philosophy of India.

[4] This was a very volatile period just before the partition of India and Calcutta was a powder-keg.

Calcutta, 19th May, 1946

Yesterday, Dakshineshwar [5]. The atmosphere is so terrific and so blissful, it seems to surpass everything I have come across so far. Sat at the Panchavati [6] first, where already tears began to come, then at the Kali temple where He worshipped. I was simply overcome and cried profusely. I had to force myself to get up. I could have stayed there happily for the rest of my life, also at His room where I sat and meditated for sometime. Ultimately I shall have to stay in such a place and sit there in solitude. There the whole world vanished. Such bliss.

Late at night I talked to Mother, I could not get my plans to go South out of my mouth in Her Presence. She evidently does not want me to go and agreed to take me with Her. I told Her if She went to another noisy place like this I would not follow Her. She said that soon it would not be so busy anymore. So She has decided for me, as I wanted Her to.

Calcutta, 20th May, 1946

Last night I felt utterly distraught and disturbed by the crowds and noise, almost to madness. Then I remembered that the external world is not my real life and that my problems are all due to my taking it seriously instead of concentrating inside. Here I hardly meditated. When I do not obey Her, what do I expect? This morning I felt better. How excruciatingly difficult it is to surrender.

Dr. Sunder Rao gave me something by Upasini Baba [7] to read about his *Kanya* worship. In his book he says that to have no personal will, to surrender at all times to the Supreme, to accept everything, is the state of a real 'woman' and also of a true *sadhaka*.

---

[5] The sacred Kali temple near Calcutta which was the abode of Sri Ramakrishna.

[6] A *panchavati* is a traditional arrangement of 5 sacred trees which is considered to be very holy and is often found in temple precincts. Sri Ramakrishna meditated there for many years.

[7] A disciple of Sai Baba of Shirdi (d. 1918), Upasini Baba (1870-1941) was a great renunciate who practised tremendous austerities. He founded an ashram for young Indian women whom he symbolically married so as to free them from what was then a mandatory social obligation in order that they might be allowed to lead a spiritual life. '*Kanya*' worship refers to the worship of the Divine Mother in the form of virgin girls.

He says a man can only attain illumination if he realizes this archetypal state of a woman. A 'woman', I have always wanted to become. But even now, how difficult it is! However if I transcend my own self willedness, nothing can touch me. Here I see how many wants the body has, the first of which is sleep, and they have to be renounced. Tomorrow I leave for Almora. Strange, I had wished to see Lewis soon and now I will.

Anandamayee Ma Ashram, Benares, 22nd May, 1946

Yesterday when Mother told me to sleep in the big hall with all the other women, I felt again like running away. It will be just as bad as in Calcutta, where I had at least a room to myself and plenty of water. In Almora I shall have the forest, but there will be other discomforts. I am still totally identified with the body and resent dirt and noise. I really am not so keen on liberation. I want comfort, though to be free from all this misery created by my own resentment would be the greatest comfort of all. Fancy not to mind anything and be always conscious of one's true luminous being! Has one to go through all this to get there? How does it help to be in circumstances that make one only resentful and bitter? When I am with this noisy crowd I feel only my ego and nothing else.

* * *

Undoubtedly one of the most important aspects of the Guru-disciple relationship is that the Guru relentlessly confronts the disciple's ego by placing it in situations in which the disciple is forced to become painfully aware of his weaknesses and shortcomings. The ashram environment serves as a laboratory for the Guru to conduct this experiment wherein all sorts of people are thrown together while simultaneously undergoing an intense inner transformation. This creates a kind of pressure-cooker that forces all manner of selfishness and the repressed underpinnings of the ego to the surface. Thus where one might remain placid and calm in one's own habitat, being in the presence of the Guru, particularly under such conditions, is a cathartic experience in which the submerged roots of the ego are exposed.

The job of the Guru is to be as a mirror to the disciple, ruthlessly revealing to him his delusions. In this sense Anandamayee Ma was truly Kali and She never shirked from Her role of destroying and purifying the sadhaka's *ego. Indeed it could be said that the relationship with Her had only begun to get serious with the onset of this powerful purification process. This, however, could be so unpleasant that not everyone was prepared to stick it out; although as She told Atmananda: "You may try to leave me, but I will never abandon you". The essential work of becoming intensely aware of what is ego and what is not, and being shown clearly when one is deceiving oneself —which is virtually impossible to do on one's own— is one of the principal functions of the Guru-disciple relationship.*

* * *

Bhadaini [8], 24th May, 1946

Yesterday at 4 a.m. had a good meditation outside of Mother's room. I experienced something that had a powerful, continuous vibration. I really love Benares better than any other place in the world. I thought to myself, whatever be the extremes of heat or cold, why really leave Benares. There is no place where one can meditate so well. The atmosphere is of gold, as Ramakrishna said.

At 11 a.m. when we were getting into the train to go to Almora, Mother's brother unexpectedly got out of the train and stopped us. We had to go back to the Ashram. I did not mind it at all and was rather amused. In the afternoon everyone went out and I had a heavenly quiet time for many hours. First I meditated in the cave [an underground meditation nook that remains cool in the severest heat] before Mother's picture and She seemed to permeate me and take possession of me. Then while sitting there, I read Upasini Baba's sayings. Later I went up on the roof [9], but as it got dark I went to sleep and slept till 10 p.m., then went down and found the others cooking. By 11 p.m. I went up again to meditate.

These people are really sweet and simple. I love their company. I feel happy only in the company of *sadhus* and *bhaktas*. That is a fact. But I myself am full of doubts and criticism. I am all the time trying to bring together the two —J.K. and Mother. In my dream J.K. told me to think of the Lord all the time and leave all

---

[8] Bhadaini is the name of the area of Benares along the Ganges where the ashram of Anandamayee Ma is located.

[9] The view across the Ganges from the roof of the ashram is exquisite.

else. Mother also says think of God all the time. I imagine Krishna as Alice Boner painted Him, far beyond everything and yet containing all.

For a second, yesterday, the two methods were one. This morning I found that I resented not having been able to go to Almora, because I had hoped so much to see Lewis. It had already taken possession of my mind. I do not live in the present, but am continually looking forward to some sensation, however subtle, in the future. My spirituality is skin-deep. It is good not to know from hour to hour where one is going. After all what does it matter where this body is if one is really keen to realize God? But I am full of desires for comfort, not for God. Mother's treatment is very good in that it has brought these things to light.

I want peace and quiet because it is pleasurable to me, but no, also because I get some inkling of the Eternal in it that I cannot get in noise. Now I am here with quite a lot of quiet and nothing on earth to do except wash my clothes. Let me see what I can do with it. I am already wondering what I am going to do with this year. I am certainly not ready to renounce all, because my attachment to the body is strong and still there is a secret wish to get security through marriage and be done with it. But that must be an illusion, just as my thought that if only I am free from work and near a great Saint I shall be on the right path, may also be.

Evening:

It seems ages since this morning with all the changes I have gone through. I was given the little room next to Mother's and spent an hour or two meditating in Her room. I had perfect quiet and peace. It helps a lot. I may try and stay in Dunga alone or in Rajpur with Deviji. Mother's Presence is almost more potent in Her Ashrams when She is absent, as there are no disturbing people. I then read Sri Aurobindo's *Riddle of this World*. He warns of so many things and pitfalls that stop the *sadhaka* in the middle of his path. This evening I sat down to meditate and again felt so abysmally ignorant —nothing at all to hold on to. Sri Aurobindo says that even the old Rishis did not discover the supramental [10].

---

[10] Aurobindian terminology for a new spiritual dimension which he claimed to have brought down into matter for the first time.

Till now it was not accessible to this world. To truly divinize all matter seems more perfect, or rather the only perfection. Again the wish comes up to go there and see for myself. It seems to me that I should spend this year partly in solitude —only meditating and reading. I am so ignorant. Then I do want to meet the Great Ones in the South of whom I have heard so much. I need solitude and freedom from every kind of duty, even from letter writing; also freedom from the thoughts of friends. I must be hidden and forgotten. At present no one knows where I am. My letters are sent on to Almora. Yesterday I was eager to stay with Earl. Now I am not any more. That also will be too binding. My time must be entirely mine.

I feel that if I have quiet, something from above that I feel pressing down on me will get a chance to manifest itself. But it needs silence of the mind and body, congenial surroundings and relaxation and compete leisure. Drop everything completely.

I do not mind this heat at all [11]. On the contrary I enjoy it. I want only peace.

Yesterday it struck me that, just as when I was prevented from going to Almora two years ago and it was one of the most lucky events in my life, so not being able to go this time also is the beginning of a new life and a very beneficial trend.

Bhadaini, 25th May, 1946

On reading over Her first instructions from my diary, I find that I misunderstood. She never asked me to just watch my breath, but rather to get into a state of stillness and light above the ordinary and in that state to hold my consciousness and to breathe quietly. One must make a steady and consistent effort. My thoughts still wander to the world. Perhaps really *japa*, the repetition of a Sacred Name, takes one out of that.

26th May, 1946

Last night talked to Umeshananda about Sri Aurobindo's Ashram. He was there for 5 years. He says the chief thing there also is the constant aspiration towards and contemplation of the

---

[11] At that time of the year in Benares the temperature stays well above 100 degrees (F).

Divine. Today went to Rajghat. How singularly empty and dead and dreary it feels after the joyful, and spiritually saturated atmosphere of this ashram. In the ashram there is really a spiritual depth and strength of joy. I wonder whether it comes from all the *puja* and *bhajan*. The food also is really pure there. At Rajghat Gopibai gave me *puri* and *kheer* and *achar* [12]. I nearly felt sick; whereas in the ashram, whatever I eat agrees with me. The ashramites are worshipping all the time, both when they cook and when they eat. It does make a difference.

Bhadaini, 28th May, 1946

Mother came yesterday. Soon we will be going to Solan after all. I am attached to L. and I suppose because of this I am not meant to see him. Am reading *Light on Yoga* by Sri Aurobindo and am thrilled. It is just what Mother tells me to do, and beautifully explained. I must read his books first and then go to his ashram at Pondy. I want to go South very badly, then go to see J.K., then go to Dehradun to stay at Mother's ashram there by myself.

I now get some good results when I meditate. I know better what to do and meditate four times a day. I bathe twice daily in the Ganges and love it —at 4 a.m. and again late at night.

Solan, 2nd June, 1946

Arrived on the 31st. This is a beautiful place in the mountains —lovely and peaceful and I have all comforts— quiet, a room and bathroom to myself and everything else. Mother is different here. She talks and can be seen alone and in small groups. Met Sharananandaji on the first day on the road.

We had *dhyan* yesterday with Mother at 11 a.m. —only a small group. She told me to meditate as much as possible. This morning when going out for a walk met Sharananandaji's *bhaktas* and went to see him. We talked for two and a half hours. It was very helpful. He said: "*If you plan to go back to work after your year leave, then keep your money; but if you want to go on with this spiritual life, throw it away when half the year is over. If you have no wish to work, then the wish to sustain yourself should also go.*

---

[12] A type of fried bread; a rich pudding made from milk, rice and sugar; a spicy pickle.

The body which you call yours is part of the world. Let Him who made it look after it. If you have a desire to live in a certain condition, then you need money; but if you have no desires, then you need nothing. If you want Eternal Life, then nothing will be difficult for you to put up with or to give up. If you really want to get out of the condition of bondage to this transitory life, you will not find it difficult to do what is necessary. You can either work for yourself and enjoy; or serve others and the world will love you; or you can renounce all and have Eternal Life. In Eternal Life the other two are included. Go about and see where you like it best and then stay in one place and do your sadhana. There are three levels of satsang : The highest satsang is to have the company of the One true Self. The second is the company of those who have realized this, the third is the company of a profound spiritual book."

Mother does everything for Haribaba [13]. Her whole programme is adjusted to his wishes.

Yesterday and today She called me for *dhyan* for half an hour with only very few others present. Today somehow it lasted over an hour. When She asked me whether I had been able to sit quietly, I said I had to change my legs three times. Then She told me to meditate in my own room. I rather minded this and will come again tomorrow and see whether She will allow me to join in.

Sharananand told me not to be disturbed about the 'not touching' rules of the orthodox ladies. He also told me that I should fulfil the *sankalpas*, the strong desires or commitments that I already had, but not to make new ones.

He said: *"Renunciation is the giving up of the idea of separateness, not the giving up of things."* He also said that to give away things is to do good works, but it is still within the ego. To renounce, means getting rid of the idea of 'I' and 'mine'.

---

[13] A *sanyasi* devotee of Krishna who became famous after organizing a group of villagers to build a dam in an area continually beset by floods. It was built as an act of worship with mud and bricks and succeeded in stopping the floods whereas previous attempts by the government had always failed. He was very devoted to Anandamayee Ma and often travelled with Her.

3rd June, 1946

This morning I went in to see Mother around 6 a.m. She was resting and Renu asked me to keep the flies off Her. I did this for two hours. How quickly the time went. It was like a meditation. I became aware of all the silly thoughts I occupy myself with.

Today during *dhyan* with Haribaba, though there were disturbances, I really got quiet for sometime. It makes all the difference. Even the noisy *kirtan* afterwards did not disturb me so much, though I think I shall go deaf slowly. I honestly believe that, being a musician, my ear has a more sensitive constitution and it is not fair for me to expose myself to such terrific noises.

4th June, 1946

When I see some of these so-called *sadhus* and other aspirants who have repressed sex and are terrified of women, I feel intensely grateful to J.K. for leading me as he did. If that kind of thing is in one's nature, it is better to go through it in the natural way instead of shouting "Ram, Ram" and secretly be obsessed with sex.

These people here unquestioningly accept the *shastric* rules according to the ancient scriptures and strictly practice them even though they don't always seem to understand them within the proper context that the ancient sages, who originally formulated them, intended. I am certainly not willing to submit to this. Kitty is quite right, it will be very difficult for me to fit in anywhere.

I am extremely tired for no reason except that I suspect that the increased time of meditation and company of saints intensifies the spiritual atmosphere and probably accounts for it. I woke up late today and therefore started meditation at 5 a.m., instead of 4 a.m., which is not nearly as quiet. I must get back to that.

Mitra told me from looking at my hand that my mind is easily influenced and therefore I feel I need solitude. But he says I must strengthen myself and become composed and stable, so as not to mind surroundings and outer circumstances. I am doing almost all my own work here, even carrying water. That is all right. I don't mind it at all.

Reading Sri Aurobindo's *Bases of Yoga*. It insists on the inner peace and stability of the mind behind the surface movement.

Evening:
Met Shiva Rao and his brother B.N. on the motor road. They treat me like a joke. S.R., though such an old friend, did not even take the trouble to come see me sooner. So much the better. Now I need not bother to see them at Delhi and will certainly not see Kitty in Simla. I am rather glad of that. So one friend after another is eliminated. Lisl is going to U.S. and S.R. and co. snub me because they do not understand my connection to Mother and feel I have abandoned J.K. Good. So all is for the best.

I wore my red silk sari and rather enjoyed the beauty of it and the feel of the soft silk. What of it? Why should it be wrong? But why then do all serious spiritual aspirants renounce such things?

5th June, 1946

During *dhyan* at 11.30 it came to me that because I refuse to let go of feeling responsible for my body and worldly affairs, I am prevented from progressing. If I make all the arrangements, then what is left for 'Him' to do? I believe in my bank balance and the kindness of my friends, so where does 'He' get a chance to take charge? How do I know that 'He' won't give me much more perfect conditions than I can possibly get for myself? Why do I take it for granted that I may have to stay in a crowd and do without the many little things that I cling to, like soap, fountain pen etc. If I, with my little intelligence, can get these things, won't 'He' provide them in plenty if I just let go. I shall then be free to do whatever work my hands find, but not for money or anything in return, as I shall possess the unlimited spiritual wealth and not require anything further. Why do I take it for granted that I shall be of no use to anyone and have to accept their charity? Only when I have let go of everything will I be of any real use because only then I shall be free and able to share this great spiritual treasure.

7th June, 1946

Again I cry getting Lewis' letter. I feel more at home with him than with anyone else. After all, to come from the same culture and to speak the same language makes a lot of difference. Not to speak of what an exquisite artist he is. Here whatever sensitivity to beauty I have is being killed ruthlessly. Haribaba's dreadful gongs and the overall starkness and bad taste and mess are making me dull. Perhaps this is a necessary *tapas* [austerity].

The *jhuta* business [14] is well nigh getting too much for me. I remember Miki who warned me that a time would come when people would shrink from my touch. It has come. And strangely it upsets me. Everyday there is some trouble about the food. I have decided to eat alone. I am sick of it.

* * *

We now come to the most difficult problem that Atmananda had to deal with in her adjustment to ashram life. She has been with Anandamayee Ma for more than a year but has only now penetrated deeply enough to come up against a fundamental barrier to her further integration into the ashram community. In 1946 the majority of Hindus were still orthodox and most Brahmins still observed the ancient rules regarding ritual and caste purity as they had done for thousands of years. Originally these were based on a highly developed esoteric science of vibrations. It is firmly believed by Brahmins that observance of these rules pertaining to the purity of food, along with the conduct of specific rituals and meditation practices, is what preserves the subtle energy field that sustains the spiritual vitality and continuity of the ancient culture, creating a matrix in which specific spiritual forces can be stabilized and incorporated into daily life.

At that time even to allow a westerner to participate in ashram activities, as Atmananda was, was already a very liberal gesture and there were many more orthodox ashrams in India that would not have let her through the gate. Orthodox sensibilities were genuinely disturbed by a foreigner's presence at religious functions as it was felt that this was fundamentally out of tune with the Hindu racial and cultural ethos. In particular they feared that this dissonance would interfere with the successful realization of specific rituals and spiritual practices which were based on the esoteric focusing of profound subtle vibrations into which only the orthodox Hindu has been initiated.

Thus though almost all forms of Indian theology, philosophy and yoga are completely universal in their outlook and theoretically open to all, participation in the outer ritualistic religious structure was carefully guarded.

---

[14] Refers to the orthodox Brahminical rules of ritual purity —*jhuta* means unclean.

The Sat-Guru, however, who both embodies and transcends the tradition, sheds his or her grace equally upon all and even the most orthodox would never dispute this.

Although Anandamayee Ma made it extremely clear that she personally was totally beyond these restrictions, she clearly felt that the proper observance of orthodox rules and rituals was important for preserving the integrity of the tradition; particularly as she was aware that Indian traditional culture was under serious threat from Western materialism and she wanted to instill in Hindus a sense of pride in their ancient ways. After all, Indians had been ruled, exploited and humiliated for most of the last two centuries by what they saw as arrogant, culturally inferior European barbarians. They were at that very moment engaged in an epic struggle to regain their independence from the British.

In light of this it was inevitable that Atmananda would experience some cultural friction. Anandamayee Ma realized her predicament and made good use of it as a tool to wear down her western ego. Over time Atmananda came to see that it was indeed an honour and a great learning experience to be allowed access to this authentic spiritual tradition and to the initiatic power it possessed which would have been impossible in a more westernized context.

* * *

Mother says I must learn cooking. I have to buy a kerosene stove and a pot and begin. I seem all the time in revolt. She wants me to cook and I want to read. But I know she is always right and I shall be glad for it later. It is again like Milarepa [15]. I am fortunate to have Sharananand here, who gives some food to the mind. Otherwise one has just to sing and obey. I wish I could stay with L. But then perhaps I would want something else? Who can tell. It is perhaps better for me not to meet him. I have become too dependant on him. I must learn to manage alone.

9th June, 1946

Mother talked to me yesterday and asked me why I cried. I told Her about the eternal 'not touching' trouble. She talked to me

---

[15] In the story of Milarepa, a great Tibetan yogi, his guru imposed various very difficult tasks on him as a means of overcoming his ego.

about the *Shastras* and traditional customs of the country. But when I ask for reasons, She won't give any. She just wants obedience and I revolt. She asked me to eat by myself and not to enter other people's houses as they may be orthodox. That is rather nice and a relief as I can be by myself. Today She ordered my food to Her veranda and made me eat in Her presence. She told me that according to the orthodox rules even my sari must not touch the *thali* [metal plate] or it becomes *jhuta*. I asked Her what is so bad in *jhuta*. She had no proper explanation. She only said that if my cloth is *jhuta*, then my seat gets also *jhuta* etc. and I shouldn't want my Guru to have to touch what is unclean. She does not seem to wish to give any satisfaction to the mind, She says to think of God and leave the rest. Last night She took a lot of trouble over me and patted me profusely and asked me not to be sad. I meant to tell Her about Lewis but got no chance.

Earlier in the afternoon she had told me: "*Let God be your husband, your child, father, mother, everything.*" But I feel restless with no man even to talk to. I can't become a Saint so easily.

I am already having a strong reaction although I have only been with Her for nine days. I feel all broken to pieces. I want to get some relaxation and don't know how. The best thing will be to go to Simla, though I am not sure about it. But I think I shall go.

It will be good for me to cook. I need some physical work. I can hardly read and can't meditate. I only want to sleep. I am again at the same point: J.K.'s 'method', though I can't understand it, attracts me, and Her 'method' demands blind obedience and I cannot see the rational value of this. I have been trained since childhood to judge for myself and though I realize the fundamental limitations of this, still I revolt and revolt, and so remain in the same muddle. So many underground desires are in the way and cause strain. I am much in the same boat as L. Ultimately I cannot accept another culture although I have abandoned my own. Here I am beginning to long for Europe. I realize that I am European after all.

It was not the noise and dirt at Calcutta that upset me, but my own state of mind. Now I have very much better conditions and yet I am more upset. It is not going to be so easy to live without the escape of fixed work and 'duty'.

234

10ᵗʰ June, 1946

This morning I prayed for light out of this muddle and got a tremendous response. The solution is to be continually immersed in the awareness of 'Him' who is the Cause of everything, and to treat all outer events as a play, as incidental and irrelevant to the inner Reality.

I take everything personally. If I have to submit to Bengali customs, I see only the trouble and personal inconvenience of it. But if I watch it as I would a play, what does it really matter? Whether I read or cook or wash clothes, the great thing is to be always merged in the thought of the Divine Presence. I am so silly. I take these things so seriously and want to know the reason for the orthodox rules etc. As if it mattered. For myself I can be apart from it and just observe it and attend to that which really matters. But for the sake of the fun of the *leela* and for those who believe it, I can observe these things when necessary. Last night Mitra said to me: "All *sadhana* is to get peace of mind." That's not enough for me. It is only the beginning. The real goal is to cease to exist and to become the Eternal.

11ᵗʰ June, 1989

Now there seems to be a definite improvement and purification. The great thing is not to identify oneself with the 'play', but to remain aloof. I always forget. I have now not so much desire to go South nor for L. I have again fallen in love with Her.

She says: *"Whatever you do without the thought of God is useless and vain."*

13ᵗʰ June, 1946

I now enjoy sitting still with closed eyes even when my mind is not completely still. The events of the day stick to my mind. How to change that so that they should only pass through without leaving a mark? I am also not sure that this stillness is really the pure consciousness called *chetana*. It has an aspect to it which does not seem desirable. To accept Mother as utterly Divine is certainly good and helpful, because without doubt She is that. But on the plane of reason I must get satisfaction. I wonder whether that is because my *buddhi* (intellect) cannot surrender? Yesterday

She talked to Billu who becomes trance-like when she does *japa*. She told her this is *jar* [phenomena] and one must go beyond that.

I <u>must</u> have satisfaction for the intellect also. There are always difficulties, the outer ones perhaps make the inner ones easier. No one can explain things like Lewis. But now I don't miss him so much —I have become used to the separation. I do want to be with him again, though. Let me be by myself for sometime and become independent first.

14ᵗʰ June, 1946

Yesterday I told Mother that if I was unable to understand something, I would not be able to accept it even if God Himself told me to do so. I felt very strongly all day that I could never surrender my own intelligence to any sort of slavish blind faith.

In the evening I went for a long walk with some Kashmiri, who has a completely materialistic mind, totally illogical and thoughtless. I marvelled for what reasons people come to Mother —he wants his illness cured!

* * *

Many people came to Anandamayee Ma for material reasons and many of them got what they came for and also much more. Along with the apparently miraculous gift or cure from her there would be the far more important gift of spiritual awareness. The atmosphere of the miraculous always surrounded her but the greatest miracle, which constantly radiated from her, was that of Self-awareness; and whatever material blessing a person might discover he had received from her would only be given as a means of helping to establish him in the highest truth. In any event these material blessings, no matter how obvious to the recipient, would always occur discretely and Anandamayee Ma would never accept any responsibility for them, insisting that it was all God's grace. Nevertheless the recipient would invariably realize a startling connection between this 'grace' and her.

* * *

In the course of the conversation I told him I did not believe in *kirtan*. He said, "Don't you believe in vibrations?" That suddenly turned on a light in my mind and I thought I must try and see what it does. In the evening I sang *kirtan* by myself in my room.

Again at night I sang. All fatigue went and I remembered what I read only yesterday in Sri Aurobindo's book where he says that sleep ought to be "a luminous silence". I felt light and purified. Perhaps I went on all night unconsciously in my sleep as I woke up with "Govinda" [16] in my mind. Then I saw that what is called *buddhi* or intelligence is only the accumulated experience of the ego and therefore quite limited. It is a much greater use of intelligence to accept as a working hypothesis the word of one whose realization and understanding is far beyond that of one's ego and then to see for oneself where it leads. If one's 'intelligence' takes one up to this point, it has done its work. The *kirtan* definitely raises one's consciousness perceptibly.

Yesterday I read in Sri Aurobindo: "*The world will trouble you as long as any part of you belongs to the world. It is only when you belong entirely to the Divine that you can become free*". It struck me that really I do belong to the world. As soon as I think of Kitty laughing at me for doing these things, I shrink back. I think that I do not care what others say and yet I have reservations and do care because my ego-mind wants to preserve itself. Like in my dream, when the coffin bearer touched me and I woke up terrified. It is the ego struggling for its existence. Let it struggle: Once the tiger (the Guru) has gripped his prey, he will never let it go.

15ᵗʰ June, 1946

Mother is giving such exalted teaching now every morning. What is a little discomfort, when one gets that. How my efforts with Hindi are being repaid a million times and more, and I wish I had put in even more time and energy into learning it.

I wonder whether my aversion to *kirtan* is partly due to the fact that as I am a musician and have a certain ego in this regard, this purely spiritual music should really have a tremendously purifying effect on me and I am resisting such a catharsis. I must go slowly but very steadily.

She is really God in a human form. She told us today that during the period of Her life referred to as Her play of *sadhana*, whenever she started some *kriya* [yogic process], she would never

---

[16] A name of Krishna often sung in *kirtan*.

stop till she got *ananda*, the bliss of realization. She said that when you know there is water at a certain spot, you go on digging until you reach it. She explained how at times when saying "Haribol"[17], Her body became stiff as a board and Her hands formed *mudras* [mystic gestures] spontaneously. She could not bend Her back even if she wanted to. She would loose complete voluntary control of Her body and then sink into *samadhi*. She said that whatever *sadhana* you do, *Kundalini* [18] must be awakened before you can get *darshan* of 'Reality' —Direct Perception or *pratyaksha*. She told us that She can have *pratyaksha* of anything that She enquires into. Yesterday She said that She cannot get angry; it is impossible for Her. Whatever She sees She becomes.

* * *

Although Anandamayee Ma was incapable of anger Herself, Her disciples would sometimes feel an awesome, overwhelming disapproval from Her when they had committed some serious error —simply by the slightest glance or gesture from her, or by the absence of such.

* * *

I feel such awe and such inspiration towards Her. At all times I try to keep myself open to Her sublime will and influence, which is the Divine *shakti* [19] Herself. I remember Sri Aurobindo's teaching: "Open yourself all the time to the Mother".

Solan, 20th June, 1946

Yesterday went to see Kitty for a few hours [20]. We got on very well. She asked about Mother and I told her. But when she asked what Her teaching is, I did not know what to say. But thinking it over on the way back, it seemed to me that it is that there is only ONE and everyone has to realize this by his own way or without any way, by His Grace. As long as we see the many, life is useless and absurd.

---

[17] A divine name; lit.: 'say Hari'.

[18] The primordial cosmic energy which lies coiled at the base of the spine. See footnote for 10th September, 1945.

[19] *Shakti*, the creative feminine power of Godhead; the consort of Shiva.

[20] Kitty and S.R. were nearby in Simla.

Today in my *dhyan* it came to me that if I am sincere in my practice of seeing this body as not 'I', the emotions as not 'I', the mind as not 'I', then what right have I to regard other bodies and minds etc. as being separate individuals. It does them a disservice, for it strengthens their own identification with their false sense of separateness. Their essential nature is not other than my own. This is why *satsang* is so important, because by associating with those who have realised the 'One', it helps us to lessen our identification with the body, etc. It is as though this truth is almost magnetically contagious from such beings.

Solan, 24ᵗʰ June, 1946

I can't get Her to talk. When I caught Her for a minute only and asked Her what She meant when She told me: *"Jo pakar lia, mat choro"* (whatever was given —as *sadhana*— before, don't leave it). She gave me quite a different reply to the Benares one and said: *"What you are doing now, that you must not drop"*. Evidently I should trust my own intuition more —my dream that fused Her with J.K.—; also my understanding now that after all, it does not matter how you get there as long as you arrive. Then there is the dream I had last year of J.K. telling me exactly to the letter what She also has told me.

I had another bust-up with my room-mate and decided to keep silence. Then I found that Mother had also imposed complete silence on the house where the others stay. It is a great help to keep silent.

In the afternoon I went to the woods alone, where I found such peace and *ananda*. I really must stay in the jungle by myself. When I came down to Her, She practically ignored me. I minded it a little, but must She not attend to those who depend on Her entirely? I must bear this. I am independent by nature and must search for myself. This afternoon I also told Her I would run away. She said: *"Where will you go?"* I said: "The world is big enough." Perhaps I should not have said this.

25ᵗʰ June, 1946

Today She gave me a good scolding for what I said yesterday and said: *"Where will you go where I am not? What is the good of enjoying food and rest like an animal, and of looking at people in a worldly*

239

way, and laughing and gossiping? That is useless. Remain centered on Him all the time, that is what you have to do."

Later when I returned from a walk, She noticed the boil. I said that I was too lazy to attend to it properly. She: *"Laziness does not lead anywhere. It is only in true peace that one can find genuine rest, but in the world you can never get it, only in Ram. Therefore think of Him all the time and you will have rest even in the midst of work."*

I am sulking. Though I am now convinced that She is God, nevertheless on the physical plane She does not always seem to give perfect advice. My laziness is not real laziness. There are many reasons for it, like my period being late and also the uncongenial company in my room and insufficient food. But also I am not willing to give up my prejudices and habits regarding things that I consider good. Today I read how Vivekananda made Sister Nivedita [21] live like an Indian woman almost in *purdah* and made her drop all her personal will etc.

I revolt and revolt. My ego doesn't want to be killed and I want to remain as I am. I want everything without giving up anything. In the long run what She teaches is no easier than J.K.'s constant awareness and unconditioning, except She forces it on me like injections, whereas he leaves one to find out for oneself and one invariably has not the grit to really do it.

26th June, 1946

Here I feel homesick. I was always used to having one congenial friend, first Malati, then Lewis, but here I am alone with no room where I can hide myself from everyone; though I get more privacy than most of the others.

27th June, 1946

This morning went to see Prabhudananda who told me beautifully: *"At all times seek to realize the One Reality and take your mind off the many. Don't mistake a piece of rope for a snake. Don't see the ugliness and badness around you. The whole world is ugly, bad and undesirable to the extent that it hides the One."*

---

[21] An exceptionally strong-willed and intelligent Irish woman who was one of the main disciples of Swami Vivekananda and was later involved in revolutionary anti-British activities in Bengal. (See her biography *The Dedicated* by L. Raymond).

I liked the Swami's presence very much. He must have at least a partial realization of what he said. It came across very well. He said: "As you see the waves, which really do not exist as separate from the ocean, so you see the world mistakenly as separate from the one Absolute Reality".

This is pure Vedanta, like Ramana Maharshi, and appeals to me very much; yet there is also the other view of the world as *leela* and Sri Aurobindo's point of view. In any case everyone tells me the same: "Put your mind on the underlying Centre of things".

Mother related how during Her *sadhana leela* [22] She was often covered with ants and mosquitoes and did not feel it. Sometimes they bit Her but She was oblivious to it, and at other times they crawled on Her and did not bite. In either case She remained absorbed in inner bliss. She also told how on occasion Her body was raised into the air and how even now exalted beings often appear and take Her away to other realms for a specific purpose in the night when Her body seems to sleep.

She wants me to go to Simla, but I would much rather stay here; but what can I do. If She asks me to go, I shall have to go.

I very much want solitude. Some time ago I wanted her company above all, but now I want solitude. I am sure I shall get it later. Probably She has a good reason for keeping me near Her.

Still many things of this world seem desirable to me. That is why I cannot effectively turn inside, because of these attractions. But once I see clearly that whatever outer beauty there is in the world is only a reflection of the Divine from which it derives its being, then the attraction will turn exclusively to the One.

Simla, 29th June, 1946

Mother is always right. I was so reluctant to come here to Simla and was angry that She made me go, and that by train. But it has all been really very good. I like it here. I wanted a bit of Europe and I got it [23]. My body revolts at Her intense 'training' and tries to be ill. Why do I not trust Her more and leave all to Her. I get periods of great faith and adoration followed by rebellion and reaction.

---

[22] See footnote for 15th June, 1946.

[23] At this time Simla was still a show place of English culture and society, the place where the Raj in full regalia spent the summer.

Simla, 30ᵗʰ June, 1946

Ilse asked Her the same question as I did: "How to decide things?" It suddenly dawned on me that that was really my fundamental problem: I have not yet decided to give myself entirely to the Divine and that is why there is still choice, still conflict.

Today I heard that the three ashram *brahmacharinis* [nuns] could not eat yesterday because I was sitting in the same room and the Brahminical rules prohibit them from eating under the same roof with non-Hindus. I again got violently upset and decided that I cannot remain in such a place. I must stay by myself and think this out. My faith is gone. If I cannot understand these inhuman rules, then how can I trust Her entirely?

Simla, 2ⁿᵈ July, 1946

As menses has begun and this restricts my participation in ashram activities due to the orthodox 'rules', I changed my plans of returning to Solan at the last moment and decided to remain here. I feel extremely sad and lost. I cannot seem to get over this. The problem started when I went to see Her in November and has yet to be solved. It is extremely difficult as I really love Her and am very reluctant to part from Her. My heart says, shut your eyes to everything and stick with it. But I cannot. I must understand. My path is not through *bhakti* but through understanding. I must understand. When I look at Her face I cannot but believe that She is utterly divine. What then can be the reason for these rules that seem so cruel to me?

Solan, 4ᵗʰ July, 1946

Arrived last night from Simla. My mind was at peace when I got here. What a profound atmosphere there is around Her. This morning during Haribaba's reading I looked at Her and it occurred to me that I love Her too deeply to leave Her. Anyway, I seem to be Hers, Heart and Soul. When I look at Her it is quite impossible to believe that She is imperfect. She must be perfect. There is no flaw. Yet all these rules, how can I reconcile them?

I feel now, as a result of this conflict, nearer to Her than before. This morning I felt that the barrier that had seemed to be between she and I has gone.

Billu told me that she has to stay in the Ashram as she has left everything and has nowhere else to go. So whether she under-stands or not, she has to obey. That does not seem satisfactory to me at all. It is like a Hindu marriage, for better or for worse. How difficult life is! I am in the same boat as L. and my vision is so clouded. But there is a higher plane, above this trouble, where I am happy and at peace; but when I stir up the mind, it is gone.

Solan, 5th July, 1946

Last night talked to Her about the incident with the food at Simla. The essence of what She said was not to bother too much about these things and just eat by myself, unless someone wanted to eat with me. She told me there are different rules in every ashram and that neither through eating alone or with others does one get God realization. She told me to throw away all disturbing thoughts that come into my mind. She does not seem very interested in those rules, but seems to want people to observe them so that those who choose to be orthodox may also feel free to come to Her.

This morning again She told me to throw all disturbing thoughts out of my mind. I said: "Have I not to go into a problem as it arises? She: *"No, leave it alone. When you read a book, you don't know the whole story until you have finished it, so whatever you don't understand now, wait and see how it turns out later"*. She also said: *"Am I to listen to you or are you going to listen to me?"* So there is an end to it. I jolly well have to swallow my pride and the right to advance by my own understanding.

She asked me whether I do enough *dhyan*. Of course I do not, and also I change my method a lot. I wonder whether that is good.

When I look at Her I just melt away. I love Her more than myself and pray that She may take possession of me and destroy my ego. Then again comes the revolt. What is the good of revolt-ing. Either I surrender or leave Her completely alone.

I cannot leave Her and I cannot surrender, and dropping my judgmental intellect is so damn difficult. Unfortunately when She holds out a helping hand, I revolt. I think this is due to my years of conditioning from J.K.

243

XIII - Diksha (Initiation)

One of the unique features of these diaries is their account of specific meditation instructions given to Atmananda by Anandamayee Ma. Over the last year and a half, she has received a variety of spiritual instructions which she has essentially been allowed to experiment with. During this period Atmananda's spiritual maturity has grown considerably and only now is she ready to enter more deeply into the ongoing process of initiation.

As an embodiment of the highest spiritual truth, Anandamayee Ma was often paradoxical. In terms of the monistic non-dual state of awareness in which she was totally absorbed there could be no question of 'another'; there was only ONE and it was this supreme oneness that assumed the role of Guru or of God when manifesting in the relative appearance of duality —the 'world', consisting of subject-object awareness. Thus she would say that she was not a Guru and that there is only the One Guru, and that is God. On the other hand she often had the *kheyal* (spontaneous inspiration or intuition) to give individuals specific spiritual instructions when she perceived that they were ready for it. She pointed out that the one Supreme Guru always found a way to transmit initiation when the disciple was prepared to receive it. The point is that she herself openly took full responsibility for giving personal spiritual instructions but at the same time covered it with a slight veil to protect it from the profane.

Mother was adamant that such instruction must be kept absolutely secret as it was one's greatest treasure. This is particularly true in the case of a *mantra*, which embodies a powerful vibrational connection with the Guru that is essential for it to be effective. Disciples were meant to practice in privacy the *sadhana* given by her as this *sadhana* was the core of one's innermost relationship with God. Thus there was little emphasis placed on group practice (particularly when she was not physically present) and

245

this was emblematic of the fundamental authenticity one experienced with her.

- II -

The problem with the orthodox rules continues to be extremely upsetting for Atmananda and is something which, even after many years, she was at best to make an uneasy peace with.

Although Yoga [1] and most systems of Indian philosophy are very universal and highly attractive to people from different cultures in today's world, they are a product of and deeply rooted in the ancient Hindu tradition and cannot be so easily separated from it without losing much of their inner power. But there is no simple solution for the modern westerner who wants to go deeply into this ancient spiritual system on its home ground.

From the traditional orthodox perspective one cannot really become a Hindu except through birth which determines one's caste. This is based on one's *karma*, the fruit of one's actions from previous lives. It is extremely precise. Thus it is believed that one is exactly where one is supposed to be based on the merits and demerits of one's actions. The upper castes theoretically observe a wide variety of spiritual injunctions and training from childhood on. Particularly the Brahmins, as the priests for the culture, traditionally lead austere lives with strict dietary regulations and extensive daily spiritual practices. This in turn is believed to have a physiologically alchemical effect on both them and their environment, rendering them pure channels for the higher spiritual forces which maintain the spiritual equilibrium of the culture. Traditionally at least there is simply no place in this for the foreigner who comes from completely outside the cosmological structure and whose physical presence is felt to disturb the spiritual harmony and thus to be, literally, polluting —upsetting the delicate and all-important balance between the Gods and man— the spiritual and the material.

The 'modern' Hindu is forced into a somewhat schizophrenic position between an exclusive tradition on the one hand and, on the other, a need to bring this tradition into the modern world.

---

[1] By 'yoga' is meant a wide variety of meditative techniques as described in the classic *Yoga Sutras* of Patanjali.

Thus the Brahmins in Anandamayee Ma's ashram were not necessarily opposed to having Atmananda join them. No doubt on some level they felt gratified to have a sophisticated cultured westerner who wanted to become so involved. In any case, it was understood that Ma is the Mother of all and no one should be excluded and She Herself made it clear to Atmananda that the door was always open. But there was also no question of the integrity of the tradition being jeopardized for the benefit of a tiny number of westerners. The solution was for the westerner to adapt to orthodox customs and to stay out of the way in situations in which his or her presence might be felt to pollute certain rituals or eating arrangements.

For Atmananda though, the problem was ultimately deeper and more fundamentally personal than mere hurt feelings based on cultural differences. In order to pursue the relationship with the Guru, who both embodies and transcends the tradition, she must be prepared to abandon her ego and make inevitably painful changes. This is the same discipline that each and every disciple regardless of caste or culture must undergo —each in his own way, and the *jhuta* rules in Atmananda's case were simply one of the means used by Anandamayee Ma to effect this process.

* * *

Simla, 5th July, 1946

Asked Her again about *sadhana*. She said: "*When you find that the happiness and pain of the world are not worthwhile, you turn within to the Atma, which although you don't really know, you still aspire to. This intense aspiration alters the rhythm of your breath and puts you in a state of 'dhyan' that turns one deeply within. That also is not the true Atma nor is the shunya* [state of emptiness] *generated through the 'dhyan', but that is how you start. Don't give any thought to anything else. Remember that all thought of the world binds you. Do only the minimum that is necessary: eating, dressing, walking, and for the rest be immersed in the search for Him. In what form He will appear to you, you don't know; but don't worry about anything else. Don't mix with the Ashram people. You are only here to see Me, and for the rest keep to yourself. Don't talk and laugh with others. Accustom the mind to think about Atma all the time, whatever you may do outwardly.*"

I very nearly asked Her whether I should do *japa* [2], but then had not the courage. The fear of taking on spiritual commitments, initiations, etc., and then later dropping them, as I did in Theosophy, is still in me. I wonder whether I should not ask Her after all. I like best the *Pranava* (Om) and Sri Krishna Govinda.

6th July, 1946

This morning meditation not so good as I was very tired. But later when reading the *Gita*, suddenly *dhyan* came spontaneously and I could hardly stop it. When I look at Her face intensely the mind goes and I become devotionally absorbed. This is now my chief *sadhana*.

* * *

This was, in fact, the chief sadhana of everyone who became involved with Anandamayee Ma. This silent communication was Her principal teaching and this was not something that could be learned from a book. It was an experience of overwhelming intensity which powerfully entrained the mind in the grooves of meditative absorption. Although one's attention was exclusively focused on something outside of oneself, i.e. Ma, the internal reflection of that concentration was something purely and uniquely one's own. It might be said to be fundamentally of the nature of grace, and to be with Ma was, in a sense, to have unlimited access to that grace. Through exposure to this flow of grace over a period of time, one experienced a fundamental transformation.

* * *

7th July, 1946

Yesterday I was able to maintain my concentration during meditation quite well. There is a trick of letting go and then *dhyan* comes by itself. If I surrender to what comes, it will be easier; but how difficult it is to give up self-will. Lewis always said I have too much will. How laborious it is to tame me.

---

[2] *Japa* refers to the repetition of a *mantra*. When given through formal initiation the mantra is esoterically tied to the occult anatomy of the practitioner via the *Kundalini* and the *chakras*, and activates a bio-energetic spiritual process which produces deep meditation; i.e., it is more than just mindless repetition of a name or a sound. However, it must be given by a qualified master.

8th July, 1946

I have fallen in love with Her so desperately, it is almost maddening. What Sri Aurobindo says about aspiring to and opening oneself persistently to the influence of the Mother, I find easiest.

She asked me this evening whether I could not sing *kirtan*. I said no. Evidently she sees that I need an outlet.

She played with Ilse's hair, perhaps She did something to her brain. Then She also got hold of my bun of hair and also Maneckbai's. Last night till about 1 a.m. I concentrated on the breath being transformed by Her. I feel that the Mother is taking possession of me, that is, *Kundalini* is beginning to rise up.

11th July, 1946

Yesterday I concentrated on the pinpoint in the heart which is supposed to be the seat of the *Atma,* and I got at something. I take Her to be *Atma* and surrender to Her.

12th July, 1946

I am still full of desires for comfort and a good time. I seem to go in waves. Sometimes I do well in *dhyan* and feel I am getting somewhere, then again I have desire for the things of this world.

Today She said beautifully in reply to a question as to why there is the opposition of God and the world: "*That opposition is itself 'samsar'* [the world]. *He who sees only the One, for him there is no 'samsar'. Therefore it is called 'duniya'* [world] *because in it there are always two.*" [3]

Yesterday I gossiped with Moti Ram about all the troublesome 'orthodox' rules. That was very wrong. Mother has forbidden me even to think of these things. At once it established a barrier. I must be careful to do what She tells me, otherwise I shall get into serious trouble.

At present I feel why go anywhere else. I cannot find anyone greater than Her. But about two days ago I thought: "At least let me live where people speak a language that I can understand and where I am not a stranger."

---

[3] A play on words in Hindi; Anandamayee Ma generally used language in a very playful and creative manner that is difficult to translate.

It also occurred to me that I must have been a Brahmin in a former life who broke all the rules without having risen above them and therefore am treated in this way now. Without this particular *karma* how could all this happen. Besides, I really am learning these rules only now, after so many years in India. When I first came, I used to get into trouble about the same thing with Kelkar.

Ma ate a fruit on the road and took off Her shoes before doing so in accordance with tradition. How utterly thoughtful and correct She always is in these matters.

13th July, 1946

Last night during *dhyan* the thought of Lewis disturbed me. On thinking it out, I discovered how foolish it is to be attached to any particular person or thing. It must be an obstacle to him also, who has no other desire but self-realization. What I love in him is this very quality, but if I bring anything personal into it this quality is lost.

Last night Mukti Baba said: "*Diksha* [initiation] means transference of spiritual power from Guru to disciple. It can be effected through touch, sound, sight or even in a dream." He also said that Mother is the *Shunya* [the great Void].

16th July, 1946

On Guru Purnima [4] for the first time I enjoyed a *kirtan*. It struck me how futile and useless it is to judge with one's little intelligence the great All, that which is beyond the pairs of opposites which define normal egoicity. How idiotic it is to judge one like Mother who has not a trace of ego and is an embodiment of 'That'. These *kirtans* take one out of that little prison, if even for a second. So they are not to be disparaged.

Mrs. Khan said the other day: "You are a musician and therefore you cannot like these out-of-tune *bhajans*". But the important thing is not the relative aesthetics of the music but that one is carried away —out of oneself. I suddenly remembered what John [5] had said: "Your music and your body and the 'Eiserne Jungfrau' [6] are in your way". It is still so. What is 'my' music?

---

[4] Full moon of July dedicated to honouring the Guru; a national holiday in India.

[5] John Cordes, her Theosophical mentor in Vienna.

[6] The medieval torture device known as the "iron maiden".

Mother went into ecstasy for a minute or two during the *kirtan* —Her eyes shut and head bent backward as though pulled forcefully and then reeling round, but came to again very quickly.

She said the other day: *"The trouble is that we think 'I' am doing sadhana. It is He who does and His grace that calls you to do it."*

20th July, 1946

I feel the separation terribly. In my meditation I concentrated on Her and felt quite madly inspired, but in the end I have to go to the unmanifested Supreme which is beyond any sense of duality. She says: *"Think of God all the time and then you will know how to get rid of desire".* Two days ago She said: *"All pain comes from desire."* I said: "the desire for God realization also brings pain". She said: *"No, it does not. There is pain because of the other desires that get in between".*

21st July, 1946

When I look at Her, that is *dhyan*. She is so unearthily beautiful. I just want to be absorbed by Her. Dr. Pannalal [7] says what one desires in Her presence is granted. I suppose She will do it in time.

23rd July, 1946

My room-mate was a terrible experience. I lost my temper so badly. Thank God this nightmare is over. Now I shall be glad to stay with anyone. Sharananandaji said today: *"If you have faith that there is God, how can you have any fear or desire. Of what are you afraid and what can you want? When you have God and are His and He yours, what is there to worry about?"*

Haribaba's house, Solan, 26th July, 1946

Mother left on the 24th. It is good that I stayed on here. I need quiet and time to digest my stay with Her. Again Shobhan, in the room next to me, sings *kirtan* and talks. I suppose I have to pay for the noise I made practicing the piano to the annoyance of so many. This morning I thought: what is the good of this comfortable life I lead, enjoying little things and minding little things, when soon I

---

[7] A important devotee of Anandamayee Ma and a prominent civil servant in both British and independent India.

have to die and then start all over again this futile existence. I still have not complete trust in Her. Strange how stubborn doubt is. Yet I love and adore Her and pray daily: "Take complete possession of my mind and heart."

28th July, 1946

I must be quick and die to this world and the next, before death overtakes me. Then L. writes and I forget all.

28th July, 1946

Behind everyone and everything there is the Eternal. That is what I am seeking. She said to Vyas: *"Be immersed in Him all the time. Then you will know how to get rid of desires".*

Lewis is also an attachment, however subtle, however much on a different plane. Again I feel like breaking it forcefully, stopping correspondence and connection. I have done it so many times before, only to find a new attachment. So I hesitate. But what is the use of that. Of course when I did it before, those concerned never really complied with my request; but he would, completely. Maybe he would be rather glad of it. If you seek the Eternal you cannot seek anything else besides. That is obvious.

Just now went to see Shanti who is supposed to be a *bhakta*, but she is obviously in love with the Swamiji. Her behaviour of trying to starve herself to death shows it fully. It is not so easy to be a *bhakta*. It means to be entirely without desire. Who is to tell if one's heart is pure until one has proved it!

Jaipur Maharaj Mandir, Brindaban, 7th August, 1946

Brindaban is wonderful. I feel at once at home here. In that way it is true that I have the taste of a *sadhu*.

* * *

Vrindaban is the principal place of pilgrimage for devotees of Krishna. At that time it was, and to some extent still is, a charming pastoral town of temples. It is here that the various exploits (leelas) *of Krishna's youth took place as narrated in the Hindu epics and scriptures concerning him. The town has an intense atmosphere of devotion and is filled with thousands of pilgrims particularly at certain seasons of the year. It is especially at night when the air is heavy with the sweet scent of jasmine that Vrindaban's uncanny mystic atmosphere becomes particularly enchanting. It was at night that Sri Krishna had his secret trysts with the* gopis, *the milkmaids, who, mad with love for him, abandoned their families and risked their reputations to be with him — their spiritual infatuation making them oblivious to all else. It is believed by the Vaishnavas, as worshippers of Krishna are called, that his* leelas *take place continually in Brindaban for those who can 'see'. The* leela *of Krishna and the* gopis *is a particularly apt analogy for the Guru-disciple relationship.*

* * *

I have decided to try and live like a *Vaishnava* as long as I am here and as much as I know how to. For me Krishna can only be worshipped as the great all-pervading God who creates and preserves the worlds with a mere gesture and yet who incarnates as a small child for the benefit of mankind.

When I arrived and saw Mother after twelve days, my breath literally stopped. She really is breath-taking.

Yesterday She gave a nice talk in Hindi and said: *"Satsang, dhyan, japa, and reading of sacred books, etc., whatever appeals most to the mind, should be kept up as long as possible whether or not one is inclined to do so, like bitter medicine.*

I still mind it when I am asked not to go here and there in the ashram because I am a Westerner. I suppose I have to be treated like that, as I would feel too grand if accepted wholly, who can tell?

Brindaban, 10th August, 1946

When going round all the temples yesterday I suddenly realized how these people here appear to live in some quite different dimension. It seems that there is something else infinitely greater and more important than the visible material plane and that it matters so little what happens in this outer world. Unless one realizes this, one will never move beyond the purely mundane.

Raipur, Dehradun, 15th August, 1946

Brindaban was wonderful. I did not mind the room with the bad smell or the flies and the heat. I got some inkling there of how that which my heart desires most is something quite apart from

253

this world and how material comforts only take one's attention away from that which alone matters.

Read *Life of Chaitanya* [8] and *Life of Mirabai* [9]. In both books it is emphasized that without the *shabda* [10] and the Guru nothing can be done. My *sadhana* seems in a rut. But to keep the constant thought of "Radha Krishna" as I am doing since Brindaban seems to help. *Atma* has not the same magic. I must ask Her about this. I wonder whether I should take *diksha* [initiation]. But on the other hand I don't want to be rushed into it, but to investigate all possibilities first. I am so unbearably ignorant of these things and need someone to explain to me in my own language.

Kishenpur, 19th August, 1946, Janmasthami [11]

Arrived here on the 17th. Had a talk with Mother at Raipur about *diksha*. She said: *"What do you want, Bhagavan or Atmagyan* [12]? *In any case I don't give diksha* [13] *so from whom will you take it. Moreover when you have taken diksha, you have to obey the Guru implicitly".* We could not get to a point of resolution before someone called Her.

Yesterday there was a series of incidents that made me feel very bitter about those rules. All the accumulated insults came to a head and I burst out with everything to Didi and cried. Then I ran away and sat under a tree. Meanwhile Mother was searching for me and called me to Her as soon as I came back. In the morn-

---

[8] The 16th century Bengali Vaishnava saint who discovered Brindaban in a vision. He was thought to be a incarnation of Krishna and was a major figure in the revival of Hindu devotionalism.

[9] A 16th century Rajput princess and poetess who was a great devotee of Krishna. Her songs are among the classics of North Indian literature.

[10] The inner sound power of the *mantra* transmitted by the Guru at initiation.

[11] The birthday of Krishna.

[12] Basically she is being asked whether she wants initiation into a *sadhana* based on devotion to God or on the non-dual awareness of the Supreme Self —both being different approaches to the same goal.

[13] At this time Anandamayee Ma did not give formal initiation into *mantra* although she often gave *diksha* in dreams. In any case true *initiation* was something quite apart from and much more intimate than any outward ceremony and Atmananda already had entered into this process.

ing She had already asked me to follow Her to Almora after some days; but meanwhile I had decided to go away, as I felt so bad about the so-called 'Hindu *Dharma*'. While under the tree I had thought out where I could go: to Hyderabad and the South and in the meanwhile to Dunga. So I told Her about my wish to see the Great Ones in the South and She said: *"All right, then don't come to Almora now, but do your travelling and then come back. Whenever you feel like coming, wherever I am, the door is always open. Wherever you are, you are mine."* She explained to me —this time to my complete satisfaction —that She Herself does not care about the touching rules, therefore does not keep them consistently because She sometimes forgets. As She wants all people to be able to come to Her, She keeps Her ashram in such a way that there may be no objection to anyone's coming and eating, i.e. that the orthodox Brahmins will feel comfortable there. It is for that reason She has Her ashramites observe so strictly the purity rules so that everyone may be able to eat there as some people come to Her whose Gurus have told them to keep the food rules very strictly. Now I understand that only out of deep love for all does She keeps those rules.

* * *

Again, one must remember that the majority of Hindus at that time were orthodox. An essential part of their caste observance had to do not only with what they ate, but almost more importantly, by whom the food was prepared and with whom they ate. An orthodox Brahmin is supposed to — and frequently does — spend a considerable part of his day in spiritual practices which are believed to significantly transform the vibrational field of the individual and ultimately of society as well. This deep conviction that the subtle vibrations of the food and the environment in which it is consumed have a crucial effect on the overall spiritual process is (or at least was) an essential part of the culture as a whole. It is not easy for an outsider to grasp how basic these beliefs are to traditional Hindus.

Anandamayee Ma encouraged the Brahmins in their strict observance of these purity rules not only for esoteric reasons but also to protect the integrity of the tradition from the onslaught of western influences. But it is one thing when such rules are observed with understanding by serious spiritual aspirants and quite another when they degenerate into superstition and fanaticism.

* * *

Mother said: *"What are these rules to me? I have eaten the leavings of a dog.* [14] *Wherever you go there will be pain of some kind. I wish you would become a 'tapasvin' and cook your own food and not mix with anyone".* She told me that She had decided to keep me with Her and to give me a separate room in the ashram where I could prepare my own food and do what I liked and come to her without disturbing the others. She said that She had talked it over with Didi at Benares and that is why She was preparing me slowly and teaching me to cook etc. I asked Her why the rules were getting more and more strict. She said that there had been lots of talk about my eating with others, particularly at Brindaban, which is particularly orthodox, and She evidently is very sensitive to the feelings of the Brahmins.

Then She explained about *diksha*. She said *diksha* may be transmitted from the Guru by touch, by teaching, by sight and by *mantra*. She said that there is the way of *bhakti* for *Bhagavan* [the personal form of God] which also leads to *Atma gyan* ultimately, and also the way of *Atma vichara* [self-enquiry] and *bodha* [wisdom]. I said I wanted *bodha*. She said: *"Then you must sit still in a lonely place. If you wish to take diksha, test the Guru for a long time. Stay with him for a year or two first. You may like him very much in the beginning and then feel sorry afterwards."*

She seems to know my past broken ties. Evidently I am not to have a *mantra*. I was also thinking to myself only yesterday that on seeing J.K. again I might feel sorry for any commitment that I may have made in the meantime. It is better to remain unattached. Mother is no attachment as She is more than any Guru.

After She finished talking to me, She embraced me and lay in my arms and stroked me as I cried on Her breast. She really <u>is</u> Love Itself.

---

[14] Anandamayee Ma was always in a state of consciousness wherein she saw the underlying divinity of all things. As she often said: *"Where is God not"*. Particularly during the period of her *sadhana leela*, she was oblivious to traditional social conventions and sometimes, almost as an experiment, would make no distinction regarding what she ate, etc with the attitude that <u>all</u> is God. Although later she respected the customs and traditions of those around her, her own consciousness remained as it had always been.

· What a fool I am to go away and yet I felt that I could not reverse my —or rather Her— decision, and so must go South. Often I have this wish and that *samskara* must be fulfilled. Now She is going to Almora where She will talk in Hindi and when I come back in December, She may go to Bengal and again I won't be able to understand Her.

She told me to stay at Kishenpur until I can arrange to go South and to make all the arrangements from here. She asked me to sleep on the spot on the verandah where She had slept and to meditate in Her room whenever I wanted to. She was so over-whelmingly gracious, I cannot help crying when I think of it.

Kishenpur, 21st August, 1946

In today's meditation it occurred to me that the easiest and most satisfactory method is to merge in Her. She is Enlightenment and Love and *Shunya* and this attitude can be kept up for 24 hours.

22nd August, 1946

I know now how cruel this so-called Hindu *dharma* has become due to complete abuse of its ancient principles. No doubt this is responsible for much of India's bad *karma*. Yesterday there was a problem over the 'rules' that upset me very much and I was imprudent enough to tell one of the *sadhus* here that obviously only Brahmins were made by God, and all others by the devil. He evidently did not like it. Later I told Girinda that I could now see why the British Raj could endure so long here and that it was well deserved. He did not like this at all. So I am, as always, standing in my own way and creating difficulties. I must not talk to others.

Yesterday while resting, I talked to Billu and she told me that the Raipur ashram was meant to be a school for children of all religions and Bhaiji,[15] who was Mother's closest and most influential follower in those days, had said that the name 'Ma' was universal and that She was indeed the Mother of the whole world.

---

[15] Bhaiji, Sri Jyotish Chandra Ray (1880-1937), regarded as Anandamayee Ma's closest disciple. He left a senior position in the British Government of East Bengal to follow Her. He is the author of *Matri Darshan (Mother as Revealed To Me)*, a unique and intimate account of Her early life. He died shortly after completing a pilgrimage with Ma to Mt. Kailash (in Tibet).

But since his death in 1937, Mother's organization has become dominated by more traditional Brahmins who do not share his modern outlook.

23rd August, 1946

Saw off Girinda yesterday and went shopping. I still enjoy this world. I studied the map and the thought of perhaps sailing round Cape Comorin by a coastal steamer thrilled me. In my meditation today all sorts of thoughts about my journey came up. I am quite excited at it, though a little frightened at the expense. To keep the mind empty bores me.

Again there is a terrible smell of lavatories coming up to my little cell. Will this *karma* never leave me?

Kishenpur, 25th August, 1946

Last night I fell on the slippery roof and soiled my clothes but was not hurt, strangely enough. Mother is evidently protecting me as much as possible so that all accidents come to nought. (Since She left a branch hit me in the face near my eye; my left arm got burnt by *ghee* while learning to make *parathas*, and now this).

Today I ate Renu's food, but my own tastes so much purer. Why should that be so? She is a Brahmin and *shudhachari* [16] and the food is offered in *puja*.

I read today in Sarada Devi's biography that it is said the body cannot be purified without initiation into *mantra*. I wonder whether that is the reason why I am kept apart? Is my leaving for the South in direct connection with my question to Her about *diksha*?

She was vague and would not enlighten me on the point. Perhaps the experiences I shall have there will enlighten me and make me to understand these rules. Reading Sarada Devi's life helps me understand the surroundings and tradition from which Mother comes. [17]

---

[16] One who observes the strictest brahminical rules.

[17] Ramakrishna and Sarada Devi, like Anandamayee Ma, were Brahmins raised in remote villages in Bengal and they have much in common both culturally and in terms of their teachings.

29th August, 1946

Reading *Ramakrishna and His Disciples* by Christopher Isherwood. It is an inspiring book. What a tremendous effort his close disciples all made even though, as Ramakrishna said, they were already *Ishwarkotis* [illumined ones]. I get frightfully tired sitting even for an hour at a time, and these people sat for twelve hours on end!

30th August, 1946

This morning it suddenly struck me that this body has only one purpose and that is as a vehicle for realization. How futile and utterly senseless is this existence within the little circle of the mind. One goes on merrily worrying about bodily needs and so-called pleasures, never giving a thought to the true purpose of our being here.

Kishenpur, 1st September, 1946

Yesterday during meditation I felt Her Presence very strongly, and then I remembered that She can't drink water when I am present [due to the orthodox rules], and that made me cry. How can She be my Mother when there is this eternal separation? How can I make her ashram my home when people have to bathe if they wash my cup? Today this trend of thought continued. In my mind I wrote Her a letter saying these things. All this makes me conscious that I am European and cannot and do not want to be a Hindu. After all, I have been born in the West for some reason. I cannot and should not make any permanent spiritual connection with anyone else, as I seem to be indissolubly linked with J.K. and his group. Besides the Christian teaching which is intensely charitable and sees all as equal, appeals to me much more in spite of its lame philosophy. I worshipped the Master K.H. [18] for quite some years and had a definite mystical experience when reading *At the Feet of the Master*. [19] All these things have a meaning. Perhaps there is really no hope for me unless and until I can understand J.K.

---

[18] Master Koot Humi, one of the principal Theosophical Masters.

[19] A little book written by the 16 year old Krishnamurti when he still considered himself very much a disciple of the Theosophical Masters.

This evening it suddenly dawned on me that it is of no importance whether or not She can drink water in my presence. After all, I take Her to be a Divine Incarnation and want to be brought to my true Self through Her contact and company. That is all. In this case all the other things don't matter in the least. The trouble arose only because I wanted to make Her into my mother, whom I miss; make use of Her ashrams as my home, as I have none, and become a Hindu. All these things are really not to the point at all. The only way is to regard Her is as a Superhuman being, whose very company and *darshan* intensely reminds one of one's goal and takes one nearer to it.

The housework combined with the three hours of *dhyan* that I am doing plus walking upstairs and downstairs many times a day are perhaps too strenuous. All the same this evening at *dhyan* there seemed real absorption. When I concentrated on the breath, suddenly the Buddha flashed through my mind and I felt on the verge of a vision or some message from on high. The crying evidently purifies one as Mother says.

It occurred to me that if I am ill, there is really only Kitty to whom I can go. No one else really can look after me. I am perhaps a little under-nourished here. I dream of eating puddings and dishes made with eggs.

Here in the ashram there is so much fuss about food and clothes —just like the fashionable ladies who take no amount of trouble over food to make it taste good and to keep slim and have nice clothes to look beautiful in. Only here it is for the sake of purity that no end of trouble is taken. But the result, that the mind dwells on food and clothes, is the same. Wherever I look I see clothes drying [as they must be rinsed several times daily]. Every view is spoiled by it. At least the fashion-conscious ladies are more aesthetic!

I am planning to go to Mussoorie [20] to see Ellen and Gabriele on the 3rd, though the rains never seems to stop. I am rather looking forward to seeing some Europeans and to eat something decent.

Highland Hotel, Mussoorie, 3rd September, 1946

Ellen has this effect on me that makes me feel what need is there to go anywhere. Anyway I cannot get away from Mother. I

---

[20] A fashionable hill-station near-by.

was interested to hear how Sri Krishna Menon told her that he could not have touched her if she were not his disciple.

I understand now many things about Lewis —that he needed a Master mind like Sri K.M. I read his Guru's little booklet. What sharpness and subtleness! I feel frightened and at the same time attracted by him. I wonder whether it is just waste of time and money to go South. In a way it is, but when I go to Mother and these troubles start again, I get doubts and seeing those places may clear them. On the other hand, it may confuse things more. Today I thought, suppose I go to Delhi and then to Almora?

I imagined that my 'Hindu' ways would disturb people but Ellen naturally arranged for a very quiet place for me and likes my saris. Really the difficulties are mostly my imagination.

4th September, 1946

Slept very little. This atmosphere does not suit me at all. Neither does the food though it tasted delicious. Perhaps really the only thing to do is to seclude myself and do *tapasya* as Mother said. I read Sri K.M.'s instructions again during the night. They seem too utterly abstract to me. I also felt terrified about my proposed tour. Is it not going to complicate matters to jump into all those adventures? If I am sincere, everything is bound to come to me of its own. The Guru is waiting for the disciple and if one is ready, He comes, either in person or in a dream, etc. I have almost cancelled my tour. I shall give myself another two or three days and then decide. Life is an abomination if one has no guidance from on high. Now I desire only to be a pure instrument of the divine.

I came here to find out about Sri K.M. and what I have discovered is the futility of travelling all over the world in search of something that lies within me. Do I seek sensation or do I want to dive inside, far away from the world. Why distract myself by new contacts, vicissitudes of travel, change etc.

Kishenpur, 7th September, 1946

Ellen told me about her wonderful dream (or hallucination) which she had when delirious in the hospital while running a fever of 105 which lasted five days. In it she had to remember and live through every incident of her life, but there was one thing she could not remember and everything depended on that. When ultimately she did remember it, her mind, the worlds and stars, began to whirl and crumble and dissolve into nothing. She screamed in terror and fell unconscious. It seems she also became violent, as when she awoke she found herself in a different room, locked up by herself. She knew that her dream had to do with Self Realization and she also thought that she had died. In this state she got up and smashed all the windows in spite of her fever and then sank back exhausted. The nurses could not hold her and a man had to be called. Finally she recovered.

Sri Krishna Menon is supposed to have said when Gordon wrote to him to ask whether Ellen might come: "Yes, I want to see her. She has not far to go anymore. She has already done most of it on her own." But what a daring and dangerous path it is.

It seems I should consider everyone with whom I get in touch is in some way a *sadhaka*. Even Marion Ashkenazi, who asked me for lunch on my last day in Mussoorie, is reading *the Light of Asia* and the *Bhagavad Gita*! Europeans really seem to be waking up now.

Today in my evening meditation at the ashram I was able to concentrate on Mother, so much that I went back to the meditation room for another 20 minutes after Billu had come to light the candle. I felt *bhakti* and a terrific longing to be absorbed.

In Mussoorie I slept very well but one night dreamt that I had married X. It was a perfect nightmare and I was terribly worried about how to get divorced quickly. I wondered why I had gotten married and could not understand it. I said: "Can't I at least keep my own name, so that no one may find out? But the police will have to know".

Since Mother embraced me, I feel safe in Her arms. The physical hug lasted only a few seconds but it remains an eternal Reality, for I consider Her not a physical person but God Herself. I feel definitely nearer to Her since I tried to run away. I always think of Her embrace and Her words: *"Wherever you go you are mine"*. Was this not *diksha*? How can I go to anyone else after that? I suppose I still have to deal with J.K. I wonder whether my dream of him of last year will come true.

9th September, 1946

I get absorbed now whenever I concentrate on Mother. The mind feels such intense bliss that it does not wander. I imagine Her seated in my heart, breathing and moving through my body. I pray to Her to envelope me completely. She is *That*, She is everything. So when I say *Tatwamasi* [21] it is also the same. When will I know Her as She is? Now I have barely caught a glimpse. But I can feel Her spiritual power. When I surrender to Her and ask Her to hold me tight in Her arms, She will see to everything. She is 'I'. She is everyone's heart and root.

10th September, 1946

Meditation much improved. I do *kirtan* for many hours in my mind. I keep on reading in all the books that this purifies the mind more than anything else. So I try. Anyway there is a great joy and love developing.

Every morning I wake up feeling uneasy. There is something wrong. I can't find out in my meditation as I get absorbed in the Mother and forget.

Today it occurred to me to concentrate on the top of the head instead of the heart. There was an immediate result. I remembered that Mother had told me that the top of the head is the root of one's being and if that is well watered with Divine Grace, then the leaves and branches of one's being also become fresh and green. If I concentrate at that point, all the energy focuses there, whereas when I concentrate in the heart, some escapes down.

14th September, 1946

I now get much nearer to Her in my meditation. I see that *Atma* and Krishna are the same. She is Shiva and Shakti and also all the *Avataras*. If I make the most of Her saying: *"Whatever you believe me to be, that I am"*, I do not need anything else. She can be the *Ishta* [22] and Guru at the same time and also J.K. I now meditate on Her. It is much more successful than meditation on *Atma* which is hard to grasp.

---

[21] Upanishadic *mahavakya* (great saying) meaning "That art thou" —implying the unification of subject and object— non-dual awareness.

[22] One's chosen deity.

17th September, 1946

The one-pointedness of the mind has increased considerably. The wish for full Self-Realization is now much keener and I don't forget about it so often. This may be due to my doing *kirtan* and trying out different Divine names in my meditation. I can also sit much longer now, though the legs go to sleep. Read Vivekananda's *Raja Yoga* which is most helpful. To my surprise I find the *sadhana* Mother recommended is very much the same.

Reading now again J.K.'s 1944 Talks. It always upsets me. His way seems entirely different from all others and very much more difficult, but also very profound. He really seems to have found something new. I feel a bit frightened of meeting him. But I have surrendered to Mother and will not leave her embrace, whatever happens. But I pray that I may be allowed to see J.K. She will arrange what is best for me.

This morning sat much longer and got absorbed concentrating on Shiva Shankara. I am beginning to think that my line is the *Shakta* one. [23]

Mother is right, I should keep to myself and cook for myself.

I am very volatile. When someone disturbs me in my *dhyan*, I feel like killing them. This is dangerous, as with *sadhana* power increases. I wonder if this is why in the stories of the ancient *Rishis* [24], they sometimes become enraged and curse people who disturb them in their meditation.

There is no sense in doing anything that does not lead to Enlightenment. Every breath and every movement should be consciously directed towards that.

A Guru is not an authority from outside [as Krishnamurti invariably insists] *but is the innermost Self disguised as an outer manifestation within the play of duality. He is really inside and appears to speak from outside only because we cannot hear the Voice of the Silence. Therefore surrender to Him must lead to becoming one's own Guru, as the inner and outer become blissfully reunited in the truth of the One.* [25]

---

[23] The way of spiritual power or *kundalini* —worshipping the Divine Mother as the supreme Deity, either by herself or with Shiva, her spouse.

[24] The *Rishis* were the original seers of the *Vedas* and the progenitors of *Sanatana Dharma* (lit., The Eternal Way) or what is today called Hinduism.

[25] Italics mine —editor.

Greenfields, Solan, 22nd September, 1946

Arrived yesterday. I feel Her so strongly all the time. My thoughts almost automatically rest on Her when I relax and am free from work. Sometimes I feel as though I am always with Her, it makes no difference where I am. My photo of Her also seems quite alive.

Then again doubts come. Is She really God Himself? Suppose She is only a *siddha*, a *deva* [26] or some being of that sort. That She is not an ordinary human being I am perfectly sure. But doubts come whether She can be identified with the very highest. Where to turn? If one entertains such doubts, the whole structure falls apart. One has to have faith. How can I find out unless I try the experiment fully. The strange thing is that I trust Lewis almost more than Her. When doubts come, I remember him saying: "You are absolutely safe with Her, She is completely realized and egoless".

Solan, 29th September, 1946

Mother came yesterday. When I see Her after having been parted from Her for some time, my heart stands still with wonder. I swear She is not a human being. She is so beautiful, one goes into trance when one looks at Her. She said She knew that I would stay at Kishenpur. What is the good of my wishing for anything. Anyway, I have to do what She wills, and that is the end of it. I wonder whether She will let me go to J.K. All my life I have been searching for true spiritual authority and now I have found it. Only I have to learn to hear Her voice from inside.

1st October, 1946

Yesterday Haribaba read from Abhaya's book about Her and She again talked about Her earlier experiences. At that time She would spontaneously assume the *asana* [position] of each particular god and would then literally become that deity. She really is the 'Nothing' that is God himself and therefore everything. At such moments I feel why should I go anywhere at all; what else is there to be seen after Her. What other *darshan* can be greater than this?

---

[26] A *siddha* is someone who has occult powers; a *deva* is a demigod or an exalted spirit.

3rd October, 1946

Yesterday I saw Yashoda Ma's [27] daughter who told me how hard her mother's rules had become after she became a *sadhu* and thus she felt compelled to leave her; however, before this her mother had seemed like God to her. At once I became frightened of what Mother may ask me to do, if and when I really surrender to Her completely. Of course the food rules immediately came into my mind and caused a flood of doubt. Really I am frightened of being separated from all friends and of not being able to meet people that I want to see, which I suppose will be inevitable if I become a full member of the ashram and keep all the rules strictly. But what of it? Besides who forces me? If I really believe that She is God and if I really want to get out of this ego, must I not leave it entirely to Her and submit to things that I may not like? I was so upset I could not meditate either last night or this morning. Who knows, it may be best for me to have no company at all.

New Delhi, 11th October, 1946

At Solan it suddenly occurred to me during the *Puja* [28] that these people may have to keep all these food rules etc. in order to fulfil their *dharma* as Brahmins, so that the country may come back to its original order. Besides some of these *sadhus* like Haribaba etc. must have deserved Her attention, or even perhaps forced it through their great *tapasya*. No doubt She has come into this world through the Hindu tradition in order to revive and revitalize it.

Abhay told me his story of how She asked him: "*Tum mere sath chaloge?*" (Will you come with me?) twice. She explained to him that this was due to Her having had a vision of him once as a sadhu in his last birth and also as a *sadhak* householder in the one before that. She seems to collect a number of young men and women. Evidently She has some purpose in doing this.

When She told everyone where they were to go from Solan, She did not tell me. At last I told Her that I wanted to go with Her. She said: "*Have you nowhere to go?*" I said: "No". She: "*Achha, abhi ao, fir jo ho jai*". (All right, come now, later whatever will happen will happen). I asked Her permission to go to Delhi a day after

---

[27] The Bengali Guru of the Englishman Sri Krishna Prem.
[28] Probably the annual 9 day worship of the Mother Goddess Durga.

Her, and so travelled with Sharananand who arranged for me beautifully in the train and also a car from Delhi station. In Solan I had a good night's rest and in my meditation realized that the apparent controversy in my mind between J.K. and Mother is really my inability to surrender to the Divine Will. Also, due to my having so many possessions, I have to give too much thought to them which is a waste of time. When I had to pack I felt like throwing away everything. I saw Sharananand that morning. He said that if you stop worrying, then your *vasanas* will go. He is really wonderful, so very loving and kind and no grain of pride in him.

Mother stayed for one day more here and left early yesterday morning. So I saw quite a lot of Her and was present at evening prayers at the *harijan* colony where She met Gandhi [29]. She asked me not to accompany Her to Brindaban, but said: "*I am leaving tomorrow morning, come at 7 a.m.*" I did not know how I would be able to come so early and also did not know the way. But as She had asked me, I was sure it must be possible. Later when I returned to where I was putting up, Mridula Sarabai, who stays with us, said that she had to go to the *harijan* colony early in the morning and so gave me a lift! I arrived at Mother's well before 7 a.m. I again asked Her if I should stay back? She said: "*Yes, Ganga and Bithu are also remaining here*". I felt very hurt, as they are ill and were not going with Her in any case. When I heard that Her whole party had gone with Her, I was still wilder. I very nearly also went. Then something made me stay. But I did not go to the station to see Her off, as I was angry.

In the evening I went to see S.C. Barber at 27 Ashoka Rd., where Mother had stayed. He told me that at the station She had talked about me for five minutes, telling about my cooking my own food and liking it so much. Then she is supposed to have said: "The foolish girl took a year's leave instead of 3 months. But there is something in her mind which won't let her settle down. She should have gone back to her work now, but she is set on doing something daring".

I was rather surprised to hear this, but later felt that actually

---

[29] *Harijans* are the lowest segment of Hindu society, outcastes for whom Gandhiji strove so hard to elevate their position. Anandamayee Ma had met Mahatma Gandhi at least once before this at his keen insistence.

I would not mind going back to Rajghat school at all now, chiefly because I want L.'s company and conversation, though until now I had forgotten about it. Also I could study Bengali and perhaps Sanskrit. Anyway I do not see myself at present throwing away everything and becoming a *sadhu*. I am prepared to ask the committee to let me rejoin school by November 1st, if She agrees to my doing it. I shall talk to Her anyhow and ask Her. In any case I am prepared to submit completely to Her will.

Whatever She asks me to do, however hard it may be, it must be for my best —though I may not understand. In any case She tells me so little and leaves —or apparently leaves— decisions to me. I think of Her all day and being angry with Her really helps because then I can't drop the thought of Her at all. I love Her desperately. I feel quite contented not to know what will happen from one moment to the next. I am ready to go at half an hour's notice like a soldier, keeping most things packed. I feel now quite at ease here also at Kitty's house. It is peaceful and I have rest and read Ramakrishna's Gospel. When I opened the book after thinking that I might just as well go back to Rajghat, I read: "It is impossible to go into *samadhi* until one has finished one's experiences of the world". This is really what J.K. says but in other words. The question is only how to live in the world in a way that will quickly finish off one's experiences.

I have changed quite a lot in these five months. There is a definite turning inwards now and outer disturbances do not affect me as they used to. There is a kind of inner centre established inside me. When I met Mother again at Solan, I felt that there was a subtle rapport between Her and me which is quite unmistakable. Whenever I meet Her after sometime, my breath literally stops with wonder. In my memory She is never as wonderful as when I actually see Her.

I heard that when She was at New Delhi station, a milkmaid passed by Her and She offered the girl a garland and caressed her cheeks. She then said that the girl was pure like a *gopi* of old. Sarkar thought that She had evidently gone to the station early just to meet this girl, and to bless her. So one never can know what Her reasons are for whatever She does. [30]

---

[30] Anandamayee Ma would often suddenly change her plans or route when travelling without any explanation, sometimes going miles out of her way to meet some simple village person etc.

New Delhi, 13ᵗʰ October, 1946

There is a severe cancer in my mind which I am unable to dissolve by my own efforts. It has to do with J.K.'s making me give up all rituals, Theosophy etc. because he said I did not have any genuine experience and only did what I was told on authority at that time. Now I have come again to a similar phase. There is still that duality and fight in my mind. Against all reason and experience, I doubt Mother. Yet I love Her most desperately and She hardly leaves my mind all day and night. I have started praying to Her to dissolve this knot in my mind so that I can surrender to Her completely. I see more and more Her absolute and unquestionable wisdom. Leaving me behind here had evidently a very good reason. I have had the most thrilling time with Mr. Sarkar, who told me about the apparition of Sri Ramakrishna [31] at Navadip and how he got *diksha* from him directly. He said that Mother confirmed that he should not doubt any of these incidents. If this manifestation was still going on I would have gone to Navadip but unfortunately it has stopped now due to the misbehaviour of some people there. His wife and daughter had received instructions from Sri Ramakrishna to cultivate the company of Mother to the utmost. He says that Mother Herself says that Sri Ramakrishna's and Sri Chaitanya's subtle bodies go in and out of Her at times.

I must ask her about my dream of J.K. telling me: "I choose you for my group". And then my other dream where I walked with J.K. through a crowded bazaar and he was a woman. This evidently means that to me, She is he. That is the solution, to surrender completely to Her and to regard Her as J.K. But I am glad I was sceptical and so had a chance to discover much about Her for myself. I must cultivate Her company and disregard all difficulties as regards food rules etc. that vex me.

Radhakund, 16ᵗʰ October, 1946

At last She called me to Govardhan. I reached there on the 14ᵗʰ and found that She had left for this place [32]. It is very lovely

---

[31] At this time Sri Ramakrishna had been dead for over 60 years.

[32] Govardhan is a sacred hill near Brindaban which the boy Krishna is said to have lifted with one hand. Radhakund is the nearby birthplace of Radha, the principal *gopi* and beloved of Krishna.

here and we are only between seven and ten people. Yesterday did the traditional *parikrama* [circumambulation] of the sacred area after bathing in Krishnakund and then we all made a seventy mile bus tour to Kamban, Nandgram and Barsana and then slept that night in a temple at Mathura [33]. I had a tiny space at Her feet just like at Bareilly last year and slept most blissfully after putting Her Feet on my head. She is really all *ananda*, one just goes mad with ecstasy in Her company. I missed half the trip yesterday as I suddenly felt giddy and almost fell down at Nandgram and had to lie on a cot by the side of the road where I soon recovered. At Barsana, which I am told is most beautiful, I rested in the bus. This morning I bathed in the Jamuna. I am learning to manage with very few things. Whatever I lack, others give me. I should have more trust and take less care for myself. This morning on returning here I washed Her clothes. These are also permeated with a most lovely atmosphere. There is no doubt about it at all, whatever She touches gets that particular vibration of holiness. Although we are quite crowded in one room, I feel very happy and this time even get occasion to rest. My body cannot stand very much. The transition from Kitty's luxurious palace means nothing to me, though there is occasionally a hankering of the body —which is suffering from the heat here— for the cool, dark airy room and the comfort of her place. Strangely I felt the spiritual atmosphere much more at Mathura than here. Perhaps this is because when we were there, we stayed just near the Jamuna ghat which has such a profound vibration. But oh how dreadful are those pandits [Brahmin priests]! Just like vultures swooping down on their prey with greedy hawk-like faces. How disgusting. This is what religion has come to. How right I was to come with Her now, where it is so quiet, no crowds. And due to the two Kashmiri ladies She talks much in Hindi. I am beginning to understand Bengali slightly.

I hardly meditate here, but feel that being with Her is one intense unbroken meditation. She is so profoundly attractive that the mind rests on Her naturally.

---

[33] The birthplace of Krishna —the site of an ancient Hindu and Buddhist city on the Jamuna River.

Bareilly, 21ˢᵗ October, 1946

We stayed at Radhakund for two more days, but one seems to traverse ages when with Her. In my meditation, while in Her presence, it came to me that I must surrender not to Her but to my own true Self. Of course She is that, but even so, for me it seems somehow wrong to focus on Her outer form.

I feel that serving others is also a prayer and Vivekananda's idea to serve the God in man appeals to me very much.

On the 18ᵗʰ morning She suddenly said She would leave for Benares and asked me where I would go in the meanwhile. She evidently did not want me to go with Her. Finally we decided on Kishenpur [Dehradun]. In the train to Delhi I somehow felt that I should change my ticket to second class [34] and stay with Her. It was infinitely worthwhile. She dictated a postcard for Kamal to me, then asked me to go to Bareilly and give a message to one of Her devotees and if I liked, to stay with them till She called me. The Kashmiri lady asked me to massage Mother's legs, which I had never dared to do before; then also She put Her feet on my chest. I got much of Her in those two hours. At New Delhi station I called up Sen and by the time we reached the platform for the connecting train to Mirzapur, he had already come and soon a terrific crowd gathered for Her *darshan*. The train was already full and Mother had no reservation. No berth was available. I felt sure that some *bhakta* would be in the train and give Her a berth. The Kashmiri lady found her sister-in-law in the train and she gave her berth to Mother!

At Radhakund when I said to Mother: "Thompson is a *sadhu*", She remarked: *"You are also a sadhu"*. Then She said: *"Do you know what a sadhu is? Someone who never gets angry. Put one drop of something sour into the milk and the whole milk is spoiled. So it is with anger. Even a little spoils everything"*.

I started learning Bengali while at Delhi for two days and realize it won't be so difficult. In Delhi Mrs. Sarkar told me that Sri Ramakrishna had told her (in a vision) the terrible fate of Bengal: that the innocent ones would die of hunger and the violent by

---

[34] At that time it was very rare for a European to ride in anything other that First Class.

272

the sword. She says what is happening now is only the beginning. She said that Ramakrishna had told her: "Very few will be saved. Flee from Bengal now and save yourself." [35]

Bareilly, 23rd October, 1946

Staying in this house was rather a painful experience. Fortunately I came at Mother's express wish, so I don't care. But the people seem anxious to get rid of me. They are fairly orthodox and yet don't know the rules well, which just makes the whole thing all the more superstitious [36]. They were most uncourteous. I am leaving tonight. The first night I slept in this room I had a dreadful dream. There is a bad influence which I have driven out by incense, the sign of the cross and *namkirtan*. Then I could sit in meditation for an hour as usual.

There is a Mouna [37] Swami from Bhallia here, an old man who gives replies by writing on a slate. Yesterday he told me to remain with Mataji always. Today he said "Don't travel about. Stay in Benares and do your work and your *sadhana* as well. Even during holidays don't go away". When I told him I still had eight months holiday, he did not like it and said: "Go back earlier, you will have an opportunity". That is rather the same as what Mataji says. I shall ask Her, when I meet Her. I must talk it over with Her and also ask Her about my *sadhana*. I feel afraid of the *shunya* [the great void] and yet do not know on whom to meditate, on Krishna in *virat swarupa* [in his all-pervading aspect] or on the World Mother. So there is always a conflict in my mind. I must talk to Her. I feel strangely at ease at the thought of going to Bikaner and being with 'my own people', who have not got these horrible touching rules. I wonder whether Mother is teaching me these things so that I may be better able to manage in Hindu society?

---

[35] This was shortly before Indian independence and the terrible partition of India. It was expected that all hell would break loose in Bengal but miraculously, due to Mahatma Gandhi's efforts, the worst was averted there only to occur more horribly in the Punjab.

[36] This is unfortunately more often the case than not —particularly in North India and particularly among the semi-Westernized town people. In the villages, where the ancient tradition thrives in a much more pure and natural way, the ancient code of hospitality in which the guest is God prevails.

[37] One who has taken a vow of silence.

The Mouna Swami said: "Don't go to see anyone. Stay by yourself. Do your work and your *sadhana*." Mother also told me the same.

Bikaner [38], 27th October, 1946

I like this desert here. It seems to remind me of something, as if I had wandered in it before. I ran out into it this morning and such joy entered my heart.

But I am powerfully affected by surroundings. These people dwell on the things of this world as if that were all, and it affects me. G. refuses to be happy because thousands suffer. I used to be like that but now realize how futile it is.

Bikaner, 31st October, 1946

I'm glad that Malati seems to have discovered Lewis at last. It was right I did not go to Benares now. It is not an attachment and yet it is a peculiar relationship that I have to Lewis. He is like a son to me and also like a teacher in the highest sense.

2nd November, 1946

Reading yesterday in Lewis' letter that his health is again poor and he has lost weight, I was quite upset. I had felt so relieved that he could look after himself or had perhaps found someone else to help him. It is always a temptation to go back and do the necessary for him as I have a very deep affection for him. I must find out in detail what Mother meant when She said: "*It is my wish that you should cook your own food and do tapasya*". What She wishes matters, not what I feel. Talking to Gaby I also remembered how Mother told me the first time: "*Keep your mind on the Eternal, Changeless. That is all. That is tapasya. Don't ever forget that for a moment*".

5th November, 1946

Leaving for Delhi today. Bikaner has lovely old houses with beautiful trellis work. The Fort is beautiful and contains a fine collection of Rajput paintings (the library was closed). Devikund, the tombs of the Maharajas, has a fine peaceful atmosphere. Saw the Lakshmi Narayan and Raban Bihari Temples. I am allowed in everywhere now. Someone took me for a *Banya* [merchant caste]

---

[38] Then a princely state in Rajasthan; today noted particularly for its bird sanctuary.

lady! Felt no particular atmosphere at the Lakshmi Narayan Temple except at the shrine of Hanuman [39], to whom I prayed to for *bhakti*. I now enjoy going to temples and bowing to images. Strange how I have changed! The *pandits* here don't bother anyone for money. What a difference to Mathura, Brindaban etc. The princely states have their advantages. What beautiful clean hospitals, wonderful public buildings, and schools.

Read Ramana Maharshi's biography, *Self-Realization*, again. I notice many things that I did not notice before. Again I feel like going there; to sit quietly in such a presence is a great help. He also seems to advise many not to give up the world.

Vindhyachal, 11th November, 1946

Mother asked me to stay here in retreat, to talk only when absolutely necessary and to sit still for meditation for two hours, from 8 to 9 and 3.30 to 4.30 on the verandah of Her house.

* * *

Atmananda now records the detailed instructions given to her by Anandamayee Ma regarding the practice of mantra *repetition. Although she has neglected to mention the events leading up to this, it is clear that she has received some sort of initiation directly from Anandamayee Ma in this regard. At this time Ma did not usually give formal* mantra *initiation although she sometimes did so in dreams in an unmistakable manner (later on she appointed her mother, then a* sanyasini, *to give* diksha *and, after her mother's death in 1971, she had one of Her monks officiate at the initiation ceremony over which she presided).*

Atmananda is one of the rare individuals to have received a mantra *from Anandamayee Ma directly as is implied here. Mantra initiation esoterically binds one to the subtle energy of the Guru through the transmission of a powerful subtle sound vibration* (shabda Brahman), *though the Guru must be a fully awakened Master for this to be effective. Atmananda is careful not to mention here the* mantra *or the name of the deity for whom it is intended as such things are of sacred intimacy. In any case, as Anandamayee Ma points out, the goal of this practice is to*

---

[39] The monkey god who was especially devoted to Lord Ram and is considered to be the embodiment of devotion or *bhakti*.

ultimately experience the oneness of the Guru, the deity, and the practitioner (and indeed all else), and the mantra *effects this transformation through the esoteric power of the* shabda Brahman. *Atmananda seems to have had a special connection with Vindhyachal as she also had a very important experience there with Mother during the Kali Puja of the previous November.*

* * *

Mother told me:

"Do japa of 'G... [40]. Imagine that 'G' is the name for Atma, for Shiva, for Ma, for everything in the world including yourself and also for the shunya. Ask yourself: 'Who am I?' Even though you do not know who G. is, by sticking to the name, He will appear in whatever shape is right for you or if He does not appear in any particular form, then everything is His shape —trees, flowers, animals, men etc. When sitting for 'dhyan' face either East or North. Do 'pranam' by touching the earth with your head. First fill yourself with His power to purify yourself while inhaling, then dedicate everything to Him when exhaling and do 'pranam'. Dedicate your body, your desire, your dislikes, so that nothing remains of you and you also become 'shunya'. With every breath think of the name. While inhaling call down His power into yourself and then, exhaling, dedicate yourself again, thinking of the name. G. is 'bodh', Buddha, Atma. Breathe slowly and quietly and go on doing japa when you sit for meditation. But if the japa stops of its own accord, let it stop and remain still like a stone. If you are called back to the world either by a thought or by a noise, start the japa again. Go on doing this as long as possible, first thing in the morning and also when you lie down to sleep. When you walk, also do the japa. Today is Monday, Shiva's day. Start the japa today and always keep a partial fast on Monday, eating only one meal in the middle of the day. For the rest of the day drink only water if you feel thirsty or hungry. If anyone asks you whether you have taken diksha, say: 'Whatever is necessary, God will do for me'. Don't tell anyone what japa you are doing. If you don't feel inclined to do japa, do it nevertheless and think that it is the name for everything".

---

[40] Atmananda uses the letter 'G.' to denote her *mantra*, as she does not want to disclose the actual 'word'.

* * *

Contrary to the typically Western tendency to want to advertise, if not proselytize, one's spiritual affiliation, either to assuage one's insecurity or to enhance one's self-importance (letting it be known one is 'saved' etc.), the fundamental authority of a true mystical path often precludes even the mentioning of the Guru's name, much less the actual sadhana *one is practicing. Very often the more vocal a person is about their teacher etc., the more superficial or neophyte the relationship tends to be, and is all the more suspect if this is done in an overtly public manner.*

* * *

I asked Her about my head going back during *dhyan*. She said: "This is a very good sign that your 'kriya'[41] comes naturally from within. Don't put the head back, leave it straight unless it goes naturally back by itself. When your legs go to sleep leave them for a few minutes longer and then change the position".

Last night I told Her that I am very tired, that sleeping in other people's houses is tiring and I have no home of my own. She said: "Indeed you have a very large house, the whole world is your home and all people are your people". I was rather moved and tears came to my eyes.

Mother was extremely gracious today and yesterday. She came several times to the house where I am staying and made all arrangements about my food etc.

Sitting from 3.30 p.m. for an hour I noticed a great difference because of the *japa*.

Reached Delhi on the 6th. The atmosphere was very gloomy due to the communal trouble[42] and I disliked being there. I reached Vindhyachal only on the 9th midday. I am glad to be in a quiet

---

[41] *Kriya* : Literally, action or process. The fact of its being natural implies a specific awakening or movement of *Kundalini* as a result of the transference of *shakti* (spiritual power) given through initiation. This may manifest differently in different people according to their make-up and intensity of practice. Anandamayee Ma maintained that all yogic processes, *asanas*, *mudras*, etc. should ideally come about spontaneously from within —as they did with Her— to be truly correct and effective.

[42] She is referring to the explosive 'Partition' situation.

place. My wish to see Mother for a few days and then retire into solitude was correct. I must be alone and quiet. Now I feel I really have got something definite. To live without worry for tomorrow pays very well. The six months have not been in vain. Strange that all these things always happen in November.

XIV - The Experiment Continues

Vindhyachal, 14ᵗʰ November, 1946

I get much *ananda* from doing *japa*. What does it matter whether one earns a living etc. All that matters is to concentrate at all times on one's goal, to rise out of this petty mind into the All, the *Atma*. Everything else is only relevant in as much as it contributes to this.

I feel that I should not return to Benares now. I have taken leave, so let us see how far I can go in these eight months that remain, however difficult it may be afterwards —what does it matter. Work as such means nothing except in so far as it leads me to my goal.

I do four hours meditation daily now. In the first sitting, early morning, I can sit still for fifty minutes without moving, then another forty-five minutes and in the afternoon the same —also without having to change my position and another hour before sleep. This morning I bathed in the Ganges. It is so exhilarating. I got up at 4.30 a.m. which was a definite improvement, but must make it 4 a.m.

18ᵗʰ November, 1946

This afternoon I had quite a good, deep meditation due to reading in the *Bhagavad Gita* how to draw the breath in and concentrate in the heart. This morning went for a lovely walk to the Kali temple and the other morning to the Krishna temple. On both mornings I went to the Ganges. The baths are exhilarating.

19ᵗʰ November, 1946

I am longing for some outer stimulation. I am not yet fit for a hermit's life and require some occupation. I get restless. But it is a useful experiment and I feel like prolonging it, just to see what will happen. Sri Aurobindo's insistence on spiritually transforming the world seems rather more satisfactory than the *mayavada* [1] position of the strict Vedantist. I still wish to go to Pondicherry.

Vindhyachal, 22nd November, 1946

This afternoon during *dhyan* suddenly got into a frenzy, feeling how can one go on living not knowing who 'I' am. What an impossible state of affairs. How can one be interested in anything else till one knows? And how to know? Through enquiry, removing the various layers of what we falsely think of as 'I'? But until I have truly succeeded in this, how do I <u>know</u>? But I do know that I have come nearer to Mother and that must certainly be also nearer clarity.

This evening I asked Her in my mind: "Should I go to Benares"? She seemed to say: "Yes, tomorrow", but I wanted to wait for an outer sign. In the evening Kamlakant came with word from Her confirming my inner feeling. So I can trust my intuition quite well. Also I knew intuitively when I heard the train that Kamalakant had come; but I always doubt my intuition.

This evening went for a walk in the forest. How wonderful it is to be in nature and I wasted so much time on the bazaar!

Bhadaini, Benares, 25th November, 1946

Arriving at Mother's ashram on the 23rd by boat from Ramnagar, I felt intensely thrilled. Benares feels just heavenly. Of course it was the obvious thing to come here and not to Rajghat, which stupidly I still consider mine. To my delight I find that Rajghat has practically come to Mother. The first person I saw in the ashram was Krishni, on the roof [2]. Malati also came with A.K., Ambika and a bus full of boys. There is no place like Benares in the whole world.

Today Lewis came and talked to me. I now see him differently and very much more detachedly. Mother has led me perfectly. How good it was that I did not meet him for these seven months. If I stick to Her and obey Her all things necessary will come to me and everything will fulfil itself. Lewis said on seeing me that I am com-

---

[1] The Advaita Vedanta position of the world as having no inherent reality and thus being an illusion or *maya*.

[2] The roof of the ashram is an open terrace overlooking the Ganges.

pletely changed and that whereas I was quite centred in the physical formerly, now I have some solid spiritual training behind me and have become quite ethereal and more subtle. So that is what Mother has done to me. Malati is also much changed, quiet and truly in touch with Mother now. I feel very happy about this. Lewis seems to have broken with everyone except me. It flatters me, but now I am indifferent even to his company.

Last night I felt intense attraction for Mother and seemed to meditate all night during sleep. She was extremely gracious and came to see whether I had enough bedding.

Rajghat, 27th November, 1946, evening

When I came here today I saw so clearly the spiritual emptiness of this place. Whatever beauty and cleanliness there is here is almost solely on a physical plane. The hall was beautifully arranged and superbly clean and the *kirtan* well done, but the children were mostly bored and many went to sleep. Their bodies are looked after and their emotions not suppressed, but what is best in them is not given any positive help to come out —which is a much worse kind of suppression. The set up here is purely European. There is no real feeling for Hindu tradition at all at Rajghat, or very little. Strange that I, the only westerner in the school, should be the one to notice these things and be the first to object to it.

Now I also see why She was so adamant in keeping the orthodox Hindu rules so strictly with me, so that I may experience the spiritual essence of the ancient culture to the full. Now I shall know both: the European worship of the physical and the Indian worship of the subtle —is it spiritual? Whatever it is, it certainly furthers *sadhana*.

Bhadaini, 5th December, 1946

Last night while meditating I suddenly had a peculiar sensation of the breath having changed into something subtler. 'He' breathes and I watch Him breathing through me, then where is the Ego? The Watcher and the Actor are both impersonal, the ego does not exist at that moment. A great joy and peace accompany this. This seems to have to do with *Kundalini* and my consciousness has risen beyond its usual centre.

Lewis was here for two nights. He seems all in pieces and voiced Alain [Daniélou]'s opinion that Anandamayee Ma is dangerous etc.[3] How extraordinarily absurd! What a fantastic view of things. Strange. But one has to get beyond doubt and that is only possible by illumination and inner perception, which is beyond all discussion and argument.

Fancy, Cohen wanting to come to Mother as well. All people in any way connected with me seem affected by my having joined Her.

Bhadaini, 18th December, 1946

Mother has been away and I had a very unsettled time in Her absence. It seems also partly due to the fact that L. had an outburst of rage when I was at Rajghat on the 8th or 9th, after Mother left. He said quite mad things that rather hurt me and I decided not to see him again. But the day before yesterday when he saw me again at Rajghat, he apologised so profusely and touchingly that I had to let go of it. It has brought us nearer again. He behaved somewhat like Anandamayee Ma after I had run away to Kishenpur —first talked for a long time and at the end hugged me, which he had never done before. Still there is a kind of break, because I cannot help feeling that he is insane. He is so delicate and cannot bear to be criticized at all.

Played the piano at Rajghat. I can still play. Lewis listened for quite a while. When we both sat there I suddenly realized how tragically impossible it is to have any really valid relationship with anyone as long as there is ego, how one really cannot be of any real help to another as long as one is still identified with the ego.

---

[3] Although a renowned interpreter of Indian culture, Daniélou had at times a rather eccentric understanding of the deeper aspects of Hindu mysticism and admitted to being afraid of yogis and saints. Nevertheless at the end of his life in his autobiography, after a scathing and often unjust criticism of many of the leading holy men of the period, he has the following to say about Anandamayee Ma: "Her radiance was such that agitated and unhappy people were soon pacified, their anguish dissolving like the morning mists of the River Ganges; all their religious, metaphysical, existential problems would suddenly cease to be. Once their troubles were gone, these people would melt away into a beatific state...", *The Way to the Labyrinth*, p. 213.

I have so much trouble here in the ashram about food etc. and feel humiliated all the time. Even though theoretically I have the same rights as others, I feel as though I have to beg. Suddenly this evening it occurs to me that I am fond of having authority and this has been enhanced by my position at Rajghat. That is why Mother is applying this painful humbling medicine all the time. Is there anything more dangerous than the sense of power?

Bhadaini, 7th January, 1947

In all this time I haven't written at all. I seem to run away from myself through work. I am almost as busy as at Rajghat. She discovered that I could sing "Bhajo Radha Krishna" and made me sing it during public functions for a few days. Then Bhupendra made a slighting remark to me and I lost my temper and complained to Mother. The next day I went to Ramnagar with the Rajghat children on a steamer without telling Her. Well, since then there seems to be a deadlock. I also got ill. Now She never looks my way. Also I am fed up with listening to Bengali all the time which I still don't understand very well. I am not meditating regularly and am altogether fragmented. Do I need a change? Or is it partly L.'s influence. He came yesterday at my bidding. Perhaps it was wrong to ask him as he has a particularly destructive aura of doubt about him these days.

. The other day he came and read to me when I was ill in bed and I found it delightful. The next day a young American came. No one seemed to understand his questions except Mother, of course. But it was refreshing to me to see a Western face. When I am ill I feel more homesick. I am also longing for comforts. This ashram life is so wearing and I really do not have the energy to bear all the discomforts and the strangeness of India. I wish I had a home. Sometimes I long to live with people who haven't all these beastly rules and who are clean and neat. Now I don't even care to sit by Her. I wonder what has happened to me. I seem fit for no kind of life at all. Work I dislike, marriage is not for me either, and I do not seem to be capable of being a real *sadhu*. Best thing would be the Ganges! But that is no solution.

When I had to do *kirtan* all night and could not get a wink of sleep or even lie down for a minute, it was too much for me. Since then I am knocked out.

Rai Bahadur Mukerji read out from the *Gita* to me yesterday and today. I love it. He says 'Govinda' means the cowherd, also 'he who controls the senses' and also 'Lord of the world'.

I wonder what I shall do next; whether I have to go back to Rajghat. It seems so senseless —but what else to do?

Vindhyachal, 16ᵗʰ January, 1947

Arrived here on the 14ᵗʰ. One day in Benares Mother said to me: *"What is worrying you?"* I could not even tell what was worrying me, but consequently I found out. She said: *"You are meditating very little. You have no responsibilities in the outer world and have seen enough of it. You must meditate more."* That was true. So I started at once. The result was that I felt I need solitude. What worries me is that I am incapable of surrendering, and that means I have to go back to Rajghat. I talked to Her before leaving and told Her this. She said: *"Don't resign your job, but spend your weekends at the ashram."* I do not see how I can be a *sadhu* and there also seems no sense in it as I cannot meditate all day. I have to do some work as well. Physically also I am not too well. I cannot stand too much of roughing it.

Since I have come here to Vindhyachal, I feel that there is a definite change in consciousness. When I repeat the *mantra* there is a clear response or presence and sometimes such a wild joy that I can hardly bear it. Lewis told me that he had a clear experience of *Kundalini* rising to the heart and consequently became quite mad with *ananda* [joy]. He said the only way he could describe it was as a golden wave that had a great force. This happened the night before his birthday due to a happy conversation he had with Raymond [Burnier] and to meeting a boy in the bazaar who strongly reminded him of Krishna. L. says he always felt that I would come back to Rajghat and that it does not matter what one seems to do outwardly as long as one can keep up the inner concentration.

I am acutely aware of the fact that I have barely five and a half months of freedom left and that I have not a minute to lose. Whatever I may do when it is over, unless I have achieved a definite and lasting change (and accomplished what J.K. told me in my dream two years ago: "Think of the Lord all the time and drop all else.") it will hardly have been worthwhile taking this year off. I must not waste time on friends, letters, comforts, etc.

Vindhyachal, 18ᵗʰ January, 1947

This morning I woke late at 5:45. My physical condition is also very low, probably due to a reaction after having been with Mother for some weeks. Still there is by sheer habit the tendency to keep the *mantra* in my mind and the feeling that the mind is being turned vertically, which I feel is somehow connected with the upward movement of the *Kundalini*.

Suddenly as I was trying to meditate it dawned on me that it is 'HE' who does everything through me and not 'I'. How can 'I' exist apart from 'HIM'? What an illusion that there are many separate 'I's! How to realize this? This is the object of life! All activities, thoughts and feelings are based on this illusion of the many —the great lie of separateness— and therefore they are all in vain unless one thinks of HIM all the time as the sole doer behind the appearance of the many.

20ᵗʰ January, 1947

All thoughts, actions, feelings are rooted in the idea of the separate 'I', and therefore vain and useless. It is necessary to drop them all and let HIM work, think and feel through one. That is, one must become <u>conscious</u> of That which is really doing everything. Then one becomes conscious of who one really is.

21ˢᵗ January, 1947

Could sit for nearly two hours. There cannot be anything but God. When one is fully absorbed in this realization, then all activities and thoughts —whatever they may be— are right. Until then the only activity which is not in vain and useless, but rather of the utmost importance, is a dogged, determined, desperate and relentlessly one-pointed aspiration toward that realization. This is called *sadhana*.

Having had a good meditation this morning, at both sittings, the reaction of the ego fighting back follows at once and this evening meditation was flat. The fact that I went to the bazaar to eat sweets did not help any.

24th January, 1947

Getting stale again. I am definitely not ready for a hermit's life as yet. Read in Lin-Yu-Tang's *Between Tears and Laughter* that ritual and music are most essential as they keep the emotions in order, and he suggests government by music. Perhaps I am missing music. I started singing *kirtan* this afternoon. It struck me that Mother also gives such a prominent place to singing and ritual and practically leaves all the rest to take care of itself. Evidently one cannot do without some kind of creative expression. Cooking and cleaning are my only occupation besides *sadhana*. I think it will be best —as She suggested— that I return to Rajghat.

2nd February, 1947

A few days ago I wrote to Malati to ask whether I could return to the school now. Then I tore the letter up and decided to continue with this experiment. Again today I feel I ought to do some work. My time has not come for complete renunciation. My obligations are not over. Though there is a change of consciousness, I feel I cannot do without work. A few days ago Lewis' poem "The Simple Vision" made me quite crazy with joy. This lasted for about three days. I think of him too much. In this condition *sadhana* becomes difficult or impossible. What to do? That *sadhu* at Bareilly was right. But there has been no chance to go back, has there?

3rd February, 1947

I did write to Malati. Suddenly yesterday I got so restless and said to myself: "What really am I doing here?" I am also getting so desperately involved in thoughts of L. Last night I got quite frightened at the dimensions this is taking and turned to Mother for help. There was such an unmistakable response, as if She were there physically and took me into Her arms and made me quiet. I was amazed at the reality of Her power and my nearness to Her. I don't take advantage of this enough.

It gives me such satisfaction to converse with L. He expresses himself in such beautiful and exact language which I clearly understand and appreciate, and it is a stimulating opportunity for me to express myself in return. I miss this so much at the ashram. I do not fit in there in any way really. It is a mistake to live there as I am an outsider. When my time comes I shall find a more congenial place. But these things come of their own. Did not Lewis come without my moving a finger? Was I not taken to Mother in the same way? The best things happen of their own accord and unexpectedly, one need not struggle so much and worry. Let go and trust God. I found such beautiful passages about the meaning of *kavi* [poet] and about "vedic poetry" and "decorative poetry" in Coomaraswamy [4]. It dovetailed so well with what L. wrote in his last letter. How I love Meister Eckhardt. His quotations always transport me.

8th February, 1947

I notice with surprise that my thinking and expression has become very much freer and more lucid. The intense occupation with L.'s poem and his world seems to have effected a communion with a new subtler plane within myself that I could not function on before. But this is primarily due to the meditation that I am doing daily for at least three and a half hours. I notice that I can concentrate more effectively on the ordinary things that I have to do and that I have increased intelligence.

13th February, 1947

Reading Marco Pallis' *Peaks and Lamas* makes me see Mother's insistence on keeping the orthodox laws and injunctions of the *shastras* in a new light. Pallis makes an appeal to return to tradition, as is still the case today only in Tibet, [5] and describes the destructiveness of Western influence on the great cultures of the East. I wonder what J.K. would say to this book, he who decries all tradition and considers himself the greatest of revolutionaries. In light of this book, the ashram 'rules' do not seem so offensive to me anymore. I see that Western ways have already had a detrimental effect on Indian life. Perhaps it is good to make India conscious of her cultural heritage and these rules serve as a kind of bastion against this contamination. But unfortunately modern In-

---

[4] Ananda Coomaraswamy (1877-1947), renowned orientalist and philosopher.

[5] The ongoing brutal suppression and destruction of Tibetan religion and culture and the genocide of the Tibetan People by the Chinese since 1950 is, of course, one of the greatest crimes of all time against humanity.

dia seems to have completely lost its once great aesthetic sense, as for example in these terrible sentimental pictures of the Gods etc., and the horrid film music.

It occurs to me that what Mother told me: *"It is my wish that you should cook your own food and do 'tapasya'"* is now coming true. So Her wish is an order whether one considers it so or not. I find that I like cooking and eating my own food so much that I don't like the idea of having to eat what others have cooked. Strange transformation!

I now have come to like the solitude and quiet very much and dread returning to the senseless crowds again.

It is really a tremendous privilege that I am allowed to live in the midst of orthodox and undiluted Hinduism. I do not appreciate it enough. Few Westerners have this chance. I should stop fighting it and let go of my European habits and conditioning. The West will not go entirely out of my blood in any case. I really enjoyed the two loaves of bread that I got after one full month of only Indian food. They seemed like the greatest delicacy. Strange how strong the habits of childhood and youth are.

17th February, 1947

Today I read in Sri Aurobindo's *Words of the Mother* that thoughts are formations that have a power of their own. A retreat with so much letter writing is no retreat. S.R. must have received my letter today and Kitty, reading it, probably got wild again about my 'escaping' etc. Perhaps I should not have written: "One feels so much less lonely in solitude. Why has one to live in crowds?" I must be much more circumspect and less revealing. What a strange muddle my relationship with Kitty is! Will it ever get clear?

Vindhyachal, 19th February, 1947, Shivaratri

I feel the influence of this holy day of Shiva. I have been feeling rather dull and unable to concentrate, but today there was a peculiar uplift and I was wondering why since the moon is waning. Then I remembered that it is Shivaratri. Reading *Words of the Mother* which is comprised of sayings of Mother Mira [6]; it is full of useful knowledge and inspiration. She speaks about "listening in

---

[6] The French woman also known as the Mother of Pondicherry (1878-1973). She was the principal disciple of Sri Aurobindo.

silence" when something is said, instead of hearing only what is going on in one's own head. Also she talks about illnesses that come about through the practice of yoga because sometimes during the transformative process, the body cannot keep pace with the other parts of the being. I have of late backache and great stiffness in the legs and knees. I feel that these troubles, as well as the menses problem, are due chiefly to the resistance of the body to the rarefying effect that Mother, and my meditation, have had on me. Perhaps I have to go back to work mainly because the body simply cannot keep pace with the intensity of this process. Most likely Mother is so strict about food rules because the body has to be dragged along and pure food is evidently a great help.

Vindhyachal, 20th February, 1947

This morning was enveloped in *ananda* during meditation. There seems a definite change of consciousness, an acceptance of my attempt at surrender, as if I were being taken up into something which is indescribably blissful. Again in the evening I seemed to be taken up in this Bliss, but suddenly a mouse (attracted by the *ghee* that I had smeared on my feet) tried to bite my big toe which sent me into such a state of fright that I had to steady myself again. I hope I shall soon be able to go to Kishenpur. I am longing for solitude. I have very little time left now until July and cannot waste it. Leaving for Benares tomorrow.

Bandh, 5th March, 1947

Was in Benares for two days only. On the 23rd Mother suddenly asked me to go to Delhi by the morning Mail train. It meant going to Rajghat at once and catching the 3 a.m. train. She sent me to tell Sarkar that She was arriving the next day. When She arrived, we went to the station and while driving back in Sarkar's car, suddenly a horse ran across the road and to avoid an accident Sarkar slammed on the brakes. Mother hit Her forehead against the car and got a bump. Sarkar naturally felt desperately sorry about this. Later he related to me that She told him that he was to have had a very serious accident at that very hour and it could not have been avoided in any other way other than Her taking the *karma* on Herself in this manner.

Bandh is quite a fascinating place. Haribaba is more authoritative here in his own surroundings. Here there is a huge crowd. But I get much more solitude than I did at Calcutta. I have a solitary place where I can sit morning and evening. I now find that sitting quietly twice a day has become a necessity. I feel miserable without it, like a drunkard without alcohol. Even if the mind wanders, still it is extremely refreshing.

As soon as I came here I wanted to run away. I went so far as even to ask Mother whether I should go. Mother said: *"Didi is leaving on Tuesday."* I did not really want to leave so quickly, but I suppose I shall go in a couple of days now. Strange how attached I am to comfort. The food is heavy, the string cot uncomfortable, and there are bugs in my bed; we wade in dust and are always dirty and there are thousands of flies. But what does it matter as long as I am near Her? I know nothing and am getting old. I have not much time left. I see how old age breaks in upon one and makes one more inflexible unless one has lifted oneself out of all attachment. I dread going back to Benares, but why worry. My life is Her responsibility now. I also see how judging and criticizing others is an escape from seeing oneself and is an outlet for one's own discontentment.

There is perpetual *kirtan* here for one whole month with bells and drums and I am staying fairly near the *kirtan* hall. I mind it much less than I did at Solan though. The other day I attended Haribaba's *kirtan* where he reels around beating his gong. I was rather touched at the complete sincerity and abandonment that he and many of the villagers have. For them it is perhaps like the 9th Symphony where they forget all their petty quarrels and feel one in Rama and Krishna. It is really very interesting here, but I feel why waste my time on outer things when I should concentrate inside.

She is right that meditating in solitude is so important for me. Even that Brighu pandit [7] told me the same thing five years ago, and Bhallia and Rama Rao also. It seems to be a medicine for all evils.

---

[7] See entry for 4th July, 1942 in chapter III.

Rajghat, 16th March, 1947

Mother was marvellous beyond words at Bandh and again talked about Her experiences during Her *'sadhana leela'* like at Solan. What is it that drives me here and there? Why on earth did I leave? What else matters when I can be with Her who is everything that I aspire to?

Yesterday in the train I heard that there are riots in Benares and by a strange coincidence, I arrived here at Rajghat [which is outside of the town] instead of at the ashram, although that was not my intention. The person who is really delighted to see me is Lewis. Did I come for that? With curfew and the courts closed etc. it is really the worst moment I could have chosen to be here. And why did I not ask Mother whether to proceed with this beastly naturalization? It simply did not occur to me. Is it believable? The devil must be riding me to be so blind.

Rajghat, 17th March, 1947

Wrote to Mother by express mail for Her decision in the matter of the naturalization and said: "It is difficult for me to let go and give up the habit of acting by my own judgement, but I will from now on obey you absolutely and without any reserve. Please accept this and give me your blessing for all times. With *ashtang pranam* [full body prostration], Yours, Atmananda."

Rajghat, 18th March, 1947

Writing the aforementioned suddenly changed everything. I found yesterday that not only could I meditate but that it was difficult to stop. In the afternoon I went and sat under a tree near the Mohammedan Saints' *samadhi* [grave of a holy person]. I meant to read but began to meditate and remained in a state of elation and concentration for quite a long time. Then I continued in my room. L. came and said mockingly: "What a holy atmosphere in this room", and teased me. What he actually meant I don't know. He now has a rather dampening influence on me.

I see that the whole problem is complete surrender. Mother explained in Bandh that when She does *pranam*, She gives Herself back to the One from which all comes. That is all that is wanted.

Mother told me in Bandh when I said to Her that my mind

291

does not want to stay put anywhere: *"Do dhyan as much as possible. That will open everything. That is your path. Do your work and when it is over, do 'dhyan'"*. Also She asked me to read good books if I am unable to do much sitting. The joy of complete abandonment to Her is incomparable. It cuts off all worry and one feels so utterly light and carefree. Yet, again I still have doubts about Her at times. Complete obedience and dependence on Her actually gives one complete independence.

18th March, 1947

Again this afternoon I did not know whether to stay at Rajghat or at the ashram; well, perhaps it is irrelevant. What matters is to sit in *dhyan* as much as possible, nothing else. Now I can sit much stiller and concentrate better.

I could perhaps really have returned to work at the school rather than spending all my savings travelling around and sitting here in Benares —which I love by the way. Meditation seems easier here than anywhere else and I must admit I love Rajghat also and the wild jungles surrounding it. I sat for meditation under a tree again today. It is so beautiful there.

20th March, 1947

Today during a very noisy, nay deafening *kirtan* at the ashram, I realized that likes and dislikes are only painful if one judges and looks at them from the ego's point of view which wants to survive by asserting its imagined superiority. After all, destruction is also good. I understood Sharadananda's teaching: "Don't look at other's faults". I could do it for the first time. It is a question of surrender. If you keep concentrated on the thought: My body, soul and mind belong to Him and He can do what he pleases with them, you neither suffer nor enjoy. You just become an impersonal spectator, quite indifferent. All is the same. This indifference is not something dull but, on the contrary, intensely profound and satisfying. Later, as I was eating I saw how absolutely essential it is to realize that it is 'He' who eats through me, not I. The point is that 'I' don't do anything, I neither feel nor think but let myself be done, felt and thought. That dissolves the I-ness. If I eat for enjoyment it works contrary to this. Therefore these food rules are necessary to make me conscious of the process of eating. This is very important as the weight of the physical is the greatest problem. Saw Girinda by chance. He has been living in a cave-like cell in the ashram for the last two months. He looks transformed and very beautiful. He does not talk and remains completely aloof.

Stayed with Malati for the night. She talked to me for a long time and said she felt much lighter afterward. I wonder whether I came chiefly for the sake of Lewis and Malati or because I am restless without work. Yes, I must work again. But now I am different; the work won't eat me up. I must use these three months that are left well, and become thoroughly detached. The last few days I feel a distinct change. I try to always keep the thought in mind that 'He' breathes through me and every breath transforms me to be entirely His. Surely this is awareness.

More than ever I want to completely surrender to Her. It is like a Hindu marriage where you give up choice entirely and self-will. This is the only thing that gives one peace. I can now meditate much better and longer due to this. I have no cares, though sometimes I forget. Off and on I get immersed in *ananda*.

Rajghat, 21st March, 1947

At Bandh I told Mother: "If I don't sit for meditation regularly, I feel so uncomfortable like a tea drinker without tea." She answered: *"Excellent, that is how it should be."*

I wish Mother would tell me to drop the naturalization work so I can leave. I badly want to sit still in Dehradun. I see now that my irritability about noise is due to the noise, discontent and restlessness within my own mind.

Kishenpur (Dehradun), 26th March, 1947

She did tell me to go to Dehradun! Arrived here yesterday. But the place is not quiet and the neighbours are quite terrible, but the *Dhyan Mandir* [meditation temple] is marvellous. I wish I could obey Her better. That requires a special kind of intelligence and is not easy.

I have now only three months left. Meditate, meditate, meditate! What is the good of saying 'I must get there before I die'? Why not at once? Where is the fun of living in this state of separation?

Kamal also, like Atul, lives happily on Rs. 15 per month and his skin shows no blemish —he looks well fed, almost stout and very peaceful and happy. He says that science has only helped to increase our wants. It is quite true. As soon as one dedicates one's life to Him, no vitamins, no extra protein, are needed. Any old rice and *dal* will feed one.

Lewis again apologized for his madness. He never apologizes to anyone else. After all, our relationship is not, cannot be, 'pure' and therefore is a weakness. As long as you are an ego, how can there be right relationship.

Kamal is reading the *Gita* aloud in the morning and Mother's Life, *Matri Darshan*, [8] in the afternoon. He explains in Hindi and in English. That is good. I am lucky. But I cannot get the quiet of Vindhyachal here and I miss it a lot. I was so fortunate in the train, for many hours all alone in the compartment lying still.

How to get rid of this driving power of 'I-ness'? Why do I lend my ear to the noises of the road? This is worse than Bandh, almost like a city. But it won't do to run away. There is a shouting boy next door, just like in Rajghat. People on the road talk incessantly. It disturbs me a lot. It evidently is necessary for me to overcome this so as to be able to live in solitude under any conditions.

Now that I am used to doing everything for myself, carrying water etc., I find people who are willing to help, like Atul and Kamal. Likewise when I have learned to put up with noise, perhaps I shall have more quiet. This is *tapasya*. I wish Mother would come soon. I believe She will, at least sometime this summer.

When Kamal read to us yesterday from *Matri Darshan* how Mother, when doing *Kali Puja* in 1926, began to put flowers on Her own head as well as on the head of the image of Kali, it occurred to me that perhaps She Herself is the Kali whom Sri Ramakrishna worshipped. Sarkar told me that She had told him what Her relationship to Sri Ramakrishna was, but of course he would not tell me.

---

[8] *Matri Darshan* by Bhaiji, translated into English as *Mother as Revealed to Me*, published by the Sri Sri Ma Anandamayee Sangha, India.

Kishenpur, 27th March, 1947

Going to Raipur today it struck me what terrible madness this world is and how very powerful its driving force; how everyone is fascinated by the spell of it and moves under it, struggling to keep the body intact. All these shops filled with unnecessary things to buy and eat and to distract oneself with (and yet I bought some!). One's whole life is utter nonsense. Even what one learns is mostly only 'to earn a living'. How extraordinarily ugly the *memsahibs* [Western ladies] are with their obscene frocks and empty faces. I saw what J.K. means when he says: "You only decorate your cages."

Then arriving at Raipur one is confronted with the austere, destitute life of the *sadhus* —the reaction to this madness and therefore not the real thing either. They are rightly disgusted with the utter insanity of *samsar* [the world] and want to have done with it at all cost. But is not being compelled to go to the opposite extreme also bondage, like D., who is always ill and dissatisfied and who says: "In spite of my bad leg I must go for *bhiksha* [9] or else I shall starve." And he is always worried about his illness. I see the madness of the shops and cinemas and the strolling *memsahibs* busy with nothing, and yet I am not so different. I also spend much time shopping, cleaning, cooking, washing etc. —all this just to look after the body. How all worship the body! Mother said: "*Do 'dhyan'. With that everything will open; this is your path.*"

I feel like a mouse that is looking for a hole to hide itself in when I go to the city. It reminds me of the time when as a child I hid between the wide black skirts of my grandmother! I was reminded of Ramakrishna today, who would run away and hide in a tree when worldly people came near.

Going to the bazaar and shops etc. is definitely poisonous to meditation. I should have kept the mind turned within while in the shops but I got flustered. I see how wise Mother is to keep the girls [10] in *purdah*. It serves as a great help for their *sadhana* and it is foolish to feel sorry for them. After all, what do they miss? I must

---

[9] The daily ritual of begging food.

[10] The women who lived exclusively in the ashram under Ma's guidance like nuns were referred to as the 'girls'.

keep quiet if I have to go out and keep up concentration. My days are numbered now; I must not get sunk into the ordinary again! But I see now what a tremendous amount there is that has to be transformed —quite impossible to do it in the world. But Rajghat is a good place for this and there is jungle nearby and also L. who, after all, has left worldliness behind. Reading René Guénon is extremely clarifying.

Kishenpur, 10th April, 1947

Today a man from Sindh whom I hardly know at all —a Theosophist— offered me Rs. 1200 to enable me to spend another year in this way! I feel rather pleased at this, but I see that I haven't the courage to accept it. It seems wrong to accept so much when I can't do anything in return. Anyway it is for Mother to decide. But it seems that She wishes me to work for the present. However, I should very much like to drop the radio work and my visits to Delhi. The *sadhu* at Bareilly also told me to stay in Benares and not move about.

Having just had a desperate letter from Casella, I wonder whether I could not ask this man to help her out to relieve me from the necessity of earning money at the radio for her. I am mainly reading the *Gita* at present and thereby learning quite a lot of Sanskrit at last.

11th April, 1947

I now feel that there is definitely something happening when I sit for *dhyan*. There seems to be something enveloping me and drawing me up but I feel afraid of it. I repeat the *mantra* but who is it, what is it? I wonder whether somehow it is this very fear which creates the outer distractions like noise and other disturbances that will not let me 'go off' properly. My faith wavers. I felt this evening that *Nirguna* [the formless] is after all the best for me. However difficult it may be, it is perhaps the only safe way for me. What was my past that I feel afraid of and cannot have complete trust in any Being however great? Was it my life as a Buddhist? Or is it the 'guardian of the threshold' to the Sanctuary that is holding me back? Only when the heart is entirely pure can one enter. Mother says *japa* purifies the heart.

Again doubt creeps in about Mother. Is it Dick's book on J.K. that disturbs me? I almost believe so and yet it has such a peculiar attraction. <u>Who</u> is J. Krishnamurti? Why does his teaching have such a destructive quality for me?

When I went off my guard this evening in my meditation, my head went back so much that it hurt horribly when I came back to ordinary consciousness again.

17th April, 1947

It seems to me that my troubles arise because I lack faith. I do not know how to surrender. I have doubts about Mother. Is She really the absolute *"Purna Brahma Narayan"* [11]? I cannot fathom it, it is too big for me. *Yet if I don't have full faith in Her the whole structure of sadhana tumbles down.* Half and half will not lead anywhere. I cannot and will not leave Her. I have seen from my own experience that if I leave everything to Her all becomes well at once, even in the most unlikely situations.

In concentrating on Her in *dhyan* I get such *ananda* that my mind cannot wander, but often it becomes so intense that I just can't bear it. I want to dance, jump, embrace someone. I feel quite unbalanced and get frightened. I get taken out of myself, quite unhinged —like a lover with unbearable longing. Yet I feel the time has not come, I must first become much more purified. That is why She is sending me back to work I suppose, to work out my attachment there.

Today letter from L. He says: "It is quite clear to me that you have become more radiant, conscious, balanced and detached". Fancy!

18th April, 1947

Today I felt as if She had taken me into Herself. She is already transforming me as far as possible.

I have a dim fear that I shall have no control over my behaviour. Once one is out of the ego one is bound to behave in a queer manner. It seems inevitable and I am not prepared to face it. I still believe in properness and respectability. Lewis is quite right when he says I have to go mad. Now I see what he means.

---

[11] The ultimate and complete manifestation of God. See entry of 22th June, 1952.

297

21st April, 1947

Mother says what has been written in the sacred Scriptures [*Shruti*] is all true, but that it is only part of the Truth. Sri Aurobindo also says that not all Truth is in the Scriptures. When Mother told me not to drop J.K., why did I not ask Her to tell me how to live his teaching? I insisted that I could not do it. It never struck me until now —my mistake was that I talked to Her as if She were a limited being.

3rd May, 1947, Mother's Birthday

At times it seems I don't really believe in what I am doing. I am divided between Buddhism and the *Bhagavad Gita*. Of course it is probably all the same, but I take it as an excuse for doubt and disturbance. Yesterday I read some of the *Cloud of Unknowing* [12]. There also it is said, "Empty your mind of everything except God and Love".

4th May, 1947, Vaisakh full moon

Last night I had the idea of staying up all night and meditating. It had a tremendous effect. It seems to have taken me out of a rut. How lovely, peaceful and blissful a solitary moonlit night is! I sang *kirtan* by myself till 12 p.m., then felt tired and wanted to lie down but had a feeling as if Mother was keeping me from it. So I sat in the garden and on the roof and went to sleep only from 4 to 6 a.m. I must do this more often. All these festivals and rules seemed to be designed particularly to break the dominance of the body. How naturally quiet and undisturbed one can be keeping awake in the night and sleeping for some hours during the busy day, instead of trying to concentrate at the more normal times when noise and distraction are all round.

Had a letter from Joan Dorna saying that Sidney has gone into solitude in the bush. It occupied me quite a lot. Strange how many of my old friends want to come to India: John, Casella and now Joan.

Too much sleep heats the body and only makes one more *tamasic* and greedy for food. To eat and sleep as little as possible is quite essential.

---

[12] Medieval English mystical work with many striking similarities to Indian spirituality.

8th May, 1947

Today it is Mother's birthday according to the lunar calendar. [13] Sat in the *Dhyan Mandir* sometime between 7.15 and 8 p.m. and had a sudden but very fleeting realization of Her Greatness (although this is not the word). She is tremendous Being, All Pervading, and only seems to be a human being in a body. It was just the faintest glimpse.

Both Lewis and Malati went to see Her on or about Her birthday. She was especially gracious to them both. They were quite impressed.

---

[13] In India the lunar date is considered very much more astrologically significant than the solar one and all spiritual festivals and events are celebrated according to this.

XV - A New Mantra

Mother came on the 18th. As I have voluntarily given up my room, I have no place. I was determined to bear everything in order to be with Her. The more I see of Her the more I realize that She is pure Love, nothing else. Again the conditions I live in reminds me of Milarepa —very little sleep, no privacy, much work, tedious people, and everyday some new trouble because of their idiotic 'orthodoxy'. It is quite a severe *tapasya*.

One day there was some talk about surrendering one's head, i.e. mind. She said: *"You have given your head, so let Him play football with it if He pleases, what is it to you?"* and She looked at me particularly. Last night I slept outside by myself and strangely missed Her nearness, though it was much more airy and comfortable where I was. Off and on I have had a little realization, but no inclination to write it down as my things are in one room and rest time in another etc.

Last night She said to me: *"So you have come to sleep here again?"* She evidently minded my leaving Her the night before for the sake of a cooler place. Yesterday there was a painful incident with B. He deliberately contradicted and disobeyed Her and would not apologize. She visibly suffered so much and went on asking his forgiveness repeating many times: *"Baba, maf karo"* [Baba, forgive me]. I felt quite sick over it. In the muddle he attacked me on top of it. I feel still quite shattered.

It seems to me that She plays up to orthodoxy in order to make it possible for some of the stricter Hindus to be helped by Her who otherwise would not be able to get near Her. Perhaps it is Her function to save just those people. The trend of the world is against them. J.K. has nothing to say to them. Even his not knowing any Indian language prevents him from doing so. Equally She knows no European language. Evidently it is impossible to teach everyone at the same time. Meanwhile the killing is increasing in the Punjab and Bengal.[1] It seems to me that the creation of Pakistan is the only possibility under the circumstances. It is all very puzzling.

31ˢᵗ May, 1947

Fred came this morning. When I tried to introduce him, She at once said: *"But I know him, I have seen him before"*. He broke out into tears. He says I look much younger than when he saw me last November.

1ˢᵗ June, 1947

Last night translated a private [2] for Fred. Got so much out of it, breathtaking. There are no words in any language to express a tiny fragment of the sublimeness that She is. Today Fred asked about *avatars*. She said: *"There is no coming and no going. All are Atma. There is no question of an Avatar descending into the world. He is always there, but takes shape for the 'bhakta'."*

I hardly sit for *dhyan* these days. There is no time. I can't tear myself away from Her, and then there is housework and I have to rest. But looking at Her is more than *dhyan*.

Anand Chowk, Dehradun, 7ᵗʰ June, 1947

As usual, I cried my eyes out on the eve of my birthday. By mistake I set my foot on the veranda in an area where I am not allowed and thus polluted the eating arrangements for the *sanyasis*. Mother asked me to sit near Her last night in the *kirtan* and tried to comfort me. I did feel quite peaceful after some time, but the trouble started again this morning. I do not understand. If *sanyasis* behave this way, what is the use of all their *sadhana*? I do very little meditation when I am with Mother and perhaps that is why

---

[1] As the British prepared to pull out, the devastating partition of India between Hindus and Muslims began in which thousands would perish.

[2] The term used to denote a private interview with Anandamayee Ma. Throughout her long life, Anandamayee Ma remained very accessible to people's individual needs and problems, giving public *darshan* for many hours daily and private interviews long into the night.

I get so upset. I feel like drowning myself in the Ganges. Anyhow it is unbearably hot.

I see from my diary that a very similar thing happened in Solan last year. I am so tired and my mind does not work; but I worship Her and cannot leave Her. Though She has of Her own accord promised me that I can always come to Her, I am afraid that if these people around Her have so much power they may prevent me from doing so. But what nonsense it is! If She is Divine, who can prevent me, who can possibly have the power. I must not look on Her as a person.

8th June, 1947

Yesterday evening She took me for a drive and I completely calmed down. From what I heard afterwards the whole painful affair was just because of my silly remark. It was magnified and that caused the uproar. I should never talk about these beastly rules and just keep quiet. It is a point on which the West and India can never meet and it must be left alone.

Kishenpur, 11th June, 1947

Surrender means to let go of one's cherished opinions. The other day the young Bengali, who eats with me and who abhors caste rules, asked me what I thought about them. I replied: "I have stopped thinking as thought is by its very nature conditioned, and thus unreal."

When I meditate the only thing that keeps my mind fairly in tact is to concentrate on Her, to become utterly absorbed by Her.

15th June, 1947

I meant to ask Her the meaning of my *mantra*. Haribaba explained it yesterday in the meeting. It has many meanings, like 'Ruler of the earth', 'Ruler of the *indriyas* [senses]', 'Imparter of the Vedas' in short, it means 'God'.

A few days ago a Christian Padre and another Christian teacher came to convert Her. I had a long talk with them afterwards. I was rather amazed at the way they listened to me. Writing letters to friends I also find to my astonishment that my words carry a certain amount of weight. After all something is happening by my association with Her, only I myself don't notice the progress. Lately however there is a particular concentration when I sit for *dhyan*. She seems to pervade me more and more. I concentrate best by remembering Her face first of all. That gathers my thoughts at once in one point.

17th June, 1947

Today during *dhyan* I got some result and did not stop as usual after one hour. I realized that my trouble is that I look for happiness or satisfaction in this world. I always want to improve things —cleanliness, order etc., which are totally irrelevant to the deeper Reality I am seeking. Nowadays when I look at Her face my mind gets absorbed in 'That'.

Kishenpur, 18th June, 1947

Mother gave a little talk to a small group in which every word was meant for me. As a matter of fact she answered some of the questions I meant to ask. She said: *"Learn to laugh heartily with your whole being. Don't take offence at what anyone may say. If it bothers you, ask yourself why. Analyse your feelings. When you get angry, it is because you are thwarted in your desire. When you don't get food in time, you get restless and hanker after it. That means you depend on food. Why should hunger and habit rule you. The same with sleep. Keep awake for a night now and again and don't let sleep rule you."*

Unfortunately I found no time to write this down immediately. Again another time She was talking about anger and said: *"You do 'sadhana' for so many days. Once you get caught up in anger, the whole effect is gone. You have to gather up all the threads again. This 'shrishti' [creation] is 'dukhrupi' [full of suffering]. The friction which is caused through its constant movement also causes the suffering. Turn inside and you will find happiness."*

I am under so much strain and am resentful all the time. Today She made a rule that the conch has to blow at 4.30 a.m. and all must get up. I told Her that three hours sleep was not enough for me. She said: *"Go to bed at 10 and sleep till 12, then do 1/2 hour's dhyan and sleep again, till 4.30".* Later when I told Her I needed more sleep, She said that I could sleep in the afternoon from 12 to 4. It seems that sometimes what She says is not meant to be taken so hard and fast.

This place is getting very unhygienic with all the crowd and no organization —drains giving way and getting putrid, a child with high fever in Deviji's room and all the flies increasing daily. I also have a bad foot, something has gone deep into it somehow and there is neither place nor energy to look after it.

When I looked at Her face and my mind went, She smiled several times.

My clothes are in tatters, but She does not offer to give me any. I suppose many people would want clothes. What is She to do?

Kishenpur, 21st June, 1947

Getting up at 4.30 is after all very nice, so quiet and lovely in the morning; only I have to go to sleep early and miss sitting by Her at night. My health is not too good. I shall rest at Rajghat. Perhaps after all this strain work there will seem light? Last night suddenly I realized that as I have given myself to Her —mind, breath and body— She can do what She likes with me and it is senseless to feel hurt over a 'thing' that does not belong to me. The noise also —if She chooses to keep me in noise— how is it my concern? I have a strong habit to resent dirt, noise, disorder and inconsiderate behaviour of others.

Now I have at least a little cell for my luggage and I can sit somewhere alone, though it is hot in the day. What a relief to have a little hole to crawl into! I feel like going into the jungle and not seeing the face of any human being —and at Rajghat again I have to live with a crowd of noisy children.

I understand something now about concentrating on a sacred NAME —that it takes the mind away from everything else and has the magic quality of bringing one into touch with Reality. It is easier than abstract meditation —which is difficult to do without the mind wandering— and ultimately produces the same effect.

At the moment I am sitting in my cell and no one is shouting. What bliss! What relaxation! Yesterday a short letter came from

Lewis, apologizing again for having said: "You always irritate me". This letter sounds almost like a love letter and rather amuses me. I replied at once.

23rd June, 1947

I am getting more and more strained. Shall I ever be able to understand the mentality of this country? No one is straight, one can never depend on anyone's word. And with three hours sleep it is almost unbearable. Who knows!

Yesterday Dr. Pannalal told me how he felt when he helped to sponge the child with typhoid and how this helped him to understand how the orthodox people must be feeling about me. First he washed his hand in disinfectant, then also his feet, then his face and head. But he still felt uncomfortable, so he had a bath and changed his clothes. Then he felt all right. This is really how it is. If I had not experienced this for myself, I should have never believed that such a way of thinking is possible.

Kishenpur, 29th June, 1947

I am dead tired and want only to sleep and eat. All the same, off and on I realize something profound, utterly beyond the mind. Ah, I want rest and peace and solitude and nothing on earth to do. Just to lie still.

Kishenpur, 30th June, 1947

This afternoon doing my hour of *akhanda japa* [3] I got an inkling of the *rasa* [divine nectar] that is in the name and lost all fatigue. It was so intoxicating that I wished my replacement would not come.

Mother related today how when She was doing *sadhana* it never struck Her that She had to eat or to sleep because that would interfere with Her absorption. Her smile is so utterly irresistible. One cannot escape its charm.

Kishenpur, 1st July, 1947

This evening somehow all my complaints against the dirtiness of the surroundings and of people's bad habits etc. came out.

---

[3] *Japa* done for 24 hours or more with people taking turns keeping vigil. In this case it was being done for the sick child.

Now probably everyone hates me, but they won't throw dirt about anymore. I see that *shudh* [purity] and cleanliness (as Westerners understand it at least) are really opposites. The clean person waits until he can dispose of waste in a satisfactory way, like spitting and blowing one's nose into a handkerchief and keeping fruit peels and seeds in a paper, whereas the *shudh* [4] person disposes of it at once and throws it on the earth which according to their belief cannot be polluted. The teachings of the ancient *shastras* regarding purity were written for people living in sparsely populated rural environments, not for modern city dwellers. Now new *shastras* are required.

Talked to Mother and asked Her why the world is such a fundamentally miserable place. I could not really understand but She said: *"No, it cannot be made better. It* [its inherent imperfection] *is 'ananta'* [endless].[5] *You should do your sadhana and remain aloof from others."* I told Her about Kishindas' offer of money. She said that if someone offers to help in order to make it possible to do my *sadhana*, I could accept it. Again She told me to spend any free time I may have by myself after I return to school.

I could not finish speaking with Her as someone came. I feel that often now it is really much more satisfactory to dive inside and discover for myself what to do rather than to always ask Her.

Today when I told Her that it is useless for me to do any *sadhana* as my anger only increases, She said that anger doesn't spoil <u>all</u> the results of *sadhana*. Words really only hide Her true meaning.

2nd July, 1947

Today She said: *"If you want to change your mantra, do so tomorrow on Guru Purnima. Come in the morning after bathing and meditation. You can take any 'rupa'* [form of God] *you like best".* She agreed that I can take Her form also. She made me repeat the *mantra*, but did not say it Herself.

---

[4] One who keeps orthodox Hindu purity rules.

[5] i.e. the world, by definition, is endless nescience caused by a fundamental flaw in individual perception and until this is removed there must be suffering —as the Buddha also taught.

Kishenpur, 3rd July, 1947, Guru Purnima [6]

After 8 a.m. I brought flowers, fruits and incense and did *dandavat pranam* [full length prostration] for the first time. She stroked my head. She asked me to do *japa* briefly as a blessing before each meal, repeating the *mantra* at least four times and preferably at least twelve times. She said: *"Think of the three highest chakras as corresponding to Atma, Paramatma, and Guru."* I asked about concentrating on the heart centre. She said: *"All right, do that also. That is 'Param Shiva'. Begin with the lower chakras and move upwards, always ending with the highest chakra and never with the lower. Pray to God to remove your anger and pain and whatever takes you away from the thought of Him."*

Kishenpur, 4th July, 1947

I feel a very great difference. I get immense *ananda* repeating the *mantra* and simply can't stop. I slept a little in the evening but then went on till about 2 a.m. while lying down, and I don't feel any more tired than usual this morning. It seems to have immense power. I wonder whether I should still have gone back to work if I had received this six months earlier. I wonder how I shall be able to live at school again. Yesterday I discussed with Dr. Pananlal a passage from *Sad Vani* where She says: *"If circumstances are against you in your sadhana, make the utmost effort to stick to it regardless, and these obstacles will change by themselves"*. I suppose that will be the case at Rajghat.

---

[6] The full moon in July on which the Guru is venerated throughout India.

XVI - Back at Rajghat

Rajghat, 8th July, 1947

Arrived on the 5th. The place here is all right, especially when there are no children, but the atmosphere is so different. At times I feel strange repeating the *mantra* here in J.K.'s domain, but it is a great help. So many people at school and so much talking makes me quite dizzy. I am remembering always how Mother told me to keep to myself. She is so right.

This morning when I was asked to take a class I got almost frantic. Why have I come back here? Yet, if one is not 100% certain that one is completely finished with this world, it is better to make sure first before taking the final step. This year I shall do exactly that.

I am wearing frocks since I came back, partly because of the heat, partly because I have not enough saris. But I would prefer to wear some sort of monastic garment that would set me off from the world. It is so important to remain hidden.

19th July, 1947

Having to reply to Walther's letter regarding Ashokananda's scepticism about Mother, I felt at first uncomfortable but it has strengthened my faith in Her. I had to think over the whole thing again. Of course one cannot really know anything, but some things are sure: Her influence has been utterly beneficial, She never gives me any instruction other than what comes from my own innermost being, and She is all LOVE. There is no motive to Her actions.

Also, I realize that if I do not look at J.K. as the "World Teacher" —that is, the only possible teacher— but see my contact with him as part of my *sadhana*, then the whole perspective changes and it becomes extremely valuable. Previously I was so prone to accept authority because of the *tamasic* element in my nature, but the years of doubt and utter uncertainty and rebellion caused by J.K. have given me added strength and courage to examine things before accepting them.

The other day I got angry for an imagined reason and it disturbed my meditation. Is it worth it, even if the reason be 'real'? Ultimately it seems to be always due to misunderstanding the motives of another. But whatever the reason may be, if it takes my mind off the centre, it is harmful. I cannot be concerned with both outer things and inner things at the same time, so that means leave off the outer.

I find teaching not irksome so far. I remain concentrated within and continually try to put my ego into the background. Thus the work does not assume such proportions as it used to. But I do notice that I am already being carried away by it; that my thought is prone to dwell on the time I play the piano for the children or on the library, which I like. I have to be careful to keep all this on the surface.

Lewis does not seem to have quite the beneficial influence he used to. This is partly due to my not worshipping him anymore. The deep conflict within him is awful and destructive. I also see how intense criticism however perceptive ruins the mind, particularly when it is cultivated and given excessive importance. There is a certain conceit, pride and feeling of superiority in constantly judging and keenly seeing the subtle defects of people and things. Mother said: *"You should not look at people's faults, but remain secluded and give all your time to what truly matters."* I am not obeying Her as much as I should and am getting tempted to talk to people unnecessarily. I have no true *satsang* here.

23rd July, 1947

Mother's advice about anger was another "egg of Columbus" [ingenious revelation]. Now whenever I am about to get angry I remember that it takes me away from the Supreme. However much justification there may be, it is not worth it. Sometimes I get angry all the same, but merely out of habit, and I see this now. She always hits the mark!

I now understand something of what a 'personal' God or 'Saviour' is, through having been with Her, and that it is a much easier and quicker way than *nirguna* meditation which is really impossible at this stage. I alsò see that it is really the same as meditation on the formless, only a sort of 'condensation' of the formless in order to have something for the mind to grasp which at the same time transforms it. Now I see what She means by saying *Bhagavan* (God with form) is like ice in water.

30th July, 1947

As I get more engrossed in school work I find my meditation becomes more shallow. The mind is definitely getting externalized. I find my meditation getting less and less successful with the result that I have less control over the children. If I am concentrated inside and let the work do itself, giving it only a minimum of attention, it is of much better quality. As I put myself more into the work it looses something.

Mother was due here on Monday and I spent a night in the Ashram. The atmosphere on the roof of the women's side is far superior to that on the men's —where there are no restrictions on people going in and out. But I find Rajghat really a very good place also.

Lewis gave D.P. a piece of his mind, calling him a liar and worse, and is leaving. I have a feeling that this will be much better for him.

10th August, 1947

Mother arrived on July 29th evening and I did not know till the 31st. I am staying at the ashram several nights a week. I had a big quarrel with Her over always being chased away from certain areas due to the "rules". She said: *"All right, I shall leave Benares and you stay comfortably at Rajghat"*. She pulled this out of my mind, because I had really thought to myself why go to the uncomfortable ashram when Rajghat is much nicer. Then She also said: *"Why do you take it that I am your enemy?"* That also was something that cured me. Whatever She does is best for me. Yesterday I got a sudden glimpse of Her sublimity. Her body is both a body and not a body, it is a most mysterious affair.

Yesterday I took Kamala Sahai to Her. She spoke with her and to her question: "How does one know that one has surrendered?" Mother replied: *"When you are hungry and you eat, you are satisfied and so you know that you have eaten; just so when you surrender, you are satisfied."* She then sang a little. Her voice is so utterly childlike and touches one to the core. There is no artifice at all in it. This cannot be a fraud. This cannot be imitated.

The Annapurna [1] *murti* from the Dacca Ashram has been transferred to this Ashram because Dacca will now become part of Pakistan. The *murti* has a very powerful vibration that attracts me greatly.

Lewis is really much better off in Alice's house and teaching at the Bengali Tola School.

Rajghat, 18th August, 1947

The other day when Mother spoke to me, She also said: *"None can be angry with me for long, no one can fight with me."* I said: "I shall go away." She said: *"You cannot leave me, the more you try, the more you will stick to me."* It is quite true.

Yesterday again I ran away. I got unwell and I always get impatient with the difficulties there due to my ambiguous situation. In the morning I told Her that I was going because when it rains there would be no place to sleep. She said: *"Now it is not raining, so why do you want to go. You can go when it rains."* So I stayed till the evening. But then also I should not have gone. When I came here I realized it. I understood something of why I must learn to keep all these rules. There is something about it that denies all personal comfort and convenience of the ego. It is always the love for comfort and my nice cosy room at Rajghat that makes me leave Her. It was again so this time, but I had the pretext that I was a nuisance to everyone there.

One day someone put *chandan* [sandalwood paste] on my forehead [2]. She said: *"You look very beautiful with this mark."* Without thinking anything at all, I said: "All right, if it is beautiful I shall put it on every morning." It is a mystery to me why I said this. She at once nailed me down and said: *"Good, buy yourself a stone and a piece of sandalwood, mix the powder with Ganga jal [Ganges water] and apply it every morning after your bath, for God —and with that it would be good to wear a 'mala' [rosary] of rudraksha around your neck."*

---

[1] A form of the Mother Goddess in the aspect of "She who feeds all"
[2] A traditional Hindu custom.

311

Then She corrected Herself and said: *"No, those who have a Krishna mantra should wear tulsi* [3] *or crystal. Rudraksha is for Shaktas."* [4]

But as it was now Her order, I at once got the sandalwood and stone from the bazaar and put the mark on my forehead the next morning, which was Independence Day [5] and Sri Aurobindo's birthday. I find it has a very good and concentrating effect. I was indeed amazed to find this, and I like it immensely. To carry out Her order is always beneficial.

The day before yesterday I came in the evening after all the functions were over. It was August 16th —my Mother's death day, and the day I stopped playing the organ at Huizen. She said: *"So you have come"* and gave me a very sweetly scented garland from around Her neck. Later in the evening She asked: *"Are you well?"* I said "Yes, why, don't I look it?" She: *"Yes, you look quite beautiful."* I wondered why She had asked about my health. During the night I got unwell.

John [6] is coming here. He has nowhere else to go. It seems he may get work at the College and take L.'s place. That would be splendid. Strange how things work. Lewis left about the day John started on his journey. L. is much better off, though he has no proper food arrangement. He will now write for the "Perspective".

28th August, 1947

Yesterday morning asked Mother what to do, as concentration is lessening and the mind turning more and more outward. She said this was due to *"bahar ke sang"* [outside associations] and that I should sit still in one place and not go here and there. She asked: *"How do you do the mantra? Do you do it with the Pranava [Om]?"* I said: "No." She said: *"Sit morning and evening for dhyan. First repeat the mantra 20 times going up and down the chakras from the heart to the top of head. Then mentally repeat the Pranava with every inhalation, and be absolutely still while exhaling. Sit still without*

---

[3] Beads from the wood of the sacred basil plant.

[4] Those who worship the Goddess. *Rudraksha* is a seed sacred to worshippers of Shiva also.

[5] After more than 150 years of British domination, India obtained full independence from Great Britain on this day.

[6] John Cordes —her old Theosophical mentor from Vienna. He must have been at least 70 years old at this time.

moving." When I said that I cannot sit completely still, She at once said: "*Then lie down*". She also said: "*Repeat the mantra all day while you work.*" She sat still, closed Her eyes and showed me how to breathe with the *Pranava* and also made me do it with Her. When I told Her that I do the *mantra* sometimes only superficially, She said: "*Even that is beneficial.*"

Rajghat, 30th August, 1947

Yesterday morning during study time I went upstairs and meditated for an hour with good concentration and great *ananda*. There is a marked improvement since I have started repeating the *Pranava* according to Her instructions.

The life of Sri Chaitanya [7] is something so fascinating, I must either get the *Chaitanya Charitamrit* in Hindi or else learn Bengali.

4th September, 1947

John arrived today. It suddenly struck me how necessary J.K. was for me. In what a fortress John lives, even though it has its own profundity! But what of it. When I saw all his things and my room stock full with books, pictures and what not, I truly felt for the first time like taking *sanyas*! If one does not do so, then society expects one to do this, that, and the other. Only the saffron robe protects one from all these demands. If I really seriously want to be a *sadhaka* I must not be disturbed by anything. Again this evening I felt Mother's presence very strongly and miss Her so badly. She has said though: "*Do everything as a service*", and "*Until you cannot work at all because you are totally absorbed in God, you should not drop it*".

10th September, 1947

Took John to meet Her. His presence was at first a great strain, but has since somehow become balanced. She was most extraordinary the day he came with me. I had more contact with Her than usually. She looked me straight in the eyes for a longer time than She has ever done before as far as I remember. I could not take my eyes and mind off Her and got deeply absorbed. John's positive attitude made it easier for me to go and stay with Her for

---

[7] 16th Century devotional saint regarded as an *avatar* of Krishna.

three nights and two days at *Janmasthami* [8]. Some people covered Her with garlands when John was there and She gave one to everyone present. When I thought no garlands were left and was not looking Her way, She threw me a piece of a garland with two large flowers on either end. I looked at it saying: "What is this?" Mother said: *"Mai aur tum"* [Me and you]. I could not hear Her properly and it had to be repeated three times to me. I thought it was particularly appropriate as I had been feeling somewhat oppressed by my past which had come up again due to John's visit. I suppose what is in one has to come to light in order to be unravelled. She was especially gracious to me that night.

Lewis told me that Sri Krishna Menon had told him that it had taken him 3 days to undo the ties with his (L.'s) disciples from his former birth when he was supposedly a Tantric. It shows what all these Beings in their infinite compassion take on themselves when accepting a disciple. Mother must have seen all that in my past which bound me to John and has now undone it. This is why surrender to a true Guru is so supremely important.

Being unwell I went back to bed and, instead of *dhyan,* fell asleep. This made me heavy and drowsy. I must not give in to it. John told me that yogis say sleep wears away the body. During *Janmasthami* in the ashram I got very little sleep and though very tired in the morning sat for *dhyan* and found the body very light and the *dhyan* very restful. It occurred to me that not being able to think properly due to sleepless nights might be an advantage in that it prevents the mind from being active in its accustomed way.

Didima[9] taught me a song in the small hours on *Janmasthami* night.

15th September, 1947

Mother left on the 13th. At the ashram while sitting near Her it suddenly occurred to me how the Divinity chooses to manifest Itself in a body like Hers and how it is utterly different from every ordinary body; how the *leela* of that body is enacted and the body made an appropriate vessel by all the *sadhanas* etc. Unfortunately I didn't have my diary to write this down then and now it is not so clear.

[8] The festival marking Krishna's Birthday.
[9] Anandamayee Ma's mother, who was greatly revered and later ook sannyas under the name Swami Muktananda Giri.

When She left She said: "*Anand raho*" [Be blissful]. I said: "How can I be in *ananda* when You are away?" She pressed my hand and said: "*Jap, dhyan karo, anand raho*" [Do *japa* and *dhyan* and be happy].

25ᵗʰ September, 1947

Saw Lewis. It is always a joy to see him. He is so utterly pure, like spring water, transparent and untouched by worldliness. He will probably have to leave Benares soon.

27ᵗʰ September, 1947

Mother came suddenly the day before yesterday. As if by miracle I was informed and got a bus to go to the ashram in the evening and a car back here in the morning. Again saw Her off in the afternoon at Ramnagar. Her short stay however meant much to me. I somehow realized that my work is irksome because it is 'I' who do it. The moment I drop that idea and leave everything to Him there is no friction. What a joy it was to see Her again!

29ᵗʰ September, 1947

Now that John is leaving, I have to be nice to him. I may never see him again and somehow feel that by looking after him I may be able to pay whatever debt I have to my own father, as John has been like a spiritual father to me.

Rajghat, 9ᵗʰ October, 1947

Mother arrived on the 3ʳᵈ night. I spent the weekend at the ashram.

J.K. must have arrived in India. I do not feel a great urge to see him as I did even last year. I would not go to Madras but if he comes here then of course it is different. I do not think he can or will upset me now. She seems completely to have taken his place.

14ᵗʰ October, 1947

Mother left yesterday for Calcutta. By way of farewell She said: "*Do dhyan.*" I said: "I can't." She insisted.

Yesterday morning there was a discussion. A man of 74 said he wanted to go into *samadhi*. She said: "*Then you must be at your*

315

sadhana for 24 hours a day. Doing just a little bit won't get you there.
At your age you should be doing dhyan and japa for 12 hours daily.
Those over 50 should practice for 9 hours, below for 6 hours a day
and those who have jobs for at least 3 hours —nothing less than that.
In addition to the formal sitting, meditation should be done at all
times, during meals, when walking, bathing, dressing etc."

In parting when I said: "Now I must go!", She said: "*No, you*
can't. Even if you try to leave me you can't." At Sarnath She told me
again: "*You cannot leave me.*" When I said that I had already run
away several times, She said: "*That is not running away; with tears*
in your eyes, your mind was with me." Someone asked: "Is a Guru
necessary?" She said: "*The Guru is always with you. When the ne-*
cessity arises 'Prakash ho jaega' [Light will come]. *You need not do*
anything. You only need to concentrate on God in whichever form you
please, but do it all the 24 hours."

I brought Lewis back here to Rajghat as he was ill and had no
one to do anything for him. But now I feel such a relief to have
him. I am the winner not he. For the bit of food he gets from me, I
get infinitely more. The atmosphere is quite changed now and I
have a room to myself.

16th October, 1947

Today it occurred to me that the outer form meditation takes,
like concentrating on a *mantra* etc., is only purely formal. The great
thing is to realize that meditation means returning to oneself, going Home so-to-say, whereas involvement in anything else is simply a forgetting of one's true purpose. It is imperative to contemplate this fact all the time. All meditation is in some way simply
"Who am I?" If one is serious about this, how can one ever get
tired or bored. But how stupid to indulge in physical enjoyment
and well-being, in fact in anything that takes one away from this
intense search. *Satsang* is evidently a great help.

23rd October, 1947

John left yesterday. I realize that there is nothing to justify
my identifying myself with the Blanca who at 16 or 18 was so
fascinated by him. I cannot possibly regard that girl as myself.
What is individuality? What is it that binds the various experi-

ences together? Just the body? But this also is not the same. Every atom must have changed since then. But there is a pattern working itself out which maintains a certain form. If I cannot identify myself with the Blanca of years ago, it follows that what I appear to be now is equally temporary and not at all the essence. But then what remains?

I asked L. He says: "Of course the individual is purely an illusion. It ceases to exist when one realizes that there is no continuity. It is like the Buddhist example of the burning stick that when rotated at great speed produces a circle of light which really does not exist, but we can't perceive its non-existence unless the movement is stopped."

Today a letter came from Walter asking whether one's individual judgement should ever be abandoned. I replied that once one has found a Guru one must do just that. After all, what is individual judgement but a facet of the ego and thus based on limitation, fear and ignorance. A Guru that is 'another' and therefore an authority is not a Guru. The Guru is my true self actually and not a separate person or individual. The Guru is all. He is myself perfected, the whole. He knows at every moment my past and future, where I (as ego) only see a tiny fragment.

In my meditation I feel the most important thing is to keep my thought on Mother constantly, to become utterly immersed in Her. If I remain focused on the thought of <u>Her</u> will, not mine, and keep open to that, what else do I need?

I find that repeating the *mantra* at all times does have a great effect. Suddenly I get an illumination like the one about the illusion of continuity. All this makes me understand J. K. better.

Reading Sanjiv Rao's [10] autobiography I realize how much I have changed in this year of leave. When I went with Mother at first I had so many problems troubling me; for instance, how to reconcile Her instructions with J. K.'s teaching. Now this is no problem for me at all. I trust Her implicitly and She will lead me there.

Whether Theosophical Masters and disciples exist or not is not of the slightest interest to me. She exists and will lead me to Enlightenment. Nothing else is relevant. What is the use of a Mas-

---

10 Her close friend who was the founder of the Rajghat School.

ter who lives far away? [11] There can be no justification for a Guru who is totally inaccessible or in some other realm. One must have direct contact with the Guru. In any case he is always present in the heart.

From Sanjiv Rao's book I see how Providence arranged the acquisition of Rajghat. But what has it really become?

Lewis is a tremendous help. He at once makes my mind more keen and alert. The other day I observed his face closely. The right half is intensely beautiful, the left seems hard and cold and non-human, rather like a snake or lizard. He is quite out of the ordinary.

I now feel that it was very worthwhile having John here. It has given me a much clearer view of things just when J.K. is due, and now that it is over I've forgotten the trouble and inconvenience. J.K. was quite right when he said to John years ago regarding his continued involvement in Theosophy: "You are not doing my work". J.K.'s work points straight to the highest and rightly rejects preoccupation with organizational matters and what not.

Rajghat, 26th October, 1947

At the Chinese temple at Sarnath the Buddha image is a mysteriously attractive focus for concentration. Looking at it the mind gets absorbed. While meditating before it I was watching the thoughts floating on the surface of the mind, but there was deep concentration going on underneath. Unfortunately I had to leave too soon. Must go there again and try this experiment. Day and night at Sarnath most beneficial. I can concentrate more easily there.

Returning I found the Hakinsonsins in L's old room. One cannot escape one's fate. I was waiting for John to leave so as to be able to do my 3 hours of *dhyan* regularly. One has to do it in spite of circumstances.

Read an old "Star Bulletin". How childish all the stuff about the World Teacher. Lewis seems to have taken me right out of this stupidity. The Theosophical world has become utterly remote to me.

---

[11] The Theosophical Masters were thought to live in the Himalayas and were rarely, if ever, seen by their disciples.

Kitty's letter to John shows that she has exactly the reverse of my experience with old friends: While I cannot at all identify myself with the girl that was friendly with John, she feels as of old with Fritz and Hugh.

Evening *dhyan*. Was able visualize the Buddha image of the Chinese Temple amazingly well for about half hour, then concentration slackened. I remember that when Mataji asked me 2 years ago at Vindhyachal whom I would like to worship, I very nearly mentioned the Buddha but somehow suppressed it.

This present attraction to the Buddha may be connected with J. K.'s arrival in India.

27ᵗʰ October 1947

I see why Mother told me repeatedly to keep a diary about meditation. This will discipline the *sadhana* and prevent one from dreaming.

I must write in this diary immediately after each time I sit, so that I see what actually happens and whether there is any progress. She told me to keep a diary like a miser keeps a record of his money.

Dharma, so often falsely and inaccurately translated as 'religion', seems to be more correctly the particular method or way by which each one finds his own liberation.

During the day I become definitely affected by the people around me, who believe that the illusory outer world with which they are so preoccupied is the only thing that matters. Trying now to be more secluded with the front windows shut now that the weather is cooler.

There are now Hakinson's two noisy babies next door. One really has no control over circumstances.

31ˢᵗ October, 1947

L. is on my mind. He is penniless and it makes me miserable to know he is starving. It disturbs my meditation. I have decided to help him more substantially, though I have no money myself. Suddha Tilak says from L.'s horoscope that by 15ᵗʰ November there will be a radical change for the better. Reading *The Mystics of Islam* by R.A. Nicholson. Excellent book. The Sufis attract me greatly.

1ˢᵗ November, 1947

In the afternoon I noticed my mind getting steady and going into a deeper level as was the case also when I did *japa* while stitching. At 6 p.m. I meditated on Mother's picture and found this a very great help. Could sit without moving for quite some time. Got very calm and collected though the surface mind kept wandering, but I felt a strong pull to a deeper level.

At midday a note came from Daniélou asking me to play the piano accompaniment for a visiting Italian singer. I am so unconscious that I did not refuse. Now it strikes me that I should have been more clear. Have I not left music for good and should I not shun worldly company? Have I time to waste on such adventures. I accepted mostly perhaps because I have been feeling bored and arid lately and such a 'change' may help.

3ʳᵈ November, 1947

It was right after all that I did not refuse Daniélou's offer. I met Monod Herzen of Pondicherry there and managed to introduce him to L., who was very glad to meet him. The concert was quite enjoyable. I cannot lead a totally contemplative life at present.

Today Mulk Raj Anand [12] gave a talk at school and said that accumulated hate, passion etc. can work itself out through drawing and painting. It struck me that perhaps I have to work physically because of all the *vasanas* that are still in me.

Lewis' attitude of not bothering about money and going ahead with his interests has proved quite effective. His asking Tilak to do his horoscope made me understand much about him and I feel more than ever like helping him. When he has solved all his difficulties and gotten rid of his ego he will publish much and his books will be of lasting value they say. How noble that he will not now be forced to prostitute his gift by writing for money. I again feel very great affection for him. It always increases when Mother isn't here. Suddha T. says from his horoscope that a lady with large eyes will always look after him. I feel as if he were my own child and it gives me intense satisfaction to care for him. Now I literally seem to keep him alive. He hasn't a penny.

---

[12] One of modern India's most renowned novelists.

This evening after the Italian's concert an expert Indian classical singer sang some of Mirabai's [13] *bhajan's*. For the first time in my life I realized that Indian music means more to me now than European! This signifies a definite change. Mother has made me really Indian.

Today when teaching it suddenly struck me how receptive to learning the children are when I am able to communicate love to them. But what I've written here is in no way as profound as was the insight when it occurred. It was as though I was on a plane beyond the ordinary mind which cannot be expressed in words.

The real purpose of my meditation is to become ever more in tune with Mother. At the same time the outer work seems necessary. It helps to untie knots and bring certain things within me to the surface. Both things are necessary for me at present.

4th November, 1947

This morning felt completely out of sorts. Perhaps it was due to having created discord at the faculty meeting by my objection to calling our school "Theosophical College". All day I felt lonely and in a state of dissatisfaction that I have not known for sometime. Sitting in meditation, after a few minutes I suddenly noticed my breath changing and with that the calm and collectedness returned. I noticed first intense joy and well-being, then a sate of calm. I wonder whether the feeling of loneliness is not chiefly due to loosing touch with some layer in myself that lies beyond the ordinary mind and that one contacts when sitting for *dhyan*.

6th November, 1947

This evening there was a certain concentration and when the breath changed there was complete peace and the absence of desire.

7th November, 1947

Watching the children move and shout aimlessly, it occurred to me that their natural restlessness is a mirror of any ordinary mind.

---

[13] Mirabai was an 16th Century Rajput princess who was a great devotee of Krishna and composed many devotional songs to him which are among the classics of Indian Literature.

8ᵗʰ November, 1947

P.K. Rajagopalan, L's friend, impressed me quite deeply. He has a presence of extreme calm and detachment, as one who is in constant meditation. He says J.K.'s way is very direct and also that one must be a witness and see oneself as a corpse. He says if you try to escape an experience it only comes again with double the force. It gets strength from your resistance. He is the manager of a business and works 9 hours a day. His staff of 42 members is thoroughly inefficient, so he has to see to everyone's work; but he has not lost his temper for 3 years and takes the work as a *sadhana* in how to develop detachment. When he comes home in the evening he keeps still for 5 minutes and has his bath. After that he feels as fresh as if after a good's night sleep.

His father recently died and he has come to Benares to perform the last rites. He travelled here 3ʳᵈ class from Bombay and upon arriving went directly to put his father's ashes into the Ganges, then to the temple after taking the ritual bath in the Ganges. He then came to Rajghat after walking all over Benares. L looked fagged and worn out when they got here at about 6 p.m., but P.K.R. is calm and fresh as if he had lived here all his life. Lewis must have been right when he said that his friend is very near Realization. This is real renunciation.

This kind of detached attitude to work is exactly what I have to learn. I think my restlessness is partly due to liver trouble. *Satsang* means much to me. Sitting and talking to P.K. Rajagopalan this evening I sensed that atmosphere of detachment and awareness which makes so much difference to me.

9ᵗʰ November, 1947

Lewis held forth on the protestant reaction J.K. calls out in people because they listen to <u>his</u> words only, whereas he is the flower of a whole civilization. They put him in a sort of vacuum, as if nothing of the sort had ever been said before. This is particularly true for most Westerners who in any case have very little sense of the elaborate depth and structure of Indian culture and philosophy. But then J.K. virtually forces people to do this by his many 'don'ts' and his insistence on denying all authority (other than his own).

322

Lewis said how perfect Mother is, how free, and how She does not speak but speaks one's Self, and this awakens one's innermost spiritual being. Whereas J.K. asks people to go up to the roof without a ladder. His great seriousness and the insistence on talking seems an impurity —a lower level of realization.

All this was a Godsend to me. J. K. in India —even far away in Madras— has a very disturbing effect on me.

13th November, 1947, Diwali

Yesterday Gordon sent Sri Krishna Menon's book. In the evening P.K.R. came with Lewis and both were very very delighted to see it. They slept here and P.K.R. left early the next morning. Last night being Kali Puja [14], I hardly slept but did not feel at all sleepy this morning. This is evidently a favourable constellation for me. God knows where I was in the night.

Through reading in Sri K.M.'s book that *Atma* is entirely apart from body and mind, I suddenly saw that even when there is neither body nor mind, the 'I am' is still there, so why be afraid to leave these impediments behind.

17th November, 1947

Mother came on the 15th early morning. I had already come to the Ashram the night before. I was with Her for two full days and nights till 10.30 this morning. I feel permeated by Her. Cannot get enough of Her face. She is enchanting from every angle.

But even so meditation is not always easy. I see now why She encourages activities like *kirtan*, *puja* etc., so as to prevent people from falling asleep. Stillness must be intense inner activity, or else it is simply sleep or death. As Sri K.M. says: "When objective awareness disappears it is not nothingness that remains, but Consciousness."

18th November, 1947

I feel intensely drawn to Her. When I concentrate on Her there is so much *ananda* that I can go on and on. Whatever She has told me to do has particular value due to Her command, as well as because of what it is in itself. Moreover doing it in this spirit keeps

---

[14] The night on which the annual festival of the Goddess Kali takes place.

323

me perpetually in Her Presence. The mind takes the shape of its thoughts. So what more do you want.

20th November, 1947

Mother left for Bombay this morning. The other day I was holding Her shawl for Her, but just as She went out on the terrrace, Bhaskerao came and I asked him why he had not brought Malati etc. When I went back to Her She took the wrap from me and said: "*Are you going to give it to me or will you wear it yourself?*" I replied: "I am so bad. I talked to someone and forgot you". I must not do that. When I am about Her work, I must be completely focused.

24th November, 1947

"*If you are aware of the immensity of being, then there is silence; its very intensity brings tranquility.*" (J.K., 1945 Talks). This is what Mother's Presence does and this is what should happen in meditation. The thought of *Om* should transport one into that immensity.

Last night I dreamt of Kitty. We were discussing the fact that there was no one to show the way to the Real. I wanted to say I had found Anandamayee, then suppressed it, thinking after all I cannot say that as I have not really gotten 'there' yet.

29th November, 1947

Spent yesterday at the Ashram. It occurred to me that I have falsely interpreted Her order to keep to myself when my work is over to mean to do as little work as possible. This question of learning how to work without feeling that I am the doer and without wanting to achieve anything for myself is urgent.

I am very interested in learning Bengali these days.

Lewis came on the 27th and stayed the night. I got quite annoyed that he uses the money John sent so carelessly. As a matter of fact it is nearly finished. Girinda says he has no sense of the world because he is a *sadhu*.

Today Malati sent some newspaper accounts of J.K.'s Talks in Madras. I felt again very fascinated. Somehow I don't feel troubled because I remember Mother saying: "*The more you try to leave me, the more you will stick to me*". So I am quite safe there. I should really love to give J.K. another chance — if he comes. I shall not go to Madras though.

7ᵗʰ December, 1947

Yesterday went to give Lewis 20 rupees which P.K.R. had sent and fell and hurt my knee on the way. Then I lost both my big and small leather bags with umpteen things on the way back. It is quite troublesome to have no address book, sunglasses etc., but it is good to have such an experience to get rid of attachment. I feel so dissatisfied and disgusted and I am getting white hair, so how much time is there left? And what use is it to continually move in this circle of ignorance?

But the root of it all is my mind dwelling on what J.K. says and wondering whether the practice of *mantra* repetition is any use after all. He says it dulls the mind, Mother says it purifies it. From my own experience though I know that I have greatly changed and have been happy due to Her contact these two and a half years. And this conscious repetition of the *mantra* does make the mind more alert and aware. So in this he is definitely wrong. I wish J.K. would come here so I could finally resolve this conflict and surge ahead. I am somewhat out of touch with Mother, but on the other hand I often feel that I am safely in Her arms. She said: *"Wherever you go, you are mine."*

9ᵗʰ December, 1947

I remembered that She told me: *"If thoughts come into your mind when trying to concentrate, think that they are also He."* So this is not 'exclusive' concentration as J.K. calls it. After all, even if the surface mind keeps flitting about, something seems to grow underneath as a result of regular practice and perhaps one day when it is strong enough it will break through all this upper scum.

12ᵗʰ December, 1947

This morning during meditation, towards the end of the hour, I suddenly realized that I got somewhere where the mind neither exists or matters. This is the object of the practice — to get beyond the chattering mind. On its own level the mind can only wander, but somehow one arrives at a deeper level. I at once understood why Mother says: *"Sit as long as you possibly can."* The body that cannot sit still for a long time is an obstruction —thus the need to establish the habit of sitting. I decided to sit for 2 hours in the evening. There seems to be something inside that grows in spite and regardless of the outer life. All one has to do is to get in touch with it more and more and that is why one has to sit in meditation. Very likely that is why I am so sensitive to noise, because something in me wants to turn inside and listen to the inner sound.

19th December, 1947

Last night I dreamt of Mother. She was dissatisfied with me and told me to use the long quiet nights for *sadhana* instead of sleeping so much.

22nd December, 1947

The other day Mrs. Hakinson told me how it was the vagabond in her husband that had attracted her but how by marrying and having the responsibility of keeping a family this side of him vanished more and more. She said that one day she will burn everything and be free again. I felt sympathetic. How one must not judge people. There is a tragedy in everyone.

24th December, 1947

Reading more of J.K.'s recent Talks in Madras I feel that I don't want to listen to him. It would be more or less useless to me and probably even disturbing. I feel there is something lacking in him. He does not give the Whole, but stresses only one aspect, very likely as a reaction to present day conditions, but it is misleading. He takes you some distance and then leaves you running on empty without any support. After all, it is his own intensity and experience that brings what he says across and when he is gone it gradually wears off and you go back virtually to your former state of mind, prompted and influenced by your surroundings which are all against you.

Mother seems to have a much greater sense of reality, of what actually works, when She urges people to keep to their traditional *dharmic* prescription. India is threatening to become a cheap imitation of Western 'civilization', which in its contemporary materialistic manifestation is not civilization at all because it is born only out of the superficial, not out of the depth of the profound realization of the *Rishis*, as is Indian culture. It is here that the basis for a new culture must be found.

Education these days is all Western except the one given by a true Guru to his disciple. It is not true as J.K. says that this is based on authority. It only seems so, but it is really based on overwhelming love and complete surrender which effects the annihilation of the ego with its inherent limitation and ignorance.

It is not merely an emotional satisfaction that binds the disciple to the Guru. This most intimate love, which is really the revelation of one's own innermost Self, absorbs your mind and you become That. Therefore the Guru is a vehicle that brings you up more and more to His level and then your entire perspective changes —you become deconditioned—free.

Anyway if one finds such a great Being that calls out one's love, one would never bother with what J.K. says and perhaps that is why he never gets confronted with such a situation, because having found such a One, why would one ever bother to discuss with him.

Malati wants to go to Bombay to hear J.K. But her position is different. She does not listen dogmatically to his words, but takes what is meant for her and there is a clarity in him that will probably influence her in the right manner. She, for instance, takes any amount of trouble over Ravi's Thread Ceremony [15] or bows to Mother profusely etc. etc. and does not care that J.K. scoffs at all this. In this she is like most Indians whose consciousness is naturally in their timeless culture and who thus easily absorb all surface contradictions. Westerners are incapable of this. She does, as Mother said to her, get her honey from many flowers like the bee.

Bhadaini Ashram, 29th December, 1947

Saw Mother off till Mugalsarai. Talked to Her yesterday. She said: *"If you get sleepy, meditate with open eyes. Fix your gaze on one point. If you feel like sleeping, do so for a while and then try again. If things come into your mind, think that they are also 'He'. In no case*

---

[15] The traditional Hindu rite of giving a Brahmin boy the sacred thread to wear which confirms him as one of the 'twice born'.

give up your practice. If you can't get satsang, read good books. The dryness comes from the outer work you are doing." As to my question regarding what happens to the *vasanas* and *samskaras* etc., She said they vanish through *dhyan*.

To Malati She said: "*Your going to Krishnamurti will not estrange you from me. If you wish to go because you think that it will clear your mind, then attend those discussions, but along with it continue your individual practice.*"

Bhadaini Ashram, 30th December, 1947

I noticed that it makes a difference to be absolutely quiet, no movement except the breath and heartbeat. I got into a state of stillness this morning so that I did not feel inclined to talk afterwards. I see how painful noise and people are when one is in this kind of state. Here in the ashram it is much easier to go within due to the spiritual atmosphere. This evening Lewis came and we talked. I asked him about Coomaraswamy's statement that reincarnation does not really exist. He used the same simile as Mother did yesterday: The one sun reflects infinite suns in the waves of the water. As long as one considers this reflection as real it continues as such. So one must take one's gaze entirely away from the reflected suns in the water and look up to see the true sun. That is what I suppose happens through meditation: the water gets still and one perceives only one sun.

Rajghat, 4th January, 1948

I feel that I am just marking time as long as I am here. But I suppose I have to work off this *karma*. So the only thing to do is to learn to work impersonally, "dedicated" as Mother puts it; to do everything as a service to the Divine.

This evening's meditation again put me right a good deal. J.K. says: "You believe in God, because you are told there is God". This is not true. I cannot conceive that there is not an ultimate cause.

15th January, 1948

Yesterday Mother came to the ashram and stayed for the night. I had a dreadful time. I told Her, as She asked, that I am not well and that evidently brought out the whole problem that is still in me. I cannot get on with my *sadhana,* because I have doubts in my mind about Her! When I read J.K. I get attracted and I feel that in many ways he is right. For instance, what have I to do with all these *pujas* and *kirtans?* On the other hand the supreme thing is really <u>She</u>: that She is guiding me and that Her Love is moulding me, no matter what result I feel my meditation has. Surely I can be quite safe in her arms.

After She had left I felt thoroughly upset and thought to myself that when I open *Sad Vani* [16] I shall find the solution. I read the first bit which ends with: *"When the goal is to become absorbed in Truth, then whatever is necessary will come of its own."*

I feel this is really the case. I need not initiate any thing. For instance, when I told Dr. Pannanlal yesterday that Kussum is always rude to me, he said: "This is Mother testing you. She told me so". This made me realize that if I take everything that happens to me as sent by Her, I will have to react by making the best of it.

16th January, 1948

The essential thing in the relationship with a Guru is <u>obedience</u>. This is the real *sadhana.* Whether what the Guru asks has any result or not makes no difference at all. The whole object is to annihilate one's own ego entirely. One has nothing to do but to surrender. The Guru does everything and is responsible for everything. <u>Surrender is more than obedience</u>. There can be no personal judgement. One has to love completely and loose oneself in that love.

21st January, 1948

Reading *Milarepa* [17] moves me to tears. It makes a lot of difference to me to read the lives of saints. I must continue to do so.

I feel that having found Mother I must not initiate action, so there would be no point in my trying to see J.K. If I am to see him it will happen of its own accord and I shan't be able to avoid it. I now feel quite indifferent towards this.

---

[16] The little book of Ma's sayings.

[17] Great medieval Tibetan yogi whose biography and songs are classics of world religious literature.

Allahabad, Kumbha Mela [18], 1st February, 1947

Arrived here yesterday. Left just after Mahatma Gandhi was assassinated. No one allowed me in their tent so I slept in Mother's.

Dreamt that Mother told me that I must cook rice and dal daily and offer it to God. Then my sister [18] came with some questions which she asked me to ask Ma but I got no chance to do so. There was a very tall house. Someone was letting down huge artificial birds from the top story. They moved so beautifully, by mechanical means, that I was not sure whether they were real or not.

The night before I came to the *mela* I dreamt that it was pouring hard and I could not reach there. It was a muddled disagreeable dream. As it turned out I was nearly prevented from going because of Gandhi's death and the ensuing chaos.

I feel very dissatisfied and out of sorts. I haven't really surrendered. I feel sceptical about *kirtan* and *japa* etc. and I often forget my commitment to obey Her implicitly. My liver being out of order also badly influences my mind.

Yesterday Dr. Pananlal asked Her whether if someone stayed with Her and just enjoyed himself without any deeper spiritual interest, if this was a burden to Her. She said: *"Yes, however if it is my 'keyal', such a person could come to know the nature of pleasure — that although of itself it has no inherent reality, yet it also can be seen as one of God's many forms.*

* * *

Anandamayi Ma could take any human sentiment — be it noble or base — and transmute it into a profound learning experience according to the temperament of the individual with whom she was dealing. This did not come across in the form of verbal didactics but rather through a direct experience. Whether an individual desires what is good or bad, it still remains within the

---

[18] A huge religious festival attracting millions which is held every twelve years in accordance with a specific astrological conjunction. An enormous tent city is erected at the convergence of three rivers — the Ganges, the Jamuna, and the mystic Saraswati (no longer visible)— near the city of Allahabad to accommodate the literally millions of pilgrims and thousands of Mahatmas and sadhus who consider it their duty to preside over this auspicious event.

[19] Her sister died when she was seventeen.

nature of duality —of ego. Both, from the highest sense, are equally false. As a teacher, Anandamayee Ma was able to experientially break down the fundamentally dualistic nature of desire, giving the individual a direct experience of the unwavering inner Truth beyond the relativity of subject-object awareness. Only the very greatest spiritual masters can teach in this way.

It is significant that she says here: "If it is my kheyal". 'Kheyal' is a key term which was the basis of her doing or not doing something. Although difficult to define, it signified a spontaneous upsurge of Divine Will from within her. As Anandamayee Ma had no personal will in the egoistic sense and no personal desire for anything whatsoever, she said that her actions were determined by her 'kheyal'.

* * *

She went on to say that a *sadhaka* should do only that which facilitates his *sadhana*.

Rajghat, 4th February, 1948

Returned this morning from the Kumbha Mela. Before leaving at 3.30 a.m. I sat for a while in the *akhand kirtan* [24 hour devotional singing]. I realized how much better nights are than days for this. In the train suddenly I got a glimpse of what *kirtan* does while reading the 11th chapter of the *Gita*. One becomes immersed in the immensity of the Divine and the world of the sense impressions fades.

How changed I am even after 4 days with Her. It is quite a different world. But I also see that as I get immersed in that world I become unfit for the work I am doing here. She foretold this in my first meeting with Her at Sarnath.

How difficult it is to leave Her. I sat in Her tent last night till 12.40 a.m.

I told Her about my dream and She said: *"Cook rice and dal once and offer it. Clean the place where you put the thali* [20] *and imagine God partaking of the food. Then eat the 'prasad'.* [21] *And every day whatever food you get, even what you have not cooked yourself, offer it thus".*

---

[20] A metal plate.

[21] Prasad is food that has been offered to God and thus blessed by Him.

She also said in response to my having said that I had told Kussum he would be a *bhogi* [22] in his next life for having teased me, that if one strikes out when someone does one wrong it comes back on oneself. *"If you have to be angry, be angry with me. So the root of anger will go soon"*. This is what She does. She draws out people's negativity and takes it on Herself and eats it up. That is why people get so selfish and negative in Her presence sometimes. Her transforming intensity pulls the repressed negativity out of them.

7ᵗʰ February, 1948

Krishni returned. She looks really clear. It seems to me that J.K. must really be one of the Great Ones after all, a Guru par excellence. She says once you ask a question, he won't let go until you have seen. You have to drop everything and remain in confusion until then, suddenly, there is light.

I found that I could meditate singularly well after having spoken with Krishni. I was thinking that I haven't really bound myself to anything, but I can't let go of Mother. I see that all desire and attachment has concentrated itself on Her. That is Her method, Her way of effecting transformation. Why need I worry about this? If I meet J.K., it will be Her doing. To surrender to 'what is' means to take everything as a manifestation of the Divine and therefore not to judge and criticise anything.

8ᵗʰ February, 1948

Meditation definitely better in spite of menses. Mother attracts all the undesirable qualities in people to Herself, so as to destroy them. I feel that She is much above J.K. He has his own way no doubt, but She is far beyond that.

Bhadaini Ashram, 12ᵗʰ February, 1948

Yesterday Malati spoke with Mother who told her to try and remain in a state of meditative awareness all day long. That somehow gave me light. I see now that the repetition of the Name is only a means that leads to that awareness of stillness at all times, in which the breath remains altered as in meditation. This morn-

---

[22] Someone who lives only for sense pleasures (as opposed to a yogi); not exactly a compliment when applied to a fellow-seeker.

ing I had quite a successful meditation outside Mother's room. Towards the end it was as if I was being consumed by Her and vanished inside Her.

This morning some secondary school girls came and asked Her questions: "People say that God causes everything that happens. Why then is there evil?" She: *"You don't know that. You are only repeating what you have heard. When you know who God is and who you are, then you will know. For him who knows, evil doing is impossible. Find out for yourself"*.

Question: "If people become indifferent to the world, how will the world continue?" She: *"Just see whether it continues or not. Your job is to become established in Truth awareness, then you will know how God looks after his creatures"*.

Question: "God has created this world for us so why should we not enjoy it?" She: *"Oh, so he has created it for you? Your father and mother have made a home for you and given whatever else you may need. Without them would you be able to enjoy any of these things? Likewise find out who it is that made the world, only then will you know how to truly enjoy it. As long as you identify with the world there can be no lasting happiness. 'Duniya' [world] means 'do' [two] Where there are two there will be conflict and opposition. When you realize wholeness —the One without another— only then can there be true happiness. Then there is no coming and going and therefore no birth and death. If you merely strive to enjoy the world, your desire — which can never be fully satisfied— will make you come back again and again to birth with its inevitable suffering."*

Question: "What happens after death?" She: *"After death you reap the fruits of what you have sown during life. If you have studied well, you get a first class etc., if not, you fail. So it is also after death."*

Question: "Is there such a thing as heaven and hell?" She: *"Just as you have your own place in this world so there will be a place according to your merit after death, and then whatever remaining desire you have will bring you back to this world again. But if you leave everything to God, you will go straight to Him"*.

Then She said: *"Do something to get near God. Some people like prayer, some like japa and some like to enquire: Who is He? Who made the world? Whatever you like best, do that. Fix a time every day and if you have no time, then take it away from your sleep. But if you should*

333

miss one day, do double the next. Do it secretly, otherwise people may laugh and dissuade you from it. But if you have courage, don't bother about others and if people laugh, laugh with them".

I asked Her about my *sadhana*. I said that meditation on *Om* [pranava] produces great intensity but then I shan't want to continue working. She said: *"That is very good. From the pranava you will get illumination of the Atma. Om and Atma are closely connected."*

Then I asked Her about what we had discussed previously concerning the offering of food before eating: "To which form of God should it be offered?" She: *"Whatever form comes into your mind, or no form; it makes no difference"*.

The *sadhu* at Tiruvannamalai who attracted me so much, also told me to think of *Om* eternally.

Rajghat 16ᵗʰ February, 1948

These days I am able to observe my mind almost effortlessly. I told Mother that the *mantra* goes on by itself automatically now.

18ᵗʰ February, 1948

Dream: I am at a gathering I believe at Kitty's house. All the people there are European, a great crowd. I sit down on the carpet as do the others. I feel that I should not mix with such a crowd. They have all come to decide on something that has to be done regarding the refugee problem. [23] They have to be given rooms also. The back part of the house, which is rather nicer with a view onto a garden, is decided on. We sit in a sort of a hall ante-room. Kitty says the cupboards will have to be brought here as they are black and match with the rest of the furniture. I say there is very much work to be done, but it can be done if it is organized well. When the meeting is over we get into a sort of a *tonga* [horse drawn cart]. Suddenly Kitty hears banging in her room and says to me: "Jump out and shut my window". I obey and go to her room but cannot at once find the window which is rather hidden. Some cupboard doors are open too. I shut those and then see the window. This done I go outside, but there is no sign of the *tonga*.

---

[23] After the partition of India in 1947, it was flooded with refugees from Pakistan and what is now Bangladesh.

I run down the street (which looks like it is in Vienna) but can't catch up. Finally I get to Zolkergasse. There I see a rickshaw but I say to myself that as it is near I shall walk to Kandeg. The way leads over rocky places uphill. A gentleman helps me up. He begins talking to me. He seems a nice, clean and intelligent looking European. Finally he says: "Come in here" and takes me into a house. We sit down in a large room with all sorts of furniture and also a small harmonium and a 'Bastle' [wicker] table. I say: "So you are a musician". He says: "Well, we have found each other, so we must have need of each other. Why part"? I suspect His motives and look at him reproachfully. But he says: "I don't mean anything like that". After sitting there for a while I see the clock shows 9:30 or so. A couple comes to visit. I take the opportunity to go. He sees me out and I expect he will ask when he can see me again, but he does not. On the road I see a car and other vehicles. I shout for a cycle rickshaw. It comes. I ask him to take me to Kandly and then I woke up.

19th February, 1948

Last night I dreamt that Dr. P. gave me a huge cake. We were in a very large room. He locked it from the inside and put the key into his pocket and said: "Alone at last". I made a terrific fuss and said "I shall shout and make a scandal. I shall jump out of the window if you don't open the door at once." He was very reluctant but finally he opened the door and left. Then a lady brought me another cake. I had not eaten since morning and it was now evening, but did not feel hungry. However, I finally ate. I wanted to tell her about Dr. P., but she said "I was in the next room and heard every word."

25th February, 1948

Going out and missing *dhyan* is very bad for me. Saw the film "Mira" at the cinema yesterday. It was a mistake in spite of the spiritual subject matter.

This evening instead of looking at Her picture, I visualized Her within. The result was *ananda*. She is One, She is All.

8th March, 1948

I am quite dried out. I believe I miss music. Should I begin playing again?

I have been disobedient to Mother. She has told me to write into my diary daily, but I do it so rarely.

Eckhart, who I'm presently reading, is always so wonderful.

14th March, 1948

Since two or three days marked improvement in *dhyan*. I seem to get contact with something that is more 'myself' than what I have contacted so far. Even if I get at it for only a moment it fills me with intense happiness and takes away all craving for anything else. Have been reading the Maharshi's talks. I tried His *Aham-Aham* (I-I) —the objectless awareness of 'I' to the exclusion of all else— which was effective. I am also sitting 3 times daily now, so that the intervals are shorter.

But going to Sohasini's party was a bad idea. It is not worth it. I must be careful not to get caught in social obligations.

This afternoon on looking at a Swiss magazine "Friedeuns Worte" I noticed how it interfered with the quality of awareness I am striving to maintain. It is really not right for me to touch these things. One can do only one thing at a time.

21st March, 1948

Under some pretext or other I am not keeping up with this diary and that is bad as writing in it helps me to become more conscious. I am being eaten up by the school work now. During *dhyan* thoughts about my lessons come into my mind and I work out really good ideas —only this is not the time for it. Yesterday, Saturday, out of pure indolence and habit I decided to go to the Ashram and to return in the evening. Dr. Vyas gave me a French article about Mother to translate into English. I did it this morning. It was a great joy. It made me feel frustrated that I don't use my linguistic abilities more often in this way [24].

This evening and also a few nights back I felt very vividly Mother's Presence.

---

[24] Atmananda was fluent in English, German, French and would soon master Hindi and Bengali.

336

22nd March, 1948

When sitting this evening at Clark's Hotel waiting for Miss Sydney I realized that there is nothing of this world at all that is of any importance other than one's own *dharma* —doing that which must be done to arrive at the supreme Truth, the sole purpose of our existence. To the extent that one is in harmony with one's *dharma*, one's actions will be beneficial —otherwise not. Improvement or reform of the outer world will come automatically, if necessary, when one has become established in 'Reality'. One should not care about anything else. Noise, etc. is also of the 'world' and therefore should be ignored rather than reacted to. I noticed I got annoyed with a bearer at the hotel because he said: "Why sit alone upstairs. It is more comfortable here in the lobby." It irritated me, but why should I expect him to conform to my need or standards.

So in some ways a change is quite refreshing, even if only to confirm that nothing real can be found anywhere outside oneself.

3rd April, 1948

Mother was here for 3 days and left yesterday. The first night when I slept on the roof perhaps 5 or 6 ft away from her, I had such an intense feeling of happiness, it was quite overwhelming. I realized that She does not sleep, but works intensely during the time Her body is at rest. She seemed to draw me into Herself and I prayed: "Don't leave anything behind, take all". Then the question arose in me: "Even that little bit of duality that is necessary to enjoy the happiness of being absorbed?" And the answer came at once: "Yes (emphatically), that as well". It was a peculiar experience and I did not want to sleep but keep awake in this intense bliss. In the morning I noticed that I felt as light as a feather, as if I had lost 20 lbs.

One evening sitting by Her I suddenly realized that She is totally an incarnation of Divine Grace, nothing else. All are alike to Her and She gives equally to the deserving as to the undeserving. Dev Giri of Uttar Kashi, a famous 86 year old *mahatma* was at the Ashram for these 3 days. He is a very wonderful person, all love and benevolence and there is a deep peace and realization of another State of Being about Him. I was very impressed by him.

But it also occurred to me how utterly unique Mother is. She belongs to no denomination and thus to all and is an incarnation of each and every individual's 'atma' —an event without precedence in history.

I find that I have changed a good deal. For one thing I am centred in the realization that this world is of little importance and that most things don't matter, as the real changes must come from inside. Therefore I try not to meddle so much with others and keep more to what is my business. It is a waste of energy to try and reform things all the time that are anyway in constant flux. Better to live beyond the surface and watch whatever goes on outside dispassionately. To the extent that one's inner awareness is perfected, one's relationship with the outer will reflect this.

At times I feel extremely happy and light, and without any burden.

15th April, 1948

Mother came here on the 10th, but I did not know till the 13th. I was very upset about this, but I think it must have been because I got so engrossed in school work, preparing the children for the exam. I enjoy teaching and it is difficult to manage both this and the ashram at the same time. But the company of these restless children in my room does not help me.

I have a veritable aversion to writing this diary.

Rajghat, 21st April, 1948

Spent three days and four nights at the Ashram and yesterday also came back only for school. Once I get into the rhythm there I forget about this place and everything. The heat and discomfort that I have to bear also are part of the benefit I get from being here. I need less food and less sleep there and feel much lighter. One night Mother said in reply to a question: *"When you really meditate, the rhythm of the breath becomes one with the flow of thought, a perfect asana will form itself and you will not have pain or feel uncomfortable. One can be for hours at perfect rest sitting for meditation without changing one's position if the breath and the mind become one"*.

Question: "When people do *pranam* to you, do you see from the way they do it what their interior motive is?"

Mother: "*Certainly. But there are two ways. One is to see all the different mental attitudes of people, and the other is to perceive each and every individual as yet another of His infinite forms. In the latter there is no good or bad as all are 'He'. But this is difficult to understand*".

XVII - "All One Has to Do is Surrender Ever More Perfectly"

Benares Ashram, 24th April, 1948

Yesterday morning at Rajghat meditation was so poor that I stopped in despair after a half hour and gave it up. What is the good of repeating one thing all the time? It bores me to death and nothing will ever happen, I thought. I must ask Mother about this. In the evening Sharanananda came to the Ashram. There I got the answer. Someone asked him about his life. He said: "*As a boy my mother taught me to respect sadhus, to do pranam to them and eat their prasad. So I came to have faith in sadhus. Later I was very keen to become a wakil* [lawyer]. *But as I had become blind in the meanwhile, this was impossible. So I thought, if I can't be a wakil, I can be a sadhu. But then my parents were still alive and a sadhu whom I met told me not to leave them against their wishes. After some time they both died. Then that sadhu appeared again and said: 'If you are to go, come now.' So I went. Then he said: 'Repeat "Ram"'. I told him that I had no faith in this. He then asked me: 'Have you faith in God?' I said: 'Yes'. He: 'That is quite enough. Then surrender to Him'. This was my diksha* [initiation], *my instruction and my sadhana.* [1] *I never did any sadhana. When you surrender it hurts you if there is still chinta* [mental preoccupation] *about anything. Once you have fully surrendered, true love arises within and from this love comes smaran* [Divine remembrance]. *Through this one attains darshan* [vision of God]."

This was my reply. Strangely, I read yesterday in Maharshi's Gospel the same thing: "*If you believe in God, surrender yourself to Him. If not, find out who you are.*" Sharanananda said: "*Lie in Mother's lap if you are able, but if you can't, then vichara* [self enquiry] *is*

---

[1] When such seemingly 'simple' instructions are given by a qualified Guru, a certain power or grace is transmitted which greatly helps the recipient to become absorbed in the spiritual process.

the thing. *If this also is impossible for you, then serve the world. If you have once surrendered, then it does not matter how many sins you committed in the past, Mother will clear them up. Only trust Her completely. You have to give up your own ideas about how things should be done."*

Rajghat, 2nd May, 1948

When Mother saw that I was upset, once again, about the orthodox restrictions in the ashram, She said to me: *"Why do you bother about these things? Into whatever condition or circumstances He, to whom you belong, puts you, you should be satisfied. What does it matter to you? If you are made to stand in the sun, do so. It makes no difference. When you cry and shout you get your own wishes fulfilled. Why don't you fulfil mine instead? Now speak!"*

I said: "You always win. Now I have to keep quiet".

Mother: *"If I did not win, what would you come here for?"*

If I did not make so much fuss, I would not get this much teaching. She threw flowers at me which I tried to dry, but took so many days over it that the servant threw them away.

Yesterday reading in Maharshi's Gospel the chapter on "Guru and Grace" helped me much. Meditation is not repetition of anything or concentration on one thing, but a state —*bhava* [feeling or attitude]— where one remembers one's true Being. Surrender means that. <u>Meditation is simply awareness of one's surrender</u>. That should be the case always, but since activity often disturbs and eats up this awareness, one has to go and sit in solitude to get it back. My whole trouble is that I can't completely surrender. I want comforts for the body or some other desire that then takes the shape of doubt. If I take Mother to be only a person then I can't surrender and start to wonder whether Her orders are right for me or not. This is totally unproductive for my *sadhana*. I must see only God in Her!

Benares Ashram, 6th May, 1948

Mother sent word to me to go to Delhi directly on the 12th. I was furious to be made to stay in the heat when She is in the mountains at Solan and I have a holiday. If She had not told me the other day to submit to "wherever the One to whom I have surrendered puts me", whether it is hot or cold, I should have gone to Solan. But under the circumstances I dared not go. However it has been cool here since then. I also feel perhaps it is good for me to be alone here without work, to better understand what a state I am in. I have been extremely restless of late. I believe it is partly due to Kitty being with J.K. and partly because he is coming to Benares in November. Also I see that my position in Rajghat is getting extremely weak. Madhu asked me yesterday to take charge of children in the hostel next year. I refused. I take it all to mean that I shall have to make a definite choice soon between J.K. and Her. But is there a choice? Why can't I surrender?

Solan, 9th May, 1948

On the 6th evening I heard that Mother was still in Solan and would not go to Delhi until the 17th. So I suddenly decided to come here. I started early at 3 a.m. on the 7th and reached here yesterday at 11 a.m. All night at Rajghat I had misgivings about leaving and thought that even cool mountain air also would not give me peace if I disobeyed Her orders. I very nearly went back to the ashram but in the end decided to go. I had a terrible journey. Even at Kashi station I was wondering whether to return to the ashram. In the train it was terribly crowded and especially hot, but in spite of it all I reached here safely although I had less than five hours sleep last night.

I was afraid Mother would scold me when I arrived, but She did not. She was very sweet. All the same I understand that She wants me to give up worrying about my personal comforts. I wanted to talk to Her and ask Her what to do about my doubts and how to live; whether to practice 'self enquiry' in Ramana Maharshi's way or simply to throw myself on God. She did not grant me an interview but this morning just before leaving She said, putting the whole problem into a nutshell very simply: "*Your body is His and so is your mind. So give your body and mind to Him to whom it belongs in any case. By going here and there at will you enlarge your self-love. With Him there is no 'abhava' [lack] of any kind, there you need nothing. So remain with Him at all times. Fill your mind with Him and do His service with your body. Do you understand?*"

Yesterday also when She asked me to sing *kirtan,* I had forgotten the tune and said: "My brain does not work due to fatigue in the train and sleepless nights". She: *"You have grown old sleeping so much! What harm will two sleepless nights do?"*

This morning She said to some people: *"Work with your hands and keep your mind on Him all the time. That will purify your own mind as well as the place in which you work and also the person who gives you the work. This is necessary for all".*

Solan, 10ᵗʰ May, 1948

Yesterday saw A. and told her how I seem unable to have complete faith. She said: "You need not. If you believe that there is some Divine Power that also resides within you, just concentrate on that. In Mother's presence one gets help for this, that is why I go to Her." Perhaps she is right. In any case Mother rarely gives me a definite order. She always says: *"Keep your mind on God".* That is the key to everything.

In general I see that I have changed for the better through Mother's influence. I used to expect people to do all sorts of things for me, but now I don't —I am quite happy to do everything for myself and to make do with whatever comes; whereas I used to make elaborate arrangements for my own comforts.

Solan, 15ᵗʰ May, 1948

Last night I dreamt that J.K. was in my room and insisted on showing me the yoga exercise of the shoulder stand [*sarvang asana*]. He lay down on a small carpet in front of my bed and put up his legs, but they kept going apart and would not become straight and I said: "Oh, I used to know how to do this much better than you but now I have grown old and am out of practice."

This morning suddenly Lewis turned up. So it is not altogether wrong that I came here. This evening had a long talk with him. He explained about *kirtan* and *japa,* that the name of the Infinite ought to definitely have a harmonizing effect on one's whole being and every repetition is bound to effect this. Then he said that of course there can be no complete realization without intelligence. That is where J.K. comes in. I somehow understood that J.K.'s and Mother's way represent two sides of me that are com-

343

plementary and have both to be developed. Lewis is most useful in explaining things this way. So what I need comes to me even if I try to run away from it. I could have talked to him about this even at Benares.

Solan, 17th May, 1948

Yesterday Lewis gave me a long lecture about how we don't really exist in time and that it is utterly false to imagine ourselves extending into the future and to make elaborate arrangements. And sure enough I had to postpone my going to Delhi, even though I had already booked my seat.

Solan, 18th May, 1948

L. is always most helpful and it is an experience to be with him. This evening he told me how busy he is inside himself and therefore every outer activity, like washing clothes, seems a terrific effort. He told me how to control the mind by rejecting all unnecessary thought movements caused by fluctuating *prana*. This prevents the mind from identifying with its usual fantasies of past and future. If this is done persistently, the mind finally becomes still. However it cannot be forced from resting on outside impressions, but rather by the detached observation of the flow of thoughts one cuts identification with them and enters into that stillness which is beyond the superficial mental flux and is so much richer than any outer activity. The mind then loses interest in the outer as the inner is so much more absorbing. This meditative richness is so irresistibly attractive that one becomes absorbed in it and the meditation goes on automatically. But just as it is impossible to explain to any one how to go to sleep, so one cannot describe how to go into meditation.

Solan, 20th May, 1948

Lewis says the right behaviour for a *sadhu* is never to talk of worldly things and to observe silence even if someone speaks to him. The person will then either be drawn into the silence or go away. This, he says, will automatically ensure the *sadhu*'s solitude. But as long as one has to work in the world, one can at least try to limit all conversation to what is absolutely required.

New Delhi, 23rd May 1948

Arrived on the 21st and went directly to Mother. The heat is negligible [2]. I don't feel anything —I have changed a good deal. I don't mind mess and dirt anymore. The place where I am staying is incredibly filthy, but I shrug my shoulders at it. Yesterday went to see S.R. I was interested to see how empty, painfully empty, I found the house. This strict cleanliness seems sterile to me now. It really has no object, no inner support. I felt uncomfortable there after the richness of Mother's presence here. I miss all the *japa*, *puja* etc. that is going on in the ashram which produces a rich, vibrant atmosphere.

26th May, 1948

During *kirtan* Mother went into a sort of *bhava* [exalted state] and I found Her face even more absolutely peaceful, radiant and intense than usual. I simply could not take my eyes off Her. The mind became completely absorbed. Since then the attraction has greatly increased. Again I see that Her body is not a body, but only appears to be. It is all light.

Yesterday I had a fight with Lewis who attempted to justify Her heartless way of treating me. Then I realized that I myself believe in caste or at least in fundamental differences between types of people and try to keep aloof from people and things that are distracting. This morning, while sitting by Her for three hours, it occurred to me that Love and seeing God everywhere (or seeing the Divine essence within all things) are identical. Then I remembered my conversation with J.K. when I said: "I don't know what Love is", and he replied: *"Perhaps you will find out"*. At least I am slowly on the way to it.

The need of sleep is decreasing wonderfully, at least when with Her, and it does seem to make the body lighter. In sleep perhaps the body strengthens its own illusion while it is left to itself. So, therefore, perhaps only conscious sleep can be right rest.

Yesterday She suddenly reclined on my lap and to my great surprise She is almost light as a feather.

---

[2] Delhi is unbearably hot at this time of the year.

345

Nainital [3], 6th June, 1948

Arrived on the 29th May. It is lovely here and very much more comfortable than at Dehra, but I have to eat with everyone and also to deal with my host's excitement and anger. I don't like it. If I had obeyed Her when She asked me not to eat with anyone, I should have been better off. After all one cannot live in society and seriously meditate at the same time. One has to keep aloof.

I don't like the way the wealthy people here who are hosting Mother treat Her —as though they own Her. I gave them a good piece of my mind about this which has created a rather tense atmosphere. So be it. I simply expressed what everyone here has been feeling but is afraid to say.

Almora, 16th June, 1948

Arrived here yesterday. In Nainital it became worse daily. The atmosphere was genuinely hostile towards the end. Everyone was quarrelling with everyone else. I think I should avoid staying in other people's houses and stick to ashrams etc.

I could no longer tolerate the irreverent way in which I felt our hosts were treating Mother —as though She were there for their convenience and that of their friends. It made my blood boil. Finally there was a big bust-up with them and they threw me out of the house, which made me feel strangely happy. I felt that if the world throws me out, God will take me in. Then Mother insisted on making up the tiff and they asked me to come back. But of course it remains true that I should not stay in the house of people who treat Her as they did. Before leaving yesterday I said to Her: "One should not speak the truth so much. It only gets one into trouble; better to keep quiet". Mother said: *"No, just as you spoke the truth, so should it be spoken."* I felt extremely happy that after all She had agreed with my boldness.

Several misunderstandings and misinterpretations made these people think that I was a liar and that I was wicked. It was interesting to see how appearances deceive one and how one can never judge another. It is a great lesson. Also I must keep things to myself and not talk to everyone about what moves me. It was inter-

---

[3] A mountain resort situated on a lake, near Almora.

esting though how so many things were unearthed. I had been so keen to go into *mouna* [silence] but Mother did not agree. It seems almost that She intended this trouble to make things come out onto the surface.

Never plan or worry ahead. Lewis is perfectly right. I thought much of him when I spoke my mind boldly and was thrown out. I cried a great deal, but not because I was thrown out, but because I could not prevent these roughians from crucifying Mother as it seems to me that they were doing. Fancy telling Her: "You must sit from 7 or 8 p.m. whether there is one person or ten present. It doesn't look nice when an official comes and has to wait or go away without seeing you".

Since I came here to Almora I feel very happy. For one thing the air here agrees with me. It is not as comfortable, costs more and is not so cool as Nainital, but how much nearer heaven. Since yesterday I am learning a great lesson: Even if I have made no previous arrangement, God arranges for me so much more lavishly than I could do. So why ever give even a minute's thought to one's physical needs!

Mother told me to stay in the *dharmashala* or dak-bungalow for the night. I went to the dak-bungalow alone but no room was available. Then I mentioned the *dharmashala*. A stranger was standing nearby and said that it was very dirty and noisy there and asked me if I would not like to stay with him and his wife. I said: "Who are you?" And he answered: "A Mussalman". I rather liked this straight reply. After some thought, I agreed to go [4]. I remembered how Mother had once told me when I said that I had no home: "All houses are yours, all people are yours" and I thought that this must be the arrangement She has intended for me. I found a very clean sitting room and a small bedroom and a bathroom given to me. It is a very nice family —a wife, a married daughter and her husband and several children. The son-in-law had seen Mother once and had promised to come again tomorrow with his wife and mother. I was so moved by their kindness. I would have thought it a sacrilege to offer them a present in return. What a

---

[4] At this time tension between Hindus and Muslims was still high due to the bloodbath that had occurred between them in the Punjab as a result of the partition of India and the creation of the Islamic state of Pakistan.

boon to have been thrown out by the people in Nainital!

In the afternoon, after a bath —my host fetched the water himself— I walked out of the house and immediately ran into Sorrensen [the Danish *sadhu*, Sunya Baba]. He took me to Miss Sydney. She gave me a lavish tea, got her servant to do my shopping and invited me for breakfast. She said I could have shared her room for the night. Then Monika also said the same. My host insisted on giving me tea in the morning and I had to eat *paratha* [5] and biscuits as well, then coffee and toast and fruit at Miss Sydney's. On leaving for the ashram I found that a bus was just starting so I saved two-thirds of the walk back to town. When I leave arrangements to God, I get overwhelmed. It looks as if my own attempts to arrange things are only an obstacle.

Anandamayee Ma's ashram, Almora, 22ⁿᵈ June, 1948

Mother was away for three days. I felt much out of sorts and irritated about everything. Last night when She came back, I felt far away from Her. I had spent a whole day with Earl [Brewster]. Perhaps that put me off, though I enjoyed it a lot and admired his paintings, especially the ones of Lewis and Captain Baines.

Now I see that I have to empty myself of everything —thought, activity, feeling— to let Him take charge. If I judge people or things with my own mind I just strengthen the ego.

Almora, 24ᵗʰ June, 1948

Made a big scene with Mother because of the 'rules', but Her verdict was: "*As long you have desires you will have suffering. If you go somewhere else you will have other difficulties. You can't get peace as long as there is desire. Bear these things laughingly like Haridas* [6] *who followed Sri Chaitanya in spite of all the difficulties, refusing to have any special privileges for himself. But Chaitanya took him to his heart and embraced him. If you contemplate God, the desires will go.*"

---

[5] A fried unleavened bread often stuffed with potato.

[6] Haridas was a Muslim government official who became a close follower of Sri Krishna Chaitanya, the 16th century Bengali Hindu devotional saint. In spite of his tremendous devotion, there were still certain things Haridas could not participate in because he was not born a Hindu, even though Chaitanya himself was quite liberal regarding caste distinction.

Stupidly, perhaps, I told many people in the ashram about my staying with the Muslim family and now they are all talking about it. No doubt because of this She felt compelled to mention it to me and said: "*Although for me all are the same, nevertheless Muslims have different customs regarding food and it is better for you not to eat with them.*" Then She also said: "*I give you privileges that I don't give to other Europeans. I let you stay very close to me.*" [7]

This morning while sitting in front of Her door I could not meditate at all. Then it occurred to me that the only way for me is to do exactly as She tells me and to consider this submission itself to be liberation. After all it truly is.

I cannot doubt that She is a realized being and therefore it is useless to criticise what She does or says, even if I cannot understand it. As Gordon says, one has to do things not because it appeals to one but because the Guru has asked one to do it.

The other night some men came and asked questions. She said: "*Think of God in whatever shape He appeals to you and dedicate all your work during the day to Him. At least morning and evening, like winding a clock, dedicate yourself to Him and pray that all your work may be done by Him, as it is in any case. The little freedom you have in choosing your activity, use in meditating on Him. In the evening ask His forgiveness for whatever you have done that was not offered to Him.*"

They asked about Brahma, Vishnu and Shiva. She said: "*They are the three forms of His creation, preservation and dissolution, but ultimately there is only the One. As long as there are two there must be desire and pain. Turn to Him and you will know yourself. Peace is only found beyond pleasure and pain.*"

Almora, 1ˢᵗ July, 1948

Got very upset this morning because Mother objected to my staying in the Mohamedan's home [8]. She did it in a subtle way.

---

[7] See explanation in commentary after 10th July 1948.

[8] Undoubtedly the reason for this objection was to try to protect Atmananda from the dissension in the ashram which her actions had unwittingly stirred up. She was still relatively naive regarding the byzantine complexities of modern Hindu society and its impact on ashram life. Anandamayee Ma was brilliant at gauging these problems and at defusing potentially explosive situations within the ashram community.

Then later I saw that probably She has a good reason. How can I judge? How difficult it is to obey!

The American lady dancer who had come to see Mother yesterday told me she had seen her picture ten years ago and worshipped Her as the World Mother and was determined to meet Her, and now She has finally done so.

From last Friday till this morning I observed *mouna*. I found it a great thing. I immediately became oriented inward and it cut the connection with the world. I found I could concentrate and watch my thoughts all the time. For the first day or two I was unable to become angry. Nothing seemed to concern me and therefore there was nothing to be upset about. At the same time I felt relaxed and energy was conserved. It was like getting a real holiday at last, like coming home. Then I got angry and my whole mood changed. The anger was more painful than usual because since I was still maintaining silence it had no outlet. To keep quiet is like fasting, very refreshing. I found that I had to keep aware in order to keep up the silence. All together it is an experience worth repeating. Mother said: *"If you were not doing work I would ask you to keep this silence continually i.e. for five days every week."* But She asked me to keep it on Sundays as often as possible, at least once a month.

Benares, 10ᵗʰ July, 1948

Arrived on the 3ʳᵈ afternoon and have slept every night at the ashram. I told Mother about my having been upset at Her asking me not to stay in the Mohammedans' house. She said: *"Make up your mind whether you will obey Me or not. If you obey you will get peace, if not, there will always be scenes, crying and private talks."* I asked for an explanation. I said that I am ready to obey but please explain to me. She said that I could not understand but She did talk to me and told me that Hindus, even if some no longer keep the purity rules, have only very recently dropped them. But their families have lived according to these laws for millenniums and thus have maintained their caste and the spiritual lineages therein purely, whereas the Muslims have no sense of this tradition and do not observe these things. Then She said: *"You have the right intention but are not a caste Hindu. In order to keep you in My ashram where puja etc goes on, I have to insist on these things from you."*

350

* * *

Again we see that although Hindu philosophy is fundamentally univer-sal, the Atman *being the indwelling Divinity within all men, the power of this realization is sustained (at least in part) by the body of the tradition, and is nurtured on precise ritual and devotional observances that have been carried on for millenniums. Anandamayee Ma was very concerned with the big picture in which the cultural matrix of Hinduism had to be maintained if the living reality of the esoteric wisdom which it sustained was to remain viable.*

A basic tenet of the Hindu religion is that the higher castes trace their descent, both racially and spiritually, from the Rishis —the ancient seers and revealers of the Vedas— *who are considered to be the progenitors of the culture. Caste rules are beleived essential to preserve the purity of this unbroken lineage through which it is felt that a direct channel of spiritual transmission is maintained. It is particularly because Atmananda is in such close personal contact with Anandamayee Ma and her ashrams (i.e. she is not just another temporary visitor from abroad) that it is imperative for her to pay careful attention to these rules. This is not only because they are very important to the orthodox Hindus who would otherwise be offended by her (and through association, by Anandamayee Ma herself), but even more importantly because the inner alchemy of her own spiritual practice is intimately connected to the subtle vibrations inherent in the Hindu tradition. Ultimately the distinction is not racial or cultural, but is based on arcane principles of esoteric yoga.*

It should be borne in mind however that this applies specifically to the special situation of Atmananda. People from all faiths (including Islam) counted themselves as serious devotees of Anandamayee Ma and felt that she illumined the soul of their respective traditions for them in a much more intense way than they had ever experienced before. Anandamayee Ma clearly took delight in meeting people from all faiths and there could be no question that all were equal before her. Nevertheless she strove to maintain the esoteric purity of the Hindu tradition within her ashrams and saw no contradiction in this.

Hindu India had been dominated and oppressed by a minority of predominantly foreign Muslim invaders for over 500 years before the advent of the British. During this period virtually every Hindu temple in North In-dia had been repeatedly razed by successive intolerant Muslim regimes (who often built mosques on the sites of the more important temples). In spite of this a degree of mutual respect and accommodation had gradually arisen between the two communities. But this relative harmony had recently been shattered at the time when Atmananda wrote these entries by the so-called partition of India and its violent aftermath. Given the great volatility of the period, it was important for her, particularly as a foreigner, to be especially sensitive to the prevailing political and social realities.

* * *

I have been feeling a bit uneasy these days because I find it difficult to obey blindly. But yesterday when I went to the ashram after a day's interval I felt how utterly divine She is and how merely to look at Her is to experience the direct presence of God within oneself. This morning I sat outside of Her room meditating, concentrating on Her. That at once raised the mind out of the ordinary and seems to be <u>the</u> thing. The whole *sadhana* depends on surrender to Her. Once one has accepted a Guru, all one has to do is to surrender ever more perfectly.

Samant gave me a copy of J.K.'s Madras talks. I find that the very presence of the book upsets me. But when I started reading it today I became so disturbed as to feel almost mad. So I see that I must not have anything to do with it. What I shall do when J.K. comes, Mother only knows. I like Rajghat much better than the congested ashram. I am a creature of nature, which is abundant here. But perhaps I should go ahead and pay the Rs. 500 that Didi wants for that tiny cell upstairs above Dr. P.'s room in the ashram. It will give me a refuge if I have to leave Rajghat.

Rajghat, 14th July, 1948

On Sunday I kept *mouna*, which I found extremely pleasurable and useful. It drives the mind inside effortlessly. But somehow I always find something to fight and get upset about. When these things occur I get serious doubts about Mother. Then I see that I love Her desperately. What to do? I am afraid I have become too dependent on Her. This is an unhealthy state to be in. I feel that if I stay with Her I can do so only if I rigorously do what she has told me, namely to meditate and not to bother about anything else. Also what is the need of asking so many questions and creating problems. If I don't bring Her attention to what are basically non-essential things, She will leave it to me as to how to deal with them. These things are of minor importance and I make myself miserable by sheer wilfulness. Why did I ask Her whether I could stay with the Mohammedan. I need not have mentioned the matter but once it became public, she probably had to respond as she did.

If I could only see Her in Her divine aspect exclusively, there would not be so many problems. Of course reading J.K.'s talks only makes things much worse. His method is to invite the Divine through carefully observing what is, and Hers is to contemplate the Divine by ignoring all outer phenomena —or perhaps this is merely a preparation, an exercise to strengthen the faculty of spontaneous observation?

* * *

Atmananda's rigid distinction between the 'methodology' of Krishnamurti and Anandamayee Ma is to a certain extent her own mental creation — at least in this case. Anandamayee Ma certainly did not have a problem with Krishanmurti's teachings on self-awareness, observation and analysis; but for her this was one of many important spiritual practices whereas for him it would seem to have been the only way.

* * *

Rajghat, 25ᵗʰ July, 1948

Meditation begins only when the mind stops. It suddenly dawned on me that it is useless to try to meditate with the mind — that only causes strain and makes the mind wander more. That is why Ma said to Dr. Panalal: *"As long as you do puja or japa, you have not done it; only when you let Him do it, is it done."* That is the secret: to keep silent and to let Him work, think and feel through one.

I sent J.K.'s talks to Lisl thinking, let them be gone far away. The very next day I received another copy sent by S.R. Now I shan't try to send them away again. I evidently cannot escape J.K. —let happen what must.

3ʳᵈ August, 1948

Lewis returned and I saw him at the ashram yesterday. He looks most extraordinary, so different from everyone else. No wonder he can't pull on with anyone. I had almost forgotten him, but felt very happy to see him. There is a great affection for him and I have to force myself not to do things for him. He looks like such a saint, it is impossible to see anything else in this rarefied person.

Dick sent me his pamphlet: "There is yet time". I find it thought provoking but not deep enough. I doubt whether such pamphlets are of much use. I am so off this line of political thinking that I can hardly be a judge.

10ᵗʰ August, 1948

Spent two days at the ashram. When I am here at Rajghat I feel restless and want to go there; when I am there —except on holidays— I worry about my work here. I became upset yesterday about not being allowed in certain parts of the ashram due to the rules and She then said many things to me. First She asked me to pick sweet smelling flowers for Her and then gave me some of them and said: *"With this fragrance make your mind pure."* Then I said to Her: "If I notice outer defects and critisize, you say to me that this makes my mind become impure." She said: *"Of course it does. You should say to yourself that this is the way this person is and accept it and not find fault."* Then She said: *"What red hands you have."* I said to Her: "That is my colour, what is to be done." She: *"No, this is why you have come here. There is a sign on your feet also. You don't know it, but there is."* Later I asked Her: "What is a Hindu?" She said: *Everything is everywhere; there is only One. By doing sadhana you will know this. Where are you not allowed? In my room?* I said: "Of course," (pointing to Mother's room). Mother replied: *"That is not my room and neither is this verandah, nor this* (pointing to Her own chest). *My home is here and here* (She pointed to my heart and to everyone else's in the room)."

I also objected to not being allowed on the verandah upstairs. She said that sometimes there is water there. But I told Her that I always look before going in. This morning I asked Savitri whether there was water there and she said "No". Later Mother said: *"Why did you ask Savitri? Have you no faith in what I say?"* That is just the crucial point. I have no proper faith. I thought to myself why does She not either throw me out or accept me? Then suddenly it came to me that this is the exact mirror of my state. Neither can I drop

Anandamayee Ma surrounded by Her devotees
(photo by Richard Lannoy)

Her, nor accept Her completely. But which is the cause and which is the effect? My state or Her play? I thought perhaps it would be better to pay for the room in the ashram and so have a place there. But then again it struck me that if I have a room, there will probably be all kinds of new restrictions, so I shall jump from the frying pan into the fire. Last night I also told Her that I often think that She treats me like Marpa treated Milarepa. [9]

Yesterday I saw Lewis. It was most interesting and helpful. He told me that he had a dream which made it clear that he had to do three things: 1) Protect his solitude 2) study the *Shastras* deeply 3) Go beyond the mind. The Rani of Varanasi has given him a room near the palace. Perhaps she will look after him! Then he explained to me why Mother did not want me to stay in the house of a Muslim. The psychic atmosphere there is so different and clashes with Hers. He said that after all one cannot go in all directions at the same time and Her mission is particularly amongst Hindus. So She appears to be a Hindu but what She does on other planes is totally beyond our comprehension. His explanation pleased me.

16th August, 1948

Something seems to be happening in my meditation all the same, through the magic of the *Pranav* (OM) I suppose. When I sat today and last night, I had a sensation as if light was coming out of my head. I usually concentrate on the lotus centre and imagine light there.

18th August, 1948, Jhulan Purnima [10]

Last night at the ashram it suddenly occurred to me that if Her true dwelling place is my heart, as She said, then is it really

---

[9] In the classical biography of the Tibetan yogi, Milarepa, his Guru, Marpa, was constantly having him do virtually impossible tasks. Later it was revealed that this was the only way to purify him from the effects of previous bad *karma*.

[10] Full moon of August in which the mystic lila of Krishna and Radha is celebrated by placing statues, pictures, or sometimes even children dressed up like them in a swing and swinging them. It was on Jhulan Purnima that Anandamayee Ma underwent her self-initiation during the period of her 'sadhana-lila'. This was often commemorated on this day in the ashram by a midnight meditation with Ma.

necessary to be with Her physically so much? It has become a bad habit. I should search for Her inside. Physical contact is very helpful but ultimately one has to go beyond that. I noticed last night, standing far away from Her at the back of the crowd, that I got more from Her than sometimes when I am sitting very close to Her. *Satsang* is necessary but it must go on continually inside rather than only on the physical plane.

20th August, 1948

Yesterday at the ashram a number of things happened that made me feel that it is not fair for me to accept the special privileges given to me in that I am allowed to stay there even though I am a foreigner. It really makes things very difficult for the ashramites, as at times it is impossible to avoid spoiling their lengthy preparations by unwittingly breaking one of the rules or straying into the wrong area. But the whole thing is rather too much for me —to be such a constant disturbance to everyone. Today I felt relieved to be back here at Rajghat where I can move about without creating trouble all around me. But in the evening I felt very bad and cried again. This feeling hurt cannot be helped as long as one is identified with one's body. But I feel sort of heart broken. If only I can realize Her subtle presence within me at all times, I will become indifferent to being with Her physically.

23rd August, 1948

Last night meant to spend the night at Malati's but when going to the ashram to pick up my bedding, I found that Mother had returned. She had been away for a day only. So I stayed. Today I did not go but I find it so difficult to be apart from Her that I can hardly bear it. I have to give in and go to the ashram and bear all the troubles and humiliation.

When Malati told me about the many romantic entanglements of the people around J.K., I wondered how Mother gets all Her people through without this sort of thing happening. I see that it is simply that She takes everything on Herself and is everyone's beloved. That is no doubt why so many behave so strangely and why the girls especially have to obey so implicitly. With me it must be also the same. I have to work out attachment in this way. It is quite true that I cannot leave Her.

Bhadaini, 27th August, 1948

This morning a young girl student asked: "I want peace but I don't get it."

Mother: *If you sit at home and say 'I want to pass an exam', nothing will happen. You have to undertake the necessary steps. Then you must walk on the road that leads to peace.*

Questioner: Then what to do?

Mother: *Satsang, and if you have a Guru obey His instructions.*

Questioner: How to find a Guru?

Mother: *If you are keen to study you find a teacher. So here also if you are eager in your heart, you will find a Guru. When you call God, do it only for His sake and for nothing else. When you have found Him you have found all and you want nothing else at all.*

29th August, 1948

I have spent these last 4 days here at the ashram. Mother evidently wants me here, but I have to be so extremely careful as food and water are carried everywhere at all times. I cannot help feeling the pinch of being an outcast. She wants me to get over this. But because I am Jewish I have already got that stigma on myself and can never loose it in this life, here or in Europe. The only thing is to drop entirely identification with the body.

2nd September, 1948

Mother left on the 30th night. I joined Her train at Kashi and spent the night at Mugalsarai with Her, not sleeping or even lying down. It was wonderful to be alone with Her for several hours. Didi and Bhupen were in the waiting room together with me, but they slept soundly. Mother has an extraordinary attraction. She told me to save money for the hut at Dehra.

She is right. Also I must not worry about the orthodox rules and not complain about it either. Anyway She does what She pleases with me and it makes no difference what I do. She does not move an inch and I have to obey. There are difficulties everywhere, even at Rajghat, though of another sort.

7th September, 1948

Stayed at the Ashram for two days. One night when repeating the *mantra* I got into a state of calm above the usual level. I dreamt that night that I went to the Maharshi and touched his feet with my head very reverently. He said; "Do you really believe that I can help you?" I said full of conviction: "Of course I do". He: "Don't you see how beautiful this is?". That's all I remember, but the dream was quite impressive and seemed very real.

That afternoon I spent with Malati. She told me that Mano [11], also (like Krishni!) had said: "J.K. is not as perfect as Sri Ramana and Anandamayee Ma; he is still in the process of becoming." I was extremely amazed at this and somehow very pleased that others also felt this way. Very possibly there will be no problem at all when and if he comes here (Malati still doubts it).

But what rather disappointed and almost disgusted me was that J.K. had immediately discussed with Mano the possibility of marrying again and tried to take away the inhibitions she might have on the matter. It seems the only thing he does is to induce people to either get married or fall in love. It helps up to a point, but not very far, and entangles one; whereas Mother draws all the suppressed love unto Herself which induces a profound state of spiritual surrender through which one's innermost divinity is awakened. She does not leave you in a hole but takes you up.

15th September, 1948

Lewis came yesterday and stayed for 24 hours. He is always most helpful. He hit the nail on the head with his response to my complaint that I simply can't manage the class: "Don't worry about it, you are doing your best. In the modern world ways have to be found to keep *sadhus* of various kinds alive".

Lisl wrote that Gerty Beamt got to know a man in the concentration camp who grew so fond of her that he voluntarily went to the gas chamber with her. This throws a new light on her story and causes me to think again over the fate of all those who had to suffer so cruelly. Perhaps these catastrophes happen because people's accumulated *karma* is inescapable. Things are not always as they appear on the surface.

---

[11] Wife of the late Rama Rao, one of Krishnamurti's closest associates.

20ᵗʰ September, 1948

Spent the day at Sarnath yesterday. Met Mrs. Ananda Jennings who was with Mother and Bhaiji at Kishenpur 11 years ago. It was an interesting experience. She is no doubt not an ordinary person. There is quite a deep peace about her, quite unusual for an American. But it also showed me how dangerous it is not to have a Guru who keeps you in your place. Ananda Jennings has no doubt had some kind of a realization and now believes herself to be one of the saviours of mankind, to be blunt about it. She calls J.K. "a dear" and "a very good friend" and she evidently can't fathom the depth of Mother at all. She parted with Her chiefly because of the caste problem. Ananda Jennings is a good woman and knows something, and this is just the danger, because spiritual pride comes in. Instead of looking for guidance to take her further, she has a 'group' and evidently teaches them.

Bhadaini Ashram, 18ᵗʰ October, 1948

Was unwell for five days and then could not leave Rajghat until the 9ᵗʰ after C.J.'s [12] talk and tea. He was quite sensible. He remarked that Pestalozzi said: "No one should be a teacher who does not love children". I don't. They only worry and upset me and I have no understanding for their noisiness and capriciousness. I have never been a child myself and don't remember my childhood. Perhaps that's why I have to be among children.

Reading *Maha Yoga* and Sri Ramana's Souvenir Birthday Book got me into a strange state which makes me feel very near him. Reading some very moving articles by others about Him, I had to cry. I felt as if he were here in the room and somehow I could sit longer than usual for meditation. I felt such a longing to see Him and remembered the time when I cried so hard because I could not go there. But then I thought Mother is best for me and if I am meant to go there it will happen. Besides, everyone there knows that I belong to Mother now and expects me to stick to Her only. When one is married, one should not look at other men.

---

[12] C. Jinarajadas was president of the Theosophical Society at this time.

Rajghat, 19ᵗʰ October, 1948

This morning woke up at 3.45 a.m. and sat for two hours for *dhyan* with almost no interruption and was not tired. But it made me ask myself how much longer am I to do this useless and irksome school work?

I wonder what really my way is: '*Neti, neti*' or '*wohi, wohi*' [13]? That is, *jnana* or *bhakti*? Sri Ramana always impresses me so much. No need to go there; once one has made contact, He is everywhere.

21ˢᵗ October, 1948

There is definite progress in my meditation —a deepening of consciousness and a certain joy in sitting for *dhyan,* and there seems to be a change in breathing. Consequently there is no reluctance to sit now, but rather I take joy in it.

Reading *Maha Yoga* I find that the author says God, the Soul and the World are an inseparable trinity within the dream or illusion of life. As long as one accepts one, the others are inevitable.

26ᵗʰ October, 1948

Mother came on the 23ʳᵈ and left this morning. I do not depend on Her physical nearness so much now as I feel her more inside. In a way I seem nearer to Her when alone and in meditation than when with Her in a crowd.

Rajghat, 8ᵗʰ November, 1948

On the 6ᵗʰ I went to the Ashram for a while and on my way back visited L. who took me to see Charlie Chaplin's new film "A Comedy of Murders" [14]. The film is surely excellent but it upset me. It is bad for me to go into a crowd and worse to keep my mind on all these mad pictures of Europe etc., for they do stick to my mind. It disturbs my *dhyan.* Have I time for these things? However exquisite the film, it is not worth disturbing my solitude. I have not reached the state where nothing can affect me. Mother

---

[13] '*Neti... neti*' —'not this... not this... '— The negating method of inquiry into 'who am I'?
'*Wohi... wohi*'—'all is he' [lit. 'this is He, this is He']— The method of seeing God in everything.

[14] Later retitled "Monsieur Verdon".

has told me to do my work and meditate for the rest of the time. Death is certain, but the hour of death is not. Lewis came again today. He has gone through most of his money already in five and a half weeks. I see now how right Mother is to make me save. (Why should I waste my money on a 'Danaiden Fass'?) I manage quite well on the amount She has allowed me. For how many years have I to do this work?

Menses being late does not add to my balance. I am not ready to live without money. Without being completely absorbed in God so that one does not feel hunger and the need of anything, one cannot give up the world. But in order to get absorbed I seem to require leisure and solitude and there lies the vicious circle.

Jhusi, 16th November, 1948

Came here 14th morning. Mother is lovely and so full of love and humour with everyone. But all the people round Her are not a help to my meditation. I was getting into an awful state, eaten up by school work.

About *Atmagyan* [knowledge of the Self] She said: *"In an incomplete state of Realization one may have 'Atmagyan' only at certain times whereas a fully realized person has it at all times so that there is no ego left".* (17th February, 1949: the prior case seems to apply to J.K.)

She also said: *"'Bat' [speech] creates 'badha'[obstacle] because when one speaks he can only speak from one point of view and there will be an opposite point of view which on some level is equally true. But there is a state where speech goes beyond these".*

Rajghat, 5th December, 1948

Since the 2nd the school Anniversary Celebrations have been going on. The Governor General of the school has presided and his praise of the unexplored possibilities of combining movement with percussion instruments has inspired me to new ideas of rhythmic exercises. These come into my meditation spontaneously and I have written them down. Perhaps that will put my mind at rest.

Today keeping *mouna* after five or six weeks is intensely blissful. For the first time it is not at all difficult even here at Rajghat. Silence is a surprising help and automatically promotes detachment.

XVIII - Krishnamurti Returns

16ᵗʰ December, 1948

Mother came yesterday. I felt Her more wonderful than ever.
I again very strongly felt, looking at Her, that She is not a body
but just light. One gets the impression that Her body is only an
illusion made visible to us, that actually there is no person. She
looked at me straight for some time and seemed to see through
me with all my shortcomings. This morning I felt as light as a bird.
With Her I feel no need to sleep or eat.

Mother met J.K. in Delhi. He was staying at Kitty's house and
the meeting took place in her garden. Mother told us all about it
(in Bengali). She related how She told J.K.: "*Pitaji, why do you speak
against Gurus? When you say one does not need any Guru, sadhana
etc., you automatically become the Guru of those who accept your view,
particularly as large numbers of people come to hear you speak and are
influenced by you.*" He: "No, if you discuss your problems with a
friend he does not thereby become your Guru etc. If a dog barks in
the dark and alerts you to a snake, the dog does not thereby become your Guru!" At the end he took Her hand in both his and
said: "I hope to meet you again soon".

She commented yesterday: "*Paramananda and others say that
he* [J.K.] *has one 'dosh'* [fault]: *While his way is certainly valid he does
not accept the validity of approaches other than his own —which is one
of vichara* [self-inquiry]."

I feel very happy that She met him, it seems to make everything so much easier for me. I need not explain anything to Her.

* * *

*In her authoritiative biography of J. Krishnamurti, Pupul Jayakar
describes the meeting between Krishnamurti and Anandamayee Ma which
took place in the Delhi home of Kitty Shiva Rao: "They met in the garden, as
the Mother never entered the home of a householder. She did not speak English,*

363

and spoke through a translator [Krishnamurti no longer spoke any Indian language]. She had a radiant smiling presence. She said that she had seen a photograph of Krishnaji many years before and knew that he was very great". A description of the conversation already narrated by Atmananda follows with the difference that Anandamayee Ma has the last word, gently insisting that in the act of setting himself up as a public spiritual authority, he cannot avoid the responsibility of being a Guru, the very thing he rails against. After this: *"He held her hand gently and did not answer."*

Pupul Jayakar continues: *"Many visitors came and prostrated them-selves at the feet of K. and Anandamayee Ma. Anandamayee Ma accepted their greetings, but Krishnaji was embarrassed. As always, he would not permit them to bow down, but sprang to his feet and bent down to touch the feet of the seeker of blessing. Later, after Anandamayee left, Krishnaji spoke of her with warmth and affection. There had been communication, though much of it had been wordless."* [1]

Anandamayee Ma was always extremely respectful and deferential in the presence of mahatmas, often referring to herself as a simple, uneducated child. But this did not in any way however inhibit her from asking them direct and penetrating questions, particularly if She did not agree with them on a particular point.

In this description of their meeting, and particularly in the portrayal of their different responses to dealing with the public, is revealed an essential difference between Anandamayee Ma and J. Krishnamurti. Anandamayee Ma made no distinction whatsoever between herself and those bowing before her. She saw everything as *"God interacting with God"*, as she would sometimes say. In any case, to bow before a respected and revered figure in India is as common a gesture of elementary respect as shaking hands in the West. Anandamayee Ma had no desire to do away with tradition but on the contrary wanted to revitalize it, bringing out the fundamental spirituality upon which it was originally based. She often pointed out that in the act of bowing down (making pranam), particularly to an exalted spiritual personage, a profound transmission of spiritual energy takes place —something utterly beyond the mind that is the antithesis of anything debasing or humbling. But whereas she is in a state of absolute non-duality, aware only of the all-pervading Divinity in herself and others, Krishnamurti is self-conscious here,

---

[1] *J. Krishnamurti: A Biography*, Pupul Jayakar, p.149

'embarrassed', admitting to a sense of separation, no matter how genuinely humble and humanistically expressed, between himself and others.

* * *

18ᵗʰ December, 1948

Again there was a discussion about J.K. and it affected me adversely. J.K.'s influence upsets me. I feel a little bit like before I went to Ramanashram. I am rather terrified of J.K. On the other hand it must be right for me to meet him. So it certainly must be for the best. It will no doubt clear up my past.

19ᵗʰ December, 1948

Last night felt that I should not do anything about J.K. without asking Her. So I did. She said: *"Attend the meetings and also his talks. Afterwards if you find it disturbing, you can always stop going. What does it matter to listen to him? Abhay and others went to see him at Delhi. He was very nice to me and I liked his behaviour very much. He wants to see me again. What is there to worry about? He only wants the 'samadhan'* [proper understanding] *of thought. This won't disturb your dhyan."* I was rather in a funk until I decided to leave the whole matter entirely to Her. This morning I feel light and full of peace and joy. I slept only for four and a half hours but don't feel at all tired. I am now looking forward to J.K.'s coming, since I have put it in Her hands entirely.

Bhadaini, 20ᵗʰ December, 1948

Yesterday at Rajghat we had a long meeting about preparations for the camp that is to be arranged for J.K.'s lectures here. Since She asked me to join in this work it is now quite a different and impersonal affair. I find myself now looking forward eagerly to J.K.'s coming. It is interesting to see how quickly fear changes into desire. I feel now quite excited at the prospect of the camp.

Bhadaini, 25ᵗʰ December, 1948

It seems to me that on this path of total surrender, one accepts whatever comes as coming from God, rather than trying to make distinctions.

I have no desire even for liberation. In a way to have found someone to whom one can completely surrender is potential liberation. I have no more worries, as I leave all to Her. It is not my body, but Hers, not my mind, but Hers. So, like Milarepa's Master, She can just deal with me as She pleases.

Dunga, 1st January, 1949

Arrived at Raipur on the 29th. Got unwell in the train. When I lie in bed and think of Her I feel such an ecstatic thrill that I can hardly bear it. For me thinking of God is keeping Her in my mind always and it is so wonderful that one cannot leave it. If I could really succeed at this I think I should have to drop the school-work entirely, as I would find it impossible to think of anything else.

Yesterday I was exhausted because still unwell and lay in bed from 3 p.m. Had really a wonderful time all by myself quietly dreaming of Her. Today during *dhyan*, which was exceptionally successful, it came to me that surrendering to Her as a person is not my way at all. I have to struggle and fight every inch of the way —I am not really a *bhakta*. But this realization came while I was surrendering entirely to Her. Herein lies the paradox.

She talked for a long time this afternoon, about how *sadhana* of some sort is absolutely essential and how one has to leave the affairs of this world and turn to the Real. When one's hair gets grey near the temples it is a warning that one should turn to one's true home and away from the earthly one which is about to end. Otherwise one has to build yet another earthly one when this one is finished. Whatever has most weight in one's mind will get the upper hand at the moment of death when one is half unconscious and these thoughts will determine the nature of one's rebirth; therefore turn your mind to God.

Rajghat, 6th January, 1949

When I sit for *dhyan* I now surrender my mind, heart and body to Her and then keep still. This is so blissful that I can hardly leave it. I imagine Her looking into my eyes and I dissolve in this gaze. At Dehradun I actually felt love for everyone off and on. Ah, to have Her always with me, to exist only to be conscious of Her.

8th January, 1949

Now I feel Her embrace of love all the time. It is so delightful that I can hardly bear it. Though my liver is upset and I feel sick often and have pain sometimes, this does not affect my mood at all. Today when teaching the 5th class which is my hell, I realized how ridiculous it is to loose my temper. The children are right to laugh when I do so. But when two periods later I had the same trouble in the 4a class I was less equal to it. There are always these mad children who disturb everything in every class. I thought, well it must be the *karma* of the others to have this disturbance since I cannot stop it.

Now my condition seems like what Sharananandji describes in his book *Sharanagati Tattwa*. She is at the back of my mind all the time and the moment my work is over, it automatically turns to Her, though the chattering on the surface goes on all the same. If this minor chattering was not there the bliss would be quite unbearable and then I might go out of the body altogether. I leave everything entirely to Her. Sometimes I wonder whether She does not even arrange my desires and only seems to let me do what I want. I feel very happy that Her presence is so potent with me now, just before J.K. is coming, and I pray that it remains so. It is like being in love, only ten times as wonderful.

From Kitty's letter to Malati I feel that however great her experience has been with J.K., it is not of the greatest depth. One does not feel from J.K. that something one gets when Mother and Sri Ramana glance at one. It seems all on the surface. What J.K. talks about so elaborately, they communicate with a glance in the fraction of a second.

Rajghat, 9th January, 1949

It occurs to me that I make the mistake of thinking of Her too physically. I identify myself with the physical and therefore also Her. It is so natural to me that I am often not even aware of this. What I have to do is to keep in mind that Her physical body is only an apparition, so-to-say, for our convenience and that She is really intangible spirit. There is a great peace with me now. It remains at the background while I am busy, but its presence is there. The moment I turn inward there is a response, just as if you flick a

367

switch and there is *ananda*. When I sit for meditation I feel this immediately.

Bhadaini, 15ᵗʰ January, 1949

J.K. is to arrive this morning. I feel quite panicky and would like to hide myself in a rat hole. In vain do I reason with myself that whatever is inevitable must be a blessing in disguise. What I hear about J.K. since Sanjiva has come makes me only wish more that I could avoid him.

Rajghat (later):

J.K. has arrived. I find myself comparing him spontaneously with Mother and of course She gains infinitely. He seems nothing like on that level of complete perfection. But one cannot of course really judge like this. I feel that he is, of course, the Theosophical Messiah. His behaviour is graceful and quite perfect and at ease. We scrutinised each other. I purposely did not say anything polite as I do not want to be on a conversational basis with him. That does not interest me.

Bhadaini, 16ᵗʰ January, 1949

J.K.'s first talk at Ramacha. My impression of yesterday is intensified. The whole of him isn't worth a fragment of Mother's finger nail. His voice is strained, ugly and disagreeable. He is aggressive and sort of drives nails into people. He makes unnecessary remarks like: "We shall have these talks for six weeks, whether you like it or not". Then he keeps on saying things like: "This is stupid", and "This is absurd". When someone asked, "What is your mission?", he replied: "You want to know whether I am the World Teacher or not"? Fancy talking of being the World Teacher when there are beings like Mother and Ramana Maharshi etc. Altogether he has done me a great service already by making me turn much more to Mother. He still is a Theosophist, however he may fight it. How I have changed in these 10 years! One can hardly believe it.

Bhadaini, 22ⁿᵈ January, 1949

Mother leaving for Vindhyachal today. I have been with Her every free moment. No question of going to hear J.K. It seems quite ridiculous to waste precious moments that I can spend with Her on him. I have lost all feeling for him. I ask myself: What have I been after all these years? I believe that J.K.'s criticizing everyone and everything has spoiled his beauty. Where are his beautiful eyes, where is his love? At his talk I noticed a complete absence of *prem* and *ananda*. [2] There is of course great concentration and a certain peace and clarity of mind —but still <u>mind</u>. His group now comes regularly to Mother and pesters Her with questions. She sent me to invite him to come to the ashram and see Her. His reply was: "I do not want to go about seeing people". That completely stunned me. I have not set my eyes on him since he said that.

When Mother, years ago, referring to my saying that I had dropped him, said: *"Whatever you have begun, you should not leave"*, She was right, for then I was not ready to do so; but now he has simply fallen away. I see now that I had not pledged myself to him, but to the search for truth, so there can be no question of loyalty to a person in this case.

Rajghat, 26th January, 1949

Went to Vindhyachal with Mother on the 22nd January and returned last night. Had a most heavenly time. To do *japa* and concentrate in the Lotus Chakra [the esoteric centre at the crown of the head] is such intense *ananda* that I can hardly bear it when in Her radiant Presence. It now happens automatically. My love for Her has increased immensely and flows over to others as well. Now perhaps I am about to realize what J.K. said to me 10 years ago: "When you love one, you love all". My relationship to Her is now infinitely sweet since I have surrendered without reserve. This is already potential liberation, as it makes for desirelessness and the dropping of all worry. I feel that having found Her and being close to Her is such infinite bliss that nothing at all matters, no difficulty, no hardship. To die at Her Feet is Bliss. Whatever suffering comes is merely superficial. The body still goes on with its needs (food, sleep, etc.) out of habit, but even these are minimized. Surrender to Her is such intense meditation and utter onepointedness that there is no room for anything else, no wish for anything, no regret, no worry. All is in Her hands. Now also

[2] Love and joy.

the trouble with the orthodox rules no longer matters, as it is so small compared to the Bliss of being close to Her. It mostly worried me because it used to raise doubts about Her in my mind, but there is no room for doubts now, since J.K. has come. His advent has, like a flash of lightening, lit up the whole landscape and changed the balance infinitely in Her favour.

26th January, 1949

Attended J.K.'s first Rajghat discussion. It annoyed me intensely. His voice, though, was mellow and his eyes more beautiful than the other day. Frydman [3] is terribly cynical and destructive and tears down everything. Evidently J.K. has this effect on him. He can't always have been like this.

The other day it occurred to me that if I do not go along with J.K., it does not mean that I have to clear out of here [Rajghat], on the contrary. Surely I am as intense as anyone in my search, and in the end it is the same. It is not a question of being loyal only to persons but of a total commitment to an ideal.

When I left the talk I decided not to speak to anyone, but found Mrs. Parik and Akka in my room and immediately burst out with all that I have been through and how wrong J.K. is in many things he says and how miserable he leaves everyone. Then Malati began to talk to me and so the day goes and I wish I had remained with Mother at Vindhyachal. Fortunately Malati afterwards came and told me not to talk so much and to be by myself and to keep *mouna*. That I am most grateful for, as it is mainly due to her that I am so occupied with talking. Now I can just lock myself in, without being impolite.

I have a bad cough and feel very tired. Mother always makes me well and J.K., ill. I miss Love in him. Is it a role he plays? A supreme sacrifice of a very fervent *bhakta* ?

---

[3] Maurice Frydman was a Polish engineer who spent most of his life in India. He was in the inner circle of Krishnamurti; however today he is best remembered as the discoverer of Sri Nisargadatta Maharaj (died 1981), a great Maharastrian *jnani* who lived in a poor section of Bombay. Frydman thought so highly of him that he learned his dialect and was the editor and translator of a collection of his discourses called *I am That*. The book attracted many serious seekers, both Indian and foreign, to Sri Nisargadatta in the 1970's.

27th January, 1949

J.K. upset me terribly yesterday. Today I woke at 5.30 a.m. so had only one and a half hours for meditation. At the end I find that I have a problem after all: How to surrender completely and do only one thing —to be aware for 24 hours. At present I am doing two or three hours of meditation and spend most of my time looking after my body. The main part of my day goes in earning money, cooking, washing clothes etc. and only a very small part in *sadhana*. I am afraid to be without security and feel I can't live without a minimal income etc. So after all J.K. has a function and has to give something to me also. When he said to me yesterday: "If you are honest you must clear out or?" There was an alternative, but I did not hear it.

28th January, 1949

This morning could not meditate well but after nearly two hours I cried. J.K. always makes me cry. Quite clearly it seems to me that I shall have to clear out from here. Fourteen years is a cycle with me. He has evidently come —as far as I am concerned— to show me the way out of Rajghat. Today while doing my house work while the others were attending his morning talk, I was quite peaceful, thinking out how I have to stand alone now and not listen to him. If he is the 'World Teacher' or even a teacher, he will teach me without words. If not, I shrug my shoulders. I have found the greatest jewel anyone can find, what more do I want? His liberation does not interest me. Mother will see to all I need. Of course I still like bread and butter (and plenty of fruit with it) but I won't sell my birthright for it. Rather die at Her feet than live a lie.

I have fought Sri Ramana and he conquered me, the same holds with Mother. If he is great, I challenge J.K. to do the same. If not, I am not interested. This way is not my way and I have chewed and rechewed it to sickness. It does not matter whether one listens to J.K. or to anyone else, but whether one is really eager to find oneself. Surely I have not played with the matter, I have been serious all along. If not how did God let me find Thompson and now Mother.

30ᵗʰ January, 1949

Today meeting about Rajghat Community. I enjoyed being with J.K. for the first time since he came. For a few minutes he looked again as I had known him —beautiful, refined with liquid eyes. He evidently gets overshadowed by something. But this is not constant. I also changed my mind about Frydman. Many things he said were much to my liking. I felt very near Mother during the meeting and had the impression that She wished me to keep Her in mind strongly, so as to make Her presence felt.

1ˢᵗ February, 1949

Among all the Great Ones, the great Gurus, there is something in common, though the methods may vary —but J.K. attacks every one of them. *Does his way lead to God or deeper into a subtler form of the ego?* I cannot forget how I sat very near him thinking of the most sacred word which is recognised by <u>all</u> and it seemed to irritate him intensely.

They will call the new community '*Sangha*'. It seems a beautiful name. I must tell Mother all this. I hear She is coming tomorrow. I felt sure She would as I want Her badly here and so do others. My cold is so bad I could never have gone to Vindhyachal.

Kitty also is due tomorrow. But as I do not intend to return from the ashram before the 4ᵗʰ and then will be here only briefly before returning there again in the evening, I may hardly see her. I must confess I feel a revengeful joy, as she so consistently ignored me of late whenever I was in Delhi. Of course I am not going to Club to play bridge and never would, whatever she may have done to me.

I have pain in the chest and the cough is rather uncomfortable. But I don't mind this in the least. I am intensely happy. There is no happiness equal to surrender.

2ⁿᵈ February, 1949

Suddenly last night it occurred to me that my illness must be due to my fight with J.K. I don't remember having had such a bad cough ever in my life. I have been fighting alone, keeping aloof. I am beginning to wonder whether it was wrong, whether it was only pride and conceit that have made me so critical of him. She has always asked me not to find fault with others *"Dosh mat dekho"* [Don't see faults] is always Her order. She had expressly told me that J.K.'s way would not disturb my *dhyan*. Besides, where is 'my *dhyan*'? It is only an attempt. I need not accept J.K. wholesale, but surely there must be much I can learn from him.

However I need not blame myself, for I cannot help being bitter toward him after all that I have been through. Besides my way is to resist to the utmost. At the first talk I got angry and said that I have no problem. But of course I have problems: How to do *sadhana* more intensely? How to obey Mother implicitly? How to make my work a service? How to conquer anger? How to make my life a single whole? How to have complete faith so that I need not worry about earning money?

Bhadaini, 3ʳᵈ February, 1949

When seeing Mother this evening after having been in J.K.'s presence for the last week, it felt like plunging into clear spring-water after having wallowed in a muddy, scummy pond. What a clear and pure joy it is to set my eyes on Her. My cold is bad enough but already much better by seeing Her. When She asked me about J.K. and his lectures in front of three or four others and I said: "I did not attend because I didn't like them", She said: *"Dharmik bat sunna chahiye"* [One should listen to *dharmic* discussions]. I said: "Is it *dharmic* ? When I can listen to you, why should I listen to someone else?" She shut me up. Anyway I must talk it over with Her.

When one is with Her, it seems as clear as daylight that J.K. cannot be an *Atmagyani*. His is a much lower level, which is certainly a good deal above the ordinary. (The 'lucidity' Malati claims to receive from listening to him and about which she is so fascinated is due to a temporary stimulation of her consciousness, which is very misleading and will die down again). Lewis is also intensely critical and sceptical about him.

Bhadaini, 6ᵗʰ February, 1949

Yesterday spoke to Mother about my experiences at J.K's talk. I told Her that the atmosphere set up by my *japa* seemed to irritate him; also that he considers himself the World Teacher and does not recognize either Sri Ramana, nor Sri Aurobindo, nor anyone else. I feel he is not an *Atmagyani* and that his teaching amounts much to the reverse of what She teaches. As a matter of fact, the day before She had already given me the answer to whether I should attend his talks by saying: *"Whatever time you spend in thinking of God is well spent, all other time is wasted."* She told me not to attend the talks if I did not feel like it. She said She had told me to listen because, as I listen to so much talk, why not listen to this also. Then I asked Her whether, since thought of Her comes to me spontaneously, I should not simply do *japa* and *dhyan* of Her? She said: *"The Ishtadev is the sacred word"*. [4] Then She told me that Shiva and Parvati (or Shakti) are seated in the heart and that going up and down from the heart centre to the head centre in meditation is itself a kind of *mala*. She said at the end: *"Do not remain without japa, be at it all the time. If due to your present bronchitis you can't do the japa in rhythm with the breath, do it only in your mind without the rhythm, but don't leave it."*

I feel that J.K.'s coming here was necessary for me to make my position quite clear. Today Sri Chunilal and Mrs. Parak came to Mother after J.K.'s Talk. Mother asked what it had been about. Sri Chunilal said that he had talked about how self-analysis was one's worst enemy, as what is wanted is stillness of the mind. She said: *"That is exactly what our Shastras say"*. Then Mrs. Parak said: "There was talk about Love also. J.K. said, that one should not talk about it but experience it". Mother: *"That is not Love either. If there is experience then there is both the experiencer and that which he experiences; but Love is 'Svayam Prakash'* [Light of the all pervading Self] *in which there can be no division"*. It seemed to me that She wanted thereby to explain J.K.'s state. He has a certain experience, but that is not full Realization.

I again felt the great difference between the pure atmosphere of this Ashram, and the muckiness and muddle of J.K.'s talk.

Rajghat, 7th February, 1949

Returning here I feel rather out of place and not happy. I wish I had enough money to quit work and live at the Ashram. We had

---

[4] The *mantra* is the sound form of the Deity. *Dhyan* (meditation) is an integral part of the practice of *japa* when the latter is done correctly.

a meeting about the new experiment to be tried for the school. I have become an outsider by not attending J.K.'s Talks. I cannot go into this experiment wholeheartedly. I feel I am too old and have almost done with the world. I have no time to acquire a new family of children and manage a house. Impossible. But for the wretched money question I should leave. Everyone at Rajghat has imbibed a tremendous lot of enthusiasm and wants to work it out now. But I have not, of course. Most likely I shall have to leave. I may help them to plan the whole matter, but I can't participate in it. Well, it all lies with Mother. She said: *"Don't remain without japa!"* I must obey Her.

10ᵗʰ February, 1949

Everyone is saying that J.K.'s Talks are so wonderful. I attended today's public talk, but what I enjoyed was the *kirtan* that could be heard clearly from another compound. The talk and discussion were on such a low level, simply political, quite amazing. I can't have any quarrel with this; it simply does not concern me. It again made me feel more strongly how desperately necessary it is to have a Guru and how I must stick to Mother at all costs and how lucky I am to have found Her.

The level of the meeting seemed to be at the solar-plexus and, trying to concentrate on the Lotus [crown] *chakra*, I felt a pressure in my head. J.K. definitely believes himself to be the World Teacher and that is rather serious. Instead of dissolving the Order of the Star [5] he should have left it to its fate and gone into the jungle to meditate. Frydman evidently is extremely swollen-headed and believes himself just one step below the world teacher. See how dangerous J.K.'s teaching is, as he does not teach humility and reverence for the Guru.

Bhadaini, 13ᵗʰ February, 1949

Last Friday J.K. in his talk spoke in a sneering manner about Mother and my relation to Her. It was petty and ridiculous. He seems obsessed with sex. He always makes dirty allusions about it, quite disgusting. D.P. and others questioned him and his teach-

---

[5] Branch of the Theosophical Society, dedicated to the propagation of Krishnamurti as the World Teacher, which Krishnamurti dramatically dissolved in 1929.

ing. He responded in a peculiar way saying that he has no followers and cannot be responsible for them. He said in a furtive, frightened way: "Surely that has nothing to do with me. I am out of it, I am out of it." Then he made a remark about the Buddha, saying: "Not that I want to be the Buddha. I don't care two pence."

16th February, 1949

Attended the morning talk on 11th February. As J.K. came in and I looked at him from a distance I noticed that his face still looked very refined, so I hoped for a good talk. He started out on an interesting topic, but after a little while he just could not proceed. He also attacked me and through me Mother in a rather petty, ridiculous and ill-tempered way. I was rather amused. D.P. gave him his reward by bursting out: "Sir, your teaching is useless, your followers haven't changed, they intrigue... etc." Then a number of others attacked him. I cannot help feeling that I am a focus for opposition. He speaks for people who are confused and naively open. I am not confused and cannot be blindly open to him as I once was.

J.K.'s influence draws people out and keeps then working on the surface, rather then driving them within as Mother and Sri Ramana do. They say they keep an inner stillness but I do not think it is very deep. Very likely there is *shunya* (void) between every two stages and that stillness, though beyond the ordinary everyday mind, is on a comparatively low level.

Evening:

Suddenly it occurs to me that I have not been fair to J.K. I insist that he must be as he was, as he repeats the same words. Besides even then I did not see him as he truly was, but as he appeared to me. Now I am really afraid that he may upset me again, which does not do him justice. Even the devil becomes God if you look for God in him, since there is no devil except in our minds. If I admit his purity of intention, and I must in fairness do that, he cannot hurt people really. After all, he teaches out of love or compassion, even if unconsciously he taints it by his shortcomings. It is pride that makes me have nothing to do with anyone but the highest. It is easy to see God in Mother, but that is not enough. Real relationship means to see only God in the many different shapes and forms. He has only confirmed me in what I am doing. How can I know that he won't confirm me a thousand times more if I approach him without fear? If I can manage to be in a meditative mood instead of in critical one, he may not become aggressive. I am wondering whether I should not give him one last chance and approach him naturally as I would other people and forget all the suffering that I have been through due to him. For years I had taken him to be my Guru.

Rajghat, 17th February, 1949

After writing the above at about midnight last night, I suddenly had a glimpse of something and saw that what J.K. means by 'true relationship' is really "*wohi, wohi*" ['He is that' —i.e., all objective consciousness is God] —the same as She always says. Unless you see God in all including yourself, how can you have the right relationship? J.K. takes you with him into that state so that you get the experience. It seems extremely difficult to keep it up as one has to avoid the natural reaction to the "other" person and remain always poised in stillness, that is, really in constant meditation. I also saw that Mother and he are essentially one in their effect. She says to serve others without attachment and J.K. also says the same thing.

I did not go to sleep till 1 or 1.30 a.m. and cried quite a lot, then cried again in my morning meditation. J.K. always makes me cry. Some hard knot was dissolved and I then talked with him in my mind and told him all my grievances and tried to make peace with him. I thought perhaps I should go and talk to him but later all this was gone again!

I thought, shall I let him leave Benares and be an utter stranger after all these years of intense love, for what else can I call it? I see now that my bitterness is also due to this love. I also saw for a second that it is wrong to compare Mother and him and to see them on different 'levels'. The question of level does not come in as his message is apart from his person, and what is worth seeing is only God —not the barriers.

I did not tell anyone about my experience of last night. I feel I must keep it protected like an unborn baby that must not be exposed to the gaze of others.

My challenge to him —to teach me without words if he is a true teacher— seems to have evoked a response. He is teaching me quite a lot. So I must humbly apologize for much I said about him. I am now feeling more friendly since yesterday and have begun to see the similarities between him and Mother. She also is in surroundings that repelled me at first. She also has difficult people around Her.

19th February, 1949

Malati told me that J.K. said yesterday: "To leave that perfect stillness is death". That is the same as Mother says. Now Her telling me to spend all my time in thought of God has a different meaning. Also I feel there is no need to protect myself around him. It is like when *japa* turns into *dhyan*. I feel now I need not be afraid of him. It seems that he deliberately crucifies himself every time he encounters a new group of people and then lives out in his own body their state and their transformation, and so literally takes their limitations on himself. He then pulls them straight into the stillness that he speaks of. But he insists that meditation must not be done in isolation, alone in one's room, but in relation to every activity and encounter in ones life. I have no life apart from the Search, no other activity interests me and it is there where I have no place in his teaching. "To leave this Stillness is Death" is exactly what Sri Ramana says: "By identifying yourself with the mind you kill the true Self, it is worse than suicide".

19th February, 1949

I feel so miserable at school, it just kills me. I wish they would turn me out so it can end at last. This work never suited me, but I was here for the sake of the congenial surroundings. Now this has also gone. What more? Why can't I stay with Mother?

J.K. evidently does lead one into that stillness of which he speaks. Even though I am no longer really a follower, I definitely get it. The moment I am by myself, I am in it. Mother was right when She said: *"It won't disturb your dhyan"*. It definitely helps meditation. I now see why I could not attend his talks: I distrusted him intensely because of the negative experience I had had with him and I used Mother and *japa* as an armour to protect myself against him. I treated him as though he might be the devil. So what could he do but throw me out! I cannot blame myself either for I just could not afford to go back to the hell into which he had thrown me. If people are not ready to understand, then he just makes them worse. Now it even seems to me that he did not really attack Mother, but only insofar as I had made Her into my armour. He cannot help people as he wants unless he breaks down these barriers, so from his point of view he was quite right. Also I now see that he cannot afford to recognise Mother or Sri Ramana as very likely he feels that this would detract from the effectiveness of his mission. I wonder how tomorrow's meeting will strike me?

20th February, 1949

Before beginning his talk J.K. looked around at his audience and seeing the change in me, gave me a smile and a twinkle. I now feel quite friendly. Because his intention is pure he can't really do lasting harm. With Mother to back me I need not have used all this armour. He is not so formidable as all that. Again I had the same impression: the top structure is missing. He leads up to a point and then...? He did say some nice things. But he takes too much for granted. He has found a way to lead one up to a glimpse of Reality, but he gives no hold or support or method how to get there again. He is like a house without a roof, very beautiful, but it does not really give one shelter or protection. His teaching is not Buddhism, though it is nearer to that than to any other teaching, I believe. I was reading yesterday in the book *The Buddhist Bible* how the Buddha is permeated by *Atmagyan* —every word is full of it— but J.K. is not. He has reached a stillness, but it fades. It is not that Stillness which nothing at all can touch and where even speech either does not matter or is virtually impossible. At least that is how it seems to me.

Later he talked to the teachers. He says that the school should create a "totally integrated child" (What presumption —as though perfection can be so casually concocted!). He mentioned the importance of diet. He knows all about American educational experiments, but ignores completely the side that Mother stresses —spiritual practice. He spoke about the importance of leisure for the teachers, but he had no constructive advice how to spend it. He suggested 3 things: (1) Art —paint a picture or write a poem—, which is impractical for most. (2) Fall in love —dangerous advice. (3) Get magazines about other countries! Never a suggestion of diving deep within. Always keeping everyone on the surface. He attaches great importance to what happens all over the world and its implications to general knowledge, but his teaching is really two dimensional. He never really got to integration —or just at the end of his talk— so vaguely one could not catch it.

This is not for me. I find myself praying to Mother: Get me out of here, somehow make it possible; but not to new work. I can't teach any more, not even one child at a time. Later on when I have come to know from inside, teaching may come spontaneously —that is different and that is not yet. Isn't it time at 45 to retire? For seven years I have tried in vain to do this.

XIX-"Are These Dreams Only Dreams?"

J.K. left today. I am in bed with the flu. What a blessing this is. I need rest and quiet. J.K. is like an earthquake. He violently shakes one's rigidity into chaos and lets the pieces fall where they may. It is the *japa* that keeps me intact and gives me whatever vision or realization I get. This and J.K.'s influence combined are effecting a tremendous clarification, so much so that I can hardly keep pace. It is like a storm overwhelming me. I am beginning to see that his and Mother's teaching are not diametrically opposed. How can they be when they are on different levels altogether?

Yesterday we teachers met with J.K. for a few minutes. It was a washout. But I said: "We would like to meet you more informally". He: "Yes, I know what you mean, but I have had so many commitments". Then I said: "Would you sing for us?". All the time I realized how much like Hugh he looks, even his voice is similar. This puzzles me. Does he really resemble him, or is this only for me because Hugh was to me both guide and beloved? Strange that this should come up again, so long forgotten. That must be the hidden content of the subconscious.

It has also occurred to me how Mother has absorbed all my frustrations: I had no mother, no home, no husband, no child; She has put all this right by Love. She set my health right and taught me to be totally independent and self-sustaining through simplifying my life in general..

Yesterday I began to think out what education means. What we have to do is educate the child through its environment. That is, education starts with the origins of individual life and ends when one has become an *Atmagyani*. Life itself is the fundamental education process. The dignity of labour has to be elevated. There should be merely a difference of function (caste), not of value. In the Ashram there is a perfect classless society of the old Hindu system where all are equally respected within their caste-determined function. I remember how J.K. told me in 1929: "You don't know what Hinduism is." Now I do.

I am beginning to see a strange thing. I have no difficulty in simplifying my physical standard of living because I have the greatest luxury of all: Mother's company. I suppose that's why he attacked me —not Her—, because I am so attached to my treasure. He is really terribly destructive.

I also see that as fighting is my way, it is best for me to fight. As mother says: *"Let every one go along his own line"*. By fighting J.K., I get much more than by running after him. But this is also not the way. The ideal way is surrender. In this Mother and J.K. are the same. One has no choice, one has to be where one is meant to be and by surrendering God will reveal the right thing. So if I am meant to work here, I won't be able to go anywhere else.

Rajghat, 24th February, 1949

Since I am ill in bed it occurred to me this morning to call in some of my students and ask them to share my work between them. They were most eager and did very well. Then Lewis came.

I now see things quite differently. J.K. really opens up new vistas. The mind has become lucid and I see connections not seen before. I see people and things from a different level. There is a renewal. It is most interesting to see how really alike L. and J.K. are. Only Lewis being Western prefers the Eastern way, and J.K. being Eastern prefers the trappings of Western psychology and humanism, etc.

L.'s two poems which he brought me today are also typical of J.K.: One describes Benares as seen by the sensitive artist in him who spends his leisure looking at the river and the sky.

Mother was also right when She said: *"This* (seeing J.K.) *won't disturb your meditation"*.

My broken arm is also a blessing: Normally I depend solely on my body, rather than on my true Self. This illness forces me to allow others to help me at a time when the servants are half on strike. It forces me to surrender —to give the Universal Oneness a chance to look after me through others. There is such lucidity in the mind. I can hardly keep pace with all that comes down. Ages

seem to pass between morning and evening. The more I fight with
J.K., the more he captures me. My resistance is really turning into
love although my greatest comfort is that Mother said: *"You are
mine wherever you go"* and also: *"Where will you go? There is no place
where I am not".* She is always with me, my very breath. I feel Her
very near now. Her home is, as She told me, in everyone's heart.

25th February, 1949

Frydman came and talked to me last night. He says we must
have study classes for the teachers before we can reform the work.
He is right, this is *satsang*. Also he wants to first build houses for
the proposed new community which I am becoming ever more
interested in.

Perhaps this was the significance of my dream on 12th February 1945 when J.K. said: "I choose you for my group". There was
one other European and three Indians present in the dream. Surely
this has to do with this place.

I see now why J.K. says: "If you realize something [i.e. have
some 'spiritual experience'], forget it!" Forget it because it prevents you from going further and causes one to see everything
exclusively in the light of this new revelation, which is after all
only a passing experience and not the final goal. Mother says the
same: *"Whatever experiences you have, don't attach much importance
to them, but go on."*

Trying to write letters to John and Ellen I find that I cannot
express myself. I am speechless. Just as one cannot show the child
in one's womb to anyone, so one has to hide what one realizes till
the time is ripe. Yesterday I found that I could not even tell Lewis
all I wanted. There is now no one to whom I can tell everything. I
find myself becoming more and more attracted to J.K in spite of
myself. There is a new meaning in his words of ten years ago:
"When you love one, you love all". There is no such thing as final
'understanding'. Consciousness is continually evolving and each
new step renders the previous one incomplete.

I am again falling into this elation and expansion of love that
I used to get when I was with J.K. He smiled at me so knowingly
when we went to see him on the eve of his departure. This smile
has penetrated deeply inside me. There is no choice, no question

of it. Mother and he complement each other in the most marvellous, fascinating way.

Rajghat also seems a place I cannot leave. If we really have an ashram here as everyone is now planning (even though it may not be called an ashram), why should I not build a house for Mother with my own hands and ask Her to stay in it sometimes. Surely She will come.

When I think of all the things we do here that we imagine to be so important but are really done only to run out the clock, it reminds me of the Chinese Poem by Po-Chu I :

"Realizing the Futility of Life"

> *Ever since the time I was a lusty boy*
> *Down till now when I am ill and old,*
> *The things I have cared for have been different at different times*
> *But my being busy, that has never changed.*
> *Then on the shore —building sand-pagodas;*
> *Now, at Court, covered with tinkling jade.*
> *This and that —equally childish games,*
> *Things whose substance passes in a moment of time!*
> *While the hands are busy, the heart cannot understand;*
> *When there is no Attachment, Doctrine is sound.*
> *Even should one zealously strive to learn the Way,*
> *That very striving will make one's error more.*

27th February 1949

It also strikes me that J.K.'s reforming the world is only a game, because our generation thinks in this mode. Actually it is only another modern method of dissolving one's conflicts by activity, just like modern psychology analyses children and gives them the right activity to resolve their frustration. This Mother does also.

To be completely concentrated in the Centre, at least as far as I know the Centre, is the one work I have to do. If I can keep it up for 24 hours it does not matter what I do outwardly. There can then be no question of earning or worrying about money. I see now how right Lewis is. In this state, I need not economize or bother and can have all I need and trust that all will be provided.

This afternoon I felt so intensely happy. I am really in meditation all the time when I am alone and also even with others. To assume a particular yoga posture for meditation does not really help any more as it is not required. Now when writing this I also feel I am turned inward and concentrated. I must ask Mother about this. I can now keep it up quite well, even lying down, even when I doze off I get a feeling that the meditation goes on. My breath seems to have changed. There is a strange elation and a certain degree of Love <u>has</u> come into being.

28ᵗʰ February, 1949

I sleep now with *Milarepa* under my pillow. "Architecture is frozen music", I remember someone said. Frydman said yesterday that an architect has to be a sculptor. It reminded me that an astrologer once told me that I am gifted with regard to sculpture as well as music. Maybe the music that is crystalizing in me for lack of expression will take shape in building. The root of all art is one. Music is ethereal, architecture all solid. My difficulty is in the physical. My family name [Schlamm] itself means 'clay' and this has to be formed and modelled. It strikes me that Milarepa, who wrote innumerable songs, was a composer. Kitty may in the end be right that I shall end up by composing music! The fact that I want to prepare a house for Mother here is symbolic of the fact that She has to reside in my heart if things are to happen rightly. She is the beginning and She is the end. The physical is only the outermost fringe of creation. All outer happenings are but symbols of what really IS.

When I am in tune with the students, they work well also. Coming to Class after a week's interval, which I spent mostly in bed, I feel dimly how artificial everything is. Nothing seems real. One's real work is that which helps one most to be oneself, to turn more and more to one's centre. All other work is not only useless, but harmful. It must be dropped.

I am seeing now for the first time how much nearer to Truth Lewis' attitude to money is than is mine. Lewis came and told me how a *bhakta* of Krishna got him a room and even money. So Krishna looks after his devotees [1], however many mistakes they

---

[1] Thompson was very fond of Krishna, one of his very few possessions being an image of Gopal —Krishna as a small child.

may seem to make. I have decided not to worry about anything but to leave everything to God: little things and big things.

L. is really growing even more wonderful in my eyes as I now understand better what I used to dismiss as merely his eccentric behaviour. Today he told me how he dealt with a very aggressive and blunt student in whom he saw possibilities, and how he was able to awaken the boy's fine potential. It made me understand how Mother, by simply looking deeply into my eyes takes a great burden on Herself —how She deals with all one's problems and draws them into Herself, thus awakening one to *bhakti*. She literally <u>does</u> carry the world on Her head. I also felt deeply ashamed of my criticizing J.K., as for all I know he has taken a good deal of my dirt on himself also. But my behaviour was most useful. I need to be humbled. It was good to sneer and shout in public against him, and thereby humble myself before all, as I see now.

When I pray to Mother to absorb me into Her, the prayer immediately becomes a fact and I feel Her permeating every pore of my skin and every atom of my body such that all my emotions and mind reaches out to Her. In this way every difficulty becomes a means to get nearer, because such things make one's fervour greater when one prays. So J.K., by intimidating me, drove me to surrender completely to Mother, which I was never able to do before. In this way danger and fear are actually a blessing!

1st March, 1949

Learnt a new meaning of surrender as a result of last night's talk with L. It is for Her to deal with all my problems and for me to renounce all sense of being the 'doer'. I wonder whether my left arm got disabled from the rickshaw accident because I have to allow Her to deal with my left side. Unconsciously I used to keep this buried. J.K. and L. are teaching me that there is no high or low, one cannot divide life. Sri Ramana also told me when I told him about my two sides —the peaceful, happy one and the doubting, restless one—: *"Both are you."*

One can never criticise another. I said J.K. was not a teacher at all. Now I say he is the Teacher of Teachers, after Mother, and I fall down flat at His Feet.

Are These Dreams Only Dreams?

Yesterday went to the Ashram and also saw L. in his lovely new room in Kumaraswamy Math behind the Kedarnath Temple. It makes me so happy to see him in these harmonious surroundings. I have given up worrying about him altogether and feel that God is arranging for all his needs. I now see how his reckless generosity is much finer than my reasoning economy.

He read his latest poems to me. "The Black Angel" especially is a complete Masterpiece and unique. I do not think anything of this sort has been written in this age, neither in English, nor in any other language. I feel that in his very different way —Art, Tantra, Magic— he has achieved something very similar to J.K.'s vision. He has united all his many sides that were in such conflict with each other: immense learning, wisdom, yoga, tantra, mantric power, extreme beauty, culture. The poem also shows how Eros has the highest possibility and how it <u>has</u> to be integrated. It is altogether immense. He was right. He is now 40 and he knew he would find himself only at 40. To publish things before now would have meant to take the baby out of the protecting womb of its mother before its time. I feel intensely happy about this.

How wonderful my own *karma* must be to meet at close quarters these giants of our time. How necessary these years of frustration were for me in order to allow the essential gestation to take place undisturbed. How I misjudged J.K.!

In the evening I sat in Mother's room on the roof of the Ashram. Never have I been able to pray to Her with such fervour, such passion as I do now spontaneously. It suddenly strikes me that *bhakti* includes every dimension of love and this gives it an intensity and richness that makes one burn from head to foot to be Hers. I sat from 9 to 11.15 and the mosquitoes were eating me up. As much as I could I refrained from chasing them away with my hands or from scratching, but sometimes blew them away with my breath —though that also stopped for a while. I thought that this is my test —how serious am I when I pray? "Do what you like with me, cut my body into pieces (as Milarepa said to Marpa), only do not let me be separated from you." And I cannot even bear a few mosquitoes?!

---

[2] Included in *Black Sun. The Collected Poems of Lewis Thompson*, Hohm Press, 2001.

I caught Her eyes, as She gazed at me at Bareilly while She was going round during the *kirtan* and I was completely captured by them. They exercise such attraction that I cannot take my mind off them. This is madness. I feel drunk with emotion and happiness and longing, and the mind is held in breathless adoration of a mystery of frighteningly awesome divine beauty which Her eyes seem to conceal and yet invite me to penetrate.

When early this evening I sat quietly on the banks of the Varuna, it was wonderful —pure spontaneous meditation.

8th March, 1949

My mind goes on dreaming about the centre here. I just can't stop it. I dream of a temple of the new age that I want to build. A poet would be inspired to write there, a musician to compose, a *sadhu* to go into *samadhi* etc. Of course such a structure should be made of marble or at least of stone, with sandalwood for doors and windows etc. I would like to spend all my savings for it. I would sell the piano, so it would be literally made 'from music'. My work would be to act as the *chowkidar* [caretaker], to keep the temple clean and intact on all planes. I would use my free time to sit in *dhyan* there and would live nearby in a small hut. It should be surrounded by an exquisite garden of sweet-smelling flowers, holy shrubs and trees, no vegetables but lots of *tulsi, bel, mango, horsinghar, chameli, juiphul, amla* etc [3]. I picture the building looking somewhat like a Greek temple of the most perfect proportions, with lofty pillars and the rooms in the centre hidden from the gaze of intruders. It should look out on the Ganges. That is what I want! I don't want a house! I want to be the keeper of a temple of Mother.

Are these dreams only dreams? Am I going to build the true house for Mother only in my heart which, as She said, is Her true home; or will I also build one of earth and cement? It really does not matter, but these dreams make me intensely happy. Sanjiva Rao built this place dreaming like this and that is how these things come off. For 14 years I have fought for a sensible diet and now we are going to have it, for servants to be treated humanely, for salad to be grown, for classes of not more than 12, for *satsang* for teachers, not only children etc. etc. Now it is almost coming true.

---

[3] Various sacred fruits and plants.

10th March, 1949

Attended Frydman's study group. I actually got something out of it. He does produce that Stillness. He really uses Sri Ramana's way of argument and it really does produce a profound atmosphere that slows down the breath, as in *japa*. One gets into that Stillness. J.K. is converting me slowly. But it is the mixture of Sri Ramana and J.K. that does it, not J.K. alone. I could never have seen the point unless Mother had prepared me and shaken me out of my conditioning.

12th March, 1949

Last night at the Ashram, while immersed in the purity of the atmosphere there, I thought: After all, what difference does it make where I am? As long as my *sadhana* goes on, the setting is of little importance. I have lost now that fear that I won't get proper food or a solitary place if I do not arrange for it. Is not God rich enough to give me whatever I need and more. Surely it is only my lack of faith that makes me arrange, and that prevents Him from providing. What matters is the intensity of my concentration, the fervour of my *bhakti*, nothing else. "Think of Me and leave all else!"

Talked to Gurtu [4] by chance. He is a changed man. What power J.K. has! It is truly a miracle. We talked for nearly two hours. I forgot the time. He did not even wince when I told him that money would come if only the experiment were truly tried.

15th March, 1949

There is a certain sense of discord between Frydman and me. Today at the study group (which by the way I find very helpful for meditation and always discover something new in it) he made a statement to which I objected. I feel that J.K. encourages a narrow iconoclasm in his followers which keeps them rather smugly closed to all forms of spirituality other than what they perceive to be his way. This is really the crux of my fight with J.K.

---

[4] Pandit Iqbal Narayan Gurtu, a much respected Benares Brahmin who was one of the principal directors of the school and who had initially been opposed to the radical changes now being proposed.

I wonder whether after all, as I felt in the beginning of J.K.'s stay, that he had come to turn me out of Rajghat. May be. Anyway I am completely indifferent now.

I feel that unless Mother definitely tells me, I shall not leave until circumstances send me away. Just as the work I wanted to give up has now left me, so if I am to go, it will come about naturally. There will be no choice.

19th March, 1949

Mother arrived on 17th. After a few hours with Her everything here seems different. The atmosphere is so infinitely more rarefied at the ashram. Even my writing is quite changed I see. I wonder whether I need build a home for Her? Anyway I am building Her house in my heart. Here at Rajghat everything is on a lower level where the physical dominates. There it hardly matters.

21st March, 1949

Spent Sunday (yesterday) with Mother in *mouna* [silence]. It seems to me so much a waste of time to continue working here at the school, doing work that my heart is not in, only to get money. So I should like to resign my job and say to them: "Pay me what you like, I will do what I feel is right and leave the rest to God."

30th March, 1949

Mother left on the 28th. Coming back to Rajghat from the ashram makes me more acutely aware of the heaviness of the atmosphere here. I wonder whether this has become even more so because of J.K.'s visit, as he has taken away all the things like *kirtan*, *puja* etc which had a purifying effect.

I haven't slept here since 17th March and have been mostly very near Mother on the upper roof of the ashram —the last few nights in the same room with Her, next to Her bed about a yard or less from Her Feet. That makes a tremendous difference.

Mother said when I mentioned that it is just four years since I met Her at Sarnath: "*Yes, I went there to get you, now I have you, I need not go there anymore.*" It is true I would not have been able to get in touch with Her anywhere else at that time with all the *kirtan* and activity around Her in the ashram etc.

390

When I heard Mithu has T.B. I got a great shock and thought to myself: "Is it worthwhile doing anything except strenuous *sadhana* when death is so near at hand, even for young people?" Since I had slept in the room with her, I imagined what I would do if I became infected: of course, spend every minute in meditation and leave all other activities.

I was much impressed by Udas, who sits now in Mother's room in meditation from 4 a.m. till 12 p.m. and eats only once at 12 p.m. There is quite an atmosphere in that room. I cannot help admiring her now. It is reminiscent a bit of Milarepa.

1st April, 1949

J.K. appears in a worse light now. The whole experiment here at Rajghat seems mostly castles in the air and now everyone is complaining again as usual. I wish I could clear out. J.K. gives one an experience, but it seems ultimately to leave one worse off than before.

Bhadaini, 10th April, 1949

At first I thought Rajghat would become a place of true spiritual synthesis, but now that Telangs and consorts are getting most of the power, it looks as if I had been wrong. It will be J.K.'s place and what have I to do with that? Surely I have lost interest. His way —if it is a way— to the Ultimate is not my way.

Rajghat, 12th April, 1949

Felt Mother very strongly whilst sitting for meditation in the school garden. A tree is worship by being exactly what it is intended to be. So we also can become all worship by remembering at all times who we are.

It occurred to me that much of what I had thought was progress in meditation was really only being absorbed in the creations of my own mind, which fascinated me because their content was somewhat on a new plane due to J.K.'s influence.

No need to resign. When the need arises it will become possible or even unavoidable, even in the middle of the year.

Reading Sri Aurobindo's *The Synthesis of Yoga*, which V. Sydney brought me.

20ᵗʰ April, 1949

Lewis slept here last night. His presence is definitely helpful, amazingly so. He is really very much more extra-ordinary than one admits. His mask is so clever that even I am partly deluded. This is his protection.

I did write to Mother two days ago after all and asked Her about this place.

This morning I woke at 3 a.m. due to a storm and therefore sat up for meditation at 4 a.m. It makes all the difference.

XX - A Devastating Departure

Kishenpur, 1st May, 1949

Arrived here this morning. Was not well in the train and I got here exhausted. No accommodation except in tents hot as hell. Feel like running away. Neither have I any of the comforts of Rajghat nor Mother's Presence, and I feel afraid of the hardships at the Ashram. How attached I am to the body and how useless it is to try to run away from anything. It only makes it worse. So what is the point of leaving here again. The only refuge is really to trust in God and take everything to be God, also pain. But how easy to write this down!

Kishenpur, 6th May, 1949

Got all right and really better than before within three days. I always want to run away when I first arrive and now I like it here. Have a nice room with a Sikh family. I spend half the time busy with my possessions and when I haven't got them I am really much happier and manage easily without them.

9th May, 1949

Yesterday at the *Dhyan Mandir* meditation rather better. But what of it? J.K. has upset me again, I feel restless and wondering how to proceed. Mother was asked yesterday why we should worship God as Mother? Why not as brother or father etc? She: *"Only the Mother can do the right thing for her child and if someone else can, then he is also the Mother."*

13th May, 1949

Mother is All, God Herself. What right have I to be unhappy, when I sit face to face with Her. What more do I want?

It was a fine experience to stay as a guest of a Sikh family, Shiv Dev Singh at Gandhi Nagar. How hospitable, simple and really religious these people are —reading their scriptures for hours in their free time.

I met Helen Dhillon who picked me up on the road, took me to her house and within two days confides her troubles to me and then has a private with Mother. Then there is the Punjabi lady who ran away from home and came here on foot. Even though I do no work at the Ashram, this is also service to help these people out of their mess.

Sharanananda is here. He spoke beautifully: *"If you are truly suffering, you will find Him. This does not mean to have a headache etc but to be agonizingly aware of one's own nothingness. Usually we think of our own qualities and of others' shortcomings. This is the wrong way round."*

18ᵗʰ May, 1949

Mother appears ever more DIVINITY ITSELF. Why do I still crave food, drink, sleep, comforts? Why do I still get irritated? When She sings and someone talks, I get wild. Mother told me: *"It is a great sin to be violent. Ask for forgiveness."* When I got into the car that took Her out for a drive, She said: *"Have you hurt your foot?"* (I had hurt it slightly). I said: "Why?" She: *"Can't you walk?"* I felt bad, because so many people get into Her car, why should not I. But last night I really hurt my foot badly and did not go to Raipur with Her today. The rest did me good though. I need rest sometimes. She knows it and provides for it. I sat up all night on Her birthday and the fatigue remained in my bones. Since She scolded me I have felt sad. At such times I feel I must serve and start sweeping and cleaning everything. I also washed Her clothes lately. I suppose cleaning everything means really cleaning up one's own inner dirt. That's perhaps why one has to work.

Kishenpur, 29ᵗʰ May, 1949

On 24ᵗʰ May Mother asked Sewa (Dr. Sharma) to drop her work. She declined. I said: "Why don't you say this to me?" She: *"All right, leave everything and spend your time looking after the Sahib."* (the old Frenchman, Satyananda). I: "But if he gets cross with me?" She: *"Ah, there should be no fights, you'll have to give up anger."*

Afterwards I asked Her to talk to me privately about the matter. She: *"What is there to talk about? If you can do all his work, it will be good".* Then I told Her my doubts as to whether he will agree, that he will be more angry if he has to pay for my service etc. She said: *"Wait for a few days."* On 26th She told me to remain in silence from the next day. So I insisted on talking to Her then about this matter and told Her: "If it is your order, I shall drop my work and do his service, money or no money." She said: *"No, don't resign; when I go to Benares you can talk it over with me. Just now do nothing of the sort, but look after him as long as you are here and I shall see how well you can do it".*

It seems to me the whole matter was a test to show me how small my faith is and how great my love of comfort and security. Though I am so eager to get out of Rajghat, I at once began to worry about how I might get ill if I have to live on the insufficient food of the Ashram, how I shall not be able to bear the strain of constant travelling, how I shall be bound without a holiday and not be able to get away by myself, no privacy etc.

Today She explained how everything we see is a manifestation of the Divine. She began by saying that a Doctor and a *Vaidya* [practitioner of traditional Indian herbal medicine] see disease in two different forms: the doctor as a germ, the *Vaidya* as a *murti* [entity]. She said: *"There is only He, but we see different shapes according to our samskaras.*[1] *So therefore it is possible that two different individuals may see two entirely different forms when looking at the same thing".* Someone asked: "Where is God?" Mother: *"Where is He not?"*

She again and again advises *satsang* and to do *japa* all day long, so as to keep God's company in your mind all the time.

Solan, 23rd June, 1949

I Have an aversion to writing in this diary and am living in a sort of daze and craze after Mother. On the 14th June at Kishenpur made a big scene because H. monopolizes Mother and does not even let Her breathe. I had to drag her away by the arm and hurt it slightly and there was a long excited controversy afterwards. But it had an amazing effect; she has improved by 50%.

---

[1] Tendencies from previous lives that determine our present mental disposition.

395

Today there was a big and final clash with my French 'father'. He called me 'cobra' in front of Mother. So that makes it quite clear that my job with him will never come off. It was quite good that all this happened. So back I go to Rajghat. Never mind about the future, it will shape itself.

Today Mother said to one of the ashramites to stop being cross and to see Krishna everywhere (he is a worshipper of Krishna). He replied that he could not possibly get on with the particular person he had just been angry with. She said: *"To remain calm in the solitude of your room is easy enough. It is when with others that you have to prove your faith."* This is J.K.'s teaching!

Solan, 27th June, 1949

The 'untouchability' again gives me much trouble. It is good that I am in *mouna*, so I can just view the whole thing without being able to object. But my faith gets shaken when I see all this. Also no one really keeps the traditional injunctions properly, they don't even know them.

There is no perfection in this world, not even in Her's. I suppose it is the nature of the world to drag even the Divine into its mire. This is also Her teaching: *"Don't ever expect happiness or peace from this world. Its swarupa [nature] is pain."* So it is an utterly useless undertaking.

Solan, 29th June, 1949

This morning during *Devi Path* it suddenly dawned on me how nothing matters but the intense desire to get beyond, to be enlightened, not to exist anymore in a state of separateness. When that desire is really born nothing else is needed —no *puja*, no *sadhana*, the very intensity is its own *sadhana*. This is where J.K. is right. Also, then no outer circumstances, difficulties or trials matter or are even noticed. That is what Mother means when She says: *"Go on with your sadhana and don't bother about little things."*

Later:

After the reading was over I received the news of Lewis' passing away together with a letter from him and a poem, significant in its being the last I shall ever receive from him.

"Dark Heart"

The heart that beats,
The mad, the stammering heart,
For all beneath it as for all above,
The ruinous touch of pleasure or of thought —
Dark heart, the body's night,
Beating against the sun,
Your nest of cunning holds
Against assault.
Yet in a day not yours,
Drowned or pierced through
By infinite passionate light,
Anguish and love are healed
In the peace by which they bleed:
"All that throbs is untrue".

I have not yet taken in the loss —what it will mean to me not to be able to discuss my troubles with him, not to have his unfailing judgement of books etc. I can't even really feel sad, though it was the last thing I expected. But what I feel is: life or death really makes no difference to him. He was not made for this world and evidently had worked out all there was for him here. It seems the perfection he aimed at cannot be gained down here. He was always doubtful whether it was worthwhile to bother about producing things. If I had been in Benares, he would not have died. He did not die of heat stroke, as they say, but of starvation as I well know, or rather of overeating for a few days after having been starved for so long. Fate did not allow him to die five years ago but kept me there to save him —and kept me away this time because evidently he was not to live. Since he returned from Bombay in the middle of the hot season, penniless, his fate was sealed. I must find out from Rajagopalan exactly what happened at Bombay. Shall ask Mother whether to apply for a few days leave.

This time the *mouna* was of great value. It is such waste of energy to talk so much useless stuff. Really where is the time for this nonsense? Lewis was right. He was so concentrated every minute and never compromised one bit. Ah, I shall miss him. There has never been one like him! What a rare, rare being he was. One of the greatest privileges of my life was to know him closely.

Delhi, 4ᵗʰ July, 1949

Had a heart to heart talk with Kitty last night in the dark — after perhaps fifteen or twenty years. It made me see something I had never before seen: how the Guru is more than a person and guides everyone according to their own way and reveals himself in each one whenever and however needed. She and I really agree and have come to very much the same place, starting from different angles. But in the unreality of day-light which reveals only the outer covering of life, this had become hidden and overcast. It was good and necessary I stayed for the night. Only in the night one can talk like this.

Rajghat, 7ᵗʰ July, 1949

Arrived here 5ᵗʰ morning. Only since coming here have I taken in that Lewis is really gone. I have never known what death can mean. I remember how J.K. behaved when Nitya died. [2]

I am quite broken, I can't pick myself up. Our relationship was so much deeper and closer because it had no name. Names are false and limiting. I cannot get over the sadness. I cannot get over the feeling that somewhere he failed. He understood everything except the physical plane. The physical is imperfect by nature and he would not have it. He wanted Truth here also. I feel his imperfection was that he could not tolerate the inherent imperfection of this material universe.

11ᵗʰ July, 1949

I have now collected myself to some extent. I have secured all Lewis' journals and card registers and notes on Sri Krishna Menon's sayings etc. Everyone is asking for manuscripts. There aren't any except the poems. What is the use now of all the things he so carefully copied from books, all the collections of beautiful pictures. They are more a bother than anything else. Was his life really only *sadhana* as he insisted? Was he not deceiving himself?

---

[2] Krishnamurti's beloved brother Nitya died in 1925. This was the great tragedy, as well as the great turning point, of his life.

Would not perhaps the spiritual exercises his Guru asked him to do have been a shortcut through everything and taken him straight to the end? I feel there was a misunderstanding in him somewhere. The subtlety of his rare mind itself became a hindrance. The very perfection with which he did everything became an obstacle because no one else could come up to his standards and he could not tolerate clumsiness.

P.K. Rajgopalan seemed to have lost faith in him, judging from his letter of the 7th July. Lewis was such a powerful personality and has left much unfulfilled. But surely as a mother's intense prayer protects her child, so his intense faith must have protected him. Though I wonder how much really God protects anyone? Perhaps He is not at all concerned with the little undulations in this world of illusion. Perhaps it is our own thought, our own faith, our prayer itself, that generates the power which we erroneously call 'God'.

Very likely Lewis could not do much more in this life, except in the line of an artist, which was after all not his deepest aim. Having written and collected so much, he had perhaps created the circumstances that would have forced him into an artist's 'career', which he wanted to avoid at all cost as it would have distracted him from his goal of Realization. Very likely there was no other way out for him. He must now be with his Guru. I remember when Ma met him first, She talked to him and asked him: "*Are you doing sadhana?*". And She always asked him whether he had been to see his Guru.

Mother said at Solan: "*Whether you think of Him or not, the Guru is always holding your hand*". So Lewis evidently made a fatal error when he thought that his Guru had withdrawn because he [the Guru] refused to talk to him. The Guru need not talk, whatever he does, he remains the Guru.

At Solan I asked Mother about the use of a *mala*. She told the following story: A *sadhu* once thought he would give up using his *mala* to do *japa* and do *japa* in his mind only. He threw his *mala* down and the string broke. The beads scattered and suddenly he saw that every single bead had become an image of his chosen deity.

Mother asked me to learn the *sloka* [Sanskrit verse] which is the *pranam* [self-offering] to the Guru.

399

18th July, 1949

For the last day or so I have had the feeling that L. is happy now and free and has expanded and pervades everything. I feel him very near all the time. Perhaps he has now overcome the pangs of the birth into a new state and has been able to solve his tangle with his Guru. Or is it all imagination?

That little Krishna seems quite marvellous, full of life... [3] I wish I could keep it. It fills the room with peace and love and life. I do not feel the need now to run after Mother so constantly. I feel happy in my quiet room, away from the children.

Rajghat, 23rd July, 1949

Last Tuesday Gangadi's mother died at the Ashram. Ma presided over her departure from this world. It was very impressive. As she breathed her last, Mother touched her from head to foot as though releasing her life at the moment of death. I had brought Mother a garland and as there was no other one, She put it around the dying woman's neck. Afterwards commenting on this She said to me: *"You had to come"*. In fact I came just in time to see her die. It moved me very much as I could not help remembering how Lewis died without anyone to help.

Last night again it suddenly struck me that I could have saved L., if not from dying, at least from being hungry. I have Rs. 500 in my account. What a shame to have money and let your best friend die of starvation. It burns in my hand. There it lies unused, while it might have saved someone's life. Saving money is surely wrong.

Rajghat, 29th July, 1949

Had fever for half a day. It is mostly due to strain. I can't collect myself. L.'s affairs and his loss are on my mind. Last night read his last diary and I see now that this life was altogether impossible for him. The only solution would have been to withdraw completely into the spiritual realm and leave this world to take care of itself. This really is my solution also and what Mother

---

[3] Thompson had an image of Krishna as a child (Gopal) which he was very fond of. This was ultimately given to Atmananda and she cherished it as one of her few possessions for the rest of her life.

always says. His problem of immanence or transcendence was really solved by his death into transcendence. His living on the edge all the time could not have gone on much longer; and what for?

For me also this must be a lesson. It is useless to expect anything from this world. Only withdrawal can bring peace and then perhaps one may rise to the level where one sees nothing but God, like Mother. What a sublime state that must be, far beyond Lewis' —who after all was still identified with being an artist and, for all his sense of beauty and perfection and humanity, was still not at the point where all is equally 'That'.

In the Ashram the untouchability gives me much trouble, but now my understanding of Brahminical purity has made me keenly aware of the 'filth' of so-called civilized European habits where there is no sense whatsoever of the spiritually subtle. It really disgusts me and I prefer the 'untouchability' to this. So I must stop objecting to it. There is no other way than to obey Her and spend my time on *sadhana* and not on reforming the world. This was really L.'s problem also, in spite of his denial, because he refused to take the world as it is —nor would he completely renounce it— but demanded it conform to his standards. He refused to compromise and his solution was to live in his own self-created *satya yuga* [mythical golden age].

Later:

It is interesting to see that in every way I am wanted here at Rajghat because J.K. is unable to give the right lead, and so my close connection with Mother gives the necessary counterweight. M.K. says she wants me here because everyone else looks up to her and she can't carry it off unless there is someone who is capable of giving intelligent criticism. I see more and more how dangerous J.K. is, particularly if one has not had the benefit of meaningful contact with a spiritual teacher greater than he.

Democracy is absurd and impossible except amongst people who can think for themselves. Those who let their mind wander all day are swayed by every wind and adopt the opinion of the one who has the strongest personality amongst them. Therefore it is quite irrelevant what these people decide.

4th August, 1949

I was just remarking that, whatever happens, the only safe course is to stick to one's Guru at all cost, when Mother told me that for the next six months I shan't be able to use the tap, bathroom and latrine in the ashram that I had been using up to now. She did make some other arrangements which are adequate, if uncomfortable, but I went quite mad over this new restriction. It made me feel quite desperate. L. is gone and now the difficulties of seeing Mother have increased tenfold and my health is giving way. Since he died I simply cannot pick myself up. Mother talked to me very nicely afterwards, trying to appease me.

Sharananandji whom I saw the day before yesterday said: *"Laugh at all these rules. Difficulties are good because they wake you up."* I suppose the two things do not go together anymore: Rajghat and the Ashram, but I haven't the courage to leave the comforts I have at Rajghat altogether. I feel the burden will be too great, and yet, perhaps it will lessen the strain.

11th August, 1949

This evening while trying to meditate on the roof I suddenly felt Lewis very near and he seemed to convey that I could contact him when meditating since he is now no longer limited by the physical. While it is true that I cannot talk with him as before, I can get even closer to him by ascending to the plane where he is when I meditate. It just means adjusting myself to his present state, there is really no loss —there need not be— on the contrary, it can be a gain. I felt extremely happy suddenly. It is just stupidity and rigidity that made me feel so uncomfortable for so long. As he has always helped me, so his now being removed to an inner world should help me to turn more deeply inside.

19th August, 1949

Since I got hold of L. I can meditate again and I have an urge to do so. These days when I think of Lewis my breath seems to change at once and I am drawn inside. I have the impression that he has now withdrawn to an inner plane, which is his real home or at least very much nearer to it than what he used to be in during life and even immediately after death. I feel that he is in a deep and intense *samadhi*, utterly concentrated, his whole being collected in a single point. "In this intensity peace and pain are one", as his last poem runs.

This is a great help to me. He helps me in my *sadhana* even more than he did when he was here physically.

Yesterday there was a letter from Sri Krishna Menon dated 12th August. The steps I undertake in Lewis' affair seem all guided. The Guru also seems to have complete trust in me in this matter. Yesterday evening in my meditation I felt that Sri K.M.'s papers should be sent to him as soon as possible. Much later I heard he is leaving for England in October or November. There was also a letter from Ella Maillart yesterday. Matters are beginning to get cleared up.

At the Ashram I realized how necessary all these hardships like fasting and lack of sleep and material comfort are. Though very irksome they help to make one free from the bondage of the body and I am really much better for it when I undergo them for a few days.

It occurred to me that Mother is testing me through the hardships I undergo in the ashram because if I want Her, which is RE-ALITY itself, I must be prepared to forego everything else, even seemingly justified needs.

There seems a close connection —at least as far as I am concerned— between Ma and L.; that is, he is sort of my little Guru or Her assistant in rearing me, and I depend much on him and on the state he is in. I feel an ever deepening love for him. The very thought of him drives tears into my eyes, not anymore for grief over his loss, but due to joy as I have found him again, so beautifully that I would not have him return to this miserable existence.

Someone asked Mother: "Surely the birthdays of Rama and Krishna are occasions for great rejoicing. Why should we not eat well instead of fasting on those days?"

Mother: "*You eat everyday. On those special days we refuse to take enjoyment from the world. We celebrate the birth of an avatar by being absorbed in the thought of Him, refusing even food and sleep and saying: 'Rather will I die than accept anything from the world', at least on those days. Or else —there is another way— if the hardship is too great, you may say: 'I will eat a little, just enough to keep up my medi-*

tation', just as the Lord Buddha had to eat milk-rice before he could get enlightenment because his body had become too weak from the great austerities he practised. Whatever you enjoy of the world takes away from your nearness to God. *The two don't go together*".

27th August, 1949

Yesterday some foreigners asked Mataji questions.

Questioner: How can I get Self-Realization?"

Mother: *The Self is Swayam Prakash* [self-illuminated], *so you need not do anything.*

Questioner: But have we not to make an effort towards it?

Mother: *Yes, there is a veil over the Self and you can remove it by your effort.*

Questioner: What is the process towards this?

Mother: *Do you really want it? Then will you do without questioning what I tell you?*

Questioner: (hesitates) I came to India for this purpose and I regard Ramana Maharshi as my Guru.

Mother: *Then you must do exactly as He tells you. If you want Self-Realization and nothing else, you shall find a way. There is no doubt about it.*

This is really the point and justifies what J.K. said: "If one is in dead earnest, this very seriousness becomes the Guru." But who is in dead earnest?

Kishenpur [Dehradun], 1st September, 1949

On Sunday 28th August, seemingly by chance, I went into Mother's room at 2 p.m. and found Her discussing the arrangements for the old Frenchman's journey to Dehradun. It struck me to say to Her: "I feel bad because you had told me to serve him and now he is ill. If I had done as you asked me he would be all right". Mother at once caught me and said: *"All right, take one month's leave and go with him. He has no one and no one here can really look after him properly."* So my fate has brought me here unexpectedly.

Kishenpur, 5th September, 1949

There are so many difficulties here. I feel quite ground under. But today looking at Her pictures I feel one must keep continually

Her in mind —then one can bear it. She takes the most difficult people and puts them together and there is clash after clash, no doubt to work off their *karma* with each other.

In Benares I began to like my Gopal Krishna *vigraha* [4] so much, quite ridiculously so. I must find out what is in it really —only a piece of metal? It cannot be. There must be an invisible being enshrined in it that wants to be loved and worshipped and which blesses in return.

I suppose humanism does not go together with *Deva* worship. Europe is more human for all its cruelty, the only God they know is man. But here one serves the Godhead and neglects human beings terribly. I can't help condemning this although perhaps I am wrong.

When Mother is not here there is no *satsang*. The old man talks only about nonsense, his greatness, and abuses everyone else. He loves only those who flatter him.

Kishenpur, 23rd September, 1949

Today Mother said: *"This world means the constant change between happiness and pain. There can be no stability here, no 'nitya'* [eternity], *no 'sthiti'* [absoluteness]. *That is only in Him. There cannot be both 'samsar'* [the world] *and God. On the way there seem to be both, but when you have reached God, there is no 'samsar', there is only He."*

Kishenpur, 2nd October, 1949

Yesterday was Dussehra [5]. This time I could really join in the spirit of the festival and enjoyed it for the first time. Formerly I just used to put up with it. I watched the fascinating process of the *murti* of the Goddess being made from bamboo and straw and earth etc, all according to an esoteric procedure which makes use of *yantras* and *mantras* until finally it takes on a very life-like appearance and is beautifully dressed in silk and richly worshipped with sumptuous food offerings etc. Finally at the end of the tenth day it is consigned to the river where it dissolves back into the formless from where it came. It gives one a sense of the transiency of all

---

[4] The image she had inherited from Thompson.

[6] The tenth day of the annual fall festival to the Mother Goddess.

405

things and of *leela* [life as the play of God]. After the *Vigraha* [image] is gone, only the devotion and the love remains and one traditionally embraces everyone in token that She is everywhere. The image was merely a help towards this realization.

I feel that Lewis is gone altogether, that he has dissolved his individuality and is utterly oblivious of his affairs here. I now miss him again. Sometimes I feel so desperate, I wish I were where he is. There is no place on this earth where I can really be at ease.

Rajghat, 9th October, 1949

Returned here on the 6th after one day at Lucknow. Have a swollen leg, perhaps due to eating food paid for grudgingly by Satyananda [the old Frenchman].

Yesterday packed L's things. There is so much strain in dealing with them. Again I do not know what to do with his diaries and meticulously organized notes. Perhaps it would be best to go to Bombay and see Sri Krishna Menon and get his advice. It seems such a responsibility to have these things. I wish he had left a will! I suppose he did not care much what would happen in that case; it all happened so fast.

I wonder whether he died because all these activities, however wonderful and extraordinary, were side-tracking him from the true goal —to attain Self Realization— which he persistently postponed. If, as we all feel, he belonged to a non-human species, some kind of *deva*, and took this incarnation only to attain *Atmagyan* [knowledge of the true Self], he should have obeyed his Guru promptly and explicitly and not played about so much with writing and what not.

I ought not to miss Lewis, having Her. But I do.

17th October, 1949

Debu [6] left on the 15th taking Lewis' books to England to his mother. I spent a few days studying L's things and have changed my mind completely. I found the manuscript of his 'Autobiography', which explains his life. It makes me see him in a new light. It is such a great work of art, entirely consistent and harmonious and even his death was not really premature but part of a wonderful

---

[6] Thompson's friend, the poet and musicologist Deben Bhattacharya.

design. He writes: "My life must be as short as possible". What seemed an undesired responsibility to me, now appears as a sacred trust. The work he did is not lost. In his card registers and journals there are as yet untapped treasures of deep, unique, original thought. Debu says that he told him: "It is all there. If I had money you could be my secretary and we could work it all out".

He had already long ago entrusted his card registers to me, which evidently encompass his main work, and I shall surely find the right people to work it out.

I still feel that Rajghat is the best place for me. It is lucky Satyanand behaved as he did, so as to leave no doubt that I cannot do that work. Rajghat gives a frame to my life and a home to those manuscripts which I treasure like a mother her unborn baby.

With this swollen leg of mine I shall not be able to see so much of Her as I used to. Anyway I want some time to go into Lewis' work.

This coincides with a letter to the Rajghat Trust by J.K. where he says that Rajghat should not be his place, but a centre of education, which means the transformation of the individual. So I can with clear conscience remain here. And certainly L.'s work is very much on J.K.'s lines.

19ᵗʰ October, 1949

What seems of great importance to stress in a 'foreword' when his writings are published, is that he did not 'write' like other writers. He did no <u>work</u>. He despised work. He <u>lived</u>. He refused to do formal *sadhana* because he felt that the <u>whole</u> of life must be *sadhana*. The realization, intuitions, illuminations, call it what you will, that came to him in the course of his life (*sadhana*), he jotted down and arranged according to the headings under which they came —not for the sake of producing something, but to keep his mind clear, for the sake of order. It was a spontaneous activity. Each of his poems also marks a living experience, a step in his life —*sadhana*.

5ᵗʰ November, 1949

When I went to pay for the copy of Plato's *Republic* for Lewis on October 29ᵗʰ, his last debt as far as I know, I felt as if he thanked

407

me profusely. From what Sri Krishna Menon is supposed to have said about L's death and his "intense struggle" for a month after he left his body, my feelings about his transition are confirmed. Even the fact that he was in a body of light, I knew. I wrote on August 10th to his mother (but did not send the letter): "He must now be garbed in nothing but light".

Now I feel he is always with me, never leaves me for a moment. Also he seems to constantly draw me towards where he is, draw me and push me. He is not in the world of the dead, as he has gone beyond birth and death; and if I merely die without having attained to his state, I shall not be a hairbreadth nearer him than I am now. I feel a kind of anguish, a restlessness, no time to loose. Why attend do anything that does not lead beyond! I must be quick.

14th November, 1949

Mother evidently wants me to learn to obey blindly. Anyway we are blind and we think we see, so it is very likely better to let someone who really sees decide for us. But I just can't seem to learn this.

I feel out of sorts. In Dehradun at the Durga Puja I prayed: "Let me die soon". It came naturally from my heart. Though I felt then I should not have prayed like that, this wish comes often now. That is why I am ill and haggard, as I have no wish to live. Since Lewis died there is no comfort in life and I don't see why I must live. What for? I could not pull on with J.K.'s teaching. Now I can't with Mother's either. I get hurt all the time at being kept out and not being able to talk freely with Her.

The other night someone saw me make my bed on the verandah outside of Ma's room. He asked: "Do you feel too hot inside?" I: "No, but some of them won't allow me inside". "Why?". "Because I was not born in this country". Next day he brought a bundle of new blankets and asked Didi to give me one. It is quite useful as it is getting colder and I freeze bitterly going to the ashram in early morning by rickshaw. I do get so many presents. Since I have no money to buy clothes everyone gives me something. No need to buy at all.

25th November, 1949

Dream at 3.30 a.m.: I go to see my grandmother with another person. For breakfast she gives us first a sweet dish then Kartoffel puree with Blutwurst [mashed potatoes with sausage]. I say it is too much so early in the morning, but she says: "You are going out and won't have lunch, so eat now." I wonder why she does not offer us fruit, but then remember that she may not have the money to buy it. We then go somewhere, I have forgotten that part of the dream, except that I climb down a rocky incline which suddenly turns into a steep cliff and I have not much of a foothold. I first consider sliding down but then reflect that the distance is too great and I may smash my body. So I hold on with both my hands and began to shout: "Help, help, save me, save me Lord". Then a lady comes and smilingly gives me a hand and easily draws me up. We walk back to my grandmother's house. I now remark how steep and difficult the path is —I did not notice this the first time and I wonder how my grandmother can manage to get up there, especially in winter when there is ice. The house is quite lonely and I wonder how she gets by there. Then there is some talk of a relative who is a doctor, and of my grandmother going somewhere to earn money. I am shocked —at her age? But she says: "Why not?" Then I feel I ought to help her with funds. The lady (who saved me) asks me: "Have you only loved women or has there also been a man in your life?" I feel surprised at the question and first think she is talking to my grandmother. She says: "No, I am talking about you". With that I woke up, feeling I must write this dream down, but am too lazy as it has suddenly grown cold this night.

The other day Mother said to me: "You have suddenly grown old in such a few days." It is true, since Lewis died I have hardly a wish to live and my health has deteriorated. I get headaches and my leg is still swollen. I as yet cannot go for walks. I suddenly look 10 years older. L. meant even more to me than I realized and now I feel almost frantic to join him —though I know that mere dying will not bring me any nearer to him. He has gone beyond birth and death and only by going there myself will I solve the problem. It is almost as if now he has realized the Truth and is dragging me along to that Reality.

28ᵗʰ November, 1949

Reading Sri Aurobindo's *Lights on Yoga* I wonder whether my attitude of sulking since L's death is not a snare of the ego. After all, attachment is attachment. Sri Aurobindo says: "The love of the *sadhaka* should be for the Divine. It is only when he has developed that fully that he can love others in the right way." My dream also points to that I suppose. I was wondering why I did not wake up when I was dangling between heaven and earth and shouting for help. But no, a lady drew me up easily and the same lady then asked me: "Has there been a man in your life?" That question made me wake up, because this would seem to be the point which I want to escape. The man evidently is L., because I ask in the dream: "Do you mean my grandmother?" —which must signify my past— that does not concern me; but the lady says: "No, I mean you". The fact that our relationship was not the ordinary attachment between man and woman but was more that of Guru and disciple only makes it subtler and more difficult to get out of. This rut I have gotten myself into and the feeling that I shall die soon is quite wrong and destroys my will. I suppose I shall soon find myself hanging on the edge of a cliff as in my dream, unable to draw myself up. But then it is easy enough to get Mother's help if I only call out. Then though, I have to go back to my grandmother. Why? And the way seems very steep this time.

I seem to have drawn away from Mother to some extent. When I do *pranam* it seems hypocritical. There is really no surrender. Just like the old Frenchman who *pranams* profusely but it really means nothing. I feel very bitter about him still and he about me. I suppose he feels I ate too much at his expense!

1ˢᵗ December, 1949

Reading Sri Aurobindo's *Lights on Yoga* it suddenly occurred to me that what we know —that is, the physical-emotional-mental— is such a small fragment of the whole. Lewis really knew this and was awake on deeper levels and intensely busy there, but most of us merely exist on the surface. I felt this so strongly, but did not write it down two days ago. Now the realization of it has faded. Mother insists so much on *sadhana* to quicken the deeper levels.

Last night I fell and hurt my right knee. Now both are swol-

410

len. My inner dissatisfaction and crookedness makes for outer ailments and disasters these days.

I suspect more and more that my attachment to L. was an escape. Attachment is attachment however subtle, and the subtler it is, the more difficult to detect. When I first met Mother She told me: *"You are attached, whether it is father, mother, brother or sister, it is an obstacle to sadhana."* It never struck me till now that She must have meant Lewis. How subtle She is. My whole being is really shattered because he is gone and I am only dimly aware of it. And now he has nothing to do with this life, he seems utterly beyond.

I am attached to Mother also. I suppose that is why She makes it so difficult for me. As long as one sees the Guru as a person it is attachment.

9th December, 1949

Yesterday I sat outside Her window while She was in the Shiva Temple and all were meditating. When She came out She turned round to me and said: *"The more you can increase your meditation the better."*

10th December, 1949

Yesterday I wanted to ask Mother about meditation, but then found out without asking. I realized that one cannot meditate with the mind, but must negate it through *'neti... neti'* [7] and so go beyond the mind. Then suddenly I could sit quietly.

Sri Krishna Menon's letter is really a commentary on Mother's attitude in not allowing me to help L. I was only prolonging his agony. His ego could evidently not be destroyed without contacting his Guru and it seems he was unable to do this after such a long break, and so had to die physically to complete the process.

16th December, 1949

Yesterday at the Ashram after an absence of four days, I found Mother's health rather worse. She had a far-away look and suddenly the thought occurred to me that She also may intend to

---

[7] 'Not this... not this' —the process by which one inquires into 'who am I?'; it is likened to peeling off the layers of an onion.

slowly withdraw. It never had struck me before. Perhaps for my own good She is trying to wean me away from her. How long can I so entirely depend on Her? I must find Her inside.

Whatever I may do, if the desire to achieve illumination in this life is strong and persistent, it must get me there and thus destroy the ego.

Why can't I get in touch with L? If a person is egoless, what remains? Surely there must be something that remains eternally? Just as there is consciousness when thought stops, there must be something when the individual stops.

19th December, 1949

Spent the weekend at the Ashram. She definitely tries to wean me from being too attached to Her. I asked Her about Premanand [8] who had written to me. She said to tell him: *"That which is most dear to you, with that remain always. And this is also for you"*. I started crying when I heard this. She said: *"When one cries, one's inside becomes cleansed, just as water cleans the outside."* I said: "I am unable to do what you tell me to do. I simply do not know how. The only thing I can do is cry." She: *"By this all will be achieved"*. Yesterday during the *satsang* I recalled that from time to time I have these periods of crying. Before I met Lewis in 1942-43 I cried so much, and now it seems to start again. I am at a loss —perhaps this suffering is necessary. I do not know how to obey completely, so the *sadhana* also does not take me as far it should. I cannot be bothered to discipline myself, and when Mother deals with me and treats me severely I resent it. It is a desperate situation, I cannot fit in anywhere. In the Ashram I feel ever a stranger and at Rajghat I do not like it either. What do I expect from the world that it never gives? I am not deeply happy within, as I used to think I was. It depends on Mother, on my being with Her, and, very much more than I thought, on Thompson. Somehow he and Mother seemed closely connected in my case, and since he is gone my relationship to Her has also changed.

---

[8] Collin Turnbull, the renowned anthropologist and author who as a young man studied in Benares.

22nd December, 1949

The atmosphere in the Ashram is marvellous in spite of the noise and the loudspeaker. The mind gets clear and lucid there. I was singing *kirtan* in the morning for several hours. It cheered me up a lot. Where there is nothing but HE then there is meditation.

She has given me a place in the entrance of the Ashram to sleep. Someone said to me: "Hanuman [9] was Ram's gate-keeper and you are Mother's".

23rd December, 1949

This morning it occurred to me during the *kirtan* that *kirtan* is nothing but crying for God. Only the intense dissatisfaction with everything can produce 'real' *kirtan* and its result. That is why Haribaba's frantic beating and shouting is awe inspiring. Unless one is at it day and night it can produce only a very mild result.

26th December, 1949

Spent two days at the Ashram. The atmosphere is really tremendous. Many things do get clear. It occurred to me that if Mother does not allow me in Her room, which is a very painful punishment indeed, it is very likely the mildest way of getting me through the suffering that I no doubt have to undergo. Surely no one could imagine that She could give pain to anyone unless somehow it was for their benefit. It is quite out of place that I should be angry.

I wonder whether I have deserved this treatment by disobeying Her. Although She had asked me to spend at least three hours daily in meditation, I consider sitting by Her or even just waiting for Her to come out as more important and more satisfactory. The dreadful thing is that I cannot ask Her all these things, partly because of the language and partly because I feel too awed by Her. She seems so far away. When I make up my mind to talk to Her, as soon as I see Her I just can't. When L. was still here I could go to him. Now I have no one. I miss him terribly.

Yesterday in the lecture Swami Akhandananda said there are two ways: 'Neti... neti' where one negates everything, or the way of 'Om' —where one sees Him everywhere and nothing else. So

---

[9] Hanuman —the so-called 'monkey' God who is devotion incarnate.

the latter is evidently my way, but how far I am and how impatient, because of the dreariness of life and the continuous suffering. How can one get to *'Atmananda'* if one lingers or is satisfied with anything less than that! But to stand outside and peep through a crack in the shutter when everyone else is in Her room and She talks is quite a torture, nothing less than that. But after all She probably takes as much of my *karma* as possible on Herself and lets me work out the rest through this suffering. Again I think of Milarepa, how he was thrown out and left to cry outside when his Master called all the other disciples and how his Master refused to give him any teaching time after time. Finally he had to go into retreat <u>alone</u> and meditate to realize. One cannot stay with one's Guru all the time.

On December 23rd I heard from Debu that Edith Sitwell [10] cabled: "You sent me a poet of genius whose loss is immeasurable. Have no fear, we will get him published". So Lewis will be famous. In a way it is better for his work that he died. His "perversity" [11] and unworldliness and uncompromising superiority, and his love of "the way of blame" won't be in the way. Those who will deal with the publication can be much more businesslike than he could have been. For him there was evidently no other possibility but to slip away quietly. But for his friends it is utterly painful.

---

[10] Renowned literary critic and author whose opinion carried great weight in intellectual and publishing circles.

[11] 'Perversity' and 'the way of blame' are key terms in Thompson's philosophy of what he called 'the other half of the circle'. They have a Zen-like connotation. The radical sincerity with which he adhered to this philosophy would have made worldly success untenable.

XXI - The Process Deepens

Last night or rather early this morning, Trivenipuri Maharaj, a great *mahatma* from Khanna came. Mother arranged a roaring welcome for him. It was so touching, it drove tears into my eyes. Why do we not receive Her like this? We should —every time. It was like Mary Magdalene putting the most expensive rose oil on the Christ's feet, there being no question of expense and no effort too great to honour a Blessed One. Mother Herself put garlands on both sides of the path from the Ashram Gate. Fabulous lighting arrangements were made. Flags and *kirtan* greeted his car as he drove up. She Herself walked out on the road as soon as someone came running to announce his arrival. Conches blew and a shower of flowers rained over him wherever he walked. She had posted people on the verandahs above and on both sides of his way for this. It was really most extraordinarily impressive. I came back only reluctantly to Rajghat today. The atmosphere in the Ashram makes me electrified.

Yesterday Mother rebuked me harshly for ordering someone around. This was very painful for me but it made me realize what a self-centered life I lead. It also made me feel suddenly that whatever She says or does or asks me to do is for my best. I felt: "Whatever you do, I shall stick to you". The hurt helps me as much as the affection or perhaps more. She treats me harshly to teach me and to purify my ego which is what I want more than anything else. My body consciousness is so strong. I also see how right L. was when he objected to my being so 'good' and 'proper', how necessary it is for me to be 'mad'. Now I see that just being good and virtuous will never get you there. Yes, unless you are mad and ready to do something drastic to break this comfortable illusion, you can go on forever with your *sadhana*.

Austerities <u>are</u> necessary. Lewis used to say: "One must be ruthless with oneself and never allow oneself to rest until one gets there. Never let up." This is true. That is why Mother drives people as She does, so very hard. Even if they get ill —isn't illness an integral part of every *sadhana*, a means of purification?

23rd January, 1950, Vasant Panchami

The recent *yagya* [1] at the ashram was wonderful. I saw Alice [Boner] and she commented on the *yagya* saying: "No one is pure enough according to the *shastras* to perform such rituals in the *Kali Yuga*" [2]. It dawned on me that this is very likely the reason why Mataji is so very strict about the orthodox rules. Probably these rituals are necessary to counteract the evil forces of this age and to speed up the coming of a better one. They seem to have a profound effect on the purification of the atmosphere that calls down a strong spiritual presence. No doubt it is for this that She has people strictly observe these ancient Brahminical injunctions. Obviously She cannot jeopardize this only for the sake of my western ego. I was the only Westerner who stayed in the Ashram throughout the *yagya*, though there was a Polish painter, Mr. Topolovsky, who visited, as well as the Dutch Sufis, Baron and Baroness van Tuyl.

It is difficult to get Her attention these days and I find I can only approach Her when I do some service for others. For instance, when the Dutch people came I could get near Her; or after I had brought twenty-two children and teachers from Rajghat. I talked to Her two days ago but She won't be pinned down to saying anything. It makes me miss Thompson more painfully. Premanand has returned from his tour to the South and tells very interesting things about Pondicherry which again makes me want to see it.

Two nights ago I dreamt that I had to bless some people. Didima [3] corrected me and told me how to hold my hand; then I did *pranam* to her, without touching her feet, (which I have also never done in waking) and she put her hand on my head and pressed it strongly. Since then I seem somehow nearer to her.

---

[1] Traditional Vedic fire sacrifice.

[2] One of the four cyclic divisions of time in Hindu cosmology. The *Kali Yuga* is the lowest and most debased period.

[3] Anandamayee Ma's mother.

To sit in the rooms of the visiting Mahatmas, Dev Giri and Triveni Puri, was a great help.

24th January, 1950

This morning I translated for the Dutch Sufis. I had a feeling that I would get the reply to my own questions and I did. Mother was really wonderful. She told them several times to meditate along their own line more and more, and to first attain full realization themselves before trying to 'teach' others. She told Premanand [Collin Turnbull] when he asked about his friend —an American who studies sociology but feels that life is purposeless and useless—: *"Tell him to sit absolutely still for sometime every day and meditate on 'Who am I'. He should go into this inquiry deeply and try to find the answer. Light will come. He should not move at all, neither his eyes nor his limbs, and should only change his position when he cannot bear it any longer so as to increase his capacity to bear discomfort."* This is 100% what Ramana Maharshi says. She also said that this practice is good for Premanand and myself.

The Dutch people think they are saviours of mankind and have come to spread the message of their Guru in India. He had told them that India was not ready for it during his life-time, but that they, his disciples, must go there for this work. So, as they consider him the latest *Avatar*, they take themselves to be modern Saint Pauls. They want the blessing of Indian saints for this, which J.K. would call exploitation.

They said that they considered this time ripe for mankind to receive the message that all religions are one and the world should acknowledge it. Regarding this Mother said: *"Whatever has to come about, will come about. If anyone's desire is 'Sat' [the truth] then it must be fulfilled. If it is not fulfilled it is evident that it was not God's will"*. She told them again and again: *"Meditate and become absorbed so that people will sense the 'ras' [Divine sweetness] in you, then you will have success"*.

It was so interesting how subtle Her ways are. J.K. would have treated them entirely from the negative side and told them they were conceited and what not; but She takes the positive side and encourages them in their personal practice saying: *"Talking and being with people are a waste of time. Life is so short. Meditate,*

meditate, try to find yourself. Try to know for yourself that there is only One. As you are called father, friend, son, husband by different people but are really one and the same, so He also is only One though He has many names and shapes. The Blessing of God is always pouring down on you, but if you hold your cup upside down you cannot receive it. Therefore fill your mind with the Divine, day and night, then you will have God's Blessing in full measure". She had a little basket on Her bed and used it to illustrate what She was saying.

29th January, 1950

I see now why I can't get at Lewis. He has withdrawn from the physical plane whereas I am centered in it; as soon as I get into touch with my real Self he will be there also. In *samadhi*, where the mind is completely absent, I will find him.

Mother left for Vindhyachal on the 27th. Yesterday Premanand came and stayed for six hours. After talking to him I came to realize as never before that however exalted Pondicherry [i.e. Sri Aurobindo's ashram] is, it is still very much of this world. The attempt there to divinize matter is really irrelevant to the ultimate Realization which has nothing whatsoever to do with time and space. Suddenly my wish to go there vanished. It would no doubt be interesting to go but ultimately quite irrelevant. Mother is beyond all that and She points to Self-Realization only —and to nothing else. I feel that to make the physical more perfect would be a help in one way but also a hindrance in another. The more that life becomes beautiful and harmonious, the less incentive there is to go further; it would be too soothing, too comfortable —what would be the incentive then to continue searching? Of course at Pondy they are out for both together; but there is something 'Theosophical' about the whole affair.

Mother's last words to me before She left for Vindhyachal were: *"Look after him"*, meaning Premanand [4]. No sooner has L. gone than She provides me with another sensitive young Westerner. She seems to want me to be in touch with at least one other foreigner. I suppose I need that. He is a nice fellow. When he talked to me yesterday, suddenly for a second, I noticed his beautiful blue clear eyes. There was a sudden instantaneous recognition. He told me some incidents from his life that are strangely parallel to mine: How he

---

[4] Colin Turnbull, who would become a renowned anthropologist and author.

went fishing, and when seeing the first fish caught with the hook violently stabbed through its mouth, he threw down the rod and ran away in terror. Just like I, when the chicken that I had looked after and personally cared for was cooked and brought to the table and I refused to eat it. From that day really my vegetarianism began. Also he adores Chopin and Bach and wanted to be a musician but his parents would not allow it, so he came out here to Mataji. He is also an only child as his brother died in the war.

Before Mother left She seemed friendly again and very attentive. She asked me to teach Premanand cooking and related something I had told Her previously in a jovial way. I suppose She wanted me to feel at ease before She left. Somehow I don't miss Her as She seems always with me. But I cannot really meditate these days. All the same I set my alarm for 4.30 a.m. and sit as still as I can.

Reading only a page of J.K upset me. It is better to avoid him completely. Anyway, he is in my blood, no need to emphasize him.

Rajghat, 31st January, 1950

Putting Lewis' letters into chronological order and reading them over again brings to memory the stress and anxiety in which he lived. It really was agony for him and it makes me feel ever so grateful that it is over —for good "ausgelitten". What intense joy to know that he has gone utterly and completely beyond identifying himself with any of that, even with his poems or anything at all. This is a lesson in what it means to go beyond identification. Before I only understood this in theory but it never was practical to me. So he is still teaching me even now. There are wonderful passages in his letters about poetry etc. but I do not know how to file them so that I can find them again easily.

3rd February, 1950

Today there was a rumour that Ma had come. I almost found it disturbing as I feel I need some time to collect myself. I have been so much with Her that it is like drunkenness and I must come to myself.

Even though at times I feel completely unable to meditate, my saving grace is that I feel obsessed to reach the goal —like a wood-worm that never stops. It struck me in my meditation that the divine name should not merely be repeated mindlessly but with great intensity and desperation until the Truth which it embodies shines forth. Meditation is only the elimination of all activity that distracts one from the sole purpose of life which is to find HIM = One's Self. So although this search should go on continuously day and night, nevertheless at least for sometime during the day it should be exclusively focused through formal sitting to the exclusion all else.

4th February, 1950

This morning after meditating for one and a half hours, something changed and I seemed to get a touch of Him, and of great Peace. I then sat for another hour and the pain in the leg did not bother me at all. It was such bliss. I felt truly changed afterwards. But at food time I got angry with Ramsamaj and that troubles me. It leaves a mark at once.

6th February, 1950

Yesterday at the Ashram felt at once the beneficial influence of so many *sadhaks* [spiritual practitioners]. There it is easier to concentrate. But again, there is so much physical noise. I felt very strongly that I must persist in creating my own inner vibration and practising divine remembrance all the 24 hours. To keep this up is my contribution to Rajghat, not the teaching. *"Never be without Him"*, as Ma said.

I find that devotional singing helps enormously in concentration. I must cultivate singing. It is evidently necessary for me, has a loosening, harmonising effect which I cannot do without.

If I put the *Pranav* [Om] before each *mantra* it definitely helps in drawing the mind inside.

8th February, 1950

Dream:

I stay in a strange town with a family and am in charge of a boy of 11, good looking and intelligent. He runs away and returns after two days. Meanwhile I have been out in the town to look for him but cannot find him as he has already returned home. However I find the book he had taken with him in a little hut where one waits for conveyance. There is a strange lady there who packs the book into her bag, but when I ask for it returns it. I then get into the train and meet a girl I know. I ask her whether the boy has returned. She says, yes, Tutu has returned. I get quite angry and say: "Who wants Tutu?" She says: "Oh that other boy, he won't return." I take it to mean that something mysterious has happened to him, perhaps he is dead. I have forgotten the name of the street where I am staying and that girl tells me. When I get home I embrace the boy's mother in numb sympathy, taking it that the boy is not there; but later I find that he has come home. No one seems to know where he had been. I feel frightened and say: "How can I look after him, if I go out with him he may vanish again. " There is an air of mystery and fright about the dream.

10ᵗʰ February, 1950

Yesterday Mother came for two days from Vindhyachal. It is such delight to see Her again. She is pure Light, no heaviness, no earth to Her at all. After having been away from Her for a few days one feels it even more.

11ᵗʰ February, 1950

Last night Kamla Mohanlal's brother, a government official, asked some questions to Ma. There had been a theft in his house and he said: "I thought I had too many things so God has relieved me of some".

Mother: *Yes, somebody's needs have been fulfilled. No one can have more things than are due to him. God has given you the things and has taken them away again. We think we have enemies, that there are thieves etc, but in reality they are all our brothers.*

Then there is also another thing to be considered: It is better to loose one's possessions than one's life. The attack might have been on your life, so from that point of view you have been fortunate.

Question: Some *sadhus* refuse to go to Mathura [5] because *ganja* [6] has been forbidden there. Why should *sadhus* who are after God use intoxicants?

---

[5] An ancient city which is the birthplace of Krishna.

[6] Marijuana, traditionally used by some sects of India's wandering ascetics —theoretically as an aid to meditation.

Mother: *There is something to be said for them also. If the intoxication takes them to God and leads them into dhyan, the ganja will go and God remain, there will be no question of intoxicants any more. This was the original idea. But nowadays people use it only for the pleasure and forget about the original purpose. Even so, there are still some who use it as a serious part of their sadhana.*

Then the conversation passed on to different religions:

Mother: *You don't know who you are, you think of yourselves as Hindus, Muslims, Christians etc, but really, I am telling you the truth, there is only the ONE. If you read the Vishnu Purana, it is said that Vishnu is the Greatest of all, the same is said of Shiva in the Shiva Purana. How can that be? Or if it is so, then as there can be only <u>one</u> greatest, Vishnu and Shiva must be the same. There must be Vishnu in Shiva and Shiva in Vishnu. They are different functions. If you see only the One, there is no question of Shiva, Vishnu, Buddha, Jesus, etc. But as long as there are two* ['duniya'] *then there is 'dukha'* [suffering], *'dwandwa'* [opposition] *and all the rest.*

The world implies movement and thus death, because its nature is to change constantly. But if you find your true Self, the transcendent <u>One</u>, then all remains unchanging despite outer appearances. Where the one becomes two, there is the play of Shiva and his Shakti, Krishna and Radha etc. [7] *This is necessary to produce the 'leela'*[the 'play' of life, the world, the many]. *The Prakriti* [the ever-changing outer world of form and matter —the feminine principle] *is ever attracted to the Purusha* [the sole, unchanging unmanifest male principle] *and vice-versa. So it is also in marriage, which is meant to be for the sake of helping one another to realize the highest. One's wife is one's 'swadharmini'* [life partner], *not as it is nowadays.*

First you must know yourself, then there will be no pain, no differences, no sense of separateness.

Question by Shambhu, who wishes to take *sanyasa*: "How is one to get the final realization as fast as possible?"

Mother: *When you really want the Supreme Truth, then your mind becomes incapable of thinking of anything else at all, it becomes 'ekagra'* [one pointed]. *As long as there is 'granthi'* [8], *there can be no realization. The granthis have to be dissolved.*

---

[7] God (in various forms) with his inseparable consort.

[8] *Granthi*, lit. a knot —that which binds the individual mind to false identification with the world and the ego.

12th February, 1950

Yesterday translated a private for Premanand. I find myself becoming fond of him. It started the other day when he talked to me. Yesterday when he laid his soul bare before Ma I found him delightful, so pure and fresh and sincere and full of joy. He is simple and not at all complicated like Lewis was; he seems much healthier and there is not so much conflict in him. Ma evidently wants me to have some human relationship as She always gives me someone to look after, perhaps to counteract my tendency of being too cut off.

Mother said that there are two basic methods of meditation: One is to concentrate on the breath observing each inhalation and exhalation. Then when the mind has become stilled in this manner, one should practice *vichara,* inquiring "Who am I?" until the true Self is revealed. She said that in this way one becomes a light unto oneself. The second way is to think of one's *mantra* (or any name of God) with each inhalation and exhalation, feeling that both the Name and the Breath are none other than God Himself —the very breath of life— thus becoming fully absorbed in this devotional awareness. The first way is one of *jnana* and the second of *bhakti.*

Again She told me to think of the *Pranav* [Om] as much as possible. She said: "*It must become so automatic that you cannot breath without remembering it. Do your personal mantra when you sit for meditation and the rest of the time the Pranav*".

I always get much when I translate for others, perhaps more than when I ask for myself, because I am too involved then and not a witness.

I feel that I can do so much for Rajghat by just being utterly intense! Already it has had its effect. The fact that there is someone here who considers that nothing else is of value but Self-Realization must influence the children unconsciously all the time. It does not matter much whatever else I may teach. It is our responsibility as teachers to give them the correct foundation upon which they will build their lives.

20th February, 1950

Reading the *Isha Upanishad,* with commentary by Shankaracharya and Sri Aurobindo, shows into what a forest one looses oneself if one becomes caught up in intellectual polemics. Even two such great ones as these have such a difference of opinion. Sanskrit, though, is fascinating —more the sound than the meaning. Sound is basic and therefore nearer the Truth than meaning, which is of the mind. This is why *japa* has such a profound effect.

27ᵗʰ February, 1950

On *Shivaratri* I fasted and my general health at once recouped. I decided to stop eating in between meals. That simply ruins my health and also makes me sleep too much. I was able to stay awake all night without lying down until 5.30 a.m. without any fatigue whatsoever. It is wonderful in the night, especially in the open. Ma is right —one must keep awake some nights. The day after of course I was tired, but not so badly. Food and sleep are obviously closely connected.

This morning I could sit for two and a quarter hours without fidgeting.

Yesterday started Bengali lessons with Debu's brother as a means of helping him, as he lost his tuition; but it will also be a great asset to me. I know already quite a lot and perhaps will yet learn to understand Ma in Bengali.

Yesterday had a letter from Ellen to whom I sent L.'s poem "Black Angel". She appreciated it deeply and senses the man through his work. She gives the clue to his life by saying: "He once said to Prema: "I want to realize like Ravana or not at all [9]".

This brought home to me again what a strange and wonderful being he was and what a privilege it was to be his friend. It makes me feel that what have I to worry about when I am so close to him, to Mother, to J.K. etc. I am really quite safe. There is no question of going off the track; I shall immediately be brought back. Since Lewis died and went evidently into *'Nirvana'*, which really is from our point of view 'Non Being' (as I now see), I have a much clearer idea of what the goal of human existence is.

---

[9] Ravana was the great enemy of the *Avatara* Rama in the epic the *Ramayana*. A great ascetic and yogi, he was told that he could either reincarnate as a devotee of Rama and get liberation in several lifetimes or he could incarnate as his arch-enemy and be liberated in one lifetime. He chose the latter and his hatred of Rama became so intense that his mind never left the thought of Him for even a moment. Thus Ravana ultimately became totally absorbed in Rama and was liberated when he was finally killed by him in battle.

Bhadaini, 1ˢᵗ March, 1950

Since Malati has returned from being with J.K. I talk to her instead of writing my diary. That is a pity. I see however how changed she is. Formerly her room was messy and felt bourgeois. Now this is not so. It feels clean and empty, almost better than mine. I must admit that J.K. does have a way and if one has the patience to go into it, he shows people a method which has a quick effect and clears out the mind. I notice there is even a regret in my mind that I cannot go that way. But I realize that I can only do what Ma tells me. I have surrendered to Her and leave the results to Her. It is no longer my problem. Surrender means that one cannot do anything of one's own volition and also there is no need to do so. The finding of someone to surrender to is already the final fulfilment in embryo. As the fruit is in the seed, so the achievement is already potentially there.

* * *

The language of spiritual surrender can be very easily misunderstood by anyone not deeply involved in an authentic spiritual process, the goal of which is stilling of the individual will before God —the innermost truth of one's being. The Guru is the essential intermediary in this process and guides the disciple through the desperate attempts of the ego to thwart its fulfillment. For this he must be a pure channel of the Divine, accepting the devotion of the disciple as a means to externalize and thus structure what is actually a purely internal process within the disciple, leading to the final realization that in Reality there are not two.

* * *

2ⁿᵈ March, 1950

Today when telling Miss Sydney that the physical is of necessity '*dukh rupa*' [suffering] as it is by nature constant change which implies constant death, it suddenly came to me what Mataji means by saying this and by telling everyone not to cling to the material world. There is nothing permanent in 'this' (the world) to hang on to, and this fact is in itself a guarantee of THAT which is beyond the created. This is probably what J.K. means also. By realizing the nature of 'this', you get 'THAT'.

Anandamayee Ma surrounded by Her devotees - 1954 (photo by Richard Lannoy)

7ᵗʰ March, 1950

Reading Sri Aurobindo's Letters —most fascinating. It again revives my wish to go to his ashram in Pondy. Different *sadhanas* seem to lead to different goals. Yet I take it that each individual has his own way and goal and one really has very little if any choice at all in the matter.

Malati's and my ways are so entirely different —they seem diametrically opposed in their method— she going into 'this' [the outer world], though always standing apart as a witness —and I leaving 'this' and concentrating on 'That' [the transcendent]. It can almost be called extrovert and introvert. But we tolerate and respect each other.

Mother seems such a unique incarnation, with no comparison and no antecedent, as Krishna was —complete and whole and always perfect, quite incomparable.

20ᵗʰ March, 1950

I get now into an altered state when I meditate, but it takes time. Then however it is so attractive that I don't want to stop. But when I miss it in the morning as I did today, I feel out of sorts.

30ᵗʰ March, 1950

Ma is here since the 25ᵗʰ. I spent four days and five nights at the Ashram. At Rajghat the atmosphere is extremely strained, mainly due to Maurice Frydman being here and upsetting all the teachers with his talk about 'transference'[10] etc. It seems so petty.

When I am at the Ashram I am quite different altogether. It is like heaven there. I never feel hungry and eat just one good meal a day. Here it's enough to drive one to smoking and drinking. To have three Europeans here quite upsets me. I have become so attuned to the subtleness of the Brahminical vibration that I find the Western one quite jarring. For the first time I realize how these orthodox Hindus must be feeling when they have me there mixing with them. It is really quite a problem. It is good for me to realize it.

Not to obey Her really creates terrible problems. When She told me: *"My wish for you is to do tapasya* [spiritual disciplines] *and*

---

[10] A key term in psychoanalysis.

you should also prepare your own food", I blatantly refused; and now I am suffering the consequences. Also when She wanted to give me the upstairs room, I should have simply accepted.

Mother was very gracious this time. She called me into Her room and said: *"I had this door leading from the terrace to my room made specially for you and Premanand. There is not a hair's difference between you and the others as far as I am concerned"*. At that time I could have seized the opportunity to ask Her about 'the rules'. But I was not quick enough to make up my mind and someone else burst in.

31st March, 1950

Ma left this morning for Vindhyachal. Kitty arrived at midday. I really like her a lot. She has a clear mind and what she does, she does well [11]. She is evidently in her right surroundings and I in mine.

Strange that the fate of Rajghat is now being decided in my quiet hermitage where Mother's influence is strongest.

In meditation I feel a great peace and I go beyond the ordinary physical level. Noise seems somewhere far away and does not disturb me as it once did.

11th April, 1950

Maurice Frydman says I give him hell. I was rather surprised to hear it. So it is mutual.

In M.F. I resent my own identification with Polish Jews. I feel responsible for his nastiness because we are both of the same caste. I seem to put my foot into things I should not bother about. Is it my business what outwardly happens? I seem to interfere quite unnecessarily. Mother has told me to do *sadhana* and my work, nothing else.

21st April, 1950

Yesterday there was Shiva Mandir *pratishta* [12] at the Ashram. It was wonderful. I took leave for the day. Mother was around

---

[11] At that time Kitty Siva Rao was one of the principal trustees of the organization governing Krishnamurti's educational institutions.

[12] Consecration of the Siva temple.

practically all the time. The two stone *lingas* [13] were bathed in *ghi*, honey, *panchamrit*, ground bel leaves and gallons of Ganges water. I put some of this holy liquid on my head and face and felt a definite effect of being drawn inwards and the mind becoming peaceful.

Dr. Syed [14] was there. He is very sceptical about J.K. A famous *sadhu*, Krishnanand Puri, gave quite a good talk. Five people took formal religious vows of renunciation and became *sanyasis*. Nepalda is now Swami Narayananand. When he came out of the *havan*, the ritual fire sacrifice, I touched his feet and was moved to tears by his blessing. The other night Nepalda was distributing all his possessions and gave me a bowl. It felt lovely and I was envious. I wished I could do the same as he and be free, depending on God alone. Why can't I? The only thing that matters is to be really engrossed in God always.

Ma does not take any notice of me these days, except that occasionally She gives me little jobs to do. Last time when She came in March, as soon as I arrived She made me distribute *prasad*. This time when I went out on the road to meet Her (on April 15th), She did not wait till I could do *pranam*, but at once asked me to take a heavy box from Kamla and carry it to the Ashram. She evidently does not want me to just sit about like some others, but to be helpful. When I do *pranam* She takes no notice, but then I also feel a bit ridiculous, feeling that in any case I have surrendered, so what is the use of doing it over and over again; it is more a formality than anything else.

25th April, 1950

Mouna on Sunday was again a great help. It always drives the mind inside and gives a certain realization. Now Mother again appears extraordinarily radiant to me. When I live too much outside I cannot get at Her. That is perhaps why She is often inaccessible to Westerners.

I feel the heat much less this year and I remember I hardly felt the cold in winter. No doubt that is a result of *sadhana*, which causes

---

[13] The abstract stone symbol of Shiva in which he is universally worshipped throughout India.

[14] A Muslim professor who was very devoted to Anandamayee Ma.

these outer things to become ever more unreal. The physical needs less and less as one decreases one's attention to it, and this allows one to live more intensely within.

27ᵗʰ April, 1950

Ma left today for Calcutta. The other day I suddenly got at something that I cannot put into words. When I was sitting very near Her in Her room suddenly I sensed Her as a great Stillness, a Void in which there is a complete Peace and in which the mind gets wholly absorbed. Just to look at Her and be charmed is not enough. What I experienced goes much deeper (but very likely even this is still far from a real *darshan* —the experience of Her complete Presence). Again today when I sat very near I could sense this overwhelming peace. It remained with me when I was alone in the rickshaw and while sitting at the station.

At the teachers' meeting when we discussed the children I suddenly realized with a shock that I really know nothing about them. It is I who 'throw' things at them as M.F. puts it. How can one teach without contacting the true nature of the child, only then can one really discover what he needs. If I can see the Divine in the child rather than my own limited concept of who he is, then God Himself will inspire me to find the right way to help him. These meetings are now very nice. They proceed very much like a spoken group meditation.

28ᵗʰ April, 1950

I feel painfully aware of limitation in my meditation. I get to a stillness when I sit but then what? Also I do not really know Mother. What I perceive of Her is surely not She, but only a tiny glimpse of a fragment of Her. If I think of Her as a PRESENCE beyond that perceived by the senses it has certainly a greater reality than Her physical form and is not subject to Her physical nearness but rather to the capacity of my mind to remain in that PRESENCE, which I have experienced through Her again and again.

Rajghat, 1ˢᵗ May, 1950

Drawing up plans for the next school year. All this outer activity does not agree with me. If I get caught in it and keep my mind on it, it creeps into my meditation. I don't really know how to reconcile the going inwards with outer activity. If I feel that I must first of all keep the <u>Presence</u> with me always, as Mother says, it should be impossible to take a breath without it. As I was told in my dream over five years ago: "Think of the Lord at all times and leave everything else". At the same time I seem to be karmically bound to this outer work as I can't do without it. I need some activity to keep balanced —so what to do? How to discuss this with Mother —I do not know how to put it to Her; but I feel that a solution must come. When Mother is not here it is difficult to maintain the clarity that comes automatically in Her presence.

Rajghat, 15ᵗʰ May, 1950

Yesterday in my meditation I experienced a tremendous blessing. It made me realize how absolutely necessary it is to keep up regular practice at all costs, and in complete solitude. I feel very uneasy and disturbed when I don't meditate. I notice that I then depend on the company of others and on activity. But if I set apart some time for meditation, it stills the restlessness and the anxiety. There is then a balance and composure. Also I notice that if I don't meditate properly in the evening I wake up with a feeling of discomfort in the morning.

26ᵗʰ May, 1950

Mother is always near me, I only have to cling to Her. Surrender would mean that whatever happens is the same to me, because it all comes from God.

Puri, 3ʳᵈ June, 1950

Arrived here on May 30ᵗʰ morning after spending one day at Calcutta. Mother had replied to my letter that if I don't mind all the discomforts here in Puri I may come. I was fortunate to have *darshan* of Jagannath [15] (in the open) on the full-moon day; but

---

[15] The famous Jagannath Temple in Puri. Once a year the image is pulled through the streets of the town on a huge chariot attended by thousands of people. The temple is strictly off limits to non-Hindus and so it is only on this festival day that she would have had the opportunity to see this image of Krishna which is quite unique.

since then I am again resting. I have a rash which looks quite nasty and is spreading. All the same I feel better mentally here than at Benares. I feel Mother near. I lie or sit and watch the sea and enjoy the sea breeze day and night. It seems I <u>have</u> to keep still these days. Every time I get an illness it nails me down in one place. Non-identification with the body would solve all troubles. But I feel afraid of this beastly itch and how long it will torture this body. Sometime ago I remember I had an impression that I would get ill this summer and was wondering who would take care of me. It is always the Lord who does so. So no need to worry.

Calcutta, 11th June, 1950

Mother insisted on my going to Calcutta to see a doctor on the 6th. So I came here on my birthday. I don't mind being here as it appears I cannot be with Mother at present. I am better, but still far from well. My hosts do much for me and so do people of the Ashram. Mother really arranges perfectly. No need to have a home even when one is ill. It is only the fearful imagination that causes one to think otherwise.

I realize again how different the Indian outlook is to ours. We want to be happy by having all sorts of comforts and enjoyments that we consider our right, whereas the Indian accepts whatever life provides him as the right thing for him —knowing that happiness is not based on the outer, the material. By submitting thus to conditions as they present themselves he is content and happy because he has not the illusion that happiness depends on outer circumstances.

Reading Sister Nivedita's *The Master as I saw him*. Most interesting about Vivekananda.

12th June, 1950

Have been reading how Sister Nivedita [16] always imagines when speaking to someone that she is addressing their mind rather than their ear and how much more response she gets from this. She does this as an exercise to practice the awareness that man is not a body.

---

[16] An Irish woman, Margaret Noble, who spent many years in India and was a close disciple of Swami Vivekananda.

20ᵗʰ June, 1950

Returned to Puri on 16ᵗʰ. One day Mother said: *"I have the 'kheyal' that you should do puja to your Gopal* [17]*."* She then asked me to learn the appropriate *mantras* from Didima and Didi, and said: *"Start tomorrow, Monday morning"*. She asked me to offer sandal paste, water, fruit, flowers and incense sticks and gave me a *chandan* [sandalwood] *mala*. I find, though I have not yet really mastered it, that it has an extraordinarily concentrating effect, even more than sitting for *japa* and *dhyan*. Of course one cannot yet know because every new thing is effective at first. In the train from Calcutta when waking up in the morning I suddenly remembered that in 1929 when I left the Theosophical centre at Huizen I said that I would never do ritual ceremonies again! So without noticing I have fallen into the same thing once more. But I feel it is better to go into it, since it has come of its own accord and moreover I have to obey Mother's orders in any case. But I still felt upset when I remembered this prior resolve. But doing the *puja* one really becomes oblivious to the physical and is hardly aware of noise at all. Also I find that half an hour of this seems at least as effective as sitting quietly.

It is significant that L., who was so much on J.K.'s iconoclastic line, should have left me this ritual inheritance. By going into it seriously I will find out all about it and will also know Hinduism from inside.

Calcutta, 22ⁿᵈ June, 1950

Spent twenty hours at Nawadwip [18] with Mother at the Govinda Mandir. I am beginning to see that with all the *puja* in this place there is simply no time and no energy to deal with order on the physical plane —cleanliness or anything. The people are simply engrossed in another level and take physical life as a necessary evil. They have no interest to improve it.

Part of me feels very critical about this at present. But I must concede that in spite of the physical disorder, it makes for a lovely atmosphere whereas our European physical order and cleanliness does not in itself make anyone happy.

---

[17] The image of Krishna as a small child that she had inherited from Thompson.
[18] A famous devotional centre for devotees of Krishna in Bengal.

Rajghat, 8ᵗʰ July, 1950

Came to Benares with Mother on June 30ᵗʰ and stayed in the Ashram till the 5ᵗʰ. Coming back here to Rajghat I feel the contrast between the restlessness here and the harmony there. The *puja* keeps me in trim in this atmosphere. I am interested especially in the *mala*. I find it definitely helps concentration. Reading again what Sri Aurobindo says about 'Krishna consciousness' —that it is inseparable from the direct personal experience of Krishna Himself. L. knew this and felt it deeply. I am conditioned like most Westerners to believe more in the abstract formless divinity — Judaism, Buddhism and J.K.— because it is intellectually safer and more acceptable to our rather sterile 'modern' sophistication. So perhaps it is necessary for me to experience the other side, the *saguna*, the personal aspect of God.

24ᵗʰ July, 1950

Mother came two days ago. When I saw Her I felt transported at once. Madhavacharya has been teaching me *slokas* [Sanskrit verses from sacred texts] which I like immensely. Especially the *'Gayatri'* [19] thrills me. All these days I was extremely keen to get permission from Mother to recite it, however when I saw Her I felt: "What else do I need —She is everything, the remembrance of Her is all that is required." But when She is not here physically, I want these things. The *puja* helps me when at Rajghat, but as soon as one gets to the Ashram one feels like in heaven and everything else falls away. Then I feel that learning Sanskrit is also beside the point. These *slokas* do have a profound effect though. The *Saraswati* [20] *Stotram* has a vibration of pure whiteness that appeals to me immensely.

3ʳᵈ August, 1950

Mother came here to Rajghat yesterday. Her visit (just as three years ago) made me painfully aware of our own emptiness at the school and our pride in our lifeless beauty, organization etc, and our attaching values to things that have no value. Our songs were

---

[19] One of the most sacred *mantras* of the Hindus. This hymn to the solar deity is repeated daily by all devout upper-caste Hindus at sunrise and sunset.

[20] Goddess of wisdom

empty and boring. The principal's speech was almost tactless in its typical organizational egotism. And Mother is expected to give Her blessing to this nonsense! This is exploitation. Yet She did give what was necessary for us to see how empty our love of *samsara* [the world] is. I felt very humbled. I was in favour of the principal speaking because I imagined he would say what I felt: That we are trying to bring up children in a way as to make this place a living temple of Gopal, the Divine Child; but as we are incompetent to live up to this, we ask the Mother of mothers to give us Her Blessing, Her Wisdom and Her guidance in all our steps. We pray that with Her coming into our midst a new era of harmony may start, that She may help us to forget all our petty purposes and put us on the path which leads straight to the Eternal. That is what I was hoping for but in any case what he actually said seemed utterly irrelevant.

In Her talk to the teachers Mother told us: *"Whatever you do must be done for God, otherwise it binds you. Go after 'amrit'* [Divine nectar], *that which does not decay."*

She sang *"He Bhagavan"*. All in all Her presence here just pointed out our weakness —our godlessness. We have so much, but what of it if the only thing that matters is missing.

20ᵗʰ September, 1950

Last night dreamt of Sri Krishna Menon for the first time. I told Tapasi yesterday that I have wanted to meet Him for a long time, but unless He came North I could not; so now he has come to me anyway. Tapasi told me today how she met J.K. and how he changed her life. It was very beautiful. She evidently feels that he is the Christ though she did not say it quite like that. She calls him "a pure light". She is a beautiful soul and I like having her in the house. My first impression of her in the Ashram several weeks ago as someone very striking, extraordinary and independent was correct. It is perhaps not without significance that I meet so many people who are deeply impressed by J.K. She seems to feel that I am a main stay of this place in spite of my defiant attitude towards him.

Somehow I played the piano for several hours three times this week. I find that my past is still all there, not blotted out. I can play quite well. Perhaps I would still fit in the West very well,

provided I find the right people. My Hindu present has not re-
placed my Western past, but is only an extension of it. On the
other hand music has no attraction for me any more. I have really
worked this out entirely. The attachment is gone.

Premanand is, or was, torn between music and India. It is
significant that so many Europeans interested in *sadhana* seem to
be musicians. But although music, at least western music, does
not take one as far as the silence which comes through meditation,
yet it is perhaps the best introduction.

Rajghat, 29ᵗʰ September, 1950

Long talks with Tapasi lately. It is most interesting to find at
last someone who is utterly smitten by J.K. and who claims to live
entirely by his teaching. But she refuses to see that she has this
adhikara [spiritual ability] as a result of her meditation of fourteen
years and her life as a *sanyasini* for seven years, as well as through
her contact with Mother and other Gurus. However, perhaps I
have been too hasty in judging J.K. Let the question remain open.
The main thing is that she and I have in essence the same *sadhana*,
that of surrender —I to Ma, she to J.K. As long as one is able to
find God in someone, what does it matter in whom. J.K. advises
people to be involved in the world as part of their *sadhana*, whereas
Mother feels that it is by nature an illusion based on faulty perception and that the *sadhaka* should completely detach himself from
the world —which She calls "slow poison". In both cases it's a
question of observing the true nature of things.

Rajghat, 4ᵗʰ November, 1950

Went to Bikaner on 17ᵗʰ October and from there to Delhi on
29ᵗʰ October. Felt extremely reluctant to write in my diary, partly
because I had no pen. Returned this morning at 4 a.m. and meant
to go to see Mother in the evening but somehow felt too lethargic;
then later felt extremely sorry as She will stay for only a very few
days. It is really my Gopal that prevents me from going to the
Ashram easily, because his *puja* takes time and arrangements and
forethought and so it gets late.

In Bikaner Fred said that I have changed, but not for the better; he finds me too contented, without having my mind clarified.

(Since he is muddled himself, how can he judge!) I cannot be upset all the time. I have had more than enough of it. Besides there is a strong sense of certainty in me that I am at all times being driven towards my goal. That was really always so, even in my worst times, though now I am much more aware and certain of it.

In Delhi I stayed with S.C. Sarkar and his wife. Mrs. Sarkar told me of her visions of Vishnu when she was under chloroform for an operation, and again when she was very upset after having taken *diksha* of a *nirakara* [abstract or formless] *mantra* which her husband objected to. At that time she had the vision of Vishnu and He spoke to her saying: "Why do you worry? You are on the right path. I am both *saguna* [with form] and *nirguna* [formless]".

When talking to Sarkar it occurred to me what an immense advantage it really was to go through the ordeal of having my life broken to pieces by J.K. After that there could never be a dualistic belief like he has in which one lives forever in blissful contemplation of his deity. He does not even conceive of the death of the personality, that complete annihilation of separation which I envisage as the supreme goal of life. Of course, it is not only J.K. but also Mother who has really established me in this attitude.

Rajghat, 3rd December, 1950

Mother left on November 27th. She said so many inspiring things but somehow I never get time or leisure to write them down.

A few days ago for a fraction of a second I got a glimpse of what one really worships in *puja*. Obviously it is not at all merely worship of a piece of stone (which is just a focus), but is meant to teach one to do all actions in the right way, namely for God and not for oneself. This is an important teaching.

The new American, Jack Unger, seems dissatisfied and complains about all the crowds around Mother. [21] I also had that wish

---

[21] He ultimately became so impressed with Anandamayee Ma that he left everything to remain in her ashram for several years. The story has it that he was in the American Merchant Marines on a ship in the Indian ocean when he had an extraordinary vision (or dream) of a supernaturally beautiful woman who said she was waiting for him in Benares. When the boat docked in Calcutta he jumped ship and upon reaching Benares discovered Anandamayee Ma to be the woman in his vision. Years later when he returned to America, it is said that Anandamayee Ma had to request the Prime Minister, Nehru, to prevail upon the U.S. authorities to get the ex-seaman off the hook.

for a Guru who would teach me privately, not in crowds and noise, but now I have no particular desire for this and I just go on.

When Mother left She stroked my head and told me: *"Jap, dhyan karo!"* [Do *japa* and *dhyan*].

Seeing Jack Unger for the first time I at once liked him immensely. It must be a link from before.

7th December, 1950

Sri Aurobindo's passing away on December 5th was a great shock. I wonder whether it means that he has given up what He meant to achieve or whether through his death he effected a release of spiritual power that will help to hasten what he worked for. Anyway it must mean that all is not well with the world. Premanand also feels that. I wonder whether J.K.'s retiring for a year is also on the same line?

18th December, 1950

Last night Basu told me that Sri Aurobindo's body remained completely intact for over one hundred hours after he passed away. The flesh was soft and fresh and an intense golden light came out of the body and suffused the whole room. Even during the burial the light was still there. Basu maintained that it was the supramental light, as it is a totally miraculous event for a body to be intact for more than forty hours after death.

Reading some of Lewis' things I see how much I miss him, how it has lowered my standard not to have him near. I feel he has left the earth-consciousness all together; but then he never quite entered it.

24th December, 1950

Some days ago a letter came from Ellen to say that Sri Krishna Menon wants to make it clear that, when L.'s poems are published it should be stated that they were written before L. became his disciple. At first I got into an awful funk about this, but it is true that the subject of the "Black Angel" is a most perilous one and the fact that this is his master-poem makes it much worse. Finally I decided to write to Debu about this and also to send a copy to Sri Krishna Menon. I got a strange feeling of entire surrender to him

438

during this process. It came on its own. I wonder what my relationship to him is and whether we shall ever meet in the flesh.

26ᵗʰ December, 1950

Yesterday I suddenly realized how meditation absorbs one's entire being into a vibration of profound harmony. This must be the stream of pure consciousness of which Ma speaks.

Rajghat, 16ᵗʰ January, 1951

So long as one is always turned towards the Light, it does not matter what happens. This came as a revelation. *Sadhana* is the turning towards the Light, the gradual surrender of one's whole nature to that Divine Light. L. used to call it vertical activity (as opposed to horizontal activity which is on the levels of the ego and does not really lead anywhere). In this regard I see how stupid I am at school when only keen to make the children learn or behave, which is totally secondary to the importance of keeping my mind turned upwards all the time. This is my real contribution to the school: To keep my gaze fixed on the all-pervading Truth and thus transmit it to the best of my ability.

The statement of Sri Krishna Menon to the effect that Lewis was not his disciple when he wrote the "Black Angel" [22] disconcerted me a good deal, but now that I have replied to Levi and written to Debu, it is out of my mind. It is of course true that I myself told L. that most likely if he did the practices that Sri K.M. had told him to do he would not have felt the necessity to express himself 'artistically' in this particular manner as a means to correct his mental balance. But then of course, as Sri K.M. rightly surmises, he would have never written the "Black Angel". It would have been a loss to art, but would it really? Since Lewis was no doubt a genius he might have written something much more inspiring as a result of an even deeper vision, instead of what he wrote. But anyway he could not obey Sri K.M. All the same he got 'There'. So what does it really matter now.

---

[22] This poem, which brought Thompson considerable posthumous recognition, was written well after his rift with Krishna Menon. Although 'difficult', it is hard to see why the 'Guru' found it so objectionable. The poem is a hymn to the dark, Kaliesque side of divinity. (See her description of it in the entry for 2ⁿᵈ March, 1949).

26th January, 1951

Ma came today or rather yesterday from Vindhyachal and I was at the Ashram for a few hours. It is two months since I saw Her last. The impression was quite overwhelming. She is indeed LIGHT Itself, an Incarnation of THAT and definitely not a human being. It is so futile to criticize Her because no standards can possibly apply to Her. It is stupid to judge anything She does. One can just obey *and that is a very great privilege.* When one tunes into Her presence, one becomes overwhelmed with the feeling that nothing has any value other than to surrender entirely to That (the Supreme Reality) which She IS. What does it matter if one ruins one's health or even one's life if it brings one to Her.

It makes all the difference how one does *pranam* to Her. When I pranamed to Her as the Supreme Light, what an extraordinary response I got!

3rd February, 1951

More Westerners have come and I have had the privilege of translating. It is marvellous because it gives me a chance to really know Her teaching and get Her alone, to be very near in an intimate situation. I had an experience of how tremendous She is, that She is <u>The Thing</u>, the Achievement Itself. She said: *"The one thing to aim at is to know Oneself. Everything else is quite useless. Therefore all practice must be done in that Spirit, to know Oneself."*

She also said: *"Om is the root of all sounds. Every other sound is contained in that, and it is used to take one beyond all sound. Surrender is to the 'One' who is one's true Self, and not to another."*

I also translated for an American who makes strange involuntary movements when he meditates. She wished to help him and told Jack to tell him that all these practices must be done according to *niyam* [23] otherwise they may lead to disturbances in mind and body. When She actually talked to the boy, She would not tell him anything directly but sent him to one of the swamis whom he considers his Guru, to ask whether this was in fact true and whether these practices were dangerous. Later She gave me to understand that She could not give him advice as he goes here and there for it and does not really regard anyone as his Guru. She only told him

---

[23] Traditional ethical and moral precepts that are the basis for all yogic practices.

to keep to himself when he did these movements.

Yesterday a French Jew, Dr. Weintraub [the future Swami Vijayananda] came. It was most fascinating to translate for him. He was greatly impressed by Ma at first sight. This I believe is due to the fact that he has practised meditation for fifteen years. She told him that it was not without danger to concentrate on the spot between the eyes as long as the mind is not completely *sattvic*, for as long as there is the possibility of lower vibrations like anger or lust the strain could cause nervous disturbance. Therefore the ordinary person is asked to concentrate in the heart, because from there the energy can either go up or down without danger. If the meditation is successful the focus rises of its own accord to the forehead.

She also said quite definitely: *"There is no other Guru but God."* To me she said long ago: *"If anyone asks you whether you have taken diksha* [initiation] *say 'Whatever is necessary for me God arranges'."* Mother does not like people to advertise their relationship with Her as it is always something intimate and totally personal.

It seems to me that people who have already done some *sadhana* immediately find Mother attractive and She is of particular help to those that are inclined towards meditation and solitude.

It has been most worthwhile for me to learn languages (how right my father was!) and I must spend my free time learning more Hindi and Bengali. Being able to translate I get more and more teaching from Her and my knowing French and German also allows me to be of service to many people who otherwise would be unable to speak with Her.

Malati writes that she had a tremendous experience with Mother on 1st February and has since given up Rajghat altogether. Mother told her that this was inevitable.

17th February, 1951

Went to Vindhyachal but got unwell on the way so Mother sent me back the next day. Still, I sensed the charming influence of Devi [the Goddess] there and it somehow had a refreshing influence, in spite of my condition. Travelling in a station wagon with the six Westerners I could feel how serious and concentrated these people are.

Mother asked me to come to Patna for three days, so I went on the 10th night and returned on the 14th morning. It was very strenuous but gave me a keen sense of the fact that I am half asleep, not really knowing what *sadhana* is. True *sadhana* begins when one is unable to forget the goal even for a minute, when one is aspiring to the Supreme with one's whole being at every moment. When translating for Weintraub I thought: "How many things he has tried and how much pains taken." Mother asked him if he had remembered what She had told him to do and She then asked me also. I felt that I should be much more serious; I am drifting. I asked Her if I could talk to Her in Benares. She agreed.

I feel that my *sadhana* consists in discovering Her ever more completely, in surrendering ever more to Her. I do it in thought and words but then I go on as before most of the day. When I am with Her, though, this remembrance remains much stronger.

It is really very important to either segregate oneself or stay with serious *sadhakas*. Yet there is now *Om* in my breath every time I turn my mind to it, so it <u>is</u> going on as a constant undercurrent.

At Patna Mother reproached me for wearing a sari with a pretty border. I asked: "What's wrong with it?" She: "*Then why don't you dress up and paint your face also?*" It must have been because both Premanand and Weintraub met me at the station and brought me to Her. There is a subtle pleasure in my mind at being attended to by Europeans who have proper manners, in contrast to the people here who are full of disregard for women. Perhaps Mother saw that.

With the advent of Westerners at Ma's Ashram a gap that I have always felt has been filled. I missed the congenial and intelligent company of people from my own culture.

Rajghat, 22nd February, 1951

Premanand left two days ago and I translated his last talk with Mother which lasted for about two hours. I got a glimpse of him as Mother sees him and of the enormous volume of teaching She gave him behind the few words She said:

"*Meditate on God all the time, whatever you do, wherever you are. Remember that whatever you see, whatever you hear, is HE alone.*

Pain exists because you believe yourself to be separate. Don't consider anyone as separate from yourself. Regard everyone as your friend. Remember that you are God's 'yantra' [24] *and that He is moving you. Dedicate yourself entirely to Him, feel all the time that it is He who is doing everything through you. Even when you walk, feel that He is moving your legs. Whatever work you do, offer it to Him, then you will be incapable of any baseness; for how can you offer anything ugly to your Beloved.*

"Surrender entirely to Him". *What does this mean? The little knowledge you have, you give up to Him and in return, because you have emptied yourself, He will give you All. Remember that you are out to know who you are. The japa is the Sound of Brahman, His own 'swarupa'* [essential form]. *So when you do japa you are with Him, that is Satsang. Therefore keep it up all the time, either japa or meditation. Meditate on the Oneness of all, of everything. There can be nothing outside Him. Everything that is, is necessary to make up the world. If only one finger is missing you say 'he is a cripple!' So don't see anything as apart from Him, who is your own self. Then you will be incapable of anger. How can you be angry with your Beloved, who is none other than your real Self?*

"Feel that you have been with God in your meditation, though you do not know it. Keep a place separate for your meditation and, just as the perfume of the flower spreads through the air, so will the fragrance of God produced by your daily practice be transported on the wind into the world at large."

Question: Why should onions and garlic be avoided?

Mother: *They take the mind in the wrong direction, down instead of up.*

Question: Meat?

Mother: *Meat also. You are already flesh —if you eat flesh, you become more of the flesh. It keeps you down to worldliness, whereas you are aspiring to the Divine.*

Questioner: Is there immorality involved in eating meat?

Mother: *Yes, certainly, killing is 'pap'* [sin].

Question: Only for the *sadhak* or for all.

Mother: *For all.*

Question: I am going back to avoid pain to my parents. But

---

[24] Esoteric geometric diagram considered to be an embodiment of the Deity.

how far should I comply with their wishes? They expect me to settle down and get married.

Mother: *If you wish to get married you may do so though you may get caught in the movement of the world; but remember that all the Rishis of old were married. Together with your wife go on aspiring towards the Divine. But if you do not wish to get married, no one can force you. If you can keep your mind pure without marriage, so much the better.*

Question: Should I take up work for my father's estate and property or welfare work for Indians and Africans?

Mother: *As you are going back, there is no harm in working. But don't take up work that will bind you.*

Questioner: Should I give talks in clubs and societies about Indian Philosophy and mysticism etc if asked?

Mother: *Yes, certainly you should. And before talking, offer yourself to God as His instrument, do pranam to Him mentally and make it clear in your talk that just as there are different ways of earning a living, so in India the different sects and philosophies are various ways to Self-Realization.*

She was very emphatic and I felt that Premanand will work in England; and though he may come here many times, it will only be to take with him Her light to the West. Suddenly I got a glimpse of how Europe will be influenced through people like Premanand, who is utterly devoted to Her. She told him to regard me as his *'didi'* (older sister). I am indeed lucky to have a brother like this and to get all Her teaching now in such abundance after having been kicked about and in everyone's way for so long. And how right my father was to make me learn languages. How my life has been guided all the time and I did not know it!

In the morning I translated for Rappold who says he finds Indian conditions very trying and gets ill because of faulty nourishment here. But I feel it is also because he is obviously too attached to the comfort of his life in America. She called him 'Dhyananand' which means the bliss of meditation. He suddenly asked: "If my health gets bad should I return home, for there I get well very quickly". Mother: *"No, don't go in a hurry. Try to keep well here. Since India is favourable to your meditation try to live here. Only if your body gets so weak that it disturbs your meditation you* should go home. But even then try to get well and come back. Whatever is congenial to your meditation, that should guide your steps".

Question: Can the body ever be weak enough to disturb meditation?

Mother: *If your mind could rise beyond the body you would not get ill. But as yet your mind is dependent on the body, if the body is too weak the mind gets restless.*

Question: Is it then ultimately a question of the mind?

Mother: "*Yes, entirely. There is nothing, no problem outside of the mind*". She again spoke of how pain and happiness are due to identification and said: "*The same situation will produce pleasure or pain according to one's mental disposition.*" (She gave the example of politics).

Strangely, yesterday I had a letter from my old teacher, Helene Ueberall (Avriel), from Bucharest —where her son is ambassador for Israel. A voice from the past and just when my mind has turned to the West due to my translating for so many Westerners.

26ᵗʰ February, 1951

Last Thursday Miss Merston told Mother that she sometimes forgets to meditate. Mother told me to remind her! Most embarrassing task. Then she told us both to go to Dehradun and sit there and do *sadhana*, I should remind her to meditate and she should give me food in return. I at once got terrified and revolted —so much for surrender! Anyhow the old lady will never submit to this, fortunately.

Yesterday morning Mother said: *If there must be duality, then let it be between God and his devotee. Consider yourself the 'das'* [servant] *of the Lord and everything you do to be His work. By offering everything unto Him one loses the false sense of 'I am the doer'. The true bhakta is a perfect servant who ultimately becomes one with the Master.*

Today I translated a private for Cecile who asked: "I don't know whom to worship, no form seems quite right. If I turn to Christ, I feel it should be Krishna or Buddha etc."

Mother: *Worship Him who is 'All in All' through whichever focus appeals to you most. Even if one takes the attitude that there is no God whatsoever, then here is Atmaprakash* [Light of the Self] *because in reality there is only One.*

Slowly I am getting a slight glimpse of what it means to offer Him everything. In the Ashram I am much more aware of this. I get carried away into that sublime atmosphere.

31st March, 1951

Reading Brother Lawrence's *The Practice of the Presence of God*, which Walter sent me, makes all the difference. His teaching is almost identical with Mother's. What matters is to love God in all things; to practice seeing Him in all things; to be alone with God; to practice that all forms are His. Then no one can annoy one. Also to realize that all one's shortcomings come from the fact that one forgets Him. But I have not come to the stage where I can think of Him in the midst of a lot of people all wanting things from me, especially when Mother is not here.

7th April, 1951

I am being eaten up by school work. Somehow having no counterweight, as when Mother is here, I put too much intensity into my work and the children have become so fanatically interested in English that they nearly kill me, coming to me at all times and wanting books, copy books etc. Almost every child has suddenly begun to write and to read furiously. It is like Krishni's arithmetic class.

This evening on the roof it suddenly struck me how wonderful it would be to take *sanyas*. How much help one would get out of literally dropping one's old life, dying to the world and living only on what God sends; to give away all one's things, money, clothes, books and literally depend on God for everything —to start anew quite naked; just to drop everything at a stroke. This seems so much easier than to go gradually by stages. All temptations would fall away in one shot.

XXII - "Are You Not Mine ?"

I woke up lying on my back, stiff with cold, feeling I must write down this dream; but already most of it is gone. I had fallen in love with the son of someone I know. I receive a letter from him, which has crossed mine, but cannot read the signature and I have forgotten his name. I have to do *puja* and while grinding the sandalwood I begin thinking about this man and in my thoughtlessness grind an entire vessel full. I say to myself: "I can't throw it away." so I keep it in the vessel and wonder whether it will be all right. I smear some of it on the forehead of a dog, a black dog who is friendly with me. Then I go with some people in a car. The car stops on the way. I ask the driver what the matter is, and he says: "Now it is difficult, but later I shall go at great speed." I say, by then I shall have gotten out as I am only going a short distance. The man says: "I was going to ask you to come with me." He has to see a doctor and he wants me to help him. He says he will bring me back in the car in a short while. I have to do my *puja* and I don't want to go with him, but wonder whether it is proper to refuse. Just as the others are getting out at the place I had wanted to, I hear that Ramana Maharshi has come and so I say I can't go with him as I must go and see Ramana. I feel very happy about this. I set off at once. He is in an amphitheatre. One has to go very many steps down and he is sitting at the bottom in the middle. I am a bit worried because I have no flower or anything to bring him, but enter all the same. On the way I see Lewis sitting up at the top of the steps (I am several steps lower down already) and I feel I must go to him. Then I debate within myself whether I should first see the Maharshi, but am afraid Lewis will mind it and so I go to him. He is dressed in European clothes and looks fairly ordinary. I ask him why he never came to see me and he makes some empty excuse that he could not. He seems to be quite

447

cracked. I wonder how it is that he is not dead after all, only half mad. Then I start to go down to the Maharshi after telling L. that He has come and that Mother will also come soon. On my way down there are a few steps where the railing is broken and I slip and have some trouble, but proceed. Some lady makes remarks about my clothes fitting well, I seem to be wearing European clothes. As I go down the steps I think, one cannot rely on Lewis' Guru because he gave such precise details about L.'s death and now he is not dead after all. As I think this I wake up and thus never get to the Maharshi. [1]

Hoshiarpur, 8th May, 1951

Arrived here on 6th. Leaving tomorrow for Jullundhur.

Ma said yesterday: *"A vigraha* [a sacred image] *is not a stone. If you see Shiva in it, then you don't see the stone. If you see the stone, you don't see Shiva"*. This, then, is the secret: to see only Him in all. Then one would not get angry or worry, or be caught up in the illusion of this world.

Jullundhur, 9th May, 1951

The absurdity of keeping hours for *sadhana* and of having a time-table etc occurred to me. If one really wants to find oneself how can one do anything else at all. So all these helps are preliminaries to get one to the stage where one can do nothing else but search. Then only does real *sadhana* begin and the way must of itself open out. In that sense J.K. is right.

Ma said yesterday: *"If you go on scrubbing a dirty vessel its own swarupa* [true form] *gradually gets revealed, then you find out whether it is copper, brass, silver etc. So by repeating God's name your own swarupa becomes revealed. Therefore do it all the time, whether you feel like it or not."*

Jullundhur, 11th May, 1951

The mind wanders because one does not desire the One, but takes delight in all sorts of things. The moment one really becomes deeply interested in the One, all desire and wandering thought would stop at a stroke.

---

[1] Sri Ramana Maharshi had died a few months before this.

Mother ordered me to learn *asanas* from Pushpa and to do them every morning before meditation. She (Pushpa) showed me the *Surya Namaskar* and some *asanas* which I had done before, but also some others which I doubt I can learn at my age.

Amballa, 19ᵗʰ May, 1951

Was in Doraha for three days, all the time very near Mother. This time I am staying with the other lady devotees and everyone eats with me as it seems Punjabis do not pay much attention to orthodox observances. Somehow many take me to be the Mataji and do *pranam*. In Jullundhur wherever I stood a crowd collected. It is very embarrassing.

Jullundhur, 24ᵗʰ May, 1951

After coming here I felt very bad to have left. I don't know why I get these fits of running away even now. My other side is still so strong. If I was really aware of what Mother is, I could never leave Her of my own free will, whatever the circumstances.

In Doraha Ma sat near the canal every afternoon. One day a *sanyasi* asked Her:

"Some ladies here tell me that they feel very bound by their outer circumstances and asked what they are to do? I told them I am also bound by the Guru, by the *dharma* etc."

Ma: *"No, dependence is due to fear. As long as you are afraid, you are bound. But the moment you are fearless, you are independent. The householder is bound by laws and rules. But the sanyasi, who should be fearless, is free".*

I am reading Guru Nanak's Life with great interest. The Sikhs are very hospitable and have a great sense of service.

25ᵗʰ May, 1951

Mother, as if She had known I would leave, was very sweet to me the night before I left. She playfully hit me several times with a sweet smelling garland and then gave it to me. I said: "You are right to beat me, I have been very angry today". She said: *"You call it beating when I just wanted you to smell the flowers".* As I pranamed to Her, She gave me a light slap on the back. She said: *"Now I am beating you to remove the anger".* Then when I told her it was so hot there, day and night, She said: *"Why can't you bear it when the others can. You should try."* But I would not listen. Strange why I was so adamant that I must have my minimum comforts.

Last night, Mother's birthday, I should have stayed up all night, but then I thought that the next night there will also be little opportunity to sleep so I got up at 2.30 a.m., had a wash and sat in meditation from 3 a.m. to 4 a.m. I prayed to Mother to destroy my own personal will and to make me like a flute on which She plays —mind, heart and body— so that it will become impossible for me to do anything that is not Her will. Let there be only Her and no me at all. Let it be now and forever. I cannot wait any longer.

Amritsar, 26th May, 1951

There is a response to my prayer to Mother. The *japa* combined with meditation on Her has become extremely intense and absorbing. When I sit I get great bliss. The spine straightens of itself and it feels as if a rod of wood was inside me extending from the bottom of my spine to the top of my head. There is a feeling of light around my head. Today when I did *japa* my fingers seemed to have lost their solidity and felt etheric.

I get the impression that what Mother wants me to do is to stay in meditation all the time. Everything else is irrelevant. I wonder whether I shall still be able to carry on with the school work.

Mandi, 10th June, 1951

We went to many beautiful places: first Tarana, a Kali temple near here. There I knew She wanted the song "Mahavidya" sung, and so I sang it.

Then we went to Rewalsar [2] for a whole day where there is a fine Buddhist temple in Tibetan style and a Gurdwara where we stayed. On the 7th we went to Kulu and Manali. Mother is quite enchantingly beautiful. I felt so happy there with the wild virgin jungle, the roaring river, the rocks and huge trees. I walked all alone down from Vasishtakund, where we bathed in hot sulphur

---

[2] Also known by the Tibetan name Tso Pema. It is a place sacred to the great Indian *siddha*, Padmasambhava, who is credited with establishing Buddhism in Tibet.

springs, and I felt myself again. I could hug the whole world at such moments, but when I am with people all day, I loose my temper. Too much *'satsang'* is not good for me. Glorious nature is God's own *satsang*. There I automatically am with God. I wish I could stay at Manali all by myself for sometime. Vijayananda also felt the same way and he looked quite 'verklärt' [transformed]. Yesterday I walked and sat by myself for an hour or more by the side of the mountain stream. It at once healed me inside.

Since I have come back to Mandi I feel very exhausted. I cannot shake off a cold I caught in Baijnath, probably bathing in the stream there. This morning everyone has gone to Gita Bhavan and I stayed here alone and went for a walk up the hill in the palace garden. The moment I am alone in nature I feel refreshed, but people upset me. I think that I must spend my next holiday in a solitary place doing *tapasya*. But when the time comes I always get tempted to go with Mother.

Kishenpur, 1st July, 1951

Mother ordered me to leave Mandi on 13th June for Kishenpur. We went to Jogendranagar and Barod up to 9000 ft and then the next day down into the boiling heat. But I had wanted to be by myself and so I have been until Mother came here on the 22nd June. I did quite a lot of meditation. One day I went to Rishikesh in the Raja of Mandi's car. It is a most charming place. I now feel like going up to Badrinath. The bus now goes quite a way and one has only to walk the last forty-five miles.

Today I had a good meditation in the *Dhyan mandir*. I found that the only way is to open oneself completely to Mother and then remain still. To disobey Her is fatal, because one then feels one's surrender to be untrue and becomes stuck. It does not matter what She demands, but what matters is the giving up of self-will so that the Divine Will may shine through one.

I intend leaving for Benares tomorrow.

Rajghat, 15th July, 1951

Was with Mother from 3rd to 10th at the Ashram. It was very cool here until She left Benares on the 10th. Now it is terribly hot. When She is here I can never manage to meditate much as there is no time, but being with Her is much more than meditation. I now love to sing *kirtan*.

To my great surprise I am not so eager as I used to be to sit and gaze at Ma. I wonder whether that is because She has really gotten inside me.

Whether I feel I am progressing or not I remain fully committed to my *sadhana* with Her —come what may. All that is needed really is intense longing, nothing else. Of course Mother is quite clear that this longing is intensified and cultivated precisely by having fixed daily periods of meditation which one must adhere to whether one feels like it or not.

31st August, 1951

When Mother is here I live in a kind of intoxication. I have no time for anything and yet cannot leave off going to the Ashram even for a day. Frydman asked me today what had happened to me in the course of this year and I could not reply. I am only aware of the present moment filled with Her presence. It is perhaps wrong to go on with this schoolwork as it gives me a kind of escape from the rigours of the Search. If I could get by on four hours of sleep I should not be so rushed.

Rajghat, 19th October, 1951

During the Durga Puja holidays I was with Mother at the Ashram for over a fortnight. I got unwell but enjoyed myself thoroughly all the same. One day Patalda gave me a sweet from Mother's mouth. As I swallowed it I had a sensation as if my body was being diffused with Light, which produced a deep meditative condition in my mind.

One morning someone asked Mother: "Is it any use taking *diksha* from a Guru who does not show the signs that the *shastras* [scriptures] have laid down for a real Guru?"

Ma: "*There are two points here. One is 'taking' a Guru and the other is, that the Guru is the Guru. There can be no question about it, no 'taking' and no 'leaving' as the Guru is the Self. If he is not, he may show you a path but he cannot take you right to your goal, to enlightenment, because he is not there himself. You may make someone your Guru and then leave him, but in this case I say you have never had a*

Guru. The true Guru cannot be left. He is the Guru by his nature and he naturally fulfils all that is lacking in the disciple. As the flower gives its fragrance naturally, so the Guru gives diksha —by sight or hearing or touch or teaching or mantra or even without any of these, just because he is the Guru. The flower does not make an effort to give its fragrance, it does not say: 'Come and smell me'. It is there. Whoever comes near it will enjoy the scent. As ripe fruit falls from the tree and is picked up by man or eaten by the birds, so the Guru is all that is needed for those who are his own, whoever they may be.

There are false Gurus and many get caught by those. It is said you must give body and mind to the Guru, but that does not mean that the Guru may take advantage of you. If he tries to do that, you must leave him and very often also the mantra he has given you, because it is associated with him and brings him to your mind. Then I say, go and bathe in the Ganges and start afresh with another mantra. A mantra is that which protects [there is a play on words here in Hindi]. *If it does not do that, it is not a mantra."*

26th October, 1951

Last night dreamt of Sri Ramana Maharshi. I believe Frydman and Kitty were also in it. At the end I did *pranam* to Him. The atmosphere is still with me, a meditative quiet and physical well being. Yesterday I was very weak after severe diarrhoea.

12th December, 1951

Yesterday when I said good-bye to Mataji, She said: "*Do all your work for Him. Whatever you do is a mudra* [mystic gesture] *in His worship. When you eat, offer it as an oblation to the Self."*

Sharanananda was here last week. I saw him three times and liked immensely both the quality of spirituality he conveys and his replies to questions. He said that *tyag* [renunciation] means non-attachment, not only with regard to others, but first of all towards one's own body and mind —not to consider anything one's own.

Then he said that there are three things one has to do in one's approach to God: First to think of Him, then *sambandh karna* [create a relationship with Him] and then to have *vishwas* [faith]. The last one is the most difficult and is based on the other two. Where there is real faith, there is no more desire.

453

26th December, 1951

This morning I remembered what Mataji had told me on leaving, that whatever work I did was a *mudra* in His *puja*. For a little while when working I thought: It is not my hand but His, not my foot etc. If I could keep up this *smriti* [remembrance], it would be all that is wanted. Perhaps this is J.K.'s 'awareness', if it really becomes an experience, not only a thought.

This time preparing a folk-dance for the school anniversary, I had much less trouble than I used to have. It was because although I had planned not to do anything, the children insisted that I must; so I was completely detached and not ambitious. All the same I thought: "This is also His work", and put in quite a lot of care. The costuming happened almost by itself this time, I had no quarrel, there was no expense, and I believe it was better than last year's.

18th January, 1952

Now that I am trying to write an article about Ma for an ashram publication, I could tear out my hair with grief that I have not written down all that I heard Her say this autumn. Such pearls of wisdom and sometimes in a small group when no one took notes. The opportunity that is lost does not return. Now I shall always keep a notebook and pencil with me.

21st January, 1952

Spent weekend at Ashram. This mad eagerness about the book on Ma [3] continued there. In the night I seemed to work out my whole article. It came on its own spontaneous flowing. I was half asleep and half awake. But I did not write down anything as I felt it is not yet ripe. Let it come slowly. But now I shall have to start writing. It is a strange feeling like being pregnant and it has to be laboured out now. After having been wildly inflamed with eagerness to show Mother to the world for what She is, a great reaction has now set in and I feel where is the need for all this publicity. Why throw such a pearl before swine. In any case, those who can

---

[3] This book was an anthology comprised of articles written by devotees of Anandamayee Ma entitled: *Mother as Seen by Her Devotees*, published by the Shree Ma Anandamayee Sangha.

benefit from Ma will come to Her, and the world at large can only be a disturbance.

I keep on praying that I may not write anything but what Mother wishes to be written and that my work might be an offering of faith to Her and nothing else. If it isn't public, so much the better.

23rd January, 1952

Trying to write about Ma has at least the good effect that it makes me realize more than ever how beyond all words and thoughts She is and how small my understanding. How little in spite of everything I value my contact with Her, otherwise would I even notice how I am treated; would I allow my body to get the better of me and leave Ma in order to be more comfortable as I did at Amballa? Isn't it better to die at Her Feet than to live away from Her. I cry now every day because contemplating Her invariably drives tears into my eyes. How unworthy I am of Her Grace and Mercy.

24th January, 1952

If only I had obeyed Ma and written down daily my inner experiences I should have ample material for the article. But I feel I cannot possibly write about Her. All I can do, if that, is to describe my own interaction with Her. How really appropriate the simile is of the ant that crawls about on the slopes of Mt. Everest. It cannot even have an inkling of that wonderful giant peak and yet the mountain provides all its needs. It lives and feeds on It.

A new meaning of *japa* and *kirtan* has dawned on me: When one realizes one's own nothingness, one's own incapacity, then nothing is left but to turn to Him —then only one is ready to surrender. Surrender is only possible when you discover that your own intelligence is quite incapable of solving the problem, that your own effort is only the impotent ego struggling —and it is precisely this egoistic struggle that has to go.

Bhadaini, 28th January, 1952

When Mother was in Rajghir recently some people there asked Her: "What is the use of *sadhana*, as in any case one has to reap the results of one's past actions *(karma)."* Ma said: *"Karm kar? (Whose karma?) The moment you understand that <u>He</u> is the actor and is doing <u>everything</u> Himself, the problem is solved."*

1st February, 1952

Ma was here for two days for Vasant-Panchami. Vijayananda asked me to tell Her that all are Her children, but Westerners are her step children. She said: *"Sant ka bachha hai, achha hai, sat ke bachche hain"* [You are holy children, that's good, you are the true children]. I thought it was so deep, so full of meaning to say this. She fed us Jagannath *prasad.*

Since I began translating Vijayananda's article and working on the book I feel Her very near —even when I am physically separated from Her— almost more than when in Her physical presence. But now after being with Her for a while I again feel how important it is to be with Her. One changes so much, even physically in Her proximity. After all, as long as She is among us it is better to be with Her as much as possible.

Someone said: "Ma, a mouse has eaten the garland you gave me". Ma said: *"God in the form of the mouse has taken it."* Someone else: "The mouse is the vehicle of Ganesh." Ma: *"I don't know about Ganesh, but God the rat has eaten it."*

3rd February, 1952

Yesterday saw Ma off at Mugalsarai. She said something which I did not catch. Mira said it was: *"Kirtan karo"* [Do *kirtan*]. Last night we therefore sang *kirtan.* I woke up singing "Ram nam". The whole day I have been in a peculiar state of elation, feeling a special benevolence toward the children while I was on duty in the 2nd hostel. It seemed very easy, the children did not trouble me at all. This morning during my meditation I was getting ideas about what to say regarding Ma's teaching for the article, but did not write it at once and so forgot. I only remember one thing: "Her words are not, as with ordinary mortals, mere expressions of ideas and mental concepts, but are vehicles of light and power. They enlighten the mind so that there is an ever deepening understanding of all they imply and they give the questioner the power to carry them out in his life."

The Kashmiri, Mrs. Mehta, came and was rather upset about Prabhudat Brahmachari [4] and his way of making people swear by the Ganges to support the Hindu *dharma* against Nehru. She had heard an unfounded rumour that Ma supports him. Of course there is no truth in this, as Mother will have nothing to do with politics. But even if She did support him, who are we to judge Her actions. It changes absolutely nothing.

11th February, 1952

Some people feel that Mother is greater than any *avatar* that has ever existed, but I feel that there is no ground for this exaggerated feeling; though in a sense it is true, in that every divine incarnation must be unique. But how do we know exactly what Sri Krishna was like? Even now, when She is here with us, we know so ridiculously little about Her. So how can we possibly know anything at all from accounts of centuries ago. And what does it matter if She is different from all former examples. What difference does it make. I feel that this tendency of some people to exclusivity will have the wrong effect, just like Dr. Besant's announcement of J.K. as <u>the</u> World Teacher. That did not help but rather hindered. People must find out these things for themselves.

When we have taken refuge in Ma we must live Her famous maxim: "*Jo ho jayega*" [whatever happens, happens (as the Divine will)].

Sharananand said the mistake we make is that we think it is possible to fulfil our wishes, but very difficult to reach God. The very reverse is a fact: our wishes can never be fulfilled as ever new ones spring up, but God is nearest of all.

Hardwar, 16th February, 1952

While sitting with Mataji on a large rock in the Ganges, She said to us: "*Though He is everywhere and everything, still in his play He makes us believe that He is far from us. Isn't it wonderful? Any karma [work] or kriya [action] we do brings a result, but it can never take us to Him. But if He attracts us, then He sweeps us along like the*

---

[4] A famous swami and upholder of tradition who was very opposed to Nehru's 'secular' socialism (which many felt to be a euphemism for anti-Hinduism) and ran against him for Prime Minister on several occasions.

ocean and no one can alter this. Just as it is the natural result of digging to find water at some stage, just as it is natural that there should be a spark if one goes on rubbing two sticks together, so it is natural that the regular practice of cultivating His 'abhav' [state of total voidness] *should take us to Him. When meditation or japa is done it is to get a touch of Him. The joy we receive from this contact only emphasizes our awareness of the pain caused by our ultimate separation and this will inspire us to make even greater efforts to unite completely with Him. But the result of meditation is still not He as long as it remains within the realm of experience. Only when the experiencer is wholly dissolved in the experience is the supreme Truth revealed."*

Later She said to the Raja of Tehri's daughter-in-law: *"He attracts you through any form that appeals to you. It is like water and ice. Ice looks different from water but actually it is nothing but water. Krishna, Shiva etc are like the ice i.e. different forms of what is really only pure formlessness. When you have become attracted to and get in touch with a particular Divine form, as you become more absorbed in it you one day find out that He is indeed the formless. Then you see that He is sakara* [with form] *as well as nirakara* [without form] *as well as beyond both"*.

Since She Herself is that Supreme Formlessness in a Form, this teaching becomes intensely alive in Her presence.

This evening it struck me how to entitle my article: "Ma —the supreme paradox". She is the most universal and yet the most orthodox. She affirms all paths and yet She says: *"There is no path as all action, all effort, is done by He alone."* She also says: *"He both is and is not, neither is He not nor is He."*

This morning She said to me: *"Anger appears to me also as one of His beautiful forms"*. So I said: "If this is so, then where is the need to change it?" Ma: *"Because it is full of pain for the one who gets angry, not for anything else"*. I: "But if one also sees it as one of His beautiful forms?" Ma: *"Long before one can do that anger will have left one."* I: "What about the Rishis who could be so very angry and sometimes curse people?" Ma: *"That is different. They had the power to create and so could destroy. Even a Rishi is only at a particular stage"*.

Avadhutji [5] gave a talk today on Mother's saying *"Jo ho jae"* [what-

---

[5] A great ascetic who had lived for years high up in the Himalayas practising austerities. He was very devoted to Anandamayee Ma.

ever happens happens (as His will)] as being the end of all wisdom because only when you see God in whatever happens can you have perfect equanimity. He also said: "God is the source of both pain and happiness. Without pain we could never find ourselves for it is only that which turns us away from the world to God."

Hardwar, 17ᵗʰ February, 1952

This evening during *mouna* it occurred to me that real *mouna* means that the ego keeps completely silent and only He speaks. Spontaneously I prayed to Ma: "Let me become utterly silent to You, so that You can speak through me".

Avadhuthji spoke about the virtue of *Mahamantra* ⁶ this evening and said that it is especially powerful during the *Kali Yuga*. It destroys all sin and *dosh* [imperfections] and takes one towards God.

This afternoon Vijayananda came to see where I stay and I talked with him about Mother for one and a half hours. Nowadays She has relaxed Her restriction about our talking together.

18ᵗʰ February, 1952

Last night when I went to bed, between waking and sleeping, I experienced some of that *viraharas* [intense longing] which must be the root of true *kirtan*. I was really shouting "Ma, Ma" from my heart. But I fell asleep all the same and in the morning it was gone. It was only a glimpse.

Today Ma gave a long talk to someone whom the Raja brought. But not taking it down at once, a lot of it has gone from my memory. What I do remember is the following: *"Even when the mind wanders, never mind, go on doing 'sadkarm' [spiritual practice]. The result will come. Just as fire dries wet wood and then burns it, because this is its 'svabhav' [inherent nature], so 'sadkarm' —japa, meditation, scripture study etc— purifies the mind. You do it in order to get 'pratyaksha' [direct perception]. At present you don't know anything about God, it is all hearsay and from books, but not experience. The 'swarupa' [true form] of the mind is He himself. That is why the mind is restless, because it has to find Itself and it can't get lasting peace until it has found its true nature."*

---

⁶ The well known *mantra* praising both Ram and Krishna.

459

Today I again spoke to Ma about some of the orthodox rules. She said: "*Yes, God's rules need to be obeyed*". I said: "Is it God's or man's". She said: "*Admi kaun hai?*" [(find out) who is man].

So She teaches all the time. She continued: "*There is only God and to realize that is the only thing that has to be done. There are many ways, as many ways as there are people, but the ways in themselves do not lead to God. That lies with Him alone and does not depend on your effort. All you can do is to remove the curtain, the 'durbudhhi', which creates the illusion of separateness from God, whereas actually He is always there. As long as you consider yourself the doer, you cannot go beyond karma. It is only when you realize the ONE that action and non-action cease.*

Pain and happiness are in the mind, not in action; the same action can be painful to one and joyful to the other, depending on identification." She gave the example of Mahatma Gandhi's murder saying it was a source of joy to his enemies and agony to his friends.

Hardwar, 23rd February, 1952, Shivaratri

Ma was discussing the *puja* for the Shiva *prathishta* [consecration] with the Raja of Solan [7] and said: "*How many mantras the pandits use to make sure that none of the other deities should put any obstacles in the way of the puja. The chief thing is to make the 'pratishta' in oneself —on that which is— so that there may be prakash [light] and for this one has to eliminate all inner obstacles, all one's negative tendencies.*"

It seems to me that part of Ma's work is to establish spiritual centres that will go on for thousands of years. That is why She is ever willing to be present at these consecrations. [8]

Today I heard about Her recent spontaneous visit to Bhawanipur —a remote village that somehow called out to Her as She passed by in the car. Although well off the main road and com-

---

[7] One of Anandamayee Ma's greatest devotees, known affectionately as Yogibhaiji (brother Yogi). He was the first president of the Shree Ma Anandamayee Sangha.

[8] To this end Anandamayee Ma has over 30 ashrams in India and Bangladesh, each having one or more temples consecrated by Her. Today these are managed by the Shree Ma Anandamayee Sangha.

pletely out of the way, She suddenly ordered the driver to go there without offering any explanation. She then got down and, to the villagers' amazement, embraced two trees —afterward instructing the people gathered there to worship and revere them always. She began the worship Herself there on the spot and distributed fruits as prasad. She told the woman who had planted the trees: "*I am your daughter*". Clearly Ma had a divine insight into this situation that is totally beyond our comprehension.

Since I am trying to translate Mother's sayings, I seem to be walking on air. I am gripped by it so strongly, it goes on day and night. Inspiration comes at all times, especially when I sit quiet or lie down to rest.

Benares, 22nd March, 1952

Went over the Bengali to be translated with Kamalda last night. Stayed up till 1 a.m. in order to write down what he told me so as not to forget.

24th March, 1952

Today it is seven years since I first spoke to Ma at Sarnath.

It seems to me that I am becoming too obsessed and ambitious about this translation work. I feel exhausted and have slight heart trouble. Is it really necessary or even desirable to make such an effort? This is due to the idea that 'I' must do.

It is now five years since I took a year's leave. I said then: "One should take a year off every 5 years, but next time I shall go for good". Now again I feel it would be the perfect thing to take one year to study Bengali and Sanskrit thoroughly, and English of course, so as to prepare myself for this translation work.

Rajghat, 9th April, 1952

Shiva Rao was here for a day. It strikes me that gratitude implies separation and different actors. The moment one accepts that everything is His Will, where is there room for gratitude and to whom is one to be grateful? And equally it is quite wrong to expect gratitude from anyone.

10ᵗʰ April, 1952

This morning A.'s 'correction', i.e. mutilation, of Mother's translation arrived. I was so upset I could not eat. I at once ran to the Ashram in the middle of a very hot day. I did not feel the *loo* or anything. I felt like a mother that has borne a child and someone goes and cuts off its limbs and puts on dog's and frog's paws and claws in their place. Fortunately A. did not only ruin the translation but perverted and distorted Mother's teaching to such a degree that I shall be able to get his influence eliminated altogether from anything that has to do with Mother's publication.

How subtly the ego prolongs its life! How attached I have become to this work and how deeply hurt I felt. But I also feel like Arjun who was told by Krishna [in the *Bhagavad Gita*] to fight. At first I thought one should just let them stew in their own ignorance and do what they like. But how can I look calmly on as Mother is kept away from everyone? It is enough that we Westerners are kept out by the orthodox rules (which are after all to a great extent imposed on Her by these people), but is Her teaching also to be denied us, guarded by those vultures? If this is indeed Her wish —well then, the West simply has not deserved Her. The few who have to come to Mother need to learn Bengali. Certainly I will do that now with all my might and will-power. Everything is His, everything is He —this incident included, and it shows me how attached I am.

Isn't it strange that all my fights are on this issue of how I feel that Mother is used by others —same as at Nainital. But this seems more serious by a long way. Mother's words still ring in my ears: *"One must speak the truth."* That was worth all the trouble a million times.

When I fought Frydman in the teacher's meeting I made myself ridiculous, but that finished him for our school. Malati at once promised that he would not be allowed in any meetings again. Similarly Kamalda promised that A. won't have any more say in the translation matter. [9]

---

[9] The work she was doing at this time ultimately appeared as the book *Words of Shree Anandamayee Ma*.

15th April, 1952

I asked Mother three questions last night:

1) Do you wish your teaching to be translated?

Mother: *"Nothing comes to me to say about this."*

2) A. made a mistake in section No. 7 of the translation and therefore reversed the meaning of what You said, mistranslating "Pray to Him who has given you worldly possessions for His own sake and not for what he may give you" as "Pray to Him for these things".

When the passage was read to Mother, She said: *"No, the meaning is 'Pray to Him for His own sake'"*. Then She said to me: *"Why do you get angry? You should feel pleased that you have understood rightly"*. *"So jao!"* [Go to sleep now]. I said: "No, Mother, I shall not sleep. I shall fight."

3) You use mostly the impersonal form and not the imperative when you give advice and also you use no verbs. In English this makes the sentence very awkward. Must the impersonal form be kept?

Mother: *"This body* [10] *speaks according to its 'kheyal'. You have to see from the context whether the personal form can be used"*. Section No. 1 of the translation was read to Her in Bengali and She was asked how the last sentence was to be translated. She said: *"This is personal advice, and should be in the personal form"*. From this test case I conclude that we have done it correctly.

I insisted on reading my translation in English [which she did not understand] to Mother, but She was not very willing to listen. So I said: "If you don't want it, I shall not read". Then She said: *"Tumhara kam karo!"* [Do your work]. So I read. She said: *"The words are very beautiful"*. I: "Is it your words or the work of my mind?" She looked at me with a peculiar look and said smiling: *"It is yours"*. I: "Then it must be all wrong." Mother: *"Are you not mine?"*

This was so touching and implied so much, even now I cannot keep tears from my eyes when I remember it. Now I understand why She does not give me inspiration on a platter but lets me labour for every word, so that I may become its meaning; oth-

---

[10] Anandamayee Ma usually referred to herself as "this body" or "this little girl" etc.

erwise where will the *sadhana* be. It is the effort that is the important thing, not the outcome.

"Response"
by Violet Sydney

As on the stillness of the waters
is reflected the silver of night
and the gold of noon day,
so my soul dreams at Thy passing.

As the slumber of the waters is
lightly broken by trailing zephir
and laughing breeze,
so my soul stirs at Thy touch.

As the surface of the waters is
rent by a great wind, is uplifted
and falls deep, so my soul
wakes at Thy call.

As in the mirage the waters are
one with the Heavens —undefined,
inseparate— so my soul
rests in Thy presence.

Khanna, 7th May, 1952

Arrived here this morning. Mother said to me: *"I am always with you. Sometimes in the shape of anger!"*

10th May, 1952

Yesterday Mother went for a walk to a new place. We came to a cluster of houses and trees and were told only *sadhus* stayed there. Mother sat under a peepal tree which had a brick platform around it and we sat on the ground. The tree had lovely green leaves. Mother remarked on it and then began to tell us about the trees at Her ashram at Dacca. She said: *"There is a tree of Madrasi mangoes there and these don't normally grow in Bengal, but because so many Mahatmas have lived there, it has grown. Someone may have once eaten a Madras mango there and thrown away the stone. The leaves of that tree shed honey. It was found that so much honey dropped from the tree that it filled a jar. Some say the tree is not a tree, but a*

464

Mahatma in the shape of a tree. There is also a jackfruit tree there that gives fruit all the year round. Where so much kirtan is sung all sorts of things become possible.

In Shahbag [11] *very, very much kirtan was sung. There are two trees near the room where this body lived and the wood of those ordinary trees has turned into sandalwood. Not only does it smell of sandal, but people use it to make sandalpaste for their puja."* Someone asked: "Are there any sandal trees near about?" Mother said: *"No, no sandal trees grow in Bengal".*

Khanna, 11th May, 1952

Yesterday only a small number people went for the daily walk with Ma as there was a meeting of the Sangha [12]. We found a nice clean place to sit on the sandy ground. Someone brought a plant out of whose fruit comes a silky cotton —like fibber, and it was remarked that it has specific healing properties. Sadhananda said that one could use the cotton of that plant to become invisible.

Mother observed: *"That is all right if you know how to wield this power properly so that you may become visible again at will. But if you are not quite expert, you may not be able to come back to your ordinary state again. These kind of things require tremendous concentration. You see, whatever you do, you must do with all your might, if you are to succeed. You must put your whole being into it and not be swayed by blame or praise. When someone reproaches you, you have doubts and when you are patted on the back you feel encouraged. That means you are not really committed, but are looking for the approval of others".*

Sadananda replied: "We are all like that". Mother said: *"Why do you shield yourself by saying this! How is it your business to see what others do? Improve yourself."* Then turning to me She said: *"Sometimes when I reproach you for something you say: 'Why only me? So many others do the same and you allow it.' But I say, turn your criticism on yourself, improve yourself, don't look to other's mistakes for justification".*

---

[11] The garden estate in Dacca where Mother lived with Bholanath at the time she first began to become known. (See p. 20)

[12] The Shree Ma Anandamayee Sangha, the principal organisation responsible for the maintenance of Anandamayee Ma's many ashrams, temples, schools, hospitals and charitable institutions.

Solan, 6ᵗʰ June, 1952

Mother said to me: *"You see 'dosh'* [defects] *in your surround-ings because there is 'dosh' in your mind. All is God's 'sundar rup'* [beautiful form]. *Satsang purifies the mind. Think Sri Krishna to be everything."* Then She said regarding a blow-up over the rules I had had recently: *"Throw away anger. It may be the dharma of a scorpion to bite but even a scorpion* (referring to me?) *that strives for ahimsa should not sting."*

During the silence at 8.45 p.m. I felt strongly how Ma is all-pervading and that all one has to do is to get out of the way; She does all the rest.

Two or three days ago I was feeling resentful that Avadhutji talks so much and Mother not at all. I told Her so and She scolded me; but from that day on She has started talking for hours literally.

Solan, 7ᵗʰ June, 1952

This evening when someone asked Avadhutji about Christ, whether or not He was an *avatar*, he said that he did not know. As to Ramakrishna he remarked: "It is not said in the *shastras* so he might be a great yogi, but not an *avatar*. A yogi can have very great power, enough to create a universe." About Gandhi he said definitely that he was limited etc. Avadhutji is a bit too orthodox for me.

8ᵗʰ June, 1952

This morning (quite late) I went to Ma's room and while doing *pranam* I thought "Take me and bless me that I may be yours", and I felt an immense blessing from Her. Immediately someone asked: "Ma, what is *ashirvad* [blessing]? Ma: *"When you do pranam to a mahatma, you surrender yourself to him completely and this induces a current of love from him that takes away your men-tal obstacles and obstructions and fills you with auspiciousness. A con-tact is made that establishes an inner harmony which gives one great strength to attain one's goal. Just as watering a tree causes its fruit to grow, so the blessing that pours down on one through pranam exalts one's spirit."*

For the last day or two I felt all out of tune, but today I feel wonderful because I have established a contact of love with Her

466

that I had forgotten about. If I cultivate that contact all the time it just carries me away. Then it struck me that when I was doing the translation work I was constantly praying to Her to do the work through me. I realize that if I maintain that attitude in whatever I do, it is bound to have the result of establishing Her constant presence within me.

Solan, 15ᵗʰ June, 1952

Avadhutji said one day: "When we see our *Ishtadev* [13] only in one form we belittle Him. Unless we see Him everywhere, and nothing but Him, we don't see Him at all."

---

[13] The form of God to which one is personally devoted.

XXIII - "Everything Is He, He Alone Is."

Mother has been talking daily about Her *sadhana leela* [1]. She underwent so many extraordinary mystical experiences during that period from Her early to late twenties, but She emphasized that these did not come from outside Herself as She found that the entire universe was contained within Her. At the time She would observe long periods (months on end) of complete silence during which she said the world literally ceased for Her. In this state there was no question of conventional subject-object perception but only an absolute Oneness. She explained that this play of *sadhana* was not done by Her in order to realize anything in particular, as Her consciousness had been immersed in non-dual awareness (which Yogis practise austerities for lifetimes to achieve) from birth. Nevertheless She spontaneously submitted to this esoteric process in which the most sacred divine mysteries unfolded through Her. She said that from Her childhood She had always been aware of an almond-shaped light between Her eyebrows that was ever present. It strikes me that in some way the whole thing was a kind of descent for Her —to better understand how the ONE takes on the appearance of the many.

22ⁿᵈ June, 1952

Today She told an amazing story of how once in the early days, when She was absorbed in deep meditation, Her brother-in-law had angrily reproached Her for not doing the housework. As he came toward Her he was suddenly struck by an invisible force that knocked him back as if he had received a powerful electric shock. In terror and awe, he said: "Who art Thou?" (addressing Her with the formal *'aap'* rather than the customary *'tu'*).

---

[1] See pages 19-20.

She replied: *"Purna Brahma Narayan"* [Supreme Absolute Godhead].[2]

The room became filled with an uncanny spiritual power. A family friend who was also present said: "You are *Shaitan*" [Satan]. *"Yes"*, She replied smiling: *"whatever you say, that I am"*. So he kept quiet!

The friend then said: "If you are *Purna Brahma*, then give Bholanath illumination." Without any hesitation Mother touched Bholanath's head and he immediately sat up straight and went into *samadhi*.

At that point She herself was totally unaware of Her surroundings, as though in another dimension, and Her sari had fallen down from Her shoulder. In the midst of all this Bholanath's little nephew, who was living with them, arrived home from school. When he saw Ma and Bholanath in such a condition he thought they had gone mad and began to cry. Then the friend beseeched Ma to return Bholanath to his ordinary state, which She did by touching him lightly. On coming round he said he had experienced supreme ecstasy!

She also told how once a thief vandalized the Kali Temple at the ashram in Dacca and broke the wrist of the Kali image by twisting it. Although Ma, who was far away at the time, had not received news of this, She kept on twisting Her wrist and said to Didi: *"Bring an axe, I must cut off my hand"*. Like a child She pleaded and kept on twisting Her wrist. She told us: *"For me, cutting off my hand was like cutting off a tree stump, no more"*.

She related another incident that occurred around the same time: One of Her devotees became ill while travelling with Her and remained behind when She went on to another place. Not long after, arriving at Her new destination, Ma asked for a fire to be made, and before anyone knew what was happening, She thrust Her hand into it and only with difficulty were those with Her able to remove it. The next day word was received that the devotee who had remained behind had died and his body had been cre-

---

[2] Anandamayee Ma normally did not go about proclaiming Herself to be God. To the contrary she always referred to herself in the third person —usually as "this body" or "this little girl". But in this instance it would seem that "That" with which she was wholly merged chose to make itself known.

mated at precisely the moment Mother had put Her hand into the fire. Once we surrender to Her, She really becomes one with us in every way.

Solan, 23rd June, 1952

The presence of some old devotees from Dacca here seems to have inspired Mother to relate more and more incidents from the old days. Today She spoke of Bhaiji[3], whom everyone agrees was Her closest disciple. Once while travelling with Bholanath Mother received the news that Bhaiji was very ill and the doctors had given up all hope for his recovery. Bholanath said immediately that they must go to him at once. On the way there Ma had a vision of Bhaiji with his head in Her lap and his wife standing by sadly. On telling Bholanath about this he was very pleased and said: "Then Bhaiji won't die". When they reached there Bhaiji was spitting blood and was very weak and unable to stand, so he knelt when Mother came. She had never before seen his head from above, as he never sat in Her presence. As he was kneeling She said to Bholanath: *"See, he has a yogic sign on his head"*, and She touched the spot which was just at the *sahasrarachakra* [4]. Bhaiji became ecstatic at this and his condition was at once dramatically improved. Bholanath, who had a great love for Bhaiji, was overjoyed at this miraculous recovery and in a state of exaltation he picked him up in his arms and circumambulated Mother as the deity. He then placed Bhaiji, as an offering, in Her lap, saying: "This is your *'dharma putra'* [spiritual son]."

Bhaiji remained in an ecstatic state for days afterward and later, when he was fully recovered, he asked Mother whether he could have photos made to record this incident which he deemed the greatest moment of his life, a true spiritual rebirth. She told him he would have to ask Bholanath's permission for this. Bholanath enthusiastically agreed and called a photographer at once, arranging personally the positions to be photographed of Mother, Bhaiji and himself exactly as he remembered them.

---

[3] Jagdeesh Chandra Ray (d. 1936). He was a high-ranking government officer and a man of profound universal vision.

[4] The highest of the esoteric bodily centres, or chakras, the 'opening' of which induces enlightenment.

Bhaiji cherished these photos and kept them carefully in a special box. Once when he was away on a journey, his wife, who had become jealous of her husband's spiritual attachment to Ma, found the pictures and became incensed, particularly when she saw the one with Bhaiji's head in Mother's lap. In her distorted jealousy she had the photo redone, taking away Bholanath, who was shown standing next to Mother in the original. She then circulated the altered picture amongst some college students who used to go to Ma, saying: "See, this is the Mother whom you worship". One boy showed the photo to his mother who was a devotee of Ma. She immediately ran to Ma and told Her the story, crying disconsolately [5]. Mother tried to comfort her.

When Bholanath heard what had happened he was aghast. But when Bhaiji discovered what his wife had done he became deeply disgusted with the world and said: "If this woman who has lived with me for twenty-seven years and seen the way I am inclined —I have never even smoked a cigarette— can still think of me in this way, then what remains for me in this world? Ma is everywhere, I need not be near Her body". He was so upset that Bholanath was afraid he might renounce everything there and then and vanish entirely. So Bholanath sent Kamalakant to him with a request for him to come the next morning. "If he gives you his word", Bholanath instructed him, "you may come back, but if he does not reply, stay with him and don't let him out of your sight". Bhaiji came as requested and eventually the problem was resolved.

Benares, 24th July, 1952

Went to Delhi with Mother. Arrived there on 28th June and stayed with Kitty till 1st July. To my surprise Kitty of her own accord asked whether she could see Ma. The day she went it was very crowded and there was no place to sit so she stood for ten or fifteen minutes and looked intently at Ma. She afterwards told me that Mother stared directly into her eyes for several minutes. That was all I wished for Kitty. She was quite impressed. She said that Mother had eyes like deep wells. We talked a great deal those

---

[5] Within the context of the strict traditional mores of the period whereby Indian women were highly restricted and never allowed to be alone with men outside their immediate family, this could have potentially caused a serious scandal.

three days and nights and found that essentially we do not really disagree, though our approaches are very different. It was interesting to see that we are still such good friends in spite of our seemingly very opposite ways of life (but of course this difference is only outward). Kitty told me how when in a department store in New York, she suddenly saw the whole madness that manufactures all those unnecessary goods and ran out in terror (although she sent someone else to buy the things for her!). She also told me that she had lost all interest in clothes and I noticed that she did not wear make-up even when she had guests for a formal dinner.

Mataji was here in Benares for Guru Purnima on 7th July and stayed through the 16th. One day She asked me to buy fruits and garlands and have a blessing ceremony done for my new room in the ashram. This was done but I felt very nervous doing the *arati*. In any case everyone enjoyed it. The best part was that the *Kanyapith* [6] lent me their silks from the temple and Didi gave me Ma's own vessels to put the fruits on.

One evening while I was doing *puja* Ma walked into my room and removed one mango from the offering plate. As I was sitting with closed eyes doing *japa*, I did not notice anything. Then She said loudly outside the room that Gopal had given Her one of the two mangoes which I had offered to him. I opened my eyes and smiled when I saw that the mango had vanished. When I finished the *puja*, I brought Her the other mango. She returned the first one to me and tasted the second, giving the rest to Dr. Gopal Das Gupta. Then I brought out a number of mangoes I still had and She threw them for people to catch as a small crowd had gathered.

In the night She told me to write down to whom I wanted to leave my things when I die. I said I had nothing in particular except the money She had made me save and the piano which I explained that I needed for my school work.

Afterwards I remembered that I also had a golden locket containing pictures of the Theosophical Masters and my Mother's wedding ring. Now I feel I should give away whatever I don't need. I still have some art books and my sheet music as well as books on music.

---

[6] Traditional Vedic School for girls within the ashram.

5ᵗʰ August, 1952, Jhulan Purnima

Last night was *Jhulan Purnima* and Ma devised a wonderful play in which all present (mainly the girls from the *Kanyapith*) participated. Each person was given a role to play representing a saintly or mythological figure, and as part of the play they then had to actually do a *sadhana* based on their particular character. Thus some participants were engaged in worshipping Krishna, others Shiva or Durga, and one of the *brahmacharinis* was dressed up as Adi Shankaracharya surrounded by his disciples. In the midst of all this Ma appeared dressed up as *Tirtha Vasini Ma*, an old lady who provides whatever is necessary for the spiritual aspirants gathered at various holy places to fulfil their *dharma*. Thus she gave a drum to one, an incense burner to another, a sacred book to another etc. At a certain point the lights were put out and everyone became absorbed in deep meditation for some time. Then the lights came back on and the rest of the evening was spent singing *kirtan*, chanting the *Ramayana* [7], etc.

The performance was really an enactment of the *leela* of Ma's life that She is playing at every moment in which all the different spiritual paths are brought together within one ashram —one transcendent Truth. This is really the true spirit of Hinduism and She wishes to strengthen this so that it may have the power to renew the whole world. She is the 'Tirthavasini Ma' who stays in sacred *tirthas* and provides everyone with whatever they need to perfect their *sadhana*, as well as to renew the ancient spiritual power of such places. In fact any place becomes one of pilgrimage by Her presence there. Wherever Mataji goes people's minds are turned toward spirituality —toward the Reality of their own innate Divinity. And She is always ready to give whatever may be needed to facilitate this realization. Everyone who comes is drawn into Her *leela* and must play their own unique role, even Europeans of whom there were three present, Jay, Vijay and myself.

This morning I could easily meditate. The atmosphere was so wonderful last night. We hardly had any time to sleep, but as Avadhutji said today: "It is difficult when one is alone to keep to a self-imposed discipline but when Brahman itself is here incarnate in front of you in the form of Mataji, nothing is impossible".

---

[7] The great Hindu spiritual epic dealing with the exploits of the God-king Rama.

Benares, 23rd September, 1952

Mother is leaving soon for the Durga Puja which is to be held this year at Allahabad. I asked Her what my attitude should be towards J.K. since he will come while She is away. She said: *"Listen to him with the sense that he is not opposed to Ma, but that it will help you in your sadhana. He teaches through the watching of the mind and makes you drop your preconceptions and conditioning. I also say you should watch the mind, it is a good thing to do. But it is certainly not the only way. When you do japa, the mind becomes fully absorbed in the inner sound of the mantra through the ras [spiritual nectar] it generates which ultimately leads one into samadhi.*

Don't worry about anything regarding your sadhana. Whatever is to happen to you will come about of its own accord. These different ways of sadhana lead to the same goal. The way that is right for you will become paramount and in that you will find everything. There will no longer be any doubt as to which to follow."

24th September, 1952

There was an incident involving the orthodox 'rules' over which I became hysterically upset. I really felt it was too much to bear. Afterwards Ma talked to me privately and said: *"Look, whatever is necessary I do for myself. You, as well as the others here are none other than my very Self."* I realize that there is no question of reasoning or criticizing. Since I have entrusted Her with the job of killing this 'I', I have to submit to whatever method She chooses to use.

Sometimes I feel that the Guru has to take limitations on Himself in order to provide the circumstances that will eradicate the disciple's *karma*. It is we who make Her seem imperfect and then we doubt. But that one sentence She said: *"What I do, I do for myself"*, cuts out all argument. As long as we see the many, we cannot possibly judge Her who is the One. The only thing one can do really is to resist as little as possible and leave everything to Her. But to accept everything is not so simple —to really accept, not merely to resign oneself to the inevitable. I find now that reading a little in J.K.'s new talks of 1952 does really help me in my *sadhana*. This time very likely it will be good to see him. Anyway with Her directions I feel quite safe. I need not be on my guard like last time.

Benares, 7th October, 1952

Mataji left on 1st October evening. That day I came down with a fever although I still went to Rajghat to bring my luggage there and then saw Her off to Mugalsarai, fever and all. Then when I got back I had a bath and went to bed and have not gotten up ever since. But now I am OK.

This evening somehow the whole humiliation of these seven years that I have lived in orthodox Hindu society arose before my eyes and I feel sore all over, like someone whose whole body has been scalded —as if I could never bear any of it ever again. How have I been able to put up with this, day and night, for all these years? But evidently it was necessary for me. By Her Grace alone can this be born.

However much I may have cried at the time, now I see I hardly felt any pain because I was so engrossed in Mataji, but it was there underneath and now it has come up. No human being can bear such humiliation day and night. I have no quarrel with Ma. What-ever She has done, She had to do. I have no doubt about it. On the contrary, She may have made it infinitely milder and borne the major share Herself. In fact I am sure of this.

How much of a nuisance I have been to everyone. And yet it had to be. In Kishenpur six years or so ago Didi told me: "You don't know how much extra work I have because of you", and I wanted to leave but Mother would not let me. I had to stay and bear it.

Recently She said to me: *"How can you become Atmananda unless you can endure? You must have the power to bear what comes. Let the girls be frightened of you. That is their work. Your work is to laugh".*

17th October, 1952

In the evening this thought came to me: just as in any scien-tific investigation one has to observe the rules exactly, so it is with ritual. One observes the rules but without feeling that one is supe-rior or inferior due to this. It is our perverted idea of high and low that has to go, not the fact of a social order in which each one has his or her own allotted place. Mother teaches that ritual has to be done precisely if it is to be effective. Unity is not of the physical.

The world (the many) ceases when there is Oneness. But within the relative context of the many, each one has a different function —which is not to say that one part is any less divine than another.

The European is educated to feel that his world is superior to other cultures, but in India he learns otherwise. Here he is outside of the prevailing social order and must be kept apart. Mixing is not really permissible because the two different cultures combine no better than do water and oil and to force them together without mutual respect for the integrity of their differences is to dilute the quality of both. It is a great art for two such different worlds to learn to be together in perfect love and goodwill in a way that each may retain its own unique qualities. Already it is tragic to see how much Hindu culture has deteriorated through contact with the West.

Perhaps I am not ready to move into the ashram yet because I have not completely finished my *karma* with J.K. It is time that I face him and come to grips with him and be clear about what my position is —not just to hang on to Mother's skirts and hide between the folds as I used to in my granny's black skirts when I was a child. What She told me certainly seems to point to that.

9th November, 1952

Nowadays I get into a great stillness during my *puja* which gives deep satisfaction and which I like to prolong. It is not true that *japa* makes the mind dull (as J.K. says), on the contrary it makes it quiet so that consciousness can then function freely.

I am reading *Shakta and Shakti* by Sir John Woodroffe [8], which is extremely interesting. He writes: "Concentration on the breath drives the mind inward, away from distraction, to its own root."

---

[8] Sir John Woodroffe, a leading British jurist of his day as well as an initiate into the esoteric yoga teachings of the Tantra about which he wrote a number of books.

XXIV - "Isn't That the Way of Love?"

Rajghat, 6th December 1952

J.K. arrived yesterday. I feel very quiet and collected. I do not expect anything from him, as I get all I want from Ma. If he can teach me anything so much the better, if not it does not matter as I am so sure that Ma will in any case provide whatever is necessary for me. He still looks like the Messiah of the Theosophical Society, but rather softer than four years ago. I notice his very extraordinary face and especially the beautiful sensitive mouth. Today I spent all day running up and down for guests, but my meditation after 8 p.m. was so restful that I feel completely refreshed now. I notice that J.K.'s presence —in spite of the commotion due to the school anniversary tomorrow— helps my meditation.

This evening Miss Merston's letter about Ma's visit to Tiruvannamalai and Bangalore came. I feel quite homesick for Ma since reading it. A few days ago I moved into the upstairs room over the sick room here at Rajghat. The solitude I get here is so luxurious and so restful, I really get a chance to recuperate.

19th December, 1952

This evening music in J.K.'s room. This was real art after a long time. If the children can have this, ritual may be dispensed with. He has such a marvellous, deep, rich voice. And how wonderfully he recited from the *Vedas* and the *Gayatri*, tremendously powerful —a perfect Brahmin.

Mother was right when She said the *japa* will become automatic and the mind absorbed in it. I find the moment my mind is free it goes on automatically repeating the *mantra*.

near Ahmedabad, 11th January, 1953

After J.K. left I had to see Ma whatever might happen. This was the next step —I could not proceed until I had seen Her. I had already written to Swami Paramananda and on the fourth night I got a wire calling me to Ahmedabad for the 9th. In Delhi I stayed at Kitty's house where I was put up in the room that J.K. had vacated only the day before. The Working Committee meeting concerning the new work in Rajghat was very much on my mind and Kitty is an expert on this. After being with J.K., I feel this kind of social work is something I can really devote myself to whole-heartedly.

Actually when I began my work as Secretary of the Working Committee I felt utterly thrilled as if I had now really found something worthwhile, particularly as I have always felt the need to do social work. [1] But I also noticed the pride I took in doing 'such wonderful work' and I felt afraid of that pride.

When I arrived here today, the first question to Ma that arose in my mind was this: how to do the work without feeling I am the doer? In the *satsang* this morning Ma said: *"We think we do sadhana, but actually we can't do anything. We can cry out to God but even that is actually done by God"*.

Yesterday we came here to this very charming Ashram. I feel so much more comfortable in an Ashram than in a house, particularly a luxurious one like in Delhi. I find simplicity is so much more congenial.

Last night Avadhutji talked and I actually listened, remembering J.K.'s saying: *"If you know how to listen and especially if something is said that is true, you will find an extraordinary thing taking place."* Actually I got much out of his talk.

During the *dhyan* with Mother it suddenly occurred to me: How could I have real *darshan* of Ma as long as my ego remained? I felt very apprehensive about this and wanted to speak with Her. Later, as She was going to Her room She looked me straight in the face as She walked by, as if to give me a chance. So I said: "I want to talk to you alone." She said: *"When?"* I: "Whenever you tell me to." She told me to come immediately and took me into a corner. I asked Her about what I had been thinking and She said: *"You have not had real darshan as long as the 'I' persists"*, and walked away. I said: "I have much more to tell you", meaning the problems that arose from listening to J.K. She said: *"Later"*.

---

[1] At this time the Krishnamurti Foundation began undertaking large scale charitable and educational activities, particularly at Rajghat.

This morning I woke early and went up on the roof to meditate. After sometime it occurred to me that the very certainty which I have of Mother's Divinity is still only a mental concept and this proud belief prevents me from going beyond the mind and having Her true *darshan*. All conceptions of Her must be abandoned.

I then said to myself: "So what remains? If I don't know anything, then to whom do I do *pranam* ? To the concept of my mind? Do I merely worship my mind, not God? But then I thought: Still love remains, gratuitous love, the love that attracts me to Her without thought of Her greatness or Her helping me towards my goal.

In this regard what J.K. said was an eye-opener: "When you drop the respect, which basically is fear, the relationship still remains". That there is fear in me I have experienced lately, intensely. Before I only knew it intellectually.

Ahmedabad, 13th January, 1953

Today had a short talk with Mother. It is almost impossible to explain to Her in Hindi about J.K. Besides She is so far beyond all that he is trying to do that it hardly concerns Her. In response to my question about my inner conflict as to whether to observe the mind (as J.K. advises) or to do *japa*, She said: *"If you can watch your mind, it does not matter whether or not you do the japa"*. I: "When I sit quietly, *japa* comes spontaneously along with the breath". Ma: *"Then you are not doing anything. It happens by itself."*

I then explained to Her that since J.K. has forbidden all ritual at Rajghat, I did not feel right about doing formal *puja* of L.'s Gopal as long as I remain there. She agreed that I should drop it, however not at once but on a special day that She would tell me later. I said if I don't do the formal *puja*, the real *puja* in the mind will increase. Ma: *"Yes, do it secretly in your mind."* I then said that in any case my work with the children is really a kind of Gopal *puja* —to which She agreed.

I: "Ma, now you have thousands of children, we can hardly get a chance to see anything of you".

Ma: *"What else do you want? Keep me in your heart"*.

When I had tea with Ashish he told me how much nearer one is to Mataji when She sends one to do work for Her, than when actually sitting by Her. That made me think that if only I can be quite sure that my work at Rajghat is Her work, I shall be with Her fully, just as when I did the translation work.

14th January, 1953

J.K. is really a terrible destroyer, Shiva himself. After being with him this time I feel almost as desperate as when I had to leave him at Rishi Valley 14 years ago. Then at other times I feel quite all right. But I don't even know what to ask Ma. Only last night I offered the whole work at Rajghat to Her with tears streaming from my eyes, and now I wonder what is it all about.

At times I feel quite mad. I don't know anything any more —who or what Mother is, though it cannot be denied that whenever one looks at Her one feels overwhelmingly: This is truly God. One can't help feeling it. In any case at least I know that I love Her. But how can I even say that when I don't know what love is or what She is. How can I go on living like this? Until one truly knows oneself —the 'I'— one cannot know anything at all.

Lord, have mercy upon me! How many times has one to wash one's feet in the blood of one's own heart. No, this is the last time. I realize that what I have done up to now is basically to deify my own ego and call it Mother. I mistook the picture I made of Her for the Reality that She is.

* * *

The philosophical intensity which produced such profound anguish in Atmananda was remarkable and drove her throughout her life to search for ever deeper levels of inner awareness. The sadhana *process, the relationship with the Guru, inevitably induces a profound psychological catharsis as it ruthlessly reveals the fundamental falseness of the conditioned conceptualizing mind through which one defines oneself and the world. The constant chipping away of the conditioned ego, constitituting what seems like an unending number of little ego deaths, means that each new hard-won realization, as soon as it becomes a possesion of the ego — something to enhance rather than dissolve its importance— must be discarded.*

In this instance Atmananda is having to come to terms with one of the fundamental deceptions of the religious mind: the deification and worship of the idea, the mental concept of God and religious authority, which ultimately guarantees the preservation of the ego — sustained through fear of the (mind created) 'Lord' etc. This indeed is a great danger of an incomplete spiritual experience, as what originally may have been an authentic revelation is taken over by the ego and used as a means to preserve its own dominance. It is precisely for this reason that the guidance of the Guru is so absolutely essential.

One cannot help but be struck by the integrity and tenacity with which she submits to authentic spiritual giuidance. Her close association with both Anandamayee Ma and J. Krishnamurti — each in their own way — ensured that her inner intensity was brought to a fever pitch.

* * *

17th January, 1953

To a question from a girl as to whether she should earn money as a teacher Mother replied: "*The modern attitude is such that people think they must look after themselves and so they go and take up a teaching job. They do not realize that the very act of sharing knowledge with their students automatically generates the arrangement for their sustenance. Knowledge must not be sold.*"

This was a revelation to me and I suddenly understood that the solution to my problem with 'earning' a living lies not in dropping work and doing nothing, but in dropping the business attitude of selling my labour. Do service as an end in itself and then take whatever you are given as coming from God and make do with it.

This idea consumed me and I could not sleep all night, but did not feel at all tired in the morning. When the *Gita* was read I had new insight into much of the meaning, it had become altogether new. I decided not to take money anymore but to continue the work I am doing and leave it to up to the Committee what they would give me, and then to resign in July.

In the evening Mother noticed that I had been crying and Didi called me in to Her. I told Her I was not going to accept money anymore for my work. She said: "*How will you eat?*" I: "Food I shall get in any case". "*Suppose you want to come to me and live permanently in the ashram?*" I: "I shan't come". Ma: "*Do*

481

you not wish to come?" Twice I said: "Yes, I want to come". But when She said: *"All right, I shall arrange for it.",* I got frightened and said, "No, no". To this She replied: *"You said yes twice, if you had said it three times it would have come about".*

She then told me not to do anything about the money question at present but to wait and talk to Her in Benares. When I objected and said: "For once I have understood something and you won't allow me to act on it, She said: *"Wait till an auspicious day comes and Thakurji* [the Lord] *appears to you in a dream and tells you".*[2]

Also I told Her again that I felt it was not right for me to do *puja* while at Rajghat as J.K. is so adamantly opposed to such things. She agreed that I may drop it but said to keep the little Krishna with me as I did before and to keep the *mala* in my box along with my devotional pictures etc. She said: *"Do japa in the mind, do meditation."* I said: "Will you really talk to me in Benares". She: *"Thora sa"* [A little bit] showing a tiny bit of Her finger. I: "You do with me as you like". Ma: *"Isn't that the way of love? —to be completely surrendered".* I: "Do with me what you like".

Late at night She answers questions daily. To my question as to how to get rid of the sense of "I am the doer", She said: *"When total surrender comes, one feels continually that God does everything through one as through an instrument. One's body and mind become like a piece of cloth blown by the wind —it is the wind that moves it, not the cloth moving of its own volition."*

I was too tired to understand everything She said but what was clear was that until the state of *sharanagati* [total surrender] is reached, all self-motivated activity is useless. One might just as well do nothing at all.

Last night someone asked: "What is 'Harikatha'[3]? Ma: *"Harikatha is that narration through which all sorrow is destroyed."*

This morning in the *satsang* I again cried. When the crowd lined up to do *pranam* to Ma I thought: "I have done this millions of times but it has never been a true *pranam*. The 'I' still remains.

---

[2] Dreams played an important part of Anandamayee Ma's relationship with her followers.

[3] A traditional form of devotional singing that narrates the life of Krishna.

Rajghat, 22ⁿᵈ January, 1953

I feel more and more that I have to leave this place. In any case I can't do this teaching work any more. I am a *sanyasi* by nature and need to spend my time in meditation. Obviously I can't do this here. When J.K. was here there was *satsang*, Sanjiv Rao also is still *satsang*, but there is nothing of substance with the rest. J.K. told me so clearly: "You can't build together if you have to go to your 'lady guru'". Since I cannot drop Her, it is really quite simple: all the rest must be dropped. "Think of me alone and leave all else", as I was told in my dream eight years ago, and not even now have I done it. Now that Sanjiv Rao has taken charge there is no need for me here anymore.

Rajghat, 30ᵗʰ January, 1953

On the 26ᵗʰ January Ma arrived in Vindhyachal. I was with Her practically the whole day. She sent me up and down and made me sweep, wash clothes etc, kept me fully busy all the time. I knew She would be coming to Benares the next day and I told Her that I could not stay at the ashram that night because I had to attend the Working Committee meeting. She said: *"Now you have become really great. That's fine, do service."* The next day I felt so miserable at Rajghat, I just could not bear the thought of Her being in Benares and I not able to be with Her. I could not teach I was so upset, quite mad. In spite of not having any money with me I just went to the Ashram by rickshaw, thinking I would walk back. Instead I got a lift in a car all the way home.

I feel now very strongly that I should not remain here after July. J.K. has come to throw me out after all —for my own and everyone's best.

Bhadaini, 17ᵗʰ March, 1953

This evening an abnormal or half-mad young man came and asked Ma to keep him. He had one crippled hand and one crippled foot and could not talk properly. He kept on saying to Her: "Keep me with you". Ma said: *"No, go back to Calcutta to your mother"*. He said: "Not unless you come with me". Finally Ma said to us: *"Is there anyone here who is ready to serve such a man in the way you serve your Thakur [Lord], to give your life to him? Any-*

one who does so would never need money, because God will arrange for him. But there is no one. Some people might join in and pay to engage someone to look after the sick person, but that won't be the same; for with money it cannot be done properly". Someone said: "Vibhu said he would serve him". Ma called Vibhu and said: *"If I relieve you from all other duties, can you give your life to this?"* Vibhu said: "What you tell me I can do". But it was obvious that he would not of his own choice. Ma said: *"From such an undertaking one would become purified, but no one is willing to do it. So it is better to send him to his mother. Here, when so many come, who knows how he will be looked after in the crowd?"*

I felt the tragedy of it and thought: In Europe there are institutions etc for such people and yet the atmosphere is horrible. There it is not done from love, but from some imposed sense of social responsibility dictated by the modern cult of political humanism.

22nd March, 1953

Tonight Dr. Pannalal asked the question which I had discussed with him regarding J.K. saying that *puja* presupposes duality and is therefore stupid. Mataji gave such a subtle answer, obviously far beyond J.K.'s level. First She said: *"For him who says thus, it is all right. For instance, Ashish won't do puja because he is an advaitist. Some say that doing puja is just playing with dolls. But when one has the question in one's mind: 'Why do puja?' one is actually a dualist. For in advaita [non-duality] there is no distinction whatsoever between subject and object, and there in that state of absolute wholeness, whatever comes is only that which alone is. So criticism of doing or not doing could never arise."* This is really the last word on the matter.

Hardwar, 28th May, 1953

With regard to a question about *mantra*, Ma said:

"There is power in the mantra, in the 'akshara' [the indestructible essential vibration of the letters], and it is possible at any time for that state to be revealed —which in any case is always there— in which the seer, the seeing and the seen are one. Then added to this there is the power of the Guru. The Guru plants a seed in you and

484

Atmananda speaking with Anandamayee Ma on the roof of the Benares ashram (photo by Richard Lannoy)

there is no doubt that the fruit will come forth some day. Whether you notice it or not it grows inside you. Your task is to obey his orders so that the seed may grow properly. The spiritual seed of the mantra cannot be spoiled; it is there and it must bear fruit at some point. Even if the Guru does not appear to have obtained the full 'siddhi' of the mantra, you cannot know how far he has attained in the inner worlds and it may bear its visible fruit in the disciple and not in the Guru."

Hardwar, 29th May, 1953

Kamlakant: We listen to so many beautiful things said...

Ma: *Beautiful? As long as you distinguish between beautiful and ugly you have not listened.*

Kamlakant: ...and some things we understand...

Ma: *"We understand" —that is useless in so far as he that understands and that which is understood still remain separate.*

Kamlkant: And some we forget...

Ma: *"Forget"? Forget the forgetting. Death must die.*

Kamlakant: And some we remember...

Ma: *Remember? That means you keep it in your mind. Throw it away. Lay it at His Feet. I say keep satsang. Satsang means "Sat-swarup ka prakash hona"* [being in the light of Truth —that which is]. *Remain in the shade of the 'trees', the seekers after Truth, who do not call anyone nor send anyone away. Listen to them. Who knows when you will learn to listen and hear the 'Shabdabrahma'* [4] *so that there will be no listener and no listening. With darshan it is also like that. People come and go, but true Darshan means you can never be separate from the vision of truth any more.*

Dr. Pannalal: Can a human being be reborn as an animal?

Ma: *'Manush'* [human] *means 'Man hosh' —consciousness of that which you truly are. At present you are unconscious, 'behosh'* [and thus not really human].

Dr. Pannalal: After death, can we have meetings like this?

Ma: *If you say 'we'* [ham log], *in that there is 'I' and others. But when you realize that all are in you, when you know that, then this question does not arise.*

---

[4] The primal sound of the Absolute.

1st June, 1953

During Mother's birthday last night I sat on the roof for meditation. I was worrying about the garland of flowers I had ordered which had not yet arrived. Then I thought: "Why a garland? One has to offer one's body and mind". It then occurred to me: "What is there to offer, and to whom is it offered and by whom?" *And suddenly, there was no body, no mind and no Mother.*

Today I was reflecting on what J.K. means by 'idolatry'. Looking at Mother and thinking of Her as a body seems quite absurd. In my *'darshan'* on the roof last night I saw that She is not that which I identify Her with. I understood that Her body and all She does is a kind of sham, really a *leela* —theatre just to attract human beings to something that is in reality completely other. She is really something totally different from Her body. That is what J.K. wants me to find. It was a startling experience to see that.

Kishenpur, 8th June, 1953

Question: How to get faith?

Ma: *Keep company with those who have faith. Travel with a traveller on the path. Sit in the shade of the 'tree'. But you never sit, your mind goes here and there, even your eyes wander.*

Question: How does the state of *'ajapa'* [*japa* which occurs spontaneously] come?

Ma: *First put all your 'I-ness', your power, your effort into japa, dhyan etc, and then ajapa will come. Then the Divine Swarupa will be revealed.*

With some the breath becomes so completely identified with the japa so that they cannot breathe without simultaneously repeating the mantra. Only this can be called 'ajapa'.

Mother spoke for about twenty minutes like a waterfall without stopping and then said: "*Truth will speak out. And you will not find a thing in this against the shastras, even though this body has, of course, never read such things.*

God comes to you as the Ganges, He comes in forms that you <u>can</u> get in touch with. Take the opportunity."

Kishenpur, 9th June, 1953

Question: We often hear You say: "Think of God". But surely, God is unthinkable and formless. What can be thought of must have name and form and therefore cannot be God.

Ma: *Yes, undoubtedly He is beyond all thought, form and description, but all the same I say 'think of Him' as long as you have the sense of 'I'. Why? Since you are identified with the ego, since you think you are the doer and thus you get angry, greedy etc, therefore you have to apply your 'I-ness' to thinking of Him. True, He is formless, nameless, immutable etc. Nevertheless He has come to you in the form of 'Shabda Brahma' and 'Avatar Shabda'* [5]*. These are also He Himself and consequently if you contemplate His name and think of His form the veil which is your 'I' will fall off and then He, Who is beyond thought, beyond form, will shine forth.*

You think you do the sadhana, but actually it is He who does everything. Without Him nothing can be done. It is not that one does so much and thus will get so much in return. God is not a merchant, there is no bargaining with Him.

New Forest, Dehradun, 11th June, 1953

Last night Mother Herself chose a place for me to sleep —at Her Feet! As I lay down I was seized by a veritable frenzy of spontaneous self-surrender. It was like a state of madness, burning and effortless. I slept very little during the night and was fanning Her part of the time. In the morning She came to the *satsang* tent and was giving garlands and flowers to everyone. After some talk and jokes She took up a twig of bougainvilla and said: *"How beautiful! The leaves are gerua".* I said: "In my country all trees become gerua in autumn". Ma: *"Your country? Which is your country?"* I: "Where I used to be before". Ma: *"Before? What does that mean? And before that where were you?"* I: "With you". Ma: *"With me? How do you know?"* I: "You know". Ma: *"How do you know that I know?"* I: "I don't know". Ma: *"How do you know that you don't know?".* I: "I don't know anything, I am a fool". Ma: *"How do you know you are a*

---

[5] *'Shabda Brahma'* and *'Avatar Shabda'* refer to the primordial divine sound vibration symbolized by Aum (and other *mantras*) and its incarnation in human form, the *'avatar'* — as per the famous passage from the Gospel of St. John: "And the Word became flesh and dwelt among us."

fool?" I: "Now I shall have to become silent". Ma: *"And what will be the good of the silence?"* I: "At least stupid words and nonsense will not be said". Ma: *"And to what good?"* I: "I don't know". Ma: *"You don't know? Is one who does not know anything able to become angry? One who knows is angry because this or that is not as it should be. But the fool cannot be angry, because he does not know how things should be. Remember that you are a fool and therefore you cannot become angry. It is the false 'I' that becomes angry and that is exactly what you have to drop. If you can do that you will be transformed from a 'buddhu'* [fool] *into a 'Buddha'* [enlightened one]." I: "No, no, I am a fool". Ma: *"All right, then remember that you know nothing and so you can't become angry. Then the 'I' will go and 'Atmananda' will be revealed. Take this twig of bougainvilla and take off all the flowers that are gerua, dry them and keep them."* [6]

Raipur, 1st August, 1953

Question: Ma, we don't find peace, the mind is restless and disturbed.

Ma: *Become immersed in the repetition of God's name. Do not even entertain the possibility of considering whether you are at peace or not, just cling to the Name at all times.*

Rajghat, 18th August, 1953

I had a very vivid dream after reading *Ashtavakra Gita* for about an hour and half and then going to sleep: I had received a brand new blue suitcase with all sorts of papers in it. I enter a shop with Dr. Pannalal. The suitcase slips from my hand and falls on a large counter and vanishes into it. I open the counter and try to find it. All sorts of other things are there but no sign of a suitcase. Other items appear and I say to Dr. Panalal: "Would you believe this if we had not seen it with our own eyes". "Never, it is like magic". I go on looking for the suitcase, but it is nowhere — it can't be recovered. A lady comes into the shop and someone says: "Tell Her". I say: "I feel ashamed, no one will believe such a story". I go on searching all over the counter but this time it seems to be made of layers of old wet paper. I feel quite desperate at

---

[6] I found these flowers dried and pressed on the next page of this diary entry more than 40 years later.

this magic, all the while keeping an eye on my handbag —also dark blue with a zip. But now that also disappears and I feel very worried about it. I tell myself not to mind about the other things but about the handbag I feel exasperated. I feel I can't proceed. There are other handbags though. One of them looks like mine and I take it up, but on opening it I find it filled with very dainty things that can't possibly be mine. Someone says it belongs to the American lady who has gone upstairs to be treated and who will return in a few minutes. I say it can't be mine and that when the lady comes she will claim it. Abruptly like in a cinema words appear written on the screen: "You have just seen the beauty of the illusion of? [sic] in six acts —now the next act will follow which is...?" I forget. I feel very surprised and say: "It is like in a dream", but am convinced of the reality of what is happening. At that I wake up.

Now when writing it comes to my mind that it may allude to Lewis' box containing his writings which may have gotten lost in the post. My letter to Ella Maillart was understamped and returned by the dead letter office after ten days, so it will never reach her before the box arrives.

My eyes just shut by themselves and prevent me from writing. But I feel the dream has a deep significance showing the futility and unreality of all concrete things, which is the message of *Ashtavakra Gita*.

31st December, 1953

Today at noon J.K. arrived. I had no impression at all of him. There was nothing to look at. The children sang a song to 'Devi' [the Goddess] which seemed awfully funny to me. Of course in a way J.K. is Kali, the one who destroys. Now, by the evening I begin to feel his very powerful presence that seems to penetrate every particle of the air. I have a feeling of discomfort, a slight sensation of being strangled. Leave all to Ma. She will arrange. The last few days I have been crying out for Her. Somehow J.K. always drives me closer to Her. She is expected on 3rd or 4th January and will be here right through the time of the J.K.'s talks. Who knows whether I shall still be at Rajghat then?

5ᵗʰ January, 1954

Yesterday was J.K.'s first talk and immediately after it was over Ma arrived by car from Mugalsarai. We went to the bridge to have Her *darshan*. That one second just swept away everything. Again like five years ago I saw, but this time much more clearly, that they are on such very different levels. There is no question of a choice. J.K. is just part of my training —just as I go to Gopinath Kaviraj [7] for my translation work. Why take so seriously what J.K. says when I know it is partly false.

In the evening I went to the Ashram. Again my memory had failed me. I had not remembered how wonderful She is! —how utterly beyond all conception— each time a completely new revelation. It happens again and again —and that's what J.K. calls useless repetition! How absurd. This time I did not ask Her whether or not to listen to him, it is on so different a level. Sanjiv Rao said to me: "Since Ma has come, there will be divided attention." I said: "No, for me there is no choice."

I stayed the night at the ashram and slept only four hours, but felt very fresh this morning —a changed being after absorbing Her for these few hours. All that J.K. tries to get across and infinitely more, one gets just by glancing at Her for a second. All fear is gone. In the face of such a miracle of what can one be afraid? Life has become worthwhile for that one glance. What is the whole world compared to Her radiance?

6ᵗʰ January, 1954

Last night I came back and slept here at Rajghat, but the atmosphere here is not congenial. This morning I felt like clearing out altogether to the Ashram. But after doing *pranam* to Mother in my *puja* and saying within: "I am prepared to give up everything but you", I attended to J.K.'s talk.

From it I understood for myself that I must go my own way, which is through Mother; but I can still learn a lot from J.K. I see much clearer this time: there is no comparison, each has his place. As he said: If you compare B with A, you destroy B when you

---

[7] The renowned Benares pandit, authority on the Tantras, and philosopher who spent his final years in Anandamayee Ma's ashram in Benares.

491

expect him to be as good as A. So by expecting J.K. (unconsciously) to be like Ma, I do him a great wrong.

29ᵗʰ March, 1954

On 24ᵗʰ March, exactly nine years after I spoke to Ma for the first time, Sanjiva Rao asked me to ask Her if She would allow me to stay permanently in the ashram as it is not fair to Rajghat for me to stay here as I do, disliking the work etc. He insisted that he was not asking me to leave and said that he would personally miss me very much, but that this could not come in the way of the work that has to be done. He suggested my taking leave for three months, but he obviously meant for me to go; though he put it very nicely. [8] This was really already achieved when J.K. shouted at me last year: "Break dependence". It always takes time for things to work themselves out.

The first day or two after Sanjiv spoke to me I felt rather sorry to leave this place and noticed what a tremendous attachment has grown up in me in the 19 years I have been here. But then I came to feel that already there is an arrangement for me, the most perfect one possible, and I am not even curious to know what it is.

---

[8] In a letter from Sanjiv Rao to Atmananda, dated January 29, 1952 he says, after speaking of his personal closeness to Anandamayee Ma: "Pure love — this tremendous power of transformation— this is what I saw in Ma." He goes on to say: "Blanca, you have been so identified with Ma that for me you are that Love."

XXV - "Blood of Your Blood, Bone of Your Bones Am I"

Ma refused to talk to me about my resignation, obviously because She wanted to first find out what arrangements were presently possible in the ashram. I felt quite upset, but after reminding Her twice more She called me last night. At first She seemed opposed to my quitting and said: *"How will you eat?"* I: "Whatever God gives me. I shall try to live like a *sanyasi*". Ma: *"Are you then prepared to beg?"* [1]. I hesitated and said: "I don't know, if necessary I shall have to. But I shall not be idle, I shall do as much service as I can and eat what I get. You once said when someone [a teacher] passes on their knowledge to others, the arrangement for his or her upkeep is already made. They need not do anything about it".

Ma: *"What about your temper? There will be cause for anger and people will say all sorts of things"*. I: "My anger has decreased quite a lot. The translation work is a *sadhana* and helps me very much and I believe it is a service to others as well". Ma did not say much as I hardly gave Her a chance, but She called in Swami Paramananda and had me repeat everything to him. He agreed that I could live in the Ashram and work for the "Ananda Varta" [2]. I felt extremely happy when Ma finally gave Her permission. I hope I have not forced the situation, as whenever that happens with Her things do not usually work out well.

Today I got a letter from Bodhgaya [3] with a leaf from the Bodhi tree. I wonder what it is that has linked me to Rajghat so power-

---

[1] Begging is an honoured and fundamental part of the renunciates' training in accepting whatever they may be given as coming from God.

[2] The ashram magazine of which she was the editor for the next 30 years.

[3] The Holy of Holies for all Buddhists, where the Buddha attained enlightenment while sitting under a tree —henceforth known as the 'Bodhi Tree'.

fully all these years. Am I really finally going to break with it? Anyway, whatever comes I shall accept it. With Mother's Grace everything is possible.

Almora, 6ᵗʰ June, 1954

Question: If you have business dealings with someone and he cheats you by not giving you your money's worth, should you go to court or keep quiet over it?

Ma: *Some may feel, if I don't give this person a lesson, he will do more cheating and so they go to court. But there is another way of looking at it: Who is it that has cheated me? In all forms it is only He. What has been taken from me was not evidently meant for me to keep, so He has taken it. Then there is a third way: once a thief came to a sadhu and stole whatever he could. He was just running away with the load on his head when the sadhu discovered him. He quickly ran after the thief and shouted: "Wouldn't you like a few more things? Take this also and this!" The thief was so moved that he gave up stealing and became a sadhu himself.*

Then there is yet a fourth way: "Is it my business to punish the evil doer?" Once a bhakta of Krishna was walking intoxicated with the love for his adored one and, without noticing, trod on newly washed clothes. On seeing this the dhobi [washerman], who had just spread the clothes out on the ground to dry, got furious and said: "Have you no eyes?" and he took hold of a stick and was about to beat the devotee. At that very moment Lord Krishna was having his meal with his beautiful wife, Rukmini. Suddenly he jumped up without further explanation and ran off, but returned after a short while. Rukmini asked him where he had been. He replied: "My bhakta was being attacked by a dhobi, so I went to save him, but as soon as I got there I saw that he had already picked up a stone and was ready to throw it at the dhobi. So since he could take care of himself, there was no need for me to intervene and I at once returned."

There is still another way to consider this matter: Once a sadhu was being abused badly by someone. He thought: "What a terrible punishment will be his for this grave offence". So he gave him a light slap to avert a more severe punishment.

Which ever of these ways seems most correct to you, according to that you should act.

Question: If one takes the first mentioned view, that the evil-doer must be taught a lesson, does one not thereby injure oneself, especially when a *sadhaka* ?

Ma: *Yes, for by acting thus one's ego will be enhanced.*

8ᵗʰ June, 1954

Private talk with Mrs. M. [a western woman].

Mataji started by telling her: *"Last night I saw you as a girl of about sixteen. You were very beautiful, fair and pure. The other day when you came to me for the first time, I saw you also in the same way and this caused that deepest, truest part of you to respond. That is why you cried and were so moved."*

Mrs. M. then told her story. When she was about twenty years old she went into a kind of *samadhi* on two different occasions. Then she studied medicine so that she could come out to India with a Christian mission, but eventually she fell in love and married and therefore postponed her journey till now. In the meantime she had three children, one of whom died and two daughters who are now married.

Mrs. M. asked what the Christian doctrine of salvation through faith in the crucified Christ really means.

Mataji: *There is happiness and pain, sin and virtue, life and death: the pairs of opposites —and that is the cross to which Christ was nailed. But His is the eternal ecstatic Truth beyond duality, and thus he smiled on the cross. This is what we have to do. That is our saviour. This is also the Hindu way. The ideal of the Rishi is also this.*

Meditate on the Christ as the Light of the World, the inner light as well as the outer light of the sun and moon. All are in Him and He is in all. He is the light between your eyebrows. If during meditation you get visions of Kali, Durga, Ma, Shiva, regard them also as forms of Christ, not as separate from him. If you meet any great spiritual person, say to yourself: "It is Christ who has revealed Himself to me in this form". All forms are His form. He is not small, not limited only to the form of Jesus. Regard your house as the House of the Lord. Burn incense and keep a special seat for meditation. Meditate and read sacred books. Let your children live their own life and you spend yours in contemplation.

495

Almora, 9th June, 1954

My room looks out over the valley to the mountains. This morning when I woke up, before I was fully awake, I seemed to see a wall with panels where the door should have been. Somewhat alarmed I thought: "From where has this wall come?" Then I opened my eyes wide and the familiar landscape returned. At once it flashed through my mind: "Is this how it is?" The illusory nature of the world: we see a wall and actually there is nothing at all, it is pure illusion. It was a peculiar experience.

Nainital, 28th June, 1954

On the 25th night Mataji talked till 1 a.m. Someone said to Her: "When you go away we shall feel very lonely; how shall we manage?"

Mataji: *I never leave. Why do you want to push me far away? I am always with you.*

"Then do you dwell in our hearts?"

Mataji: *In your hearts? Why do you want to confine me to a particular place? Blood of your blood, bone of your bones am I. This is the truth, I don't tell lies.*

The next night the hall was packed, mostly with women. At the end Mataji led the *kirtan* and sang [4] *He Bhagavan* and *Sita Ram, Prana Ram.* Then again someone said: "We have been coming to you daily. Now that you are going away our lives will feel empty without you. What are we to do?"

Mataji: *Why do you say I am going away? I am your little child and am always with you. Remember this, that I am always with you. I am not asking you to hold your breath, to sit up straight, to purify yourselves. Just as you are, I am with you. A child stays with his parents, whatever they may be like.*

Someone said: We regard you as our mother, not as our child.

Ma: *Well, then if you say Mother, that also is right. But does a Mother ever leave her children? Never.*

One day Ma told the following story:

Once the Rishi Narada came to Sri Krishna and said: "What actually is this maya of yours?" "Maya?" said Krishna, "All right, come

---

[4] Anandamayee Ma had an inspired, ecstatic manner of singing devotional songs for which she was well known.

for a walk with me!" They went and walked for a long time. When a village came into sight Krishna said: "I am thirsty. Bring me a glass of water". Narada went into the village, while Krishna waited for him. Narada asked for water at the first house he came to. The housewife who came to the door sent her beautiful daughter to fetch the water and when she returned with it, the woman said: "Why don't you marry my daughter?" Narada, totally enchanted with the lovely girl, readily agreed. They got married and had two children, a son and a daughter, and lived very happily. All went well till one day torrential rains caused a flood. When the water penetrated into their house, they climbed up on some furniture. But it kept on rising and finally they were forced on to the roof. Still the water rose and rose. At last Narada had to hold on to his whole family in order to keep them from being swept away. Then the mother-in-law lost her grip and drowned. Narada thought: "She was old and she might have died anyhow!" But next his daughter let go of him and fell in the water. He thought: "At least my son is still alive!" But soon the son also succumbed. He was greatly upset but consoled himself thinking: "As long as I have a wife, I may have other children." But then his wife too was swept away. He himself was gasping for breath and about to give up when he found himself standing again next to Krishna, still panting. Krishna said: "What is the matter with you. Where is my glass of water?" Narada replied: "Now I know what your maya is".

Benares, 19th July, 1954

Mataji arrived on the 14th morning by the same train that Kali Prasad (Richard Lannoy) was to leave on, thus graciously fulfilling his great desire to say good-bye to Her before returning to England [5]. On Guru Purnima She told me to observe silence, except for two hours daily when I may talk. This is a wonderful arrangements which suits me perfectly for it cuts out all useless talk and superficial conversation. I can do all my work this way and energy is not wasted on idle words. My mind is already getting more lucid and the silence helps my work. It helps me to lis-

---

[5] Richard Lannoy later became a noted photographer and author of books about India. His most recent works include a pictorial biography of Anandamayee Ma: *Anandamayi: Her Life and Wisdom* (Element Books, 1996) and a monumental photographic study of Benares: *Benares Seen from Within* (Callisto & Indica Books, 1999).

ten within and find the right words for the translation as though coming directly from Mataji. Afterwards She also told me not to make any hand gestures or to write messages. At the railway station She again repeated this.

I have begun to translate *Sad-Vani* [6]. It is a great joy —most interesting and not very difficult to do. I am daily gaining speed in translating.

Life in the ashram so far has been very pleasant, no hardships. At Rajghat I was always hungry despite all the good food I got. Here I feel satisfied and so far am well and fit on much more simple fare. At first I found it difficult to eat the dry *rotis* [Indian bread], and was longing for richer food but already I do not even want to eat outside the ashram. The food is so pure here, it makes a lot of difference to one's state of mind. I have not even bought a single sweet in the bazaar. Whatever I get here is given with love and tastes delicious. I buy only fruit and raw vegetables. The heat also even, without a fan, is not so trying. The atmosphere here is so happy and congenial, I feel freer than anywhere else. No one takes any notice of me and I have a very secluded life, in spite of the close proximity of so many people and the nearness of the bazaar.

20th August, 1954

This has changed into the reverse since Mataji asked me to vacate the room on the top floor. I feel strangled now, having no place without noise practically all day. I have also started quarrelling with people and the problem with the orthodox rules makes itself felt almost daily. When I went to Rajghat for a visit, I felt so relaxed sitting under the neem tree in front of Krishni's room, all by myself in such quiet. I miss the wide open fields and green trees at Rajghat and the quiet above all. Ultimately however one gets what one wants.

Ma arrived here on the 9th from Dehradun. The girls performed a play about Krishna for *Janmasthami* [7] that was held in the open. All the trees and plants in the courtyard were transformed into the sacred geography of Krishna's childhood home —even the drain became the Jamuna river! After the *puja* Ma showered

---

[6] The little book of Ma Anandamayi Ma's sayings compiled by Bhaiji.

[7] The birthday of Krishna.

rose petals on all the trees and plants and on all present, saying: *"All these trees and flowers are Gopal, tonight everyone is Gopal"*. The next morning She said again: *"These trees and plants have come here to perform the puja, they are not ordinary trees"*.

The wife of the *pujari* who had previously been doing *puja* to the new Gopal image before it was acquired by the ashram came. She is blind. Bhatuda brought her and told the story of how the image of Gopal had found its way to the ashram. The man who had been paying for the *puja* had lost all his money in Pakistan due to partition and for three years the *pujari* and his family had paid for everything from their own pocket. But one night the son of the *pujari* dreamt that Gopal said: "My *puja* is not being done properly". They then decided to either find someone who could afford to do the worship correctly or else to put the image into the Ganges. [8] Then the son of the *pujari* again dreamt that Gopal told him: "Don't remove me from Kashi [Benares]". Mataji heard about this and said She would take care of the image. The *pujari* agreed and Mataji at once sent Kantibhai in the ashram car to fetch it. It was put on the terrace and worshipped as soon as Ma came. It is very beautiful with a profound spiritual presence about it.

Benares, 4th September, 1954

Mataji returned here yesterday morning after one day in Calcutta, having spent two nights (going and coming) in the train. Last night when I did *pranam* to Her I did so from the side. She did not see me and stepped on my back full force. Incredibly, I discovered that She has no weight at all. It was a tremendous surprise. Her full weight was not even as heavy as a hand that someone puts lightly on your shoulder. Altogether it was very strange. I seemed to loose consciousness for a fraction of a second. She said: *"Did it hurt you very badly?"* I said: "Not at all, Ma. How little you weigh!" *"Very light, isn't it?"* she replied, and walked away.

Vindhyachal, 27th September, 1954

Arrived here on the 25th. Here also the trouble has begun. People in this Ashram are so differently conditioned, we don't

---

[8] This is traditionally done when an image that has been formally worshipped becomes damaged or for some reason can no longer be properly looked after.

speak the same language. It is true I have been in India for 19 years continuously, but Rajghat was not really India. The Theosophists there are creating something which combines aspects of Eastern and Western civilization. It seems to be the only congenial place for me and I feel it will be very difficult for me to live anywhere else. Those people are really my family. How free and at ease I feel at Malati's and how strained at the Ashram. I am not able to fit in. Mataji was more than right when She hesitated to allow me to leave Rajghat. I wanted to ask Her whether I should ask the authorities at Rajghat to take me back; but if I am to go it will happen by itself, since everything is His will only.

Benares, 9ᵗʰ October, 1954

It seems to me that all my troubles are due only to my not obeying Her 100%. I am only 50-50 and that is why I get into all these scrapes. In spite of everything this fortnight at Vindhyachal has done me immense good. I have become more inward turned. Now that I am again with Ma, all troubles seem so petty and silly —it is all on a different plane; but when She is not there one falls back into the old patterns to some extent. I shall have to put up with the hardships if I want to stay with Her.

Benares, 24ᵗʰ December, 1954

On the 4ᵗʰ December evening we left for Bhimpura. It is a beautiful place on the Narmada River, more beautiful than even Vindhyachal. One morning Mataji suddenly said: *"You like this place, don't you? Stay here for 2 or 3 years and meditate"*. I said: "How can I do the *Ananda Varta* work from here?" Mataji: *"Drop the work and do sadhana"*. I did not reply as I was not willing. At Bhimpura I had a tent, hardly high enough to sit up straight in, and had I remained there my accommodations in the ashram would have been extremely primitive. On the 10ᵗʰ we went to Ahmedabad. There I had my old little verandah, cold but sunny and solitary. A minor incident occurred there that caused me to loose my temper and make a scene. Mother was not at all pleased with my behaviour but I am unable to control these outbursts. This transition into the ashram is really very difficult for me.

It is exactly twelve years since the first time I resigned from

Rajghat and was going to Tiruvannamalai. Then I was really desperate, much more so than now. Although I sometimes find my outer circumstances almost unbearable, meditation is going on inside me all the time and I am calling Ma continuously. In that way I am very much more steady.

Benares, 28th December, 1954

My difficulty is like Lewis' in that I can't surrender my judgement. On the one hand I say She is my Guru and I have no doubt as to Her omniscience and yet I still use my own discrimination rather than unquestioningly obeying Her. What is the use of doing *pranam* when my head is still in charge? I need solitude in nature and to sit still in one spot and find myself.

30th December, 1954

This morning I did *pranam* on the terrace when Ma came out to pick some flowers. As She walked by Her shawl caressed me as I got up. It seemed to take away all the gloom in less than a second. Strange! After having felt desperate and without hope, I feel suddenly all right —quite at peace. Ultimately one gets what one desires, one has only to be a little patient. I also feel that it was right for me to leave Rajghat. Even if Ma takes no notice of me, what does it matter? After all, She will not put me aside and however She may choose to behave, ultimately I am Hers.

Kitty has arrived as well as John Plot. [9]

31st December, 1954

Malati came in the car and took me to see Kitty. Actually we have nothing much to say to each other, but we are still very close. Rajghat feels nice with J.K. there. When I returned there I again felt that it was a paradise lost. But I had no choice. One has really no choice, things just happen.

Although Ma seems to take no notice of me these days, neither looks at me nor talks to me, I feel Her near all the time. She is always with me. What a game She is playing! Who knows, perhaps She does not want to attract me outwardly because of the

---

[9] John Plot was a professor of philosophy and the author of several books including the multi-volume *Global History of Philosophy*.

scene I made at Ahmedabad. But that also I could not help. I had no control, it was like an earthquake. My path is not an easy one. When I want to ask Ma about inner things the answer invariably comes from within. But with regard to outer matters, I still have to ask Her.

7th January, 1955

Mataji flatly refused to give me a quiet place. She called me to talk to Her for a minute though before She left. As to another room, She said She could not give me one. I would have to do my work in the noise. *"Choose times when it is quiet, but not the night. That is for your sadhana. I am not asking you to do the work, but if you wish to do it, you will have to do it under these conditions".*

This is very disappointing. I now see why J.K. sneered at me when I said: "She means everything to me". And now I want a proper room, quiet, congenial companions and other comforts that I consider a necessity. So where is my love? She is really putting me to the test.

To live in this crowd is nothing less than a torture. I have also lost interest in my work already. I ask myself: Does it really help anyone? Anyway Europeans can't surrender, they are not fit for this life, we are too materialistic, it is too difficult. In any case it is not so much what She says as the power behind it and that can't be put into words. So does it really come off in print?

Since J.K. has returned to Benares I am in this awful condition. I meant to hear a talk, but now I feel I haven't the energy to go. Let's see whether someone fetches me in a car. In any event surely such a close connection of so many years standing can't be dissolved. He is a part of me. Whether I go there or not makes little difference. Anyway it was really J.K. who drove me out of Rajghat. And he was right too. I was using him as an escape from Ma. Now I see what it means to say: "I can leave everything but Her." Can I?

5th February, 1955

Yesterday and the day before went to hear J.K. It is always the same story. The first talk I liked immensely, he was wonderful and there was nothing one could object to; so I went again. But at once he began to get aggressive and attack: "You want to be loved by your mother... or by your Guru who is as ugly as everyone else". As usual these two visits have made me feel how flawless Mataji is: no question, it is not at all on the same level. And how right it was for me to leave Rajghat and come to Her. Whatever the difficulties, it is worth it. One can't sell oneself for comforts and beautiful surroundings.

18th February, 1955

This morning Jack returned from U.S.A. [10] I felt so happy as if my own son had come. I almost cried with joy.

Today Ma gave a marvellous talk about *pranam*, or rather *namaskar* as She called it. She said: *"To do namaskar means to put one's head in its rightful place, namely at the Feet of God. The Feet of God are everywhere and therefore one can do namaskar anywhere and to any-one or anything —remembering the Feet of God. It means to open oneself to the Divine Power which is always streaming down on everyone. But we close ourselves against it. To pranam means to give one's mind to Him ('Na man'), and to give oneself ('Na main') so that there should be only the 'one' and not the two i.e. no other. If you can do nothing else at least do namaskar. It should be done with the whole body or when that is not practical, at least with the mind. First, with the intaking of the breath, one receives His power into oneself and then with the exhalation one bows down and breathes out the 'I-ness' and remains like this as long as possi-ble in 'kumbhak' —with the breath naturally suspended. This is dhyan. When doing namaskar to a vigraha* [consecrated image] *or to a living Guru which is also a vigraha, one should always first look at it (him), so as to get the adhikar* [inner conviction] *to do namaskar.*

When this body was playing the play game of sadhana, the hand that offered the food while doing puja became one with the oblation and the act of offering, and the body remained as if frozen like this for hours. Lots of big red ants would collect and eat the food and crawl all over this body and get entangled in the hair, but never a single ant bit it. When the body came to, it felt God had come and partaken of the offerings in the form of ants who were running about on it. God in the form of ants was walking, jumping and playing all over this body; like this it had become the Kingdom of God! That is what I felt, not disgust that insects had

---

[10] See footnote for entry of 3th December, 1950.

come and eaten the prasad. *When doing pranam offer all of yourself,* punya [good deeds] *as well as pap* [sin]."

Yesterday an American couple from the Hollywood film industry came. The woman was young and beautiful, he elderly in his 60's. She had done some meditation practice for three years. She asked the following:

Question: I know that certain people with whom I work have a bad influence on me, yet I am unable to extricate myself from this. How can I save myself?

Ma: *Keep less company with them.*

Question: How can we avoid it? Our work forces us not only to be with them but even to eat and live with them.

Ma: *Then you won't be able to avoid their influence. If you go near fire won't you feel the heat? If you put ice on your hand, won't it freeze?*

The woman seemed to understand what Ma said on an inner level and appeared greatly relieved. She said: We feel very honoured to have met Ma.

Ma: *Honoured you feel when you meet another. But when you come to your self you feel only joy.*

The lady then asked her husband: Are you at peace now?

He: Completely. When I came I was worried about something concerning my business. Now it is gone.

Solan, 23rd May, 1955

Mrs. Mason asked: "Mataji, please explain to me what exactly is purity and impurity?"

Mataji: *Purity is an attitude of the mind. Some people think that if everything is very clean, looks very clean, then it is also pure. But take for instance germs. A place may look perfectly clean and yet be full of germs. Germs mean illness, although you cannot see them. Likewise, neither can you see mental qualities and tendencies. But it is their mental qualities that make a person pure or impure. Whatever a man touches takes on something of his own unique vibrational quality.*

A thing is pure when it is not mixed, when it is unalloyed, true to itself. When mixed with another substance it is called impure. Suppose someone brings you water from the tap in a perfectly clean vessel. The water is physically clean, but it bears something of the imprint of the vibrational quality of the person who brought it. This is why Brahmins were asked not to drink water that was touched by anyone else. A Brahmin's duty is to seek Self-Realization, to find 'Brahman'. Therefore he should not mix with anyone who is engaged in other pursuits. A deep sensitivity to subtle vibrations arises in one who practices intense sadhana. The primary duty of a Brahmin is to transform himself for the benefit of all society. For this he must live in a strictly controlled environment. [11]

Actually purity means truth, that which is. Whatever helps you to come nearer to that Reality, towards the realization of Truth, may be called pure and whatever retards that is impure.

To another question along the same line She said:

Hindus believe that the Ganges is pure. Others say its water is filthy and filled with germs. It is a matter of angle of vision. From your point of view you are right. But essentially purity and impurity lie in the mind. There is only one Atma. Filth and sandal paste are both that ONE. When you have realized the ONE, there is neither purity nor impurity. Today you eat pure food and tomorrow it becomes your excrement. But some creatures feed on it. A putrid corpse floats down the Ganges. The vulture swoops down on it and eats of its flesh; it is his food and he thrives on it. Life is one. What is dirt to one creature may be sustenance to another. We must reach the stage where we know only the ONE and everything is His form. There is only ONE Brahman without a second.

Solan, 6th June, 1955

Kussum asked: How is it possible to teach someone who is under the sway of the delusion of the world true discrimination and renunciation?

Mataji: *If you like rasgula* [a juicy Indian sweet] *and you find it interferes with your sadhana, give it up for a day or two. Say to yourself: I can always get it again, but for these two days I shall leave it. This will break the habit. When a student is intelligent and eager to study, there is no problem. But when he is dull and unwilling he can still be made to pass by a good teacher. In the worldly field there are people who are simply too dull to learn, but where the spiritual is con-*

---

[11] In general this holds true for anyone involved in an intense spiritual process. Likewise a Brahmin who is not more or less exclusively involved in spiritual activity is not a true Brahmin.

cerned there is no alternative because everyone has to ultimately reach the goal of human existence. The important thing is to find a true spiritual teacher (Sat Guru).

Sometimes a fortuitous combination of events will cause someone to renounce bad habits. For instance at the Ashram smoking is forbidden. Once when a bhakta from Delhi was staying at the Kishenpur ashram with this body, he went on the road to smoke a cigarette. Just as he was lighting his cigarette, I called him. He put it out and came inside. When our talk was over he again went outside for a smoke. It so happened just as he lit his match, I had the kheyal to call him. By some coincidence the same situation repeated itself eleven times. The 11th time he threw away his cigarettes and never smoked again. When his friend heard the story it struck home and he also left off smoking.

Where these things happen by Grace, as it were, nothing need be done. But one can also achieve results by effort as well.

Solan, 11th June, 1955

Yesterday Ma told the following story: "*Once Maharattan brought a blanket for me as we were going up in the mountains to Nainital. I kept it folded on my bed. I saw (in a vision) a large animal, a kind of goat standing before me and understood that the blanket had been made from its wool. Like this whenever you wear something from an animal's body it is connected with it. Likewise suppose someone goes to the bazaar and sees something he would very much like to purchase but can't afford. A clairvoyant can see that very desire in the vessel long after the person has gone. Like this there are many subtle things, invisible yet there.*"

Solan, 17th June, 1955

Question: Is it good to often call a dead person by his name and keep his picture?

Mataji: *If one mourns for the person and regrets the loss of the worldly enjoyment one had together with him, it is bad both for the departed and for oneself. But if the remembrance is done as an act of worship in which the deceased is thought of as a manifestation of the Divine, then that Supreme Reality is attracted both to the departed one and to oneself. If you have this attitude and keep your spouse's picture, then it may be beneficial for both of you.*

506

Solan, 22nd June, 1955

A few days ago in meditation I had a faint glimpse of a vast consciousness. Since then there is a change in me. The sense of I-ness has become much less. The other day Mataji said: *"There is no such thing as 'jiva'* [individual self]". That somehow struck home and produced this experience. All that has to be gotten rid of is the idea that one has a separate existence of one's own, which is as fundamentally mistaken as if the eye or the ear or the hand thought it was somehow independent of the body and acted from that point of view. But how strange that this false sense of separateness is so powerful and rules one's whole life. The *maya* of the Creator is really a most fascinating and intricate invention.

Solan, 9th July, 1955

Vijayananda asked: Can one reach Self-realization by intensifying emotion such as love?

Mataji: *Yes, prema, love for God, is a way. But what the world calls 'love' is <u>moha</u> [delusion]. There is no true love between individuals. How can one get pure love from one who is not pure, who is limited by selfish egoicity and possessiveness? People come to me and say: 'My love for such and such a person is real love, not worldly love.' But they are deceiving themselves. Moha invariably is love for that which is mortal and therefore leads to death. If you can't get the object of your love, you want to kill it or die yourself. Whereas love for God, 'prema' leads to the death of death, to Immortality. For this reason it is said that to regard the Guru as limited to a human body is a sin. The Guru has to be considered as God.*

I know of a woman who wanted to commit suicide when her Guru died. I said to her: "Does a Guru die? Because he has left the body it does not mean that the Guru is dead. The Guru is everywhere and never leaves his disciple. If you want to take your life because he has passed away, it shows that you love him as a person, not as a Guru." It does happen that people fall in love with their Guru, but if he has reached the stage of a real Guru he can sublimate their love and turn it towards the Divine. But if he is himself not beyond personality, then difficulties will arise.

There are many cases when inexperienced girls or young widows, even married women, have been led into the wrong path. It is said that one has to surrender one's whole being, body, mind and heart to the

507

Guru. To surrender one's body means to surrender one's desires to him so that they may be obliterated, but it does not mean to surrender the body in the physical sense. If it is misunderstood or abused in this way, then I say, although you may have received diksha, that person is not your Guru. You should then bathe in the Ganges and purify your-self and start afresh. Sometimes it is necessary even to give up the mantra, because it has been closely associated with the memory of the false Guru. In such a case it is appropriate to practise another mantra.

Solan, 10ᵗʰ July, 1955

Question: How can one conquer sleep?

Ma: *Sleep cannot be conquered, it goes by itself. Within the 24 hours of the day some time has to be given to sleep. Why? When you are in deep sleep, the activities of the senses are at rest and, although still under the veil of ignorance, you touch your true Self. Without that you can't go on. But as you progress with your sadhana, the senses get more and more rest. The nearer you get to your Self the less will sleep be necessary. When you have reached the state of Atmananda —the Bliss of the Self— there is no more question of work, of experience or of sleep, because there is only One. Then sleep goes by itself. A Yogi may conquer sleep through the Divine Energy that awakens in him through his yoga. When you have become established in your Self there is no question of sleep.*

Benares, 30ᵗʰ October, 1955

Some days ago I fell early in the morning in the dark and sprained my ankle. Since then I have been hardly able to walk and could not go down to the satsang hall. I feel very weak physically. In the midst of all this however I had a wonderful experience in meditation of Ma's constant Presence within me which remained for sometime. I remembered how She took me into Her arms once at Kishenpur, saying: *"You are mine, wherever you go!"* I sometimes forget this, otherwise I would not feel as bad as I do, but without solitude and nature it is hardly possible for me to exist.

Benares, 13ᵗʰ December, 1955

A young girl who often comes for Mother's *darshan*, greeted me and introduced me to her mother. "I am confined to bed", said the old lady, "and cannot walk; but last night I dreamt that I must go and see Mataji. I said to my daughter, I must go and have Mataji's *darshan* and look, now I am walking!"

Benares, 15ᵗʰ December, 1955

Question: Why do many people, old and young, come to you?

Ma gave various evasive replies to the effect that She is an abandoned child and considers all are Her parents etc. But when pressed further She finally said:

"All right, look here. Is it not natural to come to your own Self, does it require a reason? The most natural thing for everyone is to come to his own Self."

Vindhyachal, 6ᵗʰ January, 1956

Today after lunch Mataji was in Her room alone with Dr. Pannalal when I went in. She was speaking about Haribaba's illness and operation and how efficient Dr. Sen and his wonderful nursing home are. Then She said: *"I always say, if you are ill go to the best doctor. It is so in all walks of life, go to the greatest. If you put yourself into the hands of the very best you can be free from worry and say: 'Whatever happens will be all right.' But it is difficult, it costs a lot. One has to give and give. Likewise when going to God (the greatest of all) one has to give everything —one's pride, one's anger, one's self-importance, and then bear insult without complaining."* At that moment Lila and her daughter came and offered garlands to Mataji who quickly gave each of them rose garlands that had been hung previously on the mosquito net posts. Dr. Pannalal said: "Achha, one does not only give, one also gets something here". Ma said: *"When you give everything you get everything".*

Vindhyachal, 11ᵗʰ January, 1956

(Day of the Star in the East [12])

See how things happen on particular days! Today I asked Ma whether I could come back to Vindhyachal as it would be most difficult in Benares now that the hall will be rebuilt. Mataji said: *"Difficulties will gradually come to an end."* I said: "Even in Benares?" Mataji said: *"Yes"*. That was a promise. So it is coming to an end. I

[12] The day that Krishnamurti was recognized as the vehicle of the World Teacher while still a boy in Madras.

felt so happy, I was nearly in tears. Twice when I did *pranam* to Her here She put Her hand on my head.

Today in the course of the conversation She said: *"Whatever anyone does has a result. For example, if you kill in the line of duty, you also have to bear the consequences. So when people say: 'Why have I these difficulties? Due to what sin?' It is certainly due to something they have committed"* [the infallible law of *karma*].

Kishenpur, 13th July, 1956

Ma has allowed me to stay here in 'Kalyanvan' near the Kishenpur ashram. It is a beautiful retreat, completely quiet, set in a large garden comprising several acres of ancient fruit trees. From here one can see the Himalayas [13]. She has assigned both Jack and myself various duties.

This morning She talked to the two of us and asked me to write down what She said: *"When you work in the garden you should serve the trees and plants and, living with them, try to become like them. Let the trees be your Gurus. A tree gives fruit and shade. When the fruit is ripe it falls down and is sweet to the taste. It gives you its wood with which you cook your food. So the tree gives itself entirely, it holds nothing back. Watch how the trees grow, make them your friends and learn from them. Also from the grass. Grass is lowly and bears everything. People tread on it, cut it and it does not defend itself. So also the earth.*

You will also be in charge of the Ashram library. Catalogue it and later on it will grow. It was Bhaiji's wish. He himself had the cupboards made.

Be friendly with the servants. Do not get angry with them, but be firm and see that they do their work."

Vrindaban, 11th March, 1957

The wife of the Dutch Ambassador and her friend, both Jungian psychologists, came to see Ma and asked the following:

Question: In psychology patients are cured by talking to them, but with you it seems that your emanation cures people without words. We are trying to help people. What is the most essential thing that we should do for them?

---

[13] This was to remain her home for the rest of her life.

Mataji: *In this world who can be said to be normal? Everyone is mad after something or other; some after money, some after beauty, others after music or their children or whatever. So no one is really quite balanced.*

Question: What then is the remedy?

Ma: *Just as one does not water the leaves of a tree but its roots, so also one has to grapple with man's disease from its root. Man's root lies in the brain. So the remedy for all ills is to still the mind. When man's mind has become quiet then all will be well with him, physically and psychologically.*

Question: How does the mind become still?

Ma: *By treading the path that leads to the realization of 'who am I?' The body that was once young and then becomes old with hair greying and teeth falling out does not last. It is not the real 'I'. So man has to find out who he really is. When he tries to do that, his mind will be supplied with the right nourishment that will calm it. The right sustenance for the mind cannot be had from anything that is of the world and hence perishable, but only from that which is Eternal. The rasa, or nectar of that Eternal, will pacify the mind.*

The universe was created out of joy and that is why you find temporary joy in the fleeting things of the world. Without joy life is an ordeal. So you must attain to that great Joy that has brought forth the world and is the essence of your own being. This is exactly what is discovered when the mind becomes still.

Question: What is the unique contribution a woman can give as apart from a man?

Ma: *A woman is essentially a mother and therefore her duty is to serve everyone as her own children. Also as you are a daughter, a wife and a mother all in one it is important to recognize the oneness of these three. But in every woman is contained a man and in every man a woman. So the woman's task is also to find the man in herself.*

Question: What is the special contribution of a man?

Ma: *Man is the reflection of the Supreme* [Purusha], *the one who upholds the universe. True manliness is divinity. But then there is the Atma, which is beyond man and woman. Everyone has to discover that Atma within himself. It is the task of every human being to unfold both the man and woman contained potentially within themselves and to realize the Atma which is beyond both.*

511

Kishenpur (Dehradun), 5ᵗʰ August, 1957

Yesterday wires were sent to Swami Paramananda, Haribaba and other close devotees informing them that Ma's health was causing anxiety. This morning Haribaba came with Avadhutji and Swarupji. Mrs. Vadera somehow managed to get onto Ma's private verandah and stood outside of the room and heard Ma say clearly to Haribaba: *"For about eight months the breathing has changed. It is of a different kind than normally and that causes all these phenomena to occur in the body. But it does not trouble me. I am always in Ananda"*.

Last night I slept at the Ashram, feeling that I should make every effort to be near Ma as long as I have the chance. The atmosphere was terrific —in the night much more than in the day— even though it is in the night that Mataji is usually in worse health.

6ᵗʰ August, 1957, Jhulan Ekadashi

Today Dr. Das Gupta, Dr. Balram and Dr. Mukerji came. Dr. Das Gupta asked Mataji what was the root cause of Her illness. I managed to get into the room and heard Her speak for the first time in several days. She said: *"For eight months there is a noise in my head and there is difficulty in inhaling. Consequently there is no sleep. In any case this body does not sleep in the ordinary sense of the word, but at least there used to be 'nidra ka asana'* [14]. *Now that also has stopped. I said before that if this continues you will see into what a condition this body will get into and now you see it. For myself, I am not at all concerned. I am always in Ananda"*. Mataji was lying down when She spoke but She seemed quite lively.

* * *

It is generally considered in India that when a saint suffers, they are taking on the karma of their devotees or are doing so for the benefit of the world. Anandamayi Ma made it very clear that what appeared to be illness with Her was something totally different than would be the case with an ordinary person and she always refused medical treatment of any kind. She would say that, just as individuals came for her darshan, *so also the so-called diseases, which in traditional Indian medicine are considered as entities.*

* * *

---

[14] A trance-like state of deep repose in which full consciousness remains.

7th August, 1957

Yesterday Mrs. Sabarwal told me that on the 7th night at perhaps 10 p.m. Mataji suddenly sat up very straight in *samadhi*. After sometime She called Didi to Her side and asked everyone, including Didima to leave the room. She talked to Didi for about fifteen minutes during which Didi was crying. The next day at midday *darshan* She was again sitting in *samadhi*, Her eyes shut, the face thin and drawn —a most awe-inspiring sight, as if this was the *samadhi* which ends in *Mahasamadhi* [the final exit]. My breath stopped when I saw her face and I thought She was never going to speak again. I had to hide my face and turn away, shutting my mouth tightly, so as not to sob aloud. I was however wrong.

Mataji lay down again and at perhaps 5 p.m. the Raja of Solan [15] arrived. He went into Ma's room with his small entourage. Mataji was sitting and talking animatedly, although Her voice had become very weak. I was standing outside and heard Her say distinctly: *"Samadhi awastha hota hai"* [samadhi was there —referring to Herself] the rest I could not hear. The Raja's servant who came out told me She had said that sometimes She feels that each breath is Her last and that Her hands and feet turn cold at times. When we had *darshan* at about 6.30 p.m., Mataji was lying still with Her face towards us and eyes open watching everyone who did *pranam*. We are now allowed to do *pranam* only from the doorstep as the doctor says the oxygen gets spoiled by too many people in the room. At 9 p.m. Haribaba came and I could hear that Mataji was talking again and explaining very beautifully about Her condition.

In the evening Mataji came out onto the verandah and sat near the hall in an armchair to watch the *arati* [16] for about five minutes. I had gone to the Dhyan Mandir to open a window. When I came out I saw Mataji coming followed by Didi, Dr. Das Gupta and Swami Paramanandaji. I sat quietly in a corner on the floor. Mataji looked extremely tired. After about five minutes She got up and walked back very shakily, supporting Herself by holding on to the wall and supported by someone on Her other side.

---

[15] A great devotee and the first president of the Anandamayi Sangha.

[16] The nightly worship in the temple.

9ᵗʰ August, 1957

This morning I am told She said only one or two words when Haribaba came and then lay still with Her eyes shut and face turned to the wall. After food I somehow managed to sneak onto Her veranda and had a glimpse of Her from the back. There was an overwhelming stillness.

Everyone feels that Mataji is getting better and there is an atmosphere of cheer and hope now in the ashram.

XXVI - Words of Wisdom

Varanasi, 10th October, 1957

An Irish journalist, Mr. Fennell, and a research student at the Benares Hindu University from Malabar (South India), Mr. Panikkar [1], came for an interview.

Panikkar: When there is only ONE why are there so many different religions in the world? What have you to say about those who insist that only one religion is the right one?

Ma: *Because He is infinite, there is an infinite variety of conceptions of Him, an infinite variety of paths to Him. He is everything, every kind of belief and also the disbelief of the atheist. The belief in non-belief is also a belief. It implies that you admit belief when you disbelieve. He is in all forms <u>and</u> in the formless.*

Panikkar: From what you have said I gather that you consider the formless (*Nirguna*) to be nearer to Truth than God with form (*Saguna*)?

Ma: *Is ice anything but water? Saguna is as much He as Nirguna. To say that there is only One Atma and all forms are illusion would imply that the formless was nearer to Truth than form. But I say every form and also the formless are He and He alone.*

1st February, 1960, Kumbha Mela

Question: Is it right to eat meat?

Ma: *You should eat according to what is helpful in your sadhana and abstain from that which hinders it.*

Question: But meat is *tamasic* [dulls the mind —making it less receptive to the spiritually subtle].

Ma: *Exactly, that is why I said what I said. You can think it out for yourself.*

---

[1] Raimundo Panikkar —a noted Catholic philosopher and Indologist, son of an Indian father and a Spanish mother. The main part of this interview, primarily Mr. Fennel's questions, has been used for the Prologue.

Question: When someone kills to eat, won't it affect him adversely?

Ma: *Certainly it will.*

Question: What about animal sacrifice? It is advocated in the *shastras* (ancient scriptures).

Ma: *This body does not comment on what the shastras enjoin or forbid. But one has to understand what animal sacrifice means: namely the sacrifice of one's own animal nature.*

Later:

Kriyananda [2]: What is the purpose and the fruit of *puja* and *japa*?

Ma: *For puja particular asanas, mudras and bija-mantras are used according to the particular aspect of the Godhead that one worships. One has to 'engage' in [the outer ritual of] puja, so that _real_ puja may come about. Just as one takes sanyasa (outwardly), in order that real inner sanyasa may come. What now is real puja? To give oneself entirely to the object of one's worship. Then the proper asanas and mudras come about spontaneously. The object of the puja is the darshan of Him whom one worships. When one's dedication becomes complete, then He reveals Himself. To find Him means to find one's Self and to find one's Self means to find Him. It is said that the worshipper has to become one with he object of his worship in order to be able to perform real puja. So the object and fruit of puja is that the one who worships and He who is worshipped become one. The purpose of japa is the revelation of the essence of Him whose name one repeats, then the japa has been fruitful. The object of engaging in the japa of Rama is the revelation of what Rama is in reality. The same holds true for every mantra, be it of Krishna, Shiva etc.*

Question: May women practise *siddhasana* [a particular meditation posture]?

Ma: *When this body played the play of sadhana, siddhasana came about of itself. Therefore it may be performed by women as well as men. When an asana comes about spontaneously as a natural expression of one's interior state, it will be perfect, that is to say the position of the legs, hands, arms, head, the gaze —everything will be exactly as it should be. Performing an asana by an effort of will can never have the same perfection. Asanas are connected with the rhythm of one's breath and the breath*

---

[2] An American disciple of Paramahansa Yogananda who later founded a number of popular Yoga communities in the U.S. and Europe.

516

with one's state of mind at any particular time. When asanas are done as a yogic practice, that is to say for the purpose of attaining to the revelation of union with the <u>One</u> which eternally exists, then only will they bear the desired result. If only done as physical exercise they will bring about health and fitness but that is all —not true union (yoga). Even when one has attained to perfection in a particular asana and its essence has become fully revealed, one should feel: I have attained to this fully, but what of it? It is not the ultimate goal. This attitude is 'vairagya' [inspired discrimination]. One then goes on striving for the next stage and so on, further and further. One must keep up this attitude until nothing remains to be reached, then only will the Ultimate be attained. Otherwise one is apt to linger for a long time at a specific stage rather than proceeding rapidly to the final goal. Together with asanas (hatha yoga) one has to practice raja yoga [3], otherwise it is merely physical exercise.

When this body performed asanas they occurred spontaneously, the legs assumed the right positions spontaneously actuated by an inner power, which was not the power of another but Atma Shakti.[4] Once, I wilfully moved my leg and injured it thereby. The injury has remained, it is still there.

Allahabad, 2nd February, 1960

The Chinese professor of Allahabad University, Mr. Chow asked: "Once when meditating in a dark room, I had the impression that the room was full of moonlight. But when opening my eyes I found the room dark. What was this?"

Ma: *To see light is a good sign. Unless the path becomes lit up, how can one see anything? Just as in the physical world unless there is light, you cannot distinguish anything. At present there is outer light and inner darkness. When inward light comes, then this outward light seems dim and dull. Just as we see the tree, but can't see its roots as they are hidden in the earth, so we perceive Prakriti (manifested creation), but we don't know from where it originates. The root of all that we perceive is hidden within. We see the tree but we don't see the seed from which it came. However when the tree is fully developed it again yields the same kind of seed. When we look at the seed we see only the seed, yet infinite possibilities of development are contained within it.*

---

[3] Meditation and specific mental disciplines.
[4] The Divine power of the Atman —the Supreme Self.

517

The One is contained in the infinite and the infinite in the one. When light is thrown on the inner world, the outer fades into insignificance. However at that stage there is still differentiation between the inner and the outer. But there comes a state where there is no more inner and outer, but all is seen as one whole.

Vindhyachal, 19th February, 1960

Miss Ray, a young French lady, who had lived in America for four years and is now touring through India on her way home, found out by chance about Mataji from Miss Sydney, who advised her to take a taxi and see Ma at Vindhyachal. We went this morning and stayed for just two hours.

She asked: Is it one's duty to do what one's parents want one to do or live one's own life?

Ma: *If it is a life dedicated to the search of Truth then nothing else matters.*

Miss Ray: Well, it is not exactly a life of this kind. But I am asking on principle. Is it my duty to conform to my parent's wishes, or should I live my own life?

Ma: *I have already told you —this body speaks only of the Supreme Quest. There are two kinds of seekers: one wants to dedicate his life to that highest Goal and for him there are no other duties; the other wants to live a religious life but is not fully committed and thus still sees obstacles. If you choose the spiritual path and then have a bad conscience for having left your parents, your thoughts will dwell on them and you won't be able to meditate. One must make a definite decision one way or the other. Even then there will be difficulties at times, but they can be overcome if the decision has been made once and for all. But if one feels drawn in two directions one cannot proceed.*

Question: Will I ever find peace and happiness?

Ma: *Peace and happiness are found on the path to God, never in the world. In the world one gets a little happiness which is invariably followed by its shadow —sorrow.*

On parting the young lady said: "I shall never forget this day and I shall never forget what you told me!"

Ma: *Forget? It is not a question of forgetting. You must meditate. Meditate at least five minutes daily along the line prescribed by your own religion. Not less than five minutes, but if you can give more time, the more the better. Try to give at least a quarter of an hour of every day, no matter what kind of life you may choose —and don't forget your friend. This is your friend* [pointing to Herself]. *Better to think first and then act, than to act thoughtlessly and then regret it afterwards.*

Kishenpur, 23rd April, 1960

Two blind men came. One asked: "How does one get the vision of God? Tell me the easiest way to it?"

Ma: *By seeking Him for His own sake.*

Question: Which is better, devotion or the path of knowledge?

Ma: *Adhere to God's Name. Repeat His Name day and night and get engrossed in the sweetness of His Name.*

The second blind man: Mataji, give me your blessing.

Ma: *Pray to God and you will feel His blessing.*

A lady: You said: "Seek God for His own sake". But if one seeks Him with selfishness, will he also attain to Him?

Ma: *Of course, if you seek God —with whatever motive— you will get something of Him, and if you pray for anything of this world you will also get it. But these things are not worth asking for. One should not seek God with any motive, but only for His own sake. Seek God because it is your nature to do so, because you cannot remain without Him. Whether and when He reveals Himself to you is His affair. Yours is to call out to Him constantly, not to waste your energy on anything else.*

It is not right to compare and reason saying: "Such and such a person has done sadhana for so many years and yet has not got anywhere". How can you judge what is happening to anyone inwardly? Sometimes it seems that a person who does sadhana seems to have changed for the worse. But how do you know that this tendency has not always been in him and has now come out so that it may be dealt with and purified as a result of his endeavours? To say: "I have done so much sadhana but have not been transformed", is also the wrong attitude. Yours is only to seek God and call out to Him unceasingly and not look to the result of what you are doing.

The Lady: Sometimes I feel desperate because I don't seem to be able to progress.

Mataji: *You get desperate when you have desires and they remain unfulfilled. But when you aspire to God for His own sake how can you be desperate.*

Anandamayee Ma - early 1970's

Kalyanvan, 21st July, 1960

Mataji asked me to take the 1-2 a.m. meditation. Last night when I did this for the first time, I seemed to be with Her in Her embrace and remembered Her reply to the question "What does God do?": *"He eats the ego"*. I felt that this was actually happening and it was so blissful that I did not get up, but sat till 2.40 a.m. and then lay down in that mood. I felt that I had really nothing to worry about, that in any case Ma was doing everything necessary and all I had to do was to surrender. Night meditation is really wonderful, unequalled. Since Ma has come here She talked to me a lot in the *Satsang*, so I did not feel the need to ask Her for a private.

Mataji talks often to me about anger. The other day I saw that it is intrinsic dissatisfaction about myself that makes me burst out for small reasons. Whatever happens is His doing, it is for Her to look after my welfare. What does it matter to me. Whatever happens does not concern me, so why should I get angry.

One day Ma gave me first a red flower, then a white one and said: *"Safed ho jao!"* [Become white] and put Her hand on my head. Today She wanted to give me a garland, but two stuck together and She said: *"I won't give you a pair, for you did not get married. You remain alone"*. Then She gave me a garland with red and white flowers. I said: "Ma, you are again giving me red". She said: *"This red will take away the red of your anger."*

Kishenpur, 22nd July, 1960

In the course of *Satsang* Mataji said: *"It is well to remember that whatever one enjoys of worldly happiness, be it good food or whatever else, uses up that merit (punya) that one has accumulated. Therefore it is good to think always of God and to enjoy whatever comes as coming from Him. One should also remember that whatever suffering one has to go through expiates one's sins and evil deeds".*

Kishenpur, 9th October, 1960

Question: How can sadhana become uninterrupted since it is necessary to sleep?

Mataji: *When one becomes established in ceaseless practice it continues also during sleep.*

521

Question: How can one know this?

Ma: *If one meditates before retiring and wakes up in the same kind of state with which one fell asleep one can presume that it has gone on throughout the sleep.*

Question: But during sleep one does not know.

Ma: *No, not in this case. Although there is a much higher state when one is conscious even in sleep.*

Question: Should one undertake a spiritual practice or penance with the expectation that this will atone for a wrong deed or sin?

Mataji: *The best thing is to do everything only for God, for the realization of Him alone. That will blot out all sin as well. Some people acquire money by unrighteous means and then give away a large sum for charity or some other good purpose in order to be cleansed, then they start sinning all over again. In this case they will reap the fruit of their evil deed as well as of their good deed. It is like bathing in the Ganges and then smearing mud all over one's body. Therefore everything should be done with the one motive only to realize God or one's True Self.*

Kishenpur, 10th October, 1960

Question (a French lady): If everything is God's *leela*, there seems very little scope left for human freedom. It seems as if we are marionettes and He is pulling the strings. Is there any freedom for the individual and if so how much? Have we not the freedom at least to choose at every moment whether to go towards the world or towards the Truth?

Mataji: *Everything is God's leela, but because you do not know this, you ask questions; but even your questions are within His Leela. The world is gatishila [perpetual movement] and the jiva [individual] is that which is bound. But the bondage is not lasting because it is of the world, which is constant flux. You may lock your room and go away, but the lock cannot last forever, neither can the door. It is a question of perspective. Jiva is also Shiva [God]. In reality you are actually free and therefore it is natural that you desire freedom. When you are going towards God it is difficult to go also towards the world and vice-versa.*

Turning towards a young *sanyasini* [woman renunciate] who was learned in the scriptures, Ma asked:

What then is the freedom of the individual? What do the shastras say?

522

She said: The individual is like a cow tied to a post. It cannot leave the post, but as far as the rope goes it is free to move as it pleases.

Mataji: *Yes, this is a very beautiful analogy. But when the individual makes use of the whole of his will power in anything that he undertakes, he gets into touch with the Mahashakti [supreme power] and then where is the boundary? Just as when a tree is planted it is surrounded by a boundary of bricks or a fence, but when it grows strong it breaks the boundary and grows beyond it. So the cow sometimes digs up the post and runs away with it. In some cases the Guru may destroy the boundary.*

Kishenpur, 11th October, 1960

This morning a French girl, 20 years of age, arrived here from Kabul, where she had been working on a film with Arnaud Desjardins [5]. She was so impressed by a film he showed of Mataji that she decided to stop in India only to see Her. She has ten days here. She left Kabul only yesterday and took the night train from Delhi. After an hour of Ma's *darshan* —which was mostly taken up by people bringing presents and doing *puja* to Ma— followed by a half hour's talk in Hindi and Bengali of which she could not understand a word, I asked her how she found Ma. She replied: "I expected very much, but I have found much more". At the question as to whether she wanted to see anything more of India, she simply said: "No, I want to remain only with Ma".

12th October, 1960

I asked: Mataji, Mrs. Desjardins wants to know what you mean by: "Vipad dilen tini vipad haran koren" (By adversity He destroys adversity). For various meanings are possible.

Mataji: *Since you say that, first disclose which meanings are in your mind.*

I: To be an individual is by itself pain since it means bondage, separation from the One. But immersed in worldly happiness, the individual is not aware of its suffering. So God sends sorrow and adversity so that one may wake up to the fact of one's innate misery.

---

[5] French film maker, author and spiritual teacher who along with his wife spent considerable time with Anandamayee Ma.

Ma: Yes, you see that the happiness of this world is always short-lived and so you begin to search for lasting happiness. What other meaning do you see?

I: It also may mean that He sends misfortune to prevent a greater disaster.

Mataji: *Yes, it also happens at times that a great disaster is karmically inevitable, but is blotted out or mitigated by a smaller one. Then also whatever suffering is due to a person due to his karma has to be endured, but then when it is exhausted, it is finished. In this way also suffering is beneficial. Then also if a very great difficulty arises, one is obliged to turn to God, since one feels utterly incapable to cope with it. Although one may doubt whether God exists, yet he will start praying to Him in such a case.*

This again reminds me of an incident. Mr. Modi [6] *told me about. Once he was in an aeroplane and some engine trouble arose. The travellers were told that they would all be lost, since the engine could only work for fifteen minutes more. A panic broke out and people started lamenting and bewailing their ill luck. Modi said: "Why lament? You are fortunate. This is the time to pray to God. If you die with the thought of God you will go straight to Him". So everyone started praying with great fervour and somehow the aeroplane managed to land. Even though the engine was then repaired, Modi and some others got out feeling intuitively that it was better not to continue. When the plane went up again, it hit an electric wire, caught fire and instantly went up in flames with all those who were still on board.*

Kishenpur, 13ᵗʰ October, 1960

Mataji replied at length to a question. The most important point was: *"It is difficult for the householder to always find time to sit down for his prayers. It is also difficult to always cultivate the company of saints or to attend religious meetings. But it is easy and always possible to keep company with God in the shape of His name or the mantra received from the Guru. One cannot always have an image or picture of a deity in front of one's eyes, but the vigraha of God as akshara* [the indestructible Divine sound inherent in the mantra] *can be one's constant companion under all circumstances."*

---

[6] One of modern India's foremost industrialists.

Naimisharanya, 26th October, 1960

Question: It is said that in 1962 the planetary constellations are very bad and that there will be a great disaster in the world. What is the means to save ourselves from it?

Ma: *You hear people say all kinds of things and because you are full of fear you are afraid. But there is also a state in which there is fearlessness. You must take the path that leads to fearlessness. This is a pathless path. You must have recourse to the means which is no means and beyond all means. You must have recourse to that.*

Question: But what about the rest of the world?

Ma: *First become fearless yourself.*

Question: What is your opinion about this prophesy?

Ma: *This body does not reply to such questions.*

Naimisharanya, 31st October, 1960

Akhandananda Swami gave a talk on anger. He said desire was the father of anger and *abhiman* [ego] the cause of desire. Unless one surrenders to the Guru completely and serves him, anger cannot go. Anger is a fire which eats up the *rasa* [nectar] of one's *sadhana* and stops the current of it.

Mr. Modi: I have noticed that those *sadhus* who sit in places like Gangotri [7] and can do without clothes or blankets in such ice-cold places are the very ones who get most angry. How is this to be explained?

Mataji: *So long as one is not established in the state where there is no longer consciousness of 'I' and 'you', where one knows that the Self is One and all-pervading, how can anger be completely conquered?*

Question: Suppose I have a picture of Mataji and someone comes and knocks it down. Should I not get angry?

Mataji: *No, you should say: Ma herself has knocked down the picture. Whatever happens is Her doing.*

Question: Suppose I have a picture of Mother in my heart and someone insults it. Should I not be angry?

Mataji: *No, you should feel that Mother Herself has spoken. She is all-pervading. She has spoken in this way to test my endurance, to give me a chance not to get angry even when there seems to be a reason for it.*

---

[7] Site of an ancient temple, high up in the Himalayas near the source of the Ganges.

Someone quoted a *sloka* from the *Ramayana* in which it says that when someone abuses your Guru, you should not listen and avoid that person.

Mataji: *What you said is very beautiful. At a certain stage this is the right thing to be done.*

Question: When Sita [8] entered the earth after having been subjected to very humiliating tests, was her motive not anger?

Mataji: *No, there was no anger. A condition had arisen under which she simply could not remain on the earth. It was imperative for her to leave.*

Question: What exactly did Sita feel?

Mataji: *You are not playing the instrument. The reply does not come. But you yourself are Sita, you are Rama.*

Jogesh Brahmachari: No, I am not Rama nor Sita.

Mataji: *No, 'I' is not Rama. Where the 'I' is, there cannot be Rama. I did not say 'I' am Rama. There is only Rama, nothing but Rama. All is Rama.*

Om Ma, Kishenpur, 24th November, 1960

Mataji sent me here with some young *brahmacharinis* [nuns]. A letter came from Her with instructions for us, as follows: "*At every single moment try to be aware of Him, for have you not chosen this path to dedicate your lives to Him alone! Therefore when speaking, speak only of Him; when thinking, think of Him; and when listening, listen to His words. Further, each one of you must try to keep a diary, so as to check your mind from turning outwards. This may also make you watchful and be helpful to you in your endeavour. In order to make ones' lives beautiful and to fill the new life with a new current, those who are pilgrims on this path must develop great inner strength, energy, mobility and swiftness. It will not do to sit and ride in a rickety, jolting cart. At all times the mind must be intensely vigorous, energetic and alert —then only can one forge ahead with great speed. Remember that everyone has to mould his or her own life. Accept cheerfully whatever he may bestow on you or take away from you*".

These days I sit for an hour and a half at a stretch without discomfort, in spite of my sore right knee. Also as soon as I close

---

[8] The consort of the god-king Rama.

my eyes, warmth flows through the whole body. Ma said when here in October: *"Now you are able to do a bit of dhyan. I can see it from your face"*.

Today I started at last on the book. I am putting the material in order and making the index. Even if it is not at all exhaustive, it will be better than nothing. At night it is so quiet. I wish I did not have to sleep. In the day there are disturbances. I got three marigolds from Amy's garden for Ma.

Keeping a diary is perhaps like keeping accounts —one knows how much one spends and checks when it becomes too much. Here also one can check when keeping count of what one does daily.

27th November, 1960

I feel irritated again. It seems to be an essential knot of my ego. I have a desire to attend some of J.K.'s talks. Perhaps it may help me to become aware of the root cause of this. I still fail to remember that all are manifestations of the One. Today woke early, but had stomach pain in the afternoon and had to lie down with a hot water bag and fell asleep for half an hour. Work with the book proceeding satisfactorily. Immensely enjoyable and enlightening.

Kishenpur, 29th November, 1960

Early morning before *kirtan*, meditation is good, time flies. [9]

30th November, 1960

Woke before 3 a.m. and got up, so had a quiet meditation for one hour, but then got tired and lay down again until *kirtan* time, 5.30 a.m.

I do daily *asanas* for half an hour early morning. It helps to make the body an instrument.

1st December, 1960

This morning I was tired and got up only at 4.45 a.m., but meditation was not disturbed. I sat for over one and a half hours in the same posture. My knee is better. I walked down to the School for the Blind. I enjoyed the walk, but on returning my heart seems tired. Perhaps I should avoid physical exertion. After all it is not worth it to waste my energy in this way at my age. Better to keep

---

[9] This reads like a Zen Haiku (as does much of her final entries)

quiet and preserve energy for the inner search. I am enjoying the *kirtan* twice daily and the *Gita Path* (*Bhagavad Gita* recitation).

5th December, 1960

Letter from Malati to say that they may go to Varanasi to hear J.K. The letter carries J.K.'s atmosphere and makes me feel peculiar about the life I am leading.

7th December, 1960

I have been reading Lama Govinda's book, *Foundations of Tibetan Mysticism*, which I like quite a lot. At last there was a letter from Miss Sydney, but her handwriting has changed and she seems absent minded. She is still in Almora, was ill, poor old thing.

Sunday, 10th December, 1960

What a life this is, and I go on quite complacently while death is always lurking around the corner; I am satisfied with the shadows. Such dissatisfaction must be J.K.'s influence. Whenever he is in India I feel it.

Kishenpur, 13th January, 1961

It is obviously the complete concentration on and surrender to God, the "letting go", that precipitates the transformation.

I read recently *The Way of the Pilgrim* which I loved and want to read once more. It shows how when one is really intense it takes only a very short time to go very far and also live without any means or comforts in complete bliss. It makes me feel that I am not intense enough.

I have been planning to go to Delhi to see Lisl, and now I hear Mataji Herself will be there. That is also wonderful because I don't really care whether I see anyone or anything else in the world. Mataji will be there and I can perhaps take Lisl to Her. So there is some sense in my going. Also I may see J.K. I had a wish sometime ago to meet him this year.

20th January, 1961

Heard J.K. talk. It was nothing special [10]. Lisl saw Ma on Janu-

---

[10] This is her final recorded encounter with Krishnamurti.

ary 21st and said when She came in, it was as if Bliss itself was entering the hall.

New Delhi, 23rd January, 1961

Today a young American woman, Markell Brooks, asked questions. She has been in India for only twelve days.

Question: What is the cause for the sense of unreality of everything I perceive, even though I know it is good and beautiful, as for instance a sunset?

Ma: *This feeling comes from within you. Whatever is perceived is temporary, ever changing and therefore unreal. Your Atma which is eternal and real gives you this sense of unreality, of the impermanent. It is a good sign that it should come. Turn within and seek the Atma. Life in the world and all one perceives with the senses is transitory. Only by meditation and coming to know oneself can one reach the Oneness that is the only Reality.*

Question: Since the will of the individual is illusory and one does not know God's will, how can one lead a purposeful life in this world.

Ma: *By contemplating the Self one will find out. It is man's principal duty to aspire to Self-realization.*

Question: What about self-expression in art?

Ma: *This also belongs to that which is fleeting. You paint a picture, but it can't last. The most beautiful song fades away in a moment.*

Question: Presuming that the striving goes on no matter what, how can one know how to live —in relation both to human beings and one's own creative energies?

Ma: *A man who is after worldly things and is occupied with the business of this world gets satisfaction out of what he does, for otherwise why should he do it? He feels he is doing well, he gets praise and fame, money and position and his mind is always occupied with his affairs. If someone is opposed to him and puts obstacles in his way he gets angry and hostile.*

A person who strives after Self-realization will turn to Mahatmas [great souls] for advice, guidance and company. He will start reading books written by such men. He will admire them and wish to become like them and so, since he is searching for Truth, he will come to be truthful in behaviour and speech. The Self is one, so remember the One-

*ness of all. Although a dog may bite you, you will not bite back. The
man who strives after worldly goods and satisfaction is working for
death, because everything in the world is constantly dying and something else is born. The child dies to the young girl and the girl to the
woman etc. But the man who is after Self-realization is working for
immortality. When living and working in the world one's creative power
is exhausted in the pursuit of sense objects so one may come to feel
weak, tired or ill. But by striving after Self-realization one's creative
power is preserved and strengthened.*

*While the person who lives in the world takes pleasure in parties,
meeting people etc etc, the one who is out for Self-realization will take
pleasure in meditation, singing the praises of God, reading books of
wisdom, listening to discourses by great souls and mixing with those
who are pilgrims on the path.*

*Now about behaviour: The devotee will come to feel that he is the
servant of the Lord and therefore become humble, gentle and sweet.
Everyone, whatever his line of approach, should become gentle, kind
and loving, for the Self is one. The active person will do service —not
to others but with the thought that everyone is a manifestation of God
and that whomever he may serve, he serves God in that shape. This
alone is real service; this kind of service purifies the mind and is therefore also a service to the Self. The one who is striving for illumination
will reason that all are expressions of the One and so he also will be
kind and loving to all. Just as when the dry leaves fall off a tree, the new
leaves come of their own accord, so one's behaviour and relationship
will automatically change with one's attitude to life.*

*According to the status of an aspirant he will have to observe cer-
tain injunctions. So you [referring to me] with your yellow clothes* [11]
should live up to what such dress demands.

New Delhi, 21st January 1961

A French couple from the U.N.O. had a private with Ma. The
lady asked: How does the love of God come?

Ma: *Don't you make friends with utter strangers and come to
love them? To love God who is your own Self is natural. If you feel
attracted to a particular form of God, like Christ or Krishna, contem-*

---

[11] Mother had recently told her to wear only yellow saris as this colour signifies her permanent commitment to the spiritual life.

plate Him in this form, repeat His Name constantly and think of Him, occupy your mind continually with the thought of Him.

Question: If one does not feel attracted to any particular incarnation of God?

Ma: *Then sit quite still and dive into yourself, trying to find out who you are. To find yourself means to find God and to find God means to find your Self.*

Beginning of January, 1961

Ma's letter to one of the ashramites:

"By constant practice one finally achieves the goal. Everyone in the ashram should say to themselves: 'All right, as our friend has shown us the way, we shall try to follow her advice to the minutest detail'. At what moment His touch will be felt lies with Him —our duty is to continue to invoke Him at all times. Enough time has already been spent in going here and there aimlessly, leaving the Path in order to enjoy the sights of the world and to have fun in various ways in the manner of the world. Now as much time as possible should be dedicated to the attempt of finding one's Self. Vain and useless talk is of no benefit and prevents one from advancing towards Him; it is an obstacle to one's efforts. Ages and ages have been wasted in this way. Now my friend, return to your own house. By lingering on the way you only prolong the agony of having to endure the troubles and difficulties that are met with on the pilgrimage. Ever remember that one who tries to advance towards Him and practices His name, His presence, progresses whatever his condition may be. To say: 'I am not feeling His response' and therefore to seek pleasure in mundane things, can never be beneficial. Ever bear this in mind".

New Delhi, 23ʳᵈ January, 1961

Question: Is it necessary to join an ashram in order to find God or can one do it also at home?

Mataji: *God is everywhere and can be found everywhere. The home is also an ashram, namely the grihastha ashram.* [12] *People join an ashram or sit alone on the banks of the Ganges only to realize that God is everywhere, that there are no boundaries except in the mind. Everyone chooses the life that is most helpful to him in his search.*

---

[12] The second of the four classical stages of Hindu life.

24ᵗʰ January, 1961

Miss Brooks: Is freedom an illusion?

Ma: *No, man is free.*

Question: But man is an individual, an ego, and the ego is an illusion, so how can he be free?

Ma: *Yes, the outer man who is identified with the ego is not free, but actually man is free, the 'atimanesh' [true man] is free.*

Hardwar, 5ᵗʰ February, 1961

Today a party of Swiss people came. One of them can heal people by laying on hands and also from a distance by visualizing them. She said a clergyman taught her how to do this. She was afraid, however, that she was not doing it correctly as she felt very exhausted after the healing and also experienced the illnesses in herself of whomever she was curing. For instance, she was blind for ten minutes while trying to cure a blind man, although in this case she could not affect a cure. Swami Narayanananda at Rishikesh asked her to give up this healing as it would arrest her spiritual progress. She wanted to know what Mataji had to say about this. She is the mother of three children and healing is a means of livelihood for her.

Mataji: *It is true that this type of healing arrests one's going beyond the level from which the healing is affected. If one takes to the spiritual life completely, it is an obstacle. But from the point of view of the householder, who in any case has to do business or earn money in some way to support his family, you may take money for some cures and do others free as a service. People will be benefited, although some may not be cured as it does not lie in their fate [karma]. In any case some good will be done. Householders who have to provide for their children etc inevitably cannot live completely without some compromise. But for those who dedicate themselves entirely to the spiritual, for them compromise does not exist; they have to be truthful at all costs, for such persons such an activity would represent an obstacle.*

Question: We are trying to found an international spiritual centre in Europe where Yoga of all kinds will be taught, since the spiritual hunger in Europe is very acute and ever increasing. Should we go ahead with it?

Ma: *Who is to instruct in Yoga?*

Questioner: We are getting people from all over the world to come and do it.

Mataji: *If you can secure really competent teachers, then it is no doubt a good thing to found such a centre. But all depends on the capacity and* <u>inner</u> *qualification of the instructors.*

Hardwar, 5th February, 1961

Stayed with Kitty in Delhi a day and then left by taxi with Markell Brooks for here. I enjoyed staying with Kitty. We understand each other quite well. I found the room in which J.K. stayed very helpful for meditation.

Hardwar, 17th March, 1961

In the evening someone asked about the three *naistik brahmacharis* under Ma's training. They wear either yellow or gerua and follow a very strict routine. They must get up early, bathe in the Ganges, do *sandhya, japa, havan* [13], then cook their own food on the sacred fire, clean their *puja* vessels and then do another *kriya* —all before eating by which time it is at least 1 p.m. or more. In the evening they do several hours of meditation and take only milk and fruit. They are allowed cooked food only once a day. They must observe strict rules of conduct —praise, blame and even abuse should be equal to them. They have to see everyone as Brahman. All this is to prepare oneself for Self-realization. They have to stay in a place favourable to their *sadhana.* Hardwar is very good for this because of the Ganges and the walks in the open countryside.

In the evening Mother called an American visitor to sit by Her and said She would give *darshan* daily at 11.30 a.m. and 6.30 p.m.

Hardwar, 1st April, 1961

So many foreigners come nowadays. When Mataji gives *darshan* in Her room there are sometimes more Europeans than Indians [14].

---

[13] Ritual of making offerings of rice grains and ghee to a sacrificial fire constructed in a particular manner and accompanied with *mantra* recitation.

[14] Usually there were never more than a handful of Westerners around Anandamayi Ma, nor was their presence particularly encouraged by the rather orthodox ashram community. Nevertheless, as many as 30 or 40 might occasionally come to attend a specific ashram function —especially during the last ten years of Anandamayi Ma's life.

Today at about midday the Rani of Gwalior and her daughter were in Ma's room. She called me, Sukriya and an Italian lady. Later two Europeans from Rishikesh also joined. So there were five Europeans, each of a different country.

Christa asked Her: How should one meditate? Is it better to concentrate on an object such as a flower or should the mind be made blank?

Ma: *There are two basic ways: one is to concentrate on a deity like Shiva, Rama, Kali etc. This is very helpful for those who feel attracted to a particular form of God. The other way is to make the mind empty, observing thoughts as they arise and subside, not identifying with them but standing back as a witness until all thought ceases. But to keep the mind empty is very difficult for most aspirants. One can also concentrate on the inner light, the light by which one sees the outer things. Even a blind man perceives light within. Observing the movement of one's breath is another very effective way to still the mind.*

Mataji was then called outside. The Rani of Gwalior told us that she had been wanting to ask the very same question about meditation, but felt shy to do so and thought, 'perhaps Mataji will say something of her own accord' and so she received her reply through someone else's question. She said that this happened very often with Mataji.

Kankhal, 4th April, 1961

Question: Suppose a man decides to stay in a holy place, like Vrindaban, Kashi etc and to devote the rest of his life to spiritual practices and *satsang* for the purpose of attaining liberation, but in spite of doing all this he finds that he has not really been transformed. If he dies in this condition, will he be liberated?

Mataji: *That he has not been able to progress as he had hoped is due to his sankalpa [intention] not being completely pure. This is why both positive and negative aspects remain side by side within him. The influence of the holy place and the holy company will no doubt have their effect, but along with this he is reaping the fruits of his previous bad karma as well. The fruits of one's actions have to be experienced to the minutest detail.*

In any case he should not give up but continue to exert himself. It is said that in the Kaliyuga man is so weak that his mental sins are for-

given him —*he has only to bear the consequences of his actions, not his thoughts; otherwise there would be no chance at all of being liberated.*

Question: It is said that if a man dies in Kashi or certain other holy places, he will be liberated. Is that so?

Mataji: *If he dies within the sacred confines of Kashi* [Benares] *as defined in the scriptures, then it is so.*

Kankhal, 10th April, 1961

Yesterday Mr. Modi asked what was the sense of going to the doctor and having treatment, if everything was in any case ordained beforehand by Providence.

Mataji: *The fact that you consult the doctor and undergo treatment is also part of fate. Unless it is your karma to be cured, the doctor is helpless. But when it is within your karma to get well, the right treatment is given and you recover.*

Mr. Modi: Suppose one has intense faith in God and leaves everything to Him and does not consult any doctor, can one get well even so?

Mataji: *If one is in that state where one's faith is real, then it will be so powerful that God will effect the cure. But if one's faith is only superficial it will not work.*

The other way is not to pray to God for anything and to leave everything to Him, then whether one gets well or not is exactly the same.

Poona, 3rd July, 1961

To a question as to why God allows suffering in the world Ma replied: *Whatever happens in the world is His Lila, His pleasure.*

Question: Pleasure at all this misery? Where then is His love?

Mataji: *Who loves and who suffers? He alone plays His Play; who is there save Him? The individual suffers because he perceives duality. Duniya* [the world] *means du-niya* [based on duality, the fundamental root of sorrow]. *Find only the One everywhere and there will be an end to pain.*

Poona, 5th July, 1961

It has been raining hard for days, almost non-stop. This morning Ma was speaking about the weather and how much trouble everyone had to take to come to Her. Then She said: *"It is raining and raining. If your love of God would rain like this, flowing uninterruptedly, how beautiful it would be! It is said that the rainy season is conducive to love and devotion for God. Let your devotion for Him stream continuously like this rain".*

Question: Why does God allow so much suffering in the world? Ask everyone assembled here, none is happy and all want to be.

Mataji: *If you desire the things of this world you will be unhappy, and if you advance towards God you will be happy. This is how He teaches you to come to Him. If you had no troubles, you would not think of Him. But you desire all kinds of things and so you are unhappy.*

There is a story about a donkey that is an apt illustration of just how things are in this world. A dhobi [laundryman] kept a few donkeys to carry the clothes he collected for washing. Since he was poor, his house was too small to hold the donkeys and he left them outside during the night. He also could not afford enough rope to tie them all up. The donkeys would often run away and the dhobi had to spend hours trying to find them. So he thought of a clever solution. He simply touched a short piece of rope to their legs, and they, thinking they had been tied, remained standing in the same place all night. Exactly the same happens in the world. Maya touches you and you imagine you are bound. You think: how can I do without my children, my husband, my wife my parents, etc, and so you remain where you are and do not advance towards Him.

Poona, 10th July, 1961

The famous singer Hirabai Barodkar came and sang beautifully. Ma said to her: *"By singing Hari kirtan one can also get His touch. Through the melody and the rhythm He reveals Himself. Ram Prasad* [15] *realized the Great Mother only by being engrossed in singing Her praises.*

Vrindaban, 25th January, 1962

Yesterday Mataji asked us to take turns doing *japa* for twenty-four hours without a break, each of us choosing a particular time

---

[15] Ram Prasad Sen, 18th century Bengali mystic and composer of songs to the Divine Mother.

during the day. She asked a young German woman also to take one hour. The lady then asked Ma whether she could do *japa* of Christ. Mataji said: *"Certainly, there is only One"*.

Since yesterday a German family has been singing during the *kirtan* time. Yesterday they sang some German canons, today from a book of Church music four hundred years old, beautifully in three voices. Mother liked it immensely. She then told us how once when She was a child, two European missionaries came to Her village. They pitched a tent and went about singing Christian hymns very beautifully. Mataji liked it so much that tears would roll down Her cheeks. She was fascinated by their religious spirit and followed them wherever they went. She was a child and did not know the difference between Hinduism and Christianity, She only felt the religious fervour. She stayed with them until nightfall and when they retired to their tent She stood outside. The tent was closed and it was quite still, but She felt that they were praying and meditating. When it was pitch dark Mataji ran home. Nobody scolded her or said a word about her being late. Somehow they did not notice it. The missionaries were selling Christian hymn books in Bengali for one paisa each. Mataji begged Her mother to buy her one, which she did.

Question: What is the difference, if any, between prayer and meditation?

Mataji: *When you pray you ask for your wish to be fulfilled, be it the wish to be one with God or to realize Him or serve Him etc. Whereas dhyan, or meditation, means to be immersed in the contemplation of Him.*

Question: How is this possible?

Mataji: *It comes spontaneously. First you think of Him and then remember Him and you become absorbed in Him effortlessly. Just as when you sit here the thought of your home and your children comes to you automatically and you ponder over them. Likewise, the contemplation of the Divine beloved happens of its own accord.*

Vrindaban, 26th January, 1962

A German lady asked: I read in a book on Christian meditation that it is good for a beginner to concentrate on an object or symbol, such as the cross, the chalice or the light of a candle, since it is difficult to concentrate on the Supreme.

Ma: *Is that all the book said? Why not concentrate on Christ?*

Questioner: I have not the courage to do so. He is too holy and sublime. I could only do it wrongly.

Ma: *Everything that you perceive, you perceive because of light. And what anyone perceives, be he man or animal is perceived by that same light. This outer light originates from an inner light, even a blind man has an inner light. The light of the Self is the same in all. Whether you worship Christ, Krishna, Rama or Kali, you actually worship that one Light which is also in you, which pervades all things. Everything originates from Light, is essentially Light.*

An Indian lady: You always say we should constantly think of God, be immersed in Him; but in that mood the house-work gets neglected, a child comes and wants something, one attends to it hurriedly or guests arrive and they are not looked after properly. So what is one to do while

Mataji: *If you are immersed in God, why care what happens in the world? Let happen what may, you are absorbed in God.*

Questioner: But my people find fault with me. They say I neglect my duties. I am half here and half there and so neither gets done well.

Mataji: *No, you are not 'half' there, very much less than half, and with that little bit of other-worldliness you can do your work very well, even better than you could without it. Keep some hours reserved for your meditation and for the rest do your work as a service to God. By thinking of God all the time and regarding everyone as one of God's forms, your work will be done very well and everyone will be satisfied. When a man is out to accumulate wealth, he hides the little he has and even when he has accumulated something, he keeps it concealed. Keep your spiritual wealth in your heart and do the service of your family. There is no need to exhibit the little you have gained. But when you become really immersed in Him so that it is impossible to attend to your work, then nobody will blame you. People will feel the influence of the Divine in you and on the contrary be eager to serve you. If guests remain unattended, they will not mind it, they will be satisfied to have your company. But that is quite a different thing, then the world will not exist for you.*

Vrindaban, 28ᵗʰ January, 1962

In reply to a question of Mr. Modi, Ma pointed out the importance of what one thinks of at the moment of death. She said: *"Just as a leech does not leave one place until it hooks on to something else, so the soul upon leaving the body at once goes according to the state of mind a man is in. But at the moment of death one is unable to control one's thoughts, therefore the mind will dwell where it is accustomed to going and so one has to practise while one is well and strong, in order that the thought of God may come automatically when one is weak and ill."* She told a story to illustrate this.

"An old woman who had sold oil all her life was about to die. All her relatives had assembled round her and were urging her to repeat the name of Rama or Krishna. But she was hardly conscious anymore and could not hear what they shouted to her. Being used to beggars coming to her to beg for oil, she replied every time: 'Not one drop will I give, not one drop!' Saying this she passed away.

At the moment of death one's thoughts are weighed as it were. One cannot think of anything but that which has been strongest in one's mind throughout one's life. For this reason the practice of the Presence of God is so important, while one has yet control over one's mind."

Later Mataji said: *"The quality of your mind is greatly influenced by the kind of food you eat."*

Hardwar, 8ᵗʰ February, 1962

Had a dream of Mother in which She appeared as a man and urged me to live in an isolated retreat, far removed from my too numerous friends here in Dehradun. In the dream I was not too keen to do this. I remember that I once dreamt of J.K. looking like a woman after I changed over to Mataji, many years ago.

12ᵗʰ February, 1962

Much happens daily in terms of consciousness. In the afternoon went to visit Sukriya. She told me how she reacted recently when someone was prowling around the house late at night. She prayed to God to bless him since he was also God's child. He left within three minutes. To concentrate on the divine in everyone helps to solve the problem, where as reacting only increases the negativity. One should feel that whatever comes is sent by God.

Nevertheless I still get irritated at times.

In the evening I could do good work on the new book. How rich life is —so much happens in a single day, although outwardly there is nothing special. [16]

Hardwar, 6th March, 1962

A couple came who had lost their son. The man asked what was the sense of a child dying before it had lived out its life. Mataji replied that it was all the working of *karma*.

"*It was your karma to serve the child for sometime and his karma to accept your service. When it was over, God took him away. It is all God's play. Like some flowers fade and do not bear fruit, so the child was given to you by God for a time. This is the way of the world. There is bound to be bereavement and loss.*"

Question: From where is one to take to power to bear all these troubles and tribulations?

Mataji: *Remember that the Atma of the child and your Atma are one. The Atma is neither born nor dies, it eternally is. The body, like a worn garment falls away. Try not to be attached to the body and do not cry for it. Cry for God alone. Remember God, repeat His Name and contemplate Him. Read Scriptures such as the Gita, the Bhagavata and the Ramayana regularly and you will find comfort. Your grief will become much lighter. Make your life as a householder a dedicated life, as in an ashram. Blows come to remind you to turn your mind to that which alone is real.*

Kishenpur, 17th June, 1962

Yesterday one of the ashram girls asked me to ask Ma the meaning of *Bhagavat chinta* [the thought of God]. How can one think of Him if one does not know who he is?

Ma: *Sometimes you may want to buy something that you have not actually seen but only heard about and of which you have some idea, You think of it and then go to the bazaar and look for it until you finally find it. Here you are on the level of belief and acceptance of what you have been told. In fact there is nothing but God. But as you accept the authority of the Guru therefore meditate on Him according to the*

---

[16] This is Atmananda's last personal observation and is a fitting commentary on what her life had become and was to remain.

Guru's instructions, even though you do not know who or what He really is. Carry out the Guru's orders. The mantra is the seed. When you have the seed, you potentially have the whole tree. You have only to bury the seed in the earth and tend it. The tree will grow of itself. When you have found a Guru and received His instructions, you have potentially found everything; just as the seed is potentially the tree.

Mataji also spoke of people who want to commit suicide: "*When a man cannot get the woman he loves or vice versa, he does not want to live any longer. This is called identification with the body. When the body cannot get the enjoyment it is looking forward to, one wants to give it up. Then also when someone goes in search of God and cannot find Him after a long time, he may also want to commit suicide. This is also due to identification with the body. If someone really wants to find God, he considers the body to be God's temple and tries to keep it fit, so that he can do sadhana. Therefore it is necessary to eat moderately and sleep moderately, not more than is essential to keep the body well and fit.*"

19th June, 1962

This morning during *darshan* I asked Mother the following questions:

Myself: How does *sadhana* become *tivra* [intense]?

Ma: *By one-pointedness* [eklaksh]. *Tivra means to direct the tir* [arrow] *towards the goal. To aim with concentration at the goal only.*

A little later Ma said: *Although it is good to sing kirtan, recite scriptures, do puja etc, if one does it and enjoys the prestige and praise one gets, then it is an obstacle to sadhana. Suppose someone says: "How beautifully you sang! Let me copy the song" and then takes the address. A correspondence ensues, he sends some money etc. This is not sadhana.*

An ashramite: Should we then stop singing *kirtan* ?

Ma: *No, sing as much as you can, but only for God, only to get absorbed in Him. Be oblivious of whether someone praises you or not.*

Your way of doing sadhana is like travelling by bullock cart. At times the driver falls asleep and then the bullock takes the wrong road and one has to retrace one's steps. Therefore one has to be watchful and alert all the time.

June, 1962

Question: While living in the Guru's Ashram, what is better: service of the Guru or *sadhana*?

Mataji: *Whatever the Guru tells you is best. Obey the Guru implicitly. Whatever He may tell you to do, even if it be disagreeable, take it that it is for your purification.*

Question: But the Guru does not say anything.

Ma: *Then he is not a Guru.*

To do the Guru's personal service one must have the capacity for it. It is not for everyone. It is not 'seva' if one feels possessive of the Guru and jealous of others who also want to serve him. One must remember that all service, to whomever, is service to God. So many people come to the Ashram and there is no end to the opportunities of serving them in such a holy environment.

If you are able to sit in meditation continuously, nobody will expect service from you. But if you just go about aimlessly part of the time, then you should do service of some sort.

Question: What is *mantra chaitanya* ?

Ma: *The mantra that has become alive —when that which the mantra represents becomes revealed. The seed is laid by the Guru; but when the earth is not properly prepared the tree won't grow. An ordinary seed dies if it is not tended, whereas the seed that the Guru sows is immortal. But the earth has to be dug up and made soft, then the stones have to be removed and it has to be ploughed etc. When the seed is not watered, it cannot develop. The regular practice according to the Guru's instruction provides the nourishment.*

29ᵗʰ June, 1962

Question: What is *chitta shuddhi* [pure thought]?

Ma: *When the mind becomes empty and, like a clean mirror, reflects the Self.*

30ᵗʰ June, 1962

Question: Is the death hour fixed beforehand?

Ma: *In the realm in which laws of nature function, it is so and cannot be averted. But by the Will, or by the Grace, of One who has gone beyond these laws it may be altered. Normally, however, fate will have its way.*

Once upon a time there was a learned Brahmin. One night, while he and his family were asleep, a poisonous snake entered the house and bit his wife, son and daughter. Within a few moments all of them were dead. The Brahmin naturally felt sorely grieved and dejected. What to do now? He watched the snake crawl away and leave the house. In his despair he ran behind the reptile. After following it for some distance he saw the snake change into two fighting bulls. They began to fight jealously until they had killed each other. Then a beautiful young girl emerged on the spot. Two men came and started quarrelling over her; a fight ensued and they stabbed each other to death while the young beauty went on her way.

Deeply pained and puzzled the Brahmin kept close to her heels. Finally, she turned around and said: "Why do you follow me? Leave me alone!" "Not until you explain to me who you are. First you were a snake and your poisonous fangs blotted out my whole family. Then you turned into two fighting bulls that perished, and now, taking on the shape of a charming girl, you have caused the death of two men. Tell me who you are."

The young woman tried to escape, but the Brahmin would not let her go. "First disclose your identity, then you may go where you please." At long last she replied: "I am destiny. I do not kill anyone. But man, by the results of his own actions, causes his own death in some manner or other."

"If this is so", said the Brahmin, "tell me how I shall die?" "By drowning", she replied. With these words the woman disappeared. Although the Brahmin made strenuous efforts to avoid his fate, living in the mountains and taking great pains to avoid bodies of water, he ultimately succumbed as was his inalterable destiny.

Question: If someone dies pronouncing God's Name, will he escape being reborn again?

Ma: *It depends on the state he has reached. If he is in the right state of mind, it may of course happen that all his remaining karma is burnt up in a moment. Or this may also happen by the Grace of the Guru.*

Question: Is it possible to obliterate desire by the Grace of the Guru?

Ma: *It is. The Grace of the Guru always pours down on you, but you must have mercy upon yourself so that you may realize this. If your cup is turned upside down, how can it catch anything?*

543

1st July, 1962

Question: What is the right way of doing *pranam* ?

Ma: *When doing pranam to a deity or a living saint, first look intently at the whole figure, beginning with the feet, then moving to the head while inhaling slowly. Then, as you inhale, take in the power of the one to whom you are making the pranam and as you bring your head down to touch his feet, exhale, thinking that whatever is in you —good or bad— you offer to him; pour yourself out completely. When your head touches the feet, the divine power is transmitted through them into your head, which is the root of a human being. When the saint's hand is put on your head as you touch his feet, the electricity goes into you through his fingers.*

Question: I read in the paper about someone who was found dead. He left a letter to say that the woman he loved had died a few days ago and he could not bear life without her, so he had gone to join her. Can one by committing suicide really be united with a person who is dead?

Ma: *Never. One who commits suicide enters such a deep darkness out of which it is very difficult to be liberated. One may remain in it for ages, unless someone who has power has compassion and frees one from it. Suicide is a most heinous sin. In that condition one cannot meet anyone [in the after life]. The human body is born in order to enjoy and suffer the fruit of one's deeds of former birth. To try to escape from this by suicide is most foolish and only prolongs the agony indefinitely. No one who is in his senses can take his life; at the moment of doing such a thing the person is out of his mind. Suicide does not solve anything, on the contrary.*

Kishenpur, 2nd July, 1962

Question: It is said that if one thinks a certain thing is so, then it is so. For example, if I think *prasad* brings blessing, then this will be so; but not if I do not believe in this. What then is imagination and what truth?

Ma: *Imagination is one of the activities of the mind, but prasad always carries blessing whether you believe in it or not.*

Questioner (an old woman): Why is it that I never think that I am going to die? I think of other people's death but not of my own.

Ma: *Because you are afraid of death, you avoid thinking of it. But also, because in reality you are immortal, you know intuitively that you will not die. It is only the body that dies.*

544

10ᵗʰ July, 1963

Question: Ma, we do not find peace, the mind is restless and disturbed.

Ma: *Become immersed in the repetition of God's name. Do not even consider whether you are at peace or not. All the time cling to the Name.*

Kalyanvan, 12ᵗʰ July, 1963

Yesterday Ma sat on the platform under the jackfruit tree and talked about the *adhikara* [qualities] that are necessary to be able to discern correctly the biddings of the inner Guru. She said there were clear signs: *"A person who can be guided by the inner Guru should be free from krodha [anger], moha [self delusion], lobha [greed], ahamkara [selfishness], abhimana [ego] and the rest. He feels friendly towards all and not disturbed by anyone. But what most people call the inner Guru is nothing but the mind masquerading as such.*

You are out to find the Atma which is One, so until you have found it look upon all who come to you as expressions of that One and be friendly with all. When someone slaps you on one cheek, give him the other cheek also.

Kishenpur, 23ʳᵈ July, 1963

On the 16ᵗʰ evening Ma's right foot got entangled in a towel and She fell and fractured the third toe of Her right foot. Today for the first time She came out of Her room and stood for quite a long time on the verandah to give darshan. Just before this a French priest from Poitiers had a private with Her.

Question: Do you know about Christianity and what do you think of it?

Ma: *If Christianity claims a special place for itself and puts itself apart, it destroys the divine unity and universality of the all-pervading Godhead. We recognize Jesus Christ but within the unity of religions. He Himself is above this separation.*

Question: As a Christian my first duty is to search after God and also to love my neighbour as myself. There is so much poverty in India [17]. It is my duty to serve the poor. What does Ma say to that?

---

[17] There is such tremendous wealth in India —both spiritual and cultural—; but it is typical of the fundamentally materialistic humanism so prized in the West to focus almost exclusively on the economic problems, as a sort of modern substitute for a more authentic spirituality.

Ma: *Exactly the same is also said by Hindus. To serve God in every human being is certainly a path to purification of the mind* [chitta shuddhi].

Question: You say 'a way' but for us it is the only way. Do other ways [to God] exist?

Ma: *There are innumerable paths.*

Question: Is technical progress an aid to the spiritual search or rather a hindrance?

Ma: *In themselves technological inventions are neither good nor bad. Now one flies by aeroplane, in olden times also flying existed by pushplaka ratha* [18]. *This is the constant flux of the world. Anything that helps in one's spiritual search is to be adopted and whatever hinders to be eschewed.*

Question: Take for instance the invention of printing. Through books one may be helped in one's search.

Ma: *If someone really wants God and nothing but God, he has all the books he needs within himself. He needs no printed books. But there is no harm in making use of modern inventions provided they are helpful in the quest after God.*

Priest: What does Ma consider the most essential thing in life?

Ma: *To try and find out 'Who am I'. To try to know that which has brought into existence one's body and mind. This also may become the search after God. But the first thing is to conceive the desire to know oneself. Finding one's Self, one has found God and finding God one has found one's Self —the one Atma.*

Question: Are there many people who succeed in this quest?

Ma: *Quite a number attain to some siddhi* [a degree of attainment] *or mukti* [liberation], *but only one in ten millions arrives at complete Realization. It is very, very rare.*

Question: Do you think you have reached the ultimate state?

Ma: (Laughs) *Whatever you believe me to be, that I am.*

Question: From what moment did you have that Realization?

Ma: *When was I not?*

---

[18] A kind of flying machine spoken of in the ancient Hindu epics.

XXVII - The Final Years

In 1965 a Dutch devotee had a tiny but charming stone cottage constructed for Atmananda in the ashram retreat of Anandamayee Ma known as 'Kalyanvan', located near the city of Dehradun. It is situated at an altitude of around 2,500 feet in a beautiful tranquil garden surrounded by ancient pine and jackfruit trees, with a view of the mountains. This was all and more than Atmananda ever dared hope for and she remained delighted with the place until the end of her life. Every afternoon she would walk a mile or so to Ma's Kishenpur ashram to lead the *kirtan* which was faithfully attended by a group of local devotees. Dehradun is a fairly sophisticated community and she had many friends there.

By the late 60's India had become inundated with hordes of young Westerners fleeing what they felt to be the oppressive sterility of Western materialism. Although ostensibly in search of something spiritual, their fundamentally hedonistic quest often boiled down to 'doing their own thing', and although many of them imitated the vagabond life-style of the Indian *sadhu*, few had any deep sense of the underlying spirituality of it. Initially the Indians were kind and hospitable to these people (many of whom were genuinely well-meaning and idealistically motivated) but in time came to see them as incomprehensible barbarians. In general the 'hippies', as they were called, who were often unwashed and on drugs with little sensitivity to Indian tradition and customs, created a bad impression that left an indelible stigma on the many young Western seekers who came to India after them, for years to come.

A few years later a new wave of Westerners appeared on the scene who were interested in Yoga and meditation, often followers of various Indian 'Gurus' who had recently gone to the West. Although they were more serious than the 'hippies', most returned home after barely getting their feet wet. The common clichés of the period were: "I had to go to India in order to discover that it wasn't really necessary" and "In the New Age everyone is their own Guru". Nevertheless some did stay on in India, living in ashrams or on their own, pursuing their research with various teachers or institutions. Others returned to the West and took up studies at Universities which were increasingly opening up departments of Eastern Religion etc. Meanwhile the practice of meditation and Yoga was becoming very widespread, almost commonplace. [1]

When I first met Atmananda in 1972 I was 23 years old and she 68, but in spite of the age difference our meeting was like a reunion of old friends. We were both staying in the same dharmasala in Hardwar while attending the annual meditation and fasting week presided over by Anandamayee Ma known as *Samyam Sapta*. Although the program was quite demanding, Atmananda went out of her way to talk to me, sometimes late at night after returning from the ashram. It could be quite cold due to the biting wind that cuts through Hardwar at that time of the year and we would share a hot drink in my room made on the indispensable kerosene stove which she had taught me to use. I recall that she questioned me intensively about my background etc as though she were looking for someone; and I remember one particular moment when there was something like a flash of recognition —something profound seen in the periphery of one's vision that when one turns toward it, immediately vanishes.

As one of the principal themes of this book has been Westerners' spiritual involvement with India and particularly with Anandamayee Ma, it will perhaps be useful to briefly mention something of my own experience in this regard. Although I had not come to India specifically to meet Anandamayee Ma, on my first day there when I walked into her ashram in Benares, I had an overwhelming feeling that for the first time in *this* life I had finally come home.

---

[1] Today one finds a new, perhaps more sophisticated, generation of young Westerners in India who although having grown up with an exposure to a Westernized version of Indian philosophy and spiritual practices, are still finding the spiritual discovery of the East a revelation. As India becomes a major player in today's world, bringing with it its ancient culture more or less intact, it more than ever offers a truly distinctive post-modern cultural alternative. Nowhere is this more apparent than in Atmananda's beloved Benares.

Although I had been involved in yoga and meditation for several years in America, my initial interest in mysticism stemmed from an earlier encounter as an adolescent —not unlike what happened to Atmananda when as a young girl in Vienna she experienced an ecstatic oneness with all life. It was only several years later that I discovered to my amazement that Indian philosophy specifically dealt with what I had here-to-fore considered my own special secret. [2] No doubt something like this happens to many people who are irresistibly drawn to Eastern Wisdom, as it strikes a fundamental universal chord innate to humanity that is not based on any sectarian creed or belief but on a direct experience of the ground of being.

When I first approached Anandamayee Ma it was with an intense desire to enter more deeply into the spiritual quest on which I had already embarked. To say that she did not disappoint me would be a radical understatement. When I first met Her it was as though she were expecting me and almost before I could open my mouth she said: *"Don't worry, I will take care of everything."* Indeed the answers which she gave to my questions and the specific instructions she gave regarding my *sadhana* ultimately caused me to remain with Her in India for the next ten years —much of that time as a monk in her ashram.

From the beginning I was aware that to be in Her presence dramatically intensified my own inner spiritual awareness, particularly if I placed my attention on Her without any preconceptions. Indeed, the more one became attuned to Ma the more one experienced Her as an external manifestation of what was in reality a purely interior experience. The infinitely greater reality of 'transcendent' spiritual union to which Ma awakened one quickly dispersed the comparative illusion of the outer material world. One hesitates to say anything about this because words can only get in the way, but the main point is that one experienced an overwhelming spiritual intimacy with Ma and the interiorization of this was the fundamental nature of the *sadhana* process with Her.

---

[2] Once when I asked Ma about this, somewhat proudly saying that I had discovered these truths within myself, on my own, without the aid of God or Guru, She corrected me saying that such things always require God's grace and then added, almost imperceptibly: "And it was also known to Me at that time."

I embarked upon an extraordinary spiritual adventure which was characterized by an ever deepening spiritual passion, the flames of which were continually fanned by Her Divine presence.

As this process deepened I soon became aware that Her spiritual presence activated an inner awareness of what could be called my own uniquely individual spiritual archetype —some fundamental inner ideal hidden deep within the primal personality structure that is uniquely and divinely one's own— one's own unique way to apotheosis which is a *divinely transformed* mirror image of the imperfect human ego-mind personality structure. In this sense each individual *is* his or her own unique spiritual path. It became clear with Ma that authentic spirituality is not the repression of individuality but the complete fulfilment of it in which the ego abandons its limiting sense of separateness and becomes fully merged in its true identity: the one undifferentiated whole.

Still more startling and profound one saw the revelation of this uniquely personal archetype manifested externally in Ma's (one can only say) divine physical form, as well as being experienced overwhelmingly within the depths of one's being. It was the overwhelming recognition of the primordial authenticity of this 'relationship' with Ma that dispelled any possible doubt about Her supreme authority and ability to guide one. The *sadhana* process consisted in cultivating the relationship both externally and internally with this revelation which was equally Ma and one's innermost Self.

In one sense Ma's primary, if not sole purpose, seemed to have been to awaken this realization of inherent divinity in whomever She came into contact with. Without exception, every time I laid eyes on Ma this process was activated. In time my daily meditation also became nothing but an automatic interiorization of this experience. I mention these things only to testify in some small way to Ma's greatness as a Teacher. Everyone who seriously cultivated a relationship with Her had similar, if not much more profound, experiences according to their intensity and temperament, for Ma is not other than one's Self —the most essential and true part of all of us.

Through association with Ma one came to understand that energy (both as consciousness and matter) can be transformed

and 'divinized' (indeed this is of the essence of yoga, of *sadhana*[3]).
Ma's physical form was the ultimate perfect manifestation of this
phenomenon. Living and travelling with Her one particularly
became aware of the immense importance of wholly transformed
individuals (saints) and sacred places of power —the transformative shrines and pilgrimage sites that make up the mystic body
of Mother India.

To have even a glimpse of Ma's radiant physical form was
an experience of overwhelming beauty that almost defies description —a manifestation of divinely physical grace and aesthetics
that was wholly entrancing. This alone was enough to inspire
me to forsake all else and to put up with any hardship in order to
remain near Her. I simply could not get over what I felt was my
wholly unjustified good fortune at being able to have this *darshan*
and with time this feeling only became intensified. It also became increasingly clear that Ma literally knew one's every
thought (when She chose to) and could see one's mind in its en-
tirety so that it was impossible to hide anything from Her. I experienced this with Her on many occasions on which She made
it overwhelmingly clear. Each time one went before Ma it was a
wholly new and original experience, a mini ego death in which
one stood naked before the eternal truth of Being. To stay with
Her was to live wholly beyond death and the repetitious patterns of the ego.

During my years in the ashram I underwent a process of intense training under Ma's specific guidance which would be impossible, indeed unimaginable, for anyone who had not made
the commitment to remain with Her in India. The protective field
of the ashram, irradiated by Anandamayee Ma's intense physical
and spiritual presence, provided the precise 'laboratory conditions' under which the Great Work with the Guru could be ex-
ecuted. Total immersion in this process is not something that takes
place overnight but requires years of being tested and purified
by the Guru, more or less on a daily basis, as we have seen in
Atmananda's case. Only then has the prospective disciple been
weaned sufficiently from the world to enter into the more serious

---

[3] This concept is also fundamental to understanding the esoteric technology
of Brahminical ritualism and the creation of sacred space.

practice for which complete solitude is necessary. Through Ma's Grace I was in a position to have had at least a glimpse of this process which would have otherwise been inaccessible. This was definitely not something that was meant for everyone and only a very few of the many who sought Anandamayee Ma's guidance were prepared, or in a position, to make this kind of commitment. In any case she dealt with each aspirant according to their own unique needs. [4]

For most it was enough to stay with Her for a few days or occasionally weeks to feel that a profound inner connection had been made and then return home and incorporate this blessing into their lives. But for those like Atmananda who had given up everything for the quest, there was no question of having any personal life to "go back" to. The relationship with Ma, the Guru, the *Atma*, was the very air they breathed. It was on a radically different level of commitment. Anandamayee Ma was extremely clear that anyone who had a chance of avoiding entanglement in the world, which she often referred to in English as "slow poison", should by all means do so in order to devote himself fully to the cultivation of the spiritual; and it was inevitable that the more intensely one followed her, the more detached one became from what was clearly shown to be a fatal illusion.

In reply to the question: "What is real *darshan*?", Mother said: "[It is] *To see That which when seen, the wish to see anything more vanishes forever; to hear that which when heard, the desire to hear anything else is forever silenced.*" [5] When an individual's *darshan* of Ma approximated this level of intensity, there was simply nothing else that he or she could do other than passionately attempt to keep his full awareness fixed on this Supreme Reality to the exclusion of all else, abandoning completely whatever they had heretofore considered to be their lives and responsibilities in the world. This was the essential point of departure, the *beginning* of a radical spiritual life under Ma's guidance.

---

[4] Throughout this book I have attempted to highlight in the commentaries the unique manner in which Anandamayee Ma would guide people whenever Atmananda encountered these situations. See particularly entries for 6th July, 1946; 14th June, 1946; 22nd May, 1946; and Intro. to chapter 8.

[5] See entry for 1st October 1946.

I think it important to emphasize these points particularly because the value of the purely contemplative life, as encouraged by Anandamayee Ma in her ashrams, is so often misunderstood and disparaged in the modern world which equates success in life almost exclusively with material gain even with regard to so-called spiritual pursuits. Traditional societies clearly understood that the monastic contemplative or hermit was involved in the crucial work of bringing down and 'stabilizing' the spiritual within the outer physical world for the great benefit of all mankind. Even the most 'worldly' people in such cultures have a fundamental understanding and respect for those engaged in this endeavour. As has often been noted, the great tragedy of our own age is a mechanistic materialistic 'scientific' way of life that has severed modern man from his natural spiritual moorings —to the extent that to even mention the spiritual automatically puts one on the defensive.

In the ashram I saw Atmananda quite often and sometimes helped her with the ashram journal, *Ananda Varta*, of which she was the editor. She considered that translating the words of Anandamayee Ma and preparing the ashram publications was her principal *sadhana*, but she was always very humble about her role in this work for which she was completely indispensable and which she did virtually single-handedly.

The handful of Westerners who remained permanently with Anandamayee Ma were inevitably thrown together, particularly when following her around India. Between an intense meditation schedule, Ma's *darshan* —often several hours a day—, and preparing one's food (one cooked meal a day at noon), there was very little time for socializing. But Atmananda was always ready to do whatever she could to assist anyone —particularly the occasional foreigner— who might come for Anandamayee Ma's *darshan*, whatever their circumstances. This was sometimes a thankless task which was not always appreciated by some of the ashram authorities who in no way encouraged foreigners, particularly after the hippie invasion of the late 60's. But Atmananda could never remain still when she perceived an injustice and did not hesitate to do whatever she could to help those foreign seekers who had come from such a great distance and who otherwise

553

Atmananda with Swami Vijayananda - mid 1980's
(courtesy of Haripriya Dillon)

might have been ignored and become discouraged. She felt that Mother wanted her to aid these people and she was in a unique position to understand their needs and to explain ashram protocol to them.

A famous astrologer in Benares, who had done Atmananda's chart, told her that she would die at the age of 74. It is generally considered in India that such predictions are based on precise calculations and are usually accurate. Around the time of her scheduled demise, she half-jokingly mentioned this to Ma who said: *"Good, consider that your life is now over. Henceforth you shall live on my time and your life belongs to me."* She was, of course, delighted with this response and, in fact, her health and general level of energy improved noticeably from that time on.

It was during this period (1979) that Anandamayee Ma had Atmananda go to the ancient pilgrimage town of Gaya to have her death rites performed by the pandits there in the traditional manner. This was her formal entry into *sanyasa*, the final stage of renunciation in which one is completely dead to the world. She had already been wearing the ochre coloured cloth of a renunciate for sometime, but with this rite she made the final irrevocable step. Outwardly though she kept all this a secret.

Towards the end of 1981 Anandamayee Ma's health began to seriously deteriorate and she ceased eating solid food, taking only minimal liquid sustenance. Great Mahatmas came to her from all over India begging her to remain in her body as the world had such great need of Her. It was deeply believed that she could heal herself if only she had the *'kheyal'* to do so. However, it seemed at last that she had no *'kheyal'* in this regard other than to go, as she put it, into 'the *avyakta*' —the formless— which she said was calling her. Finally, on 27th August, 1982, she gave up her body at the Dehradun-Kishenpur Ashram. As per her instructions, her body was taken to her ashram at Kankhal (Hardwar) where she gave her final *darshan*. Thousands of people from around India streamed in for this last blessing. Indira Gandhi, then Prime Minister of India and a devotee of Ma since childhood, flew in by helicopter. The following obituary in the Himachal Times sums up the shock that her passing generated around the country:

A God Died Yesterday

With the passing of Ma Anandamayee an era in the annals of Indian culture has come to a close.

Ma, as she was known to Her innumerable devotees in this country and abroad, was a saint in the tradition of the greatest Indian mystics. She had, in her own particular way, stood as a formidable bulwark against the erosion of traditional Indian values and culture at a time when these had come under heavy onslaught from within the nation itself...

For millions of men and women who made the journey to her door Ma had come to crystallize the peace and universality which is so peculiar to the Indian culture. The Indians, the westerners from wherever they came —the very best minds of nearly four generations — some of them leading writers, philosophers, spiritualists, scientists and politicians — all who flocked to her luminous door were found returning to their respective niches enriched with humanity's rarest and best achievement — love.

That was Ma Anandamayee... Her spirit is as eternal, as everlasting as India herself. She was amongst the finest of Mother India's offspring.

(The Himachal Times) 29. 8. 82

During the final year of Anandamayee Ma's life, I noticed a marked change in Atmananda. While many of us were distracted by a feeling of gloom that had descended due to Ma's withdrawal, Atmananda seemed to have discovered a new inner intensity. She was always the first to arrive for Mother's *darshan* and the last to leave, blissfully absorbing every second she was able to be with Her. Clearly something special was taking place within, quite different from her more routine attitude of recent years.

After Ma's passing, Atmananda became more engrossed in her work than ever. One sensed that she felt she was working against the clock. At that time I was living not far from her, higher up in the mountains, and saw her fairly often. In late 1983 I left India and did not return until the end of 1984 and then only for a short visit. When I went to see Atmananda, she cheerfully told me that she wanted to be ready when death came for her and to this end was organizing her few possessions (she was concerned, for example, with what to do with an old pot I had once given her). I remarked that she seemed very healthy. She agreed but said that she felt death could come at any time and that, although she was not in any great hurry, she intended to be completely prepared.

It was at this time that Atmananda first mentioned her diaries to me. She told me that she had always intended to destroy them and had never shown them to anyone, but recently, as she was preparing to dispose of the diaries, she began rereading them after a very long time and had the thought that "they might be of value to someone". She was referring here specifically to the material dealing with her personal spiritual development as she had already published her more impersonal observations of Ma in 1983 in her book *As the Flower Sheds its Fragrance*. She asked me to go through the diaries and tell her what I thought and suggested that I should come and stay somewhere near-by for this work. Unfortunately this was, quite uncharacteristically, a very rushed trip for me and to my great regret I never found the time.

The last time I saw Atmananda was in mid-December of 1984. She had prepared a special lunch for myself and my wife, of whom she was extremely fond, which she served on the verandah of her cottage with great motherly affection. The meal was very enjoyable and we had a lively and intimate conversation as there was much to discuss. When finished we were careful to clean our utensils and eating area in the prescribed orthodox Hindu manner which she always faithfully observed. At length the conversation turned to the recently published book of Lewis Thompson's metaphysical aphorisms *Mirror to the Light*. She had gone through the work carefully, but from the vantage point of her spiritual evolution over the more than thirty-six years since his death, she was clearly no longer as impressed with his writings as she had once been. She then began to reminisce about him, saying what an unusual person he was and how it was he who had really brought her to Ma. She also said that in some way I had always reminded her of him. At the time this remark meant very little to me as I knew almost nothing about Thompson. (Later, as I was preparing this book, it would come back to haunt me).

When it was time to go, Atmananda realized that we still had not gotten around to looking at the diaries. I promised her again that I would come back within a few months for this work, although I still had no idea what a treasure they were.

After returning to America I made arrangements to return to India in early April, going so far as to purchase a plane ticket and acquire a visa. However, at the last minute I was forced to cancel everything. Atmananda wrote to me expressing her regret that I was unable to come and I responded that I would definitely do so by the following January as I planned to attend the Kumbha Mela in Hardwar.

* * *

On the afternoon of 24th September, 1985, when Atmananda arrived by taxi from Dehradun at the Kankhal ashram, where the body of Anandamayee Ma had recently been enshrined in an impressive marble temple specially built for this purpose, she was in an extremely debilitated condition. She was running a high fever and her throat had been acutely inflamed and swollen for the last week [6], as a result of which she had eaten practically nothing. Although quite conscious and evidently not in great pain, life was holding her by the slenderest of threads and she could only speak in a faint whisper. It is not clear whether she went first to the ashram and then to the dilapidated *dharmasala* where she was accustomed to stay on her visits to Kankhal, or whether she went directly to the dharmasala, which was about one kilometre from the ashram, and where her friend and fellow disciple of Anandamayee Ma, Melita Maschmann [7], was living.

What is very clear, however, is that she was not offered a place in the ashram (where three doctors were residing) in the recently built well-fitted ashram guest house. Instead it was decided that she should be sent to the ashram hospital in Benares that very night as it was felt that only there could she receive the proper

---

[6] It was thought she was suffering from dyptheria (from which her sister had died from at the age of 17).

[7] Melita Maschman is a prominent German writer who met Anandamayee Ma 'by chance' in the early 1960's and remained with her in India from that time on. She relates her experience of this in her book in German, *As the Tiger Sings Kirtan*.

care. This would have entailed a gruelling 20 hour train ride which would have been excruciating for her. Every effort was made to convince Atmananda to go along with this but she adamantly refused. This was undoubtedly very upsetting for her, particularly as it was almost impossible for her to speak or to withstand the slightest exertion. She had come to Kankhal to complete her final *sadhana* within the sacred precincts of her Guru's *samadhi*, but this final attachment also had to be renounced. She would have to make do with the primitive and often over-crowded arrangements in the ancient pilgrims' rest house, with Melita to look after her.

The *dharmasala* where she was taken (where I have also stayed on many occasions) is a massive run down 18th Century structure built like a medieval fortress. Its lime walls are at least 6 feet thick and its four corners resemble turrets. It fronts on a narrow lane that serves as the main avenue to the local cremation ground situated nearby on the banks of the Ganges. At various times during the day, triumphant Hindu funeral processions pass by carrying the body of the deceased on a flower decked bier, the mourners chanting: *"Ram nam satya hai"*—The name 'Ram' is truth.

The rooms, which open onto a central courtyard downstairs and upstairs onto a large open verandah, are extremely minimal, although quite large and draughty, with dirty white-washed walls and a bare cement floor. The only furnishing is a simple Indian rope bed. The windows have rusted iron bars with no glass and cracked wooden shutters. At this time the place was often used for Hindu wedding parties which are unbearably noisy and frequently go on all night. Fortunately there was nothing scheduled for that evening.

The main problem for Atmananda would have been that there was only one primitive latrine that served all of the 10 upstairs rooms (in one of which lived a family of 5), and it was located at least 120 feet from the room she occupied. Nevertheless, in spite of these physical inconveniences, the place had its own charm and she was probably much more relaxed here than she could ever have been in the ashram —particularly as Melita was there to look after her. In fact it seems profoundly fitting for someone who had renounced all and whose entire life had been nothing if not a pilgrimage, to embark on her final journey from such a humble pilgrim's rest house. There could be no doubt that the Guru's grace was also present in this. Anandamayee Ma often used to compare the world to a *dharmasala*, saying that it is merely a temporary shelter on our eternal pilgrimage.

What happened next is best described by Melita who was the sole witness to many of these events:

"It was early afternoon when someone called me out of my room. There were two young men, one from the Dehradun ashram who was accompanying Atmananda and the other was, I believe, the taxi driver. They were holding a large bundle in which, I understood, was Atmananda, although I could not see her. Together we carried her upstairs and put the bundle down on the cot in her old room and, suddenly, there she was! She spoke in a very soft voice. I spread her bedding on another cot and made it as comfortable as possible and that seemed to make her feel more at home. After that her voice became a little stronger and she said that she had had a very high fever but was now feeling a little better. I made her some tea which she drank but we did not talk much as I guess it was difficult for her. So we just sat quietly. After 2 or 3 hours, Swami Swarupananda [8] and the French doctor, Swami Vijayananda, came. The latter examined her and, as I recall, found her not to be mortally ill. Later, after dark, most of the ashram *brahmacharinis* came to visit and brought her fruits and chatted with her, but her voice was rather weak and she did not say much. Finally one of the swamis said that she should leave for Benares as soon as possible to stay in Ma's hospital there where she could get the proper treatment. But Atmananda was very much against it and it was put off for the next day.

When the guests left, I made some soup for her and we talked. She made me promise to bring out three books containing the accounts of Mother's activities (*Matri Lila*) which she had published in the "Ananda Varta" over the years. I promised to do so and this made her happy. Then she went to sleep and later on I went to sleep on the second cot. I woke up several times as Atmananda seemed to be having trouble breathing but then she always fell asleep again quickly.

---

[8] The General Secretary of the Anandamayi Sangha and president of the Kankhal ashram.

Early in the morning, around 5:00 a.m., I heard her breathing with difficulty and got up and made some tea. I was worried because she looked so pale and hardly spoke. After the tea, she seemed to feel better and I began talking in a low voice about Ma, Her beauty and Her love, and about how much we had received from Her. Atmananda also said some things along these lines but then, suddenly, I became very concerned as her voice became so soft. I ran to find the father of the family who lived in the corner room. He at once got dressed and went to the ashram to call one of the lady doctors then staying there. Atmananda was continually repeating Ma's name as she had been doing so all morning. In spite of her weakness, with my assistance, she was able to walk to the bathroom and then was able to manage by herself. I then helped her to walk back to the room and again helped her into a sitting position, holding her in my arms and softly repeating the *japa* of Ma's name along with her. When I could no longer hear her, I went on repeating "Ma, Ma, Ma..." Suddenly, I felt a strange movement in her whole body and I understood that she had given up her life. I slowly laid her down and covered her face, and kept on praying Ma's name while sitting at her side.

A long time passed and still no doctor came. So I sent someone else to notify the ashram that Atmananda had left her body. Then a big crowd arrived. The Gujarati lady doctor and myself propped her up and arranged her clothes. Later the body was brought to Ma's *Samadhi mandir* [9], where the ashram girls washed and dressed it in fresh clothes and placed her just in front of the *Samadhi*. [10] An hour later she was placed in an open vehicle, with her body seated in a crossed legged position on a chair and covered with many garlands. Then she was taken in procession, in the traditional manner for a *sannyasi*, to a special area of the Ganges reserved for the submersion of *sannyasis*. Many ashramites accompanied her and when we returned to the ashram, a *bandhara* [a ritual feast] was given in her honour —and that was that." [11]

---

[9] The Temple which houses the remains of Anandamayee Ma.

[10] This would be behind a railing in the temple where normally she was not allowed.

[11] From a letter written to me by Melita Maschman in 1996.

It was observed by those present that Atmananda's exit from this world was that of a true yogini —sitting upright repeating her Guru's name with complete composure. To the credit of the ashram, particularly to the *brahmacharinis* who made most of the arrangements, in the end Atmananda was given the full honours due to her as a Hindu *sanyasini*. To my knowledge she is the only Western woman who has ever been accorded such an honour and there can be no doubt that she was immensely delighted!

Epilogue

When I returned to Hardwar at the beginning of 1986, I found myself by chance staying in the very room in the *dharmasala* in which Atmananda had died only four months before. Not long after my arrival Melita appeared at my door with a large cloth bundle, greeting me with the words: "I believe this is meant for you." Inside were the ten hand-written volumes of Atmananda's diaries. Melita had rescued them from Atmananda's little cottage in Dehradun just before they were about to be thrown out.

By the time I received the diaries I had almost completely forgotten about them; but once I began reading it became clear that they would be the culmination of Atmananda's life work of presenting Anandamayee Ma to the West.

Anandamayee Ma's last instructions to Her followers were: "*Remain where you are*" (i.e., there is no need to change one's outer circumstances) "*and do your sadhana*" (with the sense that all one's effort should be exerted exclusively for this purpose). Her penultimate instruction, given a few days earlier at the urgent request of her devotees (who were desperately aware of the prospect of her imminent departure) was: "*Strive to be worthy of (or receptive to) the grace of your Guru.*" These two statements sum up perfectly Ma's teachings, and all who would follow Her need, in truth, no more than this. To this end life today in her ashrams in India goes on much as it always has. Mother's presence is particularly and very powerfully focussed in the Samadhi Temple in the Kankhal (Hardwar) ashram where Her body is enshrined. But most of all She is enshrined in the hearts of all those who call out to Her with sincere devotion and surrender.

Jay Ma

जय माँ

Kankhal, 21st March, 2002

Glossary

adhikar (Sanskrit *adhikāra*): Spiritual qualification, aptitude.
ahimsa (Sanskrit *ahimsā*): Non-violence.
anand (Sanskrit *ānanda*): Bliss.
asana (*āsana*): Seat for meditation; yoga posture.
arati (*āratī*): A basic Hindu ritual in which various items symbolic of the senses such as incense, light, and food items are offered to the deity.
Atma (*ātmā*): The true Self, the indwelling Divine Presence within every individual.
Atmachintan (*ātmachintan*): Thought concentrated on the Atma.
Atmagyan (*ātmajñāna*): Knowledge of the Atma or true Self.
Avatar (*avatāra*): Divine incarnation.
bhajan (*bhajana*): Devotional singing.
bhakti (*bhakti*): Spiritual devotion.
bhava (*bhāva*): Inspired mood.
bhog (*bhoga*): Food.
bhogi (*bhogī*): Enjoyer of the pleasures of the senses.
bija mantra (*bīja mantra*): One syllable mantra that denotes the essence of a particular deity.
brahmachari (*brahmācārī*): Monk or nun (*brahmācārinī*) who has yet to take the final irrevocable vow of *sanyas*. The first of the 4 stages or ashramas of traditional Hindu life.
buddhi (*buddhi*): Intellect.
darshan (*darśana*): 'Seeing', here used with the sense of being in the presence of a saint and absorbing the blessing of the one who gives *darshan*.
deva (*deva*): Demi-god, local deity.
dharma (*dharma*): Righteous action appropriate to one's station.
dharmasala (*dharmaśālā*): Rest house for pilgrims.
dhyan (*dhyāna*): Meditation.
diksha (*dikṣā*): Initiation.
ekagra (*ekāgra*): One-pointed.

567

gandharva (*gandharva*): Celestial musician.

gerua (*gerua*): The ochre or salmon color symbolic of *sannyasa* — complete renunciation.

ghee (*ghī*): Clarified butter.

gopi (*gopī*): Refers to the cow-herder girls of Vrindaban who were devoted to Krishna.

guna (*guṇa*): Any one of the 3 fundamental states of energy-matter-consciousness known as *sattva, rajas, tamas.*

iccha (*icchā*): Will or desire.

indriya (*indriya*): The physical senses.

ishtadev (*īṣṭadeva*): The form of God to which one is personally and naturally inclined, such as Krishna, Shiva, Durga, etc.

jap or **japa** (*japa*): Repetition of a mantra either audibly or mentally.

jnana or **gyan** (*jñāna*): Spiritual wisdom implying the direct cognition of non-duality as The true nature of Reality —the knowledge of the Self.

jnani or **gyani** (*jñānī*): One who has attained *jnana.*

jhuta (*jhuṭā*): Impure (ritually).

kanya (*kanyā*): virgin girl.

karma (*karma*): Action; the results of one's action; the law of cause and effects which determines the inevitable fruit of one's destiny as determined by one's actions in previous lives.

kheyal (*kheyāla*): A spontaneous upsurge of Divine Will.

kirtan (*kirtana*): Devotional singing, chanting of Divine names.

kumbhak (*kumbhaka*): Yogic process of suspension of the breath.

kundalini (*kuṇḍalinī*): The primordial cosmic energy said to be coiled like a serpent at the base of the spine, the energy of enlightenment (see footnote for 10th Sept., 1945).

leela or **lila** (*līlā*): Divine play —the world as such.

mahatma (*mahātmā*): Literally 'great soul', it is the respectful title for one of spiritual attainment.

mala (*mālā*): Rosary used for the repetition of a *mantra.*

mandir (*mandira*): A temple.

mantra (*mantra*): Sacred syllable(s) or phrases repeated as a means of entering into meditative absorption.

maya (*māyā*): The Mystery through which the one absolute Reality appears as the duality of subject-object perception within the relativity of time and space.

moha (*moha*): Infatuation, delusion.

moksha (*mokṣa*): Liberation from the cycle of birth and death.

mudra (*mudrā*): Mystic hand gesture, position of the fingers denoting a particular movement of spiritual energy.

muladhara (*mūlādhāra*): The *chakra* at the base of the spine where the *Kundalini* is coiled.

murti (*mūrti*): Sacred image.

nirguna (*nirguṇa*): Without form or qualities.

nitya (*nitya*): Eternal.

pap (*pāpa*): Sin, bad actions.

paramatma (*paramātmā*): The supreme Atma.

prakriti (*prakṛti*): In Samkhya philosophy, the female, dynamic principle of God.

prana (*prāṇa*): Life force related to the movement of the breath.

pranam (*praṇām*): A fundamental Hindu gesture of reverence consisting either of full prostration or a bow with folded palms.

prasad (*prasāda*): Food items that have been ritually offered either to a sacred image or holy person and thus blessed.

prem (*prema*): Love.

puja (*pūjā*): Ritual religious ceremony.

pujari (*pujārī*): Priest who performs formal puja in a temple etc.

punya (*puṇya*): Merit, good actions.

purna Brahma (*purṇabrahma*): The full manifestation of the supreme Godhead.

purusha (*puruṣa*): The male principle —the unmoving unmanifest aspect of God according to Samkhya philosophy. (The relationship of Purusha and Prakriti in the Samkhya system is analogous to that of Shiva and his consort, Shakti, in the Tantras).

rajas (*rajas*): The guna of action.

ras (*rasa*): Divine nectar, the subtle profound essence of that is truly aesthethic.

sadhak (*sādhaka*): Someone who does *sadhana*.

sadhana (*sādhanā*): Spiritual practice.

sadhu (*sādhu*): A person who has dedicated his life to spiritual practice and is a renunciate.

saguna (*saguṇa*): With form, with qualities.

samadhi (*samādhi*): The state of complete absorption in non-duality in which the individual consciousness is completely dissolved into the infinite indivisible Whole.

samsar (*saṁsāra*): The cycle of life and death, the world.

samskaras (*saṁskāra*): Impressions from past lives which influence one's present life, the inescapable results of *karma*.

satsang (*satsaṅga*): Association with the Truth; usually refers to keeping the company of the Saints and spiritual seekers.

satwa (*sattva*): The guna of purity, refinement.

sanyasi (*saṁnyāsī*): One who has taken formal vows of renunciation according to the Hindu tradition.

shabda (*śabda*): Sound, usually referring to the Eternal Divine sound known as *Shabda Brahman*.

shakti (*śakti*): Power or Energy, the active feminine aspect of God

Shastras (*śāstra*): Scriptures.

shraddha (*śraddhā*): Faith.

shuddhachari (*śuddhācārī*): One who keeps very strictly the laws of ritual purity.

shunya (or sunya) (*śūnya*): Emptiness or void, absence of dualistic perception.

siddha (*siddha*): one who possesses *siddhis* or occult powers.

sloka (*śloka*): A verse from the Scriptures.

tamas (*tamas*): The guna of inertia, torpor.

tapasya (*tapasyā*): Spiritual austerities.

tapasvin (*tapasvin*): One who does spiritual austerities.

thali (*thālī*): Metal plate.

vasanas (*vāsanā*): Mental tendencies and behaviour patterns resulting from past karma that create the appearance of an individual ego-self.

vichara (*vichāra*): Philosophical inquiry; here, inquiry into the ultimate nature of individual identity.

viveka (*viveka*): Discrimination.

yagya (*yajña*): Vedic fire sacrifice.

yantra (*yantra*): Esoteric diagram that is the geometric embodiment of the deity.

yoga (*yoga*): systems of spiritual techniques and discipline through which the practitioner attains union with God as specifically outlined in the *Yoga Sutras* of Patanjali as well as other Yoga and Tantric texts.

Acknowledgments

This book would not have been possible were it not for Melita Maschmann, who rescued the diaries from oblivion after Atmananda's death and then urged me to make a book out of them; Zarine Pegler, who transcribed the hand written volumes onto computer disc at a time when such a thing would have been inconceivable to me; and, especially, my wife, Parvati, who has been indispensable in this work every step of the way.

Special thanks also to the many individuals around the world who contributed in various ways to this project —in particular: Richard Lannoy for his beautiful photographs of Atmananda and Anandamayee Ma as well as for his correspondence concerning Lewis Thompson; Carol Devi of Matri Satsang for her photographs and encouragement; likewise to Hari Priya Dillon and Chandravali Schang. Many thanks also to Swami Nirvananda for photos of Atmananda, to Swami Dayananda (USA) and Swami Karunapremananda (USA) for their discerning critique, and to Richard Willis, Father Francis Tiso and Chris Pegler for their hospitality, friendship and encouragement. The same to Robert Svoboda, Fred Smith and Mark Dyczkowski.

My gratitude to Ani Tenzin Palmo, Swami Jnanananda Giri, Swami Vijayananda, and the late Br. Gadhadhar, all friends of Atmananda and 'westerners' who like her have lived an authentic spiritual life in India and with whom it has been my good fortune to be close to over the years. Many thanks also to Swami Purnanandaji of Sri Ma Anandamayee Ashram for his encouragement and inspiration while preparing this work.

It is extremely auspicious that Sri Swami Bhaskarananda, Spiritual Head and General Secretary of the Anandamayee Sangha has graced the book with his profound Forward. My deepest appreciation to Sri Swami Chidananda of the Divine Life Society, Rishikesh, for gracing the book with his thoughtful preface and likewise to Sri Swami Satchidananda of Anandashram, Khanangad, Kerala, for maintaining such a perfect oasis of peace there and for offering that most precious treasure : true spiritual friendship.

I would like to also thank Washington State University for the photo of Lewis Thompson and permission to quote from his poems; the Anandamayee Sangha for permission to quote from their publications, particularly *As the Flower Sheds its Fragrance* by Atmananda and to Sri Ramanasramam for permission to quote from their publications.

Lastly I would like to thank Indica Books for their creative vision in undertaking this project, and Govinda Baba for making the connection in holy Kashi (Benares), abode of Shiva, city of light.

Hara, Hara, Mahadeva!

Other books of related interest
published by **INDICA BOOKS:**

- **MY DAYS WITH SRI MA ANANDAMAYI**
  by *Bithika Mukherji*

- **NEW LIVES.**
  50 WESTERNERS SEARCH FOR THEMSELVES IN SACRED INDIA
  by *Malcolm Tillis. Edited with an Introduction by Ram Alexander*

- **SPIRITUAL EDUCATION**
  by *Purnima Zweers*

Distributed by **INDICA BOOKS:**

- **ANANDAMAYI : HER LIFE AND WISDOM**
  Photographies and text by *Richard Lannoy*